최근 7개년
기출문제

영어

신념을 가지고 도전하는 사람은 반드시 그 꿈을 이룰 수 있습니다.
처음에 품은 신념과 열정이 취업 성공의 그 날까지 빛바래지 않도록
서원각이 수험생 여러분을 응원합니다.

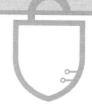

시험의 성패를 결정하는 데 있어 가장 중요한 요소 중 하나는 충분한 학습이라고 할 수 있다. 하지만 무작정 많은 양을 학습하는 것은 바람직하지 않다. 시험에 출제되는 모든 과목이 그렇듯, 전통적으로 중요하게 여겨지는 이론이나 내용들이 존재한다. 그리고 이러한 이론이나 내용들은 회를 걸쳐 반복적으로 시험에 출제되는 경향이 나타날 수밖에 없다. 따라서 모든 시험에 앞서 필수적으로 짚고 넘어가야 하는 것이 기출문제에 대한 파악이다.

영어는 9급 공무원 시험과목 중 수험생들이 가장 어렵게 여기는 과목 중 하나이다. 영어는 기출 패턴 그대로 출제되는 경향을 보이므로 최근 출제 경향인 길어지는 독해지문에 대한 읽기능력 배양, 어휘 · 숙어와 생활영어, 암기가 아닌 구조 이해를 통한 문법과 영작 등 난도 있는 문제에 대비하는 학습이 필요하다.

9급 공무원 최근 7개년 기출문제 시리즈는 기출문제 완벽분석을 책임진다. 그동안 시행된 국가직 · 지방직 및 서울시 기출문제를 연도별로 수록하여 매년 빠지지 않고 출제되는 내용을 파악하고, 다양하게 변화하는 출제경향에 적응하여 단기간에 최대의 학습효과를 거둘 수 있도록 하였다. 또한 상세하고 꼼꼼한 해설로 기본서 없이도 효율적인 학습이 가능하도록 하였다.

9급 공무원 시험의 경쟁률이 해마다 점점 더 치열해지고 있다. 이럴 때일수록 기본적인 내용에 대한 탄탄한 학습이 빛을 발한다. 수험생 모두가 자신을 믿고 본서와 함께 끝까지 노력하여 합격의 결실을 맺기를 희망한다.

S tructure

● 기출문제 학습비법

step 01 '진짜' 기출문제 풀기 with 스톱워치

step 02 기출 포인트만 쏙쏙! 정답 및 해설

step 03 고득점을 위한 PLUS 오답노트

step 04 합격을 위한 반복학습

9급 영어 출제경향

공무원 영어 출제 유형은 크게 어휘 및 표현, 생활영어, 문법, 독해로 구분할 수 있다. 최근의 출제 경향을 보면 다른 유형들의 경우, 대개 기출 범위 내에서 출제되고 있어 충분한 대비가 가능하다. 하지만 독해의 경우 지문이 길어지거나 추상적·전문적 내용이 많거나, 혹은 논리적 사고를 요하는 문제 출제 비율이 높아지면 시험의 체감 난도가 크게 높아지므로 정확한 독해와 더불어 유형에 따른 풀이 방법을 익히는 것이 중요하다.

● 본서 특징 및 구성

최근 7개년 기출문제 수록

최신 기출문제를 비롯하여 그동안 시행되어 온 9급 공무원 국가직·지방직 및 서울시 등의 기출문제를 최다 수록하였다. 매년 시험마다 반복적으로 출제되는 핵심내용을 확인하고, 변화하는 출제경향을 파악하여 실제 시험에 대한 완벽대비를 할 수 있도록 구성하였다.

꼼꼼하고 자세한 해설

정답에 대한 상세한 해설을 통해 한 문제 한 문제에 대한 완전학습을 꾀하였다. 정답에 대한 설명뿐만 아니라 오답에 대한 보충 설명도 첨부하여 따로 이론서를 찾아볼 필요 없이 효율적인 학습이 될 수 있도록 구성하였다.

C ontents

7개년
기출문제

1 다음 이메일의 제목으로 가장 적절한 것은?

> Subject:_____
>
> Inspired by the Special Olympics, this year's theme highlights competitive and charitable sports situations among Liz Claiborne, Inc., employees, their families, their friends. You might snap a shot of a friend or employee participating in a walkathon to raise funds, a five-mile run, or a company volleyball or soccer game.
>
> All Liz Claiborne, Inc., employees worldwide are encouraged to submit photos. The first, second, and third prizes will again be $500, $250, and $100.
>
> Now's the time for you to start taking pictures focused on the spirit of competition for Liz Claiborne people and friends!
>
> Because of the overwhelming number of entries last year, we're making one contest change this year. For further information call Rosemary at Extension 7645.

① The Special Olympic: Time and Place

② Annual Photography Contest of Liz Claiborne

③ Liz Claiborne's Advanced Service Quality

④ The Keynote Speech on Christmas Day

2 밑줄 친 it이 가리키는 대상이 나머지 셋과 다른 것은?

Anger makes problems for relationships when there is too much of ① it, and when people are unable to control the way they express it, and become, for instance, argumentative, aggressive, or violent. It also causes problems when people cannot express their anger and try to keep ② it hidden. It is normal, however, to feel angry at times, and it can also have useful effects. Anger can mobilize you to take action, for example, to set limits to the demands others make of you, to think about why something matters to you or to defend yourself if attacked. ③ It can be constructively expressed, and prompt you to explain what ④ it is that is distressing or alarming you, and to ask for what you need.

3 다음 글의 내용으로 보아 글의 종류로 가장 적당한 것은?

Are you embarrassed by excessive body hair or body hair in the most awkward areas? Well, you can remove unsightly, unwanted hair with laser hair removal treatment. Laser hair removal is a safe and effective medical procedure that uses laser light to remove unwanted hair painlessly within a few minutes. During the procedure, the laser passes through the skin and hits the hair follicle where hair growth originates. Thereafter, the intense heat destroys the hair follicle instantly, clearing the skin of any hair. Treat your legs, armpits, upper lip, chin, bikini line, and any other area. You can finally be free of unwanted body hair, so call our clinic today for more information.

① essay   ② novel
③ advertisement   ④ article

4 다음 글에서 필자가 주장하는 바로 가장 적절한 것은?

'Zero tolerance' is a phrase that first came to light as a description of the crackdown on trivial crime. The aim of zero tolerance is to prevent petty criminals graduating to serious crime by imposing immediate and harsh sentences for trivial offences such as under-age drinking, small-scale drug use and dealing, shoplifting or vandalism. I think 'Zero tolerance' is an innovative and effective weapon to fight against crime. It sends a clear, tough message that the state will condemn and punish rather than be soft and 'understanding'. This stance functions as an effective deterrent to potential offenders, especially potential young offenders, and also raises public confidence in the police and judiciary.

① 훈화를 통해 잘못을 개선시킴이 가장 중요하다.
② 범죄에 맞선 다양한 대처 방안이 필요하다.
③ 재활센터를 운영해 범법자가 사회에 적응할 수 있도록 도와야 한다.
④ 정부는 소소한 범죄 행위에도 강력하게 대처하여야 한다.

5 다음 글의 밑줄 친 부분 중 어법상 가장 옳지 않은 것은?

Across the nation, East Timor ① has been involved in conflicts for more than 30 years to gain independence from Indonesia. In a ② war-torn country, people with intellectual challenges are often forgotten and abandoned. Alcino Pereira, an intellectually challenged orphan from East Timor, ③ who is unable to speak, has never had access to health care. He can use one of his arms but only in a very limited way and walks with a limp. ④ Although these intellectual and physical challenges, he loves to run. In his worn-out shoes, Pereira runs every day in his home town of Dili. So he got his nickname, the "running man."

6 다음 글에 드러난 'I'의 심경으로 가장 적절한 것은?

I still remember the incident that happened last summer. We were staying at a country inn that had a small movie theater. Before every evening's presentation, my husband and I instructed our three-year-old son to sit quietly. Except for an occasional whispered question, he concentrated on the movie quietly. The soundtrack, however, was impossible to hear. That's because two children bounced on their seats, talked loudly and raced up and down the aisles. Never once did I see their parents. After several evenings of this, I followed the children to the dining room. There sat their parents enjoying a relaxed meal.

① annoyed and irritated

② regretful and apologetic

③ cold and indifferent

④ frightened and scared

7 다음 글의 제목으로 가장 적절한 것은?

A common but seriously hindering medical condition, stuttering is something that everyone wants to avoid if possible. Some people simply have a genetic predisposition towards stuttering, but there are other factors that contribute to it, though only a few are well understood. Learning a new language is often the cause for stuttering in children, but this is a rather benign form of stuttering. Some people have neurological problems that inhibit the proper brain functions regarding speech, and these problems are often the result of a stroke, accident, or some other trauma. However, the problem might be psychological, too, such as a severe lack of self-confidence or the presence of disproportionate stress. Also, behavioral disorders like autism and attention deficit disorder can lead to the speech disorder.

① The Common Symptoms of Stuttering

② Various Causes of Stuttering Conditions

③ The Factors that Aggravate Stuttering

④ The Harmful Effects of Stuttering

8 다음 글의 빈칸에 들어갈 말로 가장 적절한 것은?

Have you ever stopped and spent some time thinking about the two amazing machines located at the ends of your arms? Your hands are really incredible: they work all day, hardly ever taking a break, but they rarely get tired. And not only are your hands strong, they are also _____. Think about all the different things they do! They knock on doors and turn doorknobs. If you're hungry, they'll take the lid off a cookie jar and then put the cookies to your mouth! And if you are good at computer games, you can thank your hands for that, too. Whatever you are doing, your hands can help you.

① versatile   ② tangible

③ eligible   ④ genuine

9 다음 밑줄 친 단어의 쓰임이 적절하지 않은 것은?

Euphemisms are also problematic for English learners because they often contain more difficult words than their more direct ① counterparts. Learners of English, for instance, have to memorize that an old person can be referred to as "a senior citizen," while a police officer can be described as "a law-enforcement officer." They also have to learn to use euphemisms like "② vertically challenged" when they can get by with "short."

Despite the burden that euphemisms pose on learners of English, it is clear that euphemisms are tools which allow us to talk about all kinds of things in ③ impolite ways. As old euphemisms fall out of use and new ones come into use, English is ever ④ evolving to handle every situation, pleasant or unpleasant.

10 글의 흐름으로 보아, 주어진 문장이 들어가기에 가장 알맞은 곳은?

> She recommended better meal planning, more protein and fresh vegetables, and supplements containing B vitamins, magnesium, and F-theanine.

Angie was always anxious and impatient. She regularly skipped meals and ended up driving through fast-food restaurants to eat just as her blood sugar was crashing. (①) Then she usually felt fuzzy brained and wanted to take a nap. (②) She eventually sought the advice of a nutritionally oriented physician for her bouts of fatigue. (③) Her response to eating more protein — a rotisserie chicken and steamed vegetables on the first day — was nothing short of dramatic. (④) Several months later, Angie's sister described her as a new person — she slept more soundly and woke up feeling alert and energetic.

11 다음 글의 빈칸에 들어갈 말로 가장 적절한 것은?

> In a new study, it was found that species that live in restrictive environments such as the tropics cannot adapt to a changing climate as well as species in more diverse environments. The reason is _____. A species adapts to its environment and becomes better at surviving by undergoing physical and behavioral changes. These usually occur due to a gene mutation. If a species already has a more varied set of genes, it is more like to undergo the necessary changes. However, species in the tropics have less varied sets of genes.

① destroyed environment

② isolation from their habitat

③ attack from their predators

④ the lack of variation in their genes

12 다음 글의 주제로 가장 적절한 것은?

Scientists are currently studying the navigational systems and locomotive strategies of insects to help design the next generation of autonomous robots and vehicles. Also, researchers have recently found that the flipper of the humpback whale is a more efficient wing design than the current model used by the aeronautics industry on airplanes. They are working to apply their findings to future airplane and automotive design. Similarly, engineers have used the rough skin of the shark as inspiration in developing a ridged foil coating for the wings of aircraft, a design which has resulted in six percent less friction and improved fuel efficiency.

① Borrowing from Nature
② The Wonders of Nature
③ The Future of Aerospace Industry
④ Why We Should Preserve Wild Life

13 주어진 글 다음에 이어질 글의 순서는?

President Roosevelt openly blamed the greed of many Americans for the Depression and acted to rectify the problem. At that time, people with a lot of currency or gold hoarded them and did not put them into banks because of the fear of losing their money.

(A) It also allowed the government to seize the gold of private citizens in exchange for paper money.
(B) This made the Depression worse because banks had no money and were forced to close.
(C) In response, Roosevelt enacted the "Emergency Banking Act" which worked to shut down insolvent banks so that they could be reconstructed.

① (B) — (A) — (C)
② (B) — (C) — (A)
③ (C) — (A) — (B)
④ (C) — (B) — (A)

14 다음 글의 목적으로 가장 적절한 것은?

> Feel like a cup of tea, but don't have the time to brew one up? Take a "tea pill" instead. Indian tea scientists have produced a tea-flavored pill that can be chewed or quickly dissolved in hot or cold water. The brownish tablet weighs 0.3 grams and is composed of 80 percent tea and 20 percent their flavors. The inventors at the research center say that it peps you up just like a traditional tea. "You can suck it, chew it, or dissolve it in water the way you like to have it, and still feel the taste of a real cup of tea," they said. "As the liquid tea refreshes, this tea pill will also refresh people because it contains pure tea ingredients." They said the center had applied for a patent, and that the pill should hit the market in six months.

① 차의 성분과 효능을 알리려고
② 차의 유래와 역사를 설명하려고
③ 약 복용 시 주의사항을 알리려고
④ 새로 시판될 알약 형태의 차를 소개하려고

15 다음 중 글의 내용과 일치하지 않는 것은?

> Heart attacks, which take about 550,000 lives each year, occur when the coronary arteries that supply blood to the heart muscle become obstructed. Without oxygen and other nutrients carried in the blood, heart tissue dies or is damaged. If too much tissue is affected, the heart is so weakened that it cannot pump. But even mild damage can kill by disrupting the electrical impulses that govern the heart's rhythmic beating. Each year, stroke claims another 170,000 lives, and is also caused by impeded blood flow, this time to the brain.
>
> * coronary artery : 심장의 관상동맥

① 심장마비는 관상동맥이 막힐 때 발생한다.
② 산소가 없으면, 심장 조직이 손상을 입는다.
③ 심장 조직이 약간 손상되는 경우에는 큰 위험이 없다.
④ 뇌졸중은 매년 170,000명의 생명을 앗아간다.

16 다음 밑줄 친 부분 중, 지칭하는 대상이 나머지 셋과 다른 하나는?

It's my Aunt Grace's practice to travel by bus and to notice what ① <u>most people</u> miss. One Saturday morning the 144 bus passed a busy intersection. She saw two young girls outfitted for camping. They looked nervous. When her bus arrived at the next intersection, she saw two young men outfitted in the same manner standing by a car. They were waiting for an appointment. Grace got off the bus and approached the young men. They spoke to her in a foreign accent. Grace described the girls she had seen, and the young men left. When ② <u>the small happy band</u> returned to thank her, what she had supposed was confirmed. There had, indeed, been a mix-up! Anxious to return good for good, ③ <u>the chattering little group</u> insisted they be allowed to take her home. Grace refused. Instead, the young people crossed the avenue to gift shop and returned with a little cotton elephant. Now there is a remembrance in Grace's apartment, but there are also ④ <u>four young people</u> who are bound to remember a friendly lady.

17 다음 글의 빈칸에 들어갈 말로 가장 적절한 것은?

Despite progress in the field of child and adolescent mental health, millions of young people every year do not get proper help. Only one in five children with a serious emotional disturbance actually uses specialized mental health services. Although today, child welfare services, the juvenile justice system, and our schools often provide care to children in need, none of these institutions has as its first priority the delivery of mental health care. In addition, the complexity of promoting collaboration across agency lines of all professionals serving the same child is daunting. All too often there is no cooperation, not enough money, and limited access to trained mental health professionals — and children and their families _____.

① require their rights

② receive good health services

③ suffer the tragic consequences

④ are reluctant to go to hospitals

18 다음 글의 밑줄 친 부분 중, 어법상 가장 옳지 않은 것은?

People who are satisfied appreciate what they have in life and don't worry about how it compares to ① which others have. Valuing what you have over what you do not or cannot have ② leads to greater happiness. Four-year-old Alice runs to the Christmas tree and sees wonderful presents beneath it. No doubt she has received fewer presents ③ than some of her friends, and she probably has not received some of the things she most wanted. But at that moment, she doesn't ④ stop to think why there aren't more presents or to wonder what she may have asked for that she didn't get. Instead, she marvels at the treasures before her.

19 주어진 문장에 이어질 글의 순서로 가장 적절한 것은?

It would be hard to find anything more controversial than the subject of cloning. People find it either totally fantastic or totally frightening.

(A) But for most people, the cloning of humans is different. The idea of duplicating human beings the same way we make copies of book pages on a copy machine is terrible.

(B) In addition, it could be useful in increasing the world's food supply by the cloning of animals. Bigger and healthier animals could be produced.

(C) Cloning holds the promise of cures for what are now incurable diseases, sight for the blind, hearing for the deaf, new organs to replace old worn-out ones.

① (A) - (C) - (B)
② (B) - (A) - (C)
③ (C) - (A) - (B)
④ (C) - (B) - (A)

20 글의 흐름상 밑줄 친 부분이 문맥에 맞지 않는 것은?

Britain caused hardship in the Indian cloth industry by putting a 30 percent import tax on Indian cloth. This made Indian cloth too ① <u>expensive</u> to sell in Britain. When the Indian lost their British customers, their cloth industry was ruined. Then British cloth factories profited by selling British cloth to the Indians. The Indian people were ② <u>discontent</u> under British rule. In 1930 Mohandas Gandhi took up the cause of Indian independence. He encouraged Indians to protest in nonviolent ways. He encouraged them not to pay taxes to the British, and he ③ <u>resisted</u> a boycott of British-made product. After great struggle, both nonviolent and violent, the British ④ <u>withdrew</u>, and in 1947 India became a self-governing, independent country.

① expensive 　　　　　　② discontent

③ resisted 　　　　　　④ withdrew

21 다음 글의 제목으로 가장 알맞은 것은?

A study by the USA's Northwestern University provides biological evidence that people who are bilingual have a more powerful brain. Drs Viorica Marian and Nina Kraus investigated how bilingualism affects the brain. They found that studying another language "fine-tunes" people's attention span and enhances their memory. In particular they discovered that when language learners attempt to understand speech in another language, it activates and energizes the brainstem – an ancient part of the brain. Professor Kraus stated : "Bilingualism serves as enrichment for the brain and has real consequences when it comes to attention and working memory."

① The Effect of Bilingualism on Brain

② Tips for Learning Foreign Languages

③ The Negative Effect of Bilingualism

④ The Necessity of Learning Foreign Languages

22 다음 문장이 들어갈 위치로 가장 적절한 곳은?

> However, poor people began making their own boxes and asking employers and customers for money in recognition of their service.

> Have you ever heard of Boxing Day? It's a holiday celebrated in the United Kingdom and British Commonwealth countries on December 26 every year.
> (①) Some people say that the ancient Roman tradition of gift giving during the winter festival inspired Boxing Day, but no one knows for certain. (②) This gift giving eventually took the form of placing alms boxes in churches on Christmas Day so that people could drop coins into them for later distribution to poor people. These early "Christmas Boxes" were made of clay and had holes cut in their tops but no 'stoppers' at the bottoms. It was "smashing fun" opening them! (③) During the seventeenth century, the alms-box of giving stopped.
> (④) From that time on, it became a tradition to give money to delivery people and other service workers on Boxing Day.

23 다음 (A), (B), (C)에서 문맥에 맞는 낱말로 가장 적절한 것은?

> Companies often seek the services of well-known sports or entertainment personalities to promote their products. Although this is a good practice when the person embodies wholesome qualities, it can backfire when the person engages in scandalous or (A) [moral / immoral] behavior. In such cases, the public comes to associate antisocial behavior with the product, and will avoid buying it. It is advisable that before deciding whom to star, a complete background check be made. If a person has exhibited (B) [desirable / undesirable] behavior in the past, he will probably exhibit undesirable behavior in the future. Also, the contract should cancel automatically, should the personality bring (C) [credit / discredit] to the product advertised.

	(A)	(B)	(C)
①	moral	desirable	credit
②	moral	desirable	discredit
③	immoral	undesirable	credit
④	immoral	undesirable	discredit

24 주어진 글 다음에 이어질 글의 순서는?

The only way for different marine animals to survive in their harsh aquatic environment is to help each other. This is especially true in the case of the clownfish and the poisonous sea anemone.

(A) Other fish, fearing the anemone's poison, won't attack the clownfish there.

(B) On the other hand, the anemone benefits by eating leftover food provided by the clownfish.

(C) In return for cleaning the anemone, the clownfish, which is not affected by the anemone's poison, lives safely among the animal's tentacles.

① (B) − (A) − (C)　　　　② (B) − (C) − (A)

③ (C) − (A) − (B)　　　　④ (C) − (B) − (A)

25 다음 글의 요지로 가장 적절한 것은?

ABC Airlines uses the same scent everywhere, for instance, in the perfume worn by its flight attendants, in its hot towels, and in other elements of its service. Among the sensory elements, using a scent is a relatively recent marketing strategy adopted by many retailers. More and more research shows that smell affects consumer behavior, which stimulates the demand for scent marketing by stores, hotels, and even museums. Advertising studies in Martin Lindstrom's book Brand Sense suggest that although most contemporary commercial messages are aimed at our eyes, many of the emotional moments people remember on a given day are actually prompted by smell.

① Certain scents energize us for work.

② Sense of sight is mightier than sense of smell.

③ The demand for scent marketing is increasing.

④ Our sense of smell becomes dull over the years.

☞ 정답 및 해설 P.9

1 다음 빈칸에 들어갈 말로 가장 적절한 것은?

> Please _____ from smoking in the restaurant, as it disturbs other people.

① refrain　　　　　　　　　　② remove

③ convert　　　　　　　　　　④ exclude

2 다음 빈칸에 들어갈 말로 가장 적절한 것은?

> Initial decision-making and actions vary _____ the nature and type of the incident.

① in honor of　　　　　　　　② on behalf of

③ for the sake of　　　　　　　④ according to

3 다음 빈칸에 들어갈 말로 가장 적절한 것은?

> A : Hi Josh. How is it going?
> B : Not so good. I think I need a new job.
> A : What's the problem? Is it the people you work with?
> B : No, my coworkers are fine, but _____.
> A : Maybe you should start looking for a more interesting job.
> B : You are right. I can probably find something better.

① my workplace is too far from home

② I think my salary is too low

③ I do the same thing everyday

④ I am too busy to find free time

4 다음 빈칸에 순서대로 들어갈 말로 가장 적절한 것은?

> As a police officer, your job is to arrest those who _____ crime and protect _____ of crime.

① act − people

② experience − perpetrators

③ commit − victims

④ compare − criminals

5 주어진 설명이 뜻하는 단어로서 예문의 빈칸에 들어갈 말로 가장 적절한 것은?

> 설명 : a commission or document giving authority to do something
>
> 예문 : The police had a _____ for his arrest.

① bail
② custody
③ warrant
④ restraint

6 다음 빈칸에 들어갈 말로 가장 적절한 것은?

> Inspector Javert discovered that Monsieur Madeleine was not the mayor's real name but an _____ for Jean Valijean, the ex-convict.

① alias
② alchemist
③ apprentice
④ avarice

7 다음 두 문장의 빈칸에 공통으로 들어갈 말로 가장 적절한 것은?

> • He was sentenced _____ three years in prison.
> • When polite requests failed, he resorted _____ threats.

① in
② on
③ to
④ for

8 다음 빈칸에 순서대로 들어갈 말로 가장 적절한 것은?

> As Max Weber pointed out, we perceive power — the ability to get your way, even over the resistance of other — as either legitimate or illegitimate. Legitimate power is called _____. This is power that people accept as right. In contrast, illegitimate power called _____ is power that people do not accept as just.

① automation – dictatorship

② coercion – authority

③ dictatorship – automation

④ authority – coercion

9 다음 빈칸에 순서대로 들어갈 말로 가장 적절한 것은?

> • Global warming has led to an increase _____ temperatures and sea levels, and much less polar ice.
> • The big problem is _____ I don't get many chances to speak the language.
> • I am very careful with my money and I enjoy _____ a bargain when I go shopping.

① on – when – find

② in – that – finding

③ to – what – to find

④ with – whether – found

10 다음 빈칸에 들어갈 말로 가장 적절한 것은?

> A : Do you like Peter's new suit?
> B : Yes, I think it makes _____ handsome.

① him look

② he looks

③ him to look

④ he is

11 다음 빈칸에 순서대로 들어갈 말로 가장 적절한 것은?

> A : Mom, my stomach _____.
> B : Do you _____ a fever?
> A : No, I don't think so.
> B : Do you _____ nauseous?
> A : No, not at all. But you know, I did have potato chips and peanut butter for dinner.

① hurts – feel – have   ② feels – have – hurt

③ has – feel – hurt   ④ hurts – have – feel

12 다음 글의 제목으로 가장 적절한 것은?

> The Great Depression began in late 1929 and lasted for about a decade. Many factors played a role in bringing about the depression. One was the greatly unequal distribution of wealth throughout the 1920's, and the other was excessive stock market expansion.

① The cause of the Great Depression

② The definition of the Great Depression

③ The prospect of the Great Depression

④ The rule of the Great Depression

13 다음 글에서 밑줄 친 them이 가리키는 말로 가장 적절한 것은?

Bats fly like birds, but they are mammals. Female bats give birth to live young and produce milk. Bats are nocturnal, searching for food at night and sleeping during the day. They roost upside down in dark, quiet places such as caves and attics. People think that bats drink blood, but only vampire bats do this. Most bats eat fruit or insects. As bats fly, they make high-pitched sounds that bounce off objects. This echolocation is a kind of radar that guides them.

① people
② bats
③ high-pitched sounds
④ insects

14 다음 글의 흐름으로 보아 (A), (B), (C)에 들어가기에 가장 적절한 말로 짝지은 것은?

Cats have a memory for things that are important to their lives. Some cats seem to have extraordinary memories for finding places. Taken away from their homes, they seem (A) [able / unable] to remember where they live. The key to this homing ability could be a built-in celestial navigation, similar to that used by birds, or the cats' navigational ability could be (B) [distributed / attributed] to the cats' sensitivity to Earth's magnetic fields. When magnets are attached to cats, their normal navigational skills are (C) [enhanced / disrupted].

	(A)	(B)	(C)
①	able	distributed	enhanced
②	able	attributed	disrupted
③	unable	attributed	enhanced
④	unable	distributed	disrupted

15 다음 글의 종류로 가장 적절한 것은?

Here, you can meet people who make traditional crafts. You'll find presents that are perfect for all your friends. We have clay pottery and beautiful leather bags. Try on a pair of sandals made of straw or a wood mask used in old dances. Bamboo crafts like boxes and baskets are famous in Korea. Korea also has great artists who make things with metal like gold necklaces and brass bowls. You can even take home a stone statue. Come and visit to the Korean Folk Village!

① autobiography　　　　　　　　② novel

③ obituary　　　　　　　　　　　④ advertisement

16 다음 글에 드러난 Sally의 심경으로 가장 적절한 것은?

Suddenly, Sally heard a voice. "Good afternoon, Let's start with Afternoon of a Faun, please," the voice repeated wearily. Sally's heart began to pound. She spread her music out on the music stand slowly. A lifetime of preparation, four long weeks of intensive practice, and it all came down to this moment. She felt sweat rolling down on her back. She lifted the flute to her lips, took a deep breath, and began to play. The opening notes of Afternoon of a Faun came from her flute, but her two hands that were holding it were still trembling.

① nervous　　　　　　　　　　② relieved

③ satisfied　　　　　　　　　　④ sympathetic

※ 다음 글을 읽고 물음에 답하시오. 【17~18】

A feminist is not a man-hater, a masculine woman, or someone who dislikes housewives. A feminist is simply a woman or man who believes that women should enjoy the same rights, privileges, and opportunities _____ men. Because society has deprived women of many equal rights, feminists have fought for equality. _____, Susan B. Anthony, a famous nineteenth century feminist, worked to get women the right to vote. Today, feminists want women to receive equal pay for equal work. They support a woman's right to pursue her goals and dreams, whether she wants to be an astronaut, athlete, or full-time homemaker. Because the term is often misunderstood, some people don't call themselves feminists _____ they share feminist values.

17 윗글의 빈칸에 들어갈 말의 순서로 가장 적절한 것은?

① like - In contrast - if

② as - For instance - even though

③ to - However - as

④ in - By the way - when

18 윗글의 제목으로 가장 적절한 것은?

① Diversity of Women's Careers

② History of Feminist Movement

③ Women's Rights in the Near Future

④ What a True Feminist Is

19 다음 빈칸에 들어갈 말로 가장 적절한 것은?

> The public has every right to expect that police powers are used professionally and with integrity, irrespective of who is being dealt with. In other words, the same (㉠) should be used by police officers whether dealing with a duke or a dustman, a fellow officer or a villain. Additionally, some people who come into contact with the police may be (㉡), and officers have a requirement to support and protect them. This is especially important when (㉡) witnesses, such as victims of domestic violence, feel very frightened or inhibited — often after years of abuse — about making an allegation against an abuser.

	㉠	㉡
①	freedom	absolute
②	impartiality	vulnerable
③	prudence	adamant
④	sincerity	inquisitive

20 다음 글을 읽고, 본문의 내용과 가장 일치하지 않은 것은?

> Two women were upstairs in a townhouse when they heard their roommate, a third woman, being attacked downstairs by intruders. They phoned the police several times and were assured that officers were on the way. After about 30 minutes, when their roommate's screams had stopped, they assumed the police had finally arrived. When the two women went downstairs, they saw that in fact the police never came, but the intruders were still there. As the Warren court states in the opinion: For the next fourteen hours the women were held captive, robbed, and beaten. The three women sued the District of Columbia(D.C.) for failing to protect them, but D.C.'s highest court pardoned the District and its police, saying that it is a "fundamental principle of American law that a government and its agents are under no general duty to provide public services, such as police protection, to any individual citizen."

① 법원은 경찰에게 면죄부를 주었다.
② 괴한들이 3명의 여자가 있는 가택을 침입하였다.
③ 법적으로 경찰은 모든 시민을 보호할 의무가 있다.
④ 전화 신고를 받은 경찰은 즉시 출동하지 않았다.

※ 밑줄 친 부분에 들어갈 표현으로 가장 적절한 것을 고르시오. 【1~4】

1

In his book, Marco Polo does not mention the important invention of paper, which was first introduced by the Chinese. The Moors, having been taught by Chinese paper makers, brought paper into Europe. By the twelfth century Spain and then France knew the art of paper-making, thanks to their Moorish invaders. However, at that time, most of the European printing continued to be done on parchment, since the paper was considered too _____.

① convenient ② durable

③ fragile ④ fervent

2

Unless disposed of in a responsible way, batteries are detrimental to the environment and humans. That's because batteries sometimes contain heavy metals, which, if _____, don't really leave the organism's body.

① ingested ② disgusted

③ suggested ④ evacuated

3

The exhibitors at the trade fair _____ free samples to stimulate interest.

① pull through ② pass out

③ put aside ④ pay for

4

My mother does not like sports. That's why she walks out of the room whenever my father _____ sports.

① turns down   ② catches out

③ brings up   ④ copes with

※ 밑줄 친 부분 중 어법상 옳지 않은 것을 고르시오. 【5~6】

5

Sometimes a sentence fails to say ① <u>what</u> you mean because its elements don't make proper connections. Then you have to revise by shuffling the components around, ② <u>juxtapose</u> those that should link, and separating those that should not. To get your meaning across, you not only have to choose the right words, but you have to put ③ <u>them</u> in the right order. Words in disarray ④ <u>produce</u> only nonsense.

① what   ② juxtapose

③ them   ④ produce

6

When I was growing up, many people asked me ① <u>if</u> I was going to follow in my father's footsteps, to be a teacher. As a kid, I remember ② <u>saying</u>, "No way. I'm going to go into business." Years later I found out that I actually love teaching. I enjoyed teaching because I taught in the method ③ <u>in which</u> I learn best. I learn best via games, cooperative competition, group discussion, and lessons. Instead of punishing mistakes, I encouraged mistakes. Instead of asking students to take the test on their own, they ④ <u>required</u> to take tests as a team. In other words, action first, mistakes second, lessons third, laughter fourth.

① if   ② saying

③ in which   ④ required

7 ① 그가 전화를 하고 나서야 나는 지갑을 잃어버린 것을 알았다.

　　→I did realize I had lost my wallet until he called me.

② 그를 보는 순간, 그가 범인이라는 감이 왔다.

　　→The moment I saw him, I had a feeling that he was the criminal.

③ 그는 대통령 선거에서 누가 이기든 상관하지 않을 것이다.

　　→He won't care who wins the presidential election.

④ 초록 단추를 눌러야 한다. 그렇지 않으면 작동하지 않을 것이다.

　　→You have to press the green button; otherwise it won't work.

8 ① 당신은 그 영화를 봤어야 했다.

　　→You should have watched the movie.

② 당신을 성공으로 이끄는 것은 재능이 아니라 열정이다.

　　→It is not talent but passion that leads you to success.

③ 시간을 엄수하는 것은 모든 사람들이 갖추어야 할 미덕이다.

　　→Being punctual is the virtue everyone has to have.

④ 사람들은 나이가 들면서 엄해지는 경향이 있다.

　　→People tend to be strict as though they got old.

※ 밑줄 친 부분에 들어갈 표현으로 가장 적절한 것을 고르시오. 【9~10】

9

> A : I'll let you into a secret.
> B : What's that?
> A : I heard your boss will be fired soon.
> B : It can't be true. How is that happening?
> A : It's true. This is strictly between us. OK?
> B : All right. _____

① I'll spell it.

② I can't share that with you.

③ I'll keep it to myself.

④ I heard it through the grapevine.

10

> A : It's so hot in here! Do you have air-conditioning in your apartment?
> B : You see that air-conditioner over there? But the problem is, it's not powerful enough.
> A : I see.
> B : But I don't care, cause I'm going to move out anyway.
> A : _____
> B : Well, I had to wait until the lease expired.

① You should've moved out a long time ago.

② You should've turned it on.

③ You should've bought another one.

④ You should've asked the landlord to buy one.

※ 다음 글의 요지로 가장 적절한 것을 고르시오. 【11~12】

11

There is widespread fear among policy makers and the public today that the family is disintegrating. Much of that anxiety stems from a basic misunderstanding of the nature of the family in the past and a lack of appreciation for its resiliency in response to broad social and economic changes. The general view of the family is that it has been a stable and relatively unchanging institution through history and is only now undergoing changes; in fact, change has always been characteristic of it.

① The structure of the family is disintegrating.

② The traditional family system cannot adapt to broad social changes.

③ Contrary to the general view, change has always characterized the family.

④ The family has been a stable unit but is undergoing changes nowadays.

12

Biologists often say that the tallest tree in the forest is the tallest not just because it grew from the hardiest seed. They say that is also because no other trees blocked its sunlight, the soil around it was rich, no rabbit chewed through its bark, and no lumberjack cut it down before it matured. We all know that successful people come from hardy seeds. But do we know enough about the sunlight that warmed them, the soil where they put down the roots, and the rabbits and lumberjacks they were lucky enough to avoid? They are beneficiary of hidden advantages and extraordinary opportunities and cultural legacies.

① Success comes through the disadvantages.

② Heroes are born in bad circumstances.

③ Success arises out of the accumulation of advantages.

④ Success depends on the efforts of the individual.

※ 다음 글의 제목으로 가장 적절한 것을 고르시오. 【13~14】

13

The digital world offers us many advantages, but if we yield to that world too completely we may lose the privacy we need to develop a self. Activities that require time and careful attention, like serious reading, are at risk; we read less and skim more as the Internet occupies more of our lives. And there's a link between self-hood and reading slowly, rather than scanning for quick information, as the Web encourages us to do. Recent work in sociology and psychology suggests that reading books, a private experience, is an important aspect of coming to know who we are.

① In Praise of Slow Reading
② In Praise of Artificial Memory
③ In Praise of Digital World
④ In Praise of Private Life

14

The heavy eye make-up favored by ancient Egyptians may have been good for the eyes. Lead is usually a risk to health. But the study by French scientists published in the journal Analytical Chemistry suggests that the lead salt in the cosmetics helps prevent and treat eye illness. At very low levels, salts promote the action of cells in the immune system to fight off bacteria that can cause eye infections. The scientists from the Louvre Museum and the CNRS research institute also found that the lead salts found in the make-up could actually have a positive effect to protect people against eye disease.

① Egyptians Suffering from Lead
② Eye Make-up Has Health Benefits
③ Eye Make-up Causes Eye Infections
④ Cosmetics Attract People's Attention

15 다음 문장이 들어갈 위치로 가장 적절한 것은?

Such large numbers are necessary since blood reserves are perishable and constantly need to be replenished.

New York City Blood Center has experienced a constant shortage in blood donation. (A) To meet the needs, approximately 2,000 people need to donate blood every day to maintain its supplies. (B) One pint of donated blood can save up to three lives. (C) And one out of every three people will need a life-saving transfusion at some point in their lifetimes. (D) Donate blood through the New York City Blood Center.

① A

② B

③ C

④ D

※ 밑줄 친 부분에 들어갈 표현으로 가장 적절한 것을 고르시오. 【16~17】

16

In fact, newspapers and magazines often stress that they print the news "straight." But the big problem is that there is the variable of human observation. For example, suppose 10 people view an accident, and afterwards, they are interviewed by a reporter. Each one offers a slightly different version. The overlap and its consistencies in their views all go into reconstructing what happened. The absolute truth is impossible to discover because each one saw the accident from a different position. In conclusion, many factors make it difficult to _____ the truth.

① conceal

② disapprove

③ distort

④ discriminate

17

Although intimately related, sensation and perception play two complementary but different roles in how we interpret our world. Sensation refers to the process of sensing our environment through touch, taste, sight, sound, and smell. This information is sent to our brains in raw form where perception comes into play. Perception is the way we interpret these sensations and therefore make sense of everything around us. To illustrate the difference between sensation and perception, take the example of a young baby. Its eyes take the same data as those of an adult. But its perception is entirely different because it has no idea of what it is looking at. With experience, perception enables us to assume that _____, even when we can only see part of it, creating useful information of the surroundings.

① the whole of an object is present

② objects are impossible to identify

③ optical illusion is caused by our brain

④ our perception gives us inadequate information

18 다음 글의 주제로 가장 적절한 것은?

According to Dr. Weil, green tea is prepared in a much more gentle fashion than ordinary black tea. Green tea leaves are steamed, rolled and dried to preserve the antioxidant compounds that give us health benefits. Dr. Weil suggests this antioxidant protects our heart by lowering cholesterol and boosting metabolism, and guards against cancer by removing radicals that can damage cells and push them in the direction of uncontrolled growth. Green tea also has antibacterial properties, which help prevent and fight illness. In China, green tea has been used as a medicine for at least 400 years, and numerous studies are reporting drinking green tea brings positive aspects to their health.

① advice for curing cancer

② food choices making us positive

③ manner of drinking and serving tea

④ health advantages of drinking green tea

19 다음 글의 addax에 대한 설명과 일치하지 않는 것은?

The addax is a large antelope with long and thin spiral horns with two and sometimes three twists. Its coat is grayish brown in the winter and changes to nearly white in the summer. The addax is a desert creature and hardly ever needs water except from the drops of water it gets from eating plants. The addax prefers to travel through the desert at night in search of sparse vegetation in the desert that manages to grow during rainfall. It is believed that the female gives birth to just one calf after a pregnant period of 8 to 9 months. There are only a few hundred left in the wild. Excessive hunting for its flesh and hide seems to be the main cause of decline for the addax.

① 여름에는 털이 거의 흰색으로 변한다.
② 식물을 통해 다량의 물을 섭취한다.
③ 식물을 찾기 위해 밤에 사막을 돌아다니는 것을 좋아한다.
④ 암컷은 한 번에 새끼를 한 마리씩 낳는다고 여겨진다.

20 다음 글의 ㉠, ㉡에 들어갈 가장 적절한 것은?

In the mid to late 1990s, Brazil was one of Latin America's fastest growing economies and "was the darling of the international investment community." In particular, the country's middle class was experiencing significant work-related opportunities to improve its standard of living. _____㉠_____, the effects of late-1990 economic "meltdowns" in Russia and Asia were crippling for the Brazilian economy. _____㉡_____, the global economic turmoil resulted in a decline in sales of 27.5 percent from 1997 to 1998 for Brazil's automobile industry alone. In response to the nation's crisis, the country's president instituted a major currency devaluation. In 1998, employers eliminated over 580,000 jobs. The fortunes of the middle class became bleak as job losses found them unable to cope with the demands of financial purchases they made during the "good times."

	㉠	㉡
①	However	Nevertheless
②	However	For example
③	Therefore	Similarly
④	Therefore	On the other han

1 밑줄 친 부분에 가장 적절한 것은?

> Before she traveled to Mexico last winter, she needed to _____ her Spanish because she had not practiced it since college.

① make up to

② brush up on

③ shun away from

④ come down with

2 밑줄 친 부분과 의미가 가장 가까운 것은?

> I was told to let Jim <u>pore over</u> computer printouts.

① examine

② distribute

③ discard

④ correct

3 밑줄 친 부분과 의미가 가장 가까운 것은?

> Johannes Kepler believed that there would one day be "celestial ships with sails adapted to the winds of heaven" navigating the sky, filled with explorers "who would not fear the vastness" of space. And today those explorers, human and robot, employ as <u>unerring</u> guides on their voyages through the vastness of space the three laws of planetary motion that Kepler uncovered during a lifetime of personal travail and ecstatic discovery.

① faultless

② unreliable

③ gutless

④ unscientific

4 다음 빈칸에 들어갈 단어가 순서대로 짝지어진 것은?

> Visitors at Disneyland pay a high admission price and wait hours for rides that last no more than five minutes. Why do they respond so well to a situation that might otherwise cause great (㉠)? One reason is that the theme park provides extra service wherever they can. They lend cameras at no (㉡) to their guests at designated photo sites. People remember the fun picture with Mickey Mouse and forget the long lines. Clean facilities and friendly staff also go far to (㉢) the negative experiences.

	㉠	㉡	㉢
①	dissemination	chance	evoke
②	dissemination	charge	erase
③	dissatisfaction	charge	erase
④	dissatisfaction	chance	evoke

5 우리말을 영어로 잘못 옮긴 것은?

① 그녀는 등산은 말할 것도 없고, 야외에 나가는 것을 좋아하지 않는다.

→She does not like going outdoor, not to mention mountain climbing.

② 그녀는 학급에서 가장 예쁜 소녀이다.

→She is more beautiful than any other girl in the class.

③ 그 나라는 국토의 3/4이 바다로 둘러싸여 있는 소국이다.

→The country is a small one with the three quarters of the land surrounding by the sea.

④ 많은 학생들이 졸업 후 취직을 위해 열심히 공부한다.

→A number of students are studying very hard to get a job after their graduation.

6 밑줄 친 부분에 가장 적절한 것은?

> A : I saw the announcement for your parents' 25th anniversary in yesterday's newspaper. It was really neat. Do you know how your parents met?
>
> B : Yes. It was really incredible, actually, very romantic. They met in college, found they were compatible, and began to date. Their courtship lasted all through school.
>
> A : No kidding! That's really beautiful. I haven't noticed anyone in class that I could fall in love with!
>
> B : _____. Oh, well, maybe next semester!

① Me neither

② You shouldn't blame me

③ It is up to your parents

④ You'd better hang about with her

7 밑줄 친 부분에 가장 적절한 것은?

> A : Did you see Steve this morning?
>
> B : Yes. But why does he _____?
>
> A : I don't have the slightest idea.
>
> B : I thought he'd be happy.
>
> A : Me too. Especially since he got promoted to sales manager last week.
>
> B : He may have some problem with his girlfriend.

① have such a long face

② step into my shoes

③ jump on the bandwagon

④ play a good hand

8 어법상 옳은 것은?

① While worked at a hospital, she saw her first air show.

② However weary you may be, you must do the project.

③ One of the exciting games I saw were the World Cup final in 2010.

④ It was the main entrance for that she was looking.

9 밑줄 친 부분 중 어법상 옳은 것은?

Compared to newspapers, magazines are not necessarily up-to-the-minute, since they do not appear every day, but weekly, monthly, or even less frequently. Even externally they are different from newspapers, mainly because magazines ①resemble like a book. The paper is thicker, photos are more colorful, and most of the articles are relatively long. The reader experiences much more background information and greater detail. There are also weekly news magazines, ②which reports on a number of topics, but most of the magazines are specialized to attract various consumers. For example, there are ③women's magazines cover fashion, cosmetics, and recipes as well as youth magazines about celebrities. Other magazines are directed toward, for example, computer users, sports fans, ④those interested in the arts, and many other small groups.

10 밑줄 친 부분에 가장 적절한 것은?

Until recently many experts assumed that under the influence of universal literacy and mass media, regional dialects were being leveled. _____. Local identity and other social forces exert a stronger influence than even TV on how dialects evolve. The Inland North, the Midland, Canada, and the South are now more different from each other than ever.

① Absolutely true

② Too much so

③ Not so

④ Well enough

11 밑줄 친 부분에 가장 적절한 것은?

Body type was useless as a predictor of how the men would fare in life. So was birth order or political affiliation. Even social class had a limited effect. But having a warm childhood was powerful. It's not that the men who flourished had perfect childhoods. Rather, as Vaillant puts it, "What goes right is more important than what goes wrong." The positive effect of one loving relative, mentor or friend can _____ the negative effects of the bad things that happen.

① augment

② convene

③ vanquish

④ reinforce

12 주어진 글 다음에 이어질 글의 순서로 가장 적절한 것은?

It's amazing what a little free beer can accomplish. Samso, then known for its dairy and pig farms, would become Denmark's showcase for sustainable power, eventually going carbon-free. How that would happen, however, was far from clear, since the government initially offered no funding, tax breaks or technical expertise.

(A) So Hermansen showed up at every community or club meeting to give his pitch for going green. He pointed to the blustery island's untapped potential for wind power and the economic benefits of making Samso energy-independent. And he sometimes brought free beer.

(B) It worked. The islanders exchanged their oil-burning furnaces for centralized plants that burned leftover straw or wood chips to produce heat and hot water. They bought shares in new wind turbines, which generated the capital to build 11 large land-based turbines, enough to meet the entire island's electricity needs. Today Samso isn't just carbon-neutral — it actually produces 10% more clean electricity than it uses, with the extra power fed back into the grid at a profit.

(C) Given that almost all its power came from oil or coal — and the island's 4,300 residents didn't know a wind turbine from a grain silo — Samso seemed an odd choice. Soren Hermansen, though, saw an opportunity. The appeal was immediate, and when a renewable-energy project finally secured some funding, he volunteered to be the first — and only — staffer.

① (A) − (B) − (C)　　　　② (B) − (A) − (C)

③ (C) − (B) − (A)　　　　④ (C) − (A) − (B)

13 밑줄 친 부분에 가장 적절한 것은?

The emphasis on decoding, translated mainly as phonemic awareness and knowledge of the alphabetic principle, has led schools to search for packaged or commercially produced reading programs that help students master the skills of decoding. According to the teachers we work with, this highly scripted approach to reading instruction has produced many students who know how to sound out words, but that is where the process of reading ends for them. While the students can decode and even become fluent oral readers, they do not truly comprehend the material; they cannot read between the lines, infer meaning, or detect the author's bias, among other things. Reading _____.

① is basically decoding since phonemic and alphabetical knowledge is added to the general decoding process

② is much more complex than simply mastering phonemic awareness and alphabet recognition

③ can be more efficiently learned together with peers than either alone or with teachers

④ can be mastered when learners know how to sound out words fluently

14 다음 글의 요지로 가장 적절한 것은?

Through discoveries and inventions, science has extended life, conquered disease and offered new material freedom. It has pushed aside gods and demons and revealed a cosmos more intricate and awesome than anything produced by pure imagination. But there are new troubles in the peculiar paradise that science has created. It seems that science is losing the popular support to meet the future challenges of pollution, security, energy, education, and food. The public has come to fear the potential consequences of unfettered science and technology in such areas as genetic engineering, global warming, nuclear power, and the proliferation of nuclear arms.

① Science is very helpful in modern society.

② Science and technology are developing quickly.

③ The absolute belief in science is weakening.

④ Scientific research is getting more funds from private sectors.

15 다음 문장이 들어갈 위치로 가장 적절한 것은?

> For example, some cultural groups were often portrayed as gangsters, while others were usually shown as the 'good guys' who arrested them.

One of the challenges we face in the world today is that a lot of the information we get about other people and places comes from the advertising and entertainment we see in the media. (A) You can't always trust these types of information. (B) To the people who make television programs and advertisements, true facts and honest opinions aren't as important as keeping you interested long enough to sell you something! (C) In the past, the messages we received from television programs, advertisements, and movies were full of stereotypes. (D) Even places were presented as stereotypes: European cities, such as Paris and Venice, were usually shown as beautiful and romantic, but cities in Africa and Asia, such as Cairo and Calcutta, were often shown as poor and overcrowded.

① A   ② B
③ C   ④ D

16 내용의 흐름상 적절하지 못한 문장은?

The earth is a planet full of life. One of the reasons for this is that our sun is the kind of star that can support life on a planet. All the time the sun continues to send out a steady supply of heat and light. For our sun is a stable star. ①This means that it stays the same size. And its output of energy (heat and light) does not change much. ②Some stars are not stable. They grow bigger and hotter and then smaller and cooler. ③The heat and light they send out vary greatly. If our sun behaved like that, the earth would boil and freeze repeatedly. ④Life could exist under these great changes. We are here because a steady amount of energy pours forth from our sun.

17 다음 글의 내용과 일치하지 않는 것은?

Chicago's Newberry Library and the Brookfield Zoo were among 10 institutions presented Monday with the National Medal for Museum and Library Service by First Lady Laura Bush at the White House. The annual awards, given by the Institute of Museum and Library Services in Washington, D. C., honor institutions for their collections and community involvement, and include a $10,000 award each. The Brookfield Zoo was honored for programs such as Zoo Adventure Passport, which provides free field trips to low-income families. "Brookfield Zoo is a living classroom for local students," Bush said. The Newberry Library was also honored for its extensive collection of more than half a million maps and its role in helping African-Americans trace their family heritage.

① The Brookfield Zoo ran a program that supports free admission for low-income families.

② The Brookfield Zoo assisted African-American kids in tracing their family history.

③ The Newberry Library and the Brookfield Zoo won a $10,000 award respectively.

④ The Newberry Library was awarded the medal for an extensive number of maps.

18 피드백에 대한 글쓴이의 주장으로 가장 적절한 것은?

Feedback, particularly the negative kind, should be descriptive rather than judgmental or evaluative. No matter how upset you are, keep the feedback job-related and never criticize someone personally because of an inappropriate action. Telling people they're stupid, incompetent, or the like is almost always counterproductive. It provokes such an emotional reaction that the performance deviation itself is apt to be overlooked. When you're criticizing, remember that you're censuring a job-related behavior, not the person.

① 상대방에게 직접 전달하는 것이 바람직하다.

② 상대방의 인격보다는 업무에 초점을 두어야 한다.

③ 긍정적인 평가가 부정적인 것보다 더 많아야 한다.

④ 상대방의 지위와 감정을 고려해야 한다.

19 다음 글의 내용과 일치하는 것은?

During the nine-week summer session, services for the university community will follow a revised schedule. Specific changes for campus bus services, the cafeteria, and summer hours for the infirmary and recreational and athletic facilities will be posted on the bulletin board outside of the cafeteria. Weekly movie and concert schedules are being finalized and will be posted outside the cafeteria every Wednesday. Campus buses will leave the main hall every half an hour and make all of the regular stops along their routes around the campus. The cafeteria will serve breakfast, lunch, and early dinner from 7 a.m. to 7 p.m. during the weekdays and from noon to 7 p.m. on weekends. The library will maintain regular hours during the weekdays, but shorter hours noon to 7 p.m. on Saturdays and Sundays. All students who want to use the library borrowing services and the recreational, athletic, and entertainment facilities must have an authorized summer identification card. This announcement will also appear in the next issue of the student newspaper.

① Movie and concert schedules will be notified twice a month.

② During the weekdays, the cafeteria and the library will open at noon.

③ Campus buses will run every hour and make all of the regular stops.

④ A valid identification card is required to use the athletic and entertainment facilities during the summer session.

20 다음 글의 내용과 일치하지 않는 것은?

When the children had originally been shown what we think of as an object, like the copper tee, they pointed to an object of the same shape but a different substance, such as a plastic plumbing tee, not to the same substance with a different shape, namely a pile of copper bits. But when they had originally been shown what we think of as a substance, like the hair gel, they pointed to the same substance regardless of its shape, such as three smears of hair gel, and not to the same shape of a different substance, such an identically curved glob of hand cream. So well before children know how the English language distinguishes individual objects from portions of a substance, they distinguish them on their own, and generalize words for them accordingly. Names for solids with a noteworthy shape are taken to apply to objects of that kind; names for nonsolids with an arbitrary shape are taken to apply to substances of that kind.

① With regard to pointing to an object, the children pointed to an object of the same shape but a different substance.

② With regard to pointing to a substance, the children pointed to the same substance regardless of its shape.

③ Children can apply the names for solids with a noteworthy shape to objects of that kind.

④ Children can distinguish objects from substances only after they know how their language distinguishes them.

※ 밑줄 친 부분과 의미가 가장 가까운 것을 고르시오. 【1~2】

1

Electric cars also are a key part of China's efforts to curb its <u>unquenchable</u> appetite for imported oil and gas, which communist leaders see as a strategic weakness.

① infallible ② aesthetic

③ adolescent ④ insatiable

2

John had just started working for the company, and he <u>was not dry behind the ears</u> yet. We should have given him a break.

① did not listen to his boss ② knew his way around

③ was not experienced ④ was not careful

※ 밑줄 친 부분에 들어갈 가장 적절한 것을 고르시오. 【3~4】

3

If you are someone who is _____, you tend to keep your feelings hidden and do not like to show other people what you really think.

① reserved ② loquacious

③ eloquent ④ confident

4

How did you _____ selling cosmetics online?

① go around   ② go back

③ go down   ④ go into

5 밑줄 친 우리말 문장을 영어로 가장 적절하게 옮긴 것은?

Goods for which the marginal costs are close to zero are inherently public goods and should be made publicly available. Bridges and roads are good examples. Once society has incurred the capital costs of constructing a bridge or road, maximum benefit from the initial investment is gained only if use is not restricted by charging. 따라서 사람들은 무료로 그러한 시설들을 이용할 수 있어야 한다.

① Therefore, people freely such facilities must be able to use.

② Hence, people should be allowed free access to such facilities.

③ Therefore, people must make access to such facilities without charging.

④ Hence, people should be given freedom to such facilities' accession.

6 밑줄 친 부분에 들어갈 가장 적절한 것을 고르시오.

Unlike in the House of Representatives, representation in the Senate is equal for every state: each state has two senators. Senators serve six-year terms. The purpose of the guaranteed term is to insulate senators from public opinion and allow them to act independently. In regard to the selection, public servants in the Senate used to be _____ by the legislatures of the states they represented. It was the Seventeenth Amendment, ratified in 1913, that gave Americans the power to elect their own senators directly.

① appointed   ② applauded

③ appeased   ④ appealed

7 다음 밑줄 친 부분의 설명으로 가장 적절한 문장은?

You'll never get a fair distribution of goods, or a satisfactory organization of human life, until you abolish private property altogether. So long as it exists, the vast majority of the human race, or the morally superior part of it, will inevitably go on laboring under the burden of poverty, hardship, and worry.

(A) Private property assumes that there's nothing wrong with your being rich, when your neighbors all around you are poor. (B) When everyone's entitled to get as much for himself as he can, all available property is bound to fall into the hands of a small minority. (C) This means that everyone else is poor. (D) And wealth will tend to vary in inverse proportion to merit, since the rich will be totally useless greedy characters, while the poor will be simple, honest people whose daily work is profitable to the community.

① (A) ② (B)

③ (C) ④ (D)

8 밑줄 친 부분에 들어갈 가장 적절한 것을 고르시오.

There are ninety-two naturally occurring elements on Earth, plus a further twenty or so that have been created in labs. Not a few of our earthly chemicals are surprisingly little known. Astatine, for instance, is practically unstudied. It has a name and a place on the periodic table, next to Marie Curie's polonium, but almost nothing else. The problem is _____. There just is not much astatine out there. The most elusive element of all, however, appears to be francium, which is so scarce that it is thought that our entire planet may contain, at any given moment, fewer than twenty francium atoms. Altogether only about thirty of the naturally occurring elements are widespread on Earth.

① acidity ② rarity

③ toxicity ④ compatibility

9 주어진 글 다음에 이어질 글의 순서로 가장 적절한 것은?

Experienced travel agents of yesterday are being rapidly replaced by new ones who have less firsthand knowledge of destinations. What this new breed faces are clients who do not know much about geography but have leisure time and money at their disposal. The solution is to equip these less knowledgeable travel agents with computer and video technology to help them match clients with right destinations.

(A) The client then views video programs on those destinations that seem most appealing, and finalizes his or her vacation plan. This way, travel agencies use modern technology to compensate for the inexperience of many agents on their payroll.

(B) Responses collected are fed into a computer program to produce a list of suggested destinations and itinerary options matched to the client's preferences.

(C) The key is to ask a client about his or her preferred vacation in mind. Included might be specific requests the representatives of which are "I don't like to pack and unpack repeatedly," or "I don't like to quickly move around and see many things."

① (A) − (B) − (C)

② (A) − (C) − (B)

③ (B) − (C) − (A)

④ (C) − (B) − (A)

10 밑줄 친 부분에 들어갈 가장 적절한 것을 고르시오.

> The best way to develop ideas is through ____(A)____ with your fellow managers. This brings us back to the importance of teamwork and interpersonal skills. One of the biggest problems today is that most managers have too much information. The key to success is not information. It's ____(B)____. And those I look for to fill top management spots are eager beavers, the guys who try to do more than they're expected to.

	(A)	(B)
①	interacting	people
②	breaking	management
③	interfering	technicians
④	working	skills

11 다음 문장이 들어갈 위치로 가장 적절한 것은?

> His hiring concluded an exhaustive process that collected input from all segments of the university.

> The selection as Heoha University's tenth president of Carlos Jimenez, the current chancellor at the University of Licafornia since 2008, was announced at the board of trustees meeting on March 15. (A) He will begin his term on July 1. (B) Faculty, students, and alumni were invited to nominate candidates. An advisory subcommittee also gathered input through 40 public forums held around the country. (C) The nominations were first narrowed to 100 names, then to 20 who received interviews, and then to five finalists. Board member Jeffrey Pinorius, who headed the search committee, said that Jimenez emerged as the clear choice. (D) "The presidential search committee was responsible for finding a leader with a clear vision and proven leadership skills required for running a highly complex organization," he added.

① (A) ② (B)
③ (C) ④ (D)

12 글의 논리적 흐름에 맞지 않는 문장은?

(A) Adventure travel is a hot trend in today's tourism industry. (B) Ordinary people are no longer content to spend two weeks away from their office lying on a sunny beach in Hawaii. (C) More and more often, they are choosing to spend their vacations rafting down wild rivers, hiking through steamy rain forests, climbing high mountains, or traversing slippery glaciers. (D) People of all ages are choosing educational study tours for their vacations.

① (A)　　　　　　　　　　② (B)

③ (C)　　　　　　　　　　④ (D)

13 글의 요지를 가장 잘 나타낸 속담 또는 격언은?

The benefits of exercise extend far beyond physical health improvement. Many people work out as much for mental and spiritual well-being as for staying fit. Can being physically active make you happy? Can it help you deal with life stress? Can it lead to a more spiritual and religious life? For many, the answer is yes. Exercise, such as walking, increases blood flow to the brain. A study of people over 60 found that walking 45 minutes a day at 6 km/h enhanced the participants' thinking skills. They started at 15 minutes of walking and gradually increased exercise time and speed. The result was that the participants were found mentally sharper with this walking program.

① Practice makes perfect.　　　　② A sound mind in a sound body.

③ Experience is the best teacher.　　④ Time and tide wait for no man.

14 다음 우리말 문장을 영어로 옮길 때 밑줄 친 부분에 들어갈 가장 적절한 것은?

> 폭풍우 전에는 대체로 고요한 시기가 먼저 온다.

> A quiet spell usually ＿＿＿＿＿＿ a storm.

① pacifies   ② precedes

③ presumes   ④ provokes

15 다음 중 어법상 옳은 것은?

① Many a careless walker was killed in the street.

② Each officer must perform their duties efficient.

③ However you may try hard, you cannot carry it out.

④ German shepherd dogs are smart, alert, and loyalty.

※ 밑줄 친 부분에 들어갈 가장 적절한 것을 고르시오. 【16~18】

16

> A tenth of the automobiles in this district alone ＿＿＿＿ stolen last year.

① was   ② had been

③ were   ④ have been

17

A : How did you find your day at school today, Ben?

B : I can't complain. Actually, I gave a presentation on drug abuse in my psychology class, and the professor _____.

A : What exact words did he use?

B : He said my presentation was head and shoulders above the others.

A : Way to go!

① made some headway

② made a splash

③ paid me a compliment

④ passed a wrong judgment

18

A : Excuse me. I'm looking for Nambu Bus Terminal.

B : Ah, it's right over there.

A : Where? _____

B : Okay. Just walk down the street, and then turn right at the first intersection. The terminal's on your left. You can't miss it.

① Could you be more specific?

② Do you think I am punctual?

③ Will you run right into it?

④ How long will it take from here by car?

19 다음 글을 쓴 목적으로 가장 적절한 것은?

Last month felt like the longest in my life with all the calamities that took us by surprise. There was only one light at the end of the tunnel, and that light was you. I cannot begin to tell you how much your thoughtfulness has meant to me. I'm sure I was too tired to be thinking clearly, but each time you appeared to whisk my children off for an hour so that I could rest, or to bring a dinner with a pitcher of iced tea, all I knew was that something incredibly wonderful had just happened. Now that we are back to normal, I know that something incredibly wonderful was you. There are no adequate words to express thanks with, but gratefulness will always be in my heart.

① 어려움에 처한 사람을 격려하려고
② 아이들을 돌보아 줄 사람을 찾아 부탁하려고
③ 힘들 때 도와주었던 사람에게 감사하려고
④ 건강이 좋지 않았던 사람의 안부를 물으려고

20 밑줄 친 부분에 들어갈 가장 적절한 것을 고르시오.

Why do we reach for a candy bar at the end of a heavy meal? We certainly are not hungry. Why do we like salt and other seasoning in our food? Soldiers who have been temporarily deprived of salt report that at its maximum intensity the craving for salt is more insistent than the desire for food itself. Cows and other livestock which are not receiving enough lime eat the bones of other animals to relieve the craving. These conditions are not thoroughly understood at present but it seems certain that somewhere in the body there are receptors which respond to the chemical conditions in the blood brought about by the absence of certain substances necessary for the body. When these receptors perceive such conditions, we have _____

① an aversion to salty foods or sweets.
② an appetite for particular substances needed.
③ an ability to prevent food-borne bone diseases.
④ an ambivalent sensory receptor for digestion.

※ 밑줄 친 부분과 의미가 가장 가까운 것은? 【1~4】

1

David decided to <u>efface</u> some lines from his manuscript.

① enlighten
② appreciate
③ construe
④ recite
⑤ erase

2

Including several interviews with the residents who used to mine but now suffer from asthma, the documentary <u>delves into</u> coal mining issues in the suburban area of Ontario.

① discourse
② corroborate
③ explicate
④ converse
⑤ investigate

3

The Polish coach admits he would love to <u>emulate</u> the Frenchman by taking charge of 1,000 matches at the same club.

① imitate
② comfort
③ excruciate
④ substantiate
⑤ announce

4

> We've got a new junior assistant, fresh from law school. He s very idealistic – still <u>wet behind the ears</u>.

① an optimist

② a rookie

③ a misfit

④ a functionary

⑤ a troublemaker

※ 문맥상 빈칸에 들어가기에 적절한 것은? 【5~6】

5

> According to dental researchers, a vaccine that could significantly reduce the number of microorganisms thought to cause cavities will soon be ready for human trials. Consequently, _____.

① cavity prevention programs may soon be eliminated

② immunization of test animals will no longer be necessary

③ children will be able to consume more sugary foods and drinks

④ long-term protection against tooth decay could soon be available on the market

⑤ microorganisms related to tooth cavities will not respond to the vaccine

6

> When you observe peaceful, relaxed people, you find that when they are feeling good, they are very grateful. They understand that both positive and negative feelings come and go, and that there will come a time when they won't be feeling so good. To happy people, this is okay, it's the way of things. They accept _____ the of passing feelings.

① vengeance

② indolence

③ inevitability

④ reluctance

⑤ expulsion

7 ① At certain times may this door be left unlocked.

② Eloquent though she was, she could not persuade him.

③ So vigorously did he protest that they reconsidered his case.

④ The sea has its currents, as do the river and the lake.

⑤ Only in this way is it possible to explain their actions.

8

Sometimes there is nothing you can do ①to stop yourself falling ill. But if you lead a healthy life, you will probably be able to get better ②much more quickly. We can all avoid ③doing things that we know ④damages the body, such as smoking cigarettes, drinking too much alcohol or ⑤taking harmful drugs.

9

My ①art history professors prefer Michelangelo's painting ②to viewing his sculpture, although Michelangelo ③himself was ④more proud of the ⑤latter.

10 다음 빈칸에 들어갈 단어가 순서대로 짝지어진 것은?

Ancient navigation relied on the sun, and therefore depended on fair weather; overcast skies could mean extensive delays or worse. The contingencies of weather paired with the lack of more sophisticated navigational tools meant that the Greeks and other ancient Mediterranean civilizations were forced to (A)_____ their exploration; trade relations were mostly limited to closely surrounding islands and coasts. Eventually, sailors were able to venture farther out using celestial navigations, which used the positions of the stars relative to the movement of the ship for direction. But even then, few captains dared to travel too far beyond the sight of coastlines for fear of unfavorable currents carrying ships off course into more dangerous waters. Finally, the introduction of the compass to Europe (B)_____ the age of explorations and paved the way for future Western European empires.

	(A)	(B)
①	restrict	circumvented
②	expedite	recorded
③	circumscribe	ignited
④	ban	depicted
⑤	facilitate	spurred

11

_____ test positive for antibiotics when tanker trucks arrive at a milk processing plant, according to the Federal Law, the entire truckload must be discarded.

① Should milk   ② If milk

③ If milk is   ④ Were milk

⑤ Milk will

12

The sales industry is one _____ constant interaction is required, so good social skills are a must.

① but which   ② in which

③ those which   ④ which

⑤ what

13 다음 글에서 밑줄 친 'it'이 의미하는 것은?

For me as a person and a businesswoman every day is a challenge that needs to be faced. History has taught me that if I am to achieve my goals, I should never set limits for myself. I believe it is within each and everyone of us to achieve greatness.

① a businesswoman   ② every day

③ a challenge   ④ history

⑤ to achieve greatness

14 다음 글을 쓴 목적으로 적절한 것은?

Among the growing number of alternative work styles is flextime. Flextime allows workers to adjust work hours to suit personal needs. The total number of hours in the week remains the same, but the daily schedule varies from standard business hours. Flextime can also mean a change in workdays, such as four 10-hour days and six short days. Workers on flextime schedules include employment agents, claim adjusters, mail clerks, and data entry operators.

① To define flextime

② To describe flexible workers

③ To discuss the alternative work styles

④ To compare different jobs

⑤ To arrange flextime schedules

15 다음 ㉠~㉣을 문맥에 맞게 배열한 것은?

㉠ Mark Twain began his career writing light, humorous verse, but evolved into a chronicler of the vanities and hypocrisies of mankind.

㉡ Though Twain earned a great deal of money from his writings and lectures, he lost a great deal through investments in ventures in his later life.

㉢ Samuel Langhorne Clemens, better known by his pen name Mark Twain had worked as a typesetter and a riverboat pilot on the Mississippi River before he became a writer.

㉣ At mid-career, with The Adventures of Huckleberry Finn, he combined rich humor, sturdy narrative and social criticism, popularizing a distinctive American literature built on American themes and language.

① ㉠ – ㉡ – ㉢ – ㉣

② ㉡ – ㉣ – ㉢ – ㉠

③ ㉠ – ㉣ – ㉡ – ㉢

④ ㉢ – ㉠ – ㉣ – ㉡

⑤ ㉢ – ㉣ – ㉠ – ㉡

16

Medieval people did not distinguish between entertainment (which people expect to pay for) and general merriment, of the sort that anyone could take part in at festive times. They regarded both as 'play,' as opposed to work, and they called entertainers 'players.' The Church taught that idleness was a sin, that players were idle and that it was idleness to watch them. But the closing of theaters in Roman times had not taken away people's appetite for comedy, tricks and tunes. The most lasting effect had been to _____, so that they had to wander in search of audience.

① let the players take part in the festivals

② employ entertainers for festivals

③ teach people not to be idle

④ supply players with new ethics

⑤ deprive players of a workplace

17

Microwave works mainly by agitating or shaking the molecules of water within the food. A molecule that shakes or vibrates more has more heat energy, that is, it gets hotter. The heat energy is transferred from each water molecule to the other molecules around it. The food cooks inside, rather than from the outside inwards as in a normal oven. The process also continues for a time after the microwaves are switched off. So _____.

① microwaves made by the magnetron are led along the hollow waveguide and into the general oven compartment

② the most likely place for microwaves to escape is around the door seal when this gets loose or broken

③ food from a microwave oven is left to stand for a time afterwards to finish cooking

④ the cooking can be paused for a short period by stopping the magnetron and revolving platter

⑤ the door is locked shut and can't be opened while the oven is working

18 다음 글의 주제로 적절한 것은?

Although Albert Einstein's Theory of Relativity revolutionized physics, his mathematical models were based on the erroneous assumption that the universe is static – all the components are fixed in time and space. In order to maintain this view, when Einstein's equations predicted a universe in flux, he invented the "cosmological constant" to maintain the supposed constancy of the universe. Within ten years, the astronomer Edwin Hubble discovered that the universe was expanding, causing Einstein to abandon the idea of the cosmological constant. Almost a century later, physicists have discovered that some unknown force is apparently pushing the universe apart, leading some scientists to conclude that Einstein's "cosmological constant" may in fact exist.

① The observations of Hubble severely damaged the Theory of Relativity.

② One of Einstein's most significant discoveries was the cosmological constant.

③ Einstein's Theory of Relativity is fundamentally flawed.

④ The cosmological constant, while erroneously derived, may actually play a part in describing the universe.

⑤ Physicists today still make use of Einstein's cosmological constant to describe the universe.

※ 다음 글을 읽고 물음에 답하시오. 【19~20】

Elizabeth Barret Browning, a feminist writer of the Victorian Era, used her poetry and prose to take on a wide range of issues facing her society, including "the woman questions." In her long poem Aurora Leigh, she explores this question as she portrays both the growth of the artist and the growth of the woman within. Aurora Leigh is not a traditional Victorian woman — she is well-educated and self-sufficient. In the poem, Browning argues that the limitations placed on woman in contrast to the freedom men enjoy should incite women to rise up and <u>effect</u> a change in their circumstances. Browning's writing, including Aurora Leigh, helped to pave the way for major social change in women's lives.

19 빈칸에 들어가기에 적절한 것은?

It can be inferred from the passage that the author believes the traditional Victorian woman _____.

① wrote poetry

② was portrayed accurately in Aurora Leigh

③ was not well-educated

④ fought for social change

⑤ had a public role in society

20 밑줄 친 <u>effect</u>의 문맥상 의미와 같은 것은?

① imitate　　　　　　　　　② cause

③ result　　　　　　　　　　④ disturb

⑤ prevent

※ 밑줄 친 부분의 의미와 가장 가까운 것을 고르시오. 【1~2】

1

Babies as young as one and two months of age have the capacity to <u>discriminate</u> speech sounds.

① distinguish　　　　　　　② dislocate

③ disturb　　　　　　　　 ④ distribute

2

Students who click their ball-point pens in class <u>drive me up the wall</u>.

① distract me a lot

② annoy me greatly

③ play up to me frequently

④ take a big load off my mind

3 어법상 틀린 것은?

① Surrounded by great people, I felt proud.

② I asked my brother to borrow me five dollars.

③ On the platform was a woman in a black dress.

④ The former Soviet Union comprised fifteen union republics.

4 우리말을 영어로 가장 잘 옮긴 것은?

> 소년이 잠들자마자 그의 아버지가 집에 왔다.

① The boy had no sooner fallen asleep than his father came home.

② Immediately after his father came home, the boy fell asleep.

③ When his father came home, the boy did not fall asleep.

④ Before the boy fell asleep, his father came home.

5 밑줄 친 부분에 들어갈 가장 적절한 것은?

> A : Hi, Gus. I'm glad to see you up and about.
>
> B : Thanks. After that truck plowed into my car last month, I thought it was all over for me. I'm really lucky to be alive.
>
> A : That's for sure. It must have been quite a traumatic experience for you. Has your car been repaired yet?
>
> B : Yes, it has. But I won't be driving it anymore. I'm not taking any chances on being hit again.
>
> A : Come on, now. You can't let one unfortunate incident keep you from ever driving again. _____
>
> B : That's what people say, but for the time being, I'll be taking public transportation.

① A squeaky wheel gets the oil.

② It is better to be safe than sorry.

③ The grass is always greener on the other side.

④ Lightning never strikes twice in the same place.

6 다음 글의 요지로 가장 적절한 것은?

Supporters of positive computing make the case that technology should contribute to well-being and human potential. The real potential for positive computing to make a difference in our lives is in the next generation of wearable computing devices. One idea for how wearables might lead to increased well-being and mindfulness is in the current generation of fitness trackers and health devices. Designed to measure physical factors such as heart rate and the amount of sleep we get, they could theoretically become positive feedback devices for regulating moods. These devices would not just be ergonomically well-designed and aesthetically pleasing to the eye, but they would also lead to experiences that remove barriers to well-being.

① Wearable computing devices can contribute to well-being.
② Positive computing can contribute to national power.
③ Wearable computing devices increase living costs.
④ Positive computing develops science.

7 ㉠, ㉡에 들어갈 가장 적절한 것은?

Stress is a fact of life and can affect all aspects of our daily existence. Stress can have a negative impact on one's mental, as well as physiological, functioning. An important issue here is the way that employees handle stress. For some individuals, stress motivates and challenges them to excel; this is *eustress*. For others, _____㉠_____, excessive stress diminishes the capacity to function and can have severe medical ramifications; this is *distress*. Even though stress is inevitable, the negative and dangerous consequences associated with it are not. _____㉡_____, it is necessary to examine potential sources of stress, especially in the workforce, in order to prevent unnecessary and unhealthy outcomes for the individual as well as the organization.

	㉠	㉡
①	however	Therefore
②	in addition	Furthermore
③	thus	Nevertheless
④	for instance	Accordingly

8 밑줄 친 부분에 들어갈 가장 적절한 것은?

In recent years, some Americans have been giving their children two last names. This is a direct result of some women thinking it is sexist and outdated to take on their husband's name. It is also sexist that the child would only carry the name of one parent, especially since the unnamed parent is the one who carried the child for nine months. The only logical solution is to give the kid a split last name. As a result, we have children growing up named Elijah Sadler-Moore. As this is a recent phenomenon, we have yet to see what happens when one split-named person marries another split-named person. Does their kid _____?

① go back to the mother's last name

② insist on three last names

③ end up with four last names

④ give up the first name

※ 내용의 흐름상 적절하지 못한 문장을 고르시오. 【9~10】

9

Crying is the most powerful way that babies can let the outside world know they need something. ① It's a vital means of communication and the first way that infants establish any kind of control over their lives. ② Research shows that babies whose cries are responded to seem to become more self-confident because they realize that they can affect their own lives. ③ You may find listening to your baby cry is one of the hardest parts of being a parent. By the end of the first year, babies whose cries have brought tender, soothing care cry less and communicate more in other ways, while babies of less responsive caregivers cry more. ④ So don't be afraid of spoiling your baby by responding to her when she cries.

10

Most of us who have ever cleaned a house would be much happier if there were less dust. ① However, without dust there would be less rainfall and sunsets would be less beautiful. Rain is formed when water molecules in the air collect around particles of dust. When the collected water becomes heavy enough, the water droplets fall to the earth as rain. ② This could decrease the amount of carbon dioxide in the atmosphere, alleviating the threat of global warming. Thus, water vapor could be much less likely to turn to rain without the dust particles. ③ The water vapor and dust particles also reflect the rays of the sun. At sunrise and sunset, when the sun is below the horizon, the dust and water vapor molecules reflect the longer, red wavelengths of light such that we can see them for more time than any of the other wavelengths. ④ The more dust particles in the air, the more colorful the sunrise or sunset.

11 밑줄 친 부분의 의미와 가장 가까운 것은?

It is important to find a way to settle the issue before the meeting begins.

① resolve   ② resume

③ retrieve   ④ revoke

12 밑줄 친 부분에 들어갈 가장 적절한 것은?

Robert wasn't able to _____ so he had to ask his parents to pay his rent and utility fees.

① hit the sack   ② slack off

③ keep his chin up   ④ make ends meet

13 밑줄 친 부분 중 어법상 옳지 않은 것은?

A college girl was really ① upset with her father. She was ashamed of him because he didn't treat his workers well. She demanded that he ② shared the profits with the employees. She explained to him ③ how unfairly workers ④ were treated.

14 우리말을 영어로 잘못 옮긴 것은?

① 우리는 그녀의 행방에 대해서 아는 바가 전혀 없다.
→ We don't have the faintest notion of her whereabouts.
② 항구 폐쇄에 대한 정부의 계획이 격렬한 항의를 유발했다.
→ Government plans to close the harbor provoked a storm of protest.
③ 총기 규제에 대한 너의 의견에 전적으로 동의한다.
→ I couldn't agree with you more on your views on gun control.
④ 학교는 어린이들의 과다한 TV 시청을 막기 위한 프로그램을 시작할 것이다.
→ The school will start a program designed to deter kids to watch TV too much.

15 밑줄 친 부분에 들어갈 가장 적절한 것은?

A : What do you say we take a break now?
B : _____
A : Great! I'll meet you in the lobby in five minutes.

① Okay, let's keep working.
② That sounds good.
③ I'm already broke.
④ It will take one hour.

16 다음 글의 제목으로 가장 적절한 것은?

Anyone who wants to be a librarian must decide what type of work most interests him or her. As with any profession, it is necessary to plan ahead. A good general education is essential to someone who is going to guide and teach others. So are a good reading background and a knowledge of nonprint materials and computers. For specialist library work, training in that specialty is often required. An advanced degree is needed to teach in a library school or to run a large library. All librarians must have at least a college degree and should attend library school beyond that. Pamphlet material on library jobs and on scholarships is available in most libraries.

① How to Attend Library School

② The Librarian as a Person

③ Librarianship: Pros and Cons

④ Tips for Tomorrow's Librarian

17 내용의 흐름상 적절하지 못한 문장은?

Asian art and music have had profound influences on the West across the centuries. ①Chinese porcelain, for example, was imitated not only by Persian ceramicists, but also by English bone china designers. ②Japanese watercolors shown at Far East exhibitions in Paris in the late nineteenth century affected the compositions and palettes of Matisse and Degas. ③When Westerners collect non−Western art or view it in a museum, they probably miss much of its original context. ④Oriental musical modes also influenced composers like Mozart and Debussy.

18 밑줄 친 부분에 들어갈 가장 적절한 것은?

> When daughters react with annoyance or even anger at the smallest, seemingly innocent remarks, mothers get the feeling that talking to their daughters can be like _____: they have to watch every word.

① walking on air

② walking on a cloud

③ walking on eggshells

④ walking on the grass

19 다음 글을 쓴 작가가 장난감을 살펴본 이유로 가장 적절한 것은?

> The first hint of spring floated across the East River, mixing with the soft-coal smoke from the factories and the street smells of the poor neighborhood. As I turned the corner on my way to work and came to Sheftel's, I was made once more aware of the poor collection of toys in the dusty window, and I remembered the approaching birthday of a small niece of mine in Cleveland, to whom I was in the habit of sending modest gifts. Therefore, I stopped and examined the window to see if there might be anything appropriate, and looked at the confusing collection of unappealing objects.

① The toy smelled like the writer's niece.

② The toy was as charming as the writer's niece.

③ The birthday of the writer's niece was around the corner.

④ The writer was impressed by the low prices and wide selection.

20 다음 글의 주제로 가장 적합한 것은?

It may seem improbable that you can make money by selling to people who don't have much, but companies that have actually bothered to try are flourishing. Hindustan Lever has built a lucrative business in Africa and India selling brand-name consumer goods, from lotion to salt. Casas Bahia, a department-store chain, now sells more than five billion dollars' worth of brand-name electronics and appliances to working-class Brazilians every year. Big companies often disdain what they think of as the low-end market, because they make a lot less money on each sale than they do selling high-end goods. But, because of the sheer size of that market, they can still make a lot of money on it.

① Poor people do not have high standards for their products.

② The objectives of big companies should not be solely based on profits.

③ People in low-end markets can be a great opportunity for large businesses.

④ The individual purchasing power is still very low in the developing countries.

※ 밑줄 친 부분에 가장 적절한 것을 고르시오. 【1~2】

1

The young knight was so _____ at being called a coward that he charged forward with his sword in hand.

① aloof　　　　　　　　　　　　② incensed

③ unbiased　　　　　　　　　　　④ unpretentious

2

Back in the mid-1970s, an American computer scientist called John Holland _____ the idea of using the theory of evolution to solve notoriously difficult problems in science.

① took on　　　　　　　　　　　② got on

③ put upon　　　　　　　　　　　④ hit upon

3 내용의 흐름상 적절하지 못한 문장은?

Of equal importance in wars of conquest were the germs that evolved in human societies with domestic animals. ① Infectious diseases like smallpox, measles, and flu arose as specialized germs of humans, derived by mutations of very similar ancestral germs that had infected animals. ② The most direct contribution of plant and animal domestication to wars of conquest was from Eurasia's horses, whose military role made them the jeeps and Sherman tanks of ancient warfare on that continent. ③ The humans who domesticated animals were the first to fall victim to the newly evolved germs, but those humans then evolved substantial resistance to the new disease. ④ When such partly immune people came into contact with others who had had no previous exposure to the germs, epidemics resulted in which up to 99 percent of the previously unexposed population was killed. Germs thus acquired ultimately from domestic animals played decisive roles in the European conquests of Native Americans, Australians, South Africans, and Pacific islanders.

4 다음 글의 제목으로 가장 적절한 것은?

Everyone knows what the *Mona Lisa* and Michelangelo's *David* look like — or do we? They are reproduced so often that we may feel we know them even if we have never been to Paris or Florence. Each has countless spoofs — David in boxer shorts or the *Mona Lisa* with a mustache. Art reproductions are ubiquitous. We can now sit in our pajamas while enjoying virtual tours of galleries and museums around the world via the Web and CD-ROM. We can explore genres and painters and zoom in to scrutinize details. The Louvre's Website offers spectacular 360-degree panoramas of artworks like the *Venus de Milo*. Such tours may become ever more multi-sensory by drawing on virtual reality technology, which includes things like goggles and gloves. Lighting and stage set designers, like architects, already use this technology in their work.

① Should We Ban Art Reproductions?
② Why Are Virtual Artworks So Popular?
③ Art : More Widely Accessible Than Ever!
④ Secrets of Vanished Galleries and Museums

5 어법상 옳지 않은 것은?

① The main reason I stopped smoking was that all my friends had already stopped smoking.

② That a husband understands a wife does not mean they are necessarily compatible.

③ The package, having wrong addressed, reached him late and damaged.

④ She wants her husband to buy two dozen of eggs on his way home.

6 어법상 옳은 것은?

① China's imports of Russian oil skyrocketed by 36 percent in 2014.

② Sleeping has long been tied to improve memory among humans.

③ Last night, she nearly escaped from running over by a car.

④ The failure is reminiscent of the problems surrounded the causes of the fatal space shuttle disasters.

※ 밑줄 친 부분에 가장 적절한 것을 고르시오. 【7~8】

7

A : What business is on your mind?

B : Do you think that owning a flower shop has good prospects nowadays?

A : It could. But have you prepared yourself mentally and financially?

B : _____.

A : Good! Then you should choose a strategic place and the right segment too. You must do a thorough research to have a good result.

B : I know that. It's much easier to start a business than to run it well.

① I plan to go to the hospital tomorrow

② I can't be like that! I must strive to get a job

③ I'm ready to start with what I have and take a chance

④ I don't want to think about starting my own business

8

M : What's that noise?

W : Noise? I don't hear anything.

M : Listen closely. I hear some noise. _____.

W : Oh, let's stop and see.

M : Look! A piece of glass is in the right front wheel.

W : Really? Umm... You're right. What are we going to do?

M : Don't worry. I got some experience in changing tires.

① I gave my customers sound advice

② Maybe air is escaping from the tire

③ I think the mechanic has an appointment

④ Oh! Your phone is ringing in vibration mode

9 주어진 글 다음에 이어질 글의 순서로 가장 적절한 것은?

Thunderstorms are extremely common in many parts of the world, for example, throughout most of North America. Updrafts of warm air set off these storms.

(A) This more buoyant air then rises and carries water vapor to higher altitudes. The air cools as it rises, and the water vapor condenses and starts to drop as rain. As the rain falls, it pulls air along with it and turns part of the draft downward.

(B) An updraft may start over ground that is more intensely heated by the sun than the land surrounding the area. Bare, rocky, or paved areas, for example, usually have updrafts above them. The air in contact with the ground heats up and thus becomes lighter, more buoyant, than the air surrounding it.

(C) The draft may turn upward again and send the rain churning around in the cloud. Some of it may freeze to hail. Sooner or later, the water droplets grow heavy enough to resist the updrafts and fall to the ground, pulling air in the form of downdrafts with them.

① (A) − (C) − (B)　　　　　　② (B) − (A) − (C)

③ (B) − (C) − (A)　　　　　　④ (C) − (A) − (B)

10 다음 문장이 들어갈 위치로 가장 적절한 것은?

> We can in consequence establish relations with almost all sorts of them.

Reptiles and fish may no doubt be found in swarms and shoals; they have been hatched in quantities and similar conditions have kept them together. In the case of social and gregarious mammals, the association arises not simply from a community of external forces but is sustained by an inner impulse. They are not merely like one another and so found in the same places at the same times; they like one another and so they keep together. This difference between the reptile world and the world of our human minds is one our sympathies seem unable to pass. (A) We cannot conceive in ourselves the swift uncomplicated urgency of a reptile's instinctive motives, its appetites, fears and hates. (B) We cannot understand them in their simplicity because all our motives are complicated; ours are balances and resultants and not simply urgencies. (C) But the mammals and birds have self-restraint and consideration for other individuals, a social appeal, a self-control that is, at its lower level, after our own fashion. (D) When they suffer they utter cries and make movements that rouse our feelings. We can make pets of them with a mutual recognition. They can be tamed to self-restraint towards us, domesticated and taught.

① A

② B

③ C

④ D

※ 밑줄 친 부분과 의미가 가장 가까운 것을 고르시오. 【11~12】

11

He took out a picture from his drawer and kissed it with deep reverence, folded it <u>meticulously</u> in a white silk kerchief, and placed it inside his shirt next to his heart.

① carefully
② hurriedly
③ decisively
④ delightfully

12

The company cannot expect me to move my home and family <u>at the drop of a hat</u>.

① immediately
② punctually
③ hesitantly
④ periodically

13 다음 글의 제목으로 가장 적절한 것은?

America gets 97 % of its limes from Mexico, and a combination of bad weather and disease has sent that supply plummeting and prices skyrocketing. A 40-lb. (18 kg) box of limes that cost the local restaurateurs about $ 20 late last year now goes for $ 120. In April, the average retail price for a lime hit 56 cents, more than double the price last year. Across the U.S., bars and restaurants are rationing their supply or, like Alaska Airlines, eliminating limes altogether. In Mexico, the value spike is attracting criminals, forcing growers to guard their limited supply of "green gold" from drug cartels. Business owners who depend on citrus are hoping that spring growth will soon bring costs back to normal.

① An Irreversible Change in Wholesale Price of Lime
② Mexican Lime Cartel Spreading to the U.S.
③ Americans Eat More Limes than Ever
④ A Costly Lime Shortage

14 다음 문장이 들어갈 위치로 가장 적절한 것은?

> Print, however, with its standard format and type, introduced exact mass reproduction.

Print transformed how knowledge itself was understood and transmitted. A manuscript is a unique and unreproducible object. (A) This meant that two readers separated by distance could discuss and compare identical books, right down to a specific word on a particular page. (B) With the introduction of consistent pagination, indexes, alphabetic ordering, and bibliographies (all unthinkable in manuscript), knowledge itself was slowly repackaged. (C) Textual scholarship became a cumulative science, as scholars could now gather manuscripts of, say, Aristotle's *Politics* and print a standard authoritative edition based on a comparison of all available copies. (D) This also led to the phenomenon of new and revised editions.

① A

② B

③ C

④ D

15 다음 글의 내용과 일치하지 않는 것은?

East of the Mississippi, the land rises slowly into the foothills of the Appalachian Mountains. At the edge of the Canadian plains, the Canadian Shield, a giant core of rock centered on the Hudson and James Bays, anchors the continent. The stony land of the Shield makes up the eastern half of Canada and the northeastern United States. In northern Quebec, the Canadian Shield descends to the Hudson Bay. The heavily eroded Appalachian Mountains are North America's oldest mountains and the continent's second−longest mountain range. They extend about 1,500 miles from Quebec to central Alabama. Coastal lowlands lie east and south of the Appalachians. Between the mountains and the coastal lowlands lies a wide area of rolling hills. Many rivers cut through the Piedmont and flow across to the Atlantic Coastal Plain in the Carolinas.

① Centered on the Hudson and James Bays is a giant core of rock, the Canadian Shield.

② The Appalachian Mountains are North America's longest mountain range.

③ From Quebec to central Alabama, the Appalachian Mountains stretch.

④ The Piedmont is traversed by many rivers that flow toward the Plain.

16 다음 글의 내용과 일치하는 것은?

The WAIS-R is made up of eleven subtests, or scales. The subtests of the WAIS-R are arranged by the type of ability or skill being tested. The subtests are organized into two categories. Six subtests define the verbal scale, and five subtests constitute a performance scale. We can compute three scores: a verbal score, a performance score, and a total (or full-scale) score. The total score can be taken as an approximation of general intellectual ability. To administer the WAIS-R, you present each of the eleven subtests to your subject. The items within each subtest are arranged in order of difficulty. You start with relatively easy items, and then you progress to more difficult ones. You stop administering any one subtest when your subject fails a specified number of items in a row. You alternate between verbal and performance subtests. The whole process takes up to an hour and a half.

① The WAIS-R has eleven subtests, each of which has two main parts.

② Several subtests with higher scores among the eleven ones should be presented.

③ The items of each subtest in the WAIS-R begin from easy and continue on to more difficult ones.

④ Subjects take all of the verbal subtests first and then all of the performance subtests.

17 밑줄 친 부분에 가장 적절한 것은?

Language is saturated with implicit metaphors like "Events are objects and time is space." Indeed, space turns out to be a conceptual vehicle not just for time but for many kinds of states and circumstances. Just as a meeting can be moved from 3:00 to 4:00, a traffic light can go from green to red, a person can go from flipping burgers to running a corporation, and the economy can go from bad to worse. Metaphor is so widespread in language that it's hard to find expressions for abstract ideas that are not metaphorical. Does it imply that even our wispiest concepts are represented in the mind as hunks of matter that we move around on a mental stage? Does it say that rival claims about the world can never be true or false but can only be _____? Few things in life cannot be characterized in terms of variables and the causation of changes in them.

① proven to be always true in all circumstances

② irreversible and established truths that cannot be disputed

③ subject to scientific testings for their authenticity and clarity

④ alternative metaphors that frame a situation in different ways

18 우리말을 영어로 잘못 옮긴 것을 고르시오.

① 가능한 모든 일자리를 알아보았음에도 불구하고, 그는 적당한 일자리를 찾지 못했다.

　→Despite searching for every job opening possible, he could not find a suitable job.

② 당신이 누군가를 믿을 수 있는지 알아보는 최선책은 그 사람을 믿는 것이다.

　→The best way to find out if you can trust somebody is to trust that person.

③ 미각의 민감성은 개인의 음식 섭취와 체중에 크게 영향을 미친다.

　→Taste sensitivity is largely influenced by food intake and body weight of individuals.

④ 부모는 그들의 자녀가 성장하고 학습하는 데 알맞은 환경을 제공할 책임이 있다.

　→Parents are responsible for providing the right environment for their children to grow and learn in.

19 우리말을 영어로 잘못 옮긴 것을 고르시오.

① 그는 자신의 정적들을 투옥시켰다.

　→He had his political enemies imprisoned.

② 경제적 자유가 없다면 진정한 자유가 있을 수 없다.

　→There can be no true liberty unless there is economic liberty.

③ 나는 가능하면 빨리 당신과 거래할 수 있기를 바란다.

　→I look forward to doing business with you as soon as possible.

④ 30년 전 고향을 떠날 때, 그는 다시는 고향을 못 볼 거라고 꿈에도 생각지 않았다.

　→When he left his hometown thirty years ago, little does he dream that he could never see it again.

20 다음 글의 ㉠, ㉡에 들어갈 가장 적절한 것은?

The chimpanzee — who puts two sticks together in order to get at a banana because no one of the two is long enough to do the job — uses intelligence. So do we all when we go about our business, "figuring out" how to do things. *Intelligence*, in this sense, is taking things for granted as they are, making combinations which have the purpose of facilitating their manipulation; intelligence is thought in the service of biological survival. *Reason*, _____㉠_____, aims at understanding; it tries to find out what is beneath the surface, to recognize the kernel, the essence of the reality which surrounds us. Reason is not without a function, but its function is not to further physical as much as mental and spiritual existence. _____㉡_____, often in individual and social life, reason is required in order to predict (considering that prediction often depends on recognition of forces which operate underneath the surface), and prediction sometimes is necessary even for physical survival.

	㉠	㉡
①	for example	Therefore
②	in the same way	Likewise
③	consequently	As a result
④	on the other hand	However

※ 밑줄 친 부분의 의미와 가장 가까운 것은? 【1~4】

1

South Korea's Ministry for Foreign Affairs and Trade came under fire for making hundreds of translation errors in overseas trade deals.

① became a mockery   ② became notorious

③ caught flak   ④ was investigated

2

Lawmakers in Nevada, New Mexico, Texas and Utah are trying to pass bills that would allow the states to circumvent daylight saving time laws.

① cramp   ② maintain

③ codify   ④ reestablish

3

Moscow's annexation of Crimea last year and its meddling in the conflict in eastern Ukraine have galvanized NATO and focused particular attention on its vulnerable Baltic members.

① spurred   ② disparaged

③ appeased   ④ justified

4

The frequency and severity of <u>corporal</u> punishment varies widely. Parents who sometimes smack their children also use other positive and punitive methods.

① typical   ② physical

③ physiological   ④ psychological

※ 밑줄 친 부분 중 어법상 옳지 않은 것은? 【5~7】

5

The cartoon character SpongeBob SquarePants is ①<u>in a hot water</u> from a study ②<u>suggesting</u> that watching just nine minutes ③<u>of that program</u> can cause short-term attention and learning problems ④<u>in 4-year-olds</u>.

6

Most European countries failed ①<u>to welcome</u> Jewish refugees ②<u>after</u> the war, which caused ③ <u>many</u> Jewish people ④<u>immigrate</u> elsewhere.

7

It was ①<u>a little</u> past 3 p.m. when 16 people gathered and sat cross-legged in a circle, blushing at the strangers they knew they'd ②<u>be mingling with</u> for the next two hours. Wearing figure-hugging tights and sleeveless tops in ③<u>a variety of shape and size</u>, each person took turns sharing their names and native countries. ④<u>All but five were</u> foreigners from places including the United States, Germany and the United Kingdom.

8 어법상 밑줄 친 부분에 가장 적절한 것은?

> Most of the art _____ in the museum is from Italy in the 19th century.

① is displayed

② displaying

③ displayed

④ are displayed

9 다음 대화의 흐름으로 보아 밑줄 친 부분에 가장 적절한 것은?

> A : Do you have any vacancies?
> B : I'm sorry. _____
> A : I should have made a reservation.
> B : That would have helped.

① How many people are there in your company?

② We're completely booked.

③ We have plenty of rooms.

④ What kind of room would you like?

10 다음 대화에서 밑줄 친 'carousel'이 잘못 쓰인 것은?

> A : I'm new here at this airport. Where can I get my baggage?
> B : Please check at ① carousel number 2.
>   Do you have anything special in your baggage?
> A : I have a 500 watt microwave with a ② carousel.
> B : You didn't have to bring it. Most of the hotels have microwaves.
>   By the way, what are you planning to do first in your trip to Seattle?
> A : I'd like to ride the ③ carousel at Miners' Landing.
>   Well, what kind of clothing will be the best here at this season?
>   It's so chilly.
> B : I'd recommend you to wear a ④ carousel, then.

In books I had read-from time to time, when the plot called for it-someone would suffer from (㉠). A person would leave a not so very nice situation and go somewhere else, somewhere a lot better, and then long to go back where it was not very nice. How impatient I would become with such a person, for I would feel that I was in a not so nice situation myself, and how I wanted to go somewhere else. But now I, too, felt that I wanted to be back where I came from. I understood it, I knew where I stood there. If I (㉡) to draw a picture of my future then, it (㉢) a large gray patch surrounded by black, blacker, blackest.

11 문맥상 ㉠에 들어가기 가장 적절한 것은?

① drowsiness
② hysteria
③ depression
④ homesickness

12 어법상 ㉡과 ㉢에 들어가기 가장 적절한 표현을 순서대로 나열한 것은?

① would have, were
② had had, would have been
③ would have, was
④ have had, would be

13 다음 괄호에 들어가기 적절한 것을 순서대로 나열한 것은?

(   ) cats cannot see in complete darkness, their eyes are much more sensitive (   ) light than human eyes.

① Despite, to
② Though, at
③ Nonetheless, at
④ While, to

14

The source of this economic paralysis are somewhat different in the two countries. In Japan, a combination of highly constraining social patterns, consensus−based decision making and an ossified political process have suppressed new ideas and made the country resistant to change. In the U.S., there is no shortage of fresh thinking, debate and outrage−the paralysis is caused by _____ of consensus on how problems should be tackled. In a rich nation like the U.S., it's easy to be fooled into thinking there's always more time for problems to get solved. So it has been in Japan. The Japanese are wealthy enough that they don't suffer too much from the prolonged period of stunted growth.

① a number   ② a variety

③ a lack   ④ a ground

15

In late−twentieth−century America, perhaps in the West as a whole, human life is conceived in terms of a basic unit, the autonomous, free, self−determining individual. This is a being understood as possessing a(n) _____ selfhood, an inner entity known through a sense of immediacy and plenitude and constituted above all by a self−aware consciousness and an executive will.

① communal

② connected

③ dividual

④ undivided

16

Since William Shakespeare lived more than 400 years ago, and many records from that time are lost or never existed in the first place, we don't know everything about his life. For example, we know that he was baptized in Stratford-upon-Avon, 100 miles northwest of London, on April 26, 1564. But we don't know his exact birthdate, which must have been a few days earlier. However, we do know that Shakespeare's life revolved around two locations: Stratford and London. He grew up, had a family, and bought property in Stratford, but he worked in London, the center of English theater. As an actor, a playwright, and a partner in a leading acting company, he became both prosperous and well-known. _____, fans of Shakespeare have imagined and reimagined him according to their own tastes, just as we see with the 19th-century portrait of Shakespeare wooing his wife at the top of this page.

① Even without knowing everything about his life

② Because we know everything about him

③ Because it is impossible to understand him

④ Even though he was our contemporary poet

17 다음 글의 종류로 적절한 것은?

New York City's Department of Education plans to announce on Wednesday that it will lift the ban on cellphones in schools, a person familiar with the decision said Tuesday. The ban, which was put in place by former Mayor Michael R. Bloomberg, has been unpopular among parents, who worry about not being able to contact their children during school hours and in the time just before and after. According to a different news report, under the new policy, principals would decide, in consultation with teachers and parents, on a range of options for cellphone use.

① An advertisement

② A news article

③ A cellphone manual

④ A statement of legal disposal

※ 다음 글을 문맥에 맞게 순서대로 연결한 것은? 【18~19】

18

㉠ The Butterfly Defect addresses the widening gap between systemic risks and their effective management.

㉡ But rapid globalization has also created concerns because the repercussions of local events now cascade over national borders and the fallout of financial meltdowns and environmental disasters affects everyone.

㉢ Global hyperconnectivity and increased system integration have led to vast benefits, including worldwide growth in incomes, education, innovation, and technology.

㉣ It shows how the new dynamics of turbo-charged globalization has the potential and power to destabilize our societies.

① ㉠-㉢-㉡-㉣
② ㉠-㉣-㉡-㉢
③ ㉢-㉡-㉠-㉣
④ ㉢-㉡-㉣-㉠

19

㉠ Speaking two languages rather than just one has obvious practical benefits in an increasingly globalized world.

㉡ Being bilingual, it turns out, makes you smarter.

㉢ It can have a profound effect on your brain, improving cognitive skills not related to language and even shielding against dementia in old age.

㉣ But in recent years, scientists have begun to show that the advantages of bilingualism are even more fundamental than being able to converse with a wider range of people.

① ㉠-㉡-㉢-㉣
② ㉠-㉣-㉡-㉢
③ ㉡-㉣-㉢-㉠
④ ㉢-㉡-㉣-㉠

20 다음 글의 내용에 가장 가까운 것은?

To act well, a person needs to determine which action-guiding statements are true, or likely to be true, and which false, or likely to be false. For it seems reasonable to suppose that a person who is acting in accordance with true statements, and not false ones likely to be true, has more chance of reaching acceptable goals.

① It can be unreliable to act in accordance with statements which are likely to be true.

② Acceptable results will be guaranteed to a person acting on the ground of true statements.

③ It is equally dangerous to act on the statements that are true and on those that are likely to be true.

④ Action is one thing, and statements another; the two have no mutual dependency.

☞ 정답 및 해설 P.49

1 밑줄 친 부분과 의미가 가장 가까운 것은?

> There are some diseases your doctor will <u>rule out</u> before making a diagnosis.

① trace   ② exclude

③ instruct   ④ examine

2 다음 중 어법상 옳은 것은?

① She supposed to phone me last night, but she didn't.

② I have been knowing Jose until I was seven.

③ You'd better to go now or you'll be late.

④ Sarah would be offended if I didn't go to her party.

3 우리말을 영어로 옮긴 것 중 가장 어색한 것은?

① 제인은 보기만큼 젊지 않다.

→Jane is not as young as she looks.

② 전화하는 것이 편지 쓰는 것보다 더 쉽다.

→It's easier to make a phone call than to write a letter.

③ 너는 나보다 돈이 많다.

→You have more money than I.

④ 당신 아들 머리는 당신 머리와 같은 색깔이다.

→Your son's hair is the same color as you.

4 밑줄 친 부분에 들어갈 표현으로 가장 적절한 것은?

M : Would you like to go out for dinner, Mary?
W : Oh, I'd love to. Where are we going?
M : How about the new pizza restaurant in town?
W : Do we need a reservation?
M : I don't think it is necessary.
W : But we may have to wait in line because it's Friday night.
M : You are absolutely right. Then, I'll _____ right now.
W : Great.

① cancel the reservation   ② give you the check
③ eat some breakfast   ④ book a table

5 다음 글의 (A), (B), (C)에서 어법상 옳은 것을 모두 고른 것은?

Pattern books contain stories that make use of repeated phrases, refrains, and sometimes rhymes. In addition, pattern books frequently contain pictures (A) [that/what] may facilitate story comprehension. The predictable patterns allow beginning second language readers to become involved (B) [immediate/immediately] in a literacy event in their second language. Moreover, the use of pattern books (C) [meet/meets] the criteria for literacy scaffolds by modeling reading, by challenging students' current level of linguistic competence, and by assisting comprehension through the repetition of a simple sentence pattern.

	(A)	(B)	(C)
①	that	immediate	meet
②	what	immediately	meets
③	that	immediately	meets
④	what	immediate	meet

6 밑줄 친 부분에 들어갈 가장 적절한 것은?

> Culture travels, like people. There are Chinese and Zen gardens in cities from Sydney to Edinburgh to San Francisco. 'World Music' is enormously popular: the latest disco style breezily combines flamenco with jazz and Gaelic traditions. Dance troupes from Africa and South America routinely perform overseas. It would be impossible to disentangle strands of influence in the spaghetti western, samurai film, Hollywood action flick, Indian adventure story, and Hong Kong cinema. In the modern world, no culture, however 'primitive' and remote, remains _____. The Huichol Indians, who live in mountain villages of Mexico, make their masks and bowls using glass beads imported from Japan and Czechoslovakia.

① isolated
② interconnected
③ multicultural
④ complex

※ 주어진 글의 제목으로 가장 적절한 것을 고르시오. 【7~8】

7

> Depending on your values, different kinds of numbers may be important to you. To some, it's cholesterol count and blood pressure figures; to others, it's the number of years they've been married. To many, the sum total in the retirement account is the number-one number, and some people zero in on the amount left on their mortgage. But I contend that your per-hour worth should be among the top-of-mind numbers that are important to you – no matter what your values or priorities are – even if you don't earn your living on a per-hour rate. Knowing the value of your time enables you to make wise decisions about where and how you spend it so you can make the most of this limited resource according to your circumstances, goals, and interests. Obviously, the higher you raise your per-hour worth while upholding your priorities, the more you can propel your efforts toward meeting your goals, because you have more resources at your disposal – you have either more money or more time, whichever you need most.

① Your Time Is Money
② Maintaining High Motivation
③ Part-time Jobs Are Better
④ Living Within Your Income

8

Making mistakes is central to the education of budding scientists and artists of all kinds, who must have the freedom to experiment, try this idea, flop, try another idea, take a risk, be willing to get the wrong answer. One classic example is Thomas Edison's reply to a reporter who was lamenting Edison's ten thousand experimental failures in his effort to create the first incandescent light bulb. "I have not failed," he told the reporter. "I successfully discovered 10,000 elements that don't work." Most children, however, are denied the freedom to noodle around, experiment, and be wrong in ten ways, let alone ten thousand. The focus on constant testing to measure and standardize children's accomplishments has intensified their fear of failure. It is certainly important for children to learn to succeed; but it is just as important for them to learn not to fear failure.

① Getting It Right the First Time

② The Secret Inventions of Edison

③ Road to Creativity : Avoid Risks

④ Failure : Nothing to Be Afraid Of

9 우리말을 영어로 옮긴 것 중 가장 어색한 것은?

① 그녀는 젊었을 때 더 열심히 일하지 않았던 것을 후회한다.
  →She regrets not having worked harder in her youth.

② 그는 경험과 지식을 둘 다 겸비한 사람이다.
  →He is a man of both experience and knowledge.

③ 분노는 정상적이고 건강한 감정이다.
  →Anger is a normal and healthy emotion.

④ 어떤 상황에서도 너는 이곳을 떠나면 안 된다.
  →Under no circumstances you should not leave here.

10 밑줄 친 부분에 들어갈 표현으로 가장 적절한 것은?

> M : Excuse me. How can I get to Seoul Station?
> W : You can take the subway.
> M : How long does it take?
> W : It takes approximately an hour.
> M : How often does the subway run?
> W : _____.

① It is too far to walk

② Every five minutes or so

③ You should wait in line

④ It takes about half an hour

※ 밑줄 친 부분과 의미가 가장 가까운 것을 고르시오. 【11~13】

11

> Bringing presents for his children alleviated some of the guilt he felt for not spending enough time with them.

① relieved

② accumulated

③ provoked

④ accelerated

12

> I am not made of money, you know!

① needy

② thrifty

③ wealthy

④ stingy

13

Experienced salespeople claim there is a difference between being assertive and being <u>pushy</u>.

① thrilled   ② brave

③ timid   ④ aggressive

※ 주어진 부분에 들어갈 가장 적절한 것을 고르시오. 【14~15】

14

A growing number of people are seeking medical attention for vitamin D deficiency, a common condition among those who spend a lot of time indoors. It is well known that vitamin D deficiency can affect one's muscles, bones and immunity and is even associated with cancer. Vitamin D is produced by the body in response to skin being exposed to sunlight. A lot of women, however, wear sunscreen before they go out, and this often makes it more difficult for their body to produce vitamin D – as _____.

① many types of sunscreen may contain beneficial substances

② sunscreen can block vitamin D–producing ultraviolet rays

③ their sunscreen is professionally prescribed

④ they exercise on a regular basis

15

Muzafer Sherif's research on the autokinetic effect is a good example of the role of _____ in perception. People in his experiments were told that a spot of light projected on the wall would move and were instructed to estimate the amount of movement. Although the spot of light never actually moved, the people inevitably reported movement. When told that the spot of light would even trace out letters and words, participants began reporting words and sentences. Clearly what they thought would happen resulted in the addition of a considerable amount of information to their sensations.

① unification   ② expectation
③ competition   ④ quantification

16 다음 글의 (A)와 (B)에 들어갈 가장 적절한 것은?

Mythology was an integral part of Egyptian culture for much of its timespan. Characters and events from myth permeate Egyptian art, architecture, and literature. Myths _____(A)_____ many of the rituals performed by kings and priests. Educated Egyptians believed that a knowledge of myth was an essential weapon in the fight to survive the dangers of life and the afterlife.

There is disagreement among Egyptologists about when mythical narratives first developed in Egypt. This dispute is partly due to the difficulty of deciding what should be counted as a myth. Today, the term myth is often used in an unfavorable way to refer to something that is exaggerated or untrue. In ancient cultures, myth did not have this _____(B)_____ connotation; myths could be regarded as stories that contained poetic rather than literal truths. Some scholars separate myths from other types of traditional tale by classifying them as stories featuring deities. This simple definition might work quite well for Egypt, but not for all cultures.

	(A)	(B)
①	extinguished	immoral
②	bolstered	literal
③	underpinned	negative
④	corroborated	political

※ 주어진 부분에 들어갈 가장 적절한 것을 고르시오. 【17~18】

17

We rarely get tired when _____. For example, I recently took a vacation in the Canadian Rockies up around Lake Louise. I spent several days trout fishing along Coral Creek, fighting my way through brush higher than my head, stumbling over logs, struggling through fallen timber — yet after eight hours of this, I was not exhausted. Why? Because I was excited, exhilarated. I had a sense of high achievement: six cutthroat trout. But suppose I had been bored by fishing, then how do you think I would have felt? I would have been worn out by such strenuous work at an altitude of seven thousand feet.

① we are doing something interesting and exciting

② we get a good night's sleep and a hearty meal

③ we do household chores for our family

④ we are elevated to high altitudes

18

The 'ten-thousand-hour rule' states that expertise requires at least ten thousand hours of practice. Clearly, though, time is not the only requirement. Years of one's life spent practicing the wrong things will not lead to expertise any more than spending the same amount of time watching television. Time is a basic prerequisite, but not _____.
Layered upon time are a slew of other ingredients, life focus, precision, discipline, and desire.

① a sufficient one in itself

② a requisite for time

③ a tolerant one of others

④ a predictor of longevity

19 George Stephenson에 관한 다음 글의 내용과 일치하지 않는 것은?

George Stephenson gained a reputation for working with the primitive steam engines employed in mines in the northeast of England and in Scotland. In 1814, Stephenson made his first locomotive, 'Blucher.' In 1821, Stephenson was appointed engineer for the construction of the Stockton and Darlington railway. It opened in 1825 and was the first public railway. In October 1829, the railway's owners staged a competition to find the best kind of locomotive to pull heavy loads over long distances. Stephenson's locomotive 'Rocket' was the winner, achieving a record speed of 36 miles per hour. The opening of the Stockton and Darlington railway and the success of 'Rocket' stimulated the laying of railway lines and the construction of locomotives all over the country. Stephenson became engineer on a number of these projects and also participated in the development of railways in Belgium and Spain.

① 탄광에 사용된 초기 증기 기관과 관련된 일을 하여 명성을 얻었다.
② 1814년에 그의 첫 번째 기관차를 만들었다.
③ 시속 36마일의 기관차를 개발하여 기관차 대회에서 준우승했다.
④ 벨기에와 스페인의 철도 개발에도 참여했다.

20 밑줄 친 부분에 들어갈 가장 적절한 것은?

There are many instances in our society in which it is entirely appropriate for people to play a power role over others. _____, teachers, coaches, police, and parents all play this role. Any leader of a group of people has to have some kind of authority. Still, the right to wield power and the extent to which an authority should wield power must be questioned and negotiated lest the power be abusive and lead to injustice and unfairness.

① However
② Otherwise
③ For example
④ Nevertheless

※ 밑줄 친 부분과 의미가 가장 가까운 것을 고르시오. 【1~2】

1

> The opposition party leaders promised to <u>persist in</u> their efforts to force the prime minister's resignation.

① consider   ② continue

③ rescue   ④ stop

2

> Many people <u>were taken in</u> by his good-looking face and great manner of talking, so they gave him all their money to invest.

① were pleased   ② were shocked

③ were deceived   ④ were disillusioned

3 우리말을 영어로 가장 잘 옮긴 것은?

> 내가 저지른 모든 실수에도 불구하고 그는 여전히 나를 신임했다.

① I had made all the mistakes, though he still trusted me.

② I had made all the mistakes, moreover, he still trusted me.

③ Despite all the mistakes I had made, he still trusted me.

④ Nevertheless all the mistakes I had made, he still trusted me.

4 우리말을 영어로 잘못 옮긴 것은?

① 네가 하는 어떤 것도 나에게는 괜찮아.

　→ Whatever you do is fine with me.

② 나는 어떤 일도 결코 우연히 하지 않았으며, 내 발명 중 어느 것도 우연히 이루어진 것은 없었다.

　→ I never did anything by accident, nor did any of my inventions come by accident.

③ 사랑은 서로를 응시하는 것에 있지 않고, 같은 방향을 함께 바라보는 것에 있다.

　→ Love does not consist in gazing at each other, but looks outward together in the same direction.

④ 자원봉사자들은 그들이 가치가 없기 때문이 아니라, 매우 귀중하기 때문에 보수를 받지 않는다.

　→ Volunteers aren't paid, not because they are worthless, but because they are priceless.

5 주어진 문장이 들어갈 위치로 가장 적절한 곳은?

> That plunge in poverty levels is truly one of the greatest achievements in human history.

Welfare helps alleviate poverty. But growth can end it. Asia's example over the past half-century teaches that there are two critical ways to raise incomes: create jobs – and create more jobs. And the way to do that is to boost economic growth. (①) When nations like China set in place the market-friendly policies to supercharge their growth rates, poverty melted away. (②) In 1981, figures the World Bank, about 52 % of the population of the developing world lived on less than $ 1.25 a day. (③) By 2008 that share had shrunk to 22 %, owing largely to gains made in Asia. (④) But it isn't enough. The International Monetary Fund recently stated that nearly all economies – advanced and emerging – suffered a widening gap between rich and poor in the past three decades.

6 밑줄 친 부분에 들어갈 말로 가장 적절한 것은?

A : Finally, the long vacation begins tomorrow. What are your plans?
B : I'm not sure. Maybe I'll go on a trip.
A : Where do you want to go?
B : That's a good question. Well, I'll just take a bus and go wherever it leads me to. Who knows? I may find a perfect place for my vacation.
A : Yeah, trips are always refreshing. But I prefer to stay at home and do nothing.
B : _____. Relaxing at home can recharge your energy.

① That's not a bad idea
② I prefer a domestic airline
③ You need to work at home too
④ My family leaves for Seoul tomorrow

7 글의 요지로 가장 적절한 것은?

How do you describe the times we live in, so connected and yet fractured? Linda Stone, a former Microsoft techie, characterizes ours as an era of continuous partial attention. At the extreme end are teenagers instant-messaging while they are talking on the cell phone, downloading music and doing homework. But adults too live with all systems go, interrupted and distracted, scanning everything, multi-technological-tasking everywhere. We suffer from the illusion, Stone says, that we can expand our personal bandwidth, connecting to more and more. Instead, we end up overstimulated, overwhelmed and, she adds, unfulfilled.

① Modern technology helps us to enrich our lives.
② We live in an age characterized by lack of full attention.
③ Family bond starts to weaken as a result of smart phone development.
④ The older generation can be as technologically smart as the younger one.

8 다음 글을 통해 IQ에 대하여 유추할 수 있는 것은?

IQ is a lot like height in basketball. Does someone who is five foot six have a realistic chance of playing professional basketball? Not really. You need to be at least six foot or six one to play at that level, and, all things being equal, it's probably better to be six two than six one, and better to be six three than six two. But past a certain point, height stops mattering so much. A player who is six foot eight is not automatically better than someone two inches shorter. (Michael Jordan, the greatest player ever, was six six after all.) A basketball player only has to be tall enough — and the same is true of intelligence. Intelligence has a threshold.

① IQ is just a myth; it has nothing to do with how smart you are.
② Once your IQ is over a certain level, it may not really matter anymore in terms of intelligence.
③ The higher IQ you have, the more intelligent you must be.
④ The more you practice, the higher your IQ will get.

9 주어진 글 다음에 이어질 글의 순서로 가장 적절한 것은?

Two major techniques for dealing with environmental problems are conservation and restoration. Conservation involves protecting existing natural habitats. Restoration involves cleaning up and restoring damaged habitats. The best way to deal with environmental problems is to prevent them from happening. Conserving habitats prevents environmental issues that arise from ecosystem disruption.

(A) To solve the problem, the city built a sewage-treatment complex. Since then, the harbor waters have cleared up. Plants and fish have returned, and beaches have been reopened.
(B) For example, parks and reserves protect a large area in which many species live. Restoration reverses damage to ecosystems. Boston Harbor is one restoration success story.
(C) Since the colonial period, the city dumped sewage directly into the harbor. The buildup of waste caused outbreaks of disease. Beaches were closed. Most of the marine life disappeared and as a result, the shellfish industry shut down.

① (A) − (B) − (C)
② (B) − (C) − (A)
③ (C) − (A) − (B)
④ (C) − (B) − (A)

10 밑줄 친 부분에 들어갈 말로 가장 적절한 것은?

The majority of British people dress conservatively rather than fashionably. A small number of the upper and professional upper middle class, for example, barristers, diplomats, army officers and Conservative MPs, dress in the well-tried styles of the past 50 years or so. Many of the men still have their suits specially tailored, and are thus instantly recognizable as belonging to the upper echelons of society. Yet how they dress is wholly unrepresentative of society in general. The vast majority of people buy their clothes at the high-street stores, of which Marks and Spencer, a major British multinational retailer, must be the most famous. They wear the clothes of the British middle classes, perfectly passable but hardly stylish like the dress standards in much of Europe. Indeed, the British still have a reputation of being _____ in Europe, and they do not really care.

① the most diligent people
② the worst dressed people
③ the most arrogant people
④ the least conservative people

※ 밑줄 친 부분과 의미가 가장 가까운 것을 고르시오. 【11~12】

11

When my sister's elbow healed, her fears of never being able to play tennis were <u>assuaged</u>.

① heightened ② soothed

③ tormented ④ escalated

12

There are <u>multiple</u> opportunities each day to become upset about something, but we have the choice to let them go and remain at peace.

① various ② important

③ occasional ④ decisive

13 두 사람의 대화 내용 중 가장 어색한 것은?

① A : I don't think I can finish this project by the deadline.

  B : Take your time. I'm sure you can make it.

② A : Mom, what do you want to get for Mother's Day?

  B : I don't need anything. I just feel blessed to have a son like you.

③ A : I think something's wrong with this cake. This is not sweet at all!

  B : I agree. It just tastes like a chunk of salt.

④ A : Would you carry this for me? I don't have enough hands.

  B : Sure, I'll hand it over to you right away.

※ 밑줄 친 부분 중 어법상 옳지 않은 것을 고르시오. 【14~15】

14

The middle-class Americans who chose ① to avoid the suburban lifestyle and ② live in the central city ③ were most often those least ④ depended on central-city government services.

15

In 1778 Carlo de Buonaparte, re-elected as one of the Council of Twelve Nobles, ① was chosen to be a member of a Corsican delegation to King Louis XVI. He took ten-year-old Giuseppe and nine-year-old Napoleone with him, ② to begin their life in their new country. They spent a night in a miserable inn at the port, sleeping on mattresses ③ lay out on the floor. En route from Corsica they visited Florence, where Carlo was able to procure a letter of introduction from the Habsburg Grand Duke Pietro Leopoldo to his sister Queen Marie Antoinette. Then they went on to France. Admittedly Carlo had something to celebrate, ④ having been informed by the Minister for War that Napoleone had been granted a scholarship and a place in the military school at Brienne as 'Royal Pupil' whose expenses would be paid by the King.

16 밑줄 친 부분에 들어갈 말로 가장 적절한 것은?

The first commercially successful steam engine was built in England in 1712, but it was very slow. Then an inventor named James Watt came up with crucial innovations. His engine was faster and more efficient at driving machinery. By 1800 about 500 of Watt's steam engines were chugging and hissing in mines and factories throughout Britain. The widespread use of steam engines began when inventors put them to use in the textile mills. Using steam power instead of water power meant that factories no longer had to be built near ready supplies of water. _____, they could be located where fuel was readily available and where workers already lived. Also, factories could be built closer to roads and ports from which raw materials and finished products could be shipped.

① Unfortunately

② Nevertheless

③ Similarly

④ Instead

17 주어진 문장이 들어갈 위치로 가장 적절한 곳은?

Teaching is also one of the few jobs where you can say you are making a significant and positive impact on the world around you.

The rewards that come from teaching are numerous. (①) One of those is the emotional connections you make with your students. (②) You are constantly engaging with them on a personal level, inspiring them to strive to do the best they can and providing support when they run into problems. (③) Watching them grow from the experience and ultimately seeing them succeed because of your tuition and guidance is a feeling without comparison. (④) While other jobs may leave a more obvious mark, few can say that over the course of their career they have helped countless young people fulfill their potential and become the adults they are today.

18 글의 내용과 가장 일치하는 것은?

Polar bears are mammals that belong to the bear family. They are one of the largest animals in the Arctic and one of the largest meat-eating animals in the world. They can weigh up to 680 kilograms and can be up to 3.4 meters tall. Polar bears have thick, oily, and water-repellent fur. This fur covers their body, including the spaces between their pads on their paws. Their white fur helps them blend in with the snow and ice. They use only their broad front paws to swim through the water. As for their food, polar bears hunt and eat seals from time to time. They also eat fish, grass, or even dead animals and stranded whales.

① Polar bears have fur that is permeable to water.
② Polar bears have no fur on their paws.
③ Polar bears rely on their front paws for swimming.
④ Polar bears eat only meat.

19 글의 흐름상 가장 어색한 문장은?

Children can benefit from learning how to use context clues and guessing the meaning from the context. ①This is a strategy that children can use when they encounter unfamiliar words. ②Conversely, some researchers point out that in addition to teaching how to use context clues, children also need to be taught that context clues do not always help readers to understand the meanings of unfamiliar words. ③An example would be having a child choose between the words enormous and giant in a sentence about sandwiches. ④Children need to be taught that there are times when they will not be able to figure out the meaning from context clues.

20 글의 제목으로 가장 적절한 것은?

When we think of the people who make our lives miserable by spreading malicious viruses, most of us imagine an unpopular teenager boy, brilliant but geeky, venting his frustrations from the safety of a suburban bedroom. Actually, these stereotypes are just that — stereotypes — according to Sarah Gordon, an expert in computer viruses and security technology. Since 1992, Gordon has studied the psychology of virus writers. "A virus writer is just as likely to be the guy next door to you," she says. The virus writers Gordon has come to know have varied backgrounds; while predominantly male, some are female. Some are solidly academics, while others are athletic. Many have friendships with members of the opposite sex, good relationships with their parents and families; most are popular with their peers. They don't spend all their time in the basement. One virus writer volunteers in his local library, working with elderly people. One of them is a poet and a musician, another is an electrical engineer, and others work for a university quantum physics department.

① Unmasking Virus Writers

② Virus Writers: Gender and Class

③ Underground Virus Writers

④ Misterious Activities by Virus Writers

영어

2016. 4. 9. | 인사혁신처 시행

☞ 정답 및 해설 P.60

1 밑줄 친 부분에 들어갈 말로 가장 적절한 것은?

> The campaign to eliminate pollution will prove _____ unless it has the understanding and full cooperation of the public.

① enticing

② enhanced

③ fertile

④ futile

2 밑줄 친 부분과 의미가 가장 가까운 것은?

> Up to now, newspaper articles have only <u>scratched the surface of</u> this tremendously complex issue.

① superficially dealt with

② hit the nail on the head of

③ seized hold of

④ positively followed up on

※ 밑줄 친 부분에 들어갈 말로 가장 적절한 것을 고르시오. 【3~4】

3

A : I'd like to get a refund for this tablecloth I bought here yesterday.
B : Is there a problem with the tablecloth?
A : It doesn't fit our table and I would like to return it. Here is my receipt.
B : I'm sorry, but this tablecloth was a final sale item, and it cannot be refunded.
A : _____
B : It's written at the bottom of the receipt.

① Nobody mentioned that to me.
② Where is the price tag?
③ What's the problem with it?
④ I got a good deal on it.

4

A : Hello? Hi, Stephanie. I'm on my way to the office. Do you need anything?
B : Hi, Luke. Can you please pick up extra paper for the printer?
A : What did you say? Did you say to pick up ink for the printer?
  Sorry, _____
B : Can you hear me now? I said I need more paper for the printer.
A : Can you repeat that, please?
B : Never mind. I'll text you.
A : Okay. Thanks, Stephanie. See you soon.

① My phone has really bad reception here.
② I couldn't pick up more paper.
③ I think I've dialed the wrong number.
④ I'll buy each item separately this time.

5 우리말을 영어로 잘못 옮긴 것은?

① 나의 이모는 파티에서 그녀를 만난 것을 기억하지 못했다.
   → My aunt didn't remember meeting her at the party.

② 나의 첫 책을 쓰는 데 40년이 걸렸다.
   → It took me 40 years to write my first book.

③ 학교에서 집으로 걸어오고 있을 때 강풍에 내 우산이 뒤집혔다.
   → A strong wind blew my umbrella inside out as I was walking home from school.

④ 끝까지 생존하는 생물은 가장 강한 생물도, 가장 지적인 생물도 아니고, 변화에 가장 잘 반응하는 생물이다.
   → It is not the strongest of the species, nor the most intelligent, or the one most responsive to change that survives to the end.

6 글의 제목으로 가장 적절한 것은?

After analyzing a mass of data on job interview results, a research team discovered a surprising reality. Did the likelihood of being hired depend on qualifications? Or was it work experience? In fact, it was neither. It was just one important factor: did the candidate appear to be a pleasant person. Those candidates who had managed to ingratiate themselves were very likely to be offered a position; they had charmed their way to success. Some had made a special effort to smile and maintain eye contact. Others had praised the organization. This positivity had convinced the interviewers that such pleasant and socially skilled applicants would fit well into the workplace, and so should be offered a job.

① To Get a Job, Be a Pleasant Person
② More Qualifications Bring Better Chances
③ It Is Ability That Counts, Not Personality
④ Show Yourself As You Are at an Interview

7 글의 내용과 일치하지 않는 것은?

> Most writers lead double lives. They earn good money at legitimate professions, and carve out time for their writing as best they can: early in the morning, late at night, weekends, vacations. William Carlos Williams and Louis-Ferdinand Céline were doctors. Wallace Stevens worked for an insurance company. T.S. Elliot was a banker, then a publisher. Don DeLilo, Peter Carey, Salman Rushdie, and Elmore Leonard all worked for long stretches in advertising. Other writers teach. That is probably the most common solution today, and with every major university and college offering so-called creative writing courses, novelists and poets are continually scratching and scrambling to land themselves a spot. Who can blame them? The salaries might not be big, but the work is steady and the hours are good.

① Some writers struggle for teaching positions to teach creative writing courses.

② As a doctor, William Carlos Williams tried to find the time to write.

③ Teaching is a common way for writers to make a living today.

④ Salman Rushdie worked briefly in advertising with great triumph.

8 글의 흐름상 가장 어색한 문장은?

> One of the largest celebrations of the passage of young girls into womanhood occurs in Latin American and Hispanic cultures. This event is called La Quinceañera, or the fifteenth year. ①It acknowledges that a young woman is now of marriageable age. The day usually begins with a Mass of Thanksgiving. ②By comparing the rites of passage of one culture with those of another, we can assess differences in class status. The young woman wears a full-length white or pastel-colored dress and is attended by fourteen friends and relatives who serve as maids of honor and male escorts. ③Her parents and godparents surround her at the foot of the altar. When the Mass ends, other young relatives give small gifts to those who attended, while the Quinceañera herself places a bouquet of flowers on the altar of the Virgin. ④Following the Mass is an elaborate party, with dancing, cake, and toasts. Finally, to end the evening, the young woman dances a waltz with her favorite escort.

9 주어진 문장이 들어갈 위치로 가장 적절한 곳은?

> He dismally fails the first two, but redeems himself in the concluding whale episode, where he does indeed demonstrate courage, honesty, and unselfishness.

> Disney's work draws heavily from fairy tales, myths, and folklore, which are profuse in archetypal elements. (①) Pinocchio is a good example of how these elements can be emphasized rather than submerged beneath a surface realism. (②) Early in the film, the boy/puppet Pinocchio is told that in order to be a "real boy," he must show that he is "brave, truthful, and unselfish." (③) The three principal episodes of the movie represent ritualistic trials, testing the youth's moral fortitude. (④) As such, like most of Disney's works, the values in Pinocchio are traditional and conservative, an affirmation of the sanctity of the family unit, the importance of a Higher Power in guiding our destinies, and the need to play by society's rules.

10 글의 내용과 일치하지 않는 것은?

> Stanislavski was fortunate in many ways. He was the son of a wealthy man who could give him the advantages of a broad education, the opportunity to see the greatest exponents of theatre art at home and abroad. He acquired a great reputation because he had set high goals and never faltered along the hard road leading to them. His personal integrity and inexhaustible capacity for work contributed to making him a professional artist of the first rank. Stanislavski was also richly endowed by nature with a handsome exterior, fine voice and genuine talent. As an actor, director and teacher, he was destined to influence and inspire the many who worked with him and under him or who had the privilege of seeing him on the stage.

① Stanislavski was born with attractive features.
② Stanislavski remained uninfluential on his colleagues throughout his life.
③ Stanislavski's father was affluent enough to support his education.
④ Stanislavski became a top-ranked artist by the aid of his upright character and untiring competence.

※ 밑줄 친 부분과 의미가 가장 가까운 것을 고르시오. 【11~12】

11

> It was personal. Why did you have to <u>stick your nose in</u>?

① hurry   ② interfere

③ sniff   ④ resign

12

> Newton made <u>unprecedented</u> contributions to mathematics, optics, and mechanical physics.

① mediocre   ② suggestive

③ unsurpassed   ④ provocative

13 어법상 옳은 것은?

① Jessica is a much careless person who makes little effort to improve her knowledge.

② But he will come or not is not certain.

③ The police demanded that she not leave the country for the time being.

④ The more a hotel is expensiver, the better its service is.

14 글의 제목으로 가장 적절한 것은?

Character is a respect for human beings and the right to interpret experience differently. Character admits self-interest as a natural trait, but pins its faith on man's hesitant but heartening instinct to cooperate. Character is allergic to tyranny, irritable with ignorance and always open to improvement. Character is, above all, a tremendous humility before the facts — an automatic alliance with truth even when that truth is bitter medicine.

① Character's Resistance to Truth

② How to Cooperate with Characters

③ The Ignorance of Character

④ What Character Means

15 글의 주제로 가장 적절한 것은?

Children who under-achieve at school may just have poor working memory rather than low intelligence. Researchers from a university surveyed more than 3,000 primary school children of all ages and found that 10 % of them suffer from poor working memory, which seriously impedes their learning. Nationally, this equates to almost 500,000 children in primary education being affected. The researchers also found that teachers rarely identify poor working memory and often describe children with this problem as inattentive or less intelligent.

① children's identification with teachers at school

② low intelligence of primary school children

③ influence of poor working memory on primary school children

④ teachers' efforts to solve children's working-memory problem

16 글의 내용과 일치하는 것은?

A new study by Harvard researchers may provide a compelling reason to remove canned soup and juice from your dining table. People who ate one serving of canned food daily over the course of five days, the study found, had significantly elevated levels – more than a tenfold increase – of bisphenol-A, or BPA, a substance that lines most food and drink cans. Public health officials in the United States have come under increasing pressure to regulate it. Some of the research on BPA shows that it is linked to a higher risk of cancer, heart disease, and obesity. Some researchers, though, counter that its reputation as a health threat to people is exaggerated. The new study published in The Journal of the American Medical Association is the first to measure the amounts of BPA that are ingested when people eat food that comes directly out of a can.

① 하버드의 새로운 연구가 통조림 음식의 안전성을 입증하였다.

② 비스페놀 A와 암, 심장병, 비만의 연관성이 과장되었다는 데에 모든 학자들이 동의한다.

③ 통조림 음식으로부터 사람의 몸에 유입된 비스페놀 A의 양이 아직 측정되지 않았다.

④ 미국의 보건 관리들은 비스페놀 A를 규제하라는 압력을 점점 더 받고 있다.

17 밑줄 친 부분에 들어갈 말로 가장 적절한 것을 고르시오.

There's a knock at your door. Standing in front of you is a young man who needs help. He's injured and is bleeding. You take him in and help him, make him feel comfortable and safe and phone for an ambulance. This is clearly the right thing to do. But if you help him just because you feel sorry for him, according to Immanuel Kant, _____. Your sympathy is irrelevant to the morality of your action. That's part of your character, but nothing to do with right and wrong. Morality for Kant wasn't just about what you do, but about why you do it. Those who do the right thing don't do it simply because of how they feel : the decision has to be based on reason, reason that tells you what your duty is, regardless of how you happen to feel.

① that wouldn't be a moral action at all

② your action is founded on reason

③ then you're exhibiting ethical behavior

④ you're encouraging him to be an honest person

18 주어진 글 다음에 이어질 글의 순서로 가장 적절한 것은?

All animals have the same kind of brain activation during sleep as humans. Whether or not they dream is another question, which can be answered only by posing another one: Do animals have consciousness?

(A) These are three of the key aspects of consciousness, and they could be experienced whether or not an animal had verbal language as we do. When the animal's brain is activated during sleep, why not assume that the animal has some sort of perceptual, emotional, and memory experience?

(B) Many scientists today feel that animals probably do have a limited form of consciousness, quite different from ours in that it lacks language and the capacity for propositional or symbolic thought.

(C) Animals certainly can't report dreams even if they do have them. But which pet owner would doubt that his or her favourite animal friend has perception, memory, and emotion?

① (A) − (B) − (C)　　　　　② (A) − (C) − (B)
③ (B) − (C) − (A)　　　　　④ (C) − (B) − (A)

19 밑줄 친 부분 중 어법상 옳은 것은?

①As the old saying go, you are what you eat. The foods you eat ②obvious affect your body's performance. They may also influence how your brain handles tasks. If your brain handles them well, you think more clearly, and you are more emotionally stable. The right food can ③help you being concentrated, keep you motivated, sharpen your memory, speed your reaction time, reduce stress, and perhaps ④even prevent your brain from aging.

20 밑줄 친 부분에 들어갈 말로 가장 적절한 것을 고르시오.

A group of tribes and genera of hopping reptiles, small creatures of the dinosaur type, seem to have been pushed by competition and the pursuit of their enemies towards the alternatives of extinction or adaptation to colder conditions in the higher hills or by the sea. Among these distressed tribes there was developed a new type of scale – scales that were elongated into quill-like forms and that presently branched into the crude beginnings of feathers. These quill-like scales lay over one another and formed a heat-retaining covering more efficient than any reptilian covering that had hitherto existed. So they permitted an invasion of colder regions that were otherwise uninhabited. Perhaps simultaneously with these changes there arose in these creatures a greater solicitude for their eggs. Most reptiles are apparently quite careless about their eggs, which are left for sun and season to hatch. But some of the varieties upon this new branch of the tree of life were acquiring a habit of guarding their eggs and _____. With these adaptations to cold, other internal modifications were going on that made these creatures, the primitive birds, warm-blooded and independent of basking.

① hatching them unsuccessfully

② leaving them under the sun on their own

③ keeping them warm with the warmth of their bodies

④ flying them to scaled reptiles

☞ 정답 및 해설 P.66

※ 밑줄 친 부분에 들어갈 말로 가장 적절한 것을 고르시오. 【1~3】

1

> The two cultures were so utterly _____ that she found it hard to adapt from one to the other.

① overlapped   ② equivalent

③ associative   ④ disparate

2

> Penicillin can have an _____ effect on a person who is allergic to it.

① affirmative   ② aloof

③ adverse   ④ allusive

3

> Last year, I had a great opportunity to do this performance with the staff responsible for _____ art events at the theater.

① turning into   ② doing without

③ putting on   ④ giving up

4 ① 오늘 밤 나는 영화 보러 가기보다는 집에서 쉬고 싶다.

→I'd rather relax at home than going to the movies tonight.

② 경찰은 집안 문제에 대해서는 개입하기를 무척 꺼린다.

→The police are very unwilling to interfere in family problems.

③ 네가 통제하지 못하는 과거의 일을 걱정해봐야 소용없다.

→It's no use worrying about past events over which you have no control.

④ 내가 자주 열쇠를 엉뚱한 곳에 두어서 내 비서가 나를 위해 여분의 열쇠를 갖고 다닌다.

→I misplace my keys so often that my secretary carries spare ones for me.

5 ① 그녀가 어리석은 계획을 포기하도록 설득해 줄래요?

→Can you talk her out of her foolish plan?

② 그녀의 어머니에 대해서는 나도 너만큼 아는 것이 없다.

→I know no more than you don't about her mother.

③ 그의 군대는 거의 2대 1로 수적 열세였다.

→His army was outnumbered almost two to one.

④ 같은 나이의 두 소녀라고 해서 반드시 생각이 같은 것은 아니다.

→Two girls of an age are not always of a mind.

6

The planet is warming, from North Pole to South Pole, and everywhere in between. Globally, the mercury is already up more than 1 degree Fahrenheit, and even more in sensitive polar regions. And the effects of rising temperatures aren't waiting for some far-flung future. They're happening right now. Signs are appearing all over, and some of them are surprising. The heat is not only melting glaciers and sea ice; it's also shifting precipitation patterns and setting animals on the move.

① Preventive Measures Against Climate Change
② Melting Down of North Pole's Ice Cap
③ Growing Signs of Global Warming
④ Positive Effects of Temperature Rise

7

Few words are tainted by so much subtle nonsense and confusion as *profit*. To my liberal friends the word connotes the proceeds of fundamentally unrespectable and unworthy behaviors: minimally, greed and selfishness; maximally, the royal screwing of millions of helpless victims. Profit is the incentive for the most unworthy performance. To my conservative friends, it is a term of highest endearment, connoting efficiency and good sense. To them, profit is the ultimate incentive for worthy performance. Both connotations have some small merit, of course, because profit may result from both greedy, selfish activities and from sensible, efficient ones. But overgeneralizations from either bias do not help us in the least in understanding the relationship between profit and human competence.

① Relationship Between Profit and Political Parties
② Who Benefits from Profit
③ Why Making Profit Is Undesirable
④ Polarized Perceptions of Profit

8 글의 내용과 일치하는 것은?

> Electric cars were always environmentally friendly, quiet, clean—but definitely not sexy. The Sesta Speedking has changed all that. A battery-powered sports car that sells for $120,000 and has a top speed of 125 m.p.h. (200 km/h), the Speedking has excited the clean-tech crowd since it was first announced. Some Hollywood celebrities also joined a long waiting list for the Speedking; magazines like Wired drooled over it. After years of setbacks and shake-ups, the first Sesta Speedkings were delivered to customers this year. Reviews have been ecstatic, but Sesta Motors has been hit hard by the financial crisis. Plans to develop an affordable electric sedan have been put on hold, and Sesta is laying off employees. But even if the Speedking turns out to be a one-hit wonder, it's been an exciting electric ride.

① Speedking is a new electric sedan.

② Speedking has received negative feedback.

③ Sesta is hiring more employees.

④ Sesta has suspended a new car project.

9 콜라비에 대한 설명 중 글의 내용과 일치하지 않는 것은?

> Kohlrabi is one of the vegetables many people avoid, mainly because of its odd shape and strange name. However, kohlrabi is delicious, versatile and good for you. Kohlrabi is a member of Brassica, which also includes broccoli and cabbage. Brassica plants are high in antioxidants, and kohlrabi is no exception. Plus kohlrabi contains fiber, useful amounts of vitamin C, together with vitamin B, potassium and calcium. Kohlrabi can be eaten raw: it's delicious when thinly sliced and mixed into salads. You can also roast chunks of it in the oven, or use it as the base for a soup.
>
> *brassica : 배추속(屬)

① 생김새와 이름이 이상하여 사람들이 좋아하지 않는다.

② 브로콜리와 양배추와 함께 배추속에 속한다.

③ 다른 배추속 식물과는 달리 항산화제가 적다.

④ 날것으로 먹거나 오븐에 구워먹을 수 있다.

10 밑줄 친 부분에 들어갈 말로 가장 적절한 것은?

In an early demonstration of the mere exposure effect, participants in an experiment were exposed to a set of alphabets from the Japanese language. As most people know, Japanese alphabets look like drawings and are called ideograms. In the experiment, the duration of exposure to each ideogram was deliberately kept as short as 30 milliseconds. At such short durations of exposure—known as subliminal exposure—people cannot register the stimuli and hence, participants in the experiment were not expected to recall seeing the ideograms. Nevertheless, when participants were shown two sets of alphabets, one to which they had been previously exposed and another to which they hadn't, participants reported greater liking for the former even though they couldn't recall seeing them! These results have been replicated numerous times and across a variety of types of stimuli, so they are robust. What the mere exposure results show is that _____.

① we can learn the Japanese language with extensive exposure.

② duration is responsible for the robust results across studies.

③ it is impossible to register the stimuli at short durations.

④ people develop a liking towards stimuli that are familiar.

11 밑줄 친 부분에 공통으로 들어갈 말로 가장 적절한 것은?

• The psychologist used a new test to _____ overall personality development of students.
• Snacks _____ 25 % to 30 % of daily energy intake among adolescents.

① carry on   ② figure out

③ account for   ④ depend upon

12 밑줄 친 'your dad's character'를 가장 잘 표현하는 것은?

I began to get a pretty good sense of your father the first time I came to visit you at your house. Before my visit, he asked me some detailed questions about my physical needs. As soon as he learned about my heavy wheelchair, he began planning how he would build a ramp to the front door. The first day I came to the house, the ramp was ready, built with his own hands. Later on, when your dad found out about your younger brother's autism, he said one thing I will never forget. "If Sam can't learn in school," he told me, "I will take a couple of years off work and we will sail around the world. I will teach him everything he needs to know in those two years." That says everything about your dad's character.

*autism : 자폐증

① strict and stern

② funny and humorous

③ lazy and easygoing

④ considerate and thoughtful

13 밑줄 친 부분에 들어갈 말로 가장 적절한 것은?

John : Excuse me. Can you tell me where Namdaemun Market is?
Mira : Sure. Go straight ahead and turn right at the taxi stop over there.
John : Oh, I see. Is that where the market is?
Mira : _____

① That's right. You have to take a bus over there to the market.

② You can usually get good deals at traditional markets.

③ I don't really know. Please ask a taxi driver.

④ Not exactly. You need to go down two more blocks.

14 두 사람의 대화 중 가장 어색한 것은?

① A : Would you like to go to dinner with me this week?

  B : OK. But what's the occasion?

② A : Why don't we go to a basketball game sometime?

  B : Sure. Just tell me when.

③ A : What do you do in your spare time?

  B : I just relax at home. Sometimes I watch TV.

④ A : Could I help you with anything?

  B : Yes, I would like to. That would be nice.

※ 어법상 옳은 것을 고르시오. 【15~16】

15 ① That place is fantastic whether you like swimming or to walk.

② She suggested going out for dinner after the meeting.

③ The dancer that I told you about her is coming to town.

④ If she took the medicine last night, she would have been better today.

16 ① The poor woman couldn't afford to get a smartphone.

② I am used to get up early everyday.

③ The number of fires that occur in the city are growing every year.

④ Bill supposes that Mary is married, isn't he?

17 글의 흐름상 가장 어색한 문장은?

Progress is gradually being made in the fight against cancer. ①In the early 1900s, few cancer patients had any hope of long-term survival. ②But because of advances in medical technology, progress has been made so that currently four in ten cancer patients survive. ③It has been proven that smoking is a direct cause of lung cancer. ④However, the battle has not yet been won. Although cures for some forms of cancer have been discovered, other forms of cancer are still increasing.

18 주어진 문장이 들어갈 위치로 가장 적절한 곳은?

But the truth is, after you successfully make it through this problem, there will be another problem to face.

Some people are convinced that life is simply a series of problems to be solved. The sooner they get through with the problem they are facing, the sooner they will be happy. (①) And after you overcome that obstacle, there will be something else to overcome and there's always another mountain to climb. (②) That's why it is important to enjoy the journey, not just the destination. (③) In this world, we will never arrive at a place where everything is perfect and we have no more challenges. (④) As admirable as setting goals and reaching them may be, you can't get so focused on accomplishing your goals that you make the mistake of not enjoying where you are right now.

※ 밑줄 친 부분에 들어갈 말로 가장 적절한 것을 고르시오. 【19~20】

19

I don't know how it is for women or for other guys, but when I was young, I had a fear of _____. I thought it was a giant step toward death. So I did all I could to resist it because the idea was frightening to me. Then, one day I met Jane while I was shooting my first film. This changed everything. Jane, who was from Kentucky, was waitressing at that time, and I noticed her right away. She was really beautiful, and it took me all day to get up the nerve to ask her out. Just then a makeup man on the film snapped a photo of the two of us. About two years ago he sent it to me, saying, "Here you are asking a local girl for a date." He didn't know that that "local girl" became my wife. I still remember that day vividly.

① death
② marriage
③ making films
④ taking photos

20

One well-known difficulty in finding new things has been termed the 'oasis trap' by the cognitive psychologist David Perkins. Knowledge becomes centered in an 'oasis' of rich findings and it is just too risky and expensive to leave that still productive and well-watered zone. So people stick to _____. This is what happened to a certain extent in China over many centuries. The huge physical distances between centers of knowledge in China and the fact that the distant centers turned out to be little different from one another discouraged exploration.

① what they know
② the undiscovered world
③ their dream and imagination
④ how things are going to change

※ 다음 중 밑줄 친 단어와 뜻이 가장 가까운 것은? 【1~3】

1

Parents must not give up on kids who act <u>rebellious</u> or seem socially awkward; this is a normal stage most youngsters go through and eventually outgrow.

① passive

② delirious

③ disobedient

④ sporadic

2

He was born to a wealthy family in New York in 1800's. This circumstance allowed him to lead a <u>prodigal</u> existence for much of his life.

① perjury

② unstable

③ pernicious

④ lavish

3

Perhaps the brightest spot in the contemporary landscape of American higher education is the <u>resurgence</u> of interest in engaging students in civic life beyond campus.

① comeback

② disappearance

③ motivation

④ paucity

4 밑줄 친 부분 중 어법상 가장 옳지 않은 것은?

> He acknowledged that ① the number of Koreans were forced ② into labor ③ under harsh conditions in some of the locations ④ during the 1940's.

5 다음 대화에서 어법상 가장 옳지 않은 것은?

> Ann : Your hair ① looks nice.
> Tori : I ② had it cut by the tall hairdresser in the new hair salon next to the cafeteria.
> Ann : Not that place where I ③ got my head to stick in the drier?
> Tori : ④ Must be, I suppose. Yes, that one.
> Ann : Huh, and they still let them open.

※ 어법상 빈칸에 들어가기에 가장 적절한 것은? 【6~7】

6

> Creativity is thinking in ways that lead to original, practical and meaningful solutions to problems or _____ new ideas or forms of artistic expression.

① that generate ② having generated

③ to be generated ④ being generated

7

> It was when I got support across the board politically, from Republicans as well as Democrats, _____ I knew I had done the right thing.

① who ② whom

③ whose ④ that

8 문맥상 빈칸에 들어갈 가장 적절한 것은?

> Usually several skunks live together; however, adult male striped skunks are _____ during the summer.

① nocturnal

② solitary

③ predatory

④ dormant

9 문맥상 빈칸에 들어갈 가장 적절한 것은?

> Language and spelling change. Crystal, one of the most prolific writers on English, has helped popularize that truth. If, as internet use suggests, people are now starting to write "rhubarb" as "rubarb" _____, that, he says, may one day become an acceptable _____.

① alternative

② obligation

③ risk

④ order

10 다음 빈칸에 들어갈 표현으로 가장 적절한 것은?

> The reputation of Genghis Khan as _____ may be worse than the reality. Much of our information comes from chroniclers of the time who often exaggerated the facts. It is possible that they were encouraged by their Mongol employers to exaggerate the tales of cruelty so that the Mongols appeared more frightening to their enemies.

① an exaggerating storyteller

② a courageous emperor

③ an influential figure

④ an utterly ruthless warrior

11 다음 빈칸에 들어갈 가장 적절한 연결어를 고르면?

Our brain processes and stores different kinds of information in different ways. Think about factual knowledge. Fact memory entails learning explicit information, such as names, faces, words and dates. It is related to our conscious thoughts and our ability to manipulate symbols and language. When fact memories are committed to long-term memory, they are usually filed along with the context in which they were learned : _____, when you think of your new friend Joe, you probably picture him at the basketball game where you met him.

① In short

② For instance

③ Above all

④ In addition

12 문맥상 빈칸에 들어갈 가장 적절한 것은?

As incredible as it sounds, there are some species of insects that will _____ themselves to protect their nests. When faced with an intruder, the Camponotus cylindricus ant of Borneo will grab onto the invader and squeeze itself until it explodes. The ant's abdomen ruptures, releasing a sticky yellow substance that will be lethal for both the defender and the attacker, permanently sticking them together and preventing the attacker from reaching the nest.

① commit

② replace

③ expose

④ sacrifice

13 문맥상 빈칸에 들어갈 가장 적절한 것을 고르면?

> E-waste is being produced on a scale never seen before. Computers and other electronic equipment become _____ in just a few years, leaving customers with little choice but to buy newer ones to keep up. Thus, tens of millions of computers, TVs and cell phones are _____ each year.

① efficient – documented

② obsolete – discarded

③ fascinating – reused

④ identical – thrown

14 다음 빈칸에 들어갈 가장 적절한 것을 고르면?

> In the last twenty years the amount of time Americans have spent at their jobs has risen steadily. Each year the change is small, amounting to about nine hours, or slightly more than one additional day of work. In any given year such a small increment has probably been _____. But the accumulated increase over two decades is substantial.

① dazzling

② vulnerable

③ imperceptible

④ compulsory

※ 다음 빈칸에 들어갈 단어를 순서대로 고르면? 【15~16】

15

The country with the highest rate of crime in the world is Vatican City, with 1.5 crimes per resident. However, this high ratio is due to the country's tiny population of only around 840 people. It is likely that the vast majority of the crimes, which consist mainly of pick-pocketing and shop-lifting, are _____ by outsiders. The Vatican has a special police force with 130 members responsible for criminal investigation, border control and protection of the pope. There is no prison in Vatican City, with the exception of a few detention cells to hold criminals before trial. The majority of criminals are _____ by Italian courts.

① manipulated – sealed

② dominated – overruled

③ committed – tried

④ conducted – enforced

16

Albert Einstein's general theory of relativity is about to celebrate its 100th anniversary, and his revolutionary hypothesis has _____ the test of time, despite numerous expert attempts to find _____. Einstein changed the way we think about the most basic things, which are space and time. And that opened our eyes to the universe, and how the most interesting things in it work, like black holes.

① withstood – flaws

② resisted – proofs

③ wasted – examples

④ squandered – pitfalls

17 다음 글의 목적으로 가장 적절한 것은?

Casa Heiwa is an apartment building where people can learn some important life skills and how to cope with living in a new environment. The building managers run a service that offers many programs to children and adults living in the building. For the children, there is a day-care center that operates from 7 a.m. until 6 p.m. There are also educational programs available for adults including computer processing and English conversation courses.

① to argue for a need for educational programs

② to recruit employees for an apartment building

③ to attract apartment residents toward programs

④ to recommend ways to improve the living standard

18 다음 글을 문맥에 맞게 순서대로 배열한 것은?

ⓐ Rosa Parks was arrested, jailed, convicted and fined. She refused to pay. Her experience set off a 382-day boycott of Montgomery city buses.

ⓑ According to the segregation laws of the day, Rosa Parks, an African American, was required to sit in the back of the bus. She was accused of encroaching on the whites-only section, and the bus driver tried to convince her to obey the law.

ⓒ Instead, Rosa Parks kept both her mien and her seat. At last, the driver warned her that he would send for the police. "Go ahead and call them", Parks answered.

ⓓ On December 1, 1955, Rosa Parks took a city bus home from her job at a store in downtown Montgomery, Alabama.

① ⓑ - ⓐ - ⓓ - ⓒ

② ⓓ - ⓒ - ⓐ - ⓑ

③ ⓑ - ⓒ - ⓓ - ⓐ

④ ⓓ - ⓑ - ⓒ - ⓐ

19 다음 글의 분위기로 가장 어울리는 것은?

As Ryan Cox was waiting to pay for his coffee order at an Indiana, US fast food drive-through, he decided to try something he'd seen on a TV news show — he paid for the coffee order of the driver in the car behind. The small gesture made the young Indianapolis entrepreneur feel great, so he shared his experience on Facebook. An old friend suggested that rather than paying for people's coffee, Ryan put that money towards helping school students pay off their delinquent school lunch accounts. So the following week Ryan visited his nephew's school cafeteria and asked if he could pay off some accounts, and handed over $100.

① gloomy   ② serene
③ touching   ④ boring

20 아래 글 바로 다음에 이어질 문장으로 가장 적절한 것을 고르면?

The moon is different from the earth in many respects. First of all, there is no known life on the moon. And in terms of size, it is much smaller than the earth. You may think both of them have the same spherical shape. But strictly speaking, they are not the same. The moon is almost a perfect sphere; its diameter differs by no more than 1% in any direction. The faster an astronomical object spins, the more it becomes bulged at the equator and flattened at the poles. _____

① So spinning objects undergo some changes of their shape, except for the moon and the earth.
② Since the moon rotates more slowly than the earth, it is more nearly spherical.
③ Moreover, the moon's diameter has been varied for the last hundred years.
④ In fact, the moon's spherical shape is rather unexpected, considering its density and gravity.

※ 밑줄 친 부분과 의미가 가장 가까운 것은? 【1~2】

1

> As a salesman, you should remember that your <u>cardinal</u> rule is to do everything you can to satisfy a customer.

① definitive   ② gigantic

③ potential   ④ principal

2

> The audio of the <u>surreptitious</u> recording clearly indicates that the participants did not want to be recorded.

① clandestine   ② statutory

③ forthright   ④ seraphic

3 다음 대화 중 어색한 것은?

① A : Why doesn't this device function properly?

    B : You ought to plug in first.

② A : How long does it take from my house to his office?

    B : Hopefully, by the end of the week.

③ A : Do you know where I can rent a wheelchair?

    B : Try around at the back gate.

④ A : You're going to be present at the staff training session this weekend, aren't you?

    B : It's mandatory, isn't it?

4 밑줄 친 부분 중 어법상 옳지 않은 것은?

Allium vegetables – edible bulbs ① including onions, garlic, and leeks – appear in nearly every cuisine around the globe. ② They are fundamental in classic cooking bases, such as French *mirepoix* (diced onions, celery, and carrots), Latin American *sofrito* (onions, garlic, and tomatoes), and Cajun *holy trinity* (onions, bell peppers and celery). ③ While we sometimes take these standbys for granted, the flavor of allium vegetables can not be replicated. And neither their health benefits ④ can, which include protection from heart diseases and cancer.

5 다음 중 문법적으로 올바른 문장은?

① Both adolescents and adults should be cognizant to the risks of second-hand smoking.
② His address at the luncheon meeting was such great that the entire audience appeared to support him.
③ Appropriate experience and academic background are required of qualified applicants for the position.
④ The major threat to plants, animals, and people is the extremely toxic chemicals releasing into the air and water.

6 밑줄 친 부분에 들어갈 속담으로 가장 적절한 것은?

It's often said that _____. Actually this proverb is, for the most part, not true. For much of the history of modern neuroscience, the adult brain was believed to be a fixed structure that, once damaged, could not be repaired. But research published since the 1960s has challenged this assumption, showing that it is actually a highly dynamic structure, which changes itself in response to new experiences, and adapts to injuries – a phenomenon referred to as neuroplasticity.

① a stitch in time saves nine
② birds of a feather flock together
③ you can't teach an old dog new tricks
④ two heads are better than one

7

Research shows you'll eat less food and take in fewer calories if you eat slowly, so _____ yourself at holiday meals.

① hide
② express
③ pace
④ betray

8

The government is currently trying to find an alternative to garbage disposal to _____ environmental pollution.

① slope off
② head off
③ set off
④ run off with

9 다음 글의 요지로 가장 적절한 것은?

On a bright spring morning 50 years ago, two young astronomers at Bell Laboratories were tuning a 20-foot, horn-shaped antenna pointed toward the sky over New Jersey. Their goal was to measure the Milky Way galaxy, home to planet Earth. To their puzzlement, Robert W. Wilson and Arno A. Penzias heard the insistent hiss of radio signals coming from every direction − and from beyond the Milky Way. It was cosmic microwave background radiation, a residue of the primordial explosion of energy and matter that suddenly gave rise to the universe some 13.8 billion years ago. The scientists had found evidence that would confirm the Big Bang Theory, first proposed by Georges Lemaître in 1931.

① The light helps rule the Big Bang Theory out.
② The mysterious signal means a steady state of the universe.
③ The universe was in a steady state without a singular beginning.
④ The radiation is a residual effect of the explosion which Lemaître theorized.

10 다음 글의 제목으로 가장 적절한 것은?

If we can't directly intuit what's in our minds, then our only option is to approach the investigation of internal things (like knowledge and mental states) as we would approach the investigation of external things (like birds and planets). That is, we must formulate explicit theories in order to reach a satisfactory explanation of the facts. Since we can't look directly at what's inside the minds, our job will be to figure out what's inside on the basis of what we can observe from the outside.

① A talking analogy
② A black box problem
③ Dividing up the problem area
④ Comparisons with human language

11 글의 흐름상 가장 적절하지 못한 문장은?

The green revolution was the result of a sequence of scientific breakthroughs and development activities that successfully fought hunger by increasing food production. Basic ingredients of the green revolution were new seeds, use of chemicals and proper irrigation system. ① The green revolution resulted in an increase in production and changed the thinking of farmers. ② It improved resistance of crops to diseases and created massive job opportunities within the industrial and agricultural sectors. ③ Therefore, the environmental cost of chemical fertilizers and heavy irrigation has caused considerable controversy. ④ Self-sufficiency in food grains also affected the planning processes and gave a boost to the national self-confidence of then emerging democracies.

12 밑줄 친 부분의 의미와 가장 가까운 것은?

> When I heard the poem, some of the lines rang a bell.

① sounded familiar

② became music

③ seemed weird

④ were interesting

13 다음 글의 내용과 일치하는 것은?

> On June 23, 2016, a historic referendum took place in the United Kingdom (UK). The referendum question was: "Should the United Kingdom remain a member of the European Union or leave the European Union?" The possibility of Britain leaving the EU became known as Brexit. Over 30 million people voted in the referendum. The turnout was higher than Britain's last general election. Eligible voters were British, Irish, and Commonwealth citizens (18 and over) living in the UK. On June 23, 52% of voters chose "Leave the European Union." This shocked the world. Within hours, the value of the British pound (£) had fallen to a historic low and Prime Minister Cameron had stepped down. In the weeks following the referendum, millions of people signed a petition asking for a second referendum. The new prime minister, Theresa May, told citizens that "Brexit is Brexit." Negotiating the exit will take approximately two years. The status and rights of British nationals living in the EU and of EU nationals living in the UK are a primary concern.

① Britain joining the EU is called Brexit.

② All people in Britain participated in the vote.

③ 52% of voters wanted the UK to leave the EU.

④ The value of the Euro had risen after the vote.

14 우리말을 영어로 가장 잘 옮긴 것은?

① 나는 이 집으로 이사 온 지 3년이 되었다.

→ It was three years since I moved to this house.

② 우리는 해가 지기 전에 그 도시에 도착해야 한다.

→ We must arrive in the city before the sun will set.

③ 나는 그녀가 오늘 밤까지 그 일을 끝마칠지 궁금하다.

→ I wonder if she finishes the work by tonight.

④ 그는 실수하기는 했지만, 좋은 선생님으로 존경받을 수 있었다.

→ Although making a mistake, he could be respected as a good teacher.

15 우리말을 영어로 잘못 옮긴 것은?

① 우리는 그에게 이 일을 하도록 요청했다.

→ We asked him about this job.

② 그들은 TV 빼고는 모두 훔쳤다.

→ They stole everything but the television.

③ 식사할 때 물 마시는 게 좋니?

→ Is drinking water while eating good for you?

④ 그렇긴 하지만, 그것은 여전히 종교적 축제이다.

→ That said, it is still a religious festival.

16 다음 빈칸에 들어갈 표현으로 가장 적절한 것은?

Speaking of names, it's important to check how they are spelled – nobody wants to see their names misspelled. In English, there is often a _____ mix of ways of spelling names that are pronounced the same way: *McIntosh* or *Mackintosh*, *Stevenson* or *Stephenson*, *Davis* or *Davies*, *Frances* (female) or *Francis* (male).

① bewildering

② suasive

③ clever

④ foreign

17 다음 빈칸에 들어갈 표현으로 가장 적절한 것은?

In Book VII of "The Republic", Plato paints a picture of ordinary people imprisoned in a shadowcave, unaware of the true reality hidden from them. When a prisoner is released from the cave, he initially suffers from the sun's blinding brightness, yet as his eyes adjust he begins to see the truth. If he were to return underground to enlighten his former fellow prisoners, they would not believe him, _____. Plato's allegory is a powerful metaphor for contemplating a divide between ignorance and enlightenment — between the "visible" world and the "intelligible" realm.

① for they could be inspired by real things outside the cave

② for they couldn't imagine a world beyond the shadows dominating their existence

③ for they could drag themselves out into the light of the sun

④ for they couldn't turn away from the things which he was able to look at outside the cave

18 다음 글을 읽고 유추할 수 있는 것은?

It was November: rain fell coldly and drearily. He buttoned himself in his long raincoat and went to meet her. She had promised to wear a red carnation; the suggestion was her own, and tickled him hugely. As the pink-faced suburbanites poured, in an icy stream, into the hot waiting-room, he looked for her. Presently he saw her: she came toward him immediately, since his height was unmistakable. They talked excitedly flustered, but gradually getting some preliminary sense of each other.

① The man and woman are meeting for the first time.

② The man lived in a suburban neighborhood.

③ The man was tall and ticklish.

④ The man suggested the woman wear a flower.

19 다음 글에서 [ ]로 표시된 부분에 들어갈 글의 순서로 가장 적절한 것은?

Climate change has narrowed the range where bumblebees are found in North America and Europe in recent decades, according to a recent study, published in the journal Science. [   ] "Bumblebee species across Europe and North America are declining at continental scales", Jeremy T. Kerr, a conservation biologist at the University of Ottawa in Canada who was the lead author of the report, said at a news conference. "And our data suggest that climate change plays a leading, or perhaps the leading, role in this trend."

(A) Logic would suggest that the northern reaches of their home turf* would shift to higher latitudes by a corresponding distance.

(B) The paper suggests that warming temperatures have caused bumblebee populations to retreat from the southern limits of their travels by as much as 190 miles since the 1970s.

(C) But that has not happened, leading researchers to think that the more northern habitats may be less hospitable to them.

* turf : short, thick, even grass

① (A) − (B) − (C)　　　　　② (B) − (A) − (C)

③ (A) − (C) − (B)　　　　　④ (B) − (C) − (A)

20 다음 빈칸에 들어갈 표현으로 가장 적절하게 짝지어진 것은?

The financial rewards of owning your own business may not happen (A) _____ you put in years of hard work. The desire to make money may not be enough to (B) _____ you going through the difficult early period.

	(A)	(B)		(A)	(B)
①	until	refute	②	when	drive
③	before	reproach	④	until	keep

※ 밑줄 친 부분과 의미가 가장 가까운 것을 고르시오. 【1~2】

1

> I absolutely <u>detested</u> the idea of staying up late at night.

① defended   ② abhorred

③ confirmed   ④ abandoned

2

> I had an <u>uncanny</u> feeling that I had seen this scene somewhere before.

① odd   ② ongoing

③ obvious   ④ offensive

3 우리말을 영어로 잘못 옮긴 것을 고르시오.

① 이 편지를 받는 대로 곧 본사로 와 주십시오.

    → Please come to the headquarters as soon as you receive this letter.

② 나는 소년 시절에 독서하는 버릇을 길러 놓았어야만 했다.

    → I ought to have formed a habit of reading in my boyhood.

③ 그는 10년 동안 외국에 있었기 때문에 영어를 매우 유창하게 말할 수 있다.

    → Having been abroad for ten years, he can speak English very fluently.

④ 내가 그때 그 계획을 포기했었다면 이렇게 훌륭한 성과를 얻지 못했을 것이다.

    → Had I given up the project at that time, I should have achieved such a splendid result.

4

A : May I help you?
B : I bought this dress two days ago, but it's a bit big for me.
A : _____
B : Then I'd like to get a refund.
A : May I see your receipt, please?
B : Here you are.

① I'm sorry, but there's no smaller size.

② I feel like it fits you perfectly, though.

③ That dress sells really well in our store.

④ I'm sorry, but this purchase can't be refunded.

5

A : Every time I use this home blood pressure monitor, I get a different reading. I think I'm
    doing it wrong. Can you show me how to use it correctly?
B : Yes, of course. First, you have to put the strap around your arm.
A : Like this? Am I doing this correctly?
B : That looks a little too tight.
A : Oh, how about now?
B : Now it looks a bit too loose. If it's too tight or too loose, you'll get an incorrect reading.
A : _____
B : Press the button now. You shouldn't move or speak.
A : I get it.
B : You should see your blood pressure on the screen in a few moments.

① I didn't see anything today.

② Oh, okay. What do I do next?

③ Right, I need to read the book.

④ Should I check out their website?

6　어법상 옳은 것은?

① They didn't believe his story, and neither did I.

② The sport in that I am most interested is soccer.

③ Jamie learned from the book that World War I had broken out in 1914.

④ Two factors have made scientists difficult to determine the number of species on Earth.

7　어법상 옳지 않은 것은?

① A few words caught in passing set me thinking.

② Hardly did she enter the house when someone turned on the light.

③ We drove on to the hotel, from whose balcony we could look down at the town.

④ The homeless usually have great difficulty getting a job, so they are losing their hope.

8　다음 글의 요지로 가장 적절한 것은?

How on earth will it help the poor if governments try to strangle globalization by stemming the flow of trade, information, and capital — the three components of the global economy? That disparities between rich and poor are still too great is undeniable. But it is just not true that economic growth benefits only the rich and leaves out the poor, as the opponents of globalization and the market economy would have us believe. A recent World Bank study entitled "Growth Is Good for the Poor" reveals a one-for-one relationship between income of the bottom fifth of the population and per capita GDP. In other words, incomes of all sectors grow proportionately at the same rate. The study notes that openness to foreign trade benefits the poor to the same extent that it benefits the whole economy.

① Globalization deepens conflicts between rich and poor.

② The global economy grows at the expense of the poor.

③ Globalization can be beneficial regardless of one's economic status.

④ Governments must control the flow of trade to revive the economy.

9

Why might people hovering near the poverty line be more likely to help their fellow humans? Part of it, Keltner thinks, is that poor people must often band together to make it through tough times — a process that probably makes them more socially astute. He says, "When you face uncertainty, it makes you orient to other people. You build up these strong social networks." When a poor young mother has a new baby, for instance, she may need help securing food, supplies, and childcare, and if she has healthy social times, members of her community will pitch in. But limited income is hardly a prerequisite for developing this kind of empathy and social responsiveness. Regardless of the size of our bank accounts, suffering becomes a conduit to altruism or heroism when our own pain compels us to be _____ other people's needs and to intervene when we see someone in the clutches of the kind of suffering we know so well.

① less involved in

② less preoccupied with

③ more attentive to

④ more indifferent to

10

The Soleil department store outlet in Shanghai would seem to have all the amenities necessary to succeed in modern Chinese retail : luxury brands and an exclusive location. Despite these advantages, however, the store's management thought it was still missing something to attract customers. So next week they're unveiling a gigantic, twisting, dragon-shaped slide that shoppers can use to drop from fifth-floor luxury boutiques to first-floor luxury boutiques in death-defying seconds. Social media users are wondering, half-jokingly, whether the slide will kill anyone. But Soleil has a different concern that Chinese shopping malls will go away completely. Chinese shoppers, once seemingly in endless supply, are no longer turning up at brick-and-mortar outlets because of the growing online shopping, and they still go abroad to buy luxury goods. So, repurposing these massive spaces for consumers who have other ways to spend their time and money is likely to require a lot of creativity. _____.

① Luxury brands are thriving at Soleil

② Soleil has decided against making bold moves

③ Increasing the online customer base may be the last hope

④ A five-story dragon slide may not be a bad place to start

11

It is easy to devise numerous possible scenarios of future developments, each one, on the face of it, equally likely. The difficult task is to know which will actually take place. In hindsight, it usually seems obvious. When we look back in time, each event seems clearly and logically to follow from previous events. Before the event occurs, however, the number of possibilities seems endless. There are no methods for successful prediction, especially in areas involving complex social and technological changes, where many of the determining factors are not known and, in any event, are certainly not under any single group's control. Nonetheless, it is essential to _____. We do know that new technologies will bring both dividends and problems, especially human, social problems. The more we try to anticipate these problems, the better we can control them.

① work out reasonable scenarios for the future

② legitimize possible dividends from future changes

③ leave out various aspects of technological problems

④ consider what it would be like to focus on the present

12 다음 글의 내용과 일치하는 것은?

Taste buds got their name from the nineteenth-century German scientists Georg Meissner and Rudolf Wagner, who discovered mounds made up of taste cells that overlap like petals. Taste buds wear out every week to ten days, and we replace them, although not as frequently over the age of forty-five : our palates really do become jaded as we get older. It takes a more intense taste to produce the same level of sensation, and children have the keenest sense of taste. A baby's mouth has many more taste buds than an adult's, with some even dotting the cheeks. Children adore sweets partly because the tips of their tongues, more sensitive to sugar, haven't yet been blunted by trying to eat hot soup before it cools.

① Taste buds were invented in the nineteenth century.

② Replacement of taste buds does not slow down with age.

③ Children have more sensitive palates than adults.

④ The sense of taste declines by eating cold soup.

13 밑줄 친 부분과 의미가 가장 가까운 것은?

> At this company, we will not put up with such behavior.

① modify

② record

③ tolerate

④ evaluate

14 밑줄 친 부분 중 의미상 옳지 않은 것은?

① I'm going to take over his former position.

② I can't take on any more work at the moment.

③ The plane couldn't take off because of the heavy fog.

④ I can't go out because I have to take after my baby sister.

15 다음 글의 제목으로 가장 적절한 것은?

> Drama is doing. Drama is being. Drama is such a normal thing. It is something that we all engage in every day when faced with difficult situations. You get up in the morning with a bad headache or an attack of depression, yet you face the day and cope with other people, pretending that nothing is wrong. You have an important meeting or an interview coming up, so you talk through the issues with yourself beforehand and decide how to present a confident, cheerful face, what to wear, what to do with your hands, and so on. You've spilt coffee over a colleague's papers, and immediately you prepare an elaborate excuse. Your partner has just run off with your best friend, yet you cannot avoid going in to teach a class of inquisitive students. Getting on with our day-to-day lives requires a series of civilized masks if we are to maintain our dignity and live in harmony with others.

① Dysfunctions of Drama

② Drama in Our Daily Lives

③ Drama as a Theatrical Art

④ Dramatic Changes in Emotions

16 우리말을 영어로 잘못 옮긴 것을 고르시오.

① 그 회의 후에야 그는 금융 위기의 심각성을 알아차렸다.

→ Only after the meeting did he recognize the seriousness of the financial crisis.

② 장관은 교통문제를 해결하기 위해 강 위에 다리를 건설해야 한다고 주장했다.

→ The minister insisted that a bridge be constructed over the river to solve the traffic problem.

③ 비록 그 일이 어려운 것이었지만, Linda는 그것을 끝내기 위해 최선을 다했다.

→ As difficult a task as it was, Linda did her best to complete it.

④ 그는 문자 메시지에 너무 정신이 팔려서 제한속도보다 빠르게 달리고 있다는 것을 몰랐다.

→ He was so distracted by a text message to know that he was going over the speed limit.

17 빈칸 (A), (B)에 들어갈 말로 가장 적절한 것은?

The amount of information gathered by the eyes as contrasted with the ears has not been precisely calculated. Such a calculation not only involves a translation process, but scientists have been handicapped by lack of knowledge of what to count. A general notion, however, of the relative complexities of the two systems can be obtained by _____(A)_____ the size of the nerves connecting the eyes and the ears to the centers of the brain. Since the optic nerve contains roughly eighteen times as many neurons as the cochlear nerve, we assume it transmits at least that much more information. Actually, in normally alert subjects, it is probable that the eyes may be as much as a thousand times as effective as the ears in _____(B)_____ information.

* cochlear : 달팽이관의

	(A)	(B)
①	adding	clearing up
②	adding	disseminating
③	comparing	reducing
④	comparing	sweeping up

18 글의 흐름상 가장 어색한 문장은?

Children's book awards have proliferated in recent years; today, there are well over 100 different awards and prizes by a variety of organizations. ① The awards may be given for books of a specific genre or simply for the best of all children's books published within a given time period. An award may honor a particular book or an author for a lifetime contribution to the world of children's literature. ② Most children's book awards are chosen by adults, but now a growing number of children's choice book awards exist. The larger national awards given in most countries are the most influential and have helped considerably to raise public awareness about the fine books being published for young readers. ③ An award ceremony for outstanding services to the publishing industry is put on hold. ④ Of course, readers are wise not to put too much faith in award-winning books. An award doesn't necessarily mean a good reading experience, but it does provide a starting place when choosing books.

19 주어진 문장이 들어갈 위치로 가장 적절한 곳은?

This inequality is corrected by their getting in their turn better portions from kills by other people.

Let us examine a situation of simple distribution such as occurs when an animal is killed in a hunt. One might expect to find the animal portioned out according to the amount of work done by each hunter to obtain it. (①) To some extent this principle is followed, but other people have their rights as well. (②) Each person in the camp gets a share depending upon his or her relation to the hunters. (③) When a kangaroo is killed, for example, the hunters have to give its main parts to their kinfolk and the worst parts may even be kept by the hunters themselves. (④) The net result in the long run is substantially the same to each person, but through this system the principles of kinship obligation and the morality of sharing food have been emphasized.

20 주어진 글 다음에 이어질 글의 순서로 가장 적절한 것은?

The most innovative of the group therapy approaches was psychodrama, the brainchild of Jacob L. Moreno. Psychodrama as a form of group therapy started with premises that were quite alien to the Freudian worldview that mental illness essentially occurs within the psyche or mind.

(A) But he also believed that creativity is rarely a solitary process but something brought out by social interactions. He relied heavily on theatrical techniques, including role-playing and improvisation, as a means to promote creativity and general social trust.

(B) Despite his theoretical difference from the mainstream viewpoint, Moreno's influence in shaping psychological consciousness in the twentieth century was considerable. He believed that the nature of human beings is to be creative and that living a creative life is the key to human health and well-being.

(C) His most important theatrical tool was what he called role reversal — asking participants to take on another's persona. The act of pretending "as if" one were in another's skin was designed to help bring out the empathic impulse and to develop it to higher levels of expression.

① (A) — (C) — (B)

② (B) — (A) — (C)

③ (B) — (C) — (A)

④ (C) — (B) — (A)

☞ 정답 및 해설 P.85

※ 밑줄 친 부분에 들어갈 말로 가장 적절한 것을 고르시오. 【1~2】

1

> A : I just received a letter from one of my old high school buddies.
> B : That's nice!
> A : Well, actually it's been a long time since I heard from him.
> B : To be honest, I've been out of touch with most of my old friends.
> A : I know. It's really hard to maintain contact when people move around so much.
> B : You're right. _____. But you're lucky to be back in touch with your buddy again.

① The days are getting longer

② People just drift apart

③ That's the funniest thing I've ever heard of

④ I start fuming whenever I hear his name

2

> A : What are you getting Ted for his birthday? I'm getting him a couple of baseball caps.
> B : I've been _____ trying to think of just the right gift. I don't have an inkling of what he needs.
> A : Why don't you get him an album? He has a lot of photos.
> B : That sounds perfect! Why didn't I think of that? Thanks for the suggestion!

① contacted by him   ② sleeping all day

③ racking my brain   ④ collecting photo albums

※ 밑줄 친 부분의 의미와 가장 가까운 것을 고르시오. 【3~5】

3

Some of the newest laws authorize people to appoint a <u>surrogate</u> who can make medical decisions for them when necessary.

① proxy   ② sentry

③ predecessor   ④ plunderer

4

A : He thinks he can achieve anything.

B : Yes, he needs to <u>keep his feet on the ground</u>.

① live in a world of his own

② relax and enjoy himself

③ be brave and confident

④ remain sensible and realistic about life

5

She is <u>on the fence</u> about going to see the Mona Lisa at the Louvre Museum.

① anguished   ② enthusiastic

③ apprehensive   ④ undecided

6 어법상 옳지 않은 것은?

① You might think that just eating a lot of vegetables will keep you perfectly healthy.

② Academic knowledge isn't always that leads you to make right decisions.

③ The fear of getting hurt didn't prevent him from engaging in reckless behaviors.

④ Julie's doctor told her to stop eating so many processed foods.

7 어법상 옳은 것은?

① The oceans contain many forms of life that has not yet been discovered.

② The rings of Saturn are so distant to be seen from Earth without a telescope.

③ The Aswan High Dam has been protected Egypt from the famines of its neighboring countries.

④ Included in this series is "The Enchanted Horse," among other famous children's stories.

8 다음 글의 내용과 일치하는 것은?

Soils of farmlands used for growing crops are being carried away by water and wind erosion at rates between 10 and 40 times the rates of soil formation, and between 500 and 10,000 times soil erosion rates on forested land. Because those soil erosion rates are so much higher than soil formation rates, that means a net loss of soil. For instance, about half of the top soil of Iowa, the state whose agriculture productivity is among the highest in the U.S., has been eroded in the last 150 years. On my most recent visit to Iowa, my hosts showed me a churchyard offering a dramatically visible example of those soil losses. A church was built there in the middle of farmland during the 19th century and has been maintained continuously as a church ever since, while the land around it was being farmed. As a result of soil being eroded much more rapidly from fields than from the churchyard, the yard now stands like a little island raised 10 feet above the surrounding sea of farmland.

① A churchyard in Iowa is higher than the surrounding farmland.

② Iowa's agricultural productivity has accelerated its soil formation.

③ The rate of soil formation in farmlands is faster than that of soil erosion.

④ Iowa has maintained its top soil in the last 150 years.

9 다음 글의 흐름상 가장 어색한 문장은?

Whether you've been traveling, focusing on your family, or going through a busy season at work, 14 days out of the gym takes its toll—not just on your muscles, but your performance, brain, and sleep, too. ① Most experts agree that after two weeks, you're in trouble if you don't get back in the gym. "At the two week point without exercising, there are a multitude of physiological markers that naturally reveal a reduction of fitness level," says Scott Weiss, a New York—based exercise physiologist and trainer who works with elite athletes. ② After all, despite all of its abilities, the human body (even the fit human body) is a very sensitive system and physiological changes (muscle strength or a greater aerobic base) that come about through training will simply disappear if your training load dwindles, he notes. Since the demand of training isn't present, your body simply slinks back toward baseline. ③ More protein is required to build more muscles at a rapid pace in your body. ④ Of course, how much and how quickly you'll decondition depends on a slew of factors like how fit you are, your age, and how long sweating has been a habit. "Two to eight months of not exercising at all will reduce your fitness level to as if you never exercised before," Weiss notes.

10 다음 글의 내용과 일치하지 않는 것은?

Before the fifteenth century, all four characteristics of the witch (night flying, secret meetings, harmful magic, and the devil's pact) were ascribed individually or in limited combination by the church to its adversaries, including Templars, heretics, learned magicians, and other dissident groups. Folk beliefs about the supernatural emerged in peasant confessions during witch trials. The most striking difference between popular and learned notions of witchcraft lay in the folk belief that the witch had innate supernatural powers not derived from the devil. For learned men, this bordered on heresy. Supernatural powers were never human in origin, nor could witches derive their craft from the tradition of learned magic, which required a scholarly training at the university, a masculine preserve at the time. A witch's power necessarily came from the pact she made with the devil.

① The folk and learned men had different views on the source of the witch's supernatural powers.

② According to the folk belief, supernatural powers belonged to the essential nature of the witch.

③ Four characteristics of the witch were attributed by the church to its dissident groups.

④ Learned men believed that the witch's power came from a scholarly training at the university.

11 주어진 문장이 들어갈 위치로 가장 적절한 것은?

> Fortunately, however, the heavy supper she had eaten caused her to become tired and ready to fall asleep.

> Various duties awaited me on my arrival. I had to sit with the girls during their hour of study. (①) Then it was my turn to read prayers; to see them to bed. Afterwards I ate with the other teachers. (②) Even when we finally retired for the night, the inevitable Miss Gryce was still my companion. We had only a short end of candle in our candlestick, and I dreaded lest she should talk till it was all burnt out. (③) She was already snoring before I had finished undressing. There still remained an inch of candle. (④) I now took out my letter; the seal was an initial F. I broke it; the contents were brief.

12 다음 글의 제목으로 가장 적절한 것은?

> Fear and its companion pain are two of the most useful things that men and animals possess, if they are properly used. If fire did not hurt when it burnt, children would play with it until their hands were burnt away. Similarly, if pain existed but fear did not, a child would burn himself again and again, because fear would not warn him to keep away from the fire that had burnt him before. A really fearless soldier—and some do exist—is not a good soldier, because he is soon killed; and a dead soldier is of no use to his army. Fear and pain are therefore two guards without which human beings and animals might soon die out.

① Obscurity of Fear and Pain in Soldiers

② Indispensability of Fear and Pain

③ Disapproval of Fear and Pain

④ Children's Association with Fear and Pain

※ 우리말을 영어로 잘못 옮긴 것을 고르시오. 【13~14】

13 ① 나는 매달 두세 번 그에게 전화하기로 규칙을 세웠다.

→I made it a rule to call him two or three times a month.

② 그는 나의 팔을 붙잡고 도움을 요청했다.

→He grabbed me by the arm and asked for help.

③ 폭우로 인해 그 강은 120 cm 상승했다.

→Owing to the heavy rain, the river has risen by 120 cm.

④ 나는 눈 오는 날 밖에 나가는 것보다 집에 있는 것을 더 좋아한다.

→I prefer to staying home than to going out on a snowy day.

14 ① 그를 당황하게 한 것은 그녀의 거절이 아니라 그녀의 무례함이었다.

→It was not her refusal but her rudeness that perplexed him.

② 부모는 아이들 앞에서 그들의 말과 행동에 대해 아무리 신중해도 지나치지 않다.

→Parents cannot be too careful about their words and actions before their children.

③ 환자들과 부상자들을 돌보기 위해 더 많은 의사가 필요했다.

→More doctors were required to tend sick and wounded.

④ 설상가상으로, 또 다른 태풍이 곧 올 것이라는 보도가 있다.

→To make matters worse, there is a report that another typhoon will arrive soon.

※ 밑줄 친 부분에 들어갈 말로 가장 적절한 것을 고르시오. 【15~16】

15

Our main dish did not have much flavor, but I made it more _____ by adding condiments.

① palatable

② dissolvable

③ potable

④ susceptible

16

London taxi drivers have to undertake years of intense training known as "the knowledge" to gain their operating license, including learning the layout of over twenty-five thousand of the city's streets. A researcher and her team investigated the taxi drivers and the ordinary people. The two groups were asked to watch videos of routes unfamiliar to them through a town in Ireland. They were then asked to take a test about the video that included sketching out routes, identifying landmarks, and estimating distances between places. Both groups did well on much of the test, but the taxi drivers did significantly better on identifying new routes. This result suggests that the taxi drivers' mastery can be _____ to new and unknown areas. Their years of training and learning through deliberate practice prepare them to take on similar challenges even in places they do not know well or at all.

① confined

② devoted

③ generalized

④ contributed

17 주어진 글 다음에 이어질 글의 순서로 가장 적절한 것은?

I remember the day Lewis discovered the falls. They left their camp at sunrise and a few hours later they came upon a beautiful plain and on the plain were more buffalo than they had ever seen before in one place.

(A) A nice thing happened that afternoon, they went fishing below the falls and caught half a dozen trout, good ones, too, from sixteen to twenty-three inches long.

(B) After a while the sound was tremendous and they were at the great falls of the Missouri River. It was about noon when they got there.

(C) They kept on going until they heard the faraway sound of a waterfall and saw a distant column of spray rising and disappearing. They followed the sound as it got louder and louder.

① (A) − (B) − (C)

② (B) − (C) − (A)

③ (C) − (A) − (B)

④ (C) − (B) − (A)

18 다음 글의 요지로 가장 적절한 것은?

Novelty-induced time expansion is a well-characterized phenomenon which can be investigated under laboratory conditions. Simply asking people to estimate the length of time they are exposed to a train of stimuli shows that novel stimuli simply seem to last longer than repetitive or unremarkable ones. In fact, just being the first stimulus in a moderately repetitive series appears to be sufficient to induce subjective time expansion. Of course, it is easy to think of reasons why our brain has evolved to work like this—presumably novel and exotic stimuli require more thought and consideration than familiar ones, so it makes sense for the brain to allocate them more subjective time.

① Response to stimuli is an important by-product of brain training.

② The intensity of stimuli increases with their repetition.

③ Our physical response to stimuli influences our thoughts.

④ New stimuli give rise to subjective time expansion.

19

One of the tricks our mind plays is to highlight evidence which confirms what we already believe. If we hear gossip about a rival, we tend to think "I knew he was a nasty piece of work"; if we hear the same about our best friend, we're more likely to say "that's just a rumour." Once you learn about this mental habit—called confirmation bias—you start seeing it everywhere. This matters when we want to make better decisions. Confirmation bias is OK as long as we're right, but all too often we're wrong, and we only pay attention to the deciding evidence when it's too late. How _____ depends on our awareness of why, psychologically, confirmation bias happens. There are two possible reasons. One is that we have a blind spot in our imagination and the other is we fail to ask questions about new information.

① we make our rivals believe us

② our blind spot helps us make better decisions

③ we can protect our decisions from confirmation bias

④ we develop exactly the same bias

20

For many big names in consumer product brands, exporting and producing overseas with local labor and for local tastes have been the right thing to do. In doing so, the companies found a way to improve their cost structure, to grow in the rapidly expanding consumer markets in emerging countries. But, Sweets Co. remains stuck in the domestic market. Even though its products are loaded with preservatives, which means they can endure long travel to distant markets, Sweets Co. _____, let alone produce overseas. The unwillingness or inability to update its business strategy and products for a changing world is clearly damaging to the company.

① is intent on importing

② does very little exporting

③ has decided to streamline operations

④ is expanding into emerging markets

※ 밑줄 친 부분과 의미가 가장 가까운 것은? 【1~2】

1

Leadership and strength are <u>inextricably</u> bound together. We look to strong people as leaders because they can protect us from threats to our group.

① inseparably

② inanimately

③ ineffectively

④ inconsiderately

2

Prudence indeed will dictate that governments long established should not be changed for light and <u>transient</u> causes.

① transparent

② monetary

③ memorable

④ significant

※ 밑줄 친 부분 중 어법상 가장 옳지 않은 것은? 【3~4】

3

The idea that justice ① <u>in allocating</u> access to a university has something to do with ② <u>the goods</u> that ③ <u>universities properly</u> pursue ④ <u>explain why</u> selling admission is unjust.

4

Strange as ① <u>it may</u> seem, ② <u>the Sahara</u> was once an expanse of grassland ③ <u>supported</u> the kind of animal life ④ <u>associated with</u> the African plains.

5 대화의 흐름으로 보아 빈칸에 들어갈 가장 적절한 것은?

A : Do you think we can get a loan?
B : Well, it depends. Do you own any other property? Any stocks or bonds?
A : No.
B : I see. Then you don't have any _____. Perhaps you could get a guarantor − someone to sign for the loan for you.

① investigation   ② animals
③ collateral   ④ inspiration

6 다음 글의 주제로 가장 적절한 것은?

In 1782, J. Hector St. John De Crèvecoeur, a French immigrant who had settled in New York before returning to Europe during the Revolutionary War, published a series of essays about life in the British colonies in North America, *Letters from an American Farmer*. The book was an immediate success in England, France, and the United States. In one of its most famous passages, Crèvecoeur describes the process by which people from different backgrounds and countries were transformed by their experiences in the colonies and asks, "What then is the American?" In America, Crèvecoeur suggests, "individuals of all nations are melted into a new race of men, whose labors and posterity will one day cause great changes in the world." Crèvecoeur was among the first to develop the popular idea of America as that would come to be called "melting pot."

① Crèvecoeur's book became an immediate success in England.
② Crèvecoeur developed the idea of melting pot in his book.
③ Crèvecoeur described and discussed American individualism.
④ Crèvecoeur explained where Americans came from in his book.

7

Again and again we light on words used once in a good, but now in an unfavorable sense. Until the late Eighteenth century this word was used to mean serviceable, friendly, very courteous and obliging. But a(n) _____ person nowadays means a busy uninvited meddler in matters which do not belong to him/her.

① servile   ② officious

③ gregarious   ④ obsequious

8

A faint odor of ammonia or vinegar makes one－week－old infants grimace and _____ their heads.

① harness   ② avert

③ muffle   ④ evoke

9 밑줄 친 부분 중 어법상 가장 옳지 않은 것은?

The first coffeehouse in western Europe ① opened not in ② a center of trade or commerce but in the university city of Oxford, ③ in which a Lebanese man ④ naming Jacob set up shop in 1650.

10 다음 문장 중 어법상 가장 옳지 않은 것은?

① John promised Mary that he would clean his room.

② John told Mary that he would leave early.

③ John believed Mary that she would be happy.

④ John reminded Mary that she should get there early.

11 대화의 흐름으로 보아 빈칸에 들어갈 가장 적절한 것은?

> A : Why don't you let me treat you to lunch today, Mr. Kim?
>
> B : _____.

① No, I'm not. That would be a good time for me

② Good. I'll put it on my calendar so I don't forget

③ OK. I'll check with you on Monday

④ Wish I could but I have another commitment today

12 글의 흐름으로 보아 빈칸에 들어갈 단어를 순서대로 고른 것은?

> For centuries, people gazing at the sky after sunset could see thousands of vibrant, sparkling stars. But these days, you'll be lucky if you can view the Big Dipper. The culprit: electric beams pouring from homes and street lamps, whose brightness obscures the night sky. In the U.S., so-called light pollution has gotten so bad that by one estimate, 8 out of 10 children born today will never encounter a sky _____ enough for them to see the Milky Way. There is hope, however, in the form of astrotourism, a small but growing industry centered on stargazing in the worlds' darkest places. These remote sites, many of them in national parks, offer views for little more than the cost of a campsite. And the people who run them often work to reduce light pollution in surrounding communities. _____ astrotourism may not be as luxurious as some vacations, travelers don't seem to mind.

① dark – Although

② bright – Because

③ dark – Since

④ bright – In that

13 다음 글을 문맥에 맞게 순서대로 배열한 것은?

> ㉠ Millions of people suffering from watery and stinging eyes, pounding headaches, sinus issues, and itchy throats, sought refuge from the debilitating air by scouring stores for air filters and face masks.
>
> ㉡ The outrage among Chinese residents and the global media scrutiny impelled the government to address the country's air pollution problem.
>
> ㉢ Schools and businesses were closed, and the Beijing city government warned people to stay inside their homes, keep their air purifiers running, reduce indoor activities, and remain as inactive as possible.
>
> ㉣ In 2013, a state of emergency in Beijing resulting from the dangerously high levels of pollution led to chaos in the transportation system, forcing airlines to cancel flights due to low visibility.

① ㉡ – ㉠ – ㉣ – ㉢   ② ㉡ – ㉢ – ㉣ – ㉠

③ ㉣ – ㉡ – ㉢ – ㉠   ④ ㉣ – ㉢ – ㉠ – ㉡

※ 글의 흐름으로 보아 빈칸에 들어갈 가장 적절한 것은? 【14~16】

14

> Both novels and romances are works of imaginative fiction with multiple characters, but that's where the similarities end. Novels are realistic; romances aren't. In the 19th century, a romance was a prose narrative that told a fictional story dealt with its subjects and characters in a symbolic, imaginative, and nonrealistic way. _____, a romance deals with plots and people that are exotic, remote in time or place from the reader, and obviously imaginary.

① Typically   ② On the other hand

③ Nonetheless   ④ In some cases

15

Definitions are especially _____ to children. There's an oft-cited 1987 study in which fifth graders were given dictionary definitions and asked to write their own sentences using the words defined. The results were discouraging. One child given the word *erode* wrote "Our family erodes a lot," because the definition given was "eat out, eat away."

① beneficial   ② disrespectful

③ unhelpful   ④ forgettable

16

Modern banking has its origins in ancient England. In those days people wanting to safeguard their gold had two choices — hide it under the mattress or turn it over to someone else for safekeeping. The logical people to turn to for storage were the local goldsmiths, since they had the strongest vaults. The goldsmiths accepted the gold for storage, giving the owner a receipt stating that the gold could be redeemed at a later date. When a payment was due, the owner went to the goldsmith, redeemed part of the gold and gave it to the payee. After all that, the payee was very likely to turn around and give the gold back to the goldsmith for safekeeping. Gradually, instead of taking the time and effort to physically exchange the gold, business people _____.

① began to exchange the goldsmith's receipts as payment

② saw the potential for profit in this arrangement

③ warned the depositors against redeeming their gold

④ lent the gold to somebody else for a fee

17 빈칸에 공통으로 들어갈 가장 적절한 것은?

In some cultures, such as in Korea and Egypt, politeness norms require that when someone is offered something to eat or drink, it must be refused the first time around. However, such a refusal is often viewed as a rejection of someone's hospitality and thoughtlessness in other cultures, particularly when no _____ is made for the refusal. Americans and Canadians, for instance, expect refusals to be accompanied by a reasonable _____.

① role   ② excuse

③ choice   ④ situation

18 다음 주어진 문장이 들어갈 가장 적절한 곳은?

Instead, these employees spoke first of the sincerity of the relationships at work, that their work culture felt like an extension of home, and that their colleagues were supportive.

(①) There is a clear link between job satisfaction and productivity. However, job satisfaction also depends on the service culture of an organization. (②) This culture comprises the things that make a business distinctive and make the people who work there proud to do so. (③) When employees of the "Top 10 Best Companies to Work For" were asked by Fortune magazine why they loved working for these companies, it was notable that they didn't mention pay, reward schemes, or advancing to a more senior position. (④)

19 다음 글의 내용과 일치하는 것은?

Why Orkney of all places? How did this scatter of islands off the northern tip of Scotland come to be such a technological, cultural, and spiritual powerhouse? For starters, you have to stop thinking of Orkney as remote. For most of history, Orkney was an important maritime hub, a place that was on the way to everywhere. It was also blessed with some of the richest farming soils in Britain and a surprisingly mild climate, thanks to the effects of the Gulf Stream.

① Orkney people had to overcome a lot of social and natural disadvantages.
② The region was one of the centers of rebellion that ultimately led to the annihilation of the civilization there.
③ Orkney did not make the best of its resources because it was too far from the mainland.
④ Orkney owed its prosperity largely to its geographical advantage and natural resources.

20 다음 글의 제목으로 가장 적절한 것은?

Initially, papyrus and parchment were kept as scrolls that could be unrolled either vertically or horizontally, depending on the direction of the script. The horizontal form was more common, and because scrolls could be quite long, a scribe would typically refrain from writing a single line across the entire length, but instead would mark off columns of a reasonable width. That way the reader could unroll one side and roll up the other while reading. Nevertheless, the constant need to re-roll the scroll was a major disadvantage to this format, and it was impossible to jump to various places in the scroll the way we skip to a particular page of a book. Moreover, the reader struggled to make notes while reading since both hands (or weights) were required to keep the scroll open.

① The inconvenience of scrolls
② The evolution of the book
③ The development of writing and reading
④ The ways to overcome disadvantages in scrolls

☞ 정답 및 해설 P.95

※ 밑줄 친 부분과 의미가 가장 가까운 것을 고르시오. 【1~3】

1

During both World Wars, government <u>subsidies</u> and demands for new airplanes vastly improved techniques for their design and construction.

① financial support　　　　② long-term planning

③ technical assistance　　　④ non-restrictive policy

2

Tuesday night's season premiere of the TV show seemed to be trying to strike a balance between the show's <u>convoluted</u> mythology and its more human, character-driven dimension.

① ancient　　　　　　　② unrelated

③ complicated　　　　　④ otherworldly

3

By the time we <u>wound up</u> the conversation, I knew that I would not be going to Geneva.

① initiated　　　　　　　② resumed

③ terminated　　　　　　④ interrupted

4 밑줄 친 부분에 들어갈 말로 가장 적절한 것은?

> A police sergeant with 15 years of experience was dismayed after being _____ for promotion in favor of a young officer.

① run over

② asked out

③ carried out

④ passed over

5 밑줄 친 부분 중 어법상 옳은 것은?

> Last week I was sick with the flu. When my father ① heard me sneezing and coughing, he opened my bedroom door to ask me ② that I needed anything. I was really happy to see his kind and caring face, but there wasn't ③ anything he could do it to ④ make the flu to go away.

6 어법상 옳은 것은?

① A week's holiday has been promised to all the office workers.

② She destined to live a life of serving others.

③ A small town seems to be preferable than a big city for raising children.

④ Top software companies are finding increasingly challenging to stay ahead.

7 밑줄 친 부분에 들어갈 말로 가장 적절한 것을 고르시오.

A : How do you like your new neighborhood?
B : It's great for the most part. I love the clean air and the green environment.
A : Sounds like a lovely place to live.
B : Yes, but it's not without its drawbacks.
A : Like what?
B : For one, it doesn't have many different stores. For example, there's only one supermarket, so food is very expensive.
A : _____
B : You're telling me. But thank goodness. The city is building a new shopping center now. Next year, we'll have more options.

① How many supermarkets are there?
② Are there a lot of places to shop there?
③ It looks like you have a problem.
④ I want to move to your neighborhood.

8 글의 흐름상 가장 어색한 것은?

A story that is on the cutting edge of modern science began in an isolated part of northern Sweden in the 19th century. ①This area of the country had unpredictable harvests through the first half of the century. In years that the harvest failed, the population went hungry. However, the good years were very good. ②The same people who went hungry during bad harvests overate significantly during the good years. A Swedish scientist wondered about the long-term effects of these eating patterns. He studied the harvest and health records of the area. He was astonished by what he found. ③Boys who overate during the good years produced children and grandchildren who died about six years earlier than the children and grandchildren of those who had very little to eat. Other scientists found the same result for girls. ④Both boys and girls benefited greatly from the harvests of the good years. The scientists were forced to conclude that just one reason of overeating could have a negative impact that continued for generations.

9 밑줄 친 부분에 들어갈 말로 가장 적절한 것을 고르시오.

A : So, Mr. Wong, how long have you been living in New York City?
B : I've been living here for about seven years.
A : Can you tell me about your work experience?
B : I've been working at a pizzeria for the last three years.
A : What do you do there?
B : I seat the customers and wait on them.
A : How do you like your job?
B : It's fine. Everyone's really nice.
A : _____
B : It's just that I want to work in a more formal environment.
A : Okay. Is there anything else you would like to add?
B : I am really good with people. And I can also speak Italian and Chinese.
A : I see. Thank you very much. I'll be in touch shortly.
B : I hope to hear from you soon.

① So, what is the environment like there?

② Then, why are you applying for this job?

③ But are there any foreign languages you are good at?

④ And what qualities do you think are needed to work here?

10 우리말을 영어로 옳게 옮긴 것은?

① 내가 열쇠를 잃어버리지 않았더라면 모든 것이 괜찮았을텐데.

　　→ Everything would have been OK if I haven't lost my keys.

② 그 영화가 너무 지루해서 나는 삼십 분 후에 잠이 들었어.

　　→ The movie was so bored that I fell asleep after half an hour.

③ 내가 산책에 같이 갈 수 있는지 네게 알려줄게.

　　→ I will let you know if I can accompany with you on your walk.

④ 내 컴퓨터가 작동을 멈췄을 때, 나는 그것을 고치기 위해 컴퓨터 가게로 가져갔어.

　　→ When my computer stopped working, I took it to the computer store to get it fixed.

11 우리말을 영어로 잘못 옮긴 것은?

① 예산은 처음 기대했던 것보다 약 25 퍼센트 더 높다.

  → The budget is about 25% higher than originally expecting.

② 시스템 업그레이드를 위해 해야 될 많은 일이 있다.

  → There is a lot of work to be done for the system upgrade.

③ 그 프로젝트를 완성하는데 최소 한 달, 어쩌면 더 긴 시간이 걸릴 것이다.

  → It will take at least a month, maybe longer to complete the project.

④ 월급을 두 배 받는 그 부서장이 책임을 져야 한다.

  → The head of the department, who receives twice the salary, has to take responsibility.

12 밑줄 친 (A), (B)에 들어갈 말로 가장 적절한 것은?

The decline in the number of domestic adoptions in developed countries is mainly the result of a falling supply of domestically adoptable children. In those countries, the widespread availability of safe and reliable contraception combined with the pervasive postponement of childbearing as well as with legal access to abortion in most of them has resulted in a sharp reduction of unwanted births and, consequently, in a reduction of the number of adoptable children. _____(A)_____, single motherhood is no longer stigmatized as it once was and single mothers can count on State support to help them keep and raise their children. _____(B)_____, there are not enough adoptable children in developed countries for the residents of those countries wishing to adopt, and prospective adoptive parents have increasingly resorted to adopting children abroad.

	(A)	(B)
①	However	Consequently
②	However	In summary
③	Furthermore	Nonetheless
④	Furthermore	As a consequence

13

There is a basic principle that distinguishes a hot medium like radio from a cool one like the telephone, or a hot medium like the movie from a cool one like TV. A hot medium is one that extends one single sense in "high definition." High definition is the state of being well filled with data. A photograph is visually "high definition." A cartoon is "low definition," simply because very little visual information is provided. Telephone is a cool medium, or one of low definition, because the ear is given a meager amount of information. And speech is a cool medium of low definition, because so little is given and so much has to be filled in by the listener. On the other hand, hot media do not leave so much to be filled in or completed by the audience.

① Media can be classified into hot and cool.

② A hot medium is full of data.

③ Telephone is considered high definition.

④ Cool media leave much to be filled in by the audience.

14

December usually marks the start of humpback whale season in Hawaii, but experts say the animals have been slow to return this year. The giant whales are an iconic part of winter on the islands and a source of income for tour operators. But officials at the Humpback Whale Marine Sanctuary said they've been getting reports that the whales have been difficult to spot so far. "One theory was that something like this happened as whales increased. It's a product of their success. With more animals, they're competing against each other for food resources, and it takes an energy of reserve to make the long trip back," said Ed Lyman, a Maui-based resource protection manager and response coordinator for the sanctuary. He was surprised by how few of the animals he saw while responding to a call about a distressed calf on Christmas Eve, saying "We've just seen a handful of whales." It will be a while before officials have hard numbers because the annual whale counts don't take place until the last Saturday of January, February and March, according to former sanctuary co-manager Jeff Walters.

① Humpback whale season in Hawaii normally begins at the end of the year.

② Humpback whales are profitable for tour operators in Hawaii.

③ The drop in the number of humpback whales spotted in Hawaii may be due to their success.

④ The number of humpback whales that have returned to Hawaii this whale season has been officially calculated.

15 주어진 문장이 들어갈 위치로 가장 적절한 곳은?

> However, should understanding not occur, you will find yourself soon becoming drowsy.

Dictionaries are your most reliable resources for the study of words. Yet the habit of using them needs to be cultivated. Of course, it can feel like an annoying interruption to stop your reading and look up a word. You might tell yourself that if you keep going, you would eventually understand it from the context. (①) Indeed, reading study guides often advise just that. (②) Often it's not the need for sleep that is occurring but a gradual loss of consciousness. (③) The knack here is to recognize the early signs of word confusion before drowsiness takes over when it is easier to exert sufficient willpower to grab a dictionary for word study. (④) Although this special effort is needed, once the meaning is clarified, the perceptible sense of relief makes the effort worthwhile.

16 다음 글의 주제로 가장 적절한 것은?

It is easy to look at the diverse things people produce and to describe their differences. Obviously a poem is not a mathematical formula, and a novel is not an experiment in genetics. Composers clearly use a different language from that of visual artists, and chemists combine very different things than do playwrights. To characterize people by the different things they make, however, is to miss the universality of how they create. For at the level of the creative process, scientists, artists, mathematicians, composers, writers, and sculptors use a common set of what we call "tools for thinking," including emotional feelings, visual images, bodily sensations, reproducible patterns, and analogies. And all imaginative thinkers learn to translate ideas generated by these subjective thinking tools into public languages to express their insights, which can then give rise to new ideas in others' minds.

① obstacles to imaginative thinking

② the difference between art and science

③ the commonality of the creative process

④ distinctive features of various professions

17

There are few simple answers in science. Even seemingly straightforward questions, when probed by people in search of proof, lead to more questions. Those questions lead to nuances, layers of complexity and, more often than we might expect, _____.

In the 1990s, researchers asking "How do we fight oxygen-hungry cancer cells?" offered an obvious solution : Starve them of oxygen by cutting off their blood supply. But as Laura Beil describes in "Deflating Cancer," oxygen deprivation actually drives cancer to grow and spread. Scientists have responded by seeking new strategies : Block the formation of collagen highways, for instance, or even, as Beil writes, give the cells "more blood, not less."

① plans that end up unrealized

② conclusions that contradict initial intuition

③ great inventions that start from careful observations

④ misunderstandings that go against scientific progress

18

Before the lecture began, the speaker of the day distributed photocopies of his paper to each of the audience, and I got one and leafed through it and grasped the main idea of the text. Waiting for him to begin, I prayed in silence that this speaker would not read but speak instead directly to the audience with his own words about what he knew on the subject. But to my great disappointment, he _____. Soon I found I was mechanically following the printed words on the paper in my hand.

① was afraid of making his lecture too formal

② elaborated on his theories without looking at his paper

③ began to read his lengthy and well-prepared paper faithfully

④ made use of lots of humorous gestures to attract the audience

19

In a famous essay on Tolstoy, the liberal philosopher Sir Isaiah Berlin distinguished between two kinds of thinkers by harking back to an ancient saying attributed to the Greek lyric poet Archilochus (seventh century BC) : "The fox knows many things, but the hedgehog knows one big thing." Hedgehogs have one central idea and see the world exclusively through the prism of that idea. They overlook complications and exceptions, or mold them to fit into their world view. There is one true answer that fits at all times and all circumstances. Foxes, for whom Berlin had greater sympathy, have a variegated take on the world, which prevents them from _____. They are skeptical of grand theories as they feel the world's complexity prevents generalizations. Berlin thought Dante was a hedgehog while Shakespeare was a fox.

① behaving rationally

② finding multiple solutions

③ articulating one big slogan

④ grasping the complications of the world

20 다음 글에서 Locke의 주장으로 가장 적절한 것은?

In Locke's defense of private property, the significant point is what happens when we mix our labor with God's land. We add value to the land by working it; we make fertile what once lay fallow. In this sense, it is our labor that is the source of the value, or the added value, of the land. This value-creating power of my labor makes it right that I own the piece of land which I have made valuable by clearing it, the well I have made full by digging it, the animals I have raised and fattened. With Locke, Homo faber—the man of labor—becomes for the first time in the history of political thought a central rather than peripheral figure. In Locke's world, status and honor still flowed to the aristocrats, who were entitled to vast landholdings but were letting history pass them by precisely because new economic realities were in the process of shifting wealth to a bourgeoisie that actually created value by work. In time, Locke's elevation of the significance of labor was bound to appeal to the rising bourgeoisie.

① Ownership of property comes from labor.

② Labor is the most important ideal to aristocratic society.

③ The accumulation of private property is a source of happiness.

④ A smooth transition to bourgeois society is essential for social progress.

※ 밑줄 친 부분과 의미가 가장 가까운 것은? 【1~2】

1

> Ethical considerations can be an <u>integral</u> element of biotechnology regulation.

① key　　　　　　　　　　　　② incidental

③ interactive　　　　　　　　　④ popular

2

> If the area of the brain associated with speech is destroyed, the brain may use <u>plasticity</u> to cause other areas of the brain not originally associated with this speech to learn the skill as a way to make up for lost cells.

① accuracy　　　　　　　　　　② systemicity

③ obstruction　　　　　　　　　④ suppleness

※ 빈칸에 들어갈 단어로 가장 적절한 것은? 【3~4】

3

> Mephisto demands a signature and contract. No mere _____ contract will do. As Faust remarks, the devil wants everything in writing.

① genuine　　　　　　　　　　② essential

③ reciprocal　　　　　　　　　④ verbal

4

The company and the union reached a tentative agreement in this year's wage deal as the two sides took the company's _____ operating profits seriously amid unfriendly business environments.

① deteriorating   ② enhancing

③ ameliorating   ④ leveling

※ 밑줄 친 부분 중 어법상 가장 옳지 않은 것은? 【5~7】

5

I ① convinced that making pumpkin cake ② from scratch would be ③ even easier than ④ making cake from a box.

6

When you find your tongue ① twisted as you seek to explain to your ② six-year-old daughter why she can't go to the amusement park ③ that has been advertised on television, then you will understand why we find it difficult ④ wait.

7

Lewis Alfred Ellison, a small-business owner and ① a construction foreman, died in 1916 after an operation to cure internal wounds ② suffering after shards from a 100-lb ice block ③ penetrated his abdomen when it was dropped while ④ being loaded into a hopper.

8

A : You don't know about used cars, Ned. Whew! 70,000 miles.
B : Oh, that's a lot of miles! We have to take a close look at the engine, the doors, the tires, everything ...
A : It's too expensive, Ned. _____
B : You have to watch these used car salesmen.

① Let's buy it.

② I'll dust it down.

③ What model do you want?

④ I don't want to get ripped off.

9

The term combines two concepts—"bionic" which means to give a living thing an artificial capability like a bionic arm, and "nano" which _____ particles smaller than 100 nanometers that can be used to imbue the living thing with its new capability.

① breaks in   ② refers to

③ originates from   ④ lays over

10 어법상 가장 옳은 것은?

① If the item should not be delivered tomorrow, they would complain about it.

② He was more skillful than any other baseball players in his class.

③ Hardly has the violinist finished his performance before the audience stood up and applauded.

④ Bakers have been made come out, asking for promoting wheat consumption.

11 〈보기〉 문장이 들어갈 곳으로 가장 적절한 것은?

〈보기〉

If you are unhappy yourself, you will probably be prepared to admit that you are not exceptional in this.

(①) Animals are happy so long as they have health and enough to eat. Human beings, one feels, ought to be, but in the modern world they are not, at least in a great majority of cases. (②) If you are happy, ask yourself how many of your friends are so. (③) And when you have reviewed your friends, teach yourself the art of reading faces ; make yourself receptive to the moods of those whom you meet in the course of an ordinary day. (④)

12 글의 흐름상 가장 적절하지 않은 문장은?

Tighter regulations on cigarette products have spilled over to alcohol, soda and other consumer products, which has restricted consumer choices and made goods more expensive. ①Countries have taken more restrictive measures, including taxation, pictorial health warnings and prohibitions on advertising and promotion, against cigarette products over the past four decades. ②Regulatory measures have failed to improve public health, growing cigarette smuggling. ③Applying restrictions first to tobacco and then to other consumer products have created a domino effect, or what is called a "slippery slope", for other industries. ④At the extreme end of the slippery slope is plain packaging, where all trademarks, logos and brand−specific colors are removed, resulting in unintended consequences and a severe infringement of intellectual property rights.

※ 글의 흐름상 빈칸에 들어갈 가장 적절한 것은? 【13~14】

13

Language changes when speakers of a language come into contact with speakers of another language or languages. This can be because of migration, perhaps, because they move to more fertile lands, or because they are displaced on account of war or poverty or disease. It can also be because they are invaded. Depending on the circumstances, the home language may succumb completely to the language of the invaders, in which case we talk about replacement. _____, the home language might persist side-by-side with the language of the invaders, and depending on political circumstances, it might become the dominant language.

① Typically

② Consistently

③ Similarly

④ Alternatively

14

The notion that a product tested without branding is somehow being more objectively appraised is entirely _____. In the real world, we no more appraise things with our eyes closed and holding our nose than we do by ignoring the brand that is stamped on the product we purchase, the look and feel of the box it comes in, or the price being asked.

① correct

② reliable

③ misguided

④ unbiased

15 〈보기〉 글의 제목으로 가장 적절한 것은?

〈보기〉

Many visitors to the United States think that Americans take their exercise and free time activities too seriously. Americans often schedule their recreation as if they were scheduling business appointments. They go jogging every day at the same time, play tennis two or three times a week, or swim every Thursday. Foreigners often think that this kind of recreation sounds more like work than relaxation. For many Americans, however, their recreational activities are relaxing and enjoyable, or at least worthwhile, because they contribute to health and physical fitness.

① Health and fitness
② Popular recreational activities in the United States
③ The American approach to recreation
④ The definition of recreation

16 〈보기〉 글의 요지로 가장 적절한 것은?

〈보기〉

Feelings of pain or pleasure or some quality in between are the bedrock of our minds. We often fail to notice this simple reality because the mental images of the objects and events that surround us, along with the images of the words and sentences that describe them, use up so much of our overburdened attention. But there they are, feelings of myriad emotions and related states, the continuous musical line of our minds, the unstoppable humming of the most universal of melodies that only dies down when we go to sleep, a humming that turns into all-out singing when we are occupied by joy, or a mournful requiem when sorrow takes over.

① Feelings are closely associated with music.
② Feelings are composed of pain and pleasure.
③ Feelings are ubiquitous in our minds.
④ Feelings are related to the mental images of objects and events.

17 〈보기〉 글의 분위기로 가장 적절한 것은?

〈보기〉

I go to the local schoolyard, hoping to join in a game. But no one is there. After several minutes of standing around, dejected under the netless basketball hoops and wondering where everybody is, the names of those I expected to find awaiting me start to fill my mind. I have not played in a place like this for years. What was that? What was I thinking of, coming here? When I was a child, a boy, I went to the schoolyard to play. That was a long time ago. No children here will ever know me. Around me the concrete is empty except for pebbles, bottles, and a beer can that I kick, clawing a scary noise out of the pavement.

① calm and peaceful   ② festive and merry

③ desolate and lonely   ④ horrible and scary

18 글의 흐름상 빈칸에 들어갈 단어를 순서대로 고른 것은?

Often described as the _____ "rags to riches" tale, the story of steel magnate Andrew Carnegie's rise begins in 1835 in a small one-room home in Dunfermline, Scotland. Born into a family of _____ laborers, Carnegie received little schooling before his family emigrated to America in 1848. Arriving in Pennsylvania, he soon got a job in a textile mill, where he earned only $1.20 per week.

① quintessential – destitute

② exceptive – devout

③ interesting – meticulous

④ deleterious – impoverished

19 다음 글의 내용과 일치하는 것은?

In the American Southwest, previously the Mexican North, Anglo—America ran into Hispanic America. The meeting involved variables of language, religion, race, economy, and politics. The border between Hispanic America and Anglo—America has shifted over time, but one fact has not changed : it is one thing to draw an arbitrary geographical line between two spheres of sovereignty ; it is another to persuade people to respect it. Victorious in the Mexican—American War in 1848, the United States took half of Mexico. The resulting division did not ratify any plan of nature. The borderlands were an ecological whole ; northeastern Mexican desert blended into southeastern American desert with no prefiguring of nationalism. The one line that nature did provide —the Rio Grande —was a river that ran through but did not really divide continuous terrain.

① The borderlands between America and Mexico signify a long history of one sovereignty.

② While nature did not draw lines, human society certainly did.

③ The Mexican—American War made it possible for people to respect the border.

④ The Rio Grande has been thought of as an arbitrary geographical line.

20 다음 글을 문맥에 가장 어울리게 순서대로 배열한 것은?

㉠ The trigger for the aggressive driver is usually traffic congestion coupled with a schedule that is almost impossible to meet.

㉡ Unfortunately, these actions put the rest of us at risk. For example, an aggressive driver who resorts to using a roadway shoulder to pass may startle other drivers and cause them to take an evasive action that results in more risk or even a crash.

㉢ As a result, the aggressive driver generally commits multiple violations in an attempt to make up time.

㉣ Aggressive driving is a traffic offense or combination of offenses such as following too closely, speeding, unsafe lane changes, failing to signal intent to change lanes, and other forms of negligent or inconsiderate driving.

① ㉠ – ㉢ – ㉡ – ㉣
② ㉠ – ㉣ – ㉢ – ㉡
③ ㉣ – ㉠ – ㉢ – ㉡
④ ㉣ – ㉡ – ㉢ – ㉠

☞ 정답 및 해설 P.105

※ 밑줄 친 부분에 들어갈 말로 가장 적절한 것을 고르시오. 【1~2】

1

A : Can I ask you for a favor?
B : Yes, what is it?
A : I need to get to the airport for my business trip, but my car won't start. Can you give me a lift?
B : Sure. When do you need to be there by?
A : I have to be there no later than 6 : 00.
B : It's 4 : 30 now. _____. We'll have to leave right away.

① That's cutting it close　　　　② I took my eye off the ball
③ All that glitters is not gold　　④ It's water under the bridge

2

Fear of loss is a basic part of being human. To the brain, loss is a threat and we naturally take measures to avoid it. We cannot, however, avoid it indefinitely. One way to face loss is with the perspective of a stock trader. Traders accept the possibility of loss as part of the game, not the end of the game. What guides this thinking is a portfolio approach ; wins and losses will both happen, but it's the overall portfolio of outcomes that matters most. When you embrace a portfolio approach, you will be _____ because you know that they are small parts of a much bigger picture.

① more sensitive to fluctuations in the stock market
② more averse to the losses
③ less interested in your investments
④ less inclined to dwell on individual losses

3 다음 글의 제목으로 가장 적절한 것은?

Over the last years of traveling, I've observed how much we humans live in the past. The past is around us constantly, considering that, the minute something is manifested, it is the past. Our surroundings, our homes, our environments, our architecture, our products are all past constructs. We should live with what is part of our time, part of our collective consciousness, those things that were produced during our lives. Of course, we do not have the choice or control to have everything around us relevant or conceived during our time, but what we do have control of should be a reflection of the time in which we exist and communicate the present. The present is all we have, and the more we are surrounded by it, the more we are aware of our own presence and participation.

① Travel : Tracing the Legacies of the Past
② Reflect on the Time That Surrounds You Now
③ Manifestation of a Hidden Life
④ Architecture of a Futuristic Life

4 밑줄 친 부분 중 어법상 옳지 않은 것은?

It would be difficult ①to imagine life without the beauty and richness of forests. But scientists warn we cannot take our forest for ②granted. By some estimates, deforestation ③has been resulted in the loss of as much as eighty percent of the natural forests of the world. Currently, deforestation is a global problem, ④affecting wilderness regions such as the temperate rainforests of the Pacific.

5 밑줄 친 부분의 의미와 가장 가까운 것은?

> Robert J. Flaherty, a legendary documentary filmmaker, tried to show how <u>indigenous</u> people gathered food.

① itinerant

② impoverished

③ ravenous

④ native

6 밑줄 친 부분에 들어갈 말로 가장 적절한 것은?

> Listening to music is _____ being a rock star. Anyone can listen to music, but it takes talent to become a musician.

① on a par with

② a far cry from

③ contingent upon

④ a prelude to

7 다음 글의 흐름상 가장 어색한 문장은?

> Biologists have identified a gene that will allow rice plants to survive being submerged in water for up to two weeks—over a week longer than at present. Plants under water for longer than a week are deprived of oxygen and wither and perish. ①<u>The scientists hope their discovery will prolong the harvests of crops in regions that are susceptible to flooding.</u> ②<u>Rice growers in these flood-prone areas of Asia lose an estimated one billion dollars annually to excessively waterlogged rice paddies.</u> ③<u>They hope the new gene will lead to a hardier rice strain that will reduce the financial damage incurred in typhoon and monsoon seasons and lead to bumper harvests.</u> ④<u>This is dreadful news for people in these vulnerable regions, who are victims of urbanization and have a shortage of crops.</u> Rice yields must increase by 30 percent over the next 20 years to ensure a billion people can receive their staple diet.

8 밑줄 친 부분에 들어갈 말로 가장 적절한 것은?

A : Do you know how to drive?
B : Of course. I'm a great driver.
A : Could you teach me how to drive?
B : Do you have a learner's permit?
A : Yes, I got it just last week.
B : Have you been behind the steering wheel yet?
A : No, but I can't wait to _____.

① change a flat tire
② get an oil change
③ get my feet wet
④ take a rain check

9 다음 글의 내용과 일치하는 것은?

Sharks are covered in scales made from the same material as teeth. These flexible scales protect the shark and help it swim quickly in water. A shark can move the scales as it swims. This movement helps reduce the water's drag. Amy Lang, an aerospace engineer at the University of Alabama, studies the scales on the shortfin mako, a relative of the great white shark. Lang and her team discovered that the mako shark's scales differ in size and in flexibility in different parts of its body. For instance, the scales on the sides of the body are tapered—wide at one end and narrow at the other end. Because they are tapered, these scales move very easily. They can turn up or flatten to adjust to the flow of water around the shark and to reduce drag. Lang feels that shark scales can inspire designs for machines that experience drag, such as airplanes.

① A shark has scales that always remain immobile to protect itself as it swims.
② Lang revealed that the scales of a mako shark are utilized to lessen drag in water.
③ A mako shark has scales of identical size all over its body.
④ The scientific designs of airplanes were inspired by shark scales.

10 밑줄 친 부분 중 어법상 옳지 않은 것은?

Focus means ① getting stuff done. A lot of people have great ideas but don't act on them. For me, the definition of an entrepreneur, for instance, is someone who can combine innovation and ingenuity with the ability to execute that new idea. Some people think that the central dichotomy in life is whether you're positive or negative about the issues ② that interest or concern you. There's a lot of attention ③ paying to this question of whether it's better to have an optimistic or pessimistic lens. I think the better question to ask is whether you are going to do something about it or just ④ let life pass you by.

11 밑줄 친 부분 중 글의 흐름상 가장 어색한 것은?

Most people like to talk, but few people like to listen, yet listening well is a ① rare talent that everyone should treasure. Because they hear more, good listeners tend to know more and to be more sensitive to what is going on around them than most people. In addition, good listeners are inclined to accept or tolerate rather than to judge and criticize. Therefore, they have ② fewer enemies than most people. In fact, they are probably the most beloved of people. However, there are ③ exceptions to that generality. For example, John Steinbeck is said to have been an excellent listener, yet he was hated by some of the people he wrote about. No doubt his ability to listen contributed to his capacity to write. Nevertheless, the result of his listening didn't make him ④ unpopular.

12 다음 글의 주제로 가장 적절한 것은?

Worry is like a rocking horse. No matter how fast you go, you never move anywhere. Worry is a complete waste of time and creates so much clutter in your mind that you cannot think clearly about anything. The way to learn to stop worrying is by first understanding that you energize whatever you focus your attention on. Therefore, the more you allow yourself to worry, the more likely things are to go wrong! Worrying becomes such an ingrained habit that to avoid it you consciously have to train yourself to do otherwise. Whenever you catch yourself having a fit of worry, stop and change your thoughts. Focus your mind more productively on what you do want to happen and dwell on what's already wonderful in your life so more wonderful stuff will come your way.

① How do we cope with worrying?

② When should we worry?

③ Where does worry originate from?

④ What effects does worry have on life?

13 밑줄 친 부분에 들어갈 말로 가장 적절한 것은?

Kisha Padbhan, founder of Everonn Education, in Mumbai, looks at his business as nation-building. India's student-age population of 230 million (kindergarten to college) is one of the largest in the world. The government spends $83 billion on instruction, but there are serious gaps. "There aren't enough teachers and enough teacher-training institutes," says Kisha. "What children in remote parts of India lack is access to good teachers and exposure to good-quality content." Everonn's solution? The company uses a satellite network, with two-way video and audio _____. It reaches 1,800 colleges and 7,800 schools across 24 of India's 28 states. It offers everything from digitized school lessons to entrance exam prep for aspiring engineers and has training for job-seekers, too.

① to locate qualified instructors across the nation

② to get students familiarized with digital technology

③ to bridge the gap through virtual classrooms

④ to improve the quality of teacher training facilities

14 다음 글의 내용과 일치하지 않는 것은?

Students at Macaulay Honors College (MHC) don't stress about the high price of tuition. That's because theirs is free. At Macaulay and a handful of other service academies, work colleges, single-subject schools and conservatories, 100 percent of the student body receive a full tuition scholarship for all four years. Macaulay students also receive a laptop and $7,500 in "opportunities funds" to pursue research, service experiences, study abroad programs and internships. "The most important thing is not the free tuition, but the freedom of studying without the burden of debt on your back," says Ann Kirschner, university dean of Macaulay Honors College. The debt burden, she says, "really compromises decisions students make in college, and we are giving them the opportunity to be free of that." Schools that grant free tuition to all students are rare, but a greater number of institutions provide scholarships to enrollees with high grades. Institutions such as Indiana University Bloomington offer automatic awards to high-performing students with stellar GPAs and class ranks.

① MHC에서는 모든 학생이 4년간 수업료를 내지 않는다.
② MHC에서는 학생들에게 컴퓨터 구입 비용과 교외활동 비용을 합하여 $7,500를 지급한다.
③ 수업료로 인한 빚 부담이 있으면 학생들이 자유롭게 공부할 수 없다고 Kirschner 학장은 말한다.
④ MHC와 달리 학업 우수자에게만 장학금을 주는 대학도 있다.

15

The police spent seven months working on the crime case but were never able to determine the identity of the <u>malefactor</u>.

① culprit   ② dilettante

③ pariah   ④ demagogue

16

While at first glance it seems that his friends are just leeches, they prove to be the ones he can depend on <u>through thick and thin</u>.

① in good times and bad times   ② in pleasant times

③ from time to time   ④ in no time

17 주어진 문장이 들어갈 위치로 가장 적절한 것은?

Some remain intensely proud of their original accent and dialect words, phrases and gestures, while others accommodate rapidly to a new environment by changing their speech habits, so that they no longer "stand out in the crowd."

Our perceptions and production of speech change with time. (①) If we were to leave our native place for an extended period, our perception that the new accents around us were strange would only be temporary. (②) Gradually, we will lose the sense that others have an accent and we will begin to fit in-to accommodate our speech patterns to the new norm. (③) Not all people do this to the same degree. (④) Whether they do this consciously or not is open to debate and may differ from individual to individual, but like most processes that have to do with language, the change probably happens before we are aware of it and probably couldn't happen if we were.

18 다음 글의 내용과 일치하지 않는 것은?

Insomnia can be classified as transient, acute, or chronic. Transient insomnia lasts for less than a week. It can be caused by another disorder, by changes in the sleep environment, by the timing of sleep, severe depression, or by stress. Its consequences such as sleepiness and impaired psychomotor performance are similar to those of sleep deprivation. Acute insomnia is the inability to consistently sleep well for a period of less than a month. Acute insomnia is present when there is difficulty initiating or maintaining sleep or when the sleep that is obtained is not refreshing. These problems occur despite adequate opportunity and circumstances for sleep and they can impair daytime functioning. Acute insomnia is also known as short term insomnia or stress related insomnia. Chronic insomnia lasts for longer than a month. It can be caused by another disorder, or it can be a primary disorder. People with high levels of stress hormones or shifts in the levels of cytokines are more likely than others to have chronic insomnia. Its effects can vary according to its causes. They might include muscular weariness, hallucinations, and/or mental fatigue. Chronic insomnia can also cause double vision.

※ cytokines : groups of molecules released by certain cells of theimmune system

① Insomnia can be classified according to its duration.

② Transient insomnia occurs solely due to an inadequate sleep environment.

③ Acute insomnia is generally known to be related to stress.

④ Chronic insomnia patients may suffer from hallucinations.

19 주어진 문장 다음에 이어질 글의 순서로 가장 적절한 것은?

> A technique that enables an individual to gain some voluntary control over autonomic, or involuntary, body functions by observing electronic measurements of those functions is known as biofeedback.

> (A) When such a variable moves in the desired direction (for example, blood pressure down), it triggers visual or audible displays—feedback on equipment such as television sets, gauges, or lights.
>
> (B) Electronic sensors are attached to various parts of the body to measure such variables as heart rate, blood pressure, and skin temperature.
>
> (C) Biofeedback training teaches one to produce a desired response by reproducing thought patterns or actions that triggered the displays.

① (A) − (B) − (C)　　　　　　② (B) − (C) − (A)

③ (B) − (A) − (C)　　　　　　④ (C) − (A) − (B)

20 우리말을 영어로 잘못 옮긴 것은?

① 그 연사는 자기 생각을 청중에게 전달하는 데 능숙하지 않았다.

　→The speaker was not good at getting his ideas across to the audience.

② 서울의 교통 체증은 세계 어느 도시보다 심각하다.

　→The traffic jams in Seoul are more serious than those in any other city in the world.

③ 네가 말하고 있는 사람과 시선을 마주치는 것은 서양 국가에서 중요하다.

　→Making eye contact with the person you are speaking to is important in western countries.

④ 그는 사람들이 생각했던 만큼 인색하지 않았다는 것이 드러났다.

　→It turns out that he was not so stingier as he was thought to be.

☞ 정답 및 해설 P.111

※ 밑줄 친 부분의 의미와 가장 가까운 것을 고르시오. 【1~2】

1

The paramount duty of the physician is to do no harm. Everything else–even healing–must take second place.

① chief
② sworn
③ successful
④ mysterious

2

It is not unusual that people get cold feet about taking a trip to the North Pole.

① become ambitious
② become afraid
③ feel exhausted
④ feel saddened

3 밑줄 친 부분 중 어법상 옳지 않은 것은?

I am writing in response to your request for a reference for Mrs. Ferrer. She has worked as my secretary ①for the last three years and has been an excellent employee. I believe that she meets all the requirements ②mentioned in your job description and indeed exceeds them in many ways. I have never had reason ③to doubt her complete integrity. I would, therefore, recommend Mrs. Ferrer for the post ④what you advertise.

4 우리말을 영어로 잘못 옮긴 것은?

① 모든 정보는 거짓이었다.

→ All of the information was false.

② 토마스는 더 일찍 사과했어야 했다.

→ Thomas should have apologized earlier.

③ 우리가 도착했을 때 영화는 이미 시작했었다.

→ The movie had already started when we arrived.

④ 바깥 날씨가 추웠기 때문에 나는 차를 마시려 물을 끓였다.

→ Being cold outside, I boiled some water to have tea.

5 밑줄 친 부분의 의미와 가장 가까운 것은?

> The student who finds the state-of-the-art approach <u>intimidating</u> learns less than he or she might have learned by the old methods.

① humorous 　　　　　　　② friendly

③ convenient 　　　　　　 ④ frightening

6 밑줄 친 부분에 들어갈 말로 가장 적절한 것은?

> Since the air-conditioners are being repaired now, the office workers have to _____ electric fans for the day.

① get rid of 　　　　　　　② let go of

③ make do with 　　　　　 ④ break up with

7 어법상 옳은 것은?

① Please contact to me at the email address I gave you last week.

② Were it not for water, all living creatures on earth would be extinct.

③ The laptop allows people who is away from their offices to continue to work.

④ The more they attempted to explain their mistakes, the worst their story sounded.

8 우리말을 영어로 옳게 옮긴 것은?

① 그는 며칠 전에 친구를 배웅하기 위해 역으로 갔다.

    → He went to the station a few days ago to see off his friend.

② 버릇없는 그 소년은 아버지가 부르는 것을 못 들은 체했다.

    → The spoiled boy made it believe he didn't hear his father calling.

③ 나는 버팔로에 가본 적이 없어서 그곳에 가기를 고대하고 있다.

    → I have never been to Buffalo, so I am looking forward to go there.

④ 나는 아직 오늘 신문을 못 읽었어. 뭐 재미있는 것 있니?

    → I have not read today's newspaper yet. Is there anything interested in it?

9 다음 글의 흐름상 가장 어색한 문장은?

The Renaissance kitchen had a definite hierarchy of help who worked together to produce the elaborate banquets. ①At the top, as we have seen, was the scalco, or steward, who was in charge of not only the kitchen, but also the dining room. ②The dining room was supervised by the butler, who was in charge of the silverware and linen and also served the dishes that began and ended the banquet-the cold dishes, salads, cheeses, and fruit at the beginning and the sweets and confections at the end of the meal. ③This elaborate decoration and serving was what in restaurants is called "the front of the house." ④The kitchen was supervised by the head cook, who directed the undercooks, pastry cooks, and kitchen help.

10 다음 글의 요지로 가장 적절한 것은?

My students often believe that if they simply meet more important people, their work will improve. But it's remarkably hard to engage with those people unless you've already put something valuable out into the world. That's what piques the curiosity of advisers and sponsors. Achievements show you have something to give, not just something to take. In life, it certainly helps to know the right people. But how hard they go to bat for you, how far they stick their necks out for you, depends on what you have to offer. Building a powerful network doesn't require you to be an expert at networking. It just requires you to be an expert at something. If you make great connections, they might advance your career. If you do great work, those connections will be easier to make. Let your insights and your outputs—not your business cards—do the talking.

① Sponsorship is necessary for a successful career.

② Building a good network starts from your accomplishments.

③ A powerful network is a prerequisite for your achievement.

④ Your insights and outputs grow as you become an expert at networking.

11 밑줄 친 부분에 들어갈 말로 가장 적절한 것은?

A : My computer just shut down for no reason. I can't even turn it back on again.
B : Did you try charging it? It might just be out of battery.
A : Of course, I tried charging it.
B : _____
A : I should do that, but I'm so lazy.

① I don't know how to fix your computer.

② Try visiting the nearest service center then.

③ Well, stop thinking about your problems and go to sleep.

④ My brother will try to fix your computer because he's a technician.

12 다음 글에 나타난 화자의 심경으로 가장 적절한 것은?

My face turned white as a sheet. I looked at my watch. The tests would be almost over by now. I arrived at the testing center in an absolute panic. I tried to tell my story, but my sentences and descriptive gestures got so confused that I communicated nothing more than a very convincing version of a human tornado. In an effort to curb my distracting explanation, the proctor led me to an empty seat and put a test booklet in front of me. He looked doubtfully from me to the clock, and then he walked away. I tried desperately to make up for lost time, scrambling madly through analogies and sentence completions. "Fifteen minutes remain," the voice of doom declared from the front of the classroom. Algebraic equations, arithmetic calculations, geometric diagrams swam before my eyes. "Time! Pencils down, please."

① nervous and worried
③ calm and determined

② excited and cheerful
④ safe and relaxed

13 주어진 문장 다음에 이어질 글의 순서로 가장 적절한 것은?

Devices that monitor and track your health are becoming more popular among all age populations.

(A) For example, falls are a leading cause of death for adults 65 and older. Fall alerts are a popular gerotechnology that has been around for many years but have now improved.

(B) However, for seniors aging in place, especially those without a caretaker in the home, these technologies can be lifesaving.

(C) This simple technology can automatically alert 911 or a close family member the moment a senior has fallen.

※ gerotechnology : 노인을 위한 양로 기술

① (B) — (C) — (A)
③ (C) — (A) — (B)

② (B) — (A) — (C)
④ (C) — (B) — (A)

14

A : Where do you want to go for our honeymoon?
B : Let's go to a place that neither of us has been to.
A : Then, why don't we go to Hawaii?
B : _____

① I've always wanted to go there.
② Isn't Korea a great place to live?
③ Great! My last trip there was amazing!
④ Oh, you must've been to Hawaii already.

15

The secret of successful people is usually that they are able to concentrate totally on one thing. Even if they have a lot in their head, they have found a method that the many commitments don't impede each other, but instead they are brought into a good inner order. And this order is quite simple : _____. In theory, it seems to be quite clear, but in everyday life it seems rather different. You might have tried to decide on priorities, but you have failed because of everyday trivial matters and all the unforeseen distractions. Separate off disturbances, for example, by escaping into another office, and not allowing any distractions to get in the way. When you concentrate on the one task of your priorities, you will find you have energy that you didn't even know you had.

① the sooner, the better
② better late than never
③ out of sight, out of mind
④ the most important thing first

16 다음 글의 제목으로 가장 적절한 것은?

With the help of the scientist, the commercial fishing industry has found out that its fishing must be done scientifically if it is to be continued. With no fishing pressure on a fish population, the number of fish will reach a predictable level of abundance and stay there. The only fluctuation would be due to natural environmental factors, such as availability of food, proper temperature, and the like. If a fishery is developed to take these fish, their population can be maintained if the fishing harvest is small. The mackerel of the North Sea is a good example. If we increase the fishery and take more fish each year, we must be careful not to reduce the population below the ideal point where it can replace all of the fish we take out each year. If we fish at this level, called the maximum sustainable yield, we can maintain the greatest possible yield, year after year. If we catch too many, the number of fish will decrease each year until we fish ourselves out of a job. Examples of severely overfished animals are the blue whale of the Antarctic and the halibut of the North Atlantic. Fishing just the correct amount to maintain a maximum annual yield is both a science and an art. Research is constantly being done to help us better understand the fish population and how to utilize it to the maximum without depleting the population.

① Say No to Commercial Fishing
② Sea Farming Seen As a Fishy Business
③ Why Does the Fishing Industry Need Science?
④ Overfished Animals : Cases of Illegal Fishing

17 밑줄 친 (A), (B)에 들어갈 말로 가장 적절한 것은?

Does terrorism ever work? 9/11 was an enormous tactical success for al Qaeda, partly because it involved attacks that took place in the media capital of the world and the actual capital of the United States, _____(A)_____ ensuring the widest possible coverage of the event. If terrorism is a form of theater where you want a lot of people watching, no event in human history was likely ever seen by a larger global audience than the 9/11 attacks. At the time, there was much discussion about how 9/11 was like the attack on Pearl Harbor. They were indeed similar since they were both surprise attacks that drew America into significant wars. But they were also similar in another sense. Pearl Harbor was a great tactical success for Imperial Japan, but it led to a great strategic failure : Within four years of Pearl Harbor the Japanese empire lay in ruins, utterly defeated. _____(B)_____, 9/11 was a great tactical success for al Qaeda, but it also turned out to be a great strategic failure for Osama bin Laden.

	(A)	(B)
①	thereby	Similarly
②	while	Therefore
③	while	Fortunately
④	thereby	On the contrary

18 다음 글의 내용과 일치하지 않는 것은?

We entered a new phase as a species when Chinese scientists altered a human embryo to remove a potentially fatal blood disorder—not only from the baby, but all of its descendants. Researchers call this process "germline modification." The media likes the phrase "designer babies." But we should call it what it is, "eugenics." And we, the human race, need to decide whether or not we want to use it. Last month, in the United States, the scientific establishment weighed in. A National Academy of Sciences and National Academy of Medicine joint committee endorsed embryo editing aimed at genes that cause serious diseases when there is "no reasonable alternative." But it was more wary of editing for "enhancement," like making already-healthy children stronger or taller. It recommended a public discussion, and said that doctors should "not proceed at this time." The committee had good reason to urge caution. The history of eugenics is full of oppression and misery.

※ eugenics : 우생학

① Doctors were recommended to immediately go ahead with embryo editing for enhancement.

② Recently, the scientific establishment in the U.S. joined a discussion on eugenics.

③ Chinese scientists modified a human embryo to prevent a serious blood disorder.

④ "Designer babies" is another term for the germline modification process.

19 주어진 문장이 들어갈 위치로 가장 적절한 것은?

> If neither surrendered, the two exchanged blows until one was knocked out.

The ancient Olympics provided athletes an opportunity to prove their fitness and superiority, just like our modern games. (①) The ancient Olympic events were designed to eliminate the weak and glorify the strong. Winners were pushed to the brink. (②) Just as in modern times, people loved extreme sports. One of the favorite events was added in the 33rd Olympiad. This was the pankration, or an extreme mix of wrestling and boxing. The Greek word pankration means "total power." The men wore leather straps with metal studs, which could make a terrible mess of their opponents. (③) This dangerous form of wrestling had no time or weight limits. In this event, only two rules applied. First, wrestlers were not allowed to gouge eyes with their thumbs. Secondly, they could not bite. Anything else was considered fair play. The contest was decided in the same manner as a boxing match. Contenders continued until one of the two collapsed. (④) Only the strongest and most determined athletes attempted this event. Imagine wrestling "Mr. Fingertips," who earned his nickname by breaking his opponents' fingers!

20 밑줄 친 부분에 들어갈 말로 가장 적절한 것은?

In our time it is not only the law of the market which has its own life and rules over man, but also the development of science and technique. For a number of reasons, the problems and organization of science today are such that a scientist does not choose his problems; the problems force themselves upon the scientist. He solves one problem, and the result is not that he is more secure or certain, but that ten other new problems open up in place of the single solved one. They force him to solve them; he has to go ahead at an ever-quickening pace. The same holds true for industrial techniques. The pace of science forces the pace of technique. Theoretical physics forces atomic energy on us; the successful production of the fission bomb forces upon us the manufacture of the hydrogen bomb. We do not choose our problems, we do not choose our products; we are pushed, we are forced—by what? By a system which has no purpose and goal transcending it, and which _____.

① makes man its appendix

② creates a false sense of security

③ inspires man with creative challenges

④ empowers scientists to control the market laws

※ 밑줄 친 부분과 의미가 가장 가까운 것은? 【1~3】

1

Man has continued to be disobedient to authorities who tried to <u>muzzle</u> new thoughts and to the authority of long-established opinions which declared a change to be nonsense.

① express

② assert

③ suppress

④ spread

2

Don't be <u>pompous</u>. You don't want your writing to be too informal and colloquial, but you also don't want to sound like someone you're not—like your professor or boss, for instance, or the Rhodes scholar teaching assistant.

① presumptuous

② casual

③ formal

④ genuine

3

Surgeons were forced to <u>call it a day</u> because they couldn't find the right tools for the job.

① initiate

② finish

③ wait

④ cancel

4 대화 중 가장 어색한 것은?

① A : I'd like to make a reservation for tomorrow, please.

B : Certainly. For what time?

② A : Are you ready to order?

B : Yes, I'd like the soup, please.

③ A : How's your risotto?

B : Yes, we have risotto with mushroom and cheese.

④ A : Would you like a dessert?

B : Not for me, thanks.

5 밑줄 친 부분 중 어법상 가장 옳지 않은 것은?

His survival ①<u>over</u> the years since independence in 1961 does not alter the fact that the discussion of real policy choices in a public manner has hardly ②<u>never</u> occurred. In fact, there have always been ③<u>a number of</u> important policy issues ④<u>which</u> Nyerere has had to argue through the NEC.

6 밑줄 친 부분 중 어법상 가장 옳은 것은?

More than 150 people ①<u>have fell ill</u>, mostly in Hong Kong and Vietnam, over the past three weeks. And experts ②<u>are suspected</u> that ③<u>another 300 people</u> in China's Guangdong province had the same disease ④<u>begin in</u> mid-November.

7 글의 흐름상 빈칸에 들어갈 단어로 가장 옳은 것은?

Social learning theorists offer a different explanation for the counter-aggression exhibited by children who experience aggression in the home. An extensive research on aggressive behavior and the coercive family concludes that an aversive consequence may also elicit an aggressive reaction and accelerate ongoing coercive behavior. These victims of aggressive acts eventually learn via modeling to _____ aggressive interchanges. These events perpetuate the use of aggressive acts and train children how to behave as adults.

① stop   ② attenuate
③ abhor   ④ initiate

8 밑줄 친 인물(Marcel Mauss)에 대한 설명으로 가장 옳지 않은 것은?

Marcel Mauss (1872–1950), French sociologist, was born in Épinal (Vosges) in Lorraine, where he grew up within a close-knit, pious, and orthodox Jewish family. Emile Durkheim was his uncle. By the age of 18 Mauss had reacted against the Jewish faith; he was never a religious man. He studied philosophy under Durkheim's supervision at Bordeaux; Durkheim took endless trouble in guiding his nephew's studies and even chose subjects for his own lectures that would be most useful to Mauss. Thus Mauss was initially a philosopher (like most of the early Durkheimians), and his conception of philosophy was influenced above all by Durkheim himself, for whom he always retained the utmost admiration.

① He had a Jewish background.
② He was supervised by his uncle.
③ He had a doctrinaire faith.
④ He was a sociologist with a philosophical background.

9 글의 문맥에 가장 어울리는 순서대로 배열한 것은?

ⓐ Today, however, trees are being cut down far more rapidly. Each year, about 2 million acres of forests are cut down. That is more than equal to the area of the whole of Great Britain.

ⓑ There is not enough wood in these countries to satisfy the demand. Wood companies, therefore, have begun taking wood from the forests of Asia, Africa, South America, and even Siberia.

ⓒ While there are important reasons for cutting down trees, there are also dangerous consequences for life on earth. A major cause of the present destruction is the worldwide demand for wood. In industrialized countries, people are using more and more wood for paper.

ⓓ There is nothing new about people cutting down trees. In ancient times, Greece, Italy, and Great Britain were covered with forests. Over the centuries those forests were gradually cut back. Until now almost nothing is left.

① ⓐ − ⓑ − ⓒ − ⓓ   ② ⓓ − ⓐ − ⓑ − ⓒ

③ ⓑ − ⓐ − ⓒ − ⓓ   ④ ⓓ − ⓐ − ⓒ − ⓑ

10 글의 흐름상 빈칸에 들어갈 표현으로 가장 옳은 것은?

Contemporary art has in fact become an integral part of today's middle class society. Even works of art which are fresh from the studio are met with enthusiasm. They receive recognition rather quickly—too quickly for the taste of the surlier culture critics. _____, not all works of them are bought immediately, but there is undoubtedly an increasing number of people who enjoy buying brand new works of art. Instead of fast and expensive cars, they buy the paintings, sculptures and photographic works of young artists. They know that contemporary art also adds to their social prestige. _____, since art is not exposed to the same wear and tear as automobiles, it is a far better investment.

① Of course − Furthermore   ② Therefore − On the other hand

③ Therefore − For instance   ④ Of course − For example

11 밑줄 친 부분과 의미가 가장 먼 것은?

As a prerequisite for fertilization, pollination is <u>essential</u> to the production of fruit and seed crops and plays an important part in programs designed to improve plants by breeding.

① crucial　　　　　　　　　　② indispensable

③ requisite　　　　　　　　　④ omnipresent

12 글의 흐름상 빈칸에 들어갈 단어로 가장 옳은 것은?

Mr. Johnson objected to the proposal because it was founded on a _____ principle and also was _____ at times.

① faulty − desirable　　　　　② imperative − reasonable

③ conforming − deplorable　　④ wrong − inconvenient

※ 밑줄 친 부분 중 어법상 가장 옳지 않은 것은? 【13~14】

13

I'm ①<u>pleased</u> that I have enough clothes with me. American men are generally bigger than Japanese men so ②<u>it's</u> very difficult to find clothes in Chicago that ③<u>fits</u> me. ④<u>What</u> is a medium size in Japan is a small size here.

14

Blue Planet II, a nature documentary ①<u>produced</u> by the BBC, left viewers ②<u>heartbroken</u> after showing the extent ③<u>to which</u> plastic ④<u>affects on</u> the ocean.

15 글의 흐름상 빈칸에 들어갈 가장 적절한 문장은?

> What became clear by the 1980s, however, as preparations were made for the 'Quincentenary Jubilee', was that many Americans found it hard, if not impossible, to see the anniversary as a 'jubilee'. There was nothing to celebrate the legacy of Columbus. _____

① According to many of his critics, Columbus had been the harbinger not of progress and civilization, but of slavery and the reckless exploitation of the environment.

② The Chicago World's Fair of 1893 reinforced the narrative link between discovery and the power of progress of the United States.

③ This reversal of the nineteenth-century myth of Columbus is revealing.

④ Columbus thus became integrated into Manifest Destiny, the belief that America's progress was divinely ordained.

16 글의 흐름상 빈칸에 들어갈 단어로 가장 옳지 않은 것은?

> Following his father's imprisonment, Charles Dickens was forced to leave school to work at a boot-blacking factory alongside the River Thames. At the run-down, rodent-ridden factory, Dickens earned six shillings a week labeling pots of "blacking," a substance used to clean fireplaces. It was the best he could do to help support his family. Looking back on the experience, Dickens saw it as the moment he said goodbye to his youthful innocence, stating that he wondered "how he could be so easily cast away at such a young age." He felt _____ by the adults who were supposed to take care of him.

① abandoned   ② betrayed

③ buttressed   ④ disregarded

17 글의 내용과 일치하는 것은?

A family hoping to adopt a child must first select an adoption agency. In the United States, there are two kinds of agencies that assist with adoption. Public agencies generally handle older children, children with mental or physical disabilities, or children who may have been abused or neglected. Prospective parents are not usually expected to pay fees when adopting a child from a public agency. Fostering, or a form of temporary adoption, is also possible through public agencies. Private agencies can be found on the Internet. They handle domestic and international adoption.

① Public adoption agencies are better than private ones.

② Parents pay huge fees to adopt a child from a foster home.

③ Children in need cannot be adopted through public agencies.

④ Private agencies can be contacted for international adoption.

18 글의 흐름상 빈칸에 들어갈 단어로 가장 옳은 것은?

Moths and butterflies both belong to the order Lepidoptera, but there are numerous physical and behavioral differences between the two insect types. On the behavioral side, moths are _____ and butterflies are diurnal (active during the day). While at rest, butterflies usually fold their wings back, while moths flatten their wings against their bodies or spread them out in a "jet plane" position.

① nocturnal   ② rational

③ eternal   ④ semi-circular

19 글의 흐름상 빈칸에 들어갈 표현으로 가장 옳은 것은?

The idea of clowns frightening people started gaining strength in the United States. In South Carolina, for example, people reported seeing individuals wearing clown costumes, often hiding in the woods or in cities at night. Some people said that the clowns were trying to lure children into empty homes or the woods. Soon, there were reports of threatening−looking clowns trying to frighten both children and adults. Although there were usually no reports of violence, and many of the reported sightings were later found to be false, this _____.

① benefited the circus industry

② promoted the use of clowns in ads

③ caused a nationwide panic

④ formed the perfect image of a happy clown

20 글의 내용과 가장 부합하는 속담은?

It is one thing to believe that our system of democracy is the best, and quite another to impose it on other countries. This is a blatant breach of the UN policy of non−intervention in the domestic affairs of independent nations. Just as Western citizens fought for their political institutions, we should trust the citizens of other nations to do likewise if they wish to. Democracy is also not an absolute term−Napoleon used elections and referenda to legitimize his hold on power, as do leaders today in West Africa and Southeast Asia. States with partial democracy are often more aggressive than totally unelected dictatorships which are too concerned with maintaining order at home. The differing types of democracy make it impossible to choose which standards to impose. The U.S. and European countries all differ in terms of restraints on government and the balance between consensus and confrontation.

① The grass is always greener on the other side of the fence.

② One man's food is another's poison.

③ There is no rule but has exceptions.

④ When in Rome, do as the Romans do.

2018. 8. 25. | 국회사무처 시행

☞ 정답 및 해설 P.121

1 다음 밑줄 친 부분 중 어법상 옳지 않은 것은?

We live in a democratic age. Over the last century the world has been shaped by one trend above all others—the rise of democracy. In 1900, not a single country had ① what we would today consider a democracy: a government created by elections ② which every adult ③ citizen could vote. Today this is done by over 60 percent of all countries in the world. ④ What was once a peculiar practice of a handful of states around the North Atlantic ⑤ has become the standard form of government for humankind.

2 다음 밑줄 친 부분의 의미와 가장 가까운 것은?

He launched into the crowd to grapple his unfortunate prey.

① identify   ② avoid
③ evoke   ④ exploit
⑤ seize

3 다음 밑줄 친 부분의 의미와 가장 가까운 것은?

> <u>Conciliatory</u> gestures, such as an apology or offer of compensation, were shown to reduce anger and promote forgiveness after a conflict.

① assured   ② punitive

③ flattering   ④ appeasing

⑤ acquiescing

4 다음 밑줄 친 부분 중 어법상 옳지 않은 것은?

> ①<u>Affording a home</u> in one of Britain's opulent seaside towns has long been way out of reach, even for ②<u>the moderately rich</u>. But now it seems that house prices in two of the smartest resorts have tumbled significantly in the last year. In the boating haven of Salcombe in South Devon, prices ③<u>have fallen</u> 8.2%, according to the Halifax. And in Sandbanks in Dorset, ④<u>renowned for</u> being the UK's most expensive resort, prices ⑤<u>being down</u> 5.6%.

5 다음 밑줄 친 부분에 들어갈 가장 적절한 표현은?

> Men have always used fashion to attract attention and satisfy a desire for personal display. Women are not the only ones to turn to clothing to enhance, adorn and modify their bodies. Nevertheless, social norms have long required that men's interest in fashion be _____. Too great a concern with fashion and personal appearance may be interpreted as not only vain, but also unmanly, while too little interest is considered equally questionable.

① documented thoroughly   ② removed completely

③ carefully balanced   ④ initially ignored

⑤ fairly rewarded

6 다음 밑줄 친 부분에 들어갈 가장 적절한 단어는?

> Almost all babies start smiling at a very young age. One might think that babies learn to smile by observing others and imitating the facial expressions they see, but evidence argues against this proposal. One study compared the facial expressions of three groups of athletes receiving their award medals at the 2004 Paralympic Games. One group had been blind since birth; a second group had some years of visual experience but was now fully blind; a third group had normal sight. The study showed essentially no _____ among these groups in their facial expressions.

① difference   ② change

③ match   ④ effect

⑤ link

7 다음 밑줄 친 (A), (B)에 들어갈 가장 적절한 표현은?

> "Leisure" refers to "unobligated" time wherein we are free from work or maintenance responsibilities. (A) _____, a teacher who brings home his or her students' assignments to grade at home is not engaged in a leisure activity. Also mowing the lawn and shopping for groceries are not leisure pursuits because they are necessary maintenance tasks. (B) _____, attending a ball game, window shopping at the mall, going to the movies, and feeding the ducks at a pond are leisure activities because we are not obligated to do these things.

	(A)	(B)
①	Otherwise	On the other hand
②	Therefore	In a similar vein
③	Otherwise	For instance
④	Thus	In a similar vein
⑤	Thus	On the other hand

8 다음 밑줄 친 부분에 들어갈 가장 적절한 표현은?

> Much like in a heavy snowfall, data is piling up at a high speed and in a gigantic volume. You could think that it's good: more data means more reliable insights. But in reality, huge volumes of data don't necessarily mean huge volumes of actionable insights. Sometimes, the data you have—despite all the information it contains—statistically just isn't _____.
> For example, opinions on Twitter vs. opinions of the population on the whole. Let alone the bias of the former, it doesn't even contain the viewpoints of the entire population (for example, the elderly and the introverts often get excluded). This way, you can get wrong analysis results easily. Besides that, in such 'heavy snowfalls', it simply gets more challenging to find what you need while eliminating the data that bears no use whatsoever.

① state-of-the-art enough to find correlations with the population

② the representative sample of the data you need to analyze

③ an impediment in your way of solving the target problem

④ analyzable to come to a meaningful conclusion due to sorted information

⑤ intact because some key information has already been eliminated

9 다음 글의 내용과 가장 거리가 먼 것은?

> Maps of the world in older times used to fill in the blanks of exploration with an array of fantastic creatures, dragons, sea monsters, fierce winged beasts. It appears that the human mind cannot bear very much blankness—where we do not know, we invent, and what we invent reflects our fear of what we do not know. Fairies are born of that fear. The blank spaces on the village map, too, need to be filled; faced with woods and mountains, seas and streams that could never be fully charted, human beings saw blanks, blanks they hastened to fill with a variety of beings all given different names, yet all recognizable as fairies. Our fairies have become utterly benign only nowadays, when electric light and motorways and mobile phones have banished the terror of the lonely countryside. Used as we are to benign fairies, it is very hard for us to understand the fairies of the past.

① Human beings do not like to see things void and unfilled.

② Fairies reflect the human fear over the indecipherable things in nature.

③ There is not much historical change in our perception of the fairies.

④ The margins of maps are often decorated with fantastic creatures.

⑤ The idea of benevolent fairies is very modern.

10 대화의 흐름으로 보아 밑줄 친 부분에 들어갈 가장 적절한 표현은?

> A : Are you going to the market today?
> B : No, I'm not. I have to see my doctor today. Why? Do you need something?
> A : _____ I'll go tomorrow.
> B : No, no, I can drop by the market on my way home.

① Oh, never mind.

② Yeah. I have to see my doctor, too.

③ No, I don't need anything.

④ Can you get some eggs for me?

⑤ I would appreciate it if you could buy some eggs.

11 다음 밑줄 친 부분의 의미와 가장 가까운 것은?

> The medical resistance to death may seem entirely <u>laudable</u>, since we expect doctors to enhance health and to preserve life.

① compelling
② intrepid
③ praiseworthy
④ audacious
⑤ sagacious

12 다음 밑줄 친 부분 중 어법상 옳지 않은 것은?

> Democracy, after all, is not just ①<u>a set of practices but a culture.</u> It lives not only ②<u>in so formal mechanisms</u> as party and ballot ③<u>but in the instincts and expectations of citizens.</u> Objective circumstances—jobs, war, competition from abroad—shape ④<u>that political culture</u>, but ⑤<u>so do the words and deeds of leaders.</u>

13 다음 문장 중 어법상 옳지 않은 것은?

① Attached is the document file you've requested.
② Never in my life have I seen such a beautiful woman.
③ Should you need further information, please contact me.
④ Hardly has the situation more serious than now.
⑤ Now is the time to start living the life you have always imagined.

14 다음 밑줄 친 부분의 의미와 가장 가까운 것은?

Inertia is not a place you want to be in your life. I say this with extreme fervor because if you allow yourself to stay <u>inert</u>, I feel, you are giving up on your goals.

① distracted ② fragile

③ allured ④ irresponsible

⑤ listless

15 다음 밑줄 친 (A), (B), (C)에 들어갈 가장 적절한 표현은?

Anecdotes about elephants (A) _____ with examples of their loyalty and group cohesion. Maintaining this kind of togetherness calls for a good system of communication. We are only now beginning to appreciate (B) _____ complex and far-reaching this system is. Researcher Katharine Payne first started to delve into elephant communication after a visit to Portland's Washington Park Zoo. Standing in the elephant house, she began to feel (C) _____ vibrations in the air, and after a while realized that they were coming from the elephants. What Katharine felt, and later went on to study, is a low-frequency form of sound called infrasound.

	(A)	(B)	(C)
①	abound	how	throbbing
②	abound	that	throbbed
③	abound	that	throbbing
④	are abounded	how	throbbing
⑤	are abounded	that	throbbed

16 다음의 밑줄 친 부분에 들어갈 가장 적절한 단어는?

> If you are having trouble going somewhere or doing something, don't give up. You just haven't found the best solution or met the right person yet. Don't listen to those who say it can't be done. _____ pays off. I can't tell you how many times I've been told what I want isn't possible, only to prove it wrong later when I don't give up and keep trying.

① Anxiety

② Cooperation

③ Speculation

④ Perseverance

⑤ Convention

17 다음 밑줄 친 부분에 들어갈 가장 적절한 표현은?

> Equality and social justice are dependent on recognizing that we live and work in a diverse society, and that such diversity is an asset to be valued rather than a problem to be solved. However, this presents some degree of complication when it comes to communication. This is because communication can be seen to work best when people are similar, or at least on a similar wave length. We have to recognize, then, that there is a tension between communication and diversity. We should not be defeatists and challenge this tension. This means that the valuing of diversity is something that _____.

① is reluctant to be accepted from the perspective of social harmony

② should be pursued in different languages and cultures

③ should not be abandoned in favor of effective communication

④ forms a conflict that operates within interpersonal interactions

⑤ can work against our efforts of communication in society

18 다음 밑줄 친 부분에 들어갈 가장 적절한 표현은?

Gray, which is neither black nor white but a combination of these two opposites, is an ambiguous, indefinite color. It suggests fog, mist, smoke and twilight—conditions that blur shapes and colors. An all-gray costume can indicate a modest, retiring individual, someone who prefers not to be noticed or someone who whether they wish it or not merges with their background, like Lily Briscoe in Virginia Woolf's To the Lighthouse. When a livelier, prettier girl enters the room, the narrator reports, Lily Briscoe "became _____ than ever, in her little grey dress."

① more resonant   ② more distinguished

③ more sullen   ④ more sophisticated

⑤ more inconspicuous

19 다음 밑줄 친 (A)와 (B)에 들어갈 가장 적절한 단어는?

For many, the demands of college are the greatest challenges they have yet faced. Every day, students are exposed to a barrage of new ideas that they must grasp to meet ever present deadline. This (A) _____ process is made more difficult with schedule conflicts with work, financial difficulties, and other personal problems. Many are overwhelmed by it all, yet every year people graduate while others drop out. In most cases, only one thing separates those who graduate from those who drop out. Those who graduate have (B) _____. They won't quit when confronted by tough obstacles or even when failing. It is found in all people who succeed and it has benefits even in failure.

	(A)	(B)
①	unflinching	versatility
②	unrelenting	tenacity
③	impeccable	flexibility
④	irreversible	punctuality
⑤	unprecedented	conformity

20 다음 밑줄 친 부분에 들어갈 가장 적절한 문장은?

A person's handwriting has long been recognized as a form of human identification. This fact is the reason people are required to sign checks, wills, and contracts. _____.
For example, the serial killer Ted Bundy used several methods of killing his victims. Authorities first thought they were dealing with several different killers. With the help of handwriting identification, officials later realized they were seeking one serial killer. The Nazi war criminal, Josef Mengele, traveled to South America, and took the identity of another German man. After his death it was discovered that the handwriting of this man matched the handwriting of Mengele. Mengele had altered everything including his name, profession, and fingerprints, but he could not change his handwriting.

① Handwriting identification has played important roles in some criminal cases.

② Questioned handwriting may be found on a will, a contract, or a letter.

③ Handwriting identification is developed by forensic document examiners.

④ One type of a questioned signature is a deliberately altered signature.

⑤ There are two types of writing, request writing and non-request writing.

1 다음 글의 밑줄 친 부분 중 어법상 틀린 것은?

Recent research reveals that some individuals are genetically ①predisposed to shyness. In other words, some people are born shy. Researchers say that between 15 and 20 percent of newborn babies show signs of shyness: they are quieter and more vigilant. Researchers have identified physiological differences between sociable and shy babies ②that show up as early as two months. In one study, two-month-olds who were later identified as shy children ③reacting with signs of stress to stimuli such as moving mobiles and tape recordings of human voices: increased heart rates, jerky movements of arms and legs, and excessive crying. Further evidence of the genetic basis of shyness is the fact that parents and grandparents of shy children more often say that they were shy as children ④than parents and grandparents of non-shy children.

2 다음 밑줄 친 (A), (B), (C)에서 문맥에 맞는 낱말로 가장 적절한 것은?

South Korea is one of the only countries in the world that has a dedicated goal to become the world's leading exporter of popular culture. It is a way for Korea to develop its "soft power." It refers to the (A)[tangible / intangible] power a country wields through its image, rather than through military power or economic power. Hallyu first spread to China and Japan, later to Southeast Asia and several countries worldwide. In 2000, a 50-year ban on the exchange of popular culture between Korea and Japan was partly lifted, which improved the (B)[surge / decline] of Korean popular culture among the Japanese. South Korea's broadcast authorities have been sending delegates to promote their TV programs and cultural contents in several countries. Hallyu has been a blessing for Korea, its businesses, culture and country image. Since early 1999, Hallyu has become one of the biggest cultural phenomena across Asia. The Hallyu effect has been tremendous, contributing to 0.2% of Korea's GDP in 2004, amounting to approximately USD 1.87 billion. More recently in 2014, Hallyu had an estimated USD 11.6 billion (C)[boost / stagnation] on the Korean economy.

	(A)	(B)	(C)
①	tangible	surge	stagnation
②	intangible	decline	boost
③	intangible	surge	boost
④	tangible	decline	stagnation

3 다음 글에서 전체의 흐름과 가장 관계 없는 문장은?

The immortal operatically styled single Bohemian Rhapsody by Queen was released in 1975 and proceeded to the top of the UK charts for 9 weeks. ①A song that was nearly never released due to its length and unusual style but which Freddie insisted would be played became the instantly recognizable hit. ②By this time Freddie's unique talents were becoming clear, a voice with a remarkable range and a stage presence that gave Queen its colorful, unpredictable and flamboyant personality. ③The son of Bomi and Jer Bulsara, Freddie spent the bulk of his childhood in India where he attended St. Peter's boarding school. ④Very soon Queen's popularity extended beyond the shores of the UK as they charted and triumphed around Europe, Japan and the USA where in 1979 they topped the charts with Freddie's song Crazy Little thing Called Love.

4 (A), (B), (C)의 각 부분에서 어법에 맞는 표현으로 가장 적절한 것은?

Mel Blanc, considered by many industry experts to be the inventor of cartoon voice acting, began his career in 1927 as a voice actor for a local radio show. The producers did not have the funds to hire many actors, so Mel Blanc resorted to (A) [create / creating] different voices and personas for the show as needed. He became a regular on The Jack Benny Program, (B) [where / which] he provided voices for many characters – human, animal, and nonliving objects such as a car in need of a tune-up. The distinctive voice he created for Porky Pig fueled his breakout success at Warner Bros. Soon Blanc was closely associated with many of the studio's biggest cartoon stars as well as characters from Hanna–Barbera Studios. His longest running voice-over was for the character Daffy Duck – about 52 years. Blanc was extremely protective of his work – screen credits reading "Voice Characterization by Mel Blanc" (C) [was / were] always under the terms of his contracts.

*personas (극 · 소설 등의) 등장인물

	(A)	(B)	(C)
①	create	where	was
②	create	which	were
③	creating	where	were
④	creating	which	was

5 다음 빈칸에 들어갈 말로 가장 적절한 것은?

With the present plummeting demand market for office buildings, resulting in many vacant properties, we need to develop plans that will enable some future exchange between residential and commercial or office functions. This vacancy has reached a historic level; at present the major towns in the Netherlands have some five million square metres of unoccupied office space, while there is a shortage of 160,000 homes. At least a million of those square metres can be expected to stay vacant, according to the association of Dutch property developers. There is a real threat of 'ghost towns' of empty office buildings springing up around the major cities. In spite of this forecast, office building activities are continuing at full tilt, as these were planned during a period of high returns. Therefore, it is now essential that _____.

① a new design be adopted to reduce costs for the maintenance of buildings

② a number of plans for office buildings be redeveloped for housing

③ residential buildings be converted into commercial buildings

④ we design and deliver as many shops as possible

6 다음 글의 내용과 가장 일치하는 것은?

Child psychologists concentrate their efforts on the study of the individual from birth through age eleven. Developmental psychologists study behavior and growth patterns from the prenatal period through maturity and old age. Many clinical psychologists specialize in dealing with the behavior problems of children. Research in child psychology sometimes helps shed light on work behavior. For example, one study showed that victims of childhood abuse and neglect may suffer long-term consequences. Among them are lower IQs and reading ability, more suicide attempts, and more unemployment and low-paying jobs. Many people today have become interested in the study of adult phases of human development. The work of developmental psychologists has led to widespread interest in the problems of the middle years, such as the mid-life crisis. A job-related problem of interest to developmental psychologists is why so many executives die earlier than expected after retirement.

① 아동심리학의 연구대상은 주로 사춘기 이후의 아동이다.
② 발달심리학자들은 인간의 일생의 행동과 성장을 연구한다.
③ 아동기에 학대 받은 성인의 실업률이 더 낮은 경향이 있다.
④ 임원들의 은퇴 후 조기 사망이 최근 임상심리학의 관심사이다.

7 다음 글의 내용을 한 문장으로 요약하고자 한다. 빈칸 (A), (B)에 들어갈 말로 가장 적절한 것은?

One presentation factor that can influence decision making is the contrast effect. For example, a $70 sweater may not seem like a very good deal initially, but if you learn that the sweater was reduced from $200, all of a sudden it may seem like a real bargain. It is the contrast that "seals the deal." Similarly, my family lives in Massachusetts, so we are very used to cold weather. But when we visit Florida to see my aunt and uncle for Thanksgiving, they urge the kids to wear hats when it is 60 degree outside – virtually bathing suit weather from the kids' perspective! Research even shows that people eat more when they are eating on large plates than when eating from small plates; the same portion simply looks larger on a small plate than a large plate, and we use perceived portion size as a cue that tells us when we are full.

↓

The contrast effect is the tendency to ___(A)___ a stimulus in different ways depending on the salient comparison with ___(B)___.

	(A)	(B)
①	perceive	previous experience
②	provide	predictive future
③	perceive	unexpected events
④	provide	initial impressions

8 다음 글의 밑줄 친 부분 중 문맥상 낱말의 쓰임이 가장 적절하지 않은 것은?

Most of the fatal accidents happen because of over speeding. It is a natural subconscious mind of humans to excel. If given a chance man is sure to achieve infinity in speed. But when we are sharing the road with other users we will always remain behind some or other vehicle. ①Increase in speed multiplies the risk of accident and severity of injury during accident. Faster vehicles are more prone to accident than the slower one and the severity of accident will also be more in case of faster vehicles. ②Higher the speed, greater the risk. At high speed the vehicle needs greater distance to stop—i.e., braking distance. A slower vehicle comes to halt immediately while faster one takes long way to stop and also skids a ③short distance because of The First Law of Motion. A vehicle moving on high speed will have greater impact during the crash and hence will cause more injuries. The ability to judge the forthcoming events also gets ④reduced while driving at faster speed which causes error in judgment and finally a crash.

*severity : 심함

9 다음 글의 요지로 가장 적절한 것은?

It is first necessary to make an endeavor to become interested in whatever it has seemed worth while to read. The student should try earnestly to discover wherein others have found it good. Every reader is at liberty to like or to dislike even a masterpiece; but he is not in a position even to have an opinion of it until he appreciates why it has been admired. He must set himself to realize not what is bad in a book, but what is good. The common theory that the critical faculties are best developed by training the mind to detect shortcoming is as vicious as it is false. Any carper can find the faults in a great work; it is only the enlightened who can discover all its merits. It will seldom happen that a sincere effort to appreciate good book will leave the reader uninterested.

① Give attention to a weakness which can damage the reputation of a book.
② Try to understand the value of the book while to read before judging it.
③ Read books in which you are not only interested but also uninterested.
④ Until the book is finished, keep a critical eye on the theme.

10 다음 도표의 내용과 가장 일치하지 않는 문장은?

Majority of Americans say organic produce is healthier than conventionally grown produce

% of U.S. adults who say organic fruits and vegetables are _____ than conventionally grown produce

■Better for health　■Neither better nor worse　■Worse for health

55	41	3

■Taste better　■Taste about the same　■Taste worse

32	59	5

Note : Respondents who did not give an answer are not shown.
Source : Survey conducted May 10–June 6, 2016.
" The New Food Fights : U.S. Public Divides Over Food Science "
PEW RESEARCH CENTER

Most Americans are buying organic foods because of health concerns. ① More than half of the public says that organic fruits and vegetables are better for one's health than conventionally grown produce. ② More than forty percent say organic produce is neither better nor worse for one's health and the least number of people say that organic produce is worse for one's health. ③ Fewer Americans say organic produce tastes better than conventionally grown fruits and vegetables. ④ About one-third of U.S. adults say that organic produce tastes better, and over two-thirds of people says that organic and conventionally grown produce taste about the same.

11 밑줄 친 brush them off가 다음 글에서 의미하는 바로 가장 적절한 것은?

Much of the communication between doctor and patient is personal. To have a good partnership with your doctor, it is important to talk about sensitive subjects, like sex or memory problems, even if you are embarrassed or uncomfortable. Most doctors are used to talking about personal matters and will try to ease your discomfort. Keep in mind that these topics concern many older people. You can use booklets and other materials to help you bring up sensitive subjects when talking with your doctor. It is important to understand that problems with memory, depression, sexual function, and incontinence are not necessarily normal parts of aging. A good doctor will take your concerns about these topics seriously and not <u>brush them off</u>. If you think your doctor isn't taking your concerns seriously, talk to him or her about your feelings or consider looking for a new doctor.

*incontinence : (대소변)실금

① discuss sensitive topics with you

② ignore some concerns you have

③ feel comfortable with something you say

④ deal with uncomfortable subjects seriously

12 다음 빈칸에 들어갈 말로 가장 적절한 것은?

Although we all possess the same physical organs for sensing the world — eyes for seeing, ears for hearing, noses for smelling, skin for feeling, and mouths for tasting — our perception of the world depends to a great extent on the language we speak, according to a famous hypothesis proposed by linguists Edward Sapir and Benjamin Lee Whorf. They hypothesized that language is like a pair of eyeglasses through which we "see" the world in a particular way. A classic example of the relationship between language and perception is the word snow. Eskimo languages have as many as 32 different words for snow. For instance, the Eskimos have different words for falling snow, snow on the ground, snow packed as hard as ice, slushy snow, wind-driven snow, and what we might call "cornmeal" snow. The ancient Aztec languages of Mexico, in contrast, used only one word to mean snow, cold, and ice. Thus, if the Sapir-Whorf hypothesis is correct and we can perceive only things that we have words for, the Aztecs perceived snow, cold, and ice as _____.

① one and the same phenomenon

② being distinct from one another

③ separate things with unique features

④ something sensed by a specific physical organ

13 글의 흐름으로 보아, 주어진 문장이 들어가기에 가장 적절한 곳을 고르시오.

“Soft power” on the contrary is “the ability to achieve goals through attraction and persuasion, rather than coercion or fee.”

The concept of “soft power” was formed in the early 1990s by the American political scientist, deputy defense of the Clinton's administration, Joseph Nye, Jr. The ideas of the American Professor J. Nye allowed to take a fresh look at the interpretation of the concept of “power,” provoked scientific debate and stimulated the practical side of international politics. (①) In his works he identifies two types of power: “hard power” and “soft power.” (②) He defines “hard power” as “the ability to get others to act in ways that contradict their initial preferences and strategies.” (③) The “soft power” of the state is its ability to “charm” other participants in the world political process, to demonstrate the attractiveness of its own culture (in a context it is attractive to others), political values and foreign policy (if considered legitimate and morally justified). (④) The main components of “soft power” are culture, political values and foreign policy.

*contradict : 부인하다, 모순되다

14 다음 글의 주제로 가장 적절한 것은?

The rapidity of AI deployment in different fields depends on a few critical factors: retail is particularly suitable for a few reasons. The first is the ability to test and measure. With appropriate safeguards, retail giants can deploy AI and test and measure consumer response. They can also directly measure the effect on their bottom line fairly quickly. The second is the relatively small consequences of a mistake. An AI agent landing a passenger aircraft cannot afford to make a mistake because it might kill people. An AI agent deployed in retail that makes millions of decisions every day can afford to make some mistakes, as long as the overall effect is positive. Some smart robot technology is already happening in retail. But many of the most significant changes will come from deployment of AI rather than physical robots or autonomous vehicles.

① dangers of AI agent

② why retail is suited for AI

③ retail technology and hospitality

④ critical factors of AI development

15 다음 빈칸에 들어갈 말로 가장 적절한 것은?

"_____" is the basic understanding of how karma works. The word karma literally means "activity." Karma can be divided up into a few simple categories — good, bad, individual and collective. Depending on one's actions, one will reap the fruits of those actions. The fruits may be sweet or sour, depending on the nature of the actions performed. Fruits can also be reaped in a collective manner if a group of people together perform a certain activity or activities. Everything we say and do determines what's going to happen to us in the future. Whether we act honestly, dishonestly, help or hurt others, it all gets recorded and manifests as a karmic reaction either in this life or a future life. All karmic records are carried with the soul into the next life and body.

① It never rains but it pours

② A stitch in time saves nine

③ Many hands make light work

④ What goes around comes around

16 다음 글에서 필자가 주장하는 바로 가장 적절한 것은?

Creating a culture that inspires out-of-the-box thinking is ultimately about inspiring people to stretch and empowering them to drive change. As a leader, you need to provide support for those times when change is hard, and that support is about the example you set, the behaviors you encourage and the achievements you reward. First, think about the example you set. Do you consistently model out-of-the-box behaviors yourself? Do you step up and take responsibility and accountability, focus on solutions and display curiosity? Next, find ways to encourage and empower the people who are ready to step out of the box. Let them know that you recognize their efforts; help them refine their ideas and decide which risks are worth taking. And most importantly, be extremely mindful of which achievements you reward. Do you only recognize the people who play it safe? Or, do you also reward the people who are willing to stretch, display out-of-the-box behaviors and fall short of an aggressive goal?

*mindful : 신경을 쓰는, 염두에 두는

① 책임감 있는 리더가 되기 위해서는 보편적 윤리관을 가져야 한다.

② 구성원에 따라 다양한 전략과 전술을 수립하고 적용해야 한다.

③ 팀원들의 근무 환경 개선을 위해 외부의 평가를 받아야 한다.

④ 팀원에게 창의적인 사고를 할 수 있는 토대를 만들어줘야 한다.

※ 다음 글을 읽고 물음에 답하시오. 【17~18】

The dictionary defines winning as "achieving victory over others in a competition, receiving a prize or reward for achievement." However, some of the most meaningful wins of my life were not victories over others, nor were there prizes involved. To me, winning means overcoming obstacles.

My first experience of winning occurred in elementary school gym. Nearly every day, after the warm up of push-ups and squat thrusts, we were forced to run relays. Although I suffered from asthma as a child, my team won many races. My chest would burn terribly for several minutes following theses races, but it was worth it to feel so proud, not because I'd beaten others, but because I had overcome a handicap. By the way, I (A) "outgrew" my chronic condition by age eleven.

In high school, I had another experience of winning. Although I loved reading about biology, I could not bring myself to dissect a frog in lab. I hated the smell of anything dead, and the idea of cutting open a frog (B) disgusted me. Every time I tried to take the scalpel to the frog, my hands would shake and my stomach would turn. Worst of all, my biology teacher reacted to my futile attempts with contempt. After an (C) amusing couple of weeks, I decided get hold of myself. I realized that I was overreacting. With determination, I swept into my next lab period, walked up to the table, and with one swift stroke, slit open a frog. After that incident, I (D) excelled in biology. I had conquered a fear of the unknown and discovered something new about myself. I had won again.

Through these experiences, I now know that I appreciate life more if have to sacrifice to overcome these impediments. This is a positive drive for me, the very spirit of winning.

*asthma : 천식 *dissect : 해부하다 *futile : 헛된, 효과 없는

17 윗글의 제목으로 가장 적절한 것은?

① What Winning Is to Me

② The Pursuit of Happiness

③ Winners in the Second Half

④ Narratives of Positive Thinking

18 밑줄 친 (A)~(D) 중에서 문맥상 낱말의 쓰임이 가장 적절하지 않은 것은?

① (A)　　　　　　　　　② (B)

③ (C)　　　　　　　　　④ (D)

19 다음 글의 내용을 요약할 때 빈칸 (A),(B)에 들어갈 말로 가장 적절한 것은?

One classic psychology study involved mothers and their twelve-month-old babies. Each mother was with her baby throughout the study, but the mothers were divided into two groups, A and B. Both groups A and B were exposed to the same situation, the only difference being that group B mothers had to positively encourage their baby to continue playing with the thing in front of them, whereas the mothers in group A just had to be themselves in response to what their baby was playing with.

What were these babies playing with? An extremely large but tame python. The study went as follows: the children from group A were placed on the floor so the python could slither among them. As the fear of snakes is innate in humans but isn't activated until approximately the age of two, these babies saw the python as a large toy. As the group A babies started playing with the live python, they looked up to see what their mothers were doing. The mothers, who were told to be themselves, naturally looked horrified. Seeing the fear on their mothers' faces, the babies burst into tears. When it was group B's turn, as instructed the mothers laughed and encouraged their babies to keep playing with the python. As a result these babies were grabbing and chewing on the python, all because their mothers were supportive of their new toy.

*slither : 미끄러져 가다

↓

_____(A)_____ are learned, usually by children watching a parent's _____(B)_____ to certain things.

	(A)	(B)
①	Rules of the game	support
②	Preferences for toys	participation
③	All phobias	reaction
④	Various emotions	encouragement

20 다음 글의 밑줄 친 부분 중, 문맥상 낱말의 쓰임이 가장 적절하지 않은 것은?

According to the modernization theory of aging, the status of older adults declines as societies become more modern. The status of old age was low in hunting-and-gathering societies, but it ①rose dramatically in stable agricultural societies, in which older people controlled the land. With the coming of industrialization, it is said, modern societies have tended to ②revalue older people. The modernization theory of aging suggests that the role and status of older adults are ③inversely related to technological progress. Factors such as urbanization and social mobility tend to disperse families, whereas technological change tends to devalue the wisdom or life experience of elders. Some investigators have found that key elements of modernization were, in fact, broadly related to the ④declining status of older people in different societies.

21 다음 글의 밑줄 친 부분 중 어법상 틀린 것은?

Rice stalks lower their heads when they are mature and corn kernels remain on the shoots even when they are ripe. This may not seem strange, but, in reality, these types of rice and corn should not survive in nature. Normally, when they mature, seeds should fall down to the ground in order to germinate. However, rice and corn are mutants, and they have been modified to keep their seeds ①attached for the purpose of convenient and efficient harvesting. Humans have continuously selected and bred such mutants, through breeding technology, in order ②for these phenomena to occur. These mutant seeds have been spread intentionally, ③which means that the plants have become artificial species not found in nature, ④having bred to keep their seeds intact. By nurturing these cultivars, the most preferred seeds are produced.

*germinate : 발아하다   **cultivar : 품종

22 (A), (B), (C)에서 어법에 맞는 표현으로 가장 적절한 것은?

First impression bias means that our first impression sets the mold (A) [which / by which] later information we gather about this person is processed, remembered, and viewed as relevant. For example, based on observing Ann-Chinn in class, Loern may have viewed her as a stereotypical Asian woman and assumed she is quiet, hard working, and unassertive. (B) [Reached / Having reached] these conclusions, rightly or wrongly, he now has a set of prototypes and constructs for understanding and interpreting Ann-Chinn's behavior. Over time, he fits the behavior consistent with his prototypes and constructs into the impression (C) [that / what] he has already formed of her. When he notices her expressing disbelief over his selection of bumper stickers, he may simply dismiss it or view it as an odd exception to her real nature because it doesn't fit his existing prototype.

	(A)	(B)	(C)
①	which	reached	that
②	which	having reached	what
③	by which	having reached	that
④	by which	reached	what

23 다음 글의 밑줄 친 부분 중, 어법상 틀린 것은?

The wave of research in child language acquisition led language teachers and teacher trainers to study some of the general findings of such research with a view to drawing analogies between first and second language acquisition, and even to ①justifying certain teaching methods and techniques on the basis of first language learning principles. On the surface, it is entirely reasonable to make the analogy. All children, ②given a normal developmental environment, acquire their native languages fluently and efficiently. Moreover, they acquire them "naturally," without special instruction, ③despite not without significant effort and attention to language. The direct comparisons must be treated with caution, however. There are dozens of salient differences between first and second language learning; the most obvious difference, in the case of adult second language learning, ④is the tremendous cognitive and affective contrast between adults and children.

24 다음 글의 밑줄 친 부분 중 문맥상 낱말의 쓰임이 가장 적절하지 않은 것은?

The American physiologist Hudson Hoagland saw scientific mysteries everywhere and felt it his calling to solve them. Once, when his wife had a fever, Hoagland drove to the drugstore to get her aspirin. He was quick about it, but when he returned, his normally ① reasonable wife complained angrily that he had been slow as molasses. Hoagland wondered if her fever had ② distorted her internal clock, so he took her temperature, had her estimate the length of a minute, gave her the aspirin, and continued to have her estimate the minutes as her temperature dropped. When her temperature was back to normal he plotted the logarithm and found it was ③ linear. Later, he continued the study in his laboratory, artificially raising and lowering the temperatures of test subjects until he was certain he was right: higher body temperatures make the body clock go faster, and his wife had not been ④ justifiably cranky.

*molasses : 당밀   **logarithm : (수학) 로그

25 다음 빈칸에 들어갈 말로 가장 적절한 것은?

Saint Paul said the invisible must be understood by the visible. That was not a Hebrew idea, it was Greek. In Greece alone in the ancient world people were preoccupied with the visible; they were finding the satisfaction of their desires in what was actually in the world around them. The sculptor watched the athletes contending in the games and he felt that nothing he could imagine would be as beautiful as those strong young bodies. So he made his statue of Apollo. The storyteller found Hermes among the people he passed in the street. He saw the god "like a young men at that age when youth is loveliest," as Homer says. Greek artists and poets realized how splendid a man could be, straight and swift and strong. He was the fulfillment of their search for beauty. They had no wish to create some fantasy shaped in their own minds. All the art and all the thought of Greece _____.

① had no semblance of reality

② put human beings at the center

③ were concerned with an omnipotent God

④ represented the desire for supernatural power

※ 밑줄 친 부분의 의미와 가장 가까운 것을 고르시오. 【1~2】

1

> Natural Gas World subscribers will receive accurate and reliable key facts and figures about what is going on in the industry, so they are fully able to <u>discern</u> what concerns their business.

① distinguish ② strengthen

③ undermine ④ abandon

2

> Ms. West, the winner of the silver in the women's 1,500 m event, <u>stood out</u> through the race.

① was overwhelmed ② was impressive

③ was depressed ④ was optimistic

3 두 사람의 대화 중 가장 어색한 것은?

① A : I'm traveling abroad, but I'm not used to staying in another country.
  B : Don't worry. You'll get accustomed to it in no time.

② A : I want to get a prize in the photo contest.
  B : I'm sure you will. I'll keep my fingers crossed!

③ A : My best friend moved to Sejong City. I miss her so much.
  B : Yeah. I know how you feel.

④ A : Do you mind if I talk to you for a moment?
  B : Never mind. I'm very busy right now.

4 밑줄 친 부분에 들어갈 말로 가장 적절한 것은?

A: Would you like to try some dim sum?
B: Yes, thank you. They look delicious. What's inside?
A: These have pork and chopped vegetables, and those have shrimps.
B: And, um, _____?
A: You pick one up with your chopsticks like this and dip it into the sauce. It's easy.
B: Okay. I'll give it a try.

① how much are they
② how do I eat them
③ how spicy are they
④ how do you cook them

※ 우리말을 영어로 잘못 옮긴 것을 고르시오. 【5 ~6】

5 ① 제가 당신께 말씀드렸던 새로운 선생님은 원래 페루 출신입니다.
→The new teacher I told you about is originally from Peru.
② 나는 긴급한 일로 자정이 5분이나 지난 후 그에게 전화했다.
→I called him five minutes shy of midnight on an urgent matter.
③ 상어로 보이는 것이 산호 뒤에 숨어 있었다.
→What appeared to be a shark was lurking behind the coral reef.
④ 그녀는 일요일에 16세의 친구와 함께 산 정상에 올랐다.
→She reached the mountain summit with her 16-year-old friend on Sunday.

6 ① 개인용 컴퓨터를 가장 많이 가지고 있는 나라는 종종 바뀐다.
→The country with the most computers per person changes from time to time.
② 지난여름 나의 사랑스러운 손자에게 일어난 일은 놀라웠다.
→What happened to my lovely grandson last summer was amazing.
③ 나무 숟가락은 아이들에게 매우 좋은 장난감이고 플라스틱 병 또한 그렇다.
→Wooden spoons are excellent toys for children, and so are plastic bottles.
④ 나는 은퇴 후부터 내내 이 일을 해 오고 있다.
→I have been doing this work ever since I retired.

7

Domesticated animals are the earliest and most effective 'machines' ①available to humans. They take the strain off the human back and arms. ②Utilizing with other techniques, animals can raise human living standards very considerably, both as supplementary foodstuffs (protein in meat and milk) and as machines ③to carry burdens, lift water, and grind grain. Since they are so obviously ④of great benefit, we might expect to find that over the centuries humans would increase the number and quality of the animals they kept. Surprisingly, this has not usually been the case.

8

A myth is a narrative that embodies – and in some cases ①helps to explain – the religious, philosophical, moral, and political values of a culture. Through tales of gods and supernatural beings, myths ②try to make sense of occurrences in the natural world. Contrary to popular usage, myth does not mean "falsehood." In the broadest sense, myths are stories – usually whole groups of stories – ③that can be true or partly true as well as false; regardless of their degree of accuracy, however, myths frequently express the deepest beliefs of a culture. According to this definition, the *Iliad* and the *Odyssey*, the Koran, and the Old and New Testaments can all ④refer to as myths.

9 다음 글의 제목으로 가장 적절한 것은?

Mapping technologies are being used in many new applications. Biological researchers are exploring the molecular structure of DNA ("mapping the genome"), geophysicists are mapping the structure of the Earth's core, and oceanographers are mapping the ocean floor. Computer games have various imaginary "lands" or levels where rules, hazards, and rewards change. Computerization now challenges reality with "virtual reality," artificial environments that stimulate special situations, which may be useful in training and entertainment. Mapping techniques are being used also in the realm of ideas. For example, relationships between ideas can be shown using what are called concept maps. Starting from a general or "central" idea, related ideas can be connected, building a web around the main concept. This is not a map by any traditional definition, but the tools and techniques of cartography are employed to produce it, and in some ways it resembles a map.

① Computerized Maps vs. Traditional Maps
② Where Does Cartography Begin?
③ Finding Ways to DNA Secrets
④ Mapping New Frontiers

10 다음 글의 요지로 가장 적절한 것은?

When giving performance feedback, you should consider the recipient's past performance and your estimate of his or her future potential in designing its frequency, amount, and content. For high performers with potential for growth, feedback should be frequent enough to prod them into taking corrective action, but not so frequent that it is experienced as controlling and saps their initiative. For adequate performers who have settled into their jobs and have limited potential for advancement, very little feedback is needed because they have displayed reliable and steady behavior in the past, knowing their tasks and realizing what needs to be done. For poor performers — that is, people who will need to be removed from their jobs if their performance doesn't improve — feedback should be frequent and very specific, and the connection between acting on the feedback and negative sanctions such as being laid off or fired should be made explicit.

① Time your feedback well.
② Customize negative feedback.
③ Tailor feedback to the person.
④ Avoid goal-oriented feedback.

11 다음 글의 내용과 일치하지 않는 것은?

Langston Hughes was born in Joplin, Missouri, and graduated from Lincoln University, in which many African-American students have pursued their academic disciplines. At the age of eighteen, Hughes published one of his most well-known poems, "Negro Speaks of Rivers." Creative and experimental, Hughes incorporated authentic dialect in his work, adapted traditional poetic forms to embrace the cadences and moods of blues and jazz, and created characters and themes that reflected elements of lower-class black culture. With his ability to fuse serious content with humorous style, Hughes attacked racial prejudice in a way that was natural and witty.

① Hughes는 많은 미국 흑인들이 다녔던 대학교를 졸업하였다.
② Hughes는 실제 사투리를 그의 작품에 반영하였다.
③ Hughes는 하층 계급 흑인들의 문화적 요소를 반영한 인물을 만들었다.
④ Hughes는 인종편견을 엄숙한 문체로 공격하였다.

12 밑줄 친 부분 중 글의 흐름상 가장 어색한 것은?

In 2007, our biggest concern was "too big to fail." Wall Street banks had grown to such staggering sizes, and had become so central to the health of the financial system, that no rational government could ever let them fail. ①Aware of their protected status, banks made excessively risky bets on housing markets and invented ever more complicated derivatives. ②New virtual currencies such as bitcoin and ethereum have radically changed our understanding of how money can and should work. ③The result was the worst financial crisis since the breakdown of our economy in 1929. ④In the years since 2007, we have made great progress in addressing the too-big-to-fail dilemma. Our banks are better capitalized than ever. Our regulators conduct regular stress tests of large institutions.

13 다음 글의 주제로 가장 적절한 것은?

Imagine that two people are starting work at a law firm on the same day. One person has a very simple name. The other person has a very complex name. We've got pretty good evidence that over the course of their next 16 plus years of their career, the person with the simpler name will rise up the legal hierarchy more quickly. They will attain partnership more quickly in the middle parts of their career. And by about the eighth or ninth year after graduating from law school the people with simpler names are about seven to ten percent more likely to be partners – which is a striking effect. We try to eliminate all sorts of other alternative explanations. For example, we try to show that it's not about foreignness because foreign names tend to be harder to pronounce. But even if you look at just white males with Anglo-American names – so really the true in-group, you find that among those white males with Anglo names they are more likely to rise up if their names happen to be simpler. So simplicity is one key feature in names that determines various outcomes.

① the development of legal names

② the concept of attractive names

③ the benefit of simple names

④ the roots of foreign names

※ 밑줄 친 부분의 의미와 가장 가까운 것을 고르시오. 【14 ~15】

14

Schooling is <u>compulsory</u> for all children in the United States, but the age range for which school attendance is required varies from state to state.

① complementary

② systematic

③ mandatory

④ innovative

15

Although the actress experienced much turmoil in her career, she never <u>disclosed</u> to anyone that she was unhappy.

① let on

② let off

③ let up

④ let down

16 밑줄 친 (A), (B)에 들어갈 말로 가장 적절한 것은?

Visionaries are the first people in their industry segment to see the potential of new technologies. Fundamentally, they see themselves as smarter than their opposite numbers in competitive companies – and, quite often, they are. Indeed, it is their ability to see things first that they want to leverage into a competitive advantage. That advantage can only come about if no one else has discovered it. They do not expect, ____(A)____, to be buying a well-tested product with an extensive list of industry references. Indeed, if such a reference base exists, it may actually turn them off, indicating that for this technology, at any rate, they are already too late. Pragmatists, ____(B)____, deeply value the experience of their colleagues in other companies. When they buy, they expect extensive references, and they want a good number to come from companies in their own industry segment.

	(A)	(B)
①	therefore	on the other hand
②	however	in addition
③	nonetheless	at the same time
④	furthermore	in conclusion

17 주어진 문장이 들어갈 위치로 가장 적절한 것은?

> Some of these ailments are short-lived; others may be long-lasting.

For centuries, humans have looked up at the sky and wondered what exists beyond the realm of our planet. (①) Ancient astronomers examined the night sky hoping to learn more about the universe. More recently, some movies explored the possibility of sustaining human life in outer space, while other films have questioned whether extraterrestrial life forms may have visited our planet. (②) Since astronaut Yuri Gagarin became the first man to travel in space in 1961, scientists have researched what conditions are like beyond the Earth's atmosphere, and what effects space travel has on the human body. (③) Although most astronauts do not spend more than a few months in space, many experience physiological and psychological problems when they return to the Earth. (④) More than two-thirds of all astronauts suffer from motion sickness while traveling in space. In the gravity-free environment, the body cannot differentiate up from down. The body's internal balance system sends confusing signals to the brain, which can result in nausea lasting as long as a few days.

18 밑줄 친 부분에 들어갈 말로 가장 적절한 것은?

Why bother with the history of everything? _____. In literature classes you don't learn about genes; in physics classes you don't learn about human evolution. So you get a partial view of the world. That makes it hard to find *meaning* in education. The French sociologist Emile Durkheim called this sense of disorientation and meaninglessness *anomie*, and he argued that it could lead to despair and even suicide. The German sociologist Max Weber talked of the "disenchantment" of the world. In the past, people had a unified vision of their world, a vision usually provided by the origin stories of their own religious traditions. That unified vision gave a sense of purpose, of meaning, even of enchantment to the world and to life. Today, though, many writers have argued that a sense of meaninglessness is inevitable in a world of science and rationality. Modernity, it seems, means meaninglessness.

① In the past, the study of history required disenchantment from science

② Recently, science has given us lots of clever tricks and meanings

③ Today, we teach and learn about our world in fragments

④ Lately, history has been divided into several categories

19 다음 글의 내용과 일치하지 않는 것은?

The earliest government food service programs began around 1900 in Europe. Programs in the United States date from the Great Depression, when the need to use surplus agricultural commodities was joined to concern for feeding the children of poor families. During and after World War II, the explosion in the number of working women fueled the need for a broader program. What was once a function of the family – providing lunch – was shifted to the school food service system. The National School Lunch Program is the result of these efforts. The program is designed to provide federally assisted meals to children of school age. From the end of World War II to the early 1980s, funding for school food service expanded steadily. Today it helps to feed children in almost 100,000 schools across the United States. Its first function is to provide a nutritious lunch to all students; the second is to provide nutritious food at both breakfast and lunch to underprivileged children. If anything, the role of school food service as a replacement for what was once a family function has been expanded.

① The increase in the number of working women boosted the expansion of food service programs.

② The US government began to feed poor children during the Great Depression despite the food shortage.

③ The US school food service system presently helps to feed children of poor families.

④ The function of providing lunch has been shifted from the family to schools.

20 주어진 문장 다음에 이어질 글의 순서로 가장 적절한 것은?

South Korea boasts of being the most wired nation on earth.

(A) This addiction has become a national issue in Korea in recent years, as users started dropping dead from exhaustion after playing online games for days on end. A growing number of students have skipped school to stay online, shockingly self−destructive behavior in this intensely competitive society.

(B) In fact, perhaps no other country has so fully embraced the Internet.

(C) But such ready access to the Web has come at a price as legions of obsessed users find that they cannot tear themselves away from their computer screens.

① (A) − (B) − (C)

② (A) − (C) − (B)

③ (B) − (A) − (C)

④ (B) − (C) − (A)

☞ 정답 및 해설 P.142

※ 밑줄 친 부분의 의미와 가장 가까운 것을 고르시오. 【1~2】

1

I came to see these documents as relics of a sensibility now dead and buried, which needed to be _excavated_.

① exhumed   ② packed

③ erased   ④ celebrated

2

Riding a roller coaster can be a joy ride of emotions: the nervous anticipation as you're strapped into your seat, the questioning and regret that comes as you go up, up, up, and the _sheer_ adrenaline rush as the car takes that first dive.

① utter   ② scary

③ occasional   ④ manageable

3 두 사람의 대화 중 가장 어색한 것은?

① A : What time are we having lunch?

B : It'll be ready before noon.

② A : I called you several times. Why didn't you answer?

B : Oh, I think my cell phone was turned off.

③ A : Are you going to take a vacation this winter?

B : I might. I haven't decided yet.

④ A : Hello. Sorry I missed your call.

B : Would you like to leave a message?

4 밑줄 친 부분에 들어갈 말로 가장 적절한 것은?

A : Hello. I need to exchange some money.

B : Okay. What currency do you need?

A : I need to convert dollars into pounds. What's the exchange rate?

B : The exchange rate is 0.73 pounds for every dollar.

A : Fine. Do you take a commission?

B : Yes, we take a small commission of 4 dollars.

A : _____?

B : We convert your currency back for free. Just bring your receipt with you.

① How much does this cost

② How should I pay for that

③ What's your buy-back policy

④ Do you take credit cards

5 밑줄 친 부분 중 어법상 옳지 않은 것은?

> Each year, more than 270,000 pedestrians ①lose their lives on the world's roads. Many leave their homes as they would on any given day never ②to return. Globally, pedestrians constitute 22% of all road traffic fatalities, and in some countries this proportion is ③as high as two thirds of all road traffic deaths. Millions of pedestrians are non-fatally ④injuring – some of whom are left with permanent disabilities. These incidents cause much suffering and grief as well as economic hardship.

6 어법상 옳은 것은?

① The paper charged her with use the company's money for her own purposes.
② The investigation had to be handled with the utmost care lest suspicion be aroused.
③ Another way to speed up the process would be made the shift to a new system.
④ Burning fossil fuels is one of the lead cause of climate change.

7 주어진 글 다음에 이어질 글의 순서로 가장 적절한 것은?

There is a thought that can haunt us: since everything probably affects everything else, how can we ever make sense of the social world? If we are weighed down by that worry, though, we won't ever make progress.

(A) Every discipline that I am familiar with draws caricatures of the world in order to make sense of it. The modern economist does this by building *models*, which are deliberately stripped down representations of the phenomena out there.

(B) The economist John Maynard Keynes described our subject thus: "Economics is a science of thinking in terms of models joined to the art of choosing models which are relevant to the contemporary world."

(C) When I say "stripped down," I really mean stripped down. It isn't uncommon among us economists to focus on one or two causal factors, exclude everything else, hoping that this will enable us to understand how just those aspects of reality work and interact.

① (A) − (B) − (C)　　　　　② (A) − (C) − (B)

③ (B) − (C) − (A)　　　　　④ (B) − (A) − (C)

8 다음 글의 내용과 일치하는 것은?

Prehistoric societies some half a million years ago did not distinguish sharply between mental and physical disorders. Abnormal behaviors, from simple headaches to convulsive attacks, were attributed to evil spirits that inhabited or controlled the afflicted person's body. According to historians, these ancient peoples attributed many forms of illness to demonic possession, sorcery, or the behest of an offended ancestral spirit. Within this system of belief, called *demonology*, the victim was usually held at least partly responsible for the misfortune. It has been suggested that Stone Age cave dwellers may have treated behavior disorders with a surgical method called *trephining*, in which part of the skull was chipped away to provide an opening through which the evil spirit could escape. People may have believed that when the evil spirit left, the person would return to his or her normal state. Surprisingly, trephined skulls have been found to have healed over, indicating that some patients survived this extremely crude operation.

*convulsive : 경련의 *behest : 명령

① Mental disorders were clearly differentiated from physical disorders.

② Abnormal behaviors were believed to result from evil spirits affecting a person.

③ An opening was made in the skull for an evil spirit to enter a person's body.

④ No cave dwellers survived trephining.

9 다음 글의 주제로 가장 적절한 것은?

As the digital revolution upends newsrooms across the country, here's my advice for all the reporters. I've been a reporter for more than 25 years, so I have lived through a half dozen technological life cycles. The most dramatic transformations have come in the last half dozen years. That means I am, with increasing frequency, making stuff up as I go along. Much of the time in the news business, we have no idea what we are doing. We show up in the morning and someone says, "Can you write a story about (pick one) tax policy/immigration/climate change?" When newspapers had once-a-day deadlines, we said a reporter would learn in the morning and teach at night — write a story that could inform tomorrow's readers on a topic the reporter knew nothing about 24 hours earlier. Now it is more like learning at the top of the hour and teaching at the bottom of the same hour. I'm also running a political podcast, for example, and during the presidential conventions, we should be able to use it to do real-time interviews anywhere. I am just increasingly working without a script.

① a reporter as a teacher

② a reporter and improvisation

③ technology in politics

④ fields of journalism and technology

10 글의 흐름상 가장 어색한 문장은?

Children's playgrounds throughout history were the wilderness, fields, streams, and hills of the country and the roads, streets, and vacant places of villages, towns, and cities. ①The term *playground* refers to all those places where children gather to play their free, spontaneous games. ②Only during the past few decades have children vacated these natural playgrounds for their growing love affair with video games, texting, and social networking. ③Even in rural America few children are still roaming in a free-ranging manner, unaccompanied by adults. ④When out of school, they are commonly found in neighborhoods digging in sand, building forts, playing traditional games, climbing, or playing ball games. They are rapidly disappearing from the natural terrain of creeks, hills, and fields, and like their urban counterparts, are turning to their indoor, sedentary cyber toys for entertainment.

※ 밑줄 친 부분의 의미와 가장 가까운 것을 고르시오. 【11~12】

11

Time does seem to slow to a trickle during a boring afternoon lecture and race when the brain is engrossed in something highly entertaining.

① enhanced by
② apathetic to
③ stabilized by
④ preoccupied with

12

These daily updates were designed to help readers keep abreast of the markets as the government attempted to keep them under control.

① be acquainted with
② get inspired by
③ have faith in
④ keep away from

13

In the 1840s, the island of Ireland suffered famine. Because Ireland could not produce enough food to feed its population, about a million people died of ____(A)____ ; they simply didn't have enough to eat to stay alive. The famine caused another 1.25 million people to ____(B)____ ; many left their island home for the United States; the rest went to Canada, Australia, Chile, and other countries. Before the famine, the population of Ireland was approximately 6 million. After the great food shortage, it was about 4 million.

	(A)	(B)
①	dehydration	be deported
②	trauma	immigrate
③	starvation	emigrate
④	fatigue	be detained

14

Today the technology to create the visual component of virtual-reality (VR) experiences is well on its way to becoming widely accessible and affordable. But to work powerfully, virtual reality needs to be about more than visuals. ____(A)____ what you are hearing convincingly matches the visuals, the virtual experience breaks apart. Take a basketball game. If the players, the coaches, the announcers, and the crowd all sound like they're sitting midcourt, you may as well watch the game on television – you'll get just as much of a sense that you are "there." ____(B)____ , today's audio equipment and our widely used recording and reproduction formats are simply inadequate to the task of re-creating convincingly the sound of a battlefield on a distant planet, a basketball game at courtside, or a symphony as heard from the first row of a great concert hall.

	(A)	(B)
①	If	By contrast
②	Unless	Consequently
③	If	Similarly
④	Unless	Unfortunately

15 주어진 문장이 들어갈 위치로 가장 적절한 것은?

The same thinking can be applied to any number of goals, like improving performance at work.

The happy brain tends to focus on the short term. (①) That being the case, it's a good idea to consider what short-term goals we can accomplish that will eventually lead to accomplishing long-term goals. (②) For instance, if you want to lose thirty pounds in six months, what short-term goals can you associate with losing the smaller increments of weight that will get you there? (③) Maybe it's something as simple as rewarding yourself each week that you lose two pounds. (④) By breaking the overall goal into smaller, shorter-term parts, we can focus on incremental accomplishments instead of being overwhelmed by the enormity of the goal in our profession.

16 우리말을 영어로 잘못 옮긴 것은?

① 혹시 내게 전화하고 싶은 경우에 이게 내 번호야.

→ This is my number just in case you would like to call me.

② 나는 유럽 여행을 준비하느라 바쁘다.

→ I am busy preparing for a trip to Europe.

③ 그녀는 남편과 결혼한 지 20년 이상 되었다.

→ She has married to her husband for more than two decades.

④ 나는 내 아들이 읽을 책을 한 권 사야 한다.

→ I should buy a book for my son to read.

17 다음 글의 내용과 일치하지 않는 것을 고르시오

In the nineteenth century, the most respected health and medical experts all insisted that diseases were caused by "miasma," a fancy term for bad air. Western society's system of health was based on this assumption: to prevent diseases, windows were kept open or closed, depending on whether there was more miasma inside or outside the room; it was believed that doctors could not pass along disease because gentlemen did not inhabit quarters with bad air. Then the idea of germs came along. One day, everyone believed that bad air makes you sick. Then, almost overnight, people started realizing there were invisible things called microbes and bacteria that were the real cause of diseases. This new view of disease brought sweeping changes to medicine, as surgeons adopted antiseptics and scientists invented vaccines and antibiotics. But, just as momentously, the idea of germs gave ordinary people the power to influence their own lives. Now, if you wanted to stay healthy, you could wash your hands, boil your water, cook your food thoroughly, and clean cuts and scrapes with iodine.

① In the nineteenth century, opening windows was irrelevant to the density of miasma.

② In the nineteenth century, it was believed that gentlemen did not live in places with bad air.

③ Vaccines were invented after people realized that microbes and bacteria were the real cause of diseases.

④ Cleaning cuts and scrapes could help people to stay healthy.

18 다음 글의 내용과 일치하지 않는 것을 고르시오

Followers are a critical part of the leadership equation, but their role has not always been appreciated. For a long time, in fact, "the common view of leadership was that leaders actively led and subordinates, later called followers, passively and obediently followed." Over time, especially in the last century, social change shaped people's views of followers, and leadership theories gradually recognized the active and important role that followers play in the leadership process. Today it seems natural to accept the important role followers play. One aspect of leadership is particularly worth noting in this regard: Leadership is a social influence process shared among all members of a group. Leadership is not restricted to the influence exerted by someone in a particular position or role; followers are part of the leadership process, too.

① For a length of time, it was understood that leaders actively led and followers passively followed.

② People's views of subordinates were influenced by social change.

③ The important role of followers is still denied today.

④ Both leaders and followers participate in the leadership process.

※ 밑줄 친 부분에 들어갈 말로 가장 적절한 것을 고르시오. 【19~20】

19

Language proper is itself double-layered. Single noises are only occasionally meaningful: mostly, the various speech sounds convey coherent messages only when combined into an overlapping chain, like different colors of ice-cream melting into one another. In birdsong also, _____: the sequence is what matters. In both humans and birds, control of this specialized sound-system is exercised by one half of the brain, normally the left half, and the system is learned relatively early in life. And just as many human languages have dialects, so do some bird species: in California, the white-crowned sparrow has songs so different from area to area that Californians can supposedly tell where they are in the state by listening to these sparrows.

① individual notes are often of little value

② rhythmic sounds are important

③ dialects play a critical role

④ no sound-system exists

20

Nobel Prize-winning psychologist Daniel Kahneman changed the way the world thinks about economics, upending the notion that human beings are rational decision-makers. Along the way, his discipline-crossing influence has altered the way physicians make medical decisions and investors evaluate risk on Wall Street. In a paper, Kahneman and his colleagues outline a process for making big strategic decisions. Their suggested approach, labeled as "Mediating Assessments Protocol," or MAP, has a simple goal: To put off gut-based decision-making until a choice can be informed by a number of separate factors. "One of the essential purposes of MAP is basically to _____ intuition," Kahneman said in a recent interview with *The Post*. The structured process calls for analyzing a decision based on six to seven previously chosen attributes, discussing each of them separately and assigning them a relative percentile score, and finally, using those scores to make a holistic judgment.

① improve

② delay

③ possess

④ facilitate

※ 밑줄 친 부분의 의미와 가장 가까운 것은? 【1~2】

1

At least in high school she made one decision where she finally <u>saw eye to eye</u> with her parents.

① quarreled ② disputed

③ parted ④ agreed

2

Justifications are accounts in which one accepts responsibility for the act in question, but denies the <u>pejorative</u> quality associated with it.

① derogatory ② extrovert

③ mandatory ④ redundant

※ 밑줄 친 부분에 들어갈 말로 가장 적절한 것은? 【3~5】

3

Tests ruled out dirt and poor sanitation as causes of yellow fever, and a mosquito was the _____ carrier.

① suspected ② uncivilized

③ cheerful ④ volunteered

4

Generally speaking, people living in 2018 are pretty fortunate when you compare modern times to the full scale of human history. Life expectancy _____ at around 72 years, and diseases like smallpox and diphtheria, which were widespread and deadly only a century ago, are preventable, curable, or altogether eradicated.

① curtails

② hovers

③ initiates

④ aggravates

5

To imagine that there are concrete patterns to past events, which can provide _____ for our lives and decisions, is to project on to history a hope for a certainty which it cannot fulfill.

① hallucinations

② templates

③ inquiries

④ commotion

6 대화 중 가장 어색한 것은?

① A : What was the movie like on Saturday?

   B : Great. I really enjoyed it.

② A : Hello. I'd like to have some shirts pressed.

   B : Yes, how soon will you need them?

③ A : Would you like a single or a double room?

   B : Oh, it's just for me, so a single is fine.

④ A : What time is the next flight to Boston?

   B : It will take about 45 minutes to get to Boston.

7

Inventor Elias Howe attributed the discovery of the sewing machine ①<u>for</u> a dream ②<u>in which</u> he was captured by cannibals. He noticed as they danced around him ③<u>that</u> there were holes at the tips of spears, and he realized this was the design feature he needed ④<u>to solve</u> his problem.

8

By 1955 Nikita Khrushchev ①<u>had been emerged as</u> Stalin's successor in the USSR, and he ②<u>embarked on</u> a policy of "peaceful coexistence" ③<u>whereby East and West</u> ④<u>were to continue their competition</u>, but in a less confrontational manner.

9

Squid, octopuses, and cuttlefish are all ①<u>types</u> of cephalopods. ②<u>Each</u> of these animals has special cells under its skin that ③<u>contains</u> pigment, a colored liquid. A cephalopod can move these cells toward or away from its skin. This allows it ④<u>to change</u> the pattern and color of its appearance.

10

There is a more serious problem than ①<u>maintaining</u> the cities. As people become more comfortable working alone, they may become ②<u>less</u> social. It's ③<u>easier</u> to stay home in comfortable exercise clothes or a bathrobe than ④<u>getting</u> dressed for yet another business meeting!

11 글의 제목으로 가장 적절한 것은?

Economists say that production of an information good involves high fixed costs but low marginal costs. The cost of producing the first copy of an information good may be substantial, but the cost of producing(or reproducing) additional copies is negligible. This sort of cost structure has many important implications. For example, cost-based pricing just doesn't work: a 10 or 20 percent markup on unit cost makes no sense when unit cost is zero. You must price your information goods according to consumer value, not according to your production cost.

① Securing the Copyright

② Pricing the Information Goods

③ Information as Intellectual Property

④ The Cost of Technological Change

12 밑줄 친 부분이 지칭하는 대상이 다른 것은?

Dracula ants get their name for the way they sometimes drink the blood of their own young. But this week, ①the insects have earned a new claim to fame. Dracula ants of the species *Mystrium camillae* can snap their jaws together so fast, you could fit 5,000 strikes into the time it takes us to blink an eye. This means ②the blood-suckers wield the fastest known movement in nature, according to a study published this week in the journal *Royal Society Open Science*. Interestingly, the ants produce their record-breaking snaps simply by pressing their jaws together so hard that ③they bend. This stores energy in one of the jaws, like a spring, until it slides past the other and lashes out with extraordinary speed and force—reaching a maximum velocity of over 200 miles per hour. It's kind of like what happens when you snap your fingers, only 1,000 times faster. Dracula ants are secretive predators as ④they prefer to hunt under the leaf litter or in subterranean tunnels.

13 밑줄 친 부분에 들어갈 말로 가장 옳은 것은?

> I am writing to you from a train in Germany, sitting on the floor. The train is crowded, and all the seats are taken. However, there is a special class of "comfort customers" who are allowed to make those already seated _____ their seats.

① give up

② take

③ giving up

④ taken

※ 글의 흐름상 빈칸에 들어갈 말로 가장 적절한 것은? 【14~17】

14

> A country's wealth plays a central role in education, so lack of funding and resources from a nation-state can weaken a system. Governments in sub-Saharan Africa spend only 2.4 percent of the world's public resources on education, yet 15 percent of the school-age population lives there. _____, the United States spends 28 percent of all the money spent in the world on education, yet it houses only 4 percent of the school-age population.

① Nevertheless

② Furthermore

③ Conversely

④ Similarly

15

> "Highly conscientious employees do a series of things better than the rest of us," says University of Illinois psychologist Brent Roberts, who studies conscientiousness. Roberts owes their success to "hygiene" factors. Conscientious people have a tendency to organize their lives well. A disorganized, unconscientious person might lose 20 or 30 minutes rooting through their files to find the right document, an inefficient experience conscientious folks tend to avoid. Basically, by being conscientious, people _____ they'd otherwise create for themselves.

① deal with setbacks

② do thorough work

③ follow norms

④ sidestep stress

16

Climate change, deforestation, widespread pollution and the sixth mass extinction of biodiversity all define living in our world today—an era that has come to be known as "the Anthropocene". These crises are underpinned by production and consumption which greatly exceeds global ecological limits, but blame is far from evenly shared. The world's 42 wealthiest people own as much as the poorest 3.7 billion, and they generate far greater environmental impacts. Some have therefore proposed using the term "Capitalocene" to describe this era of ecological devastation and growing inequality, reflecting capitalism's logic of endless growth and _____.

① the better world that is still within our reach

② the accumulation of wealth in fewer pockets

③ an effective response to climate change

④ a burning desire for a more viable future

17

Ever since the time of ancient Greek tragedy, Western culture has been haunted by the figure of the revenger. He or she stands on a whole series of borderlines: between civilization and barbarity, between _____ and the community's need for the rule of law, between the conflicting demands of justice and mercy. Do we have a right to exact revenge against those who have destroyed our loved ones? Or should we leave vengeance to the law or to the gods? And if we do take action into our own hands, are we not reducing ourselves to the same moral level as the original perpetrator of murderous deeds?

① redemption of the revenger from a depraved condition

② divine vengeance on human atrocities

③ moral depravity of the corrupt politicians

④ an individual's accountability to his or her own conscience

18 글의 흐름상 가장 적절하지 않은 문장은?

It seems to me possible to name four kinds of reading, each with a characteristic manner and purpose. The first is reading for information—reading to learn about a trade, or politics, or how to accomplish something. ① We read a newspaper this way, or most textbooks, or directions on how to assemble a bicycle. ② With most of this material, the reader can learn to scan the page quickly, coming up with what he needs and ignoring what is irrelevant to him, like the rhythm of the sentence, or the play of metaphor. ③ We also register a track of feeling through the metaphors and associations of words. ④ Courses in speed reading can help us read for this purpose, training the eye to jump quickly across the page.

19 〈보기〉의 문장이 들어갈 위치로 가장 적절한 것은?

〈보기〉

In this situation, we would expect to find less movement of individuals from one job to another because of the individual's social obligations toward the work organization to which he or she belongs and to the people comprising that organization.

Cultural differences in the meaning of work can manifest themselves in other aspects as well. (①) For example, in American culture, it is easy to think of works imply as a means to accumulate money and make a living. (②) In other cultures, especially collectivistic ones, work may be seen more as fulfilling an obligation to a larger group. (③) In individualistic cultures, it is easier to consider leaving one job and going to another because it is easier to separate jobs from the self. (④) A different job will just as easily accomplish the same goals.

20 글을 문맥에 가장 어울리는 순서대로 배열한 것은?

> ○ To navigate in the dark, a microbat flies with its mouth open, emitting high-pitched squeaks that humans cannot hear. Some of these sounds echo off flying insects as well as tree branches and other obstacles that lie ahead. The bat listens to the echo and gets an instantaneous picture in its brain of the objects in front of it.
>
> ○ Microbats, the small, insect-eating bats found in North America, have tiny eyes that don't look like they'd be good for navigating in the dark and spotting prey.
>
> ○ From the use of echolocation, or sonar, as it is also called, a microbat can tell a great deal about a mosquito or any other potential meal. With extreme exactness, echolocation allows microbats to perceive motion, distance, speed, movement, and shape. Bats can also detect and avoid obstacles no thicker than a human hair.
>
> ○ But, actually, microbats can see as well as mice and other small mammals. The nocturnal habits of bats are aided by their powers of echolocation, a special ability that makes feeding and flying at night much easier than one might think.

① ㉠ － ㉢ － ㉡ － ㉣

② ㉡ － ㉣ － ㉠ － ㉢

③ ㉡ － ㉢ － ㉣ － ㉠

④ ㉠ － ㉣ － ㉢ － ㉡

1 다음 밑줄 친 부분의 의미와 가장 가까운 단어는?

> The commonest and most <u>conspicuous</u> acts of animal altruism are done by parents, especially mothers, towards their children.

① salient   ② pertinent

③ concealed   ④ contingent

⑤ rudimentary

2 다음 밑줄 친 부분 중 어법상 옳지 않은 것은?

> The neoliberal attack on the population remains intact, ①though less so in the United States than in Europe. Automation is not a major factor, and industrialization isn't ending, ②just being off-shored. Financialization has of course exploded during the neoliberal period, and the general practices, pretty much global in character, ③designed to enhance private and corporate power. ④That sets off a vicious cycle which in turn yields legislation and administrative practices that carry the process forward. There are countervailing forces, and they might become more powerful. The potential is there, as we can see from the Sanders campaign and even the Trump campaign, if the white working class ⑤to which Trump appeals can become organized to focus on their real interests instead of being in thrall to their class enemy.

3 다음 밑줄 친 부분 중 어법상 옳지 않은 것은?

At the time of writing, it remains unclear ①<u>what</u> this administration's plans are in regard to immigration policing more generally. All names are fictitious names ②<u>to protect</u> the identities of our undocumented research collaborators. These facts run contrary to the common belief that the undocumented ③<u>does</u> not pay taxes on their wages. On the contrary, undocumented workers pay billions of dollars annually in income taxes ④<u>using</u> false documents. Many undocumented workers also have a legitimate Individual Taxpayer Identification Number ⑤<u>with which</u> they pay income taxes.

4 다음 밑줄 친 부분의 의미와 가장 가까운 단어는?

The US Congress concluded that, unless the law was reauthorized, "racial and language minority citizens will be deprived of the opportunity to exercise their right to vote, or will have their votes <u>diluted</u>, undermining the significant gains made by minorities in the last 40 years."

① callous　　　　　　　　　　② restricted

③ belligerent　　　　　　　　④ contentious

⑤ preposterous

5 다음 빈칸에 들어갈 가장 적절한 표현은?

Many baby birds are fed in the nest by their parents. They all gape and scream, and the parent drops a worm or other morsel in the open mouth of one of them. The loudness with which each baby screams is, ideally, proportional to how hungry he is. Therefore, if the parent always gives the food to the loudest screamer, they should all tend to get their fair share, since when one has had enough he will not scream so loudly. At least that is what would happen in the best of all possible worlds, if individuals did not cheat. But in the light of our selfish gene concept we must expect that individuals _____.

① will feed their babies

② will get their fair share

③ will not scream so loudly

④ will tell lies about how hungry they are

⑤ will always give the food to the loudest screamer

6 다음 빈칸 (A)와 (B)에 들어갈 가장 적절한 단어는?

Last week, the World Wildlife Fund released their annual Living Planet Report, which estimated that wildlife populations (including mammals, reptiles, amphibians, birds, and fish) have fallen by 60% between 1970 and 2014. This represents a staggering and tragic loss of non-human life and ecological heritage. But the loss of wildlife means more than that, according to the WWF. "Our health, food and security depend on (A) _____," the report says, and "without healthy natural systems researchers are asking whether continuing human development is possible." Mike Barrett, one of the authors of the report, puts it more bluntly in an interview with The Guardian: "This is far more than just being about losing the wonders of nature, desperately sad though that is. This is actually now (B) _____ the future of people. Nature is not a 'nice to have'–it is our life-support system."

	(A)	(B)
①	instrumentality	negating
②	relativity	enhancing
③	dissimilarity	preserving
④	productivity	eradicating
⑤	biodiversity	jeopardizing

7 다음 빈칸에 들어갈 가장 적절한 표현은?

Consider the results of one well-known psychological study. People were read a word describing a personal attribute that confirmed, countered, or avoided gender stereotypes. They were then given a name and asked to judge whether it was male or female. People responded more quickly when _____; so people were faster to the trigger when it was "strong John" and "gentle Jane" than when it was "strong Jane" and "gentle John." Only when subjects were actively asked to try to counter the stereotype and had a sufficiently low "cognitive constraint" (i.e., enough time) were they able to overcome these automatic responses.

① they were asked to try to counter the stereotype than when they were not

② the stereotypical attribute matched the name than when it did not

③ the word was neutral to gender stereotypes than when it was not

④ they avoided gender stereotypes than when they did not

⑤ the sufficient time was given than when it was not

8 다음 글의 제목으로 가장 적절한 것은?

Science holds its theories to be 'true and proven' under specific circumstances. Science can never state anything with absolute certainty. This causes a problem for us all. We need to hold certain ideas as true and proven in order to carry out our work. Often we come to an arrangement where, for operational reasons, we accept certain things without continually questioning their status, for example we accept that the force of gravity means that objects fall to earth at a rate of $9.81m/s$. We understand that this is an average measurement. For school science it is often rounded to $10m/s$. The reality of acceleration due to gravity is that this figure will vary according to local conditions, for example it is less off the South coast of India than in the Pacific region. Your mass is approximately 1 per cent less off the coast of India when compared to the average.

① Seeking Absolute Truth
② Science as a Social System
③ What To Be Done in Science
④ The Relativity in Scientific Truth
⑤ The Structure of Scientific Revolutions

9 다음 빈칸 (A), (B), (C)에 들어갈 가장 적절한 단어는?

This is a really important part of representation-giving people who struggle to play games the ability to join in, and to be visible on screen. (A) _____ and inclusivity are different parts of the same message. It's why charities like Special Effect in the UK and Able Gamers in the US are so vital, building hardware and peripherals to (B) _____ disabled players, and advocating for better support throughout the industry. Games are now a (C) _____ element of childhood and teenage life, it is isolating for people with different abilities or backgrounds to find they can't play, and can't have avatars that represent them. It is isolating not to be thought of or considered in the culture you desperately want to consume and be part of. In a media-saturated environment, where messages of belonging are constantly transmitted via TV, social media and smartphones, inclusivity is a life buoy. If you do not see yourself on Netflix, on Instagram, in games, in forums, where are you? Do you mean anything? It matters.

	(A)	(B)	(C)
①	Accessibility	assist	habitual
②	Allegation	encourage	benign
③	Commitment	exclude	manic
④	Counterculture	pursue	terse
⑤	Misrepresentation	involve	widespread

10 다음 글의 내용과 일치하지 않는 것은?

In a study published Wednesday, researchers from Sorbonne Paris Cite University, said the consumption of sugary soft drinks—including 100% fruit juice—was "significantly associated with the risk of overall cancer." Artificially –sweetened drinks, like diet soda, were not associated with increased cancer risks, they found. The report's authors followed 101,257 adults over a five-year period, monitoring their intake of sugary and artificially–sweetened beverages. Sugary drinks were defined as beverages that contained more than 5% sugar, which included fruit juices that had no added sugar. During the study, 2,193 cases of cancer were diagnosed among the participants, the equivalent of around 22 cases per 1,000 people. The majority of those cases were among people who regularly consumed sugary drinks.

① Sugary drinks like orange juice may increase the risk of contracting cancer.

② The researchers recorded the study participants' intake of sugary and artificially–sweetened drinks for five years.

③ The researchers defined sugary drinks as beverages with more than 5% sugar.

④ Consuming orange juice with no added sugar for a long period of time may reduce the chance of getting a cancer.

⑤ During the study, about 2.2% of the study participants were diagnosed as cancer patients.

11 다음 밑줄 친 부분의 의미와 가장 가까운 단어는?

> Though they vowed that no girl would ever come between them, Biff and Trevor could not keep <u>acrimony</u> from overwhelming their friendship after they both fell in love with the lovely Teresa.

① malice   ② temerity

③ cordiality   ④ sympathy

⑤ recollection

12 다음 밑줄 친 부분 중 어법상 옳지 않은 것은?

> Michael Phelps is one of ①<u>the most decorated athletes</u> of all time. As the first Olympic swimmer to earn a spot on five Olympic teams and ②<u>the oldest individual swimmer</u> to earn Olympic gold, he's earned himself the nickname the "Flying Fish." Swimmers tend to have longer torsos and shorter legs than the average person. ③<u>Standing</u> at 6 feet 4 inches, Phelps has the torso of a man who's 6 feet 8 inches tall, and the legs of a man 8 inches shorter. Double-jointed elbows allow Phelps ④<u>to create</u> more downward thrust in the water. His large hands also act like paddles. Paired with his extra-long wingspan, his arms serve like propellers to shoot ⑤<u>himself</u> through the water.

13 다음 밑줄 친 부분 중 문맥상 낱말의 쓰임이 적절하지 않은 것은?

When students are asked about what they do when studying, they commonly report underlining, highlighting, or otherwise marking material as they try to learn it. We treat these techniques as ① equivalent, given that, conceptually, they should work the same way. The techniques typically appeal to students because they are simple to use, do not ② entail training, and do not require students to invest much time beyond what is already required for reading the material. The question we ask here is, will a technique that is so ③ complicated to use actually help students learn? To understand any benefits specific to highlighting and underlining, we do not consider studies in which active marking of text was ④ paired with other common techniques, such as note-taking. Although many students report combining multiple techniques, each technique must be evaluated ⑤ independently to discover which ones are crucial for success.

14 다음 빈칸 (A), (B), (C)에 들어갈 가장 적절한 단어는?

The present report has no other object than to call attention to the alarming fact that the Atlantic Ocean is becoming seriously polluted and that a continued (A) _____ use of the world's oceans as an international dumping ground for (B) _____ human refuse may have (C) _____ effects on the productivity and very survival of plant and animal species.

	(A)	(B)	(C)
①	sensible	imperishable	inviolable
②	indiscriminate	imperishable	irreparable
③	indiscriminate	imperishable	inviolable
④	indiscriminate	decomposable	irreparable
⑤	sensible	decomposable	inviolable

15 다음 빈칸에 들어갈 가장 적절한 표현은?

In a classic study, baby rats were placed in a sensorially deprived environment. Another group was raised in a sensory-rich environment. The sensory-deprived group suffered stunted brain development. They couldn't find their way through a simple maze and were prone to aggressive, violent social behavior. The sensory-rich rodents developed larger, better connected brains. They learned complex mazes quickly and played happily together. Rats are used in experiments like this because their nervous systems show many similarities to ours. So make every effort to create a brain-nourishing environment at home, beginning in the womb. Research by Dr. Thomas Verny and many others shows that your unborn baby will be positively influenced, for example, by listening to Mozart. Once they are born, take every opportunity _____. Lots of loving touch and cuddling is particularly important to your growing child's neurological and emotional development.

① to make them get acquainted with the history of classical music

② to create a rich and refined sensory environment for your children

③ to enhance loving touch and cuddling without sensory stimulation

④ to ensure healthy brain development by providing a safe environment

⑤ to bring your children to the educational environment for physical development

16 다음 빈칸에 들어갈 가장 적절한 단어는?

The geologists who defined the fossil hallmarks of the Permian in the 1840s must have feared Lyell's criticism, for they failed to mention the signs of mass extinction at the end of that period. It seems unlikely that they simply overlooked it. The Permian extinction obliterated ecosystems as complex as any on Earth today. On land, 10-foot-long saber-toothed reptiles succumbed, and grazing, root-grubbing, and insect-eating lizards _____, along with the plants and bugs they ate. In the ocean, reefs teeming with life were reduced to bare skeletons. The Permian even finished off the lowly trilobite—perhaps the one celebrity species of the predinosaur era.

① evolved   ② wrested

③ procured   ④ vanished

⑤ flourished

17 다음 빈칸에 들어갈 가장 적절한 표현은?

Firefighters contained a major fire at Paris' Notre Dame Cathedral on Monday. Throngs of tourists and locals gathered nearby to watch and take images of a massive fire that engulfed parts of the 12th-century landmark. Paris fire commander Jean-Claude Gallet said hundreds of firefighters were able to stop the flames from spreading to the north tower belfry, and _____. Major renovations were underway to address cracks in the foundation which inspectors think is the probable cause of the fire. The many works of art inside the cathedral include three stained-glass rose windows. A Catholic relic, the crown of thorns, was placed on display for Lent, which begins this week. "Like all our countrymen, I'm sad tonight to see this part of us burn," French President Emmanuel Macron said in a tweet; however, he said that the cathedral will be rebuilt through a national fundraising campaign.

① stunned spectators watched in horror

② the cathedral had closed to the public

③ cracks had started to appear in the foundation

④ the structure was saved from total destruction

⑤ some of the artwork had not actually been removed

18 대화의 흐름으로 보아 빈칸에 들어갈 가장 적절한 표현은?

> A : David, I am having a problem with reading this chart.
> B : What's wrong?
> A : I think I understand latitude and longitude, but I do not fully understand minutes and seconds.
> B : Well, "minutes" and "seconds" mean something different in nautical terms.
> _____.
> A : What do you mean?
> B : Well, a nautical minute measures distance.

① They are not the same as ordinary ones

② They use the various navigational techniques

③ They are different depending on how to use GPS

④ People have trained students to draw their own charts

⑤ People have used the different technology since early human history

19 글의 흐름으로 보아, 주어진 문장이 들어가기에 가장 적절한 곳은?

> For example, due to the distortion, a freely moving object that we would observe to move in a straight line would be observed by the goldfish to move along a curved path.

> The goldfish's picture of reality is different from ours, but can we be sure it is less real? ① The goldfish view is not the same as our own, but goldfish could still formulate scientific laws governing the motion of the objects they observe outside their bowl. ② Nevertheless, the goldfish could formulate scientific laws from their distorted frame of reference that would always hold true and that would enable them to make predictions about the future motion of objects outside the bowl. ③ Their laws would be more complicated than the laws in our frame. ④ However, simplicity is a matter of taste. ⑤ If a goldfish formulated such a theory, we would have to admit the goldfish's view as a valid picture of reality.

20 다음 빈칸 (A)와 (B)에 들어갈 가장 적절한 단어는?

The surge in (A) _____ rhetoric around the world is being accompanied by a rise in the introduction of protectionist measures by the world's leading economies, the World Trade Organization has warned. The WTO said in a report released on Tuesday that between mid-October of last year and mid-May of 2016 G20 economies had introduced new protectionist trade measures at the fastest pace seen since the 2008 financial crisis, rolling out the equivalent of five each week. That trend coincided with a slowdown in global trade now in its fifth year. Moreover, it was contributing to the persistent slow growth in the global economy, the WTO said, and the fact it was coinciding with a(n) (B) _____ in protectionist political rhetoric around the world ought to be worrying.

	(A)	(B)
①	hostile	plummet
②	democratic	embargo
③	emotional	initiative
④	banal	restraint
⑤	antitrade	increase

1 다음 밑줄 친 (A), (B), (C)의 각 괄호 안에서 문맥에 맞는 낱말로 가장 적절한 것은?

It's tempting to identify knowledge with facts, but not every fact is an item of knowledge. Imagine shaking a sealed cardboard box containing a single coin. As you put the box down, the coin inside the box has landed either heads or tails: let's say that's a fact. But as long as no one looks into the box, this fact remains unknown; it is not yet within the realm of (A)[fact / knowledge]. Nor do facts become knowledge simply by being written down. If you write the sentence 'The coin has landed heads' on one slip of paper and 'The coin has landed tails' on another, then you will have written down a fact on one of the slips, but you still won't have gained knowledge of the outcome of the coin toss. Knowledge demands some kind of access to a fact on the part of some living subject. (B)[With / Without] a mind to access it, whatever is stored in libraries and databases won't be knowledge, but just ink marks and electronic traces. In any given case of knowledge, this access may or may not be unique to an individual: the same fact may be known by one person and not by others. Common knowledge might be shared by many people, but there is no knowledge that dangles (C)[attached / unattached] to any subject.

	(A)	(B)	(C)
①	fact	with	unattached
②	knowledge	without	unattached
③	knowledge	with	attached
④	fact	without	attached

2 다음 빈칸에 들어갈 말로 가장 적절한 것은?

Impressionable youth are not the only ones subject to _____. Most of us have probably had an experience of being pressured by a salesman. Have you ever had a sales rep try to sell you some "office solution" by telling you that 70 percent of your competitors are using their service, so why aren't you? But what if 70 percent of your competitors are idiots? Or what if that 70 percent were given so much value added or offered such a low price that they couldn't resist the opportunity? The practice is designed to do one thing and one thing only-to pressure you to buy. To make you feel you might be missing out on something or that everyone else knows but you.

① peer pressure
② impulse buying
③ bullying tactics
④ keen competition

3 다음 밑줄 친 (A), (B), (C)의 각 괄호 안에서 문맥에 맞는 낱말로 가장 적절한 것은?

People with high self-esteem have confidence in their skills and competence and enjoy facing the challenges that life offers them. They (A)[willingly / unwillingly] work in teams because they are sure of themselves and enjoy taking the opportunity to contribute. However, those who have low self-esteem tend to feel awkward, shy, and unable to express themselves. Often they compound their problems by opting for avoidance strategies because they (B)[deny / hold] the belief that whatever they do will result in failure. Conversely, they may compensate for their lack of self-esteem by exhibiting boastful and arrogant behavior to cover up their sense of unworthiness. Furthermore, such individuals account for their successes by finding reasons that are outside of themselves, while those with high self-esteem (C)[attempt / attribute] their success to internal characteristics.

	(A)	(B)	(C)
①	willingly	deny	attempt
②	willingly	hold	attribute
③	unwillingly	hold	attempt
④	unwillingly	deny	attribute

4 다음 글의 제목으로 가장 적절한 것은?

To be sure, no other species can lay claim to our capacity to devise something new and original, from the sublime to the sublimely ridiculous. Other animals do build things—birds assemble their intricate nests, beavers construct dams, and ants dig elaborate networks of tunnels. "But airplanes, strangely tilted skyscrapers and Chia Pets, well, they're pretty impressive," Fuentes says, adding that from an evolutionary standpoint, "creativity is as much a part of our tool kit as walking on two legs, having a big brain and really good hands for manipulating things." For a physically unprepossessing primate, without great fangs or claws or wings or other obvious physical advantages, creativity has been the great equalizer—and more—ensuring, for now, at least, the survival of Homo sapiens.

*sublime : 황당한, (터무니없이) 극단적인
*Chia Pets : 잔디가 머리털처럼 자라나는 피규어

① Where Does Human Creativity Come From?
② What Are the Physical Characteristics of Primates?
③ Physical Advantages of Homo Sapiens over Other Species
④ Creativity: a Unique Trait Human Species Have For Survival

5 다음 글의 요지를 한 문장으로 요약하고자 한다. 빈칸 (A), (B)에 들어갈 말로 가장 적절한 것은?

"Most of bird identification is based on a sort of subjective impression—the way a bird moves and little instantaneous appearances at different angles and sequences of different appearances, and as it turns its head and as it flies and as it turns around, you see sequences of different shapes and angles," Sibley says, "All that combines to create a unique impression of a bird that can't really be taken apart and described in words. When it comes down to being in the fieldland looking at a bird, you don't take time to analyze it and say it shows this, this, and this; therefore it must be this species. It's more natural and instinctive. After a lot of practice, you look at the bird, and it triggers little switches in your brain. It looks right. You know what it is at a glance."

According to Sibley, bird identification is based on (A)_____ rather than (B)_____.

① instinctive impression – discrete analysis

② objective research – subjective judgements

③ physical appearances – behavioral traits

④ close observation – distant observation

6 주어진 글 다음에 이어질 글의 순서로 가장 적절한 것은?

As cars are becoming less dependent on people, the means and circumstances in which the product is used by consumers are also likely to undergo significant changes, with higher rates of participation in car sharing and short-term leasing programs.

(A) In the not-too-distant future, a driverless car could come to you when you need it, and when you are done with it, it could then drive away without any need for a parking space. Increases in car sharing and short-term leasing are also likely to be associated with a corresponding decrease in the importance of exterior car design.

(B) As a result, the symbolic meanings derived from cars and their relationship to consumer self-identity and status are likely to change in turn.

(C) Rather than serving as a medium for personalization and self-identity, car exteriors might increasingly come to represent a channel for advertising and other promotional activities, including brand ambassador programs, such as those offered by Free Car Media.

① (A) – (C) – (B)　　　　　　② (B) – (C) – (A)

③ (C) – (A) – (B)　　　　　　④ (C) – (B) – (A)

7 주어진 글 다음에 이어질 글의 순서로 가장 적절한 것은?

> There is a wonderful story of a group of American car executives who went to Japan to see a Japanese assembly line. At the end of the line, the doors were put on the hinges, the same as in America.

(A) But something was missing. In the United States, a line worker would take a rubber mallet and tap the edges of the door to ensure that it fit perfectly. In Japan, that job didn't seem to exist.

(B) Confused, the American auto executives asked at what point they made sure the door fit perfectly. Their Japanese guide looked at them and smiled sheepishly. "We make sure it fits when we design it."

(C) In the Japanese auto plant, they didn't examine the problem and accumulate data to figure out the best solution — they engineered the outcome they wanted from the beginning. If they didn't achieve their desired outcome, they understood it was because of a decision they made at the start of the process.

① (A) – (B) – (C)　　　　② (A) – (C) – (B)

③ (B) – (A) – (C)　　　　④ (B) – (C) – (A)

8 다음 글의 빈칸 (A), (B)에 들어갈 말로 가장 적절한 것은?

There has been much research on nonverbal cues to deception dating back to the work of Ekman and his idea of leakage. It is well documented that people use others' nonverbal behaviors as a way to detect lies. My research and that of many others has strongly supported people's reliance on observations of others' nonverbal behaviors when assessing honesty. (A) _____, social scientific research on the link between various nonverbal behaviors and the act of lying suggests that the link is typically not very strong or consistent. In my research, I have observed that the nonverbal signals that seem to give one liar away are different than those given by a second liar. (B) _____, the scientific evidence linking nonverbal behaviors and deception has grown weaker over time. People infer honesty based on how others nonverbally present themselves, but that has very limited utility and validity.

① However − What's more
③ However − Nevertheless
② As a result − On the contrary
④ As a result − For instance

9 다음 글의 밑줄 친 부분 중 어법상 틀린 것은?

As soon as the start−up is incorporated it will need a bank account, and the need for a payroll account will follow quickly. The banks are very competitive in services to do payroll and related tax bookkeeping, ①starting with even the smallest of businesses. These are areas ②where a business wants the best quality service and the most "free" accounting help it can get. The changing payroll tax legislation is a headache to keep up with, especially when a sales force will be operating in many of the fifty states. And the ③requiring reports are a burden on a company's add administrative staff. Such services are often provided best by the banker. The banks' references in this area should be compared with the payroll service alternatives such as ADP, but the future and the long−term relationship should be kept in mind when a decision is ④being made.

10 다음 글의 밑줄 친 부분 중 어법상 틀린 것은?

Many people refuse to visit animal shelters because they find it too sad or ① depressed. They shouldn't feel so bad because so many lucky animals are saved from a dangerous life on the streets, ② where they're at risk of traffic accidents, attack by other animals or humans, and subject to the elements. Many lost pets likewise ③ are found and reclaimed by distraught owners simply because they were brought into animal shelters. Most importantly, ④ adoptable pets find homes, and sick or dangerous animals are humanely relieved of their suffering.

11 다음 밑줄 친 (A), (B), (C)의 각 괄호 안에서 문맥에 맞는 낱말로 가장 적절한 것은?

EQ testing, when performed with reliable testing methods, can provide you with very useful information about yourself. I've found, having tested thousands of people, that many are a bit surprised by their results. For example, one person who believed she was very socially responsible and often concerned about others came out with an (A) [average / extraordinary] score in that area. She was quite disappointed in her score. It turned out that she had very high standards for social responsibility and therefore was extremely (B) [easy / hard] on herself when she performed her assessment. In reality, she was (C) [more / less] socially responsible than most people, but she believed that she could be much better than she was.

	(A)	(B)	(C)
①	average	easy	less
②	average	hard	more
③	extraordinary	hard	less
④	extraordinary	easy	more

12 다음 빈칸에 들어갈 말로 가장 적절한 것은?

A person may try to _____ by using evidence to his advantage. A mother asks her son, "How are you doing in English this term?" He responds cheerfully, "Oh, I just got a ninety-five on a quiz." The statement conceals the fact that he has failed every other quiz and that his actual average is 55. Yet, if she pursues the matter no further, the mother may be delighted that her son is doing so well. Linda asks Susan, "Have you read much Dickens?" Susan responds, "Oh, Pickwick Papers is one of my favorite novels." The statement may disguise the fact that Pickwick Papers is the only novel by Dickens that she has read, and it may give Linda the impression that Susan is a great Dickens enthusiast.

① earn extra money

② effect a certain belief

③ hide memory problems

④ make other people feel guilty

13 다음 글의 내용을 한 문장으로 요약하고자 한다. 빈칸 (A), (B)에 들어갈 말로 가장 적절한 것은?

Whether we are complimented for our appearance, our garden, a dinner we prepared, or an assignment at the office, it is always satisfying to receive recognition for a job well done. Certainly, reinforcement theory sees occasional praise as an aid to learning a new skill. However, some evidence cautions against making sweeping generalizations regarding the use of praise in improving performance. It seems that while praise improves performance on certain tasks, on others it can instead prove harmful. Imagine the situation in which the enthusiastic support of hometown fans expecting victory brings about the downfall of their team. In this situation, it seems that praise creates pressure on athletes, disrupting their performance.

↓

Whether __(A)__ helps or hurts a performance depends on __(B)__ .

	(A)	(B)
①	praise	task types
②	competition	quality of teamwork
③	praise	quality of teamwork
④	competition	task types

14 다음 글의 밑줄 친 부분 중 어법상 틀린 것은?

As we consider media consumption in the context of anonymous social relations, we mean all of those occasions that involve the presence of strangers, such as viewing television in public places like bars, ①going to concerts or dance clubs, or reading a newspaper on a bus or subway. Typically, there are social rules that ②govern how we interact with those around us and with the media product. For instance, it is considered rude in our culture, or at least aggressive, ③read over another person's shoulder or to get up and change TV channels in a public setting. Any music fan knows what is appropriate at a particular kind of concert. The presence of other people is often crucial to defining the setting and hence the activity of media consumption, ④despite the fact that the relationships are totally impersonal.

15 다음 글의 밑줄 친 부분 중 어법상 틀린 것은?

Many of us believe that amnesia, or sudden memory loss, results in the inability to recall one's name and identity. This belief may reflect the way amnesia is usually ①portrayed in movies, television, and literature. For example, when we meet Matt Damon's character in the movie The Bourne Identity, we learn that he has no memory for who he is, why he has the skills he does, or where he is from. He spends much of the movie ②trying to answer these questions. However, the inability to remember your name and identity ③are exceedingly rare in reality. Amnesia most often results from a brain injury that leaves the victim unable to form new memories, but with most memories of the past ④intact. Some movies do accurately portray this more common syndrome; our favorite Memento.

16 다음 빈칸에 들어갈 말로 가장 적절한 것은?

Much is now known about natural hazards and the negative impacts they have on people and their property. It would seem obvious that any logical person would avoid such potential impacts or at least modify their behavior or their property to minimize such impacts. However, humans are not always rational. Until someone has a personal experience or knows someone who has such an experience, most people subconsciously believe "It won't happen here" or "It won't happen to me." Even knowledgeable scientists who are aware of the hazards, the odds of their occurrence, and the costs of an event _____.

① refuse to remain silent

② do not always act appropriately

③ put the genetic factor at the top end

④ have difficulty in defining natural hazards

17 다음 글의 주제로 가장 적절한 것은?

The rise of cities and kingdoms and the improvement in transport infrastructure brought about new opportunities for specialization. Densely populated cities provided full-time employment not just for professional shoemakers and doctors, but also for carpenters, priests, soldiers and lawyers. Villages that gained a reputation for producing really good wine, olive oil or ceramics discovered that it was worth their while to specialize nearly exclusively in that product and trade it with other settlements for all the other goods they needed. This made a lot of sense. Climates and soils differ, so why drink mediocre wine from your backyard if you can buy a smoother variety from a place whose soil and climate is much better suited to grape vines? If the clay in your backyard makes stronger and prettier pots, then you can make an exchange.

① how climates and soils influence the local products

② ways to gain a good reputation for local specialties

③ what made people engage in specialization and trade

④ the rise of cities and full-time employment for professionals

18 밑줄 친 the issue가 가리키는 내용으로 가장 적절한 것은?

Nine-year-old Ryan Kyote was eating breakfast at home in Napa, California, when he saw the news: an Indiana school had taken a 6-year-old's meal when her lunch account didn't have enough money. Kyote asked if that could happen to his friends. When his mom contacted the school district to find out, she learned that students at schools in their district had, all told, as much as $25,000 in lunch debt. Although the district says it never penalized students who owed, Kyote decided to use his saved allowance to pay off his grade's debt, about $74—becoming the face of a movement to end lunch-money debt. When California Governor Gavin Newsom signed a bill in October that banned "lunch shaming," or giving worse food to students with debt, he thanked Kyote for his "empathy and his courage" in raising awareness of <u>the issue</u>. "Heroes," Kyote points out, "come in all ages."

① The governor signed a bill to decline lunch items to students with lunch debt.

② Kyote's lunch was taken away because he ran out of money in his lunch account.

③ The school district with financial burden cut the budget failing to serve quality meals.

④ Many students in the district who could not afford lunch were burdened with lunch debt.

19 청고래에 관한 다음 글의 내용과 일치하지 않는 것은?

> The biggest heart in the world is inside the blue whale. It weighs more than seven tons. It's as big as a room. When this creature is born it is 20 feet long and weighs four tons. It is way bigger than your car. It drinks a hundred gallons of milk from its mama every day and gains 200 pounds a day, and when it is seven or eight years old it endures an unimaginable puberty and then it essentially disappears from human ken, for next to nothing is known of the mating habits, travel patterns, diet, social life, language, social structure and diseases. There are perhaps 10,000 blue whales in the world, living in every ocean on earth, and of the largest animal who ever lived we know nearly nothing. But we know this: the animals with the largest hearts in the world generally travel in pairs, and their penetrating moaning cries, their piercing yearning tongue, can be heard underwater for miles and miles.

① 아기 청고래는 매일 100갤런의 모유를 마시고, 하루에 200 파운드씩 체중이 증가한다.

② 청고래는 사춘기를 지나면서 인간의 시야에서 사라져서 청고래에 대해 알려진 것이 많지 않다.

③ 세계에서 가장 큰 심장을 지닌 동물이면서, 몸집이 가장 큰 동물이다.

④ 청고래는 일반적으로 혼자서 이동하고, 청고래의 소리는 물속을 관통하여 수 마일까지 전달될 수 있다.

20 다음 글의 주제로 가장 적절한 것은?

> In addition to controlling temperatures when handling fresh produce, control of the atmosphere is important. Some moisture is needed in the air to prevent dehydration during storage, but too much moisture can encourage growth of molds. Some commercial storage units have controlled atmospheres, with the levels of both carbon dioxide and moisture being regulated carefully. Sometimes other gases, such as ethylene gas, may be introduced at controlled levels to help achieve optimal quality of bananas and other fresh produce. Related to the control of gases and moisture is the need for some circulation of air among the stored foods.

① The necessity of controlling harmful gases in atmosphere

② The best way to control levels of moisture in growing plants and fruits

③ The seriousness of increasing carbon footprints every year around the world

④ The importance of controlling certain levels of gases and moisture in storing foods

21 다음 글의 밑줄 친 부분 중 문맥상 낱말의 쓰임이 가장 적절하지 않은 것은?

Even if lying doesn't have any harmful effects in a particular case, it is still morally wrong because, if discovered, lying weakens the general practice of truth telling on which human communication relies. For instance, if I were to lie about my age on grounds of vanity, and my lying were discovered, even though no serious harm would have been done, I would have ①undermined your trust generally. In that case you would be far less likely to believe anything I might say in the future. Thus all lying, when discovered, has indirect ②harmful effects. However, very occasionally, these harmful effects might possibly be outweighed by the ③benefits which arise from a lie. For example, if someone is seriously ill, lying to them about their life expectancy might probably give them a chance of living longer. On the other hand, telling them the truth could possibly ④prevent a depression that would accelerate their physical decline.

22 글의 흐름으로 보아 아래 문장이 들어가기에 가장 적절한 곳은?

Water is also the medium for most chemical reactions needed to sustain life.

Several common properties of seawater are crucial to the survival and well-being of the ocean's inhabitants. Water accounts for 80−90% of the volume of most marine organisms. (①) It provides buoyancy and body support for swimming and floating organisms and reduces the need for heavy skeletal structures. (②) The life processes of marine organisms in turn alter many fundamental physical and chemical properties of seawater, including its transparency and chemical makeup, making organisms an integral part of the total marine environment. (③) Understanding the interactions between organisms and their marine environment requires a brief examination of some of the more important physical and chemical attributes of seawater. (④) The characteristics of pure water and sea water differ in some respects, so we consider first the basic properties of pure water and then examine how those properties differ in seawater.

23 (A), (B), (C)의 각 네모 안에서 문맥에 맞는 낱말로 가장 적절한 것은?

Here's the even more surprising part: The advent of AI didn't (A) diminish / increase the performance of purely human chess players. Quite the opposite. Cheap, supersmart chess programs (B) discouraged / inspired more people than ever to play chess, at more tournaments than ever, and the players got better than ever. There are more than twice as many grand masters now as there were when Deep Blue first beat Kasparov. The top-ranked human chess player today, Magnus Carlsen, trained with AIs and has been deemed the most computerlike of all human chess players. He also has the (C) highest / lowest human grand master rating of all time.

	(A)	(B)	(C)
①	diminish	discouraged	highest
②	increase	discouraged	lowest
③	diminish	inspired	highest
④	increase	inspired	lowest

24 다음 글의 내용을 요약할 때 빈칸에 들어갈 말로 가장 적절한 것은?

Aesthetic value in fashion objects, like aesthetic value in fine art objects, is self-oriented. Consumers have the need to be attracted and to surround themselves with other people who are attractive. However, unlike aesthetic value in the fine arts, aesthetic value in fashion is also other-oriented. Attractiveness of appearance is a way of eliciting the reaction of others and facilitating social interaction.

↓

Aesthetic value in fashion objects is _____.

① inherently only self-oriented

② just other-oriented unlike the other

③ both self-oriented and other-oriented

④ hard to define regardless of its nature

25 글의 흐름으로 보아 아래 문장이 들어가기에 가장 적절한 곳은?

> The great news is that this is true whether or not we remember our dreams.

Some believe there is no value to dreams, but it is wrong to dismiss these nocturnal dramas as irrelevant. There is something to be gained in remembering. (①) We can feel more connected, more complete, and more on track. We can receive inspiration, information, and comfort. Albert Einstein stated that his theory of relativity was inspired by a dream. (②) In fact, he claimed that dreams were responsible for many of his discoveries. (③) Asking why we dream makes as much sense as questioning why we breathe. Dreaming is an integral part of a healthy life. (④) Many people report being inspired with a new approach for a problem upon awakening, even though they don't remember the specific dream.

☞ 정답 및 해설 P.166

1 다음 밑줄 친 단어의 의미와 가장 가까운 것은?

> Although doctors struggled to <u>contain</u> the epidemic, it has swept all the world.

① include
② suffer from
③ prevent the spread of
④ transmit

2 다음 밑줄 친 표현의 의미와 가장 가까운 것은?

> If you take risks like that you'll <u>wind up</u> dead.

① blow up
② end up
③ make up
④ use up

3 다음 빈칸에 들어갈 단어로 가장 적절한 것은?

> The detectives _____ some clues of the hit-and-run accident and could successfully arrest the real criminal.

① obliterated
② distorted
③ complimented
④ scrutinized

4 다음 빈칸 ㉠, ㉡에 공통으로 들어갈 단어로 가장 적절한 것은?

> • I looked her ㉠_____ in the face.
> • To unbreak my heart was like trying to ㉡_____ a circle. That is, it was impossible.

① court

② overhead

③ square

④ trace

5 다음 빈칸 ㉠, ㉡에 공통으로 들어갈 단어로 가장 적절한 것은?

> • As this case seems to be more complicated than we have ever expected, we are to request the ㉠_____ from the police in order to work it out.
> • So far North Korea has habitually and blatantly violated the ㉡_____ by the UN, in relation to the matters of developing nuclear weapons.

① approval

② encouragement

③ neutralization

④ sanction

6 다음 문장 중 어법상 가장 적절하지 <u>않은</u> 것은?

① I'm feeling sick. I shouldn't have eaten so much.

② Most of the suggestions made at the meeting was not very practical.

③ Providing the room is clean, I don't mind which hotel we stay at.

④ We'd been playing tennis for about half an hour when it started to rain heavily.

7 다음 문장 중 어법상 가장 적절하지 <u>않은</u> 것은?

① No sooner had he seen me than he ran away.

② Little I dreamed that he had told me a lie.

③ Written in plain English, the book has been read by many people.

④ When I met her for the first time, I couldn't help but fall in love with her.

8 A에 대한 B의 응답으로 가장 적절하지 <u>않은</u> 것은?

① A : Oh, I've forgotten my phone again!

　 B : Typical! You're always forgetting your phone.

② A : Is your shirt inside out? I see the seams.

　 B : Actually, they're supposed to show.

③ A : Where can I get a cheap computer?

　 B : Shopping online is your best bet.

④ A : Would you like some strawberry shortcake?

　 B : Sure, help yourself to more.

9 다음 대화의 빈칸에 들어갈 표현으로 가장 적절한 것은?

> A : How many bottles of wine should I prepare for tonight's party? I heard there will be many guests.
>
> B : The more, the better. Unfortunately, however, I won't be able to be with you at the party because of the urgent matters in my office tonight. Instead, _____?
>
> A : Of course! You are always welcome to my world.

① can you give me a raincheck for this

② will you give my best regards to them

③ shall I go home

④ are you being waited on

10 우리말을 영어로 옮긴 것 중 어법상 가장 적절한 것은?

① 그들은 참 친절한 사람들이야!

　　→ They're so kind people!

② 그녀는 곰 인형을 하나 가지고 있었는데, 인형 눈이 양쪽 다 떨어져 나가고 없었다.

　　→ She had a teddy bear, both of whose eyes were missing.

③ 가장 쉬운 해결책은 아무 일도 하지 않는 것이다.

　　→ The most easiest solution is to do nothing.

④ 애들 옷 입히고 잠자리 좀 봐 줄래요?

　　→ After you've got the children dress, can you make the beds?

11 다음 글의 제목으로 가장 적절한 것은?

Imagine that after studying word pairs such as red/blood and food/radish, you are given red as a cue and recall that blood went with it. This act of recall strengthens your memory of the two words appearing together, so that next time you are given red, it will be easier for you to recall blood. Remarkably, however, recalling that blood went with red will also make it more difficult later to recall radish when given food! When practicing red/blood, it is necessary to suppress retrieval of recently encountered "red things" other than blood, so that your mind is not littered with irrelevancies that could interfere with the recall of the word you seek. But there is a cost to suppressing retrieval of unwanted items such as radish: they are less accessible for future recall, even to a cue (food) that would seem to have nothing to do with " redness."

① The Advantage and Disadvantage of Studying Word Pairs

② The Art of Matching Word Pairs

③ The Importance of Recalling Word Pairs

④ The Proper Way of Practicing Word Pairs

12 다음 글의 흐름으로 보아 〈보기〉의 문장이 들어갈 곳으로 가장 적절한 것은?

〈 보 기 〉

When the adversity is threatening enough or comes without warning, it can unbalance the leader at a single stroke.

There are times when even the best leaders lose their emotional balance. (㉠) Leadership brings with it responsibility, and responsibility, in times of serious adversity, brings emotional confusion and strain. (㉡) In this sense responsibility is like a lever, which can upset a leader's emotional balance when adversity presses down hard on one end. (㉢) Even a leader as great as Lincoln was floored more than once in this way. (㉣) Other times the effect is cumulative, coming after a period of sustained high tension-of pressure on one end and resistance on the other-until finally the leader's equanimity begins to give way. The point is that every leader had their emotional limits, and there is no shame in exceeding them.

① ㉠　　　　　　　　　　　② ㉡

③ ㉢　　　　　　　　　　　④ ㉣

13 다음 글의 제목으로 가장 적절한 것은?

Scientists hope to someday establish beyond a doubt that aging and all the nefarious things that go with it can be indefinitely postponed simply by reducing the amount of food and calories we consume. Take note that in the prevention of Alzheimer's disease, maintaining an ideal weight may not be enough. Studies have shown that the risk of Alzheimer's disease is more closely linked to caloric intake than to weight or body mass index (BMI). This means that a junk food junkie who is blessed with a high metabolic rate that keeps her from gaining weight may still be at a higher risk for developing a memory problem. If we consider the logic that explains how caloric restriction exerts its beneficial effects on the body and mind, this makes a lot of sense. The amount of age-accelerating *oxygen free radicals generated from our diet is related to the amount of calories we consume, not to our weight. Thus a person with a high metabolic rate who consumes greater calories may actually be producing more harmful forms of oxygen than someone with a slower metabolic rate.

*oxygen free radicals : 활성 산소

① The Relation between BMI and Alzheimer's Disease
② The Instruction of How to Reduce the Risk of Alzheimer's Disease
③ The Influence of Ingesting Calories on the Body and Mind
④ The Side Effect of Having Junk Food on Human Metabolism

14 다음 글의 빈칸에 들어갈 내용으로 가장 적절한 것은?

Life is full of hazards. Disease, enemies and starvation are always menacing primitive man. Experience teaches him that medicinal herbs, valor, the most strenuous labor, often come to nothing, yet normally he wants to survive and enjoy the good things of existence. Faced with this problem, he takes to any method that seems adapted to his ends. Often his ways appear incredibly crude to us moderns until we remember how our next-door neighbor acts in like emergencies. When medical science pronounces him incurable, he will not resign himself to fate but runs to the nearest *quack who holds out hope of recovery. His urge for self-preservation will not down, nor will that of the illiterate peoples of the world, and in that overpowering will to live is anchored the belief in supernaturalism, _____.

*quack : 돌팔이 의사

① and the number of its supporters has increased dramatically

② which caused ancient civilizations to develop into modern ones

③ which has had a positive effect on medical science

④ which is absolutely universal among known peoples, past and present

15 다음 빈칸 ㉠, ㉡, ㉢에 공통으로 들어갈 단어로 가장 적절한 것은?

One study that measured participants' exposure to thirty-seven major negative events found a curvilinear relationship between lifetime adversity and mental health. High levels of adversity predicted poor mental health, as expected, but people who had faced intermediate levels of adversity were healthier than those who experienced little adversity, suggesting that moderate amounts of stress can foster ㉠_____. A follow-up study found a similar link between the amount of lifetime adversity and subjects' responses to laboratory stressors. Intermediate levels of adversity were predictive of the greatest ㉡_____. Thus, having to grapple with a moderate amount of stress may build ㉢_____ in the face of future stress.

① resilience   ② impression

③ creativity   ④ depression

16 다음 빈칸 ㉠, ㉡에 각각 들어갈 표현으로 가장 적절한 것은?

> The most obvious salient feature of moral agents is a capacity for rational thought. This is an uncontested necessary condition for any form of moral agency, since we all accept that people who are incapable of reasoned thought cannot be held morally responsible for their actions. ㉠_____, if we move beyond this uncontroversial salient feature of moral agents, then the most salient feature of actual flesh-and-blood (as opposed to ridiculously idealized) individual moral agents is surely the fact that every moral agent brings multiple perspectives to bear on every moral problem situation. ㉡_____, there is no one-size-fits-all answer to the question "What are the basic ways in which moral agents wish to affect others?" Rather, moral agents wish to affect ' others' in different ways depending upon who these 'others' are.

	㉠	㉡
①	However	That is
②	Furthermore	Otherwise
③	To put it briefly	After all
④	In particular	Even so

17 다음 빈칸 ㉠, ㉡에 각각 들어갈 단어로 가장 적절한 것은?

> The sun is slowly getting brighter as its core contracts and heats up. In a billion years it will be about 10 percent brighter than today, heating the planet to an uncomfortable degree. Water ㉠_____ from the oceans may set off a runaway greenhouse effect that turns Earth into a damp version of Venus, wrapped permanently in a thick, white blanket of cloud. Or the transformation may take some time and be more gentle, with an increasingly hot and cloudy atmosphere able to shelter microbial life for some time. Either way, water will escape into the stratosphere and be broken down by UV light into oxygen and hydrogen. Oxygen will be left in the stratosphere—perhaps ㉡_____ aliens into thinking the planet is still inhabited—while the hydrogen is light enough to escape into space. So our water will gradually leak away.

	㉠	㉡
①	accumulating	misunderstanding
②	evaporating	misleading
③	flowing	persuading
④	seeping	expelling

18 다음 글의 흐름으로 보아 〈보기〉 문장 뒤에 이어질 글의 순서로 가장 적절한 것은?

〈 보 기 〉

Ankle and heel pain are the most common ailments seen by foot doctors, especially among runners and those who play sprinting sports, such as basketball or tennis.

㉠ Above all, it is most important to rest and take it easy until the injury fully heals.

㉡ While some injuries to the foot are serious and may require a trip to the doctor's office, most minor sprains can be treated at home.

㉢ They also suggest keeping the foot elevated when possible and making sure to wear comfortable shoes with plenty of support.

㉣ Sports physicians recommend icing the bruised area, gently stretching and massaging the foot, and taking anti-inflammatory drugs to help alleviate the pain.

① ㉣-㉡-㉠-㉢

② ㉡-㉠-㉣-㉢

③ ㉢-㉡-㉣-㉠

④ ㉡-㉣-㉢-㉠

19 글쓴이의 주장과 가장 일치하는 것은?

Some psychologists believe that insight is the result of restructuring of a problem after a period of non-progress where the person is believed to be too focused on past experience and get stuck. A new manner to represent the problem is suddenly discovered, leading to a different path to a solution heretofore unpredicted. It has been claimed that no specific knowledge, or experience is required to attain insight in the problem situation. As a matter of fact, one should break away from experience and let the mind wander freely. Nevertheless, experimental studies have shown that insight is actually the result of ordinary analytical thinking. The restructuring of a problem can be caused by unsuccessful attempts in solving the problem, leading to new information being brought in while the person is thinking. The new information can contribute to a completely different perspective in finding a solution, thus producing the Aha! Experience.

① 통찰력이 있는 사람은 보통 문제의 재구성을 통해 해결책을 찾는다.

② 문제 해결 실패의 경험들을 겪으면서 통찰력 획득이 가능해진다.

③ 문제에 집착을 하지 않을 때 그 문제의 재구성이 이루어진다.

④ 대조되는 능력인 분석적 사고와 통찰력을 갖춰야 문제를 해결할 수 있다.

20 다음 글의 빈칸에 들어갈 내용으로 가장 적절한 것은?

What was arguably the all-time greatest example of selection bias resulted in the embarrassing 1948 Chicago Tribune headline "Dewey defeats Truman." In reality, Harry Truman trounced his opponent. All the major political polls at the time had predicted Thomas Dewey would be elected president. The Chicago Tribune went to press before the election results were in, its editors confident that the polls would be correct. The statisticians were wrong for two reasons. First, they stopped polling too far in advance of the election, and Truman was especially successful at energizing people in the final days before the election. Second, the telephone polls conducted tended to favor Dewey because in 1948, telephones were generally limited to wealthier households, and Dewey was mainly popular among elite voters. The selection bias that resulted in the infamous Chicago Tribune headline was accidental, but it shows the danger and potential power—for a stakeholder wanting to influence hearts and minds by _____—of selection bias.

① encouraging others to hop on the bandwagon
② inspiring people to wag the dog
③ instigating the public to be underdogs
④ tempting American adults to be swing voters

1 밑줄 친 부분에 들어갈 말로 가장 적절한 것은?

> The issue with plastic bottles is that they're not _____, so when the temperatures begin to rise, your water will also heat up.

① sanitary   ② insulated

③ recyclable   ④ waterproof

※ 밑줄 친 부분의 의미와 가장 가까운 것을 고르시오. 【2~4】

2

> Strategies that a writer adopts during the writing process may <u>alleviate</u> the difficulty of attentional overload.

① complement   ② accelerate

③ calculate   ④ relieve

3

> The cruel sights <u>touched off</u> thoughts that otherwise wouldn't have entered her mind.

① looked after   ② gave rise to

③ made up for   ④ kept in contact with

4

> The school bully did not know what it was like to be <u>shunned</u> by the other students in the class.

① avoided   ② warned

③ punished   ④ imitated

5 어법상 옳은 것은?

① Of the billions of stars in the galaxy, how much are able to hatch life?

② The Christmas party was really excited and I totally lost track of time.

③ I must leave right now because I am starting work at noon today.

④ They used to loving books much more when they were younger.

6 밑줄 친 부분의 의미와 가장 가까운 것은?

> After Francesca <u>made a case for</u> staying at home during the summer holidays, an uncomfortable silence fell on the dinner table. Robert was not sure if it was the right time for him to tell her about his grandiose plan.

① objected to

② dreamed about

③ completely excluded

④ strongly suggested

7 밑줄 친 부분 중 어법상 옳지 않은 것은?

> Elizabeth Taylor had an eye for beautiful jewels and over the years amassed some amazing pieces, once ①declaring "a girl can always have more diamonds." In 2011, her finest jewels were sold by Christie's at an evening auction ②that brought in $115.9 million. Among her most prized possessions sold during the evening sale ③were a 1961 bejeweled timepiece by Bulgari. Designed as a serpent to coil around the wrist, with its head and tail ④covered with diamonds and having two hypnotic emerald eyes, a discreet mechanism opens its fierce jaws to reveal a tiny quartz watch.

8 우리말을 영어로 잘못 옮긴 것은?

① 보증이 만료되어서 수리는 무료가 아니었다.

　→Since the warranty had expired, the repairs were not free of charge.

② 설문지를 완성하는 누구에게나 선물카드가 주어질 예정이다.

　→A gift card will be given to whomever completes the questionnaire.

③ 지난달 내가 휴가를 요청했더라면 지금 하와이에 있을 텐데.

　→If I had asked for a vacation last month, I would be in Hawaii now.

④ 그의 아버지가 갑자기 작년에 돌아가셨고, 설상가상으로 그의 어머니도 병에 걸리셨다.

　→His father suddenly passed away last year, and, what was worse, his mother became sick.

9 밑줄 친 (A), (B)에 들어갈 말로 가장 적절한 것은?

Assertive behavior involves standing up for your rights and expressing your thoughts and feelings in a direct, appropriate way that does not violate the rights of others. It is a matter of getting the other person to understand your viewpoint. People who exhibit assertive behavior skills are able to handle conflict situations with ease and assurance while maintaining good interpersonal relations. _____(A)_____, aggressive behavior involves expressing your thoughts and feelings and defending your rights in a way that openly violates the rights of others. Those exhibiting aggressive behavior seem to believe that the rights of others must be subservient to theirs. _____(B)_____, they have a difficult time maintaining good interpersonal relations. They are likely to interrupt, talk fast, ignore others, and use sarcasm or other forms of verbal abuse to maintain control.

	(A)	(B)
①	In contrast	Thus
②	Similarly	Moreover
③	However	On one hand
④	Accordingly	On the other hand

10 다음 글의 주제로 가장 적절한 것은?

The e-book applications available on tablet computers employ touchscreen technology. Some touchscreens feature a glass panel covering two electronically-charged metallic surfaces lying face-to-face. When the screen is touched, the two metallic surfaces feel the pressure and make contact. This pressure sends an electrical signal to the computer, which translates the touch into a command. This version of the touchscreen is known as a resistive screen because the screen reacts to pressure from the finger. Other tablet computers feature a single electrified metallic layer under the glass panel. When the user touches the screen, some of the current passes through the glass into the user's finger. When the charge is transferred, the computer interprets the loss in power as a command and carries out the function the user desires. This type of screen is known as a capacitive screen.

① how users learn new technology

② how e-books work on tablet computers

③ how touchscreen technology works

④ how touchscreens have evolved

11 밑줄 친 부분에 들어갈 말로 가장 적절한 것은?

A : Oh, another one! So many junk emails!

B : I know. I receive more than ten junk emails a day.

A : Can we stop them from coming in?

B : I don't think it's possible to block them completely.

A : _____?

B : Well, you can set up a filter on the settings.

A : A filter?

B : Yeah. The filter can weed out some of the spam emails.

① Do you write emails often

② Isn't there anything we can do

③ How did you make this great filter

④ Can you help me set up an email account

12 우리말을 영어로 잘못 옮긴 것은?

① 나는 네 열쇠를 잃어버렸다고 네게 말한 것을 후회한다.

　　→I regret to tell you that I lost your key.

② 그 병원에서의 그의 경험은 그녀의 경험보다 더 나빴다.

　　→His experience at the hospital was worse than hers.

③ 그것은 내게 지난 24년의 기억을 상기시켜준다.

　　→It reminds me of the memories of the past 24 years.

④ 나는 대화할 때 내 눈을 보는 사람들을 좋아한다.

　　→I like people who look me in the eye when I have a conversation.

13 두 사람의 대화 중 가장 자연스러운 것은?

① A : Do you know what time it is?

　　B : Sorry, I'm busy these days.

② A : Hey, where are you headed?

　　B : We are off to the grocery store.

③ A : Can you give me a hand with this?

　　B : OK. I'll clap for you.

④ A : Has anybody seen my purse?

　　B : Long time no see.

14 다음 글의 제목으로 가장 적절한 것은?

Louis ⅩⅣ needed a palace worthy of his greatness, so he decided to build a huge new house at Versailles, where a tiny hunting lodge stood. After almost fifty years of labor, this tiny hunting lodge had been transformed into an enormous palace, a quarter of a mile long. Canals were dug to bring water from the river and to drain the marshland. Versailles was full of elaborate rooms like the famous Hall of Mirrors, where seventeen huge mirrors stood across from seventeen large windows, and the Salon of Apollo, where a solid silver throne stood. Hundreds of statues of Greek gods such as Apollo, Jupiter, and Neptune stood in the gardens; each god had Louis's face!

① True Face of Greek Gods

② The Hall of Mirrors vs. the Salon of Apollo

③ Did the Canal Bring More Than Just Water to Versailles?

④ Versailles: From a Humble Lodge to a Great Palace

15 글의 흐름상 가장 어색한 문장은?

Philosophers have not been as concerned with anthropology as anthropologists have with philosophy. ① Few influential contemporary philosophers take anthropological studies into account in their work. ② Those who specialize in philosophy of social science may consider or analyze examples from anthropological research, but do this mostly to illustrate conceptual points or epistemological distinctions or to criticize epistemological or ethical implications. ③ In fact, the great philosophers of our time often drew inspiration from other fields such as anthropology and psychology. ④ Philosophy students seldom study or show serious interest in anthropology. They may learn about experimental methods in science, but rarely about anthropological fieldwork.

16 밑줄 친 부분에 들어갈 말로 가장 적절한 것은?

All of us inherit something: in some cases, it may be money, property or some object—a family heirloom such as a grandmother's wedding dress or a father's set of tools. But beyond that, all of us inherit something else, something _____, something we may not even be fully aware of. It may be a way of doing a daily task, or the way we solve a particular problem or decide a moral issue for ourselves. It may be a special way of keeping a holiday or a tradition to have a picnic on a certain date. It may be something important or central to our thinking, or something minor that we have long accepted quite casually.

① quite unrelated to our everyday life

② against our moral standards

③ much less concrete and tangible

④ of great monetary value

17 다음 글의 요지로 가장 적절한 것은?

Evolutionarily, any species that hopes to stay alive has to manage its resources carefully. That means that first call on food and other goodies goes to the breeders and warriors and hunters and planters and builders and, certainly, the children, with not much left over for the seniors, who may be seen as consuming more than they're contributing. But even before modern medicine extended life expectancies, ordinary families were including grandparents and even great-grandparents. That's because what old folk consume materially, they give back behaviorally—providing a leveling, reasoning center to the tumult that often swirls around them.

① Seniors have been making contributions to the family.

② Modern medicine has brought focus to the role of old folk.

③ Allocating resources well in a family determines its prosperity.

④ The extended family comes at a cost of limited resources.

18 주어진 글 다음에 이어질 글의 순서로 가장 적절한 것은?

Nowadays the clock dominates our lives so much that it is hard to imagine life without it. Before industrialization, most societies used the sun or the moon to tell the time.

(A) For the growing network of railroads, the fact that there were no time standards was a disaster. Often, stations just some miles apart set their clocks at different times. There was a lot of confusion for travelers.

(B) When mechanical clocks first appeared, they were immediately popular. It was fashionable to have a clock or a watch. People invented the expression "of the clock" or "o'clock" to refer to this new way to tell the time.

(C) These clocks were decorative, but not always useful. This was because towns, provinces, and even neighboring villages had different ways to tell the time. Travelers had to reset their clocks repeatedly when they moved from one place to another. In the United States, there were about 70 different time zones in the 1860s.

① (A) − (B) − (C)

② (B) − (A) − (C)

③ (B) − (C) − (A)

④ (C) − (A) − (B)

19 주어진 문장이 들어갈 위치로 가장 적절한 것은?

But there is also clear evidence that millennials, born between 1981 and 1996, are saving more aggressively for retirement than Generation X did at the same ages, 22 ~ 37.

Millennials are often labeled the poorest, most financially burdened generation in modern times. Many of them graduated from college into one of the worst labor markets the United States has ever seen, with a staggering load of student debt to boot. ① Not surprisingly, millennials have accumulated less wealth than Generation X did at a similar stage in life, primarily because fewer of them own homes. ② But newly available data providing the most detailed picture to date about what Americans of different generations save complicates that assessment. ③ Yes, Gen Xers, those born between 1965 and 1980, have a higher net worth. ④ And that might put them in better financial shape than many assume.

20 다음 글의 내용과 일치하지 않는 것은?

Carbonate sands, which accumulate over thousands of years from the breakdown of coral and other reef organisms, are the building material for the frameworks of coral reefs. But these sands are sensitive to the chemical make-up of sea water. As oceans absorb carbon dioxide, they acidify—and at a certain point, carbonate sands simply start to dissolve. The world's oceans have absorbed around one-third of human-emitted carbon dioxide. The rate at which the sands dissolve was strongly related to the acidity of the overlying seawater, and was ten times more sensitive than coral growth to ocean acidification. In other words, ocean acidification will impact the dissolution of coral reef sands more than the growth of corals. This probably reflects the corals' ability to modify their environment and partially adjust to ocean acidification, whereas the dissolution of sands is a geochemical process that cannot adapt.

① The frameworks of coral reefs are made of carbonate sands.

② Corals are capable of partially adjusting to ocean acidification.

③ Human-emitted carbon dioxide has contributed to the world's ocean acidification.

④ Ocean acidification affects the growth of corals more than the dissolution of coral reef sands.

1 빈칸에 들어갈 말로 가장 적절한 것은?

> _____ occurs when a foreign object lodges in the throat, blocking the flow of air. In adults, a piece of food often is the cause. Young children often swallow small objects.

① Sore throat

② Heart attack

③ Choking

④ Food poisoning

2 빈칸에 들어갈 말로 가장 적절한 것은?

> Always watch children closely when they're in or near any water, no matter what their swimming skills are. Even kids who know how to swim can be at risk for drowning. For instance, a child could slip and fall on the pool deck, lose consciousness, and fall into the pool and possibly drown. _____ is the rule number one for water safety.

① Superstition

② Foundation

③ Collision

④ Supervision

3 밑줄 친 부분의 뜻으로 가장 적절한 것은?

A : 119, what is your emergency?
B : There is a car accident.
A : Where are you?
B : I'm not sure. I'm somewhere on Hamilton Road.
A : Can you see if anyone is hurt?
B : One of the drivers is lying on the ground unconscious and the other one is bleeding.
A : Sir, I need you to stay on the line. I'm sending an ambulance right now.
B : Okay, but hurry!

① 전화 끊지 말고 기다려 주세요.
② 차선 밖에서 기다려 주세요.
③ 전화번호를 알려 주세요.
④ 차례를 기다려 주세요.

4 밑줄 친 부분이 가리키는 대상이 나머지 셋과 다른 것은?

The London Fire Brigade rushed to the scene and firefighters were containing the incident when an elderly man approached the cordon. ①He told one of the crew that he used to be a fireman himself, as a member of the Auxiliary Fire Service in London during World War II. Now 93 years old, ②he still remembered fighting fires during the Blitz – a period when London was bombed for 57 nights in a row. ③He asked the officer if he could do anything to help. The officer found himself not ready for a proper response at that moment and ④he just helped him through the cordon. Later, he invited him to his fire station for tea and to share his stories with him.

5 밑줄 친 They(they)/their가 가리키는 대상으로 가장 적절한 것은?

> <u>They</u> monitor the building for the presence of fire, producing audible and visual signals if fire is detected. A control unit receives inputs from all fire detection devices, automatic or manual, and activates the corresponding notification systems. In addition, <u>they</u> can be used to initiate the adequate response measures when fire is detected. It is important to note that <u>their</u> requirements change significantly depending on the occupancy classification of the building in question. Following the right set of requirements is the first step for a code-compliant design.

① fire alarm systems
② fire sprinklers
③ standpipes
④ smoke control systems

6 다음 글에서 필자가 주장하는 바로 가장 적절한 것은?

> Judge Nicholas in Brooklyn supplied much-needed shock treatment by preventing New York City from hiring firefighters based on a test that discriminated against black and Hispanic applicants. At the time, only 2.9 percent of firefighters were black, even though the city itself was 27 percent black. One of the biggest obstacles to fairness has been a poorly designed screening test measuring abstract reasoning skills that have little to do with job performance. So it is time to design and develop a new test that truthfully reflects skills and personality characteristics that are important to the firefighter's job. It would be fairer if it is more closely tied to the business of firefighting and ensures all the candidates who are eligible to be hired can serve as firefighters, no matter whether they are blacks or not.

① 신속한 소방 활동을 위해 더 많은 소방관을 채용해야 한다.
② 소방관 채용에서 백인에 대한 역차별 문제를 해소해야 한다.
③ 소방관의 직무와 직결된 공정한 소방관 선발 시험을 개발해야 한다.
④ 소방관 선발 시험을 고차원적 사고 기능 중심으로 출제해야 한다.

7 다음 글의 주제로 가장 적절한 것은?

Weather plays a big part in determining how far and how fast a forest fire will spread. In periods of drought, more forest fires occur because the grass and plants are dry. The wind also contributes to the spread of a forest fire. The outdoor temperature and amount of humidity in the air also play a part in controlling a forest fire. Fuel, oxygen and a heat source must be present for a fire to burn. The amount of fuel determines how long and fast a forest fire can burn. Many large trees, bushes, pine needles and grass abound in a forest for fuel. Flash fires occur in dried grass, bushes and small branches. They can catch fire quickly and then ignite the much heavier fuels in large trees.

① 산불 확대 요인
② 다양한 화재 유형
③ 신속한 산불 진압 방법
④ 산불 예방을 위한 주의사항

8 다음 글의 요지로 가장 적절한 것은?

Perhaps every person on Earth has at least once been in a situation when he or she has an urgent task to do, but instead of challenging it head on, he or she postpones working on this task for as long as possible. The phenomenon described here is called procrastination. Unlike many people got used to believing, procrastination is not laziness, but rather a psychological mechanism to slow you down and give you enough time to sort out your priorities, gather information before making an important decision, or finding proper words to recover relationship with another person. Thus, instead of blaming yourself for procrastinating, you might want to embrace it − at least sometimes.

① Stop delaying work and increase your efficiency.
② Procrastination is not a bad thing you have to worry about.
③ Challenge can help you fix a relationship with another person.
④ Categorize your priorities before making an important decision.

9 다음 글에서 전체 흐름과 관계없는 문장은?

Social media is some websites and applications that support people to communicate or to participate in social networking. ①That is, any website that allows social interaction is considered as social media. ②We are familiar with almost all social media networking sites such as Facebook, Twitter, etc. ③It makes us easy to communicate with the social world. ④It becomes a dangerous medium capable of great damage if we handled it carelessly. We feel we are instantly connecting with people around us that we may not have spoken to in many years.

10 빈칸 (A)와 (B)에 들어갈 말로 가장 적절한 것은?

At one time, all small retail businesses, such as restaurants, shoe stores, and grocery stores, were owned by individuals. They often gave the stores their own names such as Lucy's Coffee Shop. For some people, owning a business fulfilled a lifelong dream of independent ownership. For others, it continued a family business that dated back several generations. These businesses used to line the streets of cities and small towns everywhere. Today, _____(A)_____, the small independent shops in some countries are almost all gone, and big chain stores have moved in to replace them. Most small independent businesses couldn't compete with the giant chains and eventually failed. _____(B)_____, many owners didn't abandon retail sales altogether. They became small business owners once again through franchises.

	(A)	(B)
①	in contrast	However
②	in addition	Furthermore
③	in contrast	Therefore
④	in addition	Nevertheless

11 밑줄 친 부분과 의미가 가장 가까운 것은?

> Predicting natural disasters like earthquakes in advance is an <u>imprecise</u> science because the available data is limited.

① accurate

② inexact

③ implicit

④ integrated

12 밑줄 친 부분과 의미가 가장 가까운 것은?

> The rapid spread of fire and the smoke rising from the balcony made a terrible reminder of the Lacrosse building fire in Melbourne in 2014. It also reminds us of the Grenfell Tower inferno in London. This catastrophe took the lives of 72 people and <u>devastated</u> the lives of more people.

① derived

② deployed

③ deviated

④ destroyed

13 빈칸에 들어갈 말로 가장 적절한 것은?

> Firefighters are people whose job is to put out fires and _____ people. Besides fires, firefighters save people and animals from car wrecks, collapsed buildings, stuck elevators and many other emergencies.

① endanger

② imperil

③ rescue

④ recommend

14 빈칸에 들어갈 말로 가장 적절한 것은?

A well known speaker started off his seminar by holding up a $20 bill. In the room of 200, he asked, "Who would like this $20 bill?" Hands started going up. He said, "I am going to give this $20 to one of you but first, let me do this." He proceeded to crumple the dollar bill up. He then asked, "Who still wants it?" Still the hands were up in the air. "My friends, no matter what I did to the money, you still wanted it because it did not decrease in value. It was still worth $20. Many times in our lives, we are dropped, crumpled, and ground into the dirt by the decisions we make and the circumstances that come our way. We feel as though we are worthless. But no matter what has happened or what will happen, you will never _____. You are special. Don't ever forget it."

① lose your value
② suffer injury
③ raise your worth
④ forget your past

15 주어진 글 다음에 이어질 글의 순서로 가장 적절한 것은?

In World War II, Japan joined forces with Germany and Italy. So there were now two fronts, the European battle zone and the islands in the Pacific Ocean.

(A) Three days later, the United States dropped bombs on another city of Nagasaki. Japan soon surrendered, and World War II finally ended.

(B) In late 1941, the United States, Britain and France participated in a fight against Germany and Japan; the U.S. troops were sent to both battlefronts.

(C) At 8:15 a.m. on August 6, 1945, a U.S. military plane dropped an atomic bomb over Hiroshima, Japan. In an instant, 80,000 people were killed. Hiroshima simply ceased to exist. The people at the center of the explosion evaporated. All that remained was their charred shadows on the walls of buildings.

① (A) − (B) − (C)
② (B) − (A) − (C)
③ (B) − (C) − (A)
④ (C) − (A) − (B)

16 주어진 글 다음에 이어질 글의 순서로 가장 적절한 것은?

> Trivial things such as air conditioners or coolers with fresh water, flexible schedules and good relationships with colleagues, as well as many other factors, impact employees' productivity and quality of work.

> (A) At the same time, there are many bosses who not only manage to maintain their staff's productivity at high levels, but also treat them nicely and are pleasant to work with.
>
> (B) In this regard, one of the most important factors is the manager, or the boss, who directs the working process.
>
> (C) It is not a secret that bosses are often a category of people difficult to deal with: many of them are unfairly demanding, prone to shifting their responsibilities to other workers, and so on.

① (A) — (B) — (C)　　　　　② (B) — (A) — (C)

③ (B) — (C) — (A)　　　　　④ (C) — (B) — (A)

17 밑줄 친 부분 중 어법상 틀린 것은?

> Australia is burning, ① being ravaged by the worst bushfire season the country has seen in decades. So far, a total of 23 people have died nationwide from the blazes. The deadly wildfires, ② that have been raging since September, have already burned about 5 million hectares of land and destroyed more than 1,500 homes. State and federal authorities have deployed 3,000 army reservists to contain the blaze, but are ③ struggling, even with firefighting assistance from other countries, including Canada. Fanning the flames are persistent heat and drought, with many pointing to climate change ④ as a key factor for the intensity of this year's natural disasters.

18 밑줄 친 부분 중 어법상 틀린 것은?

It can be difficult in the mornings, especially on cold or rainy days. The blankets are just too warm and comfortable. And we aren't usually ①excited about going to class or the office. Here are ②a few tricks to make waking up early, easier. First of all, you have to make a definite decision to get up early. Next, set your alarm for an hour earlier than you need to. This way, you can relax in the morning instead of rushing around. Finally, one of the main reasons we don't want to get out of bed in the morning ③are that we don't sleep well during the night. That's ④why we don't wake up well-rested. Make sure to keep your room as dark as possible. Night lights, digital clocks, and cell phone power lights can all prevent good rest.

19 빈칸에 들어갈 말로 가장 적절한 것은?

Thunberg, 16, has become the voice of young people around the world who are protesting climate change and demanding that governments around the world _____. In August 2018, Thunberg decided to go on strike from school and protest in front of the Swedish parliament buildings. She wanted to pressure the government to do something more specific to reduce greenhouse gases and fight global warming. People began to join Thunberg in her protest. As the group got larger, she decided to continue the protests every Friday until the government met its goals for reducing greenhouse gases. The protests became known as Fridays for Future. Since Thunberg began her protests, more than 60 countries have promised to eliminate their carbon footprints by 2050.

① fear the people
② give free speech
③ save more money
④ take more action

20 다음 글의 내용과 일치하지 않는 것은?

Dear Sales Associates,

The most recent edition of The Brooktown Weekly ran our advertisement with a misprint. It listed the end of our half-price sale as December 11 instead of December 1. While a correction will appear in the paper's next issue, it is to be expected that not all of our customers will be aware of the error. Therefore, if shoppers ask between December 2 and 11 about the sale, first apologize for the inconvenience and then offer them a coupon for 10% off any item they wish to purchase, either in the store or online.

Thank you for your assistance in this matter.
General Manger

① The Brooktown Weekly에 잘못 인쇄된 광고가 실렸다.
② 반값 할인 행사 마감일은 12월 1일이 아닌 12월 11일이다.
③ 다음 호에 정정된 내용이 게재될 예정이다.
④ 10% 할인 쿠폰은 구매하고자 하는 모든 품목에 적용된다.

☞ 정답 및 해설 P.182

※ 밑줄 친 부분의 의미와 가장 가까운 것을 고르시오. 【1~4】

1

Extensive lists of microwave oven models and styles along with candid customer reviews and price ranges are available at appliance comparison websites.

① frank

② logical

③ implicit

④ passionate

2

It had been known for a long time that Yellowstone was volcanic in nature and the one thing about volcanoes is that they are generally conspicuous.

① passive

② vaporous

③ dangerous

④ noticeable

3

He's the best person to tell you how to get there because he knows the city inside out.

① eventually

② culturally

③ thoroughly

④ tentatively

4

All along the route were thousands of homespun attempts to <u>pay tribute to</u> the team, including messages etched in cardboard, snow and construction paper.

① honor   ② compose

③ publicize   ④ join

5 어법상 옳은 것은?

① The traffic of a big city is busier than those of a small city.

② I'll think of you when I'll be lying on the beach next week.

③ Raisins were once an expensive food, and only the wealth ate them.

④ The intensity of a color is related to how much gray the color contains.

6 우리말을 영어로 가장 잘 옮긴 것은?

① 몇 가지 문제가 새로운 회원들 때문에 생겼다.
  →Several problems have raised due to the new members.

② 그 위원회는 그 건물의 건설을 중단하라고 명했다.
  →The committee commanded that construction of the building cease.

③ 그들은 한 시간에 40마일이 넘는 바람과 싸워야 했다.
  →They had to fight against winds that will blow over 40 miles an hour.

④ 거의 모든 식물의 씨앗은 혹독한 날씨에도 살아남는다.
  →The seeds of most plants are survived by harsh weather.

7 우리말을 영어로 잘못 옮긴 것은?

① 인간은 환경에 자신을 빨리 적응시킨다.

→ Human beings quickly adapt themselves to the environment.

② 그녀는 그 사고 때문에 그녀의 목표를 포기할 수밖에 없었다.

→ She had no choice but to give up her goal because of the accident.

③ 그 회사는 그가 부회장으로 승진하는 것을 금했다.

→ The company prohibited him from promoting to vice-president.

④ 그 장난감 자동차를 조립하고 분리하는 것은 쉽다.

→ It is easy to assemble and take apart the toy car.

8 다음 글의 요지로 가장 적절한 것은?

Listening to somebody else's ideas is the one way to know whether the story you believe about the world — as well as about yourself and your place in it — remains intact. We all need to examine our beliefs, air them out and let them breathe. Hearing what other people have to say, especially about concepts we regard as foundational, is like opening a window in our minds and in our hearts. Speaking up is important. Yet to speak up without listening is like banging pots and pans together: even if it gets you attention, it's not going to get you respect. There are three prerequisites for conversation to be meaningful: 1. You have to know what you're talking about, meaning that you have an original point and are not echoing a worn-out, hand-me-down or pre-fab argument; 2. You respect the people with whom you're speaking and are authentically willing to treat them courteously even if you disagree with their positions; 3. You have to be both smart and informed enough to listen to what the opposition says while handling your own perspective on the topic with uninterrupted good humor and discernment.

① We should be more determined to persuade others.

② We need to listen and speak up in order to communicate well.

③ We are reluctant to change our beliefs about the world we see.

④ We hear only what we choose and attempt to ignore different opinions.

9 다음 글의 제목으로 가장 적절한 것은?

The future may be uncertain, but some things are undeniable: climate change, shifting demographics, geopolitics. The only guarantee is that there will be changes, both wonderful and terrible. It's worth considering how artists will respond to these changes, as well as what purpose art serves, now and in the future. Reports suggest that by 2040 the impacts of human-caused climate change will be inescapable, making it the big issue at the centre of art and life in 20 years' time. Artists in the future will wrestle with the possibilities of the post-human and post-Anthropocene – artificial intelligence, human colonies in outer space and potential doom. The identity politics seen in art around the #MeToo and Black Lives Matter movements will grow as environmentalism, border politics and migration come even more sharply into focus. Art will become increasingly diverse and might not 'look like art' as we expect. In the future, once we've become weary of our lives being visible online for all to see and our privacy has been all but lost, anonymity may be more desirable than fame. Instead of thousands, or millions, of likes and followers, we will be starved for authenticity and connection. Art could, in turn, become more collective and experiential, rather than individual.

① What will art look like in the future?

② How will global warming affect our lives?

③ How will artificial intelligence influence the environment?

④ What changes will be made because of political movements?

10 다음 글의 내용과 일치하지 않는 것은?

The Second Amendment of the U.S. Constitution states: "A well-regulated Militia, being necessary to the security of a free State, the right of the people to keep and bear Arms, shall not be infringed." Supreme Court rulings, citing this amendment, have upheld the right of states to regulate firearms. However, in a 2008 decision confirming an individual right to keep and bear arms, the court struck down Washington, D.C. laws that banned handguns and required those in the home to be locked or disassembled. A number of gun advocates consider ownership a birthright and an essential part of the nation's heritage. The United States, with less than 5 percent of the world's population, has about 35~50 percent of the world's civilian-owned guns, according to a 2007 report by the Switzerland-based Small Arms Survey. It ranks number one in firearms per capita. The United States also has the highest homicide-by-firearm rate among the world's most developed nations. But many gun-rights proponents say these statistics do not indicate a cause-and-effect relationship and note that the rates of gun homicide and other gun crimes in the United States have dropped since highs in the early 1990's.

① In 2008, the U.S. Supreme Court overturned Washington, D.C. laws banning handguns.

② Many gun advocates claim that owning guns is a natural-born right.

③ Among the most developed nations, the U.S. has the highest rate of gun homicides.

④ Gun crimes in the U.S. have steadily increased over the last three decades.

11 두 사람의 대화 중 가장 어색한 것은?

① A : When is the payment due?

　 B : You have to pay by next week.

② A : Should I check this baggage in?

　 B : No, it's small enough to take on the plane.

③ A : When and where shall we meet?

　 B : I'll pick you up at your office at 8 : 30.

④ A : I won the prize in a cooking contest.

　 B : I couldn't have done it without you.

12 밑줄 친 부분에 들어갈 말로 가장 적절한 것은?

A : Thank you for calling the Royal Point Hotel Reservations Department. My name is Sam. How may I help you?

B : Hello, I'd like to book a room.

A : We offer two room types: the deluxe room and the luxury suite.

B : _____?

A : For one, the suite is very large. In addition to a bedroom, it has a kitchen, living room and dining room.

B : It sounds expensive.

A : Well, it's $ 200 more per night.

B : In that case, I'll go with the deluxe room.

① Do you need anything else

② May I have the room number

③ What's the difference between them

④ Are pets allowed in the rooms

13 밑줄 친 (A), (B)에 들어갈 말로 가장 적절한 것은?

Advocates of homeschooling believe that children learn better when they are in a secure, loving environment. Many psychologists see the home as the most natural learning environment, and originally the home was the classroom, long before schools were established. Parents who homeschool argue that they can monitor their children's education and give them the attention that is lacking in a traditional school setting. Students can also pick and choose what to study and when to study, thus enabling them to learn at their own pace.   (A)   , critics of homeschooling say that children who are not in the classroom miss out on learning important social skills because they have little interaction with their peers. Several studies, though, have shown that the home—educated children appear to do just as well in terms of social and emotional development as other students, having spent more time in the comfort and security of their home, with guidance from parents who care about their welfare.   (B) , many critics of homeschooling have raised concerns about the ability of parents to teach their kids effectively.

	(A)	(B)
①	Therefore	Nevertheless
②	In contrast	In spite of this
③	Therefore	Contrary to that
④	In contrast	Furthermore

14 다음 글의 주제로 가장 적절한 것은?

For many people, work has become an obsession. It has caused burnout, unhappiness and gender inequity, as people struggle to find time for children or passions or pets or any sort of life besides what they do for a paycheck. But increasingly, younger workers are pushing back. More of them expect and demand flexibility—paid leave for a new baby, say, and generous vacation time, along with daily things, like the ability to work remotely, come in late or leave early, or make time for exercise or meditation. The rest of their lives happens on their phones, not tied to a certain place or time—why should work be any different?

① ways to increase your paycheck

② obsession for reducing inequity

③ increasing call for flexibility at work

④ advantages of a life with long vacations

15 주어진 글 다음에 이어질 글의 순서로 가장 적절한 것은?

Past research has shown that experiencing frequent psychological stress can be a significant risk factor for cardiovascular disease, a condition that affects almost half of those aged 20 years and older in the United States.

(A) Does this mean, though, that people who drive on a daily basis are set to develop heart problems, or is there a simple way of easing the stress of driving?

(B) According to a new study, there is. The researchers noted that listening to music while driving helps relieve the stress that affects heart health.

(C) One source of frequent stress is driving, either due to the stressors associated with heavy traffic or the anxiety that often accompanies inexperienced drivers.

① (A) – (C) – (B)　　　　　② (B) – (A) – (C)

③ (C) – (A) – (B)　　　　　④ (C) – (B) – (A)

16 다음 글의 흐름상 가장 어색한 문장은?

When the brain perceives a threat in the immediate surroundings, it initiates a complex string of events in the body. It sends electrical messages to various glands, organs that release chemical hormones into the bloodstream. Blood quickly carries these hormones to other organs that are then prompted to do various things. ①The adrenal glands above the kidneys, for example, pump out adrenaline, the body's stress hormone. ②Adrenaline travels all over the body doing things such as widening the eyes to be on the lookout for signs of danger, pumping the heart faster to keep blood and extra hormones flowing, and tensing the skeletal muscles so they are ready to lash out at or run from the threat. ③The whole process is called the fight-or-flight response, because it prepares the body to either battle or run for its life. ④Humans consciously control their glands to regulate the release of various hormones. Once the response is initiated, ignoring it is impossible, because hormones cannot be reasoned with.

17 주어진 문장이 들어갈 위치로 가장 적절한 것은?

It was then he remembered his experience with the glass flask, and just as quickly, he imagined that a special coating might be applied to a glass windshield to keep it from shattering.

In 1903 the French chemist, Edouard Benedictus, dropped a glass flask one day on a hard floor and broke it. (①) However, to the astonishment of the chemist, the flask did not shatter, but still retained most of its original shape. (②) When he examined the flask he found that it contained a film coating inside, a residue remaining from a solution of collodion that the flask had contained. (③) He made a note of this unusual phenomenon, but thought no more of it until several weeks later when he read stories in the newspapers about people in automobile accidents who were badly hurt by flying windshield glass. (④) Not long thereafter, he succeeded in producing the world's first sheet of safety glass.

18 다음 글의 내용과 일치하지 않는 것은?

Dubrovnik, Croatia, is a mess. Because its main attraction is its seaside Old Town surrounded by 80-foot medieval walls, this Dalmatian Coast town does not absorb visitors very well. And when cruise ships are docked here, a legion of tourists turn Old Town into a miasma of tank-top-clad tourists marching down the town's limestone-blanketed streets. Yes, the city of Dubrovnik has been proactive in trying to curb cruise ship tourism, but nothing will save Old Town from the perpetual swarm of tourists. To make matters worse, the lure of making extra money has inspired many homeowners in Old Town to turn over their places to Airbnb, making the walled portion of town one giant hotel. You want an "authentic" Dubrovnik experience in Old Town, just like a local? You're not going to find it here. Ever.

① Old Town은 80피트 중세 시대 벽으로 둘러싸여 있다.

② 크루즈 배가 정박할 때면 많은 여행객이 Old Town 거리를 활보한다.

③ Dubrovnik 시는 크루즈 여행을 확대하려고 노력해 왔다.

④ Old Town에서는 많은 집이 여행객 숙소로 바뀌었다.

19 밑줄 친 (A), (B)에 들어갈 말로 가장 적절한 것은?

When an organism is alive, it takes in carbon dioxide from the air around it. Most of that carbon dioxide is made of carbon-12, but a tiny portion consists of carbon-14. So the living organism always contains a very small amount of radioactive carbon, carbon-14. A detector next to the living organism would record radiation given off by the carbon-14 in the organism. When the organism dies, it no longer takes in carbon dioxide. No new carbon-14 is added, and the old carbon-14 slowly decays into nitrogen. The amount of carbon-14 slowly _____(A)_____ as time goes on. Over time, less and less radiation from carbon-14 is produced. The amount of carbon-14 radiation detected for an organism is a measure, therefore, of how long the organism has been _____(B)_____. This method of determining the age of an organism is called carbon-14 dating. The decay of carbon-14 allows archaeologists to find the age of once-living materials. Measuring the amount of radiation remaining indicates the approximate age.

	(A)	(B)
①	decreases	dead
②	increases	alive
③	decreases	productive
④	increases	inactive

20 밑줄 친 부분에 들어갈 말로 가장 적절한 것은?

All creatures, past and present, either have gone or will go extinct. Yet, as each species vanished over the past 3.8-billion-year history of life on Earth, new ones inevitably appeared to replace them or to exploit newly emerging resources. From only a few very simple organisms, a great number of complex, multicellular forms evolved over this immense period. The origin of new species, which the nineteenth-century English naturalist Charles Darwin once referred to as "the mystery of mysteries," is the natural process of speciation responsible for generating this remarkable _____ with whom humans share the planet. Although taxonomists presently recognize some 1.5 million living species, the actual number is possibly closer to 10 million. Recognizing the biological status of this multitude requires a clear understanding of what constitutes a species, which is no easy task given that evolutionary biologists have yet to agree on a universally acceptable definition.

① technique of biologists

② diversity of living creatures

③ inventory of extinct organisms

④ collection of endangered species

☞ 정답 및 해설 P.188

1 다음 밑줄 친 부분의 의미와 가장 가까운 단어는?

> At present, in the most civilized countries, freedom of speech is taken as a matter of course and seems a perfectly simple thing. We are so accustomed to it that we look on it as a natural right. But this right has been acquired only in quite recent times, and the way to its <u>attainment</u> has lain through lakes of blood.

① procurement

② suppliance

③ requirement

④ process

⑤ delinquency

2 다음 밑줄 친 부분 중 어법상 옳지 않은 것은?

> Nanoscientists ①<u>have found</u> that, when ②<u>reducing to their smallest</u> size, certain elements (like silver, gold, and pencil lead) take on superpowers: super-efficient conductivity, super-sensitive poison detection, total odor eradication, ③<u>slaying the DNA of</u> bacteria, and making electricity from any wavelength of light. If you add a super-material ④<u>that detects</u> poisons to an ordinary material, let's say plastic wrap, you've created a new material — "smart plastic wrap," ⑤<u>capable of identifying</u> spoiled food and providing an alert with a change in the labels' color.

3 다음 밑줄 친 부분 중 어법상 옳지 않은 것은?

When we start to lift weights, our muscles do not strengthen and change at first, but our nervous systems ①do, according to a fascinating new study in animals of the cellular effects of resistance training. The study, ②that involved monkeys performing the equivalent of multiple one-armed pull-ups, suggests ③that strength training is more physiologically intricate than most of us might have imagined and ④that our conception of ⑤what constitutes strength might be too narrow.

4 다음 빈칸에 들어갈 가장 적절한 단어는?

Frank McCourt's childhood was filled with misery. There was never enough food. Their house was small, dirty, and very cold in the winter. When it rained, the floor would flood with water. Frank and his brothers yearned for a better life. Frank did, however, have ways to escape from his tormented childhood. He loved to read, and because his _____ house had no electricity, he would read under the street lamp outside his home.

① decumbent ② unraveled

③ scribbled ④ succinct

⑤ dilapidated

5 다음 빈칸에 들어갈 가장 적절한 단어는?

Prospective studies of lifetimes have often shown that some theories of alcoholism were incorrect because they confused cause with _____. For example, on the basis of current evidence, alcoholism is seen to be associated with but not caused by growing up in a household with alcoholic parents. Likewise, alcoholism is associated with but not usually caused (in men, at least) by depression, and alcoholism is associated with but not caused by self-indulgence, poverty, or neglect in childhood. Rather, alcoholism in individuals often leads to depression and anxiety; indeed, self-medication with alcohol makes depression worse, not better.

① evidence 　　　　　　② alcoholism

③ depression 　　　　　④ association

⑤ self-medication

6 다음 빈칸에 들어갈 가장 적절한 표현은?

When important events are happening around the world, most people _____ traditional media sources, such as CNN and BBC, for their news. However, during the invasion of Iraq by the United States and its allies in early 2003, a significant number of people followed the war from the point of view of an anonymous Iraqi citizen who called himself "Salam Pax."

① turn out 　　　　　　② turn to

③ turn into 　　　　　　④ turn over

⑤ turn out of

7 다음 밑줄 친 (A)와 (B)에 들어갈 가장 적절한 표현은?

More and more people and communities are changing their habits in order to protect the environment. One reason for this change is that space in landfills is running out and the disposal of waste has become difficult. _____(A)_____, the practices of recycling, reusing, and reducing waste are becoming more commonplace. In some countries the technology for disposing of, or getting rid of, waste has actually become big business. Individuals have also taken actions to reduce landfill waste; for example, people are recycling newspapers and donating clothes to charities. _____(B)_____, some people take leftover food and turn it into rich garden compost, an excellent fertilizer for vegetable and flower gardens.

	(A)	(B)
①	As a result	In addition
②	However	In general
③	Incidentally	Overall
④	Consequently	For instance
⑤	Accordingly	Particularly

8 다음 빈칸에 들어갈 가장 적절한 단어는?

The American Founders preferred the term "republic" to "democracy" because it described a system they generally preferred: the interests of the peoples were represented by more knowledgeable or wealthier citizens who were responsible to those that elected them. Today we tend to use the terms "republic" and "democracy" interchangeably. A widespread criticism of representative democracy is that the representatives become the "elites" that seldom consult ordinary citizens, so even though they are elected, a truly _____ government doesn't really exist.

① sincere   ② responsible

③ universal   ④ representative

⑤ perpetual

9 글의 흐름으로 보아, 주어진 문장이 들어가기에 가장 적절한 곳은?

This new fad is actually very old; for hundreds of years in India, a woman's friends have painted her to celebrate her wedding day.

A popular fad for many teenagers is tattooing. ① Parents are usually horrified by these permanent designs on their children's skin, but the young people see them as a fashion statement. ② In the new millennium, some parents are greatly relieved when their teenage children turn to a new fad, a temporary form of decorating the hands, feet, neck, or legs—a method of painting beautiful designs that last only about three weeks. ③ Another fad from India, however, causes parents more worry—bidis. Children and young teens are attracted to these thin cigarettes in candy flavors such as orange, chocolate, mango, and raspberry. The problem? Bidis contain more nicotine than regular cigarettes. ④ Unfortunately, many children think these are "cool"—fashionable. ⑤ So until a new fad comes along, "Indian style is hot," as one radio commentator observed.

10 다음 밑줄 친 (A)와 (B)에 들어갈 가장 적절한 단어는?

We need to think harder about narrowing the gap between those at the bottom and the top. If most people, especially lower-income individuals and minorities, keep the bulk of their wealth in housing, we should rethink lending practices and allow for a broader range of credit metrics (which tend to be biased toward whites) and lower down payments for good borrowers. Rethinking our retirement policies is crucial too. Retirement incentives work mainly for whites and the rich. Minority and poor households are less likely to have access to workplace retirement plans, in part because many work in less formal sectors like restaurants and child care. Another overdue fix: we should expand Social Security by lifting the cap on payroll taxes so the rich can contribute the same share of their income as everyone else. Doing   (A)   would be a good first step. But going forward, economic and racial fairness can no longer be thought of as   (B)   issues.

	(A)	(B)
①	neither	divided
②	both	equality
③	either	social
④	neither	income
⑤	both	separate

11 다음 밑줄 친 부분 중 어법상 옳지 않은 것은?

Not all people ①who have heart attacks have the same symptoms or have the same severity of symptoms. Some people have mild pain; ②others have more severe pain. Some people have no symptoms. For others, the first sign may be sudden cardiac arrest. However, the more signs and symptoms you have, ③the great the chance you are having a heart attack. Some heart attacks strike suddenly, but many people have warning signs and symptoms hours, days or weeks in advance. ④The earliest warning might be recurrent chest pain or pressure (angina) ⑤triggered by activity and relieved by rest. Angina is caused by a temporary decrease in blood flow to the heart.

12 다음 밑줄 친 (A)와 (B)에 들어갈 가장 적절한 표현은?

> If the police had asked for a safety licence for their new flying camera, it ___(A)___ a major crime-fighting success. Unfortunately they didn't, and as a result the young man they filmed stealing a car might go free. "As long as you have a licence, there is no problem using these machines," said a lawyer. "___(B)___ a properly licensed camera, it would have been fine."

	(A)	(B)
①	would have been	Had they used
②	will be	If they used
③	will have been	If they use
④	would be	Have they used
⑤	would have been	Had they been used

13 다음 빈칸에 들어갈 가장 적절한 단어는?

> Beyond that, my fellow citizens, the future is up to us. Our Founders taught us that the _____ of our liberty and our union depends upon responsible citizenship. And we need a new sense of responsibility for a new century. There is work to do, work that government alone cannot do: teaching children to read; hiring people off welfare rolls.

① submission   ② admonition

③ devastation   ④ preservation

⑤ mitigation

14 다음 글에서 제시하는 '정직하지 못한 이메일'의 특징으로 옳지 않은 것은?

A team at Cornell University in New York has developed software aimed at detecting lies in emails and text messages. Traditional lie detectors work by measuring a person's heartbeat. They rely on the fact that a person's pulse gets faster when they are nervous or stressed — a strong indicator that they are not telling the truth. The new software is much more subtle. It scans electronic messages and looks for various clues which indicate lies are being told. Researchers have identified a number of these clues, or 'falsehood indicators', ranging from overuse of the third person to frequent use of negative adjectives and verbs. A team of volunteers provided the researchers with both truthful and dishonest emails. By comparing them they came across a number of characteristics. They noticed, for instance, that truthful emails were usually short and written in the first person, with lots of use of 'I' to start sentences. Dishonest emails were on average 28 percent longer than honest ones because people worry about not sounding convincing, so tend to give more detail when lying. And because liars want people to fall for their stories, they tend to use more sense verbs such as 'see' and 'feel', perhaps in an attempt to gain the reader's sympathy.

① 정직한 이메일보다 평균 28퍼센트 정도 길이가 길다.
② 감각동사를 더 많이 사용하는 경향이 있다.
③ 3인칭 대명사를 과도하게 사용한다.
④ 부정적인 의미의 형용사와 동사를 더 자주 사용한다.
⑤ 자세한 설명은 가급적 회피하려고 한다.

15 다음 밑줄 친 (A), (B), (C)에 들어갈 가장 적절한 표현은?

> William Tell's home was among the mountains, and he was a famous hunter. No one in all the land could shoot with bow and arrow so well as he. Gessler knew this, and so he thought of a cruel plan to make the hunter's own skill _____(A)_____ him to grief. He ordered that Tell's little boy should be made _____(B)_____ up in the public square with an apple on his head; and then he suggested Tell _____(C)_____ the apple with one of his arrows.

	(A)	(B)	(C)
①	to bring	to stand	shot
②	bring	to stand	shoot
③	bring	stand	shot
④	bring	to stand	shot
⑤	to bring	stand	shoot

16 다음 중 글의 흐름과 무관한 문장은?

> Gorkha was a sitting target. Most of the houses in this mountainous district northwest of Nepal's capital, Kathmandu, were made of little more than stone or bricks bonded together with mud. ①That meant they were easily destroyed when tremors from a 7.8-magnitude earthquake rippled across the country just before noon on April 25, killing more than 8,000 people. ②By May 5, when TIME photographer James Nachtwey arrived in the remote village of Barpak, in the northern part of Gorkha, near the epicenter of the quake, "there wasn't much left" standing, he says. ③The tremors "basically shook the structures apart," leaving irregular piles of stone and twisted wooden frames where there were once homes. ④How do you rebuild when the ground beneath your feet could shift at any moment? ⑤Worst of all, there was more to come. After Nachtwey left Nepal, as relief and rescue teams finally spread out across the impoverished Himalayan nation, there was a second seismic blow. On May 12, a 7.3-magnitude quake erupted at the eastern end of the same section of the geological fault that had caused the earlier temblor.

17 글의 흐름으로 보아, 주어진 문장이 들어가기에 가장 적절한 곳은?

In addition, defensive pessimism has proven to be a useful cognitive strategy for some people.

① Pessimists sometimes make better leaders, particularly where there is a need to ignite social change. ② Their skepticism may make them more resistant to propaganda and false advertising. ③ The degree of pessimism felt by an individual or group can often be linked to political and economic conditions in their personal lives and their society. ④ They set their expectations low and then outperform them by preparing thoroughly for a wide range of negative outcomes in advance. ⑤

18 다음 글의 제목으로 가장 적절한 것은?

Throughout Earth's history, several extinction events have taken place. The largest one happened about 250 million years ago and is called the Great Dying. Scientists theorize that a single devastating event killed off most life-forms on Earth. It could have been a series of large asteroid strikes, a massive emission from the seafloor of the greenhouse gas methane, or increased volcanic activity, such as the eruptions that created the Siberian Traps that now cover some 770,000 square miles of Russia. When the mass extinction ended, 57 percent of all animal families and 83 percent of all genera had disappeared from the planet, and it took some 10 million years for life to recover.

① The Earth Affected by Mass Die-offs
② The Greatest Volcanic Eruption
③ The Beginning of Life on Earth
④ Massive Strikes of Meteors on Earth
⑤ The Mass Extinction of Life-forms by Volcanoes

19 다음에 이어질 글의 순서로 적절한 것은?

Reports of the demise of the world's most popular reserve currency were greatly exaggerated.

(A) But here we are, six years after the crisis, and the dollar is showing just how almighty it actually is. The dollar index, which measures its value against other currencies, recently reached a four-year high. And the policymakers who bitterly criticized the dollar show little real interest in dumping it. The amount of U.S. Treasury securities held by China, for instance, stands at $1.27 trillion, 75% more than in 2008.

(B) Ever since the 2008-09 financial crisis, predictions of the dollar's demise have come hand over fist. As the U.S. economy sank into recession, so too did confidence that the greenback could maintain its long-held position as the world's premier reserve currency.

(C) In Beijing, Moscow and elsewhere, policymakers railed against the dollar-dominated global financial system as detrimental to world stability and vowed to find a replacement. Central bankers in the emerging world complained that the primacy of the dollar allowed American economic activity to send shock waves through the global economy, roiling their own markets and currencies.

① (A) − (C) − (B)

② (B) − (A) − (C)

③ (B) − (C) − (A)

④ (C) − (A) − (B)

⑤ (C) − (B) − (A)

20 다음 밑줄 친 부분의 의미와 가장 가까운 단어는?

> The smartphone, through its small size, ease of use, <u>proliferation</u> of free or cheap apps, and constant connectivity, changes our relationship with computers in a way that goes well beyond what we experienced with laptops.

① reduction

② expansion

③ prospect

④ acquisition

⑤ utilization

1 다음 밑줄 친 곳에 들어갈 단어로 가장 적절한 것은?

A police chief argues that surveillance cameras can serve as a _____ to a crime.

① decency

② deterrent

③ delicacy

④ deviation

2 다음 ㉠, ㉡에 공통으로 들어갈 단어로 가장 적절한 것은?

(㉠) : a statement that a person makes, admitting that he or she is guilty of a crime: After a police questioned her for hours, she made a full (㉡).

① confession

② confinement

③ conformity

④ confutation

3 다음 밑줄 친 곳에 공통으로 들어갈 단어로 가장 적절한 것은?

㉠ Scientists _____ a link between diet and cancer.
㉡ It is tempting to _____ Tom with an Athenian painter of the same name.
㉢ Passengers were asked to _____ their own suitcases before they were put on a plane.

① associate

② identify

③ discern

④ recall

4 다음 ㉠, ㉡에 들어갈 말로 가장 적절한 것은?

> • Are there any matters (㉠) from the minutes of the last meeting?
> • A steam locomotive is an (㉡) device developed during the Industrial Revolution.

① ㉠ arising ㉡ ingenious   ② ㉠ arising ㉡ ingenuous

③ ㉠ arousing ㉡ ingenious   ④ ㉠ arousing ㉡ ingenuous

5 〈보기〉에 주어진 단어 중 문맥상 밑줄 친 곳에 들어갈 수 없는 것은?

> 〈보기〉
> ㉠ improvement(s)   ㉡ membership
> ㉢ agreement(s)   ㉣ ownership

> Patents are _____ between inventors and governments, giving inventors _____ of their creations for a certain period of time. U.S. patent law states that an invention is "any new and useful process, machine, manufacture, or composition of matter, or new and useful _____ to them."

① ㉠   ② ㉡

③ ㉢   ④ ㉣

6 다음 중 어법상 가장 적절한 것은?

① I asked Siwoo to borrow me twenty dollars.

② The manager refused to explain us the reason why he cancelled the meeting.

③ If the patient had taken the medicine last night, he would be better today.

④ The criminal suspect objected to give an answer when questioned by the police.

7 다음 각 문장을 유사한 의미의 다른 문장으로 바꾸어 쓰고자 한다. 어법상 가장 적절한 것은?

① He said to me, "Can I use your mobile phone?"

　→He asked me that he could use my mobile phone.

② He drank strong coffee lest he should feel sleepy.

　→He drank strong coffee so that he should feel sleepy.

③ Mt. Everest is the highest mountain in the world.

　→Mt. Everest is higher than any other mountains in the world.

④ I did not miss my wallet and mobile phone until I got home.

　→It was not until I got home that I missed my wallet and mobile phone.

8 다음 밑줄 친 부분 중 어법상 가장 적절하지 않은 것은?

When I first saw the old house, I ㉠had just moved to the area. It had been empty for about a year and ㉡was beginning to need some repairs, but the house was exactly what I wanted. But by the time I ㉢had put together enough money, I learnt that a property developer ㉣bought it and planned to turn it into a hotel.

① ㉠　　　　　　　　　　② ㉡
③ ㉢　　　　　　　　　　④ ㉣

9 다음 우리말을 영작한 것 중 가장 적절한 것은?

① 나는 그에게 충고 한마디를 했다.

　→I gave him an advice.

② 우리가 나가자마자 비가 내리기 시작했다.

　→Scarcely had we gone out before it began to rain.

③ 그녀의 발자국 소리는 서서히 멀어져 갔다.

　→The sound of her footsteps was receded into the distance.

④ 벌과 꽃만큼 서로 밀접하게 연결되어있는 생명체는 거의 없다.

　→Few living things are linked together as intimately than bees and flowers.

10 다음 A, B의 대화 중 가장 적절하지 않은 것은?

① A : Seohee, where are you headed?
　B : I am off to Gyeongju.

② A : Yusoo, let us ride the roller coaster.
　B : It's not my cup of tea.

③ A : It's too expensive. I don't want to get ripped off.
　B : It's water under the bridge.

④ A : Sohyun, have you been behind the steering wheel yet?
　B : No, but I can't wait to get my feet wet.

11 다음 표는 감염병 확산 방지를 위한 경찰의 업무와 세부내용이다. 업무와 세부 내용 사이의 관계가 가장 적절하지 않은 것은?

〈Police tasks in the operational manuals for infectious disease〉

	Tasks	Details
①	Enhancing cooperation with airport and port authorities	More cooperation with residential authorities and sharing of information
②	Sharing and distributing data with local and relevant authorities	Cooperation with the Ministry of Health and Welfare, local governments, collating and relaying information
③	Securing Chain of Command	Access control in quarantine places
④	Strengthening criminal justice	Criminal investigation of illegal activities

12 다음 밑줄 친 곳에 들어갈 단어로 가장 적절한 것은?

Imagine these two scenarios. In the first you learn that you've won a $500 gift certificate from Saks. You would feel pretty good about that, wouldn't you? In the second scenario, you lose your wallet containing $500. How unhappy would you feel about that? According to the results of risk-taking research, the intensities of your responses to these experiences differ markedly. As the result of what scientists refer to as the brain's _____ bias, the distress you're likely to experience as a result of the loss of $500 will greatly exceed the pleasure you feel at winning that gift certificate.

① positivity

② neutrality

③ possibility

④ negativity

13 다음 글의 밑줄 친 부분 중 가리키는 대상이 나머지 셋과 다른 것은?

In every culture, there are topics that are hard to talk about directly. People often speak about these topics using euphemisms. The reason why people use euphemisms is that they can hide unpleasant or disturbing ideas behind ㉠them. So, people don't have to bring up the ideas directly and upset people. However, euphemisms pose an additional burden to people who are learning English as a foreign language. Learners have to learn which expressions are appropriate in different situations. Euphemisms are also problematic for English learners because ㉡they often contain more difficult words than ㉢their more direct counterparts. Learners of English, for instance, have to memorize that an old person can be referred to as "a senior citizen," while a police officer can be described as "a law-enforcement officer." They also have to learn to use euphemisms like "vertically challenged" when ㉣they can get by with " short."

① ㉠

② ㉡

③ ㉢

④ ㉣

14 다음 ㉠, ㉡에 들어갈 말로 가장 적절한 것은?

One point of difference between the consumption of water and electricity is that water can be reused multiple times while electricity cannot. As a result, water can be classified as "consumed" or simply "withdrawn". In the former, water is removed from its source and lost through either evaporation(in the case of power plant cooling or flood irrigation), or transpiration(in the growing of biocrops). Withdrawn water, (㉠), can be returned to its original water source. The argument can be made that all water demand eventually returns as precipitation via the hydrologic cycle and therefore is not "consumed". (㉡), evaporation and precipitation are both spatially and temporally uneven. Water that is accessible, especially in arid and semi-arid regions, satisfies the immediate needs of water users, whereas future precipitation may not occur in the same location or at the desired timing.

① ㉠ on the other hand, ㉡ However
② ㉠ however, ㉡ Thus
③ ㉠ for instance, ㉡ As a result
④ ㉠ as a result, ㉡ For example

15 다음 글의 제목으로 가장 적절한 것은?

In alignment with Sir Robert Peel's Principles, policing has largely evolved with the approval, respect, cooperation, and collaboration of the public. Often referred to as "policing by consent," the police powers have the common consent of the general public rather than being imposed by the various branches of government. A belief in fairness has led to the legitimacy of the police—the general belief by the public that police should be permitted to exercise their authority to manage conflicts, maintain social order, and solve problems in the community. However, in order to maintain police legitimacy, police personnel must strive to be courteous, fair, and respectful when performing their duties. Public satisfaction with policing helps build and maintain community trust and confidence. The legitimacy of the actions of police officers and the agencies that employ them are upheld by valuing the rights of all individuals and the observation of procedural laws.

① Authority and fairness
② Policing and legitimacy
③ Consent and doctrine
④ Trust and relationship

16 다음 글의 흐름으로 보아 〈보기〉의 문장이 들어갈 곳으로 가장 적절한 것은?

〈보기〉

To characterize people by the different things they make, however, is to miss the universality of how they create.

It is easy to look at the diverse things people produce and to describe their differences. ㉠ Obviously a poem is not a mathematical formula, and a novel is not an experiment in genetics. ㉡ Composers clearly use a different language from that of visual artists, and chemists combine very different things than do playwrights. ㉢ For at the level of the creative process, scientists, artists, mathematicians, composers, writers, and sculptors use a common set of what we call "tools for thinking," including emotional feelings, visual images, bodily sensations, reproducible patterns, and analogies. ㉣ And all imaginative thinkers learn to translate ideas generated by these subjective thinking tools into public languages to express their insights, which can then give rise to new ideas in other's minds.

① ㉠

② ㉡

③ ㉢

④ ㉣

17 다음 글의 흐름으로 보아 〈보기〉 문장 뒤에 이어질 글의 순서로 가장 적절한 것은?

〈보기〉

It is easy to see how the automobile industry has created thousands of job opportunities and contributed immeasurably to our higher standard of living, but we are apt to overlook the underlying factor that made all this possible.

㉠ Without them, every single car would have to be laboriously built by hand and their cost would be so great that only the wealthy could pay the price.

㉡ It was more than just an accumulation of invention on newly invented motors, and pneumatic tires, and electrical headlights. Interchangeability and mass-production are the two basic manufacturing techniques that were combined for the first time by the automobile industry and they are the real reasons that the average wage-earner today can afford to own a car.

㉢ But by concentrating a workman's talents on turning out thousands of units all exactly alike and through the use of power and special tools, cars can be and are built by the millions.

① ㉡－㉠－㉢　　　　　　　　　② ㉢－㉠－㉡

③ ㉠－㉡－㉢　　　　　　　　　④ ㉠－㉢－㉡

18 밑줄 친 곳에 들어갈 내용으로 가장 적절한 것은?

Engels believed that nothing existed but matter and that all matter obeys the dialectical laws. But since there is no way of deciding, at any point in time, that this statement is true, the laws that he presupposed are not the same as usual scientific laws. It should be admitted that even in the case of "usual" laws in natural science the stated relationship, as a universal statement, is not subject to absolute proof. One cannot say, for example, that there will never be a case in which _____. But when the violation of such laws does occur, it is, within the limits of measurement, apparent that something remarkable has happened.

① the earth revolves on its axis

② the earth has the force of gravity

③ oxygen is the prerequisite for combustion

④ water fails to boil at 100 degrees centigrade

19 다음 글의 중심 내용을 아래와 같이 요약할 때, 밑줄 친 곳에 들어갈 내용으로 가장 적절한 것은?

Most of our societies are undergoing a process of modernization involving fundamental value changes which often contain many inherent conflicts and contradictions. The process of development, if not managed properly, will mean marginalization of the majority — resulting in poverty, overcrowding, etc. While the more dynamic members of urban society create prosperous real estate enclaves, most of the urban scene is a picture of the under privileged. The dualism is ironic, because the most disadvantaged in society invariably pay the highest price in the urban environment, largely because they have to bear most of the environmental costs. In large cities, there is inevitably an over utilization of marginal areas, sometimes beyond the safe limits and recoverable bearing capacities of the land. Low lying areas, riverbeds, swamps, etc, normally not habitable, become human habitats. Environmentally sensitive areas thus become threatened — resulting in an urban environmental imbalance which may hamper the actual development process itself.

↓

This article states that _____.

① urban areas can damage the environment

② utilization of marginal areas can reduce costs of living

③ modernization can result in the gap between the poor and the rich

④ modernization can keep the balance between urban and rural areas

20 다음 글에서 유추할 수 있는 요지를 아래와 같이 작성할 때, 밑줄 친 곳에 들어갈 내용으로 가장 적절한 것은?

Most people get trapped in their optimistic biases, so they tend to listen to positive feedback and ignore negative feedback. Although this may help them come across as confident to others, in any area of competence (e.g., education, business, sports or performing arts) achievement is 10% performance and 90% preparation. Thus, the more aware you are of your weaknesses, the better prepared you will be. Low self-confidence may turn you into a pessimist, but when pessimism teams up with ambition it often produces outstanding performance. To be the very best at anything, you will need to be your harshest critic, and that is almost impossible when your starting point is high self-confidence. Exceptional achievers always experience low levels of confidence and self-confidence, but they train hard and practice continually until they reach an acceptable level of competence.

↓

We can infer that _____.

① accepting positive feedback will deteriorate competence

② high self-confidence can broaden mindfulness

③ acknowledging weakness will lead you to a pessimist

④ low self-confidence can be the source for success

정답 및 해설

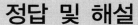

2014. 3. 8.
법원사무직 시행

---

1 ②

단어

highlight : 강조하다, ~을 밝게 비춰 드러내다
walkathon : 장거리 경보
annual : 1년마다, 매 해의, 매년

해석

제목 : 매년 개최되는 리즈 클레이본의 사진 경연대회
스페셜 올림픽의 영향을 받아 올해 주제는 Liz Claiborne사 직원, 그 가족, 친구 사이의 경쟁적이고 자선적인 스포츠 상황들을 조명합니다. 당신은 모금을 위한 걷기대회, 5마일 달리기 또는 회사의 배구·축구 경기에 참가하는 친구나 직원을 찍을 수 있을지도 모릅니다.
모든 전 세계의 Liz Claiborne사 직원들은 사진들을 제출할 것을 권장합니다. 1등, 2등, 3등 상은 전처럼 500달러, 250달러, 100달러입니다.
지금은 당신이 사진 찍기를 할 시간입니다. 경쟁의 정신에 초점 맞춰진 Liz Claiborne사 사람들과 친구들을 위하여!
작년 출품작들의 압도적인 수로 인하여 이번 해에 우리는 한 가지 경연대회의 변화를 만들 것입니다. 더 자세한 정보를 위해서는 내선 7645 로즈마리에게로 전화하세요.

① 스페셜 올림픽 : 시간과 장소
② 매년 개최되는 리즈 클레이본의 사진 경연대회
③ 리즈 클레이본의 향상된 서비스 질
④ 크리스마스에 할 기조연설

2 ④

단어

argumentative : 따지기를 좋아하는, 시비를 거는
aggressive 공격적인
mobilize : 동원하다
set limits to : ~을 제한하다
constructively : 건설적으로
prompt A to B : A가 B 하도록 촉진하다
distress : 괴롭히다
alarm : 불안, 공포

해석

분노는 관계에 문제들을 만든다. 너무 많은 ①그것이 있어서 사람들이 그것을 표현하는 방법을 조절할 수 없을 때, 그리고 예를 들자면 논쟁적, 공격적이거나 폭력적으로 될 때. 사람들이 그들의 분노를 표출하지 못하고 ②그것을 감추려고 노력할 때 그것은 또한 문제들을 야기한다. 하지만 때때로 분노를 느끼는 것은 정상이다. 그리고 유익한 효과를 가질 수 있다. 분노는 행동을 취하도록 당신을 동원할 수 있다. 예를 들어 다른 이들이 당신으로부터 만들어내는 요구들을 제한하도록, 왜 뭔가가 당신에게 문제가 되는지에 대해 생각하도록 또는 공격당하면 스스로를 방어하도록. ③그것은 건설적으로 표현될 수 있고, 당신을 괴롭히거나 불안하게 하는 ④그것이 무엇인지 설명하게 하고 그리고 당신이 필요로 하는 것을 요청하도록 촉구할 수 있다.

TIP

①②③ 분노(anger)
④ (당신을 괴롭히거나 불안하게 하는) 원인
  it은 뒤에 나오는 'that is distressing or alarming you'를 가리킨다.

3 ③

단어

excessive : 지나친, 과도한
awkward : 어색한, 곤란한
unsightly : 보기 흉한
treatment : 대우, 처리, 치료
hair follicle : 모낭
intense : 강렬한
thereafter : 차후, 그 후
originate : 발생하다, 유래하다
clear A of B : A에게서 B를 치우다
armpit : 겨드랑이

해석

당신은 과도한 체모나 혹은 가장 곤란한 부분들에 있는 체모 때문에 당황스럽습니까? 레이저 체모 제거 치료로 당신은 보기 흉하고 원치 않는 체모를 제거할 수 있습니다. 레이저 체모 제거는 몇 분 안에 고통 없이 원치 않는 체모를 제거하기 위해 레이저 빛을 이용하는 안전하고 효과적인 의료 시술입니다. 그 과정 동안, 레이저가 피부를 통과하여 털을 자라게 하는 모낭에 도달합니다. 그 후 그 강렬한 열이 모낭을 즉각적으로 파괴하여 피부에서 어떤 털이라도 제거합니다. 당신의 다리, 겨드랑이, 입술 위쪽, 턱, 비키니 라인 그리고 다른 어떤 부위든 시술 받으세

요. 당신은 마침내 원치 않는 체모로부터 자유로울 수 있습니다. 그러니 더 많은 정보를 위해 오늘 저희 클리닉에 전화주세요.

① 수필　② 소설　③ 광고　④ (신문·잡지) 기사

4 ④

단 어

tolerance : 아량, 관용
crackdown : 단호한 단속
trivial : 하찮은, 사소한
petty : 작은, 사소한
sentence : 선고, 형벌
offence : 범죄, 위법행위
shoplifting : 들치기(상점에서 물건을 훔치는 것)
vandalism : 파손
innovative : 혁신적인
deterrent : 제지하는 것, 억제력

해 석

'무관용'은 사소한 범죄에 대한 엄중 단속의 묘사로 처음 알려진 관용구이다. 무관용의 목적은 경범죄자가 심각한 범죄로 나아가는 것을 예방하는 데에 있다. 미성년자 음주, 소량의 마약사용과 거래, 상점 도둑질이나 기물파손과 같은 작은 범죄들에 대해 즉각적이고 혹독한 형벌을 부과함으로써. 나는 '무관용'이 범죄들에 대항하는 혁신적이고 효과적인 무기라고 생각한다. 그것은 국가가 부드럽고 '이해'하는 모습보다는 비난하고 처벌할 거라는 분명하고 거친 메시지를 보낸다. 이 입장은 잠재적인 범죄자들, 특히 잠재적인 어린 범죄자들에게 효과적인 억제력으로써 작용한다. 그리고 또한 경찰과 사법 제도에 있어서 대중의 신뢰를 높인다.

5 ④

단 어

across the nation : 전국적으로
be involved in : ~에 관계되다, 개입되다
independence : 독립
conflict : 갈등, 분쟁
abandon : 폐기하다, 버리다
intellectual challenged : 지적 장애
orphan : 고아
access : 접속, 접근
limited : 제한적인, 한정된
with a limp : 절룩절룩

해 석

동티모르는 인도네시아로부터 독립을 얻기 위해 30년 이상 전국적으로 분쟁에 연루되어 왔다. 전쟁으로 피폐해진 나라 안에서 지적 장애가 있는 사람들은 종종 잊히고 버려진다. 지적 장애가 있

는 동티모르 출신의 고아 알치노 페레이라는 말을 할 수 없는 사람인데, 건강보험을 이용해 본 적이 없다. 그는 한 쪽 팔을 매우 제한된 방식으로만 사용할 수 있고 절뚝거리면서 걷는다. 이런 지적 그리고 신체적인 장애에도 불구하고 그는 달리기를 좋아한다. 페레이라는 그의 다 닳은 신발을 신고 매일 그의 고향 마을인 딜리에서 달린다. 그래서 그는 "러닝맨"이라는 별명을 얻었다.

TIP

① for more than 30 years(30년 이상)의 기간 동안 개입되어(수동태) 왔으므로 has been involved(현재완료+수동태)의 형태를 취하는 것이 맞다.
② 'war-torn'이 country를 앞에서 수식하여 '전쟁으로 피폐해진 나라'를 표현하고 있다. country가 tear(-tore-torn) 동사의 주체가 아니라 '대상'이 되므로 맞는 표현이다.
③ 관계대명사 who가 이끄는 절이 삽입구(an intellectually challenged orphan from East Timor) 앞에 있는 Alcino Pereira(사람)를 수식하고 있으므로 사람을 지칭하는 관계대명사 'who'가 오는 것이 맞다.
④ although는 접속사이므로 뒤에 절(주어-동사 형태)이 와야 하는데 명사구(these intellectual and physical challenges)가 왔으므로 틀린 문장이다. 명사구를 이끄는 전치사 despite로 고쳐주어야 한다.

6 ①

단 어

instruct : 지시하다
incident : 사건
occasional : 가끔씩, 때때로
concentrate on : ~에 집중하다
bounce : 튀다
aisle : 통로
apologetic : 미안해하는, 사과하는
indifferent : 냉담한, 무관심한
frightened : 깜짝 놀란

해 석

나는 아직도 작년에 생겼던 그 일을 기억한다. 우리는 작은 영화관이 있는 한 시골의 여관에 머물고 있었다. 매일 저녁 상영 전 내 남편과 나는 우리의 세 살배기 아들에게 조용히 앉아 있으라고 지시하였다. 그는 가끔 속삭이는 질문 외에는 조용히 영화에 집중하였다. 하지만 그 소리(사운드트랙)는 들을 수 없는 지경이었다. 왜냐하면 두 명의 아이들이 그들의 자리에서 뛰고 크게 말하며 통로 위·아래로 달리기 경주를 했기 때문이다. 나는 단 한 번도 그들의 부모를 보지 못했다. 이런 몇 번의 저녁 후에 나는 식당까지 그 아이들을 따라갔다. 거기에는 그들의 부모들이 앉아서 느긋한 식사를 즐기고 있었다.

① 약이 오르고 짜증이 난
② 후회하고 미안해하는
③ 냉정하고 무관심한
④ 무서워하고 겁먹은

7 ②

단 어

hinder : 저해하다, 방해하다
stuttering : 말더듬, 구음장애
genetic : 유전의
predisposition : 성향, 경향, (병에 대한) 소인
benign : 유순한
neurological : 신경학상의
inhibit : 억제하다, 저해하다
stroke : 뇌졸중
disproportionate : 불균형의
behavioral disorder : 행동장애
autism : 자폐증
attention deficit disorder : 주의력 결핍 장애
aggravate : 악화시키다

해 석

흔하지만 심각하게 지장을 주는 질병인 말더듬은 누구나 가능하다면 피하고 싶어하는 그 무엇이다. 어떤 사람들은 단순히 말더듬에 대한 유전적인 소양을 가지는데 단지 소수의 요인들만 잘 알려져 있다 하더라도 그것의 원인이 되는 다른 요인들이 있다. 새로운 언어를 배우는 것은 종종 아이들에게 말더듬 증상을 일으킨다. 하지만 이는 오히려 말더듬의 양성 형태이다. 어떤 사람들은 말하기에 관한 올바른 뇌기능들을 저해하는 신경학상의 문제들을 지니고 있다. 이 문제들은 종종 뇌졸중, 사고 또는 어떤 다른 트라우마의 결과이다. 그러나 문제는 극심한 자신감 결여 혹은 불균형한 스트레스의 존재와 같은 심리적인 것일 수도 있다. 또한 자폐증과 주의력 결핍 장애와 같은 행동장애들이 언어 장애로 이어질 수도 있다.

① 말더듬의 일반적 증상들
② 말더듬 상태의 다양한 원인들
③ 말더듬을 악화시키는 요인들
④ 말더듬의 해로운 영향들

8 ①

단 어

incredible : 믿을 수 없을 정도의
take a break : 휴식을 취하다
doorknob : (문의) 손잡이
lid : 뚜껑
jar : 병

해 석

당신은 멈춰서서 당신의 팔 끝에 위치한 두 개의 놀라운 기계들에 대해 생각하는 데에 얼마간의 시간을 보낸 적이 있는가? 당신의 손은 정말 믿어지지 않을 정도이다. 그것들은 종일 일하고 거의 휴식을 취하지 않으면서 좀처럼 지치지도 않는다. 그리고 당신의 손은 튼튼할 뿐만 아니라 다재다능하기도 하다. 그들이 하는 모든 각양각색의 것들을 생각해보라! 그것들은 문을 두드리고 손잡이를 돌린다. 만약 당신이 배가 고프다면 그것들은 쿠키 뚜껑을 연 다음 그 쿠키들을 당신의 입으로 넣을 것이다. 그리고 만약 당신이 컴퓨터 게임에 능숙하다면 그 점에 대해서도 당신은 당신의 손에 고마워할 수 있다. 당신이 무엇을 하고 있든 당신의 손은 당신을 도울 수 있다.

① 다재다능한
② 분명히 실재하는
③ (자격 · 연령 등의 조건이 맞아서) ~을 가질 수 있는
④ 진실한

9 ③

단 어

euphemism : 완곡 어구
counterpart : 대응하는 것
be referred to : ~로 언급되다, 불리다
senior citizen : 어르신, 고령자
vertically challenged : 키가 작은
get by : 지나가다, 그럭저럭 해 나가다
pose : (위협 · 문제를) 제기하다
evolve : 진화하다, 진전하다
handle : 다루다

해 석

완곡 어구들도 또한 영어 학습자들에게 문제적이다. 왜냐하면 그것들은 그것들의 더 직접적인 ①대응어들보다 종종 더 어려운 단어들을 포함하기 때문이다. 예를 들면, 영어 학습자들은 경찰관이 "법 집행자"로 표현될 수 있는 한편, 노인들은 "고령자"로 불릴 수 있음을 기억해야 한다. 또한 그들은 "short(짧은)"이라는 단어로 그럭저럭 표현할 수 있을 때 "②vertically challenged (수직적으로 도전 받는 ─ 키가 작은)"이라는 완곡 어구를 사용하는 것을 배워야 한다. 완곡 어구들이 영어 학습자들에게 제기하는 부담에도 불구하고 완곡 어구들은 우리가 모든 종류의 것들을 ③무례한(→ polite : 예의바른) 방식으로 이야기할 수 있도록 하는 도구들이라는 것은 명확하다. 오래된 완곡 어구들이 점차 사용되지 않고 새로운 것들이 사용 됨에 따라 영어는 유쾌하거나 혹은 불쾌한 모든 상황을 다루도록 항상 ④진보하고 있다.

10 ③

단 어

impatient : 성급한
end up -ing : 결국 ~하게 되다
crash : 폭락하다
fuzzy : (모습, 소리가) 흐릿한, 어렴풋한
nutritionally : 영양상의
bout : 한바탕, 병치레
fatigue : 피곤, 피로함
protein : 단백질
supplement : 보조식품, 보완
rotisserie : 로티세리(고기를 쇠꼬챙이에 끼워 돌려 가며 굽는 기구)
be nothing short of : ~와 다름없다
soundly : 깊이, 곤히
alert : 정신이 초롱초롱한

해 석

Angie는 언제나 불안해했고 성급했다. 그녀는 자주 끼니를 걸렀고 결국 그녀의 혈당이 뚝 떨어질 때만 먹기 위하여 패스트푸드 식당을 통과해 운전하게 되었다. 그러고 나면 그녀는 대개 정신이 몽롱해졌고 낮잠을 자고 싶어했다. 결국 그녀는 그녀의 피로에 대한 병치레 때문에 영양을 중시하는 한 내과의사의 조언을 구했다. 그녀(내과의사)는 더 좋은 식사계획, 더 많은 단백질과 신선한 채소들, 그리고 비타민 B, 마그네슘, F-테아닌을 함유한 보조식품들을 권했다. 더 많은 단백질 섭취에 대한 그녀의 반응은 – 첫 날에 로티세리 치킨과 찐 채소들 – 극적이라 하기에 부족함이 없었다. 몇 개월 뒤에 Angie의 언니는 그녀를 새로운 사람으로 묘사했다–그녀는 더 푹 잤고 정신이 또렷하고 활기찬 기분을 느끼며 일어났다.

11 ④

단 어

restrictive : 제한적인
tropic : 열대 지방
diverse : 다양한
undergo : 겪다
due to : ~ 때문에
gene mutation : 유전자 돌연변이
varied : 다양한
isolation : 고립
predator : 포식자
variation : 변형

해 석

한 새로운 연구에서 열대지방과 같은 제한적인 환경 안에서 사는 종은 더 다양한 환경들 안의 종들만큼 변화하는 기후에 그만큼 잘 적응하지 못한다는 것이 밝혀졌다. 그 원인은 그들의 유전자 내 변형의 결핍이다. 한 종은 신체적 그리고 행동적 변화

들을 겪음으로써 그것의 환경에 적응하고 생존을 더 잘하게 된다. 이러한 일들은 보통 유전자 돌연변이 때문에 일어난다. 만일 한 종이 이미 더 다양한 유전자 세트를 가지고 있다면 그것은 필요한 변화들을 겪을 가능성이 더 많다. 하지만 열대지방 내의 종들은 덜 다양한 유전자 세트를 가진다.

① 파괴된 (자연)환경
② 그들의 서식지로부터의 격리
③ 그들의 포식자로부터의 공격
④ 그들의 유전자 내 변형의 결핍

12 ①

단 어

navigational : 항해의, 비행의
locomotive : 기관차, 이동의
autonomous : 자율적인
flipper : 지느러미발
humpback whale : 혹등고래
aeronautics : 항공학
similarly : 유사하게
ridged : 이랑이 만들어져 있는
friction : 마찰
fuel efficiency : 연료 효율
aerospace : 항공우주
preserve : 보존하다

해 석

과학자들은 차세대 자율 로봇들과 차량들을 설계하는 것을 돕기 위해 곤충들의 비행 시스템들과 이동 전략들을 연구 중이다. 또한 연구원들은 최근에 혹등고래의 지느러미 발이 항공 산업에 의해 항공기들에 사용된 현재의 모델보다 더 효율적인 날개 디자인이라는 것을 알아냈다. 그들은 그들의 조사결과를 미래의 항공기와 자동차의 설계에 적용하기 위해 일하는 중이다. 유사한 경우로, 기술자들은 상어의 거친 피부를 항공기 날개 부분에 융기된 포일 코팅을 개발하는 데에 영감으로 이용했다. 그리고 그 설계는 마찰을 6% 줄이고 연료 효율을 향상시키는 결과로 나타났다.

① 자연으로부터 빌리다
② 자연의 경이로움
③ 항공우주 산업의 미래
④ 왜 우리는 야생동물을 보존해야 하는가

13 ②

단어

greed : 탐욕
the (Great) Depression : 경제 대공황
rectify : (잘못된 것을) 바로잡다
currency : 화폐, 통화
hoard : (비밀리에) 비축하다
seize : ~을 꽉 쥐다
enact : (법을) 제정하다
insolvent : 파산한
reconstruct : 재구성하다, 재건하다
in exchange for : ~대신의, 교환으로

해석

루즈벨트 대통령은 공공연하게 경제 대공황에 대해 많은 미국인들의 탐욕을 탓했다. 그리고 이 문제를 바로잡기 위해 행동을 취했다. 그 당시 많은 화폐나 금을 가진 사람들은 그들의 돈을 잃을 걱정 때문에 그것들을 비축해두고 은행에 넣어 놓지 않았다.
(B) 은행들이 돈이 없어 문을 닫아야 했기 때문에 이것이 경제 대공황을 더 나쁘게 만들었다.
(C) 이에 대응하여 루즈벨트는 그것들이 재건될 수 있도록 문 닫은 파산 은행들에 작용하는 "긴급은행법"을 제정했다.
(A) 그것은 또한 지폐를 주는 대가로 정부가 개인 시민들의 금을 움켜쥘 수 있게 허용했다.

14 ④

단어

brew up : 끓이다, 만들다
chew : 씹다
dissolve : 녹다
be composed of : ~으로 구성되다
flavor : 풍미, 향료
pep up : ~에 생기를 불어넣다
ingredient : 성분, 재료
patent : 특허권
hit the market : 시장에 출시되다

해석

한 잔의 차를 하고 싶지만 그것을 끓일 시간이 없는가? 대신 "차 알약"을 먹어라. 인도의 차 과학자들이 차의 향이 나는 알약을 만들어냈다. 씹힐 수도 있고 뜨겁거나 찬 물에 빠르게 녹을 수도 있다. 갈색을 띄는 알약은 무게가 0.3그램이 나가고 80퍼센트의 차와 20퍼센트의 향료로 구성되어 있다. 그 연구 센터의 발명가들은 그것이 당신에게 생기를 불어넣는다고 말한다. 그들은 "당신이 그것을 먹기 원하는 방식으로 빨거나 씹거나 물에 녹일 수 있어요. 그리고 여전히 한 잔의 진짜 차 맛을 느낄 수 있죠."라고 말했다. 그들은 또한 "액상 차가 생기를 되찾게 하듯이 이 차 알약 또한 그것이 순수한 차 성분들을 포함하고

있기 때문에 사람들에게 상쾌한 기분이 들도록 할 것입니다."라고 말했다. 그 센터는 특허권을 신청했고, 그 알약이 6개월 안에 시장에 출시될 거라고 말했다.

15 ③

단어

coronary artery : 관상 동맥
obstruct : (진로를) 방해하다, 막다
tissue : 조직
disrupt : 지장을 주다, 방해하다
impulse : 충동, 자극
govern : 지배하다, 다스리다
stroke : 뇌졸중
impede : 방해하다, 지연시키다

해석

심장마비는 해마다 약 550,000명의 목숨을 가져가는데 심장 근육에 혈액을 공급하는 관상동맥이 막히게 될 때 발생한다. 혈액 속에서 운반되는 산소와 다른 영양소가 없다면 심장 조직은 죽거나 피해를 입는다. 만약 너무 많은 조직이 영향을 받으면 그 심장은 너무 약해져서 펌프질을 할 수 없다. 심지어 가벼운 피해조차도 목숨을 빼앗을 수 있다. 심장의 리드미컬한 박동을 다스리는 전기적 자극을 방해함으로써. 매년, 뇌졸중은 또 다른 170,000명의 목숨을 앗아가는데, 이번에는 뇌로 가는 혈액의 흐름이 지연되어 유발된다.

16 ①

단어

outfit : (특정 복장이나 장비를) 갖추어 주다
confirm : ~을 확인해 주다
mix-up : (실수로 인한) 혼동
chatter : 재잘거리다, 수다를 떨다
remembrance : 추억, 기념물
be bound to : 틀림없이 ~ 할 것이다

해석

버스를 타고 이동하다가 ①대부분의 사람들이 놓치는 것에 신경을 쓰는 것은 나의 이모 그레이스의 일상다반사이다. 어느 토요일 아침 144번 버스가 붐비는 교차로를 지나갔다. 그녀는 캠핑 복장을 갖춘 두 명의 여자아이들을 보았는데 그들은 긴장한 듯이 보였다. 그녀의 버스가 다음 교차로에 도착했을 때 그녀는 같은 방식으로 복장을 갖춘 두 명의 남자가 차 옆에 서 있는 것을 보았다. 그들은 약속을 기다리고 있었다. 그레이스가 버스에서 내려 그 젊은 남자들에게 다가갔다. 그들은 그녀에게 외국인의 억양으로 말했다. 그레이스는 그녀가 보았던 여자 아이들을 설명했고 두 남자는 떠났다. ②그 작고 행복한 무리가 그녀에게 감사하려고 돌아왔을 때 그녀가 추측했던 바가 사실임을 보여주었

다. 실제로 혼동이 있었던 것이다. 고마움을 고마움으로 돌려주기를 간절히 바라는 ③그 재잘거리는 작은 그룹은 그들이 그녀를 집에 데려다 줄 수 있게 해달라고 요청했다. 그레이스는 거절했다. 대신 그 젊은이들은 길을 건너 선물가게로 가서 작은 면 코끼리를 가지고 돌아왔다. 지금 그레이스의 아파트에는 하나의 기념물이 있지만 한 친절한 숙녀를 기억하고자 결속된 ④네 명의 젊은이 또한 있다.

17 ③

단어

adolescent : 청소년
emotional disturbance : 정서장애, 감정적 장애
juvenile : 어린애 같은, 청소년의
collaboration : 협업, 공동 작업
promote : 촉진하다, 추진하다
daunting : 주눅이 들게 하는
all too often : 너무나도 자주
consequences : 결말, 결과

해석

어린이와 청소년 정신 건강 분야에서의 진전에도 불구하고 매년 수백만의 젊은이들이 적절한 도움을 얻지 못한다. 심각한 감정적 장애를 가진 다섯 명의 아이들 중 오직 한 명만이 전문화된 정신 건강 서비스를 이용한다. 비록 오늘날 아동 복지 서비스, 청소년 재판 제도, 그리고 우리 학교들이 자주 어려움에 처한 아이들에게 보살핌을 제공하지만 이 기관들 중 어느 곳도 그것의 최우선 사항으로서 정신건강 서비스를 제공하고 있지 않다. 게다가 같은 아이를 보조하는 모든 전문가들의 기관 경계를 아우르는 협업을 추진하는 복잡성은 주눅이 들게 한다. 너무나도 자주 협조가 없고 충분한 돈이 없으며 숙련된 정신 건강 전문가들에게 제한된 접근만이 있다. — 그리고 아이들과 그들의 가족들은 비극적인 결과에 고통을 받는다.

① 그들의 권리를 요구한다.
② 좋은 건강 서비스를 받는다.
③ 비극적인 결과에 고통을 받는다.
④ 병원에 가는 것을 주저한다.

18 ①

단어

value : 가치, ~을 가치 있게 여기다
beneath : ~아래에
no doubt : 의심할 여지가 없이 ~일 것이다
marvel : 경이로워하다

해석

만족하는 사람은 그들이 삶에서 가진 것을 감사히 여긴다. 그리고 그것이 다른 사람들이 가진 것에 어떻게 비교되는지에 대해 걱정하지 않는다. 당신이 가진 것을 가치 있게 여기는 것은 당신이 가지고 있지 않거나 가질 수 없는 것을 넘어 더 큰 행복으로 이어진다. 네 살배기 앨리스는 크리스마스 트리로 달려가서 그것 아래에 있는 아주 멋진 선물들을 본다. 아마 그녀는 의심할 여지없이 그녀의 친구들 중 몇몇보다 더 적은 선물들을 받았을 것이다. 그리고 그녀는 아마도 그녀가 가장 원하던 것들 중 몇몇을 받지 못했을 것이다. 그러나 그 순간 그녀는 왜 더 많은 선물들이 없는지 생각하려고, 또는 그녀가 얻지 못한 것에 대해 무엇을 요청할 수 있었을지 궁금해 하려고 멈추지 않는다. 대신 그녀는 그녀 앞에 놓인 보물들에 경이로워 한다.

TIP

① compare to에서 to는 전치사이므로 명사구/명사절을 이끈다. others have가 오는 명사절에서 have의 목적어 역할도 해야 하므로 밑줄 친 자리에 올 수 있는 것은 what뿐이다. which는 선행사를 꾸미는 형용사절을 이끄는데, 이 문장에서는 선행사가 없으므로 which가 올 수 없다.
② 'Valuing what you have over ~ (주어)/ leads(동사) to greater happiness.'의 문장구조이다. Valuing 이하가 주어이므로 단수 취급하여 leads로 쓰는 것이 맞다.
③ 비교급 fewer가 있으므로 than을 쓰는 것이 맞다.
④ stop to-(to 부정사)는 '~을 하려고 멈추다'이고, stop -ing(동명사)는 '~하던 것을 멈추다'이다. '앨리스가 자신이 적게 가진 것에 대해 생각하려고, 혹은 의문을 가지려고 (가던 것을) 멈추지 않는다.'는 말이므로 stop to think~ or (stop to) wonder~ 로 쓴다.

19 ④

단어

controversial : 논란이 많은
cloning : 생물 복제
incurable : 불치의, 치유할 수 없는
worn out : 닳아 해진
duplicate : 복사하다
replace : 대체하다

해석

복제라는 주제보다 더 논쟁적인 어떤 것도 찾기 어려울 것이다. 사람들은 그것이 완전히 환상적이거나 또는 완전히 무섭다고 여긴다.
(C) 복제는 지금은 치료 불가능한 질병들에 대해 치료를 약속한다. 시각장애인들에게는 시력, 청각장애인들에게는 청력, 오래되어 못 쓰게 된 장기들에 대해서는 대체할 새 장기들을.

(B) 게다가 그것은 동물들을 복제함으로써 세계의 음식 공급량을 증가시키는 데 유용할 수 있다. 더 크고 더 건강한 동물들이 생산될 수 있을 것이다.

(A) 하지만 대부분의 사람들에게 인간의 복제는 다르다. 인간들을 우리가 복사기에서 책의 페이지의 복사본을 만드는 것과 같은 방식으로 복제한다는 생각은 끔찍하다.

20 ③

단어

hardship : 곤란, 어려움
discontent : 불만, 불만스러운
take up a cause : 운동에 가담하다
boycott : 거부운동, 불매운동

해석

영국은 인도산 섬유에 30퍼센트의 수입 관세를 부과함으로써 인도 섬유 산업에 어려움을 야기했다. 이것은 인도 섬유가 너무 비싸져서 영국에서 팔릴 수 없게 만들었다. 인도인들이 그들의 영국인 고객들을 잃었을 때 그들의 섬유산업은 망가졌다. 그러자 영국의 섬유 공장들은 영국의 섬유를 인도인들에게 파는 것으로써 이익을 얻었다. 인도 사람들은 영국의 지배 하에서 불만족스러웠다. 1930년에 모한다스 간디가 인도 독립운동에 가담했다. 그는 비폭력적인 방법으로 저항하도록 인도인들을 고무했다. 그는 영국인들에게 세금을 내지 말도록 인도인들을 고무했다. 그리고 그는 영국산 제품의 불매운동을 반대했다(→'지지했다'라는 뜻의 단어를 써야 전체 문맥과 맞다). 폭력적이기도 하고 비폭력적이기도 했던 엄청난 투쟁 후에 영국인들은 철수했다. 그리고 1947년에 인도는 자치적이고 독립적인 나라가 되었다.

21 ①

단어

bilingual : 2개 언어를 사용하는
fine tune : 미세 조정을 하다
attention span : 주의 지속 시간
activate : 활성화시키다
brain stem : 뇌간
enrichment : 강화, 풍부하게 함
working memory : 작동 기억

해석

미국의 노스웨스턴 대학에 의한 한 연구는 2개 언어를 사용하는 사람들이 더 강력한 두뇌를 가졌다는 생물학적 증거를 제공한다. 비오리카 마리안 박사와 니나 크라우스 박사는 2개 언어 사용이 두뇌에 어떻게 영향을 주는지를 연구했다. 그들은 다른 하나의 언어를 배우는 것은 사람들의 주의 지속시간을 "미세 조정"하고 그들의 기억력을 향상시킨다는 것을 찾아냈다. 특히 그들은 언어 학습자들이 다른 언어로 된 담화를 이해하려고 시도할 때 그것이 뇌간(두뇌의 오래된 부분)을 활성화하고 북돋운다는 것을 발견했

다. 크라우스 교수는 "2개 국어 사용은 두뇌의 강화로서 역할을 한다. 그리고 주의력과 작동기억에 관한 한 실제적인 결과들을 가진다."고 말했다.

① 2개 언어 사용의 두뇌에서의 효과
② 외국어 학습을 위한 조언들
③ 2개 언어 사용의 부정적 효과
④ 외국어 학습의 필요성

22 ④

단어

for certain : 확실히
alms : 구호품, 구호금
clay : 찰흙, 점토
smashing : 기막히게 즐거운
in recognition of : ~인정하여

해석

당신은 복싱데이에 대해 들어본 적이 있는가? 그것은 영국과 영연방 국가들에서 매년 12월 26일에 기념되는 휴일이다. 어떤 사람들은 겨울 축제 동안의 선물주기라는 고대 로마 전통이 복싱데이에 영감을 주었다고 말한다. 하지만 아무도 확실히는 모른다. 이 선물주기는 결국 구호금 상자들을 교회에 놓는 형태를 취했다. 그래서 사람들이 가난한 사람들에게 갈 나중의 분배를 위해 동전들을 그 안에 떨어뜨리도록. 이 초기의 "크리스마스 박스들"은 점토로 만들어졌고 윗면에 도려낸 구멍들이 있었지만 바닥에는 '마개들'이 없었다. 그것들을 여는 것은 "기막히게 즐거운 재미"였다. 17세기 동안 그 기부의 구호금 상자들은 멈췄다. 하지만 가난한 사람들이 그들 자신의 상자들을 만들고 고용주나 고객들에게 그들의 서비스에 대한 답례로 돈을 요구하기 시작했다. 그 시기 이후로 쭉 복싱데이에 배달원들과 다른 서비스 노동자들에게 돈을 주는 것이 전통이 되었다.

23 ④

단어

personality : 성격, 유명인
embody : 구현하다, 상징하다
wholesome : 건강에 좋은, 건전한
backfire : 역효과를 낳다
engage in : ~에 종사하다
scandalous : 가증스러운, 불미스러운
antisocial : 반사회적인
advisable : 바람직한, 권할 만한
exhibit : 보이다, 전시하다
moral : 도덕적인
desirable : 바람직한
discredit : 불명예, 신임을 떨어뜨리다

☑ 해석

회사들은 종종 그들의 제품을 홍보하기 위해 잘 알려진 스포츠인 혹은 연예인을 찾고는 한다. 그 사람이 건전한 자질들로만 이루어져 있다면 이것은 좋은 시도겠지만, 그가 불미스럽거나 (A) 비도덕적인 행동에 연관되어 있다면 역효과를 낳을 수 있다. 그런 경우에 대중은 반사회적 행동을 그 제품과 연관 짓게 된다. 그리고 그것을 사는 것을 피할 것이다. 누구에게 주연을 맡길지 결정하기 전에 완벽한 신원조사가 이루어지는 것이 바람직하다. 만약 한 사람이 과거에 (B) 바람직하지 않은 행위를 내보였다면 그는 아마도 미래에 바람직하지 않은 행위를 내보일 것이다. 또한 혹시라도 그 유명인이 광고하는 제품에 (C) 불명예를 가져온다면 그 계약은 자동적으로 무효화해야 한다.

24 ③

단어 •

harsh : 냉혹한, 혹독한
clownfish : 흰동가리
sea anemone : 말미잘
tentacle : 촉수
leftover : 잔여물, 남은 음식

☑ 해석

서로 다른 해양 동물들이 그들의 혹독한 수중 환경에서 살아남을 유일한 방법은 서로를 돕는 것이다. 이것은 특히 흰동가리와 독성이 있는 말미잘의 경우에서 그렇다.
(C) 흰동가리는 말미잘의 독에 의해 영향을 받지 않는데 그것(흰동가리)은 말미잘을 청소해주는 대가로 말미잘의 촉수들 사이에서 안전하게 산다.
(A) 다른 물고기들은 말미잘의 독을 두려워하여 거기서 흰동가리를 공격하려 들지 않는다.
(B) 다른 한편으로 말미잘은 흰동가리에 의해 제공되는 잔여물인 음식을 먹음으로써 득을 본다.

25 ③

단어 •

scent : 향기
flight attendant : 승무원
hot towel : 물수건
sensory : 감각의
stimulate : 활발하게 하다, 자극하다
be aimed at : ~을 목표로 삼다
given 특정한
prompt : 촉발하다, 유도하다
mighty : 강력한, 힘센

☑ 해석

ABC 항공은 모든 곳에 같은 향기를 사용한다. 예를 들면 그 회사의 승무원들에 의해 사용되는 향수에, 물수건에, 그리고 그 회사 서비스의 다른 요소들에. 감각의 요소들 중에서 향기를 사용하는 것은 많은 소매업자들에 의해 채택된 상대적으로 최신 마케팅 전략이다. 점점 더 많은 연구들이 냄새가 소비자 행동에 영향을 미친다는 것을 보여주고 있는데, 이는 상점, 호텔, 심지어 박물관의 향기 마케팅에 대한 수요를 자극한다. 마틴 린드스톰의 책 브랜드 감각에서의 광고 연구는 비록 대부분의 현대 상업 메시지들이 우리의 눈을 목표로 삼지만 사람들이 어떤 특정한 날에 기억하는 감성적 순간들 중 다수는 사실 냄새에 의해 촉발된다는 것을 시사한다.

① 어떤 향기들은 우리에게 일을 위한 활기를 북돋운다.
② 시각은 후각보다 강력하다.
③ 향기 마케팅에 대한 수요가 증가하고 있다.
④ 우리의 후각은 해가 가면서 둔해진다.

2014. 3. 15.
제1차 경찰공무원(순경) 채용

---

1 ①

단어 •

disturb : 방해하다

☑ 해석

식당에서는 다른 사람을 방해하므로 흡연을 삼가주십시오.

① 그만두다, 삼가다　　　　② 치우다, 제거하다
③ 바꾸다, 전환하다　　　　④ 제외하다, 배제하다

2 ④

단어 •

initial : 처음의, 초기의
decision-making : 의사결정
vary : 서로 다르다
nature : 특성, 성격
incident : (좋지 않은) 일, 사건

☑ 해석

초기의 의사결정과 행동은 사건의 특성과 유형에 따라 서로 다르다.

① ~을 기념하여　　　　② ~을 대신하여
③ ~을 위해서, ~에 때문에　④ ~에 따라, ~에 의하면

3 ③

> **단 어 ·**

coworker : 직장동료
probably : 아마도
salary : 급여, 봉급

> **해 석 ·**

A : 안녕, Josh. 어떻게 지내니?
B : 별로 좋지 않아. 새로 직장을 옮길까 고민 중이야.
A : 무슨 일인데? 같이 일하는 사람들 때문인 거니?
B : 아냐, 직장동료들은 좋아. 하지만 매일 똑같은 일만 해.
A : 어쩌면 좀 더 흥미로운 일을 찾아보는 것이 좋겠구나.
B : 그러게 말이야. 아마도 더 나은 직장을 구할 수 있을 것 같아.

4 ③

> **단 어 ·**

arrest : 체포하다, 저지하다
perpetrator : 가해자, 범인
commit : 저지르다
compare : 비교하다
criminal : 범죄의, 범인, 범죄자

> **해 석 ·**

경찰관으로서 당신의 임무는 범죄를 <u>저지른</u> 사람을 체포하고 범죄 <u>피해자들</u>을 보호하는 것이다.

5 ③

> **단 어 ·**

commission : 위원회, 수수료, 의뢰, 주문, (범행, 과실을) 저지름
authority : 지휘권, 권한

> **해 석 ·**

설명 : 무언가를 하도록 권한을 주는 위임장 또는 문서
예문 : 경찰은 누군가를 체포하기 위한 <u>영장</u>을 가지고 있다.

① 보석(금)　　　　　　② 양육, 보호
③ 영장, 보증서　　　　④ 규제, 제한

6 ①

> **단 어 ·**

inspector : 조사관, 감독관
mayor : 시장, 군수
ex-convict : 전과자

> **해 석 ·**

조사관 Javert는 Monsieur Madeleine가 시장의 실명이 아니라 전과자인 Jean Valijean의 <u>가명</u>이라는 것을 알아냈다.

① 가명　　② 연금술사　　③ 견습생　　④ 탐욕

7 ③

> **단 어 ·**

sentence : 문장, 형벌, 선고, 선고하다
polite : 예의 바른, 공손한, 예의상의, 의례적인
request : 요구, 신청, 요구하다
resort to : (좋지 못한 것에) 기대다, 의지하다
threat : 협박, 위협

> **해 석 ·**

• 그는 징역 3년 형을 선고받았다.
• 정중한 요청이 받아들여지지 않자, 그는 어쩔 수 없이 협박에 의존했다.

> **TIP**

sentence는 sentence (somebody) <u>to</u> (something) '-에게 -을 선고하다'의 뜻을 가진다. 보통 수동태의 형태로 쓰인다.
→ 'be sentenced <u>to</u> (something) : -을 선고받다'

8 ④

> **단 어 ·**

point out : 가리키다, 지적(언급)하다
perceive : 감지(인지)하다
get one's way : 제멋대로 하다, 자기마음대로 하다
resistance : 저항, 반대
legitimate : 정당한, 타당한
accept : 수용하다, 받아들이다
in contrast : 그에 반하여
automation : 자동화
dictatorship : 독재 정부(국가)
coercion : 강제, 강압
authority : 지휘권, 권한

> **해 석 ·**

Max Weber가 언급했듯이, 우리는 권력 - 다른 사람의 반대를 무릅쓰고서라도 자기 마음대로 하는 능력 - 을 정당하거나 정당하지 않은 것으로 인식한다. 정당한 권력은 <u>권한</u>이라고 한다. 이러한 권력을 사람들은 옳은 것으로 받아들인다. 그에 반해서 <u>강압</u>이라고 하는 부당한 권력은 사람들이 정당한 것으로 받아들이지 않는 힘이다.

9 ②

단어

global warming : 지구온난화
bargain : 싸게 사는 물건, 흥정, 합의, 흥정하다

해석

- 지구온난화는 온도와 해수면을 상승시키고, 빙하가 더욱 줄어들게 하였다.
- 중대한 문제는 내가 그 언어로 말할 기회가 많지 않다는 것이다.
- 나는 돈 관리에 신중하고 쇼핑할 때 저렴한 물건을 찾는 것을 즐긴다.

TIP

- increase in ~에 있어서 증가하다
- 'The problem is ~.'에서 be동사 다음은 보어(절) 자리이다. 빠진 성분 없이 완벽한 문장(I-주어/ don't get-동사/many chances~-목적어)을 이루는 절을 이끌어야 하므로 that이 오는 것이 적절하다.
- enjoy는 목적어로 동명사를 취한다. 따라서 finding이 와야 한다.

10 ①

단어

suit : 정장, 옷
handsome : 잘생긴, 멋진

해석

A : Peter의 새 정장을 좋아하니?
B : 응, 옷이 그를 멋져 보이게 하는 것 같아.

TIP

make는 사역동사로, 'make+목적어+목적보어'의 형태를 가지는데 목적보어 자리에 동사가 올 경우, 동사원형을 취한다.

11 ④

단어

stomach : 배, 복부
have a fever : 열이 나다
nauseous : 메스꺼운, 역겨운

해석

A : 엄마, 저 배가 아파요.
B : 열이 나니?

A : 아니요. 그런 것 같진 않아요.
B : 속이 메스꺼우니?
A : 아니요. 전혀 그렇지 않아요. 하지만 알다시피 제가 감자칩이랑 땅콩버터를 저녁으로 먹었어요.

12 ①

단어

the Great Depression : 대공황
decade : 10년
bring about : 야기하다
distribution : 분배(방식), 배급
excessive : 지나친, 과도한
stock market : 증권(주식) 시장
expansion : 확대, 확장, 팽창
definition : 정의
prospect : 가망, 가능성

해석

대공황은 1929년 후반에 시작되어 약 10년 동안 지속되었다. 많은 요인들이 대공황을 야기하는 데 한몫을 했다. 하나는 1920년대 전반에 걸친 불공평한 부의 분배였고 다른 하나는 과도한 주식 시장의 팽창이었다.

① 대공황의 원인 ② 대공황의 정의
③ 대공황의 가능성 ④ 대공황의 지배

13 ②

단어

mammals : 포유류
female : 여성, 암컷
nocturnal : 야행성의
roost : (새장 속의) 홰, 앉다, 쉬다
attic : 다락
high-pitched sound : 고주파
bounce off : ~의 반응을 살피다
echolocation : 반향 위치 측정

해석

박쥐는 새처럼 날아다니지만 포유류이다. 암컷 박쥐는 새끼를 낳고 젖을 만든다. 박쥐는 야행성이어서 밤에 음식을 찾아다니고 낮에는 잠을 잔다. 박쥐는 밤에 동굴이나 다락과 같은 조용한 공간에서 땅을 향하여 거꾸로 앉는다. 사람들은 박쥐가 피를 먹고 산다고 생각하지만 흡혈 박쥐만 피를 마신다. 대부분의 박쥐는 과일이나 곤충을 먹는다. 박쥐는 날아다닐 때, 물체를 살피는 고주파를 발생시킨다. 이러한 반향 위치 측정은 그들(박쥐)을 안내하는 일종의 레이더망이다.

14 ②

단 어

extraordinary : 특이한, 놀라운, 비범한
built-in : 붙박이인
celestial : 천체의, 하늘의
navigation : 항해, 항법
attribute : ~의 결과로 보다
sensitivity : 세심함, 민감함
magnetic field : 자기장
enhance : 강화하다, 향상시키다
disrupt : 방해하다, 지장을 주다

해 석

고양이는 삶에서 중요하다고 여기는 것에 대한 기억력이 있다. 몇몇 고양이는 장소를 찾아내는 특별한 기억력이 있는 것으로 보인다. 자신의 집에서 멀리 떨어져 있음에도 불구하고 고양이는 자신이 어디에 사는지 기억할 수 있는 것으로 보인다. 집을 찾는 능력의 핵심은 새가 가진 능력과 비슷하게 고양이에게 이미 탑재되어 있는 훌륭한 항법장치 때문일 수 있고, 또는 고양이의 항행 능력이 지구의 자기장에 대한 고양이들의 민감도에 기인할 수도 있다. 자석이 고양이에게 붙게 되면, 고양이는 정상적인 항행 능력에 방해를 받는다.

15 ④

단 어

traditional : 전통적인
craft : 공예, 기술
pottery : 도자기
leather : 가죽
straw : 짚, 밀짚
bamboo : 대나무
brass : 놋쇠, 황동

해 석

이곳에서 당신은 전통적인 공예품을 만드는 사람을 만날 수 있습니다. 당신의 친구에게 줄 선물로 완벽한 물건을 발견하게 될 것입니다. 우리는 흙으로 만든 도자기와 아름다운 가죽 가방을 가지고 있습니다. 짚으로 만든 샌들을 신어보거나 고전 무용에서 사용된 나무가면을 써보세요. 한국은 상자와 바구니와 같은 대나무 공예품들로 유명합니다. 한국은 또한 금속으로 금목걸이나 놋그릇을 만드는 훌륭한 예술가들이 있습니다. 당신은 돌로 만든 조각상을 집에 가져갈 수 있습니다. 한국 민속촌으로 오세요!

① 자서전   ② 소설   ③ 사망 기사   ④ 광고

16 ①

단 어

Afternoon of a Faun : 목신의 오후(드뷔시 작곡)
wearily : 녹초가 되어, 지쳐서, 싫증이 나서
pound : 요동치다
preparation : 준비
intensive : 집중적인
note : 음표, 음
tremble : 떨다, 떨리다

해 석

갑자기 Sally는 "안녕하세요, 목신의 오후로 시작해봅시다."라는 목소리가 지겹도록 반복되는 것을 들었다. Sally의 심장은 요동치기 시작했다. 그녀는 자신의 악보를 보면대에 천천히 펼쳤다. 평생의 준비, 4주 동안의 강도 높은 연습, 이 모든 것이 지금 이 순간으로 다가왔다. 그녀는 등에 땀이 흘러내리는 것을 느꼈다. 그녀는 입술로 플루트를 들어 올리고 심호흡을 한 뒤 연주하기 시작했다. 목신의 오후의 첫 음이 그녀의 플루트에서 흘러나왔다. 하지만 플루트를 잡고 있는 그녀의 두 손은 여전히 떨리고 있었다.

① 불안해하는   ② 안도하는   ③ 만족해하는   ④ 동정어린

[17~18]

단 어

feminist : 남녀평등주의자
masculine : 남자 같은, 사내다운
housewife : 주부
privilege : 특권, 특전, 특혜
the same A as B : B와 같은 A
deprive A of B : A에게서 B를 빼앗다
pursue : 추구하다
astronaut : 우주비행사
term : 용어, 단어

해 석

페미니스트는 남성혐오자, 남성 같은 여성도 아니고 전업주부를 싫어하는 사람들이 아니다. 페미니스트는 여성이 남성과 동일한 권리, 특권, 그리고 기회를 향유해야 한다고 믿는 여성 또는 남성을 말한다. 사회가 여성의 평등한 권리를 대부분 허용하지 않았기 때문에 페미니스트는 평등을 위해 싸웠다. 예를 들어, 유명한 19세기 페미니스트인 Susan B. Anthony는 여성이 투표할 권리를 얻게 하기 위해 운동했다. 오늘날, 페미니스트는 여성이 남성과 동등하게 일하는 것에 대해 동등한 보수를 받기를 원한다. 페미니스트는 여성이 우주비행사, 운동선수가 되길 원하든 혹은 전업주부가 되길 원하든 목표와 꿈을 추구하는 여성의 권리를 지지한다. 페미니스트 용어에 대한 오해 때문에, 몇몇 페미니스트는 가치관을 지지하고 있을지라도 자신을 페미니스트라고 말하지 않는다.

17 ②

단 어

by the way : (화제를 바꿀 때) 그런데

---

18 ④

단 어

diversity : 다양성
right : 권리

해 설

① 여성 직업의 다양성
② 페미니스트 운동의 역사
③ 가까운 미래의 여성 권리
④ 진정한 페미니스트란 무엇인가

---

19 ②

단 어

integrity : 진실성, 완전(온전)한 상태
irrespective of : ~에 관계없이
deal with : 처리하다, ~와 거래하다, ~을 다루다
duke : 공작, 통치자, 군주
dustman : 청소부
villain : 악당, 악인
requirement : 필요(조건), 요구
witness : 목격자, 증인
domestic : 국내의 가정의, 집안의
frightened : 두려워하는, 겁먹은
inhibited : 거리끼는, 어색해 하는
abuse : 남용, 오용, 남용하다
make an allegation : 혐의를 제기하다
absolute : 완전한, 완벽한
impartiality : 공명정대, 공평성
vulnerable : 취약한, 연약한
prudence : 신중, 조심
adamant : 요지부동의, 단호한
sincerity : 성실, 정직
inquisitive : 꼬치꼬치 캐묻는, 호기심이 많은

해 설

대중은 경찰력이 누구를 상대하느냐에 상관없이 전문적이고 진실되게 행사된다고 기대할 모든 권리를 가지고 있다. 다시 말해 통치자를 상대하든 청소부를 상대하든, 동료 경찰관을 상대하든 악당을 상대하든, 경찰관들은 동일한 공정성을 사용해야 한다. 또한 경찰과 접촉하는 일부 사람들은 약자일 수 있으므로 경찰관들은 그들을 지원하고 보호하기 위해 필요한 조건을 갖추고 있어야 한다. 이것은 가정 폭력의 피해자처럼 약자인 증인들이 수년간 여러 차례 학대를 당한 후 가해자에 대해 혐의를 제기하

는 것에 대해 몹시 두려워하거나 감정 표현을 어려워하는 경우에 특히 중요하다.

---

20 ③

단 어

upstairs : 위층으로, 위층에
townhouse : 연립주택
intruder : 불청객, 불법침입자, 강도
assure : 장담하다, 확언하다, 확신하다
downstairs : 아래층으로, 아래층에
assume : 추정하다
court : 법정, 법원
captive : 사로잡힌, 억류된
rob : 도둑질하다
sue for : ~에 대해 소송을 걸다, ~을 요구하다(=request)
pardon : 사면, 용서하다
principle : 원칙, 원리, 법칙

해 설

두 여성은 연립주택의 위층에 있었다. 그들이 룸메이트인 또 한 명의 여성이 강도들에 의해 아래층에서 폭행을 당하고 있는 소리를 들었을 때, 그들은 수차례 경찰에 전화를 걸었으므로 경찰이 오고 있을 것이라고 확신했다. 약 30분 후 룸메이트의 비명 소리가 멈추었을 때 그들은 경찰이 마침내 도착한 것이라고 추정했다. 두 여성이 아래층으로 내려갔을 때 그들은 경찰이 온 적이 없으며 강도들이 여전히 거기에 있음을 알았다. Warren 법정의 의견에 따르면 이후 14시간 동안 그 여성들은 포로로 잡혀 약탈을 당하고 두들겨 맞았다. 세 여성들은 자기들을 보호하지 못한 것에 대해 콜롬비아 특별구를 고소했지만, 콜롬비아 특별구의 최고 법원은 "정부와 그 기관들은 개개인의 시민에게 경찰 보호와 같은 공공 서비스를 제공할 일반적인 의무가 없다는 것이 미국 법의 기본 원칙이다."라고 말하며, 특별구 및 경찰들을 사면하였다.

① 병, 수술 후에 회복하다, (아주 힘든 일을) 해내다
② 분배하다, 의식을 잃다
③ ~을 한쪽으로 치우다, 제거하다
④ 대금을 지불하다, 빚을 갚다

1 ③

단 어

Moors : 무어인
be taught by : 가르침을 받다
invader : 침략군
parchment : 양피지

해 석

Marco Polo는 그의 책에서 종이의 중요한 발명에 관하여 언급하고 있지 않는데, 종이의 발명은 중국인에 의해 처음으로 소개되었다. 중국 종이 제조자들에게 가르침을 받은 무어인들은 종이를 유럽으로 들여왔다. 12세기에 스페인과 그리고 후에 프랑스는 무어인들의 침략 덕분에 종이 제조의 기술을 알게 되었다. 그러나 그 당시에, 대부분의 유럽식 인쇄는 계속 양피지에 행해졌는데, 왜냐하면 종이가 너무 약하다고 여겨졌기 때문이다.

① 편리한　　　　　② 내구성이 있는
③ 부서지기 쉬운　　④ 열렬한

2 ①

단 어

dispose of : ~을 처리하다
detrimental : 해로운

해 석

신뢰할 수 있는 방법으로 처리되지 않으면, 배터리는 환경과 인간에게 해롭다. 그 이유는 배터리는 때때로 중금속을 함유하고 있기 때문인데, 중금속들은 섭취될 경우 유기체의 몸 밖으로 거의 배출되지 않는다.

① 삼키다　　　　　② 혐오감을 느끼는
③ 제안하다　　　　④ 대피시키다

3 ②

단 어

stimulate interest : 관심을 불러일으키다

해 석

무역박람회의 출품자들은 관심을 불러일으키기 위해 무료 샘플들을 나누어 준다.

4 ③

단 어

whenever : ~할 때마다 매번

해 석

나의 어머니는 스포츠를 좋아하지 않는다. 바로 그것이 나의 아버지가 스포츠에 관한 이야기를 꺼낼 때마다 어머니가 방을 나가버리는 이유이다.

① 거절하다, 약하게 하다
② ~를 곤란하게 만들다
③ 꺼내다, ~를 기르다
④ ~에 대처하다, ~에 대항하다

5 ②

단 어

element : 요소, 성분
revise : 수정하다, 변경하다
shuffle : 섞다, 이리저리 바꾸다, 정리하다
component : 요소
juxtapose : 병치하다, 나란히 놓다
get across : (의미가 ~에게) 전달되다, 이해되다
in disarray : 혼란해져, 어지럽게 뒤섞여

해 석

때때로 문장이 당신이 의미하는 바를 나타내지 못할 때가 있는데, 왜냐하면 그 문장의 요소들이 적절한 연결성을 만들어내지 못하기 때문이다. 그렇다면 당신은 주변 요소들을 이리저리 뒤섞음으로써, 연결해야 할 것들을 나란히 놓음으로써, 그리고 연결하지 말아야 하는 것을 분리시킴으로써 (문장을) 수정해야 한다. 당신이 의미하는 바를 이해시키기 위해서는 정확한 단어들을 선택해야 할 뿐만 아니라, 그 단어들을 올바른 위치에 배치해야 한다. 어지럽게 뒤섞여 있는 단어들은 오직 난센스를 만들어 낼 뿐이다.

TIP

① say의 목적어로 명사절을 이끄는 that 혹은 what이 올 수 있는데, say의 목적절 안에서 mean의 목적어 자리가 비어 있으므로 what이 와야 한다.

② 'Then you have to revise by shuffling ∼, juxtaposing ∼, and separating ∼.'의 구조이다. 전치사 by 뒤에서 shuffling, juxtaposing, separating이 병렬구조를 이루고 있다.

③ the right words를 받은 대명사이다.

④ Words in disarray가 주어(복수형)이므로, produce가 맞는 동사 형태이다.

6 ④

단어

follow in somebody's footsteps : ∼의 선례를 좇아 나아가다
via : ∼을 통해서

해설

내가 자랄 때, 많은 사람들은 내게 나의 아버지의 뒤를 따라 교사가 될 것인지 물었다. 아이일 때 '아뇨. 전 사업 할래요.'라고 대답했던 것을 기억한다. 수년 뒤에 난, 내가 사실 가르치는 것을 매우 좋아한다는 것을 알게 되었다. 나는 내가 가장 잘 배울 수 있는 방법으로 가르쳤기 때문에 가르치는 것이 즐거웠다. 나는 게임과, 협력적 경쟁, 집단토론, 그리고 수업들을 통해 가장 잘 배운다. 실수를 벌하는 대신, 실수들을 장려한다. 학생들이 그들 혼자서 시험을 치르도록 요구하는 대신, 그들은 팀을 이루어 시험을 치르도록 요구받았다. 다시 말해 행동이 먼저였고, 실수가 그 뒤를 따르면, 그것을 통해 교훈을 얻고, 결국에는 웃을 수 있었다.

TIP

① if는 ask, know, find out, wonder 등의 동사 뒤에 쓰여 '∼인지'라는 뜻으로 명사절을 이끄는 접속사이다. 유사어로 whether가 있는데, whether는 or not과 함께 쓰기도 하고, 명사절로서 주어 역할을 하거나 전치사의 목적어로 쓰일 수 있다.

② ·remember to∼(to 부정사) : (앞으로 ∼할 것을) 기억하다
·remember ∼ing(동명사) : (과거에 ∼했던 것을) 기억하다
어렸을 때(as a kid) 했던 말이므로, remember saying이 맞다.

③ ∼I taught in the method 문장과 I learn best in the method 문장이 연결된 문장이다.
I taught in the method(선행사) which I learn best in. → I taught in the method in which I learn best.

④ required의 주어 they는 학생들을 의미하고, 이 학생들이 시험을 보도록 요구받는 것이므로 수동태인 were required가 되어야 한다.

7 ①

단어

not … until ∼ : ∼하고 나서야 …하다

TIP

① I did realize I had lost ∼ until ∼. →I did not realize ∼ until ∼.
'not A until B : B하기까지는 A하지 않다 → A하고 나서야 B하다' 구문이다.

② the moment는 '∼하자마자'를 의미하는 부사절 접속사이다.

③ who wins the presidential election은 won't care의 목적어 위치에 온 의문사 명사절이다. 선행사가 필요하고 그 자체로는 뜻을 가지지 않는 관계대명사 who와 달리, 이 문장에서는 의문사 who가 '누구'라는 뜻을 가지며 목적절 안에서 주어의 역할을 하고 있다. 선행사 또한 필요하지 않다.

④ 세미콜론(;) 뒤에 '그렇지 않으면'을 의미하는 접속부사 otherwise가 쓰였다. 세미콜론 뒤에 접속사가 오지 않도록 주의한다.

8 ④

단어

punctual : 시간을 엄수하는
virtue : 미덕
as though : 마치 ∼인 것처럼

TIP

① should have p.p. '-했어야 했는데'라는 뜻을 가진 가정법 과거완료 형태이다.

② It is …that ∼ 강조구문과 not A but B(A가 아니라 B이다) 구문이 함께 쓰였다. 'that∼ 한 것은 A가 아니라 바로 B이다'라는 뜻이 된다.

③ 동명사(Being punctual)를 주어로 쓸 수 있다.
everyone has to have가 형용사절로서 선행사 the virtue를 꾸며준다.
Being punctual is the virtue + Everyone has to have the virtue.
→Being punctual is the virtue (that) everyone has to have.

④ People tend to be strict as though they got old. → People tend to ∼ as they get old.
as though는 '마치 ∼인 것처럼'을 의미한다. '∼하면서, 함에 따라'라는 접속사는 as이다. 주절과 종속절이 동시에 일어나므로(∼함에 따라 ∼하다) 시제도 일치시켜 준다.

9 ③

on/through the grapevine : 소문으로

해 석

A : 너한테 비밀 하나 알려줄게.
B : 뭔데?
A : 너의 상사가 곧 잘릴 거라고 들었어.
B : 사실이 아닐 거야. 어떻게 그런 일이 생길 수가 있지?
A : 사실이야. 이건 철저히 우리 둘만 아는 거야. 알았지?
B : 알았어. <u>혼자만 알고 있을게</u>.

① 내가 설명해 줄게.　　② 너에게 알려 줄 수 없어.
③ 혼자만 알고 있을게.　　④ 소문으로 들었어.

10 ①

단 어 ⦁

lease : 임대차 계약
expire : 만료되다, 만기가 되다

해 석

A : 여기 매우 덥다! 너희 아파트에 냉방시스템은 있어?
B : 저기에 에어컨 보이지? 근데, 문제는 에어컨 바람이 충분히
　　세지 않아.
A : 그렇구나.
B : 그래도 상관없어. 곧 이사 갈 거라서.
A : <u>오래 전에 이사했어야 했어</u>.
B : 그게 임차계약이 만료될 때까지 기다려야 했어.

① 오래 전에 이사했어야 했어.
② 에어컨을 켜야 했어.
③ 다른 에어컨을 하나 샀어야 했어.
④ 집주인에게 하나 사달라고 했어야 했어.

11 ③

단 어 ⦁

disintegrate : 분해되다, 산산조각 나다
stem from : ~에서 생겨나다
appreciation : 감탄, 감상 (올바른) 평가, 판단, 이해, 감상
resiliency : 탄성
undergo : 겪다, 받다
characteristic : 특유의, 특성

해 석

오늘날 정책 입안자들과 대중들 사이에는 가족이 붕괴되고 있다
는 두려움이 널리 퍼져 있다. 그러한 불안감 중 많은 부분이 과거

가족의 본질에 대한 기본적인 오해와 폭넓은 사회적 · 경제적 변
화들에 따른 가족의 탄성(복원력)에 대한 이해 부족에서 비롯된
다. 가족에 대한 일반적인 관점은 가족이 역사적으로 안정적이며
비교적 변하지 않는 제도였으며, 그것이 지금 변화를 겪고 있을
뿐이라는 것이다; 사실 변화는 항상 가족의 특성이었다.

① 가족 체계가 붕괴되고 있다.
② 전통적인 가족 체계는 폭넓은 사회 변화에 적응하지 못한다.
③ 일반적인 견해에 반하여 변화는 항상 가족의 특성이었다.
④ 가족은 안정된 단위이지만 최근 변화를 겪고 있다.

12 ③

단 어 ⦁

bark : 나무껍질
lumberjack : 벌목꾼
mature : 어른스러운, 성숙한
beneficiary : 수혜자
extraordinary : 기이한, 놀라운
cultural legacy : 문화유산
accumulation : 축적, 누적

해 석

생물학자들은 종종 숲에서 가장 키가 큰 나무가 가장 강인한 씨
앗에서 자랐기 때문에 가장 큰 것만은 아니라고 말한다. 그들은
햇빛을 가리는 다른 나무들이 없었으며, 나무 주위의 토양이 비
옥했으며, 토끼들이 나무의 껍질을 갉아서 뚫지 않았고, 나무가
다 자라기 전에 벌목꾼들이 잘라내어 쓰러뜨리지 않았기 때문이
라고 말한다. 우리들 모두는 성공적인 사람들이 강인한 씨앗에
서 나온다는 것을 안다. 그러나 우리는 그들을 따뜻하게 해줬던
햇빛과, 그들이 뿌리를 내린 토양, 그리고 그들이 운 좋게 피한
토끼와 벌목꾼들에 대해 충분히 알고 있을까? 그들은 숨겨진
이점들과 놀라운 기회들과 문화유산들의 수혜자이다.

① 성공은 단점을 통해 온다.
② 영웅은 악조건에서 태어난다.
③ 성공은 이점의 축적에서 생겨난다.
④ 성공은 개인의 노력에 달려있다.

13 ①

단 어 ⦁

yield : 항복하다, 양도하다
skim : 걷어내다, 훑어보다
occupy : 차지하다, 정복하다
selfhood : 자아, 개성
aspect : 측면

디지털 세상은 우리에게 많은 이점들을 제공하지만, 만약 우리가 너무 완전히 그러한 세상에 굴복한다면, 우리는 스스로를 발전시키는 데 필요한 사생활을 잃을지도 모른다. 진지한 독서처럼 시간과 세심한 주의력을 요구하는 활동들이 위기에 처해 있다; 인터넷이 우리의 삶을 더 많이 차지해 감에 따라, 우리는 덜 읽으며 더 훑어본다. 그리고 인터넷이 우리에게 부추기듯이 정보를 빠르게 훑어보는 것보다는, 천천히 읽는 것이 자아와 더 많은 연관성이 있다. 사회학과 심리학의 최근 연구는 개인적 체험인 책을 읽는 것이 우리가 누구인지 알아가게 되는 중요한 측면임을 시사한다.

① 느린 독서의 찬양 　② 기억술의 찬양
③ 디지털 세상의 찬양 　④ 사생활의 찬양

14 ②

단 어

favor : 호의, 친절, 지지
lead : 납

해 석

고대 이집트인들에게 사랑받은 짙은 눈 화장은 눈에 좋았을지도 모른다. 납은 보통 건강에 해롭다. 그러나 Analytical Chemistry라는 학술지에 발표된 프랑스 과학자들의 연구는 화장품에 들어있는 소금납이 눈병을 예방하고 치료하는 데에 도움이 된다고 밝힌다. 매우 적은 양의 수준에선, 소금은 눈의 감염을 유발할 수 있는 박테리아를 퇴치하는 면역체계 내의 세포의 활동을 촉진시킨다. Louvre Museum과 CNRS 연구소의 과학자들은 또한 화장품에서 발견된 소금납이 실제로 눈병으로부터 사람들을 보호하는 데 긍정적인 효과를 가진다는 것을 발견하였다.

① 납으로 고통을 받는 이집트인
② 눈 화장은 건강상 이익을 가진다.
③ 눈 화장은 눈 감염을 유발한다.
④ 화장품은 사람들의 관심을 끈다.

15 ②

단 어

reserve : 비축
perishable : 잘 상하는
replenish : 다시 채우다, 보충하다
approximately : 대략
transfusion : 투입, 수혈

해 석

뉴욕시의 혈액센터는 지속적인 헌혈의 부족을 겪어 왔습니다. 수요에 맞추려면, 혈액공급을 유지하기 위해 매일 약 2,000명의 사람들이 헌혈을 해야 합니다. 비축된 혈액은 상하기 쉬워 계속적으로 보충돼야 해서 그런 많은 수의 사람이 필요합니다. 혈액 1파인트의 양은 세 명의 생명을 살릴 수 있습니다. 그리고 세 명 중 한 명은 살면서 어느 순간엔 목숨을 구해줄 수혈을 필요로 할 것입니다. 뉴욕시의 혈액센터를 통해 헌혈하십시오.

TIP

② Such large numbers는 앞 문장의 approximately 2,000 people을 가리킨다.

16 ④

단 어

stress : 강조하다
overlap : 공통부분
consistency : 한결같음, 일관성
absolute : 절대적인

해 석

사실, 신문과 잡지들은 자신들이 뉴스를 솔직하게 내보낸다고 종종 강조한다. 그러나 큰 문제는 인간의 관찰이라는 변수가 있다는 것이다. 예를 들면, 10명의 사람이 한 사고를 목격한 후 그들이 기자와 인터뷰를 한다고 가정해 보자. 각각의 목격자들은 약간씩 다른 버전을 이야기할 것이다. 그들의 관찰에서 부분적인 일치와 일관성은 모두 무슨 일이 발생했는지를 재구성하는 데 들어간다. 각자 다른 입장에서 그 사고를 목격했기 때문에 완전한 진실을 찾아내는 것은 불가능하다. 결론적으로, 많은 요인들이 진실을 식별하는 것을 어렵게 만든다.

① 감추다, 숨기다 　② 못마땅해하다
③ 왜곡하다 　　　④ 식별하다

17 ①

단 어

intimately : 친밀히
perception : 지각, 인식
complementary : 상호보완적인
interpret : 설명하다, 해석하다
refer to : ～을 나타내다, ～을 언급하다
illustrate : (삽화·도해 등을 이용하여) 설명하다
optical illusion : 착시
inadequate : 부적당한, 불충분한

비록 밀접하게 관련되어 있더라도, 감각과 지각은 우리가 세계를 해석하는 방식에 있어 두 개의 상호보완적이지만 다른 역할을 수행한다. 감각이란 촉각, 미각, 시각, 청각, 후각을 통해 우리 주위의 환경을 느끼는 과정을 말한다. 이러한 정보는 날것의 형태로 우리의 뇌로 전송되고, 거기서 인식이 작동하게 된다. 인식이란 우리가 이러한 감각들을 해석하고, 우리 주위의 모든 것을 이해하는 방식이다. 감각과 인식의 차이를 설명하기 위해 어린 아기의 예를 들어보자. 아기의 눈은 성인의 눈과 같은 정보를 받아들인다. 그러나 그 인식은 완전히 다른데, 왜냐하면 아기는 자신이 무엇을 보고 있는지 전혀 모르기 때문이다. 경험으로 인해, 인식은 설령 우리가 물체의 일부분만을 보고 있어도 물체의 전부가 존재한다는 것을 추정할 수 있게 해 주변에 대해 유용한 정보를 만들어낸다.

① 한 사물의 전체가 존재한다고
② 물체들은 구별하기 불가능하다고
③ 착시가 우리 뇌에 의해 발생한다고
④ 인식이 우리에게 불충분한 정보를 준다고

18 ④

in (a) ~fashion : 방식으로
antioxidant : 산화 방지제
compound : 복합체, 화합물
metabolism : 신진대사
radical : 기(基), 라디칼
antibacterial : 항균성의
numerous : 많은

Weil 박사에 따르면, 녹차는 보통의 홍차보다 훨씬 더 부드러운 방식으로 만들어진다. 녹차 잎은 우리에게 건강상의 이익을 주는 항산화 성분을 보존하기 위해 쪄지고, 말아져, 건조된다. Weil 박사는 이러한 항산화 성분이 콜레스테롤 수치를 낮추고 신진대사를 촉진시킴으로써 심장을 보호하며, 세포를 손상시키고 그 세포들이 무절제하게 성장하도록 하는 라디칼을 제거함으로써 암이 생기지 않도록 해준다고 한다. 녹차는 또한 항균성질을 가지고 있어 질병을 예방하고, 질병과 싸우는 데 도움을 준다. 중국에서는 녹차가 적어도 400년 동안 약으로 사용되어 왔으며, 수많은 연구들은 녹차를 마시는 것이 건강에 긍정적인 효과를 가져다준다고 보고하고 있다.

① 암 치료를 위한 조언
② 우리를 긍정적으로 만드는 음식 선택
③ 차를 마시고 차를 내놓는 방법
④ 녹차 섭취의 건강상 이점

19 ②

addax : 나사뿔영양
antelope : 영양(羚羊)
spiral : 나사 모양의
sparse : 드문, 희박한
manage to : 그럭저럭 ~하다
calf : (사슴 등의) 새끼
flesh : 살, 고기
hide : 짐승의 가죽
decline : 감소

나사뿔영양은 두세 번 꼬인 길고 가는 나선모양의 뿔을 가진 커다란 영양이다. 나사뿔영양의 털은 겨울엔 회색빛이 도는 갈색이며, 여름에는 거의 흰색으로 변한다. 나사뿔영양은 사막에서 사는 동물이며 식물을 먹으면서 섭취하는 몇 방울의 물을 제외하곤 물을 거의 필요로 하지 않는다. 나사뿔영양은 우기 동안 겨우 자라는 희박한 식물들을 찾아 밤에 사막을 돌아다니는 것을 좋아한다. 암컷은 8~9개월간의 임신 기간 후에 단 1마리의 새끼를 낳는 것으로 알려져 있다. 야생에선 수백 마리 정도만이 남아있다. 나사뿔영양의 고기와 가죽을 노린 무절제한 사냥이 나사뿔영양 수가 감소한 주요한 원인인 듯하다.

20 ②

significant : 중요한
meltdown : (주식의) 폭락, 용해
cripple : 불구로 만들다, 심각한 손상을 주다
turmoil : 혼란, 소란
institute : (제도를) 도입하다, (절차를) 시작하다
devaluation : 평가절하
eliminate : 없애다, 제거하다
bleak : 암울한, 절망적인
cope with : ~에 대처하다

1990년대 중후반경에 브라질은 중남미에서 가장 빠르게 성장하는 경제들 중 하나였으며, '국제투자계의 총아'였다. 특히 브라질의 중산층은 생활수준을 개선할 수 있는 일과 관련된 중요한 기회들을 맞고 있었다. 그러나 1990년대 후반의 러시아와 아시아에서 있었던 경제 '붕괴들'의 여파는 브라질 경제에 심각한 손상을 주었다. 예를 들면, 세계적 경제혼란은 1997년부터 1998년까지 브라질의 자동차업계에서만 27.5퍼센트의 판매 감소를 낳았다. 국가적 위기에 대응하여, 브라질의 대통령은 주요통화의 평가절하를 단행했다. 1998년엔, 고용주들이 58만 건 이상의 일자리를 없앴다. 실직으로 인해 중산층들이 "좋은 시절"에 구매했던 금융상품의 요구사항들에 대응할 수 없다는 것을 알게 되면서 그들의 운명은 암담해졌다.

2014. 4. 19.
안전행정부 시행

1 ②

단 어

practice : 연습

해 석

그녀가 작년 겨울 멕시코로 여행가기 전에, 그녀는 대학 이후로 연습하지 않았기 때문에 스페인어를 복습할 필요가 있었다.

① ~에게 아첨하다
② ~을 복습하다
③ ~을 회피하다
④ (병에) 걸리다

2 ①

단 어

pore over : ~을 자세히 조사하다

해 석

나는 Jim이 컴퓨터 출력물들을 자세히 조사해 보도록 하라는 말을 들었다.

① 조사(검토)하다
② 나누어 주다
③ 폐기하다
④ 바로잡다

3 ①

단 어

celestial : 하늘의, 천체의
vastness : 광대함
employ : (사람을) 고용하다, (기술,방법을) 쓰다, 이용하다
unerring : 틀림없는
voyage : 여행, 항해
planetary : 행성의
travail : 고생, 고역
ecstatic : 열광하는

해 석

Johannes Kepler는 언젠가 우주의 광대함을 두려워하지 않는 탐험가들로 가득 찬, 하늘의 바람에 적응한 돛을 단 천체 우주선이 하늘을 항해하는 날이 올 거라고 믿었다. 그리고 오늘날 그러한 탐험가들인 인간과 로봇이, Kepler가 평생 개인적인 고생과 희열을 주는 발견 중에 알아낸 행성의 움직임에 관한 세 가지 법칙을 우주의 방대함을 헤치고 나아가는 그들의 여행의 <u>정확한</u> 가이드로 사용한다.

① 흠잡을 데 없는
② 믿을 수 없는
③ 배짱이 없는
④ 비과학적인

4 ③

단 어

facility : 설비, 시설
dissemination : 보급
dissatisfaction : 불만족
at no charge : 무료로
designate : 지정하다
evoke : 떠올려 주다
erase : 지우다

해 석

디즈니랜드를 방문하는 사람들은 5분도 안 되는 탈 것을 위해 비싼 입장료를 지불하고 수 시간을 기다린다. 그들은 왜 다른 상황이었다면 상당한 ㉠<u>불만족</u>을 발생시킬 수도 있는 상황에 그렇게 잘 대응하는가? 한 가지 이유는 테마공원이 그들이 어디를 가든지 추가적인 서비스를 제공하기 때문이다. 그들은 지정된 사진 촬영 장소에서 손님들에게 ㉡<u>무료로</u> 카메라를 빌려준다. 사람들은 미키마우스와 찍었던 즐거운 사진을 기억하고, 긴 줄은 잊어버린다. 깨끗한 시설과 친절한 직원들 또한 부정적인 경험들을 ㉢<u>지워준다</u>.

5 ①③

단 어

not to mention : ~은 말할 것도 없고

TIP

① like는 목적어로 to부정사와 동명사 둘 다 취하므로 like 뒤에 going이 올 수 있다. not to mention N은 '~은 말할 필요 없이'라는 뜻으로 mountain climbing의 명사 형태가 왔으므로 맞다. 그러나 she does not like going outdoor에서 '바깥에'라는 부사 outdoors가 와야 하는데 형용사 outdoor를 썼기 때문에 틀린 문장이 된다.
② more ~ than any other 단수명사 : 다른 어떤 것(any other 단수명사)보다 더 ~한 →'가장 ~한'의 뜻을 가지는 최상급 표현이 된다.
③ surrounding by the sea의 수식을 받고 있는 것은 the three quarters of the land 명사구이다. 땅의 4분의 3이 바다에 의해 둘러싸여(수동) 있으므로 surrounding을 surrounded로 바꿔 주어야 한다.
④ a number of(많은) 뒤에 복수명사(students)에 맞춰 동사도 복수형(are)으로 써 주었으므로 맞는 표현이다.

6 ①

단어

neat : 뛰어난, 훌륭한
compatible : 호환이 되는, 화합할 수 있는
courtship : 교제, 연애

해석

A : 어제 신문에서 너의 부모님 결혼 25주년 기념일 발표를 보았어. 정말 근사해. 너는 부모님께서 어떻게 만나셨는지 알고 있어?
B : 응. 정말 믿을 수 없지만, 사실 아주 낭만적이야. 그들은 대학에서 만났는데 서로 잘 맞는다는 것을 알게 되자 데이트를 하기 시작했어. 그들의 연애는 학창시절 내내 계속되었지.
A : 정말이야? 그거 정말 아름답다. 나는 사랑에 빠질 것 같은 사람을 반에서 누구도 찾지 못했는데.
B : 나도 그래. 아마 다음 학기에는 가능하겠지.

① 나도 그래.
② 너는 나를 비난해서는 안 돼.
③ 그것은 너의 부모님께 달려 있어.
④ 너는 그녀와 함께 시간을 보내는 것이 좋겠어.

7 ①

단어

long face : 시무룩한 얼굴

해석

A : 오늘 아침에 Steve 봤어?
B : 응, 그런데 왜인지 표정이 안 좋던데?
A : 나는 전혀 모르겠어.
B : 나는 그가 행복할거라 생각했는데.
A : 나도 마찬가지야. 특히 지난주에 영업부장으로 승진도 했잖아.
B : 어쩌면 여자 친구와 문제가 있을지도 몰라.

① 우울한 얼굴을 하다.　　② 내 입장이 돼 봐.
③ 우세한 편에 붙다.　　　④ 멋진 수를 쓰다.

8 ②

단어

weary : 지친, 피곤한

해석

① 병원에서 일하는 동안에, 그녀는 그녀의 첫 번째 에어쇼를 봤다.
② 네가 얼마나 지치게 되든지 간에, 너는 그 프로젝트를 반드시 해야 한다.

③ 내가 본 흥미진진한 게임들 중 하나는 2010년 월드컵 결승전이었다.
④ 그것은 그녀가 찾고 있었던 중앙출입구였다.

TIP

① While절은 분사구문으로 주절의 주어 she가 생략되었다. 그녀가 일을 하는 것(능동)이므로 working으로 써준다. While she worked at a hospital, she saw her first air show. = (While) working at a hospital, she saw her first air show.
② how(ever) +형용사 +S +V : S가 아무리 V하든지 간에
③ 'one of the exciting games ~'에서 수일치 시켜야 하는 주어 부분은 one이므로 동사 were를 단수주어에 맞춰 was로 고쳐야 한다.
④ It was the main entrance + she was looking for the main entrance
→It was the main entrance(선행사) that/which she was looking for.
→It was the main entrance for which she was looking.
관계대명사 that은 전치사(for) 다음에 오지 못한다. 따라서 보기 지문의 that을 which로 고쳐주어야 한다.

9 ④

단어

not necessarily : 반드시 ~은 아닌
up-to-the-minute : 최신의, 최첨단의
externally : 외부적으로, 외면적으로

해석

신문과 비교해볼 때, 잡지는 매일 나오는 것이 아니라 매주나 매달 또는 그보다 더 드물게 나오기 때문에 반드시 최신판은 아니다. 대개 잡지는 책과 닮았기 때문에 그것들은 외형적으로도 신문과는 다르다. 종이는 더 두껍고, 사진은 보다 화려하고, 대부분의 기사들은 비교적 길다. 독자들은 훨씬 많은 배경정보들과 더 많은 세부사항들을 경험하게 된다. 주간 뉴스잡지는 많은 토픽들에 대해 보도하지만, 대부분의 잡지들은 다양한 소비자들의 마음을 끌기 위해 특화되어 있다. 예를 들어, 유명인들에 대해 다루는 청춘 잡지가 있는 것처럼, 패션, 화장품, 요리법을 다루는 여성 잡지가 있다. 다른 잡지들은 컴퓨터 사용자들, 스포츠팬들, 예술에 관심 있는 사람들, 그리고 많은 다른 소그룹을 겨냥한다.

TIP

① resemble like a book →resemble a book
resemble은 목적어를 바로 취하는 타동사이다. resemble 다음에 전치사를 쓰지 않도록 주의한다.

② 계속적 용법으로 쓰인 which절이 꾸미는 선행사는 weekly news magazines이다. 복수형이므로 which 절 안에 reports를 report로 고쳐준다.

③ there are women's magazines cover ~에서 동사는 are이다. 한 문장에 동사가 두 개 올 수 없으므로 cover 는 covering으로 바꾸어 covering fashion, cosmetics, and recipes ~가 women's magazines를 꾸미는 형용사구가 되도록 해야 한다.

④ Other magazines are directed toward (A), (B), (C), and (D). 이 문장에서 A, B, C, D가 병렬적인 구조를 이루고 있다. 또한, A, B, D가 directed toward의 대상이 되는 '사람들 혹은 단체'를 의미하고 있으므로 C 역시 '예술에 관심이 있는 사람들(those interested in the arts)'이 들어가야 내용상 어울린다. those(~한 사람들)는 대명사로, interested in the arts의 수식을 받고 있다. those (who are) interested in the arts에서 관계대명사와 be동사가 함께 생략되었다고 볼 수 있다.

10 ③

단 어

literacy : 글을 읽고 쓸 줄 아는 능력
dialect : 방언, 사투리
be level : 고저가 없다
exert : (권력, 영향력을) 가하다
well enough : 그런 대로

해 석

최근까지 많은 전문가들은 보편적인 글과 대중매체의 영향으로 지역 방언들이 비슷해졌다고 주장했다. 그렇지 않다. 지역 정체성과 여타 사회적 영향력은 방언이 어떻게 진화하는지에 텔레비전보다 더 강한 영향력을 행사한다. 북부 내륙, 중부, 캐나다 그리고 남부는 그 어느 때보다 더 서로 다르다.

TIP

③ 밑줄 친 부분 앞뒤의 문장이 서로 반대되므로 '그렇지 않다'는 내용이 들어가야 한다.

11 ③

단 어

fare : (특정 상황에서) 잘하다(well) 잘못하다(badly)
affiliation : 소속
flourish : 잘 자라다

해 석

몸의 형태는 어떻게 사람이 삶을 잘 살아가는지를 예측하는 변수로서는 유용하지 않았다. 또한 출생 순서나 정치적인 관계도 마찬가지였다. 심지어 사회적 계층도 제한적인 영향을 가질 뿐이었다. 그러나 따뜻한 아동기를 가졌다는 것은 영향력이 있었다. 그것은 잘 자란 사람들이 완벽한 어린 시절을 가졌다는 뜻은 아니다. 오히려 Vaillant가 말했듯 "잘된 것이 잘못된 것보다 중요하다." 사랑하는 친척, 조언자 또는 친구가 주는 긍정적인 영향은 발생하는 나쁜 일의 부정적인 영향을 물리칠 수 있다.

① 늘리다   ② 소집하다   ③ 완파하다   ④ 강화하다

12 ④

단 어

accomplish : 완수하다, 성취하다
dairy : 낙농장
sustainable : 지속 가능한
initially : 처음에
blustery : 바람이 거센
untapped : 아직 손대지(사용하지) 않은
furnace : 용광로
leftover : 남은, 잉여의
shares : 주식
neutral : 중립적인
grid : (전기, 가스 공급용) 배전관
at a profit : 이익을 남기고
given that : ~을 고려하면

해 석

약간의 공짜 맥주가 해낼 수 있는 것은 놀랍다. 낙농장과 돼지농장으로 잘 알려진 Samso는 결국에는 탄소가 없는 지속한 전력을 위한 덴마크의 시연회가 될 것이다. 그러나 어떻게 그러한 일이 발생할지는 명확하지 않았는데 이는 처음에 정부가 어떠한 자금과 세금 우대, 기술적인 전문성도 제공하지 않았기 때문이다.

(C) 거의 모든 전력이 석유와 석탄에서 나온다는 것을 고려하면 – 그리고 그 섬의 4,300명 주민들이 곡물 저장기로부터 나오는 풍력 발전용 터빈에 대해 몰랐다는 점을 고려하면 – Samso는 이상한 선택을 한 것처럼 보였다. 그러나 Soren Hermansen은 기회를 보았다. 그 호소는 즉각적이었고, 재생 가능한 에너지 프로젝트가 마침내 상당한 자금을 얻어냈을 때 그는 최초의, 그리고 유일한 직원이 될 것을 자원했다.

(A) 그래서 Hermansen은 친환경적이 되는 것을 홍보하기 위하여 모든 공동체나 클럽모임에 참석했다. 그는 바람이 거센 섬이 풍력을 위한 잠재력을 가졌다는 점과 Samso가 에너지 독립을 하도록 만드는 것의 경제적 이익에 대해 강조했다. 그리고 그는 가끔 공짜 맥주를 가져왔다.

(B) 그것은 효과가 있었다. 섬사람들은 열과 온수를 생산하기 위해서, 석유를 태우는 그들의 용광로를 쓰다 남은 짚과 나뭇조각을 태우는 중앙 집중식 발전소로 바꾸었다. 그들은 새로운 풍력 터빈 주식을 샀는데, 그것은 섬 전체의 전기 수요를 충족시킬 수 있는 11개의 커다란 지상 터빈을 지을 만큼의 자금을 만들어 냈다. 오늘날 Samso는 단지 탄소 중립적인 것만은 아니다. – 그것은 그것이 사용하는 것보다 10% 더 깨끗한 전기를 생산하고, 남는 전력은 이익을 남기고 배전관으로 다시 돌려보내진다.

13 ②

단 어

emphasis : 강조
decode : 해독하다
translate as : ∼으로 번역하다
phonemic awareness : 음소 인식
comprehend : 이해하다
material : 자료
infer : 추론하다
detect : 탐지하다
bias : 편향, 성향

해 석

주로 음소의 이해와 알파벳 원리에 대한 지식으로 번역되기도 하는 해독에 대한 강조는 학교들로 하여금 추구하도록 했다, 학생들이 해독하는 기술을 완전히 익힐 수 있도록 도와주는 일괄적이거나 상업적으로 만들어진 독해 프로그램들을. 우리가 함께 일하고 있는 교사들에 따르면, 독서 교육에 대해 이와 같이 완전히 원고를 읽듯 하는 접근법은 단어들을 어떻게 소리 내어 읽는지 아는 많은 학생들을 배출했지만, 거기서 독해가 끝나게 된다. 학생들이 해독할 수 있고 심지어 유창한 구어 독자가 될 수는 있지만, 그들은 그 자료를 정말로 이해하지는 못한다; 그들은 행간을 읽는다거나 의미를 추론하거나 혹은 다른 것들 중에서 저자의 성향을 알아내지 못한다. 독해는 <u>단순히 음소를 인식하고 알파벳을 아는 것보다 훨씬 복잡하다.</u>

① 음소와 알파벳 지식이 일반적인 해독 과정에 추가되는 것이기 때문에 (독해는) 기본적으로 해독하는 것이다
② (독해는) 단순히 음소를 인식하고 알파벳을 아는 것보다 훨씬 복잡하다
③ (독해는) 혼자 배우거나 선생님과 함께 하는 것보다 친구들과 함께 배울 때 더 효과적이다
④ (독해는) 배우는 사람이 단어들을 유창하게 소리 내어 읽을 수 있을 때 숙달될 수 있다

14 ③

단 어

conquer : 정복하다
push aside : 밀어 치우다
intricate : 복잡한
peculiar : 이상한, 독특한
meet the challenge : 시련에 잘 대처하다
unfettered : 제한받지 않는
proliferation : 확산

해 석

발견과 발명을 통해, 과학은 생명을 연장했고 질병을 정복했으며 새로운 물질적 자유를 제공했다. 그것은 신과 악마를 한쪽으로 밀어냈고 순수한 상상력에 의해 생산된 그 무엇보다도 더 복잡하고 놀라운 우주를 드러냈다. 하지만 과학이 창조한 그 독특한 낙원에는 새로운 문제들이 있다. 과학은 공해, 안보, 에너지, 교육, 그리고 식량이라는 미래의 시련에 잘 대처하기 위한 대중적 지지를 잃는 것처럼 보인다. 대중은 유전공학, 지구온난화, 원자력, 그리고 핵무기의 확산과 같은 영역들에서 제한받지 않는 과학과 기술의 잠재적 결과들을 두려워하게 되었다.

① 과학은 현대 사회에서 매우 유용하다.
② 과학과 기술은 빠르게 발전하고 있다.
③ 과학에 대한 전적인 믿음이 약해지고 있다.
④ 과학 연구가 민간 부문들로부터 더 많은 자금을 얻고 있다.

15 ④

단 어

portray : 묘사하다
challenge : 도전, 시험대
stereotype : 고정관념
overcrowded : 과도하게 붐비는, 초만원인

해 석

오늘날 세상에서 우리가 직면하는 도전 중 하나는 타인과 장소에 대해 우리가 얻는 많은 정보들이 우리가 보는 미디어의 광고나 오락 프로그램으로부터 나온다는 것이다. 당신은 이러한 유형의 정보를 항상 신뢰할 수는 없다. 텔레비전 프로그램과 광고를 만드는 사람들에게, 진실과 정직한 의견은 당신에게 어떤 것을 팔기 위해 충분히 오랫동안 당신의 관심을 유지시키는 것만큼 중요하지는 않다. 과거에 우리가 텔레비전 프로그램, 광고, 그리고 영화로부터 받았던 메시지들은 고정관념으로 가득 찼다. 예를 들어, 어떤 문화 그룹들은 종종 <u>폭력배들로 묘사되었고, 반면에 다른 그룹들은 보통 그들을 체포하는 '좋은 사람들'로 나타난다.</u> 심지어 장소조차 고정관념으로 표현되었다; 파리와 베니스와 같은 유럽의 도시들은 보통 아름답고 낭만적으로 나타났지만, 카이로나 캘커타 같은 아프리카와 아시아의 도시들은 빈곤하고 지나치게 붐비는 것으로 자주 비쳐졌다.

16 ④

단어

steady : 꾸준한
stable : 안정된

해석

지구는 생명으로 가득한 행성이다. 이러한 이유 중 하나는 우리의 태양이 행성에서 생명을 존재하게 할 수 있는 종류의 별이라는 것이다. 항상 태양은 계속해서 열과 빛을 꾸준히 공급한다. 왜냐하면 태양은 안정된 별이기 때문이다. ① 이것은 그것이 같은 크기를 유지한다는 것을 의미한다. 그리고 그것의 에너지(열과 빛) 방출량은 많이 변하지 않는다. ② 어떤 별들은 안정적이지 않다. 그것들은 더 크고 뜨거워지고 이후에는 작아지고 차가워진다. ③ 그들이 내보내는 열과 빛은 크게 달라진다. 만약 태양이 그와 같다면, 지구는 반복적으로 끓고 얼었을 것이다. (④ 생명은 이런 엄청난 변화 아래서 존재할 수 있을 것이다.) 꾸준한 양의 에너지가 우리의 태양으로부터 쏟아져 나오기 때문에 우리가 지금 여기에 있는 것이다.

TIP

④ 글의 앞부분에서 지구가 생명으로 가득한 이유 중 하나로 태양이 열과 빛을 꾸준히 공급하기 때문이라고 언급하였으므로 엄청난 변화 아래서 생명이 존재할 수 있을 것이라는 내용은 흐름상 적절하지 않다.

17 ②

단어

present A with B : A에게 B를 주다
extensive : 대규모의
trace : 찾아내다, 추적하다
heritage : 유산
admission : 입장
respectively : 각자, 제각기

해석

시카고의 Newberry 도서관과 Bookfield 동물원은 월요일 백악관에서 영부인 Laura Bush에게 박물관과 도서관 서비스에 대한 국가훈장을 받은 열 개의 기관들 중 하나다. 그 연례적인 상은, 워싱턴에 있는 박물관과 도서관 서비스 협회로부터 주어지는데, 기관들에게 그들의 수집품과 지역사회 관여에 대해 영예를 주고 각각 1만 달러의 상금을 포상한다. Bookfield 동물원은 Zoo Adventure Passport와 같은 프로그램들로 인해 수상의 영예를 안았는데, 그 프로그램은 저소득 가정들에게 무료 현장학습을 제공한다. Bush는 "Bookfield 동물원은 지역의 학생들을 위한 살아있는 교실입니다"라고 말했다. Newberry 도서관 역시 50만이 넘는 지도들의 대규모 수집과 아프리카계 미국인들이 그들의 가문의 유산을 찾도록 돕는 역할을 해 수상의 영예를 안았다.

① Bookfield 동물원은 저소득 가정들을 위한 무료입장을 지원하는 프로그램을 운영했다.
② Bookfield 동물원은 아프리카계 미국 어린이들의 가족사를 추적하는 것을 도왔다.
③ Newberry 도서관과 Bookfield 동물원은 각각 1만 달러의 상금을 탔다.
④ Newberry 도서관은 지도로 인해 아주 많은 수의 훈장을 받았다.

18 ②

단어

descriptive : 서술하는, 묘사하는
evaluative : 평가하는
inappropriate : 부적절한
incompetent : 무능한
or the like : 또는 그밖에 유사한 것
counterproductive : 역효과를 낳는
provoke : 유발하다
deviation : 일탈, 탈선
be apt to do : ~하는 경향이 있다
censure : 질책하다

해석

피드백은, 특히 부정적인 종류는 판단하거나 평가하기보다는 서술적이어야 한다. 당신이 얼마나 화가 나든, 피드백은 업무와 연관해서만 하도록 유지하라. 그리고 부적절한 행동을 했다고 해서 절대 누군가를 개인적으로 비난하지 마라. 사람들에게 그들이 어리석다거나, 무능하다거나, 또는 그밖에 유사한 것으로 말하는 것은 거의 항상 역효과를 낳는다. 그것은 너무나도 감정적인 반응을 유발시켜서 성과의 일탈 그 자체는 간과되기 쉬운 경향이 있다. 당신이 비판할 때, 당신은 그 사람이 아닌 업무와 관련된 행동을 질책해야 함을 기억해야 한다.

19 ④

단어

summer session : 여름 학기
revise : 변경하다
specific : 구체적인
infirmary : 병원, 양호실
bulletin board : 게시판

해석

9주의 여름 학기 동안, 대학 공동체를 위한 서비스들은 변경된 스케줄을 따릅니다. 캠퍼스 버스 서비스, 구내식당 그리고 양호실과 레크리에이션 및 체육 시설들의 하계 운영 시간에 대한 구체적인 변경사항은 구내식당 바깥에 있는 게시판에 게시될 것입니다. 주간 영화와 공연 스케줄은 끝나가고 있고 매주 수요일에 구내식당 바같에 게시될 것입니다. 캠퍼스 버스는 매 30분마다 본관을 떠나 캠퍼스 내 모든 정규 노선에 정차할 것입니다. 구내식당은 주중에는 오전 7시부터 오후 7시까지 그리고 주말에는 정오부터 오후 7시까지 아침, 점심, 저녁을 제공합니다. 도서관은 주중에는 정규 시간을 유지하지만, 토요일과 일요일에는 정오부터 오후 7시까지 단축 운영합니다. 도서관 대여 서비스와 레크리에이션 및 체육, 오락 시설 이용을 원하는 모든 학생들은 허가된 여름 신분증이 있어야 합니다. 이 공지는 학생 신문의 다음 호에서도 볼 수 있습니다.

① 영화와 공연 스케줄은 한 달에 두 번 공지될 것이다.
② 주중에, 구내식당과 도서관은 정오에 열 것이다.
③ 캠퍼스 버스는 매 시간 운영되며 모든 정규 정차 지점에 정차할 것이다.
④ 여름 학기 동안 체육 및 오락 시설을 이용하기 위해서는 유효한 신분증이 요구된다.

① 한 물체를 가리키는 것에 관해서, 어린이들은 같은 모양이지만 다른 물질인 물체를 가리켰다.
② 한 물질을 가리키는 것에 관해서, 어린이들은 그것의 모양에 상관없이 같은 물질을 가리켰다.
③ 어린이들은 주목할 만한 형태를 가진 고체의 이름을 그 같은 종류의 물체에 적용할 수 있다.
④ 어린이들은 오직 그들의 언어가 어떻게 그것들을 구별하는지를 안 이후에 물체를 물질로부터 구분할 수 있다.

2014. 6. 21.
제1회 지방직 시행

---

20 ④

단어 :

orginally : 원래
copper : 구리
plumbing : 배관
tee : T자관
substance : 물질
namely : 즉, 다시 말해
regardless of : ~에 상관없이
smear : 얼룩
identically : 꼭 같게
glob : 방울
distinguish : 구별하다, 식별하다
portion : 부분
accordingly : 부응해서
generalize : 개략적으로 말하다, 일반화하다
noteworthy : 주목할 만한
arbitrary : 임의적인

해석

구리 T배관처럼 우리가 물체라고 생각하는 것을 아이들이 처음 보았을 때, 그들은 가리킨다. 모양이 다른 같은 물질, 말하자면 한 더미의 구리 조각들이 아니라, 다른 물질로 이루어진 같은 모양의 물건. 그러나 우리가 헤어젤과 같이 물질이라고 생각하는 것을 그들이 보았을 때는 그들은 가리킨다. 세 얼룩의 헤어젤처럼 모양에 상관없이 같은 물질을. 똑같이 굽은 핸드크림 방울처럼 다른 물질의 같은 모양이 아니라. 어린이들이 영어라는 언어가 개개의 물건들과 물질이라는 부분을 어떻게 구분하는지 잘 알기 전에, 그들은 그들 스스로 식별하고, 그에 따라서 단어들을 개략적으로 말한다. 주목할 만한 고체들을 위한 이름들이 그러한 종류의 물체들에 사용된다. 정해진 모양을 가지고 있지 않은 고체가 아닌 것들을 위한 이름이 그런 종류의 물질들에 쓰인다.

1 ④

단어 :

curb : 억제하다, 제한하다
unquenchable : 채울(충족시킬) 수 없는
appetite : 식욕, 욕구
communist : 공산주의자, 공산당
see as : ~으로 생각하다(간주하다)

해석

전기자동차는 석유와 가스 수입에 대한 <u>끝없는</u> 욕구를 억제하기 위한 중국의 노력으로서 중요한 부분인데, 공산당 지도자들은 이러한 점을 전략적 약점으로 생각한다.

① 결코 틀리지 않는　　　② 심미적, 미학적인
③ 청소년　　　　　　　　④ 채울(만족시킬) 수 없는

2 ③

단어 :

not dry behind the ears : 풋내기의, 경험 없는, 미숙한
give somebody a break : ~에게 기회를 주다, 너그럽게 봐주다
know one's way around : (장소·주제 등에 대해) 잘 알다, 익숙하다

해석

John은 이제 막 회사에서 일을 시작하여 아직 <u>서툴렀다</u>. 우리는 그를 너그럽게 봐줘야 했다.

3 ①

단 어

tend to : (~하는) 경향이 있다.

해 석

만약 당신이 <u>내성적인</u> 사람이라면, 당신은 당신의 감정을 숨기는 경향이 있고 다른 사람들에게 당신의 진심을 드러내는 것을 좋아하지 않을 것이다.

① 말을 잘 하지 않는, 내성적인
② 말이 많은
③ 유창한, 연설을 잘 하는
④ 자신감 있는, 확신하는

4 ④

단 어

cosmetics : 화장품

해 석

당신은 어떻게 온라인에서 화장품 판매를 <u>시작하게</u> 되었습니까?

① go around (둥글게) 돌다, (사람들에게 몫이) 돌아가다, (자주) ~하다(하고 다니다), (소문 등이) 퍼지다, 순회하다
② go back (두 사람이 보통 긴 시간) 알고 지내다, (앞에 있었던 일 또는 말하던 내용으로) 돌아가다
③ go down 넘어지다, 쓰러지다
④ go into (어떤 직종에) 들어가다, (어떤 일이나 행동을) 하기 시작하다, (차량이) ~을 들이받다, (차량이) ~을 하기 시작하다, 검토(조사)하다, (돈, 시간, 노력 등이) 투입되다(쓰이다)

5 ②

단 어

goods : 제품, 상품
marginal : 미미한, 중요하지 않은, 경계의
marginal cost : 한계비용
inherently : 선천적으로, 기본적으로
publicly : 공공연하게
incur : 초래하다, 발생시키다
initial : 처음의, 초기의
investment : 투자
restrict : 제한하다
facility : 시설
accession : 취임, 즉위, 가입

해 석

한계비용이 0원에 가까운 재화는 기본적으로 공공재이며 대중적으로 이용될 수 있도록 만들어져야 한다. 다리와 도로가 좋은 예이다. 일단 사회에서 다리나 도로를 건설하는 데 드는 기본적 비용이 발생되면, 초기 투자에서의 최대 이익은 재화의 사용이 요금에 의해 제한되지 않는 경우에만 얻어지게 된다.

TIP

① 목적어(such facilities)와 동사(must be able to use)의 위치가 잘못되었다.
② (주어) + allow <u>people</u> free access to such facilities(allow A B : A에게 B를 허락하다)의 수동 형태로, allow의 목적어(A) people이 주어가 되면서 allow 뒤에는 free access~(B)만 남게 되었다.
③ '할 수 있어야 한다'와 must의 의미가 서로 맞지 않고, '무료'의 의미가 되려면 without charge가 되어야 한다.
④ 문장에 '무료'를 의미하는 단어가 없다. freedom은 '자유'라는 의미로 쓰인다.

6 ①

단 어

representative : 대표(자)
representation : 묘사, 표현, 대표자(대리인)를 내세움, 대의권
senate : 상원
serve : 제공하다, 차려주다
insulate : 절연(단열, 방음) 처리를 하다, ~을 보호(격리)하다
in regard to : ~과 관련하여, ~에 대하여
public servant : 공무원
legislature : 입법 기관, 입법부
amendment : (법 등의) 개정
ratify : 비준(재가)하다, 승인하다

해 석

하원에서와는 달리 상원의 대의권은 모든 주에서 동등하다. 각 주에는 2명의 상원의원이 있다. 상원의원의 임기는 6년이다. 임기 보장의 목적은 상원의원들을 여론으로부터 보호하고 이들이 독립적으로 활동하게 해주는 것이다. 선출과 관련하여 한때 상원 내 공무원들이 자신이 대표하는 주의 입법부에 의해서 <u>임명되곤 했다</u>. 미국 국민들에게 자신의 상원의원을 직접 선출할 수 있는 힘을 부여한 것은 바로 1913년에 비준된 제7차 개정헌법이었다.

① appoint 임명(지명)하다
② applaud 박수를 치다, 갈채를 보내다
③ appease 달래다, (요구를) 들어주다
④ appeal 항소(상고)하다

7 ④

> **단 어** •

distribution : 분배, 분포

abolish : 폐지하다

property : 재산, 소유물

vast : 방대한, 막대한

inevitably : 필연적으로

burden : 부담, 짐

assume : 추정하다

entitle : 자격을 주다

inverse : 반대의

proportion : 부분, 비율

merit : 가치, 훌륭함

greedy : 탐욕스러운

> ☑ **해 석** ······

당신은 사유재산을 완전히 없애버리기 전까지는 재화의 공평한 분배를 받지 못할 것이며 또한 인간으로서의 삶의 만족스러운 체계를 얻을 수 없을 것이다. 사유재산 제도가 존재하는 한 대다수의 인류, 혹은 <u>그중에서도 도덕적으로 성숙한</u> 자들은 가난, 역경, 그리고 걱정 속에서 필히 지속적으로 노력을 하게 될 것이다.

(A) 사유 재산은 이웃 사람들이 모두 가난하다고 해도 당신이 부자라는 사실에는 전혀 문제가 없다고 가정한다.

(B) 모든 사람들에게 가능한 한 스스로 많은 것을 얻을 자격이 주어졌을 때 거의 모든 재산은 반드시 소수의 손으로 들어가기 마련이다.

(C) 이것은 다른 모든 사람들이 가난하다는 것을 의미한다.

(D) 그리고 부는 **훌륭함**의 정도에 반비례해서 달라지는 경향이 있다. 왜냐하면 가난한 사람들은 그들의 매일의 일이 공동체에 유익이 되는, 단순하고 정직한 사람들인 반면에, 부자들은 완전히 쓸데없이 탐욕스러운 성향일 것이기 때문이다.

8 ②

> **단 어** •

astatine : 아스타틴(원자번호 85번의 원소)

practically : 사실상, 거의

unstudied : 자연히 터득한, 저절로 알게 된

polonium : 폴로늄(원자번호 84번의 원소)

elusive : 찾기 힘든

francium : 프랑슘(원자번호 87번의 원소)

scarce : 부족한, 드문

widespread : 광범위한, 널리 퍼진

> ☑ **해 석** ······

지구상에는 자연적으로 생기는 92가지의 원소가 있고, 이에 더해서 실험실에서 만들어져 온 20개 정도가 더 있다. 지구상의 화학물질 가운데 놀라울 정도로 거의 알려지지 않은 것이 상당

히 많다. 예를 들어, 아스타틴은 사실상 연구되지 않았다. 이것은 명칭이 있고 주기율표상에서 마리 퀴리의 폴로늄 옆에 위치하고 있지만 그밖에 다른 것은 연구된 것이 거의 없다. 문제는 <u>희소성</u>이다. 아스타틴은 그리 많지 않다. 그러나 모든 원소 가운데 가장 파악이 어려운 것은 프랑슘인데 어떠한 때에 측정해보아도 지구 전체에 20개 미만의 프랑슘 원소가 있다고 생각될 정도로 극히 적다. 모두 합쳐도 자연에서 생겨나는 원소 중 오직 약 30개만이 지구상에 퍼져있다.

① 신맛, 산성

② 진귀한(희귀한) 사람(것), 희귀성

③ 유독성

④ 양립(공존) 가능성, 호환성

9 ④

> **단 어** •

rapidly : 급속히, 신속히

firsthand : 직접

breed : 종류, 유형

geography : 지리

disposal : (무언가를 없애기 위한) 처리, 처분

equip : 장비를 갖추다

knowledgeable : 아는 것이 많은

appealing : 매력적인, 흥미로운

finalize : 마무리짓다

compensate : 보상하다

payroll : 급여 대상자 명단

feed into : ~에 반영되다

itinerary : 여행 일정표

> ☑ **해 석** ······

과거의 경험 많은 여행사들은 여행지에 대한 직접적인 지식이 적은 새로운 여행사에 의해 빠르게 대체되고 있다. 이런 새로운 종류의 여행사들이 대하는 것은 지리에 대해 잘 모르지만 돈과 시간이 많은 고객들이다. 해결책은 이러한 많은 것들을 알고 있지 못하는 직원들에게 알맞은 여행지를 고객과 잘 맞춰줄 수 있도록 도와주는 컴퓨터와 비디오를 갖춰주는 것이다.

(C) 핵심은 바로 선호하는 여행에 대해 고객에게 묻는 것이다. 특별히 요구하는 것이 있는데 이런 요구 가운데 가장 전형적인 것은 "나는 짐을 싸고 풀고 하는 것을 반복하고 싶지 않다."이거나 "나는 빨리 돌아다니면서 많은 것을 보고 싶지는 않다."와 같은 것들이다.

(B) 수집된 반응들이 컴퓨터 프로그램에 반영되어 추천 목적지 리스트와 고객의 선호에 맞는 여행 일정표를 만들어 낸다.

(A) 그러고 나서 고객은 가장 마음에 드는 것으로 보이는 목적지를 담고 있는 비디오를 보고 자신의 여행 계획을 마무리짓는다. 이런 식으로 여행사들은 (자신들이 월급을 주는) 자기 직원들의 경험부족을 보완하기 위하여 현대적인 기술을 이용한다.

10 ①

단 어

fellow : 친구, 동료, 녀석, 동료의
interpersonal : 대인관계에 관련된
spot : (특정한) 장소, 자리
eager beaver : 아주 열심인 사람, 일(공부)벌레
interact : 소통하다, 교류하다
interfere : 간섭하다, 참견하다

해 설

아이디어를 개발해내는 가장 좋은 방법은 동료 관리자들과의 소통을 통한 것이다. 이것은 우리에게 협동정신과 대인관계의 중요성을 가져다준다. 오늘날 가장 큰 문제 중의 하나는 대부분의 관리자들이 지나치게 많은 정보를 가지고 있다는 것이다. 성공의 열쇠는 정보가 아니다. 바로 사람이다. 그리고 최고의 관리자 자리를 채우기 위해서 내가 찾는 사람은 아주 열심인 노력파, 즉 예상보다 더 많은 일을 하려고 노력하는 사람이다.

11 ②

단 어

hiring : 고용, 임대차
conclude : 결론(판단)을 내리다
exhaustive : 철저한, 완전한
segment : 부분, 조각, 나누다, 분할하다
chancellor : 수상, 총장
trustee : 신탁 관리자, 이사
faculty : (타고난) 능력(기능), 교직원
alumni : 졸업생들
nominate : 임명(지명)하다
candidate : 입후보자
advisory : 자문(고문)의
subcommittee : 분과 위원회, 소위원회
narrow : 좁은, 좁아지다, (눈이) 찌푸려지다
finalist : 결승전 출전자
emerge : 드러나다, 알려지다

해 설

2008년 이후로 Licafornia 대학 총장직을 맡아온 Carlos Jimenez를 Heoha 대학의 10대 총장으로 선출했다는 소식이 3월 15일에 학교 평의원 회의에서 발표되었다. 그는 7월 1일 취임할 것이다. 그를 임명한 것은 대학 각 분야에서의 데이터를 수집하는 철저한 과정을 거쳐 결정한 것이었다. 교직원, 학생, 그리고 졸업생들에게 후보를 추천해달라고 요청하였다. 자문 소위원회도 전국에서 펼쳐진 40여 차례에 걸친 공청회를 통해 얻은 자료를 수집했다. 이 지명은 처음에는 100명으로 좁혀졌고 다음으로 면접을 받은 20명으로, 그러고 나서 최종 5명으로 압축되었다. 이번 조사위원회를 이끈 Jeffrey Pinorius 위원은 Jimenez가 확실한 선택으로 드러났다고 말했다. "이번 대학 총장 조사위원회는 분명한 비전을 가지고 있으며, 대단히 복잡한 조직을 이끄는 데 요구되는, 이미 입증된 지도력을 갖춘 지도자를 찾는 일을 맡아왔다."고 그가 말했다.

12 ④

단 어

content : 만족하는
traverse : 가로지르다, 횡단하다, 활강하다
slippery : 미끄러운
glacier : 빙하

해 설

모험 여행은 오늘날 관광 산업에서 인기가 많은 추세이다. 평범한 사람들은 사무실에서 벗어나 2주 동안 하와이의 화창한 해변에서 누워 보내는 것에 더 이상 만족하지 않는다. 이들은 점점 더 휴가를 거친 강물에서 뗏목을 타고, 열대우림 속을 여행하고 높은 산을 오르거나 미끄러운 빙하를 가로지르는 데 보내고 있다. (모든 연령층의 사람들이 휴가 동안 교육을 목적으로 하는 여행을 선택하고 있다.)

TIP

모험적인 요소가 많은 여행의 추세에 관한 내용이므로 (D)의 교육적인 요소의 모험 내용은 글의 전체 흐름과 맞지 않는다.

13 ②

단 어

extend : 확장하다, 연장하다, 포괄하다
enhance : 향상시키다, 높이다
participant : 참가자
gradually : 서서히
sharp : 날카로운, 예리한, 날렵한, 영리한
sound : 건전한, 건강한

해 설

운동의 이점은 신체적인 건강 증진보다 훨씬 더 많은 것을 포괄한다. 많은 사람들은 건강을 유지하기 위한 것일 뿐만 아니라 정신적이고 영적인 건강을 위해서도 운동을 한다. 신체적으로 건강한 것이 행복하게 해줄 수 있는가? 삶의 스트레스를 해결할 수 있게 도와주는가? 더 영적이고 신앙적인 삶으로 이어질 수 있는가? 많은 이들에게 대답은 '그렇다'이다. 걷기와 같은 운동은 뇌로 들어가는 혈액의 흐름을 늘려 준다. 60세 이상의 사람들을 대상으로 한 연구에서 하루에 시속 6킬로미터로 45분을 걷는 것이 참가자의 사고 능력을 높여주는 것으로 나타났다. 이들은 15분간 걷기에서 시작해 점차 운동 시간과 속도를 높였다. 결과는 참가자들이 이런 걷기 프로그램으로 인해 정신적으로 더욱 영리해졌다는 것이다.

① 연습하면 완벽을 이룰 수 있다.
② 건강한 육체에 건강한 정신.
③ 경험이야말로 최고의 선생님이다.
④ 세월은 누구도 기다려주지 않는다.

14 ②

> 단 어 ·

spell : 철자를 말하다(쓰다), (특정한 날씨 등이 지속되는) 한동
　　　 안(잠깐의 시기)
pacify : 진정시키다, 달래다
precede : ~에 앞서다, 선행하다
presume : 추정하다, 여기다
provoke : 유발하다

15 ①

> 단 어 ·

efficient : 능률적인, 효율적인
alert : 기민한, (정신이) 초롱초롱한

> 해 석

① 부주의한 많은 보행자들이 거리에서 사망하였다.
② 각각의 장교는 자신의 임무를 효율적으로 수행해야 한다.
③ 아무리 열심히 애를 써도, 당신은 그것을 해낼 수 없다.
④ 독일셰퍼드는 영리하고, 기민하며, 충직하다.

> TIP

① 'many a 단수명사'는 a 단수명사에 수일치를 시켜 단수
　 동사를 취한다. 따라서 many a careless walker was
　 ~ 는 맞는 표현이다.
② ~ perform their duties efficient. → ~ perform their
　 duties efficiently.
　 efficient가 동사 perform을 수식하기 때문에 형용사
　 형태가 아닌 부사 형태 efficiently로 와야 옳은 문장이
　 된다. (each officer의 경우, 성별이 정확하지 않기 때문
　 에 소유대명사로 their를 허용하기도 한다.)
③ however you may try hard → however hard you
　 may try
　 'however +형용사/부사 +S +V'의 순서이다.
④ ~dogs are smart, alert, and loyalty → ~dogs are
　 smart, alert, and loyal.
　 and 병렬구조 이므로 smart, alert와 같이 형용사 형태
　 인 loyal로 쓰는 것이 맞다.

16 ③

> 단 어 ·

automobile : 자동차
district : (특정한) 지구(지역)

> 해 석

이 지역에 있는 자동차의 10분의 1이 지난해 도난당했다.

> TIP

주어인 automobiles가 복수이고 과거 시제의 수동형이 되
어야 하므로 were가 옳다.

17 ③

> 단 어 ·

abuse : 남용, 오용, 남용(오용)하다
psychology : 심리학
head and shoulders above : 단연 빼어나게, 분명히 더 우수하게
way to go : 잘했어!

> 해 석

A : 벤, 오늘 학교에서 어땠니?
B : 탄탄대로야. 실은 심리학 수업에서 약물 중독에 관한 내용을
　　 발표했는데 교수님한테 칭찬을 받았어.
A : 정확히 뭐라고 했는데?
B : 내 발표가 다른 사람들보다 분명히 더 우수하다고 했어.
A : 잘했어!

① make headway 나아가다, 진전하다
② make a splash 깜짝 놀라게 하다, 평판이 자자해지다
③ pay a compliment 칭찬하다
④ pass a wrong judgment 잘못된 판단을 하다

18 ①

> 단 어 ·

intersection : 교차로
specific : 구체적인, 명확한
punctual : 시간을 지키는(엄수하는)

> 해 석

A : 실례합니다. 제가 남부터미널을 찾고 있는데요.
B : 아, 바로 저기예요.
A : 어디라고요? 좀 더 구체적으로 말씀해주실 수 있나요?
B : 네. 그냥 길 아래로 걸어가다가, 첫 번째 교차로에서 오른쪽
　　 으로 꺾으세요. 터미널은 왼쪽에 있어요. 분명히 찾을 수 있
　　 을 거예요.

① 좀 더 구체적으로 말씀해주실 수 있나요?
② 제가 시간을 엄수했나요?
③ 바로 그곳으로 갈 건가요?
④ 차로 여기서 얼마나 걸릴까요?

19 ③

calamity : 재앙, 재난
thoughtfulness : 생각에 잠김, 사려 깊음
whisk off : ~를 재빨리 데려가다
incredibly : 믿을 수 없을 정도로, 엄청나게
adequate : 충분한, 적절한

지난 한 달은 우리를 놀라움에 빠트린 재앙들로 인해 제가 살면서 가장 길게 느낀 시간이었습니다. 터널의 끝에 단 하나의 불빛이 있었고 그 불빛이 바로 당신이었습니다. 당신의 사려 깊음이 제게 얼마나 큰 의미가 있었는지 이루 말할 수가 없습니다. 제가 분명히 확신하기에는 너무 지쳐있었지만, 당신이 제가 쉴 수 있도록 한 시간 동안이나 제 아이들을 데려간 것이나, 또한 아이스티를 곁들인 저녁을 가져올 때마다 저는 그저 믿을 수 없이 굉장한 일이 일어났다는 것을 알 뿐이었습니다. 이제 정상으로 돌아온 지금 그 믿을 수 없을 정도로 대단한 것이 바로 당신이었다는 것을 알았습니다. 어떠한 말로 고마움을 표현해야 할지 말로는 충분하지 않지만 감사하는 마음이 항상 제 가슴에 있을 것입니다.

20 ②

seasoning : 양념
temporarily : 일시적으로, 임시로
deprive : (물건 등을) 빼앗다, (권리 등의 행사를) 허용하지 않다
intensity : 강렬함
crave : 갈망(열망)하다
insistent : 고집하는 주장하는
lime : 석회
relieve : 없애(덜어)주다, 해소하게 해주다, 완화하다, 줄이다
receptor : (인체의) 감각기
respond : 반응을 보이다
absence : 결석, 결근, 부재
perceive : 감지(인지)하다, ~을 …로 여기다
aversion : 아주 싫어함, 혐오감
appetite : 식욕
ambivalent : 반대 감정이 병존하는, 애증이 엇갈리는
sensory : 감각의
digestion : 소화(력)

우리는 왜 든든한 식사 이후에도 막대 사탕에 손이 가는가? 우리는 분명히 배고프지 않다. 우리는 왜 음식에 소금과 다른 양념을 원하는가? 일시적으로 염분을 섭취하지 못한 군인들은 염분에 대한 욕구의 최대치가 음식 자체에 대한 최대 욕구보다 훨씬 더 크다고 한다. 석회를 충분히 섭취하지 못한 소와 다른 가축들은 이런 욕구를 해소하기 위해 다른 동물의 뼈를 먹는다. 이러한 상황은 현재 충분히 밝혀지고 있지 않지만 체내 어딘가에 몸이 필요로 하는 특정 물질이 부족하여 생기는 혈액 속 화학적 상태에 반응을 보이는 감각기관이 있는 것이 확실해 보인다. 이러한 감각기관이 그러한 상태를 감지하면 우리는 필요한 특정 물질에 대한 욕구를 갖게 되는 것이다.

① 짠 음식이나 단 음식에 대한 혐오
② 특정 필요 물질에 대한 욕구
③ 음식으로 생기는 뼈 질병을 예방하는 능력
④ 소화에 대해 양면적인 감각 수용기

**2014. 6. 28.
서울특별시 시행**

---

1 ⑤

efface : 지우다, 없애다
manuscript : 원고

David는 그의 원고에서 몇 줄을 <u>지우기로</u> 결정했다.

① 이해시키다　　② 진가를 알아보다, 고마워하다
③ 이해하다　　　④ 암송하다
⑤ 지우다

2 ⑤

mine : 캐다, 채굴하다
asthma : 천식
delve into : ~을 철저하게 조사하다
suburban : 교외의

과거에는 채굴을 하곤 했으나 지금은 천식을 앓고 있는 주민들과의 몇몇 인터뷰를 포함하여, 그 다큐멘터리는 온타리오 교외 지역의 석탄광업 문제를 <u>자세하게 조사하고 있다.</u>

① 담론, 담화 ② 제공하다, 확증하다
③ 설명하다 ④ 대화를 나누다
⑤ 수사하다

③ 아이들은 더 많은 단 음식과 음료를 소비할 수 있을 것이다.
④ 충치에 대항하는 장기적인 보호물이 곧 시장에서 이용 가능하게 될 것이다.
⑤ 충치와 관련된 미생물이 백신에 반응하지 않을 것이다.

3 ①

단 어

emulate : 모방하다

해 설

폴란드인 코치는 같은 클럽에서 1,000 경기를 맡음으로써 그 프랑스인을 모방하고 싶어하는 것을 인정한다.

① 모방하다, 본뜨다 ② 위로하다
③ 몹시 괴롭히다 ④ 입증하다
⑤ 발표하다

4 ②

단 어

fresh from : ~를 갓 나온
(still) wet behind the ears : 머리에 피도 안 마른

해 설

우리가 새로 구한 조수는 법대를 갓 졸업했다. 그는 매우 이상주의적이다. – 아직 애송이다.

① 낙관론자 ② 초심자, 초보자 ③ 부적응자
④ 공무원 ⑤ 말썽꾼

5 ④

단 어

microorganism : 미생물
cavity : (치아에 생긴) 구멍, 충치
eliminate : 제거하다
immunization : 면역조치

해 설

치과 연구원들에 따르면, 충치를 유발한다고 여겨지는 미생물의 수를 현저히 줄일 수 있는 백신이 곧 인체 임상 실험 준비 중에 있다고 한다. 결과적으로, 충치에 대항하는 장기적인 보호물이 곧 시장에서 이용 가능하게 될 것이다.

① 충치 예방 프로그램은 곧 제거될 것이다.
② 실험동물에 대해 면역 조치를 취하는 것이 더 이상 필요하지 않을 것이다.

6 ③

단 어

come and go : 왔다갔다 함

해 설

당신이 평화롭고 여유 있는 사람들을 관찰하다보면, 그들이 기분이 좋을 때 매우 감사해 한다는 것을 알게 된다. 그들은 긍정적인 감정과 부정적인 감정 모두 나타났다 사라질 수 있으며 기분이 좋지 않을 때가 있을 것이라는 것을 이해한다. 행복한 사람들에게, 이것은 괜찮다. 그러기 마련이다. 그들은 흘러가는 감정들의 불가피함을 받아들인다.

① 복수, 앙갚음 ② 게으름, 나태 ③ 불가피함
④ 꺼림 ⑤ 축출

7 ①

단 어

eloquent : 웅변을 잘 하는, 유창한
vigorously : 발랄하게, 힘차게
current : 흐름, 조류

해 설

① 어떤 특정한 때에 이 문은 잠기지 않은 채로 남겨져 있을 수 있다.
② 그녀는 설득력 있었지만, 그를 설득할 수는 없었다.
③ 그가 너무 강력하게 항의해서 그들은 그의 사건을 재고하기로 했다.
④ 바다는 그것의 흐름이 있다, 강과 호수도 또한 마찬가지다.
⑤ 오직 이 방법으로만 그들의 행동들을 설명하는 것이 가능하다.

TIP

① At certain times may this door be left unlocked. → At certain times this door may be left unlocked.
시간 부사구가 문장 앞에 위치해도 주어, 동사가 도치되지 않는다. 따라서 보기에 주어진 문장은 틀린 문장이다.
② 'Though she was eloquent, ~.' 문장에서 eloquent를 강조하기 위해 문장 앞에 두었다.
③ He protested so vigorously that ~. → So vigorously did he protest that ~.
so vigorously를 강조하기 위해 문장 앞에 두면서 주어 동사가 도치된 문장이다.

④ 'as V+S'는 접속사로서, 주절의 문장 뒤에서 'S가 V하듯이'라는 뜻으로 쓰인다. 따라서 The sea has its currents, as do(=앞 문장의 have를 받는 대동사이다) the river and the lake는 맞는 문장이다.

⑤ It is possible only in this way to ~. → Only in this way is it possible to ~.

부사구 only in this way를 강조하면서 주절의 주어, 동사가 도치된 문장이다.

8 ④

단어

fall ill : 병에 걸리다

해설

때때로 당신이 병에 걸리는 것을 <u>막기 위해</u> 당신이 할 수 있는 것은 아무것도 없다. 그러나 만약 당신이 건강한 삶을 유지한다면 당신은 아마 <u>훨씬</u> 더 빨리 회복될 것이다. 우리는 흡연이나 과음, 또는 마약 <u>복용</u>과 같이 우리 몸에 <u>해를 준다</u>고 알고 있는 것들을 <u>하는 것을</u> 피할 수 있다.

TIP

① '막기 위해서'라는 뜻으로 쓰인 to부정사이다.

② much는 비교급을 강조하기 위해 쓸 수 있다.

③ avoid는 목적어로 동명사를 취한다.

④ things that we know <u>damages</u> the body → things that we know <u>damage</u> the body

that절에서 we know는 삽입절이고 damages the body가 수식하는 선행사는 things이다. 관계사절의 주어가 복수형이므로 동사 또한 수일치시켜 damage로 고쳐야 한다.

⑤ such as smoking~, drinking~ or taking~. 병렬구조이다.

9 ②

단어

sculpture : 조각

해설

나의 예술사 교수님은 미켈란젤로의 그림을 그의 조각보다 더 선호한다. 비록 미켈란젤로 스스로는 후자를 더 자랑스러워했지만 말이다.

TIP

① 명사와 명사를 연결하여 수식하는 관계를 만들 수 있다.

② prefer Michelangelo's painting to viewing his sculpture → prefer~ to his sculpture

prefer A to B에서 A와 B는 같은 형태를 취해야 한다.

Michelangelo's painting이라는 명사와 비교하고 있으므로 viewing his sculpture라는 동명사구 대신, 명사 his sculpture로 쓰는 것이 바람직하다.

③ '(그 자신) 스스로는'의 뜻으로, 앞에 있는 Michelangelo를 강조한다.

④ proud의 비교급은 prouder, 최상급은 proudest이지만, 비교급에서 'B라기보단 A하다' 뜻을 나타내기 위해 단어의 음절수에 상관없이 'more A(원급) than B'라고 쓰기도 한다. although Michelangelo was more proud of the latter (than of the former)는 '미켈란젤로는 the former보다는 오히려 the latter(=his sculpture)를 자랑스럽게 여겼지만'으로 해석할 수 있다. the latter(후자)라는 단어에서 이미 그 비교대상을 알 수 있으므로 than 이하는 생략되었다.

⑤ the latter는 '후자'의 뜻으로 맞는 표현이다.

10 ③

단어

navigation : 항해
overcast : 구름이 뒤덮인
contingency : 만일의 사태
be paired with : ~와 병행되다
sophisticated : 세련된, 정교한
celestial : 하늘의, 천체의
pave the way : 길을 닦다, 상황을 조성하다

해설

고대의 항해는 태양에 의존했다, 그래서 화창한 날씨에 의지했다 ; 구름이 뒤덮인 하늘은 지연을 더 길게 하거나 더 안 좋은 것을 의미했다. 보다 정교한 항해 도구의 부족과 병행되는 날씨 비상사태는 그리스인들과 다른 고대의 지중해 문명인들이 그들의 탐험을 (A) <u>제한할</u> 수밖에 없었음을 의미했다 ; 무역 관계는 주위의 섬과 해안으로 대부분 제한되었다. 끝내 선원들은 방향을 위해 배의 움직임에 따른 별의 상대적인 위치를 이용하는 천체의 항해술을 사용하여 더 멀리까지 모험할 수 있었다. 그러나 심지어 그 때에도 배를 항로에서 벗어난 더 위험한 바다로 데려갈 수 있는 불길한 해류에 대한 두려움으로 인해 감히 해안선이 보이지 않는 곳까지 멀리 항해한 선장들은 거의 없었다. 마침내, 유럽으로의 나침반 도입은 탐험의 시대에 (B) <u>불을 붙였고</u> 미래의 서유럽 제국의 길을 닦았다.

① 제한하다 – 피하다, 피해 가다
② 신속히 처리하다 – 기록하다
③ 제한하다 – 불이 붙다, 점화하다
④ 금지하다 – 묘사하다
⑤ 용이하게 하다 – 박차를 가하다

함을 이루는 것은 각자의, 그리고 우리들 모두의 안에 있다고 믿는다.

11 ①

> **단 어**

antibiotic : 항생제
truckload : 트럭 한 대 분량의
discard : 버리다, 폐기하다

> **해 석**

탱커트럭들이 우유 처리 공장에 도착할 때, 우유가 항생물질에 대해 양성반응이 나오면 연방법에 따라 트럭 전체에 실린 양이 폐기되어야 한다.

> **TIP**

① the entire truckload가 주어, must be discarded가 동사로서 주절을 이룬다. 따라서 앞 문장은 종속절이 되어야 하므로 접속사가 필요하다. 'If milk should test positive~'에서 If가 생략되고 도치되어 'should milk test positive~'가 되었다.
② If milk test positive~는 동사가 주어 milk에 맞춰 tests가 되어야 하므로 올 수 없다.
③ If milk is test positive~는 동사가 be동사, test 두 개가 되어 틀린 문장이 된다.
④ were, test 두 개의 동사가 되므로 틀린 문장이다.
⑤ 접속사가 있어야 한다.

12 ②

> **단 어**

social skill : 사회적 기능

> **해 석**

판매업은 지속적인 상호작용이 요구되는 하나의 사업영역이다. 그래서 능숙한 사교술이 필수적이다.

> **TIP**

② 빈칸에는 one을 수식하는 관계사가 와야 하는데 뒤에 문장이 완전하므로 관계 부사(전치사 + 관계 대명사)가 와야 한다.

13 ⑤

> **단 어**

face : 직면하다

> **해 석**

사람으로서 그리고 비즈니스 여성으로서 내게는 매일이 내가 직면해야 할 도전이다. 목표를 달성하고자 한다면, 내 스스로에게 한계를 정해서는 안 된다는 것을 역사는 가르쳐줬다. 나는 <u>위대</u>

14 ①

> **단 어**

flextime : 근무시간 자유 선택제
adjust : 조정하다

> **해 석**

작업스타일의 대안이 점점 증가하는 가운데, 근무시간 자유 선택제가 있다. 근무시간 자유 선택제는 직원들이 개인적인 필요에 따라 근무 시간을 조정할 수 있게 허용한다. 일주일에 근무하는 총 시간은 동일하지만, 매일의 스케줄은 표준 근무시간과 다르다. 근무시간 자유 선택제는 또한 근무일 안에서의 변화도 의미하는데, 예를 들면 4일은 10시간 일하고, 6일은 짧은 시간 동안 일한다. 근무시간 자유 선택제를 하는 직원들로는 고용 기관, 피해 사정인들, 편지 관리인들, 그리고 데이터 입력자들이 있다.

① 근무시간 자유 선택제를 정의하기 위해서
② 유연한 근로자들을 묘사하기 위해서
③ 대안적인 근무 스타일에 대해 논의하기 위해서
④ 다른 직업들을 비교하기 위해
⑤ 근무시간 자유 선택제 스케줄을 정하기 위해서

15 ④

> **단 어**

verse : 운문
chronicler : 연대기 작자, 기록자
vanity : 자만심, 허영심
hypocrisy : 위선
typesetter : 식자공
sturdy : 튼튼한, 견고한
distinctive : 독특한, 특징적인

> **해 석**

ⓒ 자신의 필명인 Mark Twain으로 더 잘 알려진 Samuel Langhorne Clemens는 작가가 되기 전에 식자공과 미시시피 강의 보트 파일럿으로 일했다.
㉠ Mark Twain은 가볍고, 유머러스한 운문을 쓰면서 경력을 시작했지만, 인간의 허영과 위선의 기록자로 진화했다.
㉢ 허클베리 핀의 모험을 썼던 중반기에는, 그는 풍부한 유머와 견고한 이야기와 사회적인 비판을 혼합하여 미국의 테마와 언어를 바탕으로 한 독특한 미국 문학을 대중화시켰다.
㉡ Twain은 그의 글과 강연으로 많은 돈을 벌었지만, 노후에 벤처 사업에 투자를 해서 많은 돈을 잃었다.

16 ⑤

단 어 ·

medieval : 중세의
merriment : 유쾌하게 떠들썩함
festive : 축제의
idleness : 게으름, 나태
appetite : 식욕, 욕구
wander : 헤매다, 돌아다니다
ethic : 윤리, 도덕

해 석

중세 사람들은 엔터테인먼트(사람들이 돈을 내야 할 것으로 예상하는)와 축제 기간에 누구나 참가할 수 있는 그런 종류인 일반적인 떠들썩함을 구별하지 않았다. 그들은 둘 모두를 일과는 반대되는 "놀이"로 간주했으며, 엔터테이너들을 "놀이꾼"으로 불렀다. 교회는 게으름은 죄고, 놀이꾼들은 게으르며 그들을 보는 것도 게으름이라고 가르쳤다. 그러나 로마 시대의 극장의 폐쇄는 코미디, 속임수, 곡조에 대한 사람들의 욕구를 없애지 못했다. 가장 지속적인 효과는 <u>놀이꾼들에게서 작업장을 박탈한 것이었다</u>. 그래서 그들은 관중들을 찾아서 돌아다녀야 했다.

① 놀이꾼들이 축제에 참여하도록 하다.
② 축제를 위한 엔터테이너들을 고용하다.
③ 사람들에게 게으름을 피우지 못하도록 가르치다.
④ 놀이꾼들에게 새로운 윤리를 제공하다.
⑤ 놀이꾼들에게서 작업장을 박탈하다.

17 ③

단 어 ·

agitate : 뒤흔들다, 휘젓다
molecule : 분자
inward : 안쪽으로
hollow : 속이 빈, 움푹 꺼진
compartment : 칸
revolve : 회전하다
platter : 접시

해 석

전자레인지는 주로 음식 속에 있는 물 분자를 휘저어서 흔들어 놓음으로써 작동한다. 더 많이 흔들리거나 진동하는 분자들은 더 많은 열에너지를 가진다, 즉, 더 뜨거워지게 된다. 열에너지는 각각의 물 분자에서 주위의 다른 분자들로 옮겨간다. (전자레인지에서는) 보통의 오븐에서와 같이 외부에서 안으로 요리가 되기보다는, 음식 내부에서 요리가 된다. 그 과정은 전자레인지가 꺼진 후에도 한동안은 계속된다. 그래서 <u>전자레인지로 한 음식은 요리를 끝내기 위해 한동안 가만히 놔 둔다</u>.

① 전자관에 의해 만들어진 마이크로파는 속이 빈 도파관을 따라 일반적인 오븐 칸으로 들어간다.
② 밀봉 부분이 느슨해지거나 부서졌을 때 마이크로파가 빠져나갈 가능성이 가장 큰 곳은 문 주변이다.
③ 전자레인지로 한 음식은 요리를 끝내기 위해 한동안 가만히 놔 둔다.
④ 전자관을 멈추고 접시를 회전시킴으로써 요리를 짧은 시간 동안 멈출 수 있다.
⑤ 오븐이 작동하고 있는 동안에는 문은 잠겨 있고 열 수 없다.

18 ④

단 어 ·

erroneous : 잘못된
assumption : 추정
static : 고정된
component : 요소, 부품
equation : 방정식, 동일시
flux : 끊임없는 변화
cosmological constant : 우주 상수
constancy : 불변성
apparently : 분명히
astronomer : 천문학자
fundamentally : 근본적으로
flawed : 결함이 있는
derive : ~에서 비롯되다
make use of : ~을 이용하다

해 석

앨버트 아인슈타인의 상대성 이론이 물리학에 혁명을 일으켰지만, 그의 수학적 모델은 우주가 고정되어 있다는 - 모든 구성 요소들이 시간과 공간에 묶여 있다는 - 잘못된 가정에 바탕을 두고 있다. 이러한 관점을 유지하기 위해서, 아인슈타인의 방정식이 우주가 끊임없이 변화한다고 예측했을 때, 그는 우주의 불변성을 주장하기 위해서 "우주 상수"를 발명했다. 10년 이내에, 천문학자 에드윈 허블은 우주가 팽창을 하고 있다는 것을 발견했고, 이 발견은 아인슈타인이 우주 상수라는 개념을 포기하게 만들었다. 거의 한 세기 후에, 물리학자들은 어떤 알 수 없는 힘이 분명히 우주를 떠밀고 있다는 것을 발견했고, 어떤 과학자들이 아인슈타인의 "우주 상수"가 정말로 존재할지도 모른다는 결론을 내리게 만들었다.

① 허블의 관찰은 상대성 이론을 심하게 훼손시켰다.
② 아인슈타인의 가장 의미 있는 발견들 중의 하나는 우주 상수이다.
③ 아인슈타인의 상대성 이론은 근본적으로 결함이 있다.
④ 우주 상수는 잘못 도출되었긴 하지만 실제로 우주를 묘사하는 데 역할을 할지도 모른다.

⑤ 오늘날의 물리학자들은 우주를 묘사하기 위해서 아인슈타인의 우주 상수를 여전히 이용한다.

[19~20]

prose : 산문
take on : ~에 도전하다, 떠맡다
self-sufficient : 자급자족할 수 있는
incite : 선동하다, 조장하다

해 석

빅토리아 시대의 페미니스트 작가인 Elizabeth Barret Browning은 그녀의 시와 산문을 이용하여 "여성의 문제"를 포함하여 그녀의 시대가 직면하고 있었던 넓은 범위의 문제들에 도전하였다. 그녀의 장편시 Aurora Leigh에서, 그녀는 예술가로서의 성장과 그 내면에 있는 여성의 성장을 묘사하면서 이 질문에 대해 탐구한다. Aurora Liegh는 전통적인 빅토리아 시대의 여성이 아니다 - 그녀는 고등교육을 받은 자립적인 여성이다. 그 시에서, Browning은 남성이 누리는 자유와 대조적으로 여성에게 내려진 한계가 여성들이 일어나서 그들의 환경에 있어서 변화를 유발하도록 선동해야 한다고 주장한다. Aurora Leigh를 포함하여 Browning의 글은 여성의 삶에 있어서 주요한 사회적 변화에 대한 길을 닦는 데 도움이 되었다.

19 ③

해 석

주어진 지문으로부터 작가는 전통적인 빅토리아 시대의 여성은 고등교육을 받지 못했다고 믿고 있음을 추론할 수 있다.

① 시를 썼다.
② Aurora Leigh에 정확하게 묘사되어 있다.
③ 고등교육을 받지 못했다.
④ 사회적 변화를 위해 싸웠다.
⑤ 사회에서 공적인 역할을 했다.

20 ②

단 어 •

effect : (어떤 결과를) 가져오다

해 석

① 모방하다　　② 야기하다　　③ 발생하다
④ 방해하다　　⑤ 예방하다

---

1 ①

단 어 •

capacity : (…을 이해하거나 할 수 있는) 능력, 용량, 수용력
discriminate : 식별하다, 차별하다

해 석

한 달, 두 달 된 아기들은 말소리를 구별하는 능력이 있다.

① (보거나 듣고) 식별하다, 알아듣다.
② (뼈를) 탈구시키다. (시스템·계획 등을) 혼란에 빠트리다.
③ (작업·수면 등을) 방해하다, 불안하게 만들다.
④ (사람들에게) 나누어 주다, 분배하다. (상품을) 유통시키다.

2 ②

단 어 •

drive~up the wall : ~의 이성을 잃게 하다, 몹시 화나게 하다

해 석

교실에서 볼펜 누르는 소리를 내는 학생들은 나를 몹시 화나게 한다.
① 정신을 산란하게 하다.　　② 상당히 화나게 하다.
③ 나에게 자주 아부하다.　　④ 마음의 짐을 크게 덜어주다.

3 ②

단 어 •

surround : 둘러싸다, 에워싸다
former : (시간상으로) 예전의, (특정한 위치나 지위에 있던) 과거의
comprise : ~을 구성하다
union republic : 연방 공화국

해 석

① 대단한 사람들에게 둘러싸여 나는 자부심을 느꼈다.
② 나는 형에게 5달러를 빌려달라고 부탁했다.
③ 검은 드레스를 입은 여성이 플랫폼에 있었다.
④ 과거 소비에트 연방(소련)은 15개의 연방 공화국으로 구성되었다.

TIP

① 분사구문으로, 주어인 내(I)가 둘러싸여(수동태) 있는 것이므로 surrounded로 쓰는 것이 맞다.

② borrow는 3형식 동사이므로 목적어 한 개만을 취한다. 간접목적어(me), 직접목적어(five dollars)를 취할 수 있는 4형식 동사 lend로 고쳐야 한다.

③ A woman in a black dress was on the platform. → On the platform was a woman~.
부사구 on the platform을 강조하기 위하여 문장 앞에 위치시키면서, 주절의 주어, 동사가 도치되었다.

④ comprise는 '~을 구성하다'라는 뜻을 가진 타동사이므로 바로 목적어를 취할 수 있다.

4 ①

<u>단 어</u>

asleep : 잠이 든, 자고 있는
immediately : 즉시, 즉각

✓ **TIP**

① no sooner ~ than은 '~하자마자 ~했다'라는 뜻으로 no sooner가 있는 주절은 had p.p(과거완료)를 사용해야 하며 than 종속절은 과거 형태로 사용해야 한다. 따라서 잘 옮긴 문장이다.

② 그의 아버지가 집에 들어오자마자 소년은 잠이 들었다.

③ 그의 아버지가 집에 들어왔을 때, 소년은 잠이 들지 않았다.

④ 소년이 잠이 들기 전에 그의 아버지가 집에 들어왔다.

5 ④

<u>단 어</u>

be up and about : (환자가) 좋아지다
plow into : ~을 세게 때리다, ~와 부딪치다
traumatic : 정신적 외상을 초래할 정도의, 대단히 충격적인
incident : (범죄·사고 등의) 사건
for the time being : 당분간
squeaky : 삐걱거리는

✓ **해 석**

A : 안녕, 거스. 몸이 건강해진 걸 보니 반가워.
B : 고마워. 지난달에 트럭이 내 차와 부딪친 후 난 죽었다고 생각했는데 정말 운이 좋아서 살았어.
A : 그렇구나, 그 경험으로 심한 정신적인 충격을 받았겠다. 네 차는 수리했어?
B : 응, 하지만 더 이상 운전은 안 할 거야. 다시 차에 부딪히는 경험은 안 할 거야.
A : 그러지 마. 한 번 불행한 사고가 났다고 다시 운전을 안 할 수는 없어. 번개는 결코 같은 곳을 두 번 치지 않아.
B : 사람들은 그렇게 말하지만 난 당분간 대중교통을 이용할 거야.

① 삐걱거리는 바퀴에 기름칠한다(우는 아이 젖 준다).

② 유감스러운 것보다 안전한 것이 더 낫다(나중에 후회하는 것보다 조심하는 것이 낫다).

③ 다른 쪽 잔디가 항상 푸르다(남의 떡이 더 커 보인다).

④ 번개는 결코 같은 곳을 두 번 치지 않는다(불행은 연거푸 일어나지 않는다).

6 ①

<u>단 어</u>

wearable : 착용감이 좋은, 착용하기에 적합한
theoretically : 이론(상)으로, 공론으로
regulate : 조절하다
ergonomically : 생명공학적으로, 인체공학적으로
aesthetically : 미학적으로

✓ **해 석**

긍정적인 컴퓨터 사용의 지지자들은 기술이 인간의 웰빙과 잠재력에 이바지해야 한다고 주장한다. 우리의 삶을 다르게 만들어 주는 긍정적인 컴퓨터 사용의 실제 잠재력은 몸에 착용하기 적합한 차세대 컴퓨터 장치에 있다. 웨어러블 컴퓨터 장치가 어떻게 인간의 웰빙과 마음챙김을 증진시키는지는 현재 사용되는 건강 추적기와 건강 장비에서 알 수 있다. 심장 박동수, 수면량과 같은 물리적 요인을 측정하기 위해 설계된 이러한 것들은 이론상으로 기분을 조절해주는 긍정적인 피드백 장치가 될 수 있다. 이러한 장치들은 생명공학적으로 잘 설계되었고 미학적으로도 눈을 즐겁게 해줄 뿐 아니라 웰빙의 장애를 없애주는 경험을 하도록 할 것이다.

① 웨어러블 컴퓨터 장치는 웰빙에 기여할 수 있다.

② 긍정적인 컴퓨터 사용은 국력에 기여할 수 있다.

③ 웨어러블 컴퓨터 장치는 생활경비를 증가시킨다.

④ 긍정적인 컴퓨터 사용은 과학을 발전시킨다.

7 ①

<u>단 어</u>

existence : 존재, 실재, 현존
function : (사람·사물의) 기능
physiological : 생리적인
motivate : 동기를 부여하다
excel : 뛰어나게 잘 하다
diminish : 줄어들다, 감소하다
ramification : 영향, 파문
inevitable : 피할 수 없는

✓ **해 석**

스트레스는 삶 속의 실상이며 우리의 일상적인 실재의 모든 측면에 영향을 미칠 수 있다. 스트레스는 인간의 생리, 기능뿐만

아니라 정신에까지 부정적인 영향을 줄 수 있다. 여기서 중요한 이슈는 직원들의 스트레스 해소 방법이다. 어떤 개인에게 스트레스는 보통 때보다 훨씬 뛰어나게 잘 하도록 동기를 부여하는 도전이다. 이것은 긍정적 결과를 가져오는 스트레스이다. ㉠그러나 다른 개인에게는, 지나친 스트레스가 인체 기능의 능력을 약화시키고 의학적으로 심각한 결과를 가지게 할 수 있다. 이것은 부정적 결과를 가져오는 스트레스이다. 비록 스트레스는 불가피한 것일지라도 그것으로 인한 부정적이고 위험한 결과는 피할 수 있다. ㉡그러므로 조직뿐 아니라 개인에 있어서 불필요하고 건강에 좋지 않은 결과를 예방하기 위해 특히 조직 내 직장인들의 잠재적인 스트레스 근원을 조사할 필요가 있다.

TIP

㉠ 빈칸 앞에는 좋은 스트레스에 관한 내용이며, 빈칸 뒤에는 나쁜 스트레스에 관한 내용이므로 역접의 의미인 'however'가 들어가야 한다.

㉡ 부정적이고 위험한 결과는 피할 수 있다는 내용 뒤에 잠재적인 스트레스의 근원을 조사해야 한다는 내용이 왔으므로 'therefore'가 적절하다.

8 ③

단 어

sexist : 성차별주의자
outdated : (더 이상 쓸모가 없게) 구식인
split : 분열되다, 의견이 갈리다
phenomenon : 현상, 경이로운 사람

해 석

최근 미국인들 사이에는 아이에게 두 개의 성을 붙여주는 사람들이 있다. 그것은 남편의 성을 따르는 것이 시대에 뒤처지는 것이고 성차별적이라고 생각하는 일부 여성들 사고의 직접적인 결과물이다. 아이가 한 쪽 부모의 성을 따르는 것 또한 성차별적이다. 특히 알려지지 않은 부모(엄마)가 바로 아홉 달 동안이나 아이를 품은 쪽이기 때문이다. 논리적인 유일한 해결책은 아이에게 둘로 나뉜 성을 붙여주는 것이다. 그 결과 우리에게는 Elijah Sadler—Moore라는 이름의 아이들이 생겨났다. 이런 일이 최근의 현상이다 보니 우리는 하나로 된 두 성을 가진 사람이 그와 같은 또 다른 사람과 결혼을 하게 되는 때에는 어떤 일이 일어날지 두고 봐야 한다. 그들의 아이는 <u>결국 네 개의 성을 갖게 되는 것인가?</u>

① 엄마의 성으로 돌아가야 하는가?
② 세 개의 성을 따라야 하는가?
③ 결국 네 개의 성을 갖게 되는 것인가?
④ 이름을 포기해야 하는가?

9 ③

단 어

vital : 생명 유지에 필수적인
infant : 유아, 젖먹이
establish : 확고히 하다
confident : 자신감 있는, (전적으로) 확신하는
responsive : 즉각 반응하는, 호응하는
caregiver : 돌보는 사람
spoiling : 망치다, 못쓰게 만들다

해 석

울음은 아기들이 그들의 욕구를 세상에 알리는 가장 강력한 방법이다. 그것은 의사소통의 필수적인 방법이고 유아가 그들의 삶에 대해 통제력을 확고히 하는 최초의 방법이다. 아기들은 스스로 자신의 삶에 영향을 미칠 수 있다는 것을 알기 때문에 자신의 울음에 반응을 얻는 아기는 더 자신감을 갖게 되는 것으로 보인다는 연구 결과가 있다. (당신은 부모가 되어 가장 어려운 부분 중에 하나가 당신의 아기가 우는 것을 듣는 것이라 여겨지기도 모른다.) 아기들은 첫 해가 끝나기 전 그들의 울음이 부드럽고 위로가 되는 보살핌을 가져다 줄 경우, 덜 울고 다른 방식으로 더 의사소통을 한다. 돌보는 사람이 반응을 덜 보이는 경우 더 많이 우는 반면에. 당신의 아기가 울 때 그 울음에 반응하는 것이 버릇을 망칠까 두려워하지 마라.

10 ②

단 어

molecule : 분자
particle : (아주 작은) 입자, 미립자
droplet : 작은 물방울
alleviate : 경감시키다, 완화하다
water vapor : 수증기
wavelength : 파장

해 석

집안을 청소해 본 대부분의 사람들은 먼지가 더 적을수록 많이 행복할 것이다. 그러나 먼지가 없다면 강우량도 더 적을 것이고 저녁노을도 덜 아름다울 것이다. 비는 공기 중의 물 분자가 먼지의 작은 입자 주위에 모일 때 형성된다. 물이 모였을 때 충분히 무거워지면 물방울이 비가 되어 지상으로 떨어진다. (이것은 대기 중의 이산화탄소 양을 줄여 지구 온난화의 위험을 완화할 수 있다.) 그러므로 수증기는 먼지 입자가 없다면 비로 변할 가능성이 많이 적어진다. 수증기와 먼지 입자는 또한 태양의 광선을 반사한다. 일출과 일몰은 태양이 지평선 아래 있을 때 먼지와 수증기 분자가 우리가 볼 수 있는 빛 중에서 가장 긴 빨간색 파장을 반사시켜 다른 파장들보다 더 오래 볼 수 있게 한다. 공기 중에 먼지 입자가 많을수록 일출 또는 일몰의 색이 다채로워진다.

11 ①

📑 단어

settle : (논쟁 등을) 해결하다, 합의를 보다, (마침내) 결정하다.

☑ 해석

회의가 시작하기 전에 이슈를 <u>해결하는</u> 방법을 찾는 것이 중요하다.

① (문제 등을) 해결하다
② 재개하다, 다시 시작하다
③ (정보를) 검색하다
④ 폐지하다

12 ④

📑 단어

rent : 집세, 방세
utility : (수도 · 전기 · 가스와 같은) 공익사업
fee : (조직 · 기관 등에 내는) 요금

☑ 해석

로버트는 <u>생계를 유지할 수 없었으므로</u> 그의 부모님에게 그의 집세와 공공요금을 지불해달라고 부탁해야만 했다.

① 잠자리에 들다, 자다
② (~에) 게으름을 부리다
③ 용기를 잃지 않다
④ 겨우 먹고 살 만큼 벌다

13 ②

📑 단어

ashamed : (~여서) 부끄러운
unfairly : 불공평하게, 편파적으로

☑ 해석

한 여대생은 그녀의 아버지에게 진심으로 속이 상했다. 그녀는 그녀의 아버지가 직원들을 잘 대하지 않아서 아버지가 부끄러웠다. 그녀는 아버지에게 종업원들과 이익을 나누라고 강력하게 요구하였다. 그녀는 그에게 직원들이 얼마나 부당하게 대우받는지 설명했다.

☑ TIP

② demand처럼 주장, 요구, 명령, 제안 동사가 오고 that절에는 should의 의미가 생략되어 있다면 that절에서는 동사원형이 와야 한다. 따라서 'shared'를 'share'로 고쳐야 한다.

14 ④

📑 단어

faint : 희미한, 아주 적은, 미약한
whereabout : 소재, 행방
provoke : (특정한 반응을) 유발하다

☑ TIP

④ 금지동사 deter는 'deter+목적어+from+~ing'의 형태로 '목적어가 ~하는 것을 막다, 방해하다'의 의미를 가진다. 따라서 'to watch'를 'from watching'으로 고쳐야 한다.

15 ②

📑 단어

take a break : 잠시 휴식을 취하다

☑ 해석

A : 우리 지금 쉬는 게 어때?
B : <u>좋아.</u>
A : 좋아! 5분 후에 로비에서 만나자.

① 좋아, 계속 일하자.　　　② 좋아.
③ 나는 이미 빈털터리야.　　④ 한 시간 걸릴 거야.

16 ④

📑 단어

profession : 직업
essential : 필수적인
materials : 자재
attend : 참석하다, (~에) 다니다
librarianship : 도서관원의 지위(직무)
pros and cons : 장단점, 찬성과 반대

☑ 해석

사서가 되기를 원하는 사람은 각 개인이 가장 흥미로워하는 일이 무엇인지 결정해야 한다. 어떤 직업이나 그럴듯이 미리 계획을 짤 필요가 있다. 다른 사람들을 이끌고 가르칠 사람에게 좋은 종합교육이 필수적이다. 또한 좋은 독서 배경과 비인쇄물 및 컴퓨터 지식이 필수적이다. 전문적인 도서관 업무의 경우 그 전문분야에 대한 훈련도 종종 필요하다. 높은 학위는 도서관 학교에서 가르치거나 큰 도서관을 운영하기 위해 필요하다. 모든 사서들은 최소한 대학 학위를 가지고 있어야 하고 그 이상으로 도서관 학교에 다녀야 한다. 대부분의 도서관에서 도서관 업무와 장학금에 대한 팸플릿 자료를 구할 수 있다.

① 도서관 학교에 다니는 방법
② 각각의 개인으로서의 사서

③ 사서 직무의 장단점
④ 미래의 사서에 대한 조언

17 ③

단 어

profound : (영향·느낌·경험 등이) 엄청난
porcelain : 자기(磁器)
imitated : 가짜의, 모조의
ceramicist : 도예가
exhibition : 전시회
composition : 구성
palette : (화가의) 색채
composer : 작곡가

해 석

수 세기에 걸쳐 아시아의 예술과 음악은 서구에 엄청난 영향을 미쳤다. 예를 들면 페르시아의 도예가들뿐만 아니라 영국의 본 차이나 디자이너들 또한 중국의 자기를 모방했다. 19세기 후반 파리의 극동 전시회에서 선보인 일본의 수채화들은 마티스와 드가의 구성과 색채에 영향을 미쳤다. (서구사람들이 비 서구사람들의 예술품들을 모으거나 박물관에서 그것들을 관람할 때 그들은 작품의 본래 맥락을 아마 놓칠 것이다.) 동양의 뮤지컬은 또한 모차르트와 드뷔시 같은 작곡가들에게 영향력을 미쳤다.

TIP

아시아의 예술과 음악이 서구에 영향을 미친다는 내용으로 ③은 내용 흐름상 적절치 못하다.

18 ③

단 어

annoyance : 짜증, 골칫거리
innocent : 아무 잘못이 없는, 결백한
walk on air : (너무 좋아서) 하늘을 날 것 같다(= walk on a cloud)
eggshell : 달걀 껍데기
walk on eggshells : 살얼음판을 걷다, 눈치를 살피다

해 석

아무 의미없이 하는 말에도 딸들이 짜증을 보이거나 조금이라도 화를 낼 때 엄마들은 그들의 딸들과 대화하는 것이 살얼음판을 걷는 것처럼 느껴진다. 그들은 모든 단어들을 조심해야 한다.

19 ③

단 어

soft coal : 역청탄
modest : 보통의, (크기·가격·중요성 등이) 그다지 대단하지 않은
around corner : 임박해서, 언저리에서

해 석

동쪽 강을 가로질러 봄의 첫 기운이 공장으로부터 나오는 역청탄 연기와 가난한 지역의 길거리 냄새와 섞여 떠다녔다. 나는 출근길에 모퉁이를 돌아 쉐프텔즈로 왔을 때 먼지투성이의 창문에서 낡은 장난감 수집품들이 있는 것을 보고 클리브랜드에 있는 나의 작은 조카딸의 생일이 임박했다는 것을 기억했다. 나는 조카딸에게 그다지 대단하지 않은 선물들을 보내는 습관이 있었다. 그러므로 나는 멈춰서서 적당한 것이 있는지 확인하면서 볼품없고 혼란스러운 물건더미들을 보았다.

① 그 장난감에서 작가의 조카딸과 같은 냄새가 났다.
② 그 장난감은 작가의 조카딸만큼 매력적이었다.
③ 작가의 조카딸의 생일이 임박했다.
④ 작가는 낮은 가격의 폭넓은 물건들에 감명을 받았다.

20 ③

단 어

improbable : 희한한, 별난, 있을 것 같지 않은
flourish : 번창하다
lucrative : 수익성이 좋은
consumer goods : 소비재
appliances : 가전제품
disdain : 업신여김, 무시
low-end : 저가의, 값이 싼
sheer : 순수한, 완전한
solely : 오로지

해 석

많은 것을 가지지 못한 사람들에게 판매함으로써 돈을 벌 수 있다는 것이 이상할지도 모르지만 실제로 애를 쓰고 노력한 회사들은 번영하고 있다. 힌두스탄 레버는 아프리카와 인도에 수익성이 좋은 회사를 세워 로션에서 소금에 이르기까지 유명한 소비재를 판다. 백화점 체인점인 카사스 바히아는 현재 매년 브라질 노동자 계급들에게 50억 달러 상당 이상의 전자기술과 가전제품들을 판다. 큰 회사들은 종종 그들을 저가 시장으로 생각하며 업신여긴다. 왜냐하면 그들이 고가제품을 판매하는 것보다 판매단위당 버는 돈이 더 적기 때문이다. 그러나 순전한 시장의 규모 때문에 그들은 여전히 많은 돈을 벌 수 있다.

① 가난한 사람들은 그들의 상품에 대해 높은 기준을 가지고 있지 않다.
② 큰 기업의 목표는 오로지 이익에만 기초해서는 안 된다.
③ 저가 시장의 사람들은 대기업에게 좋은 기회가 될 수 있다.
④ 개발도상국에서는 여전히 개개인의 구매력이 매우 낮다.

✓ **TIP**

마지막 부분에 주제가 나와 있다. 대기업들이 저가시장을 업신여기기도 하지만 저가시장에서 많은 돈을 벌 수 있다는 내용으로 주제는 ③이 적절하다.

2015. 4. 18.
인사혁신처 시행

1 ②

☐ **단 어** •

knight : 기사
charge : 돌격하다, 공격하다

✓ **해 석**

그 어린 기사는 겁쟁이라고 불리는 것에 <u>격분하여</u> 손에 그의 검을 쥐고 돌격했다.

① 냉담한   ② 격분한
③ 편견 없는   ④ 잘난 체하지 않는

2 ④

☐ **단 어** •

notoriously : 악명 높게

✓ **해 석**

1970년대 중반 John Holland라는 미국 컴퓨터 과학자가 진화 이론을 사용해 어렵기로 악명 높은 과학 문제를 푸는 아이디어를 <u>생각해 냈다.</u>

① (특징을) 띠다, ~를 고용하다, (책임을) 지다
② ~에 타다, 하다(지내다)
③ ~을 속이다, ~을 혹사하다
④ ~을 생각해 내다

3 ②

☐ **단 어** •

conquest : 정복, 점령지
germ : 세균
domestic animal : 가축
infectious disease : 전염병

smallpox : 천연두
measles : 홍역
mutation : 돌연변이
ancestral : 조상의
substantial : 상당한
epidemic : 유행병
acquire : 습득하다
ultimately : 궁극적으로
decisive : 결정적인

✓ **해 석**

가축을 기르는 인간 사회에서 진화한 세균들은 정복 전쟁에서 동일하게 중요했다. ①천연두, 홍역, 독감 같은 전염병들은 동물을 감염시켰던 매우 유사한 조상 세균의 돌연변이로부터 유래하여 인간에게 특화된 세균으로 발달했다. (②정복 전쟁에서 동·식물 가축화의 가장 직접적인 공헌은 유라시아의 말이었는데, 그것들의 군사적 역할은 그들을 그 대륙에서 일어난 고대 전쟁에서의 지프와 셔먼 탱크처럼 만들었다.) ③동물들을 가축화한 인간들이 이 새롭게 진화한 세균들의 첫 번째 희생자가 되었다. 그러나 그 사람들은 이 새로운 질병에 대해 상당한 저항력을 발달시켰다. ④이렇게 부분적으로 면역이 된 사람들이 이전에 이 세균들에 노출된 적이 없었던 다른 사람들과 접촉하게 되었을 때, 전염병들은 전에 노출된 적이 없었던 인구의 99퍼센트까지 죽게 만들었다. 이렇게 가축들로부터 얻어진 세균들은 궁극적으로 유럽인이 미국 원주민, 호주 원주민, 남아프리카 원주민, 그리고 태평양 섬들의 원주민들을 정복하는 데에 결정적인 역할을 했다.

✓ **TIP**

제시된 글은 가축에서 얻어진 세균이 전쟁에서 어떤 역할을 하였는지에 대한 내용이다.

4 ③

☐ **단 어** •

reproduce : 복사하다, 복제하다
spoof : 패러디한 것
ubiquitous : 어디에나 있는, 아주 흔한
virtual : 가상의
genre : 장르
scrutinize : 세심히 살피다, 면밀히 조사하다
panorama : 전경(全景), 파노라마
multi-sensory : 다중감각의
draw on : 의지하다
vanish : 사라지다, 없어지다

✓ **해 석**

모든 사람들이 모나리자와 미켈란젤로의 다비드상이 어떻게 생겼는지 알고 있다. 우리는 알고 있는 것일까? 그들은 너무 자주 복제되어 비록 우리가 파리나 플로렌스에 다녀온 적이 없음에도

불구하고 우리가 그것들을 매우 잘 안다고 느낄 수 있다. 이들에는 수많은 패러디작품 – 사각 팬티를 입은 다비드상이나 콧수염이 있는 모나리자 – 이 있다. 예술품 복제는 아주 흔하다. 우리는 지금 파자마를 입고 앉아서 웹과 CD-ROM으로 전 세계의 있는 갤러리와 박물관을 가상 관람할 수 있다. 우리는 장르별로, 작가별로 탐색할 수 있으며, 세부적인 것을 살피기 위해 확대할 수도 있다. Louvre의 웹사이트는 밀로의 비너스 같은 예술작품의 360도 전경(파노라마) 영상을 제공한다. 이런 관람은 안경과 장갑을 포함한 가상현실 기술에 의지하여 더욱 다중감각적으로 될 수 있다. 건축사 같은 조명 및 무대 설치 디자이너는 이미 이 기술을 그들의 작업에 이용하고 있다.

① 우리는 예술품 복제를 금해야 할까?
② 가상 예술작품이 왜 그렇게 인기가 있을까?
③ 예술 : 그 어느 때보다 더 광범위하게 접근 가능한!
④ 사라진 갤러리와 박물관의 비밀

5 ③

단어

compatible : 사이좋게 지낼, 호환이 되는

해석

① 내가 담배를 끊은 가장 큰 이유는 내 친구들이 모두 이미 담배를 끊었기 때문이다.
② 남편이 아내를 이해한다는 것이 그들이 필연적으로 사이좋게 지낸다는 것을 의미하지는 않는다.
③ 그 소포는 주소가 잘못 적혀있었기 때문에 그에게 늦게 도착하고 손상되었다.
④ 그녀는 남편이 집으로 오는 길에 12개짜리 달걀 두 묶음을 사가지고 오기를 원한다.

TIP

① 흡연하는 것을 멈춘 것이므로 stop –ing로 쓴 것이 적절하다. stop to smoke는 '담배를 피우기 위해 멈추다'라는 뜻이다. 또한 that절에서 친구들이 금연한 것은 그 이전에 일어났던 일이므로 had p.p(과거완료)를 썼다.
② 주어가 that a husband understands a wife(명사절)이므로 단수 취급하여 동사를 does not mean으로 써서 옳게 표현하였다. that절 이하는 주어–동사–목적어의 완전한 문장을 이루고 있으며 (the fact) that ~에서 선행사 the fact가 생략되었다고 볼 수 있다.
③ having wrong addressed → having been wrongly addressed
삽입된 분사구문의 주어는 the package이고, 수동의 의미를 가져야 하므로 분사구문에 be+p.p 형태가 와야 한다. have been p.p를 써서 주절의 동사 시제(reached)보다 앞선 시제임을 나타내고 있다. 또한

wrong은 동사구 having been addressed를 수식하고 있으므로 부사 형태 wrongly로 써 주어야 한다.
④ want A to 동사원형(A가 ~하길 원한다), on one's way(~가는 길에) 구문이 쓰였다. dozens of는 '수십의, 많은'의 뜻을 나타내지만 수사와 함께 쓰일 때는 dozen(12개)의 뜻을 가지며 복수형으로 쓰지 않는다.

6 ①

단어

skyrocket : 급등하다
reminiscent : 연상시키는

해석

① 중국의 러시아산 석유의 수입은 2014년에 36퍼센트 급등했다.
② 수면은 오랫동안 인간의 기억력 향상과 관련되어 왔다.
③ 지난 밤, 그녀는 거의 자동차에 치일 뻔했다.
④ 그 실패는 그 치명적인 우주왕복선 재난의 원인을 둘러싸고 있는 문제들을 연상시켰다.

TIP

② to improve → improving
be tied to ~ing는 '~에 연관되다' 뜻으로 쓰인다.
③ from running over → from being run over
'~을 치다'를 의미하는 run over가 수동의 의미로 쓰였으므로 수동형 동명사인 being run over로 고쳐야 한다.
④ surrounded → surrounding
problems를 수식하는 분사인 surrounded가 목적어를 취한 것으로 보아 능동관계이다. 따라서 현재분사 형태를 취해야 한다.

7 ③

단어

prospect : 전망
strategic : 전략적인
segment : 부분
thorough : 빈틈없는
strive : 분투하다

해석

A : 어떤 사업을 생각하고 있나요?
B : 요즘 꽃가게를 운영하는 게 전망이 좋다고 생각하세요?
A : 그럴 수 있죠. 그런데 심적으로나 경제적으로 준비가 됐나요?
B : 저는 제가 가진 걸 가지고 한 번 시작해 볼 준비가 됐어요.
A : 좋아요! 당신은 이제 전략적인 장소와 알맞은 부문을 선택해야 해요. 좋은 결과를 내기 위해서는 빈틈없는 조사를 해야 해요.
B : 알고 있어요. 사업을 시작하는 건 잘 운영하는 것보다 훨씬 쉽죠.

① 저는 내일 병원에 갈 계획이에요.
② 저는 그렇게는 못해요! 전 일자리를 구하기 위해 노력해야 해요.
③ 저는 제가 가진 걸 가지고 한 번 시작해 볼 준비가 됐어요.
④ 저는 제 사업을 시작하는 것에 대해 생각하고 싶지 않아요.

8 ②

vibration : 진동, 떨림

M : 무슨 소리지?
W : 소리? 난 아무 것도 안 들리는데.
M : 잘 들어봐. 난 소음이 들리는데. 아마 타이어에서 바람이 새나봐.
W : 멈춰서 한 번 보자.
M : 봐! 오른쪽 앞바퀴에 유리조각이 있네.
W : 정말? 음... 그렇네. 우리 이제 어떻게 하지?
M : 걱정 마. 내가 타이어를 교체해 본 경험이 있어.

① 나는 고객에게 지당한 충고를 했어.
② 아마 타이어에서 바람이 새나봐.
③ 그 정비공은 약속이 있는 것 같다.
④ 오! 네 전화에서 진동이 울리고 있어.

9 ②

updraft : 상승기류
set off : 시작하다
buoyant : (물에) 떠 있는
altitude : 고도
vapor : 증기
condense : 응결되다, 응축되다
bare : 벌거벗은
pave : 길을 포장하다
churn : 마구 휘젓다
hail : 우박

폭풍우는 전 세계 각 지역, 예를 들어 북미 전역에서 매우 흔한 일이다. 따뜻한 공기의 상승기류로 이런 폭풍이 시작된다.
(B) 태양에 의해 주변보다 집중적으로 데워진 지역의 땅 위에서 상승기류가 시작할 수 있다. 예를 들어 헐벗고, 바위가 많거나 도로 포장이 된 지역 위에서 보통 상승기류가 나타난다. 지열과 접한 공기는 데워지고 따라서 그 주변의 공기보다 더 가벼워지며, 더 잘 뜰 수 있게 된다.

(A) 곧이어 이 더 잘 뜰 수 있게 된 공기가 상승하며 더 높은 고도까지 수증기를 가지고 간다. 공기는 상승하면서 차가워지고, 수증기는 응축되어 비로 떨어지기 시작한다. 비가 내리면서 비는 주변의 공기를 끌어당기며 일부 아래로 향하는 기류를 회전시킨다.
(C) 이 기류는 다시 상승할 수 있으며 구름 속에서 비를 마구 흩뿌린다. 이들 중 일부가 얼어서 우박이 된다. 곧 빗방울이 상승기류에 저항할 만큼 무거워지고 그들과 함께 하강기류의 형태로 공기를 끌어들이며 땅으로 떨어진다.

10 ④

reptile : 파충류
swarm : (한 방향으로 이동하는 곤충) 떼, 무리
shoal : (물고기) 떼
hatch : 부화시키다
in quantity : 대량으로, 많이
gregarious : 떼 지어 사는
arise from : ~에서 발생하다
be sustained by : ~로 유지되다
sympathy : 동정
conceive : 상상하다
swift : 빠른
instinctive : 본능적인
appetite : 식욕, 욕구
self-restraint : 자제력
have consideration for : ~를 마음에 두다
establish relations with : ~와 관계를 맺다
utter : (입으로 어떤 소리를) 내다, 완전한
rouse : 자극하다
tamed : 길들여진
domesticated : 가축화한

파충류와 어류는 아마 무리로 발견될 수도 있다 ; 그들은 대량으로 부화하고, 비슷한 환경은 그들을 함께 모이게 한다. 사회적이고 무리지어 사는 포유류의 경우에, 단순히 외부적 힘의 군집에서만 유대가 발생하는 것이 아니라 내부의 자극에 의해서 유지된다. 그들은 단순히 서로 닮고 같은 장소에서 같은 시간에 발견되는 것뿐 아니라 ; 서로를 좋아하고 그래서 함께 지낸다. 파충류 세계와 우리 인간의 정신세계의 이런 차이점은 우리가 공감할 수 없는 것처럼 보인다. (A) 우리는 식욕, 공포, 증오 같은 파충류의 본능적 동기에서 보이는 빠르고 단순한 긴급성을 우리 안에서 상상할 수 없다. (B) 우리의 동기는 복잡하기 때문에 우리는 단순한 상태의 그들을 이해할 수 없다 ; 우리의 동기는 균형과 그 결과물이며, 단순한 긴급성이 아니다. (C) 그러나 포유류와 조류는 자제력이 있고 다른 개체와 사회적 호소에 대한 고려, 즉 낮은 수준이지만 우리 방식 같은 자제력을 가지고 있다. (D) 결론적으로 우리는 그들의 거의 모든 종과 관계를 맺

을 수 있다. 그들은 괴로울 때 울음소리를 내고 우리의 감정을 자극하는 움직임을 한다. 우리는 상호인식을 통해 그들을 애완 동물로 길들일 수가 있다. 그들은 우리를 향한 자제력을 가지게 길들여지고, 가축화되고, 교육될 수 있다.

11 ①

단 어 •

drawer : 서랍
reverence : 숭배
meticulously : 꼼꼼하게, 세심하게
kerchief : 스카프

해 석

그는 서랍에서 사진을 꺼내어 아주 경건하게 입 맞추고 하얀 실크 스카프 안에 <u>조심스럽게</u> 접어넣고 그의 심장 옆 셔츠 안쪽에 넣었다.

① 조심스럽게   ② 다급하게   ③ 단호히   ④ 유쾌하게

12 ①

단 어 •

at the drop of a hat : 즉각

해 석

그 회사는 내가 <u>즉각</u> 집을 옮기고 우리 가족을 이동시키는 것을 기대할 수 없다.

① 즉시   ② 정각에   ③ 머뭇거리며   ④ 정기적으로

13 ④

단 어 •

plummet : 곤두박질치다, 급락하다
retail price : 소매가격
ration : 제한하다, 배급을 주다
eliminate : 없애다, 제거하다
spike : 급등
drug cartel : 마약 범죄 조직
citrus : 감귤류 과일
irreversible : 되돌릴 수 없는
wholesale : 도매의

해 석

미국은 라임의 97%를 멕시코로부터 얻는데, 나쁜 기후와 질병의 결합으로 공급은 급락하고 가격은 폭등하고 있다. 지역 식당 경영자가 작년에 약 20$에 사던 라임 40-lb. (18kg) 한 상자의 가격이 지금은 120$까지 올랐다. 4월에 라임의 평균 소매가격은 작년의 두 배를 넘는 56센트에 달했다. 미국 전역에 술집과 식당들은 라임을 제한적으로 공급하거나 알래스카 항공사처럼 완전히 없애고 있다. 멕시코에서 그러한 가격 급등은 범죄를 유발하고, 재배자들이 마약 범죄 조직으로부터 그들의 'green gold(녹색의 금=라임)'의 제한된 공급을 보호하도록 강제한다. 감귤류 과일에 의존하는 사업가들은 봄철 생산량 증가가 곧 가격을 정상치로 되돌려놓기를 희망하고 있다.

① 라임 도매가격의 되돌릴 수 없는 변화
② 미국으로 번진 멕시코 라임 카르텔
③ 전례 없이 라임을 많이 먹는 미국인들
④ 값비싼 라임의 부족

14 ①

단 어 •

transmit : 전송하다
manuscript : 원고, 필사본
unreproducible : 복사할 수 없는
pagination : 페이지 매기기
alphabetic ordering : 알파벳 순 배열
bibliography : 참고문헌
textual : 원문의
cumulative : 누적되는
revised : 수정된, 개정된

해 석

인쇄술은 지식 그 자체가 이해되고 전송되는 방법을 변형시켰다. 손으로 작성된 원고는 독특하고 복사할 수 없는 물건이다. (A) 하지만, 표준 형식과 유형을 가진 인쇄술은 정확한 대량 복제를 도입했다. 이것은 거리상 떨어져 있는 두 명의 독자가 동일한 책에 대해, 특정한 페이지의 특정 단어까지 논의하고 비교할 수 있다는 것을 의미한다. (B) (손으로 작성된 원고에서는 모두 생각해볼 수 없었던 것들인) 일관된 페이지 매기기, 색인, 알파벳 순 배열, 그리고 참고문헌들을 가지고 지식은 서서히 재포장되었다. (C) 말하자면 이제는 학자들이 아리스토텔레스의 Politics와 같은 손으로 작성된 원고를 수집하고 이용가능한 모든 사본들과 비교하여 표준화된 원본을 인쇄할 수 있기 때문에 원문 연구학은 누적의 과학이 되었다. (D) 이것은 또한 신판과 개정판이라는 현상을 이끌었다.

15 ②

단 어 •

foothill : 작은 언덕
plain : 평원, 평지
shield : 순상지

anchor : 단단히 묶어 두다
descend : 내려가다, 경사지다
cut through : ~사이로 길을 내다
erode : 침식시키다
traverse : 가로지르다, 횡단하다

✓ **해석**

미시시피의 동부는 땅이 완만하게 솟아 애팔래치아 산맥의 기슭에 연결된다. 캐나다 평원 끝자락의 허드슨 만과 제임스 만의 가운데 위치한 암반의 거대한 중심지인 캐나다 순상지는 이 대륙을 단단히 고정하고 있다. 이 순상지의 돌출성이 땅은 캐나다 동부의 절반과 미국의 북동지역을 형성한다. 퀘벡 북쪽에서 캐나다 순상지는 허드슨 만을 향해 경사져 내리막이 된다. 심하게 침식된 애팔래치아 산맥은 북아메리카의 가장 오래된 산맥이고 이 대륙에서 두 번째로 긴 산맥이다. 산맥은 퀘벡에서 앨라배마의 중심지까지 약 1,500마일의 길이로 뻗어난다. 해안 저지대는 애팔래치아 산맥의 동쪽과 남쪽에 놓여 있다. 산과 해안 저지대 사이에는 구불구불한 언덕들이 놓여 있다. 많은 강들이 피드먼트 고원을 가로지르고 캐롤라이나의 대서양 연안 평원을 가로질러 흐른다.

✓ **TIP**

① 암반의 거대한 중심지인 캐나다 순상지가 Hudson 만과 James 만 중심에 놓여 있다.
② Appalachian 산맥은 북아메리카에서 가장 긴 산맥이다.
③ Appalachian 산맥은 Quebec에서부터 Alabama의 중심지까지 뻗어있다.
④ Piedmont는 평원을 향해 흘러가는 많은 강들이 횡단한다.

16 ③

✓ **단어**

scale : 등급
constitute : ~이 되는 것으로 여겨지다, 나타내다
compute : 산출하다
approximation : 근사치
administer : 관리하다
present : 제시하다
subject : 피실험자, 연구대상
in a row : 잇달아
alternate : 번갈아 나오다
take up : (시간, 장소를) 차지하다

✓ **해석**

WAIS-R은 11개의 하위 검사 또는 등급으로 구성되어 있다. WAIS-R의 하위 검사들은 평가받는 기술 또는 능력의 유형에 따라 배치된다. 하위 검사들은 두 개의 카테고리로 정리되어 있다. 여섯 개의 하위 검사는 언어적 등급을 명시하고, 다섯 개의 하위 검사는 수행 등급을 나타낸다. 우리는 세 개의 점수를 산출해 낼 수 있다; 언어적 점수, 수행 점수, 그리고 총 (또는 전체의) 점수.

총점은 일반적인 지적 능력의 근사치로 받아들여질 수 있다. WAIS-R을 실시하기 위해서 당신은 피실험자에게 11개의 하위 검사를 각각 제시한다. 각 하위 검사에 들어있는 항목들은 난이도에 따라 배치되어 있다. 당신은 비교적 쉬운 항목부터 시작하여 점점 어려운 것으로 나아간다. 당신은 당신의 피실험자가 잇달아 특정 개수를 틀리면 검사를 멈춘다. 당신은 언어적 검사와 수행 검사를 번갈아 낸다. 모든 과정은 한 시간 반까지 걸린다.

① WAIS-R은 11개의 하위 검사를 가지는데 각각 두 개의 주요 파트를 가진다.
② 11개 중에 더 높은 점수를 받은 몇몇 하위 검사들이 제시되어야 한다.
③ WAIS-R 각각의 하위 검사의 항목들은 쉬운 것으로 시작해 더 어려운 것들로 이어진다.
④ 피실험자들은 모든 언어능력 하위 검사를 먼저 받고 그 후에 모든 수행능력 검사를 받는다.

✓ **TIP**

'You start with relatively easy items, and then you progress to more difficult ones.'를 통해 알 수 있다.

17 ④

✓ **단어**

be saturated with : ~에 흠뻑 젖어들다, ~으로 가득 차 있다
implicit : 암시된, 내포된
metaphor : 은유, 비유
turn out : 판가름이 나다
circumstance : 정황
flip : 뒤집다, 젖히다
abstract : 추상적인
wispy : 몇 가닥으로 된, 성긴
hunk : 덩이, 조각
in terms of : ~면에서, ~에 관하여
variable : 변수, 변동이 심한
causation : 야기, 인과
authenticity : 진실성, 진짜임
clarity : 명료성

✓ **해석**

언어는 "사건은 물체이고 시간은 공간이다."와 같은 내포적 은유로 가득 차 있다. 사실 공간은 단지 시간만을 위한 것이 아니라 많은 종류의 상태와 정황에 대한 개념적인 매개체로 판가름 난다. 회의를 3시에서 4시로 이동시킬 수 있는 것과 같이, 교통 신호가 녹색에서 붉은 색으로 갈 수 있고, 사람은 햄버거 패티를 뒤집는 사람에서 회사를 경영하는 사람으로 될 수 있고, 그리고 경제는 나쁜 것에서 더 나쁜 것이 될 수 있다. 은유는 언어에 너무 널리 퍼져 있어서 추상적 관념에 대해 은유적이지 않은 표현을 찾기 어렵다. 이것은 우리의 성긴 생각들이 정신적 무대에서

우리가 여기저기로 이동시키는 물체의 덩어리로 표현된다는 것을 의미하는가? 세상에 대한 경쟁적 주장은 결코 진실 또는 거짓일 수 없고, 단지 어떤 상황을 다양한 방법으로 표현하는 대안적인 은유가 될 수 있다고 말하는 것인가? 변수와 그 변수들 안에서 변화의 인과관계라는 관점을 가지고 인생에서 정의되지 못하는 것은 거의 없다.

① 모든 정황에서 항상 참이라고 증명되다
② 반박될 수 없는 철회 불가능하고 확실한 진실
③ 그들의 진실성과 명확성에 대한 과학적인 실험을 받을
④ 단지 어떤 상황을 다양한 방법으로 표현하는 대안적인 은유

18 ③

단 어

suitable : 적당한, 알맞은
be influenced by : ~에 영향을 받다

TIP

① 전치사 despite 뒤에 절이 아닌 동명사구가 나왔으므로, 올바른 표현이다.
② 전체 주어는 the best way to find out if you can trust somebody이다. the best way 단수 형태에 맞춰 동사 is가 맞게 쓰였다.
③ Taste sensitivity is largely influenced by ~ → Taste sensitivity influences largely ~
보기의 우리말에서 '미각의 민감성'이 영향을 미치는 주체이므로 동사 influence(~에 영향을 미치다)가 능동태로 쓰여야 한다.
④ the environment를 to부정사(to grow and learn in)가 수식하고 있고 to부정사구의 의미상 주어로 for their children이 알맞게 쓰였다. 또한 to부정사 구에서 '환경에서' 자라고 배우는 것이므로 전치사 in을 써주었다. (in이 없으면 the environment가 grow와 learn의 목적어가 되는데 이는 의미상 적절하지 않다.)

19 ④

단 어

imprisoned : 수감된

TIP

① have는 사역동사로 목적어-목적보어를 이끈다. 목적어 his political enemies가 수감된 상태이므로 imprisoned로 써준 것이 맞다.
② unless 는 'if (주어) not ~(~하지 않으면)'을 뜻하는 접속사로 올바르게 쓰였다.

③ look forward to(~하기를 학수고대하다)에서 to는 전치사이다. 따라서 뒤에 명사 형태가 와야 하므로 동명사 doing이 쓰였다.
④ When he left ~, little does he dream ~. → When he left ~, little did he dream ~.
주절과 종속절의 시제가 일치해야 한다. 시간 부사절에서 30년 전이라고 했기 때문에 주절의 동사 does를 과거 시제 did로 써야 한다. little이라는 부정을 뜻하는 부사가 문장 앞에서 강조되었기 때문에 주절의 주어-동사가 도치되어 did he dream이라고 쓰인 것은 올바른 표현이다.

20 ④

단 어

go about : ~에 착수하다
take ~ for granted : ~을 당연시하다
facilitate : 가능하게 하다
manipulation : 조작, 속임수
aim at : 겨냥하다
kernel : 알맹이, 핵심
beneath : 아래에
further : 발전시키다
underneath : ~의 밑에

해 석

침팬지는 – 두 막대 중 어느 것도 바나나를 획득하는 데 충분히 길지 않다고 생각하여 두 막대기를 연결하는 – 지능을 사용한다. 일을 어떻게 처리할지 "생각해 내며" 사업에 착수할 때 우리 모두 또한 그러하다. 이런 의미에서 지능은 사물들을 있는 그대로 당연시하면서 그것들의 조작을 용이하게 하기 위한 결합을 이루어 내는 것이다. 즉, 지능은 생물학적 생존을 위해 존재하는 것이라 생각된다. 이성은, ㉠반면에, 이해를 목표로 한다. 이성은 우리를 둘러싼 현실의 본질인 핵심을 깨닫기 위해 표면 아래에 있는 것이 무엇인지를 알아내려 한다. 이성에 기능이 없는 것이 아니지만 그 기능은 정신적이고 영적인 존재를 발전시키는 것만큼 육체적 존재를 발전시키지는 않는다. ㉡그러나 이성은 종종 개인과 사회생활에 있어 (예측이 종종 표면 아래에서 작용하는 힘의 인식에 의존한다는 점을 고려하면) 예측을 위해 요구된다. 그리고 예측은 때때로 육체적 생존을 위해서도 필수적이다.

2015. 6. 13.
서울특별시 시행

1 ③

단 어

come under fire : 비난을 받다, 빈축을 사다
translation : 번역, 번역문
mockery : 조롱, 조소
notorious : 악명 높은
catch flak : 비난을 받다, 꾸중 듣다

해 석

남한의 외교통상부 장관은 해외의 무역 거래에서 수백 개의 번역오류를 만든 것에 대해서 <u>비난을 받았다</u>.

2 ①

단 어

circumvent : (어려움이나 법 등을) 피하다, 면하다
lawmaker : 입법자
daylight saving time law : 서머타임법

해 석

네바다, 뉴멕시코, 텍사스 그리고 유타주의 입법자들은 그 주가 서머타임법을 <u>피하도록</u> 허락하는 법안을 통과시키려고 노력하고 있다.

① cramp 피하다, 방해하다
② maintain 유지하다, 지키다
③ codify (법률 등을) 성문화하다
④ reestablish 재건하다

3 ①

단 어

annexation : (영토의) 합병, 부가
meddling : 간섭, 참견
galvanize : 자극하다, 충격요법을 쓰다
vulnerable : ~에 취약한, 연약한

해 석

작년 모스크바의 크림반도 합병과 우크라이나 동부지역 충돌에 대한 간섭은 NATO를 <u>자극했고</u> 취약한 발트 해의 회원국에 대한 특별한 관심을 집중시켰다.

① spur 자극하다, 박차를 가하다
② disparage 폄하하다
③ appease 달래다, 요구를 들어주다
④ justify 정당화시키다

4 ②

단 어

severity : 격렬, 혹독
corporal : 신체의, 육체의
smack : (손바닥으로) 때리다
punitive : 처벌적인, 처벌을 위한

해 석

체벌의 빈도와 혹독함은 대단히 다르다. 때때로 아이들을 손으로 때리는 부모들 또한 긍정적이면서도 처벌을 위한 다른 방법을 사용한다.

① typical 전형적인, 대표적인
② physical 육체의, 신체의
③ physiological 생리적인
④ psychological 심리의, 정신적인

5 ①

단 어

in hot water : 곤경에 처한

해 석

만화 캐릭터인 스폰지밥 스퀘어팬츠는 이 프로그램을 단지 9분만 시청하면 4세 유아들에게 단기 집중력과 학습 장애를 일으킬 수 있다고 제의하는 연구로 인해 곤경에 처했다.

TIP

① water는 셀 수 없으므로 부정관사 'a'를 쓸 수 없다.
② suggesting that~은 선행사 study를 꾸며주고 있다. suggesting 다음에 목적어 that절이 있으므로 능동 형태로 온 것이 맞다.
③ of that program에서 that은 (지시)한정사로 뒤에 명사 program을 수식한다. program이 단수 형태이므로 함께 단수형 that으로 쓴 것이 맞다.
④ 4-year-old는 '네 살짜리(의)'의 뜻으로, 수식을 받는 명사가 보통 뒤에 위치한다. 여기서는 따로 없으므로 s를 붙여 4-year-olds로 그 자체가 명사가 되어 '네 살짜리 아이들'이라는 뜻으로 쓰였다.

6 ④

단 어

Jewish : 유대인의
refugee : 난민, 망명자
immigrate : (다른 나라로) 이주하다

해 석

대부분의 유럽 국가들은 전쟁 후에 유대인 난민들을 환영하지
않았고, 이것으로 인해 많은 유대인들은 다른 나라로 이주했다.

TIP

④ cause가 5형식 동사로 쓰일 때에는 목적어 다음에 목적
격 보어 자리에는 'to 부정사'의 형태로 와야 한다. 따라서
'to immigrate'로 고쳐야 한다.

7 ③

단 어

cross legged : 책상다리를 하고
blush at : ~에 얼굴을 붉히다
mingle with : ~와 섞다, 어울리다
figure-hugging : (옷이) 몸매를 드러내는

해 석

16명의 사람들이 책상다리를 하고 둥글게 앉아 모여 있던 시간
은 오후 3시가 조금 지난 시간이었고 그들은 앞으로 2시간 동
안 서로 어울려야 한다는 것을 알고 낯선 타인들에게 얼굴을 붉
혔다. 다양한 형태와 크기의 몸에 꼭 맞는 바지와 민소매 탑을
입고 있는 각각의 사람들은 돌아가며 그들의 이름과 본국을 말
했다. 다섯 명을 제외한 모든 사람은 미국, 독일 그리고 영국을
포함한 나라에서 온 외국인이었다.

TIP

③ a variety of 다음에 오는 shape과 size는 가산명사이기
때문에 복수 형태로 바꿔줘야 한다. 따라서 'shapes and
sizes'로 고쳐 써야 한다.

8 ③

단 어

museum : 박물관, 미술관

해 석

미술관에 전시된 대부분의 예술작품은 19세기 이탈리아에서 온
것이다.

TIP

이 문장에서 본동사는 is이기 때문에 빈칸은 본동사 자리가
아니다. 따라서 ①과 ④는 제외시켜야 한다. 또한 display가
타동사이기 때문에 능동 형태로 쓰였다면 뒤에 목적어가 와
야 하는데 이 문장에선 목적어가 없기 때문에 수동으로 쓰는
것이 옳다. 따라서 과거분사 형태인 displayed가 와야 한다.

9 ②

단 어

vacancy : 결원, 공석

해 석

A : 빈 방이 있나요?
B : 죄송합니다. 이미 예약이 다 찼습니다.
A : 예약을 했어야 했는데.
B : 그랬으면 도움이 됐을 텐데요.

① 당신의 회사에는 얼마나 많은 사람들이 있나요?
② 이미 예약이 다 찼습니다.
③ 방이 많이 있습니다.
④ 어떤 방을 원하시나요?

10 ④

단 어

chilly : 쌀쌀한, 추운

해 석

A : 저는 이 공항에 처음 왔는데요. 제가 짐을 어디서 찾을 수 있
나요?
B : 2번 수하물 컨베이어 벨트에서 확인해 보세요. 당신 짐에 뭔
가 특별한 것이 있나요?
A : 회전대가 있는 500와트 전자레인지가 있어요.
B : 그걸 가져오지 않아도 됩니다. 대부분의 호텔에는 전자레인지
가 있어요. 근데 시애틀로 여행가서 제일 먼저 무엇을 할 계
획인가요?
A : 마이너스 랜딩에서 회전목마를 타고 싶어요. 음, 이 계절에
여기에서는 어떤 종류의 옷이 가장 좋을까요? 좀 쌀쌀하네요.
B : 그러면 carousel을 입는 것을 추천합니다.

TIP

carousel은 '회전식 원형 컨베이어, (전자레인지의) 음식물
을 놓는 회전대, 회전목마'라는 뜻으로 문맥상 옷의 종류가
나와야 하는 ④에는 carousel이 잘못 쓰였다.

【11~12】

단 어 •

long for/to : 간절히 바라다
impatient : 짜증난

해 석

내가 읽었던 책에서는 −때때로 줄거리 상 필요로 했는데− 누군가는 ㉠향수병으로 힘들어하곤 했다. 어떤 사람이 그다지 좋지 않은 곳을 떠나서 다른 곳, 즉 훨씬 좋은 곳으로 가놓고서, 그다지 좋지 않았던 곳으로 다시 돌아가고 싶어한다. 내가 얼마나 그런 사람에게 짜증이 났었는지, 왜냐하면 나는 스스로 좋지 않은 상황에 있다고 여기고 있었고, 다른 어딘가로 얼마나 가기를 원했는지 알고 있었기 때문이다. 그러나 지금은 나 역시 내가 왔던 곳으로 돌아가고 싶다. 나는 그걸 이해했고, 내가 그곳 어디에 서 있었는지 알았다. 그 때 내가 미래의 그림을 ㉡그렸더라면, 그것은 검고, 더 검고, 가장 검은색으로 둘러싸인 커다란 회색 조각이 ㉢되었을 것이다.

11 ④

해 석

① 졸림   ② 히스테리   ③ 우울증   ④ 향수병

TIP

빈칸 뒤 문장에서 어떤 사람이 그리 좋은 않은 곳을 떠나서 좋은 곳으로 갔음에도 불구하고 그 예전 곳으로 돌아가고 싶어 한다고 했으므로 빈칸에는 homesickness가 적절하다.

12 ②

TIP

과거 시제와 함께 쓰는 then이 나왔기 때문에, 과거사실의 반대를 가정하는 가정법 과거완료 구문을 사용해야 한다. 따라서 'If+주어+had+pp, 주어+would+have+pp'가 와야 하므로 ②가 적절하다.

13 ④

단 어 •

sensitive : 민감한, 세심한

해 석

고양이는 완전한 어둠 속에서 볼 수 없지만, 그들의 눈은 사람의 눈보다 빛에 훨씬 더 민감하다.

TIP

절과 절이 연결되고 있으므로 앞의 빈칸에는 접속사가 와야 한다. 따라서 전치사인 ①과 부사인 ③은 정답이 될 수 없다. sensitive는 전치사 to와 함께 쓰이므로 뒤의 빈칸에는 to가 와야 한다.

14 ③

단 어 •

paralysis : 마비
constrain : 강요하다, 제한하다
consensus : 의견일치, 합의
ossify : 경화되다(시키다)
suppress : 진압하다, 억제하다
outrage : 격분, 격노
tackle : (힘든 문제 상황과) 씨름하다
prolonged : 오래 계속되는, 장기적인
stunted : 성장을 저해당한

해 석

이 경제적인 마비의 근원은 두 나라가 다소 다르다. 일본에서는 매우 제한적인 사회적 패턴과 합의에 근거한 의사 결정과 경직된 정치적인 과정의 혼합이 새로운 아이디어를 억제하고 나라가 변화에 저항하도록 만든다. 미국에서는 신선한 사고, 논쟁, 격분이 부족하지는 않다. 즉, 마비는 어떻게 문제들이 해결될 것인지에 관한 합의의 부족으로부터 야기된다. 미국과 같이 부유한 나라에서는 항상 문제를 해결하기 위한 시간이 더 많다는 생각에 속기 쉽다. 일본에서도 그래왔다. 일본사람들은 충분히 부유해서 장기적인 성장지연으로 많이 고통을 받지는 않는다.

① a number of 많은
② a variety of 다양한
③ a lack of ～의 부족
④ a ground of ～의 근원

TIP

일본과 미국에서의 마비의 근원을 비교하고 있다. 일본에서는 제한적이고 경직된 사회구조로 인해 마비가 온다고 하였고, 미국에서는 이와 반대로 합의의 부족에서 마비가 온다고 보고 있다.

15 ④

conceive : 임신하다, 생각하다
autonomous : 자주적인, 자율적인
selfhood : 자아, 개성
entity : 독립체
immediacy : 직접성, 신속성
plenitude : 풍부함
constitute : ~이 되다, ~을 구성하다
self-aware : 자기를 인식하는, 자각하는
consciousness : 의식, 자각
executive : 실행의
will : 의지

해 석

20세기 후반 미국에서는, 아니 어쩌면 서양 전체에서는, 인간의 삶은 기본적인 단위로 즉, 자율적이고 자유로우며 자기 결정적인 개인이라는 측면에서 생각된다. 개인은 <u>분리될 수 없는</u> 자아를 소유한 존재, 즉 즉각적이고 풍부한 느낌을 통해 알 수 있고, 무엇보다도 자의식과 실행의지로 구성된 내적 독립체로 이해된다.

① communal 공동의, 공용의
② connected 연속된, 일관된
③ dividual 분할할 수 있는, 분리된
④ undivided 분리되지 않는, 완전한

TIP

빈칸 뒤에 나와 있는 'a inner entity'와 동격을 의미하므로 이를 통해 정답을 ④로 유추할 수 있다.

16 ①

baptize : 세례를 주다
revolve : 돌다, 회전하다
property : 재산, 부동산
prosperous : 번영한, 번창한
portrait : 초상화, 인물사진
woo : 지지를 호소하다, 구애하다
contemporary : 동시대의, 현대의

해 석

윌리엄 셰익스피어는 400년보다 더 이전에 살았고, 그 시대의 많은 기록들이 없어졌거나 처음부터 존재하지 않았기 때문에 우리는 그의 삶에 대해 모든 것을 알지는 못한다. 예를 들어 우리는 그가 1564년 4월 26일에 런던으로부터 북서쪽으로 100마일 떨어진 스트래퍼드 어폰 에이번에서 세례를 받은 것을 알고 있다. 그러나 우리는 며칠 더 빨랐던 그의 정확한 생년월일을 모른다. 그러나 우리는 셰익스피어의 삶이 두 지역, 스트래퍼드와 런던을 중심으로 돌아갔다는 것을 알고 있다. 그가 성장해서 가족을 가졌고, 스트래퍼드에서 부동산을 구매했지만 그는 영국 극장의 중심인 런던에서 일했다. 잘 나가는 극단에서 배우, 극작가, 그리고 파트너로서 그는 번창하고 유명해졌다. <u>그의 삶에 대해 모든 것을 알지 못하더라도</u> 우리가 이 페이지의 상단에서 셰익스피어가 아내에게 구애하고 있는 19세기의 초상화를 보는 것처럼 셰익스피어의 팬들은 그를 그들의 기호에 따라 상상하고 또 상상해왔다.

① 그의 삶의 대해 모든 것을 알지 못하더라도
② 우리는 그에 대해 모든 것을 알고 있기 때문에
③ 그를 이해하는 것이 불가능하기 때문에
④ 그는 우리의 동시대의 시인이었음에도 불구하고

17 ②

lift : (제재를) 풀다, 해제하다
consultation : 협의, 상의
disposal : 처리, 처분

해 석

뉴욕시 교육부가 수요일에 교내에서 핸드폰 사용 금지를 해제하는 발표를 할 예정이라고 그 결정에 정통한 자가 화요일에 말했다. 전임 시장인 Michael R. Bloomberg가 시행한 이 금지제도는 수업시간과 그 전후에 아이들과 연락할 수 없다는 것에 대해 걱정하는 부모들 사이에서 인기가 없었다. 다른 뉴스 보도에 따르면 새로운 정책 하에서 교장은 교사와 부모들과의 협의를 통해 휴대폰 사용 선택의 범위를 결정하게 될 것이다.

① 광고
② 뉴스 기사
③ 휴대폰 사용설명서
④ 법적 처분에 대한 성명서

18 ③

integration : 통합
vast : 방대한, 막대한
repercussion : (어떤 사건이 초래한, 보통 좋지 못한) 영향
cascade 폭포처럼 흐르다
fallout : 낙진, 부산물, 결과
address : 설명하다
systemic : 체계의, 전신적인
destabilize : 불안정하게 만들다

ⓒ 세계적인 초연결성과 증가된 시스템의 통합은 소득, 교육, 혁신과 기술 분야에서 전 세계적인 성장을 포함한 막대한 이익을 가져온다.

ⓛ 그러나 빠른 세계화는 또한 걱정을 불러일으키는데, 현재 지역적인 사건들의 영향은 국경을 넘어 폭포처럼 흐르고 재정 붕괴와 환경적인 재난의 결과가 모든 사람에게 영향을 미치기 때문이다.

ⓞ 나비 결함은 체계의 위험성과 그들의 효과적인 관리 사이에 넓어지고 있는 격차를 다룬다.

ⓔ 그것은 터보엔진이 달린 세계화의 새로운 원동력이 얼마나 우리 사회를 불안정하게 만들 수 있는 잠재력과 힘을 가지는지를 보여준다.

ⓒ에서 세계화에 대한 긍정적인 시각이 나오지만 ⓛ에서 'But'이 나오면서 반대의 내용을 다룬다. 그 다음으론 ⓞ에서 'Butterfly Defect'를 설명하고 ⓔ에서 'it'으로 'Butterfly Defect'을 받고 있다.

19 ②

bilingualism : 두 개 언어를 말하는 능력
profound : 엄청난, 깊은
cognitive : 인식의, 인지의
dementia : 치매

ⓞ 한 개의 언어로 말하는 것보다 두 개의 언어로 말하는 것이 세계화되는 세상에서 명백한 실질적 이득을 가진다.

ⓔ 그러나 최근에, 과학자들은 두 개의 언어를 말하는 능력의 이점이 더 넓은 범위의 사람들과 대화할 수 있다는 것보다 더 근본적이라는 걸 보여주기 시작했다.

ⓛ 두 개 언어를 사용하는 것은 당신을 더 똑똑하게 만드는 것으로 드러났다.

ⓒ 그것은 언어와 관련이 없는 인지적인 기술들을 향상시키고, 심지어 노년에 치매를 막아주기도 하며 당신의 뇌에 엄청난 영향을 미칠 수 있다.

ⓞ에서 두 개의 언어로 말하는 것이 실질적인 이득이 있다고 말하고, ⓔ에서는 그보다 과학자들이 밝혀내는 다른 장점을 말하고 있다. ⓒ은 ⓛ의 부가설명으로 ⓒ에서 'it'은 ⓛ의 'Being bilingual'을 의미하므로 ⓛ이 ⓒ보다 먼저 와야 한다.

20 ①

reasonable : 이성적인, 합리적인
in accordance : ~에 부합되게
unreliable : 신뢰할 수 없는
mutual : 상호적인
dependency : 의존, 종속

잘 행동하기 위해서 사람은 어떤 행동지침서가 사실인지, 사실일 가능성이 있는지, 그리고 거짓인지, 거짓일 가능성이 있는지 결정할 필요가 있다. 왜냐하면 사실일 수도 있는 거짓된 지침이 아니라 사실인 지침에 따라서 행동하는 사람이 사회적으로 용인되는 목표에 도달할 더 많은 가능성을 가진다고 생각하는 것이 합리적이기 때문이다.

① 사실일 수도 있는 지침에 따라서 행동하는 것은 믿을 수 없는 것일 수 있다.
② 용인될 수 있는 결과는 사실인 지침에 기초해 행동하는 사람에게 보장될 것이다.
③ 사실인 지침과 사실일 수도 있는 지침에 따라 행동하는 것은 똑같이 위험하다.
④ 행동과 지침은 다른 것이다. 둘은 상호 의존적이지 않다.

2015. 6. 27.
제1회 지방직 시행

---

1 ②

rule out : 배제하다
diagnosis : 진단

진단하기 전에 당신의 주치의가 배제할 몇 가지 질병이 있습니다.

① 추적하다　② 배제하다　③ 지시하다　④ 조사하다

2 ④

be supposed to : ~하기로 되어 있다
offend : 감정을 해치다

① 그녀는 어젯밤에 나에게 전화하기로 되어 있었다. 그러나 하지 않았다.
② 나는 7살 때까지 호세를 알아왔다.
③ 너는 지금 가는 것이 좋을 거야. 그렇지 않으면 늦을 거야.
④ 만약 내가 그녀의 파티에 가지 않는다면, 사라는 기분이 상할 것이다.

☑ TIP

① She supposed to phone~. →She was supposed to phone~.
'~하기로 되어 있다'의 뜻으로 'be supposed to' 구문을 쓴다.
② I have been knowing Jose~ →I had known Jose~.
know는 진행형으로 쓰지 않는 동사이다. 또한 시간 부사절에서 7살 때까지는 알았다는 뜻이므로 had p.p로 써서 과거완료 시제로 써야 한다.
③ You'd better to go now~. →You'd better go now~.
'~하는 것이 낫다'의 뜻을 가진 had better는 뒤에 동사원형을 취한다.
④ 가정법 과거형으로, if절에서 과거시제 동사, 주절에서 'would+동사원형'의 형태로 옳게 쓰였다. 또한 offend는 타동사로서 '불쾌하게 하다'라는 뜻을 나타낸다(자동사로 쓰이면 '범죄를 저지르다'라는 뜻이 된다). Sarah가 불쾌한 것이므로 수동태 be offended로 쓴 것이 맞다.

3 ④

단 어

write a letter : 편지를 쓰다

☑ TIP

① 원급 비교(as-as)에서 뒤에 오는 문장 she looks (young)에서 young이 생략되었다.
② 가주어 It에 대한 진주어로 to부정사(to make/to write)가 왔다. 또한 비교급에서 than을 중심으로 병렬구조 형태가 to부정사로 일치하므로 맞는 표현이다.
③ than이하에서 I have much money에서 중복된 부분이 생략되어 'I'만 남게 되었다.
④ Your son's hair is the same color as you. →Your son's hair is the same color as your hair(=yours).
the same – as 구문에서 그 비교대상이 일치해야 한다. 머리카락의 색을 비교하고 있으므로 you를 your hair 혹은 소유대명사 yours로 고쳐 준다.

4 ④

단 어

absolutely : 전적으로, 틀림없이

☑ 해석

M : 메리, 저녁은 나가서 먹을까?
W : 오, 좋아. 우리 어디로 갈까?
M : 시내에 새로 생긴 피자 가게 어때?
W : 우리 예약해야 할까?
M : 난 그럴 필요는 없다고 생각해.
W : 그런데 오늘은 금요일 밤이기 때문에 우리 아마 줄서서 기다려야 할지도 몰라.
M : 네 말이 맞아. 그러면 내가 지금 당장 자리를 예약할게.
W : 좋아.

① 예약을 취소하다
② 너의 계산서를 제출하다
③ 아침을 조금 먹다
④ 자리를 예약하다

5 ③

단 어

phrase : 구
refrain : 후렴
rhyme : 운
frequently : 자주
facilitate : 용이하게 하다
comprehension : 이해력
predictable : 예측할 수 있는
involve : 수반하다
literacy : 글을 읽고 쓸 줄 아는 능력
criterion : 기준
scaffold : (건축 공사장의) 비계, 발판
linguistic : 언어의
competence : 능숙함
repetition : 반복

☑ 해석

구문 교재는 반복되는 구절, 후렴, 때로는 운을 사용한 내용을 담고 있다. 게다가 구문 교재는 흔히 내용 이해를 용이하게 할 수 있는 그림을 담고 있다. 그 예측할 수 있는 구문은 제2외국어를 시작하는 사람들이 제2외국어로 읽고 쓰는 일에 즉시 몰두할 수 있도록 한다. 게다가 구문 교재의 활용은 독서를 가능하게 함으로써, 학생들의 현재 언어 능력 수준에 도전하게 함으로써, 그리고 단순한 문장의 반복을 통해 이해를 도움으로써 읽고 쓰는 능력의 발판에 대한 기준을 충족시킨다.

☑ TIP

(A) 선행사 pictures가 있으므로, 관계대명사 that이 적절하다.
(B) 부사인 immediately가 들어가는 것이 적절하다.
(C) 주어가 the use이므로, 동사는 meets가 들어가야 한다.

6 ①

단어 •

Zen : (불교) 선종, 일본식 불교
enormously : 엄청나게
breezily : 기운차게
troupe : 공연단
routinely : 일상적으로
disentangle : 구분하다
strand : 가닥
primitive : 원시 사회의
remote : 먼
glass bead : 유리구슬

해석

문화는 사람들처럼 이동한다. 시드니에서부터 에든버러까지, 나아가 샌프란시스코까지 도시에는 중국식과 일본식 불교 풍의 전통정원이 있다. '월드 뮤직은 엄청나게 대중적이다 : 가장 최근의 디스코 스타일은 플라멩코와 재즈, 그리고 게일의 전통을 경쾌하게 결합한 것이다. 아프리카와 남아메리카의 춤 공연단은 일상적으로 해외에서 공연을 한다. 서양의 스파게티, 사무라이 영화, 할리우드 액션영화, 인도의 모험담, 그리고 홍콩 영화에 미친 요소들을 구분하는 것은 불가능할 것이다. 현대 사회에서, 얼마나 원시적이고 얼마나 멀리 떨어져 있든지 간에 어떤 문화도 고립되어 있지는 않다. 멕시코의 산속 마을에 살고 있는 우이초 부족들은 일본과 체코슬라바키아에서 수입된 유리구슬을 사용하여 그들의 가면과 그릇들을 만든다.

① 고립된　② 서로 연락하다　③ 다문화의　④ 복잡한

7 ①

단어 •

figure : 수치
retirement : 퇴직
zero in : 목표를 겨냥하다, (총) 조준을 바로잡다
mortgage : 저당
contend : 주장하다
priority : 우선순위
circumstance : 상황
obviously : 분명히
uphold : 유지시키다
propel : 추진시키다
maintain : 유지하다
motivation : 자극

해석

당신의 가치에 따라, 다른 종류의 숫자들이 당신에게 중요할지도 모른다. 어떤 사람에게 그것은 콜레스테롤 수치와 혈압수치이다 ; 다른 사람들에게 그것은 그들이 결혼한 햇수이다. 많은 사람들에게 퇴직금의 총액수가 가장 중요한 숫자이고, 어떤 사람들은 그들의 대출이 남아있는 잔액에 초점을 맞춘다. 그러나 나는 당신의 가치 또는 우선순위가 무엇이든지 간에 비록 당신이 시급으로 생활비를 벌지 않더라도 당신의 시간당 값어치가 가장 우선순위가 되어야 한다고 생각한다. 당신의 시간당 값어치를 아는 것은 당신이 그것을 어디에 어떻게 사용할 것인지에 대해 명확한 결정들을 하게 해주고 당신의 상황, 목표 그리고 흥미에 따라서 이러한 제한된 자원들을 최대한 활용할 수 있게 만들어준다. 분명히, 당신의 우선순위를 유지하는 동안 당신의 시간당 가치를 높일수록, 당신은 목표달성을 향해 더욱 열심히 노력할 것이다. 왜냐하면 당신은 당신이 원하는 대로 쓸 수 있는 더 많은 자원을 가지고 있기 때문이다. – 당신이 가장 필요로 하는 것이 무엇이든, 당신은 더 많은 돈과 더 많은 시간을 가지고 있기 때문이다.

① 당신의 시간은 돈이다
② 높은 동기를 유지하라
③ 아르바이트가 낫다
④ 당신의 수입 안에서 살아라

8 ④

단어 •

budding : 싹트기 시작한
flop : 완전히 실패하다
lament : 애통해하다
incandescent : 백열성의
bulb : 전구
element : 요소
deny : 부인하다
noodle around : 시험 삼아 해보다
let alone : ~은 고사하고
constant : 끊임없는
accomplishment : 업적
intensify : 강화하다
invention : 발명품

해석

실수를 하는 것은 싹트기 시작한 모든 종류의 과학자들과 예술가들의 교육에 있어 중요하다. 그들은 실험을 하고, 아이디어를 시도했다가, 완전히 실패하며, 다른 아이디어를 시도하고, 위험을 무릅쓰며, 기꺼이 잘못된 대답을 얻을 수도 있는 자유를 가져야만 한다. 하나의 전형적인 예는 첫 번째 백열등을 만들기 위한 그의 노력에서 만 번의 실험적 실패를 애석해했던 기자에 대한 토마스 에디슨의 대답이다. "나는 실패하지 않았습니다." 그는 기자에게 대답했다. "나는 작동하지 않는 만 개의 요소들을 성공적으로 발견했습니다." 그러나 대부분의 아이들은 시험 삼아 해보고, 시험하면서, 만 번은 고사하고 열 번의 방법에서도 틀릴 수 있는 자유를 거부당한다. 아이들의 성취를 측정하고 표준화하는 끊임없는 시험에 대한 강조는 그들의 실패에 대한 두려움을 강화시켰다. 아이들이 성공하는 법을 배우는 것은 확

실히 중요하다 ; 그러나 그들이 실패를 두려워하지 않는 법을 배우는 것 또한 중요하다.

① 처음에 올바르게 이해시켜라
② 에디슨 발명품의 비밀
③ 창조의 길 : 위험을 피하라
④ 실패 : 두려워할 것이 아니다

9 ④

단 어

circumstance : 환경, 상황

TIP

① '(과거에) ~했던 것을 후회하다'라는 뜻으로 regret -ing 표현이 알맞게 쓰였다. '일하지 않았던' 시점(과거)과 '후회하는' 시점(현재)이 다르므로, have p.p(not having worked ~)를 써서 주절의 시점보다 과거의 일임을 나타내었으므로 옳은 표현이다.
② of ~ 이하가 man을 수식한다.
③ and를 기준으로 앞의 normal과 뒤의 healthy가 병렬 구조를 이루어 뒤에 오는 명사 emotion을 수식하는 형용사로 쓰였으므로 바른 문장이다.
④ Under no circumstances you should not leave here.
→ Under no circumstances should you not leave here.
부정 부사구 under no circumstances를 강조하기 위해 문장 앞에 두면, 주어-동사가 도치되어야 한다.

10 ②

단 어

approximately : 거의

해 석

M : 실례합니다. 서울역에 어떻게 가야 합니까?
W : 지하철을 타세요.
M : 얼마나 걸립니까?
W : 약 1시간 정도 걸려요.
M : 지하철이 얼마나 자주 다닙니까?
W : 5분마다 있어요.

① 걷기에는 너무 멀어요
② 5분마다 있어요
③ 당신은 줄을 서서 기다려야 해요
④ 약 30분 정도 걸려요

11 ①

단 어

alleviate : 경감하다
guilt : 죄

해 석

아이들을 위해 선물을 가져오는 것은 그들과 충분한 시간을 보내지 못한 것에 대해 그가 느꼈던 죄책감의 일부를 덜어주었다.

① 경감하다 　　　② 모으다
③ 일으키다 　　　④ 가속하다

12 ③

단 어

made of money : 엄청난 돈이 있는

해 석

너도 알다시피, 나는 돈이 많지 않아!

① 가난한 　　② 검소한 　　③ 부유한 　　④ 쏘는

13 ④

단 어

experienced : 능숙한
salespeople : 판매원
assertive : 단정적인
pushy : 지나치게 밀어붙이는

해 석

능숙한 판매원은 단정적인 것과 지나치게 밀어붙이는 것 사이에는 차이점이 있다고 주장한다.

① 황홀해 하는 　② 용감한 　③ 소심한 　④ 공격적인

14 ②

단 어

medical attention : 치료
deficiency : 결핍
immunity : 면역력
ultraviolet rays : 자외선
beneficial : 유익한
substance : 물질
on a regular basis : 정기적으로

점점 더 많은 사람들이 실내에서 많은 시간을 보내는 사람들 사이에서 일반적인 증상인 비타민 D 결핍을 위한 치료를 찾고 있다. 비타민 D 결핍은 근육과 뼈, 그리고 면역력에 영향을 줄 수 있고, 심지어 암과도 관련되어 있다. 비타민 D는 햇빛에 노출된 피부에 반응하여 몸에서 생성된다. 그러나 많은 여성들이 나가기 전에 자외선 차단제를 바르는데, 이것은 종종 비타민 D가 그들의 몸에 생성되기 어렵게 만든다. 왜냐하면 자외선 차단제가 비타민 D를 생산하는 자외선을 막을 수 있기 때문이다.

① 많은 종류의 자외선 차단제는 유익한 물질을 포함하고 있을지도 모른다.
② 자외선 차단제가 비타민 D를 생산하는 자외선을 막을 수 있다.
③ 그들의 자외선 차단제는 전문적으로 처방되었다.
④ 그들은 정기적으로 운동한다.

15 ②

☑ 단 어

autokinetic : 자동운동
perception : 지각
estimate : 어림잡다
inevitably : 불가피하게
participant : 참가자

☑ 해 설

자동운동 효과에 대한 Muzafer Sherif의 연구는 인식에 있어서 기대의 역할에 대한 좋은 예이다. 그의 실험에서 사람들은 벽에 투영된 빛이 움직일 것이라는 것을 듣고, 움직임의 양을 추정하라는 지시를 받았다. 비록 그 불빛이 실제로는 전혀 움직이지 않았음에도 불구하고, 사람들은 불가피하게 움직임을 보고했다. 그 불빛이 글자와 단어를 그린다고 들었을 때에도, 참가자들은 단어와 문장을 보고했다. 명백히 그들이 생각하기에 일어날 수 있는 것이, 그들의 지각에 상당한 양의 정보를 추가하는 결과를 초래했다.

① 통일   ② 예상   ③ 경쟁   ④ 수량화

16 ③

☑ 단 어

mythology : 신화
integral : 필수적인
timespan : 기간
permeate : 배어들다
ritual : 의식절차
priest : 사제

unfavorable 비판적인
exaggerate : 과장하다
connotation : 함축
poetic : 시의
deity : 신
definition : 정의
extinguish : 끝내다
immoral : 비도덕적인
bolster : 보강하다
literal : 문자 그대로의
underpin : 뒷받침하다
corroborate : 제공하다

☑ 해 설

신화는 오랜 기간 동안 이집트 문화의 필수적인 부분이었다. 신화의 인물과 사건들은 이집트 예술, 건축 그리고 문학에 배어들어 있다. 신화는 왕과 사제들에 의해 행해진 많은 의식들을 (A) 뒷받침한다. 학식 있는 이집트 사람들은 신화에 대한 지식이 현재의 삶과 내세의 위험에서 살아남기 위해 필수적인 무기라고 믿었다.
이집트에서 언제 처음으로 신화적인 이야기들이 발전했는지에 대해서는 이집트 학자들 사이에서 의견이 불일치한다. 이 논쟁은 부분적으로 무엇을 신화로 규정해야 하는지에 대한 결정의 어려움 때문이다. 오늘날, 신화라는 용어는 과장되거나 사실이 아닌 무언가를 지칭하기 위한 부정적인 방식으로 종종 사용된다. 고대 문화에서, 신화는 이러한 (B) 부정적인 의미를 갖지 않았다 ; 신화는 문자 의미 그대로의 사실보다는 시적 의미를 포함한 이야기로 여겨질 수 있었다. 몇몇 학자들은 신화를 신적 존재가 나오는 이야기로 분류함으로써 다른 종류의 전통적 이야기들과 구별한다. 이러한 단순한 정의는 이집트에서는 적용될지 모르지만, 모든 문화들에서 그렇지는 않다.

17 ①

☑ 단 어

trout : 송어
stumble : 발이 걸리다
struggle : 투쟁하다
timber : 수목
exhilarate : 쾌활하게 하다
cutthroat trout : 아가미 주위에 붉은 반점이 있는 송어
strenuous : 몹시 힘든
altitude : 고도
hearty meal : 푸짐한 식사
household chores : 허드레 가사일

☑ 해 설

우리가 무언가 흥미롭고 흥분되는 일을 할 때, 우리는 거의 피곤해하지 않는다. 예를 들어, 나는 최근에 루이즈 호 근처의 캐나다 로키산맥으로 휴가를 다녀왔다. 나는 내 머리보다 높은 덤불을 헤쳐 나가고, 통나무에 발이 걸리고, 쓰러진 수목들 사이

를 지나가면서 며칠 동안 코랄 호수를 따라 송어 낚시를 하였다. – 그러나 이렇게 8시간을 보내고 나서도 나는 지치지 않았다. 왜일까? 왜냐하면 나는 신나 있었고 쾌활했기 때문이다. 나는 높은 성취감을 느꼈다 ; 바로 6마리의 송어라는. 그러나 내가 낚시를 지루해했다고 가정하면, 내가 어떤 기분이었을 것이라고 생각하는가? 나는 7천 피트라는 고도에서 그렇게 힘든 일을 하고 지쳐 쓰러졌을 것이다.

① 우리는 무언가 흥미롭고 흥분되는 일을 한다.
② 우리는 숙면을 취하고 배부르게 먹는다.
③ 우리는 우리 가족의 허드레 가사일을 한다.
④ 우리는 높은 고도에 올라간다.

18 ①

expertise : 전문 기술
requirement : 필요조건
prerequisite : 전제조건
layer : 겹겹이 놓다, 쌓다
a slew of : 많은
ingredient : 구성요소
precision : 정확성
discipline : 규율
desire : 욕구
sufficient : 충분한
requisite : 필요한
tolerant : 관대한
predictor : 예측 변수
longevity : 장수, 오래 지속됨

해 석

'1만 시간의 법칙'에서 전문 기술은 적어도 1만 시간의 연습을 필요로 한다고 말한다. 그러나 분명히 시간이 유일한 필요조건은 아니다. 일생 동안 여러 해를 잘못된 것을 연습하면서 보내는 것은 같은 시간 동안 텔레비전을 보는 것처럼 어떠한 전문 기술도 이끌어내지 못한다. 시간은 기본적인 전제조건이지만, 그 자체로서는 충분하지는 않다. 삶의 초점, 정확성, 그리고 욕구 등의 많은 다른 구성요소가 시간을 두고 겹겹이 쌓이는 것이다.

① 그 자체로 충분한 것
② 시간에 필수적인 것
③ 다른 것들에 관대한 것
④ 오래 지속됨의 예측 변수

TIP

① 시간만이 아니라 다른 것들도 필요하다고 했으므로 시간 그 자체로는 충분하지 않다는 내용이 들어가야 한다.

19 ③

reputation : 명성
primitive : 원시적인
steam engine : 증기기관차
locomotive : 기관차
appoint : 임명하다
railway : 철로

해 석

조지 스티븐슨은 영국 북동지역과 스코틀랜드의 탄광에 사용된 초기 증기기관과 관련된 일을 하면서 명성을 얻었다. 1814년에 스티븐슨은 그의 첫 번째 기관차 '블러처'를 만들었다. 1821년에 스티븐슨은 스톡턴과 달링턴 철도의 건설을 위한 엔지니어로 임명되었다. 1825년 스톡턴과 달링턴의 철도가 공개되었고, 이것은 최초의 공영철도였다. 1829년 10월, 철도의 소유주들은 무거운 짐을 싣고 멀리 갈 수 있는 가장 좋은 기관차를 찾기 위한 대회를 개최하였다. 스티븐슨의 기관차 '로켓'은 시속 36마일의 기록을 달성하며 우승을 차지하였다. 스톡턴과 달링턴 철도의 개통과 '로켓'의 성공은 전국적으로 철도의 건설과 기관차의 제작을 자극하였다. 스티븐슨은 많은 프로젝트의 엔지니어가 되었으며, 또한 벨기에와 스페인의 철도 개발에도 참여하였다.

TIP

③ 시속 36마일의 기관차를 개발하여 기관차 대회에서 준우승이 아닌 우승을 했다.

20 ③

instance : 사례
appropriate : 적절한
authority : 권한
wield : 행사하다
extent : 정도
negotiate : 협상하다
abusive : 남용하는
injustice : 불평등

해 석

우리 사회에서 어떤 사람들이 다른 사람들보다 힘 있는 역할을 하는 것이 전적으로 적절한 경우가 많이 있다. 예를 들어, 선생님, 감독, 경찰, 그리고 부모님은 모두 이러한 역할을 한다. 그룹의 지도자는 어떠한 종류의 권한을 가진다. 그러나 권력을 행사할 수 있는 권리와 권한을 어디까지 행사할 수 있는지에 대한 범위는 그 권력이 남용되어 불평등과 부당함을 초래하지 않도록 의문이 제기되고 협상되어야 한다.

③ 'Despite all the mistakes (that) I had made, he still trusted me.'처럼 목적격 관계대명사 that을 생략한 문장으로 보기 문장과 그 뜻이 일치한다.
④ nevertheless는 접속부사이므로 전치사 자리에 사용할 수 없으며, 'I had made all the mistakes, nevertheless, he still trusted me.'와 같이 사용 가능하다.

1 ②

단 어 •

opposition party : 야당
persist in : ~를 고집하다
prime minister : 수상
resignation : 사임, 사직

☑ 해 석

야당의 지도자들은 수상의 사임을 강요하는 노력을 <u>고집할 것</u>
<u>(계속할 것)</u>을 약속했다.

① 고려하다   ② 계속하다   ③ 구조하다   ④ 멈추다

2 ③

단 어 •

be taken in(= be deceived) : 속임수에 넘어가다
invest : 투자하다

☑ 해 석

많은 사람들이 그의 잘생긴 얼굴과 훌륭한 태도에 <u>속아</u> 그에게
모든 투자금을 주었다.

① 반가워하다   ② 충격을 받다
③ 속다   ④ 환멸을 느끼다

3 ③

단 어 •

moreover : 게다가, 더욱이

☑ TIP

'~임에도 불구하고'라는 뜻을 나타내는 접속사에는 though,
although, even if, even though가 있고, 전치사에는 despite,
in spite of, 접속부사에는 nevertheless, nonetheless 등이
있다.
① 그가 여전히 나를 신임했음에도 불구하고, 나는 모든 실수
를 저질렀다. → 주절과 부사절의 위치가 바뀌어야 한다.
② 나는 모든 실수를 저질렀고, 게다가 그는 나를 여전히
신임했다. → moreover는 게다가, 더욱이 라는 뜻으로
문장의 내용과 일치하지 않는다.

4 ③

단 어 •

by accident : 우연히
consist in : (주요 특징 등이) ~에 있다
worthless : 가치 없는, 쓸모없는
priceless : 값을 매길 수 없는, 대단히 귀중한

☑ TIP

① 'whatever+주어+동사'가 명사절을 이루어 전체 문장의 주
어 역할을 하고 있다. 동사는 단수 형태인 is로 맞게 썼다.
② nor는 부정문 뒤에서 '~또한 아니다'라는 뜻을 나타내며
nor 뒤에서 주어-동사 순서가 도치된다.
③ Love does not consist in gazing at ~, but <u>looks</u>
outward ~. → Love does not consist in gazing at~,
but <u>looking</u> outward ~.
not A but B(A가 아니라 B이다)에서 A와 B는 병렬 관
계에 있으므로 문법적으로 통일이 되어야 한다. 생략된
문장 성분을 나타내면, 'Love does not consist in
gazing at ~, but (love does consist in) looking
outward ~.'와 같다.
④ aren't paid(보수를 받지 않는다) 수동태로 알맞게 쓰였
고, not because~, but because 또한 not A but B의
병렬구조를 따르고 있다.

5 ④

단 어 •

plunge : 급락
alleviate : 완화하다
boost : 신장시키다, 북돋우다
set in : 시작하다
supercharge : 과급하다
melt away : 차츰 사라지다
shrink : 줄어들다

☑ 해 석

복지는 가난을 완화하는 데 도움을 준다. 그러나 성장은 가난을 끝
낼 수 있다. 지난 반세기에 아시아의 예는 소득을 늘리는 대단히 중
요한 두 가지 방법은 일자리를 만드는 것과 일자리를 더 만드는 것

이라는 사실을 가르쳐주고 있다. 그리고 그렇게 할 수 있는 방법은 경제를 신장시키는 것이다. 중국과 같은 나라들이 그들의 성장률을 높이기 위한 시장친화정책을 실행했을 때 가난은 차츰 사라졌다. 1981년 World Bank의 수치에 따르면 개발도상국의 인구 52%가 하루에 1.25$ 미만으로 살아갔다. 2008년에 이르러 이 수치는 주로 아시아에서 올린 소득으로 인해 22%로 줄어들었다. 이러한 빈곤선의 급락은 인류 역사에서 가장 중요한 성과 중 하나이다. 그러나 이것으로는 충분하지 않다. 국제통화기금(IMF)은 거의 모든 국가들, 즉 선진국과 신흥국 모두가 지난 30년간 더 심각해지는 빈부격차를 겪어왔다고 최근에 말했다.

✅ TIP

④ 주어진 문장의 'That plunge'를 지문에서 찾아 그 뒤로 이어지도록 한다.

6 ①

🔲 단 어 •

refresh : 생기를 되찾게 하다, 원기를 북돋우다
recharge : 재충전하다
domestic airline : 국내선(항공사)

✅ 해 석

A : 드디어, 내일부터 긴 휴가야. 너의 계획은 뭐야?
B : 확실하진 않지만, 아마도 여행을 갈 것 같아.
A : 어디로 가고 싶은데?
B : 좋은 질문이야. 음, 일단 버스를 타고 버스가 나를 데리고 가는 곳으로 갈 거야. 누가 알겠어? 휴가를 위한 완벽한 장소를 발견하게 될지.
A : 그래, 여행은 항상 활력소가 되지. 하지만 나는 아무것도 안 하고 집에 있고 싶어.
B : 나쁘지 않은 생각이야. 집에서 휴식을 취하는 건 에너지를 재충전시켜 줄 수 있지.

① 나쁘지 않은 생각이야.
② 나는 국내선을 선호해.
③ 너도 집에서 일을 할 필요가 있어.
④ 우리 가족은 내일 서울로 떠날 거야.

7 ②

🔲 단 어 •

fracture : 균열되다, 분열되다
characterize (by) : (~로) 특징짓다
at the extreme end : 극단에
all systems go : 준비완료, 모든 시스템이 작동하다
interrupt : 가로막다, 중단하다, 방해하다
distract : 산만하게 하다, 집중이 안 되게 하다

bandwidth : 대역폭
end up : 결국 ~에 처하게 되다
overstimulate : 과도하게 자극하다
overwhelmed : 압도된
unfulfilled : 충족되지 않은
enrich : 풍요롭게 하다
bond : 유대, 끈
weaken : 약화시키다, 약화되다

✅ 해 석

우리가 살고 있는 이 시대를 어떻게 설명할 수 있을까? 너무 잘 연결되어 있는가, 그렇다 하더라도 분열되어 있는가? 전 마이크로소프트 기술자 Linda Stone은 우리의 시대를 지속적인 부분적 관심의 시대로 특징짓고 있다. 그 극단에 통화를 하고 음악을 다운받고 숙제를 하면서 순간순간 문자를 보내는 십대들이 있다. 하지만 성인들 또한 모든 시스템이 작동하는 가운데 살아간다. 모든 것을 훑어보며 어디에서나 기술적 멀티태스킹을 하면서, 방해 받고 산만한 채로. Stone은 우리가 더 많은 것들에 연결되어 우리의 개인적인 대역폭을 확장할 수 있다는 환상에 시달리고 있다고 말한다. 대신에, 우리는 결국 과도하게 자극되고 압도되어 충족되지 못한다고 그녀는 덧붙인다.

① 현대기술은 우리가 우리의 삶을 풍요롭게 하도록 도와준다.
② 우리는 완전한 관심의 부족으로 특징지어지는 시대에 살고 있다.
③ 가족 간의 유대가 스마트폰 개발의 결과로 약화되기 시작했다.
④ 나이든 세대도 젊은 세대만큼 기술적으로 똑똑해질 수 있다.

8 ②

🔲 단 어 •

threshold : 한계점
have nothing to do with : ~와 관계없다

✅ 해 석

IQ는 농구에서 키와 비슷하다. 5피트 6인치인 사람이 프로농구를 할 수 있는 현실적인 가능성이 있을까? 그렇지 않다. 당신은 적어도 6피트 또는 6피트 1인치 정도는 되어야 그 수준에서 시합을 할 수 있고, 모든 것이 동일하다면 6피트 1인치보다는 2인치가 낫고, 6피트 2인치보다 6피트 3인치가 나을 것이다. 하지만 특정한 지점을 지나면 키는 더 이상 그렇게 큰 문제가 되지 않는다. 6피트 8인치인 선수가 자동적으로 2인치 더 작은 선수보다 나은 것은 아니다. (역대 가장 위대한 선수인 Michael Jordan도 어쨌든 6피트 6인치였다.) 농구선수가 단지 충분히 크기만 하면 되듯이, 지능도 마찬가지이다. 지능은 한계점을 가진다.

① IQ는 단지 신화이다. 이것은 당신이 얼마나 똑똑한지와 관련이 없다.
② 일단 당신의 IQ가 특정 수준을 넘어서면, 지능에 관하여 문제가 되지 않는다.

③ 당신의 IQ가 높을수록, 당신은 더 똑똑할 것이다.
④ 당신이 더 연습할수록, 당신은 더 높은 IQ를 가질 것이다.

9 ②

　단 어

conservation : 보호, 보존
restoration : 복원, 복구
involve : 포함하다, 관련시키다
habitat : 서식지
restore : 회복시키다, 복원하다
arise : 생기다, 발생하다
ecosystem : 생태계
disruption : 파괴, 붕괴
sewage-treatment complex : 하수처리단지
reserve : 보호구역
species : 종
reverse : 뒤바꾸다
harbor : 항구
colonial period : 식민지 시대
dump : (쓰레기를) 버리다
sewage : 하수, 오물
buildup : 축적, 비축
outbreak : 발생, 발발
marine life : 해양생물
shellfish : 조개류

　해 석

환경 문제를 다루기 위한 두 가지 중요한 방법은 보존과 복구이다. 보존은 존재하는 자연 서식지를 보호하는 것과 연관된다. 복구는 손상된 서식지를 깨끗하게 하고 복구하는 것을 포함한다. 환경 문제를 다루는 가장 좋은 방법은 환경 문제가 발생하는 것을 예방하는 것이다. 서식지를 보존하는 것은 생태계 파괴로부터 발생하는 환경 문제를 예방해 준다.
(B) 예를 들어, 공원과 보호구역은 많은 종이 살고 있는 넓은 구역을 보호한다. 복구는 생태계 파괴를 되돌린다. Boston 항구는 하나의 복구 성공 사례이다.
(C) 식민지 시대 이래로 Boston시는 하수를 강으로 바로 버렸다. 폐기물의 축적은 질병을 발생시켰다. 해변은 폐쇄되었다. 대부분의 해양생물들은 사라졌고, 결과적으로 조개 산업이 문을 닫았다.
(A) 이 문제를 해결하기 위해서 Boston시는 하수처리단지를 건설했다. 그 이후 항구의 물은 깨끗해졌다. 식물과 물고기는 돌아왔고, 해변은 다시 개방되었다.

　TIP

② (B)에서는 주어진 글에 대한 예를 제시하고 있으며, 마지막 문장에서는 Boston시의 사례를 소개한다. (C)에서는 Boston시에 발생한 환경문제가 언급되었고, (A)에서는 이러한 환경문제를 해결하는 과정에 대하여 이야기하고 있다. 그러므로 순서는 (B)→(C)→(A)이다.

10 ②

　단 어

upper : 상류층
upper middle : 중산층
barrister : 법정 변호사
diplomat : 외교관
army officer : 군 장교
conservative : 영국 보수당원, 보수적인
MP : 하원 의원
well-tried : 충분한 시험을 거친
tailor : 맞추다
echelon : 계급, 계층
wholly : 완전히, 전적으로
unrepresentative : 대표적인 것이 못 되는
vast : 어마어마한
high-street : 시내 중심가
multinational retailer : 다국적 소매업체
passable : 그런대로 괜찮은
reputation : 평판, 명성
diligent : 근면한, 성실한
arrogant : 거만한, 오만한

　해 석

영국 사람들의 다수는 유행에 따라서 옷을 입기보다는 보수적으로 옷을 입는다. 소수의 상류층과 전문직의 중산층, 예를 들어, 변호사, 외교관, 군 장교, 보수당 하원 의원들은 지난 50여 년 동안 충분한 시험을 거친 스타일의 옷을 입는다. 대부분의 남자들은 여전히 정장을 특별히 맞추며, 그로 인해 사회적으로 상류층에 속한다는 것을 즉시 알아볼 수 있다. 하지만 전반적으로 그들이 옷을 입는 방식은 사회를 전적으로 대표하는 것은 아니다. 대다수의 사람들은 그들의 옷을 시내 중심가에서 구입하는데, 그 중 가장 유명한 것은 영국의 거대 다국적 소매업체인 Mark and Spencer일 것이다. 그들은 영국 중산층의 옷을 입고 더할 나위 없이 그런대로 괜찮지만, 많은 유럽의 옷들처럼 유행을 따르지는 않는다. 사실, 영국 사람들은 여전히 유럽에서 가장 옷을 못 입는 사람들이라는 평판을 가지고 있는데 그들은 신경쓰지 않는다.

① 가장 성실한 사람들
② 가장 옷을 못 입는 사람들
③ 가장 오만한 사람들
④ 가장 덜 보수적인 사람들(가장 진보적인 사람들)

11 ②

　단 어

elbow : 팔꿈치
heal : 치유되다, 낫다
assuage : 누그러뜨리다, 완화하다
heighten : 고조시키다

soothe : (마음을) 달래다
torment : 괴롭히다, 학대하다
escalate : 확대되다, 악화시키다

☑ 해석

여동생의 팔꿈치가 다 나았을 때, 테니스를 할 수 없을 거라는 두려움이 <u>누그러들었다</u>.

12 ①

☑ 단 어

multiple : 다수의, 다양한

☑ 해석

매일 무언가에 대하여 화가 날 <u>많은</u> 기회들이 있지만, 우리는 그것을 내려놓고 평화를 유지하는 선택지가 있다.

① 여러 가지의, 다양한　　② 중요한
③ 가끔의　　　　　　　　④ 결정적인

13 ④

☑ 단 어

take your time : 천천히 하다
make it : (시간 안에) 해내다
blessed : 행복한
chunk : 덩어리
hand over : ~을 넘겨주다

☑ 해석

① A : 이 프로젝트를 마감기한까지 마칠 수 없을 것 같아.
　 B : 천천히 해. 분명 끝낼 수 있을 거야.
② A : 엄마, 어머니의 날에 무슨 선물 받고 싶으세요?
　 B : 아무 것도 필요하지 않아. 그저 너 같은 아들이 있는 것만으로도 행복해.
③ A : 이 케이크 뭔가 잘못된 것 같아. 전혀 달지가 않아.
　 B : 네 말이 맞아. 그냥 소금 덩어리 같은 맛이야.
④ A : 이것 좀 들어주시겠어요? 제가 손이 부족해서요.
　 B : 물론이죠, <u>제가 바로 넘겨드릴게요.</u>

14 ④

☑ 단 어

suburban : 교외의

☑ 해석

교외의 생활양식을 피하여 중심도시에 사는 것을 선택한 중산층 미국인들 대부분이 중심도시의 정부 서비스에 최소한으로 의존했다.

☑ TIP

④ those (who were) least depended on central-city government services에서 depend는 능동의 의미로 사용되었으므로, depended가 아니라 능동의 의미를 가지는 현재분사 depending이 적절하다. those 뒤에 오는 주격관계대명사와 be동사(who were)가 생략되었으므로, depending과 함께 형용사인 dependent도 사용이 가능하다.

15 ③

☑ 단 어

re-elect : 다시 선출하다
council : 의회
delegation : 대표단
miserable : 비참한, 초라한
inn : 여관
port : 항구
en route : 도중에
procure : 구하다, 입수하다
Grand Duke : 대공
admittedly : 인정하건대
Minister for War : 전쟁장관
scholarship : 장학금
royal : 국왕의, 왕족의
pupil : 학생

☑ 해석

1778년 12인의 귀족 평회의 일원으로 재선출된 Carlo de Buonaparte는 루이16세에게 보내지는 코르시칸 대표단의 일원으로 선택되었다. 그는 새로운 나라에서 그들의 삶을 시작하기 위해 10살 Giuseppe과 9살 Napoleone을 데리고 갔다. 그들은 바닥에 놓인 매트리스 위에서 잠을 자며, 항구에 있는 한 초라한 여관에서 하룻밤을 보냈다. 코르시카에서 가는 도중에 그들은 Florence를 방문했고, 그 곳에서 Carlo는 Habsburg가의 대공 Pietro Leopoldo로부터 그의 여동생 Marie Antoinette에게 보내는 소개장을 구할 수 있었다. 그 다음에 그들은 프랑스로 갔다. 인정하건대, Carlo는 축하할 일이 있었다. Napoleone이 왕이 비용을 지불하는 Brienne 군사학교에 <u>장학금을 받고 왕의 장학생으로서</u> 들어가게 되었다고 전쟁장관에게 들었기 때문에.

☑ TIP

① Carlo de Buonaparte가 주어이므로 was chosen은 단수형, 수동태 모두 바르게 쓰인 표현이다.
② 목적의 뜻을 나타내는 to부정사로, 맞는 표현이다.
③ mattresses <u>lay</u> out → mattresses <u>laid</u> out
　'바닥에 놓여 있는 매트리스'라는 뜻이 되어야 하므로, lay가 mattresses를 수동 형태로 수식해야 한다. lay는 '~을 놓다'로 lay-laid-laid 형태 변화를 갖는다.

④ Carlo had something to celebrate가 주절이므로 having been informed ~는 분사 구문 형태로 알맞게 쓰였다. 소식을 들은 것이 더 이전의 일이므로 have+p.p, 정보를 '전달받은' 것이므로 수동태인 be+p.p가 함께 쓰여 having been informed~ 가 되었다.

16 ④

steam engine : 증기 기관
come up with : ~을 생각해 내다
crucial : 중대한, 결정적인
chug : 엔진이 통통 소리를 내다
hiss : 쉬익 하는 소리를 내다
mine : 광산
throughout : 도처에, 곳곳에
textile mill : 방직공장
readily : 손쉽게
ship : 수송하다

해 석

상업적으로 성공한 최초의 증기 기관은 1712년 영국에서 만들어졌지만 그것은 매우 느렸다. 그 후 발명가 James Watt는 중요한 혁신을 생각해 냈다. 그의 엔진은 기계류를 움직일 때 더 빠르고 효율적이었다. 1800년까지 약 500대의 Watt의 증기 기관이 영국 전역의 광산과 공장에서 작동하고 있었다. 발명가들이 증기 기관을 방직공장에서 사용했을 때 증기 기관의 사용이 널리 퍼지기 시작했다. 수력 대신에 증기력을 사용하는 것은 더 이상 물의 공급이 준비되어 있는 곳에 공장을 지을 필요가 없다는 것을 의미했다. 대신에, 공장들은 연료를 손쉽게 구할 수 있고, 노동자들이 이미 살고 있는 곳에 위치할 수 있었다. 또한, 공장들은 원재료와 완제품이 수송될 수 있는 도로와 항구에 더 가까이 지어질 수 있었다.

17 ④

단 어

engage with : ~와 맞물리게 하다, 관계를 맺다
inspire : 격려하다
strive : 노력하다, 분투하다
run into : ~를 만나다
ultimately : 궁극적으로, 결국
tuition : 수업, 교습
guidance : 지도
comparison : 비교
significant : 중요한, 의미 있는
impact on : ~에 영향을 주다
countless : 무수한, 셀 수 없이 많은
fulfill : 충분히 발휘하다

해 석

가르치는 것에서 오는 보상은 많다. 그것들 중 하나는 학생들과 만드는 정서적인 유대이다. 당신은 학생들에게 그들이 할 수 있는 최선을 다해서 노력하라고 격려하고, 그들이 문제를 만났을 때 지원을 제공함으로써, 끊임없이 개인적인 차원에서 그들과 관계를 맺는다. 그들이 경험을 통해서 성장하는 것을 보는 것과 결국 그들이 당신의 교습과 지도로 인해 성공하는 것을 보는 것은 비교할 수 없는 느낌이다. 또한 가르치는 것은 당신 주변 세계에 중요하고 긍정적인 영향을 주고 있다고 말할 수 있는 몇 안 되는 직업 중 하나이다. 다른 직업들이 더 분명한 흔적을 남기지만, 직업을 수행하는 동안 무수한 어린 아이들이 잠재력을 충분히 발휘하여 오늘날의 성인들이 되도록 도왔다고 말할 수 있는 사람은 거의 없다.

TIP

④ also(또한)라는 표현을 통해 이 문장 전에도 가르치는 것의 장점이 언급되었다는 것을 알 수 있고, 뒤에 오는 문장에는 가르치는 것이 중요하고 긍정적인 영향을 미친다는 것에 대한 부연설명이 나올 것이라는 것을 알 수 있다.

18 ③

단 어

mammal : 포유동물
belong to : ~에 속하다
family : 과(科)
arctic : 북극의
water-repellent : 방수가 되는, 방수 처리한
fur : 털
pad : 발바닥
paw : 발
blend in with : ~와 조화를 이루다
broad : 넓은
seal : 바다표범, 물개
strand : 좌초하다, 오도 가도 못하게 되다
permeable : 침투할 수 있는

해 석

북극곰은 곰과에 속하는 포유동물이다. 그들은 북극에서 가장 큰 동물 중 하나이며, 세계에서 가장 큰 육식동물 중 하나이다. 그들은 무게가 680kg까지 나갈 수 있고, 키는 3.4m까지 클 수 있다. 북극곰은 두껍고, 기름지고, 방수가 되는 털을 가지고 있다. 이 털은 그들의 발바닥 사이 공간까지 포함하여 그들의 몸을 덮고 있다. 그들의 하얀 털은 그들이 눈과 얼음에 조화를 이룰 수 있도록 돕는다. 그들은 물에서 헤엄칠 때 넓은 앞발만을 사용한다. 북극곰은 그들의 먹이로서 가끔 바다표범을 사냥해서 먹는다. 그들은 또한 물고기, 풀, 심지어 죽은 동물과 오도 가도 못하게 된 고래도 먹는다.

① 북극곰은 물이 침투할 수 있는 털을 가지고 있다.
② 북극곰은 그들의 발에 털이 없다.
③ 북극곰은 수영하기 위해 그들의 앞발에 의존한다.
④ 북극곰은 고기만 먹는다.

19 ③

단 어

clue : 단서
encounter : 맞닥뜨리다, 부딪히다
conversely : 정반대로, 역으로
point out : 지적하다, 언급하다
enormous : 막대한, 거대한
figure out : ~을 이해하다

해 석

아이들은 문맥 단서를 이용하는 법을 배움으로써, 그리고 문맥으로부터 의미를 추측함으로써 이익을 얻을 수 있다. ①이것은 아이들이 익숙하지 않은 단어를 만났을 때 사용할 수 있는 하나의 전략이다. ②반대로, 몇 명의 연구자들은 문맥 단서를 사용하는 방법을 가르치는 것 이외에도, 문맥 단서가 익숙하지 않은 단어들의 의미를 이해하는 데 항상 도움을 주는 것은 아니라는 것을 가르칠 필요가 있다고 지적한다. (③한 아이에게 샌드위치에 대한 한 문장 안에서 enormous와 giant 중에 고르게 하는 것이 한 예가 될 수 있다.) ④아이들은 그들이 문맥 단서로부터 의미를 이해하지 못할 때가 있다는 것을 배울 필요가 있다.

TIP

③ 이 글에서 말하고 있는 '문맥 단서를 통해 의미를 유추하는 것'과 관련 없는 예시를 들고 있다.

20 ①

단 어

malicious : 악의적인
brilliant : 훌륭한, 재능이 뛰어난
geeky : 괴짜
vent : 터뜨리다
frustration : 불만, 좌절감
virus writer : 바이러스 개발자
predominantly : 대개, 대부분
solidly : 확고하게
academic : 학구적인
athletic : 탄탄한, 육상의
peer : 또래
basement : 지하실
quantum physics : 양자 물리학
unmask : 가면을 벗기다

해 석

우리는 악의적인 바이러스를 퍼뜨림으로써 우리의 삶을 비참하게 만드는 사람들에 대해 생각할 때, 대부분이 안전한 교외의 침실에서 불만을 터뜨리는 재능이 뛰어나지만 괴짜이고, 인기 없는 10대 소년을 상상한다. 사실, 컴퓨터 바이러스와 보안기술 전문가 Sarah Gordon에 따르면 이러한 고정관념은 단지 고정관념일 뿐이다. Gordon은 1992년부터 바이러스 개발자의 심리에 대하여 연구해 왔다. "바이러스 개발자는 바로 당신의 옆집에 사는 남자와 꼭 같을 가능성이 있다."고 그녀는 말한다. Gordon이 알게 된 바이러스 개발자는 다양한 배경을 가지고 있다. 대부분 남자이지만 몇 명은 여자이다. 몇 명은 확실히 학구적이지만, 다른 사람들은 운동을 좋아한다. 많은 사람들이 이성 친구와 교제하며, 부모님과 가족들과도 좋은 관계를 가지고 있다. 대부분은 또래들에게 인기가 있다. 그들은 지하실에서만 시간을 보내지 않는다. 한 바이러스 개발자는 지역 도서관에서 봉사활동을 하며, 노인들과 함께 일한다. 그들 중 한 명은 시인이자 음악가이고, 다른 사람은 전기 기술자이며, 또 다른 사람들은 대학의 양자 물리학과에서 일한다.

① 바이러스 개발자의 정체 밝히기
② 바이러스 개발자 : 성과 계층
③ 지하의 바이러스 개발자들
④ 바이러스 개발자들에 의한 비밀스러운 활동들

2016. 4. 9.
인사혁신처 시행

1 ④

단 어

eliminate : 없애다, 제거하다

해 석

공해를 없애기 위한 그 캠페인은 대중들의 이해와 전폭적인 협력이 없다면 <u>소용없는</u> 것이 될 것이다.

① 유혹적인 ② 중대한 ③ 비옥한 ④ 쓸데없는

2 ①

단 어

scratch the surface of : 문제의 핵심까지 파고들지 않다
superficially : 피상적으로
tremendously : 엄청나게, 무시무시하게
hit the nail on the head of : 정확히 맞는 말을 하다
seize hold of : ~을 붙잡다
follow up on : ~을 끝까지 하다.

☑ 해석 --------
지금까지 신문 기사들은 이 엄청나게 복잡한 문제를 <u>수박 겉핥기</u>만 하고 있었다.

3 ①

단어

tablecloth : 테이블보

☑ 해석 --------
A : 제가 어제 여기에서 구매한 테이블보를 환불하고 싶습니다.
B : 그 테이블보에 무슨 문제가 있습니까?
A : 저희 집 테이블에 맞지 않아서 환불하려고요. 여기 영수증 있습니다.
B : 죄송하지만, 이 테이블보는 최종 세일 품목으로 환불이 어렵습니다.
A : <u>저에게 아무도 그런 얘기를 해 주지 않았습니다.</u>
B : 영수증 하단에 적혀 있습니다.

① 저에게 아무도 그런 얘기를 해 주지 않았습니다.
② 가격표는 어디 있습니까?
③ 그것에 무엇이 문제입니까?
④ 저는 그것을 저렴하게 구입했습니다.

4 ①

단어

bad reception : 좋지 못한 수신 상태

☑ 해석 --------
A : 여보세요. Stephanie, 안녕하세요. 사무실로 들어가는 길인데 뭐 필요한 것 있으세요?
B : 안녕하세요, Luke. 여분의 프린터 용지 좀 사다 주시겠어요?
A : 뭐라고 하셨죠? 프린터에 들어갈 잉크를 사다 달라고 하셨나요? 죄송한데, <u>여기서 제 전화 수신 상태가 좋지 않네요.</u>
B : 지금은 들리세요? 프린터 용지가 필요하다고 했어요.
A : 다시 한 번 더 말씀해 주시겠어요?
B : 괜찮아요. 문자 보낼게요.
A : 네. Stephanie, 고마워요. 곧 봐요.

① 제 전화 수신 상태가 안 좋아요.
② 더 많은 종이를 들고 갈 수가 없어요.
③ 번호를 잘못 누른 것 같네요.
④ 이번에는 각 물건을 따로따로 살게요.

5 ④

단어

responsive : 즉각 반응하는

☑ TIP
① 과거 일을 기억하지 못하는 것이므로 remember −ing형 태로 쓰는 것이 맞다. remember to V−는 '(앞으로) ~ 할 것을 기억하다'라는 뜻이 된다.
② take+사람+시간 : ~에게 ~(시간)이 걸리게 하다
③ blow의 목적어로 my umbrella, 부사구로 inside out(뒤집어)이 쓰인 문장이다. home은 부사어로, 앞에 전치사 to를 쓰지 않도록 주의한다.
④ It is not the strongest ~, nor the most ~, <u>or</u> the one most responsive ~. →It is not the strongest ~, nor the most ~, <u>but</u> the one most responsive ~. 'It is not A, but B'의 구문이다. or를 but으로 고쳐주어야 해석과 일치하는 문장이 된다. 'nor the most intelligent,'는 삽입구로서 앞의 It is not~ 부정문을 받아 '~또한 아니다'라는 뜻으로 쓰였다.

6 ①

단어

a mass of : 많은
likelihood : (어떤 일이 있을) 가능성
candidate : 후보자
ingratiate oneself : 잘 보이도록 하다
convince : 확신시키다
applicant : 지원자

☑ 해석 --------
취업 면접 결과에 대한 많은 양의 데이터를 분석한 후에 한 조사팀은 놀라운 사실을 발견했다. 취업이 될 가능성은 자격증에 달려있을까? 아니면 직무 경험에 달려있을까? 사실 둘 다 아니었다. 그것은 단 하나의 중요한 요소였다. '후보자가 쾌활한 사람으로 보였는지'이다. 면접관들의 마음에 든 지원자들은 일자리를 얻었을 가능성이 매우 높다. 그들은 매력을 발휘해서 성공했다. 몇몇 지원자들은 미소를 짓고 시선을 계속 마주치려는 특별한 노력을 했다. 다른 지원자들은 조직을 칭찬했다. 이러한 긍정성은 면접관들에게 이토록 쾌활하고 사회적인 능력을 가진 지원자는 회사에 잘 적응할 수 있으므로 고용해야 한다는 확신을 주었다.

① 직업을 얻으려면 쾌활한 사람이 돼라.
② 자격증이 많을수록 더 좋은 기회가 주어진다.
③ 중요한 것은 능력이지 개성이 아니다.
④ 면접에서 자신의 본모습을 면접관에게 보여라.

7 ④

단 어 •

legitimate : 정당한, 타당한
carve out time : 시간을 할애하다
scramble : (경쟁하듯) 앞다투다
land : (직장 등을) 차지하다

해 석

대부분의 작가들은 이중의 삶을 살았다. 그들은 적당한 직업을 가지고 충분한 돈을 벌었다. 그리고 그들은 자신의 최선을 다하며 자신의 글을 쓸 시간을 만들려고 노력했다. 이른 아침이나, 저녁 늦게, 주말, 휴가 등이다. William Carlos Williams와 Louis-Ferdinand Celine은 의사였다. Wallace Stevens은 보험회사에 다녔다. T.S. Elliot은 은행원이었다가 출판업자가 되었다. Don DeLilo, Peter Carey, Salman Rushdie, and Elmore Leonard는 모두 오랫동안 광고업계에서 일했다. 다른 작가들은 가르친다. 그것이 오늘날 아마도 가장 일반적인 해결방안일 것이다. 그리고 주요 종합대학과 단과대학들이 소위 창작과정을 제공하고 있기 때문에, 소설가들과 시인들은 지속적으로 자신들이 그 자리를 차지하기 위해 고군분투하고 있다. 누가 그들을 비난할 수 있는가? 월급이 많지는 않겠지만, 직업은 안정적이고 시간이 좋다.

① 어떤 작가들은 창작과정을 가르치는 자리를 잡기 위해 분투한다.
② 의사로서 William Carlos Williams는 작품을 쓰는 시간을 찾기 위해 노력했다.
③ 오늘날 가르치는 일은 작가들이 생계를 유지하는 일반적인 방법이다.
④ Salman Rushdie은 광고업계에서 짧게 일했으며 큰 성취를 이루었다.

TIP

Salman Rushdi, Elmore Leonard 모두 오랫동안 광고업계에서 일했다고 언급되어 있다.

8 ②

단 어 •

acknowledge : 인정하다
Mass : (특히 로마 가톨릭교에서) 미사
rite of passage : 통과의례
assess : 평가하다, 가늠하다
maid of honor : 들러리, 시녀
altar : 제단
elaborate : 공들인, 정교한
toast : 축배, 건배

해 석

어린 소녀에서 여성이 되는 가장 큰 통과의례의 축하연 중 하나가 라틴아메리카와 히스패닉 문화에서 열린다. 이 의식은 15세를 의미하는 La Quinceañera라고 불린다. ①이 의식은 젊은 여성이 결혼에 적당한 나이가 되었음을 인정하는 것이다. 이 날은 보통 감사의 미사로 시작한다. (②우리는 한 문화의 통과의례를 다른 문화의 통과의례와 비교함으로써 계층 간의 차이를 가늠할 수 있다.) 젊은 여성은 흰색이나 파스텔 색의 긴 드레스를 입고 남자 에스코트와 여자 들러리 역할을 하는 14명의 친구, 친지들의 시중을 받는다. ③그녀의 부모와 대부모는 제단의 맨 아래에서 그녀를 둘러싼다. 미사가 끝날 때 다른 젊은 친지들이 참석자에게 작은 선물을 주고 Quinceañera 자신은 처녀의 제단에 꽃다발을 올려놓는다. ④미사 후에는 춤, 케이크, 축배가 있는 멋진 파티가 펼쳐진다. 마지막으로 그 밤을 끝내기 위해 젊은 여성은 그녀가 좋아하는 남자 에스코트와 왈츠를 춘다.

9 ④

단 어 •

draw : 이끌어내다, 얻다
dismally : 음울하게, 쓸쓸하게
redeem : 회복하다, 되찾다
demonstrate : 증명하다
profuse : 풍부한
archetypal : 전형적인
submerge : 잠수하다, ~속에 잠기다, 깊이 감추다
beneath : 바로 아래에
ritualistic : 의례적인
fortitude : 불굴의 용기
affirmation : 긍정, 확인
sanctity : 존엄성, 신성함

해 석

디즈니의 작품은 동화, 신화 그리고 민속 문화에서 많은 것을 차용하는데 여기에는 전형적인 요소들이 풍부하다. 피노키오는 이러한 요소들이 어떻게 표면적 현실주의 아래에 파묻히지 않고 강조될 수 있는지를 보여주는 좋은 예이다. 영화 초반부에서 소년이자 인형인 피노키오는 진짜 소년이 되기 위해서 용기 있고 진실하며 이기적이지 않다는 것을 보여야 한다는 이야기를 듣는다. 이 영화의 세 가지 주요한 일화는 의례적인 시험을 나타내는데, 젊은이의 도덕적 용기를 시험한다. <u>그는 처음 두 번은 비참하게 실패하지만 마지막 고래 일화에서는 만회를 하게 되는데 이 일화에서 그는 용기, 정직, 그리고 이기적이지 않음을 확실히 보여준다.</u> 이와 같이 대부분의 디즈니 작품처럼 피노키오의 가치관은 전통적이고 보수적인데, 이는 가족의 신성성에 대해 확인하며 우리의 운명을 인도하는 데에 신이 중요한 역할을 한다는 것을 보여주고, 사회의 규칙에 따를 필요가 있다는 것을 밝힌다.

10 ②

단 어 ·

exponent : 대표적 인물
falter : 비틀거리다
inexhaustible : 다할 줄 모르는
endow : ～에게 주다
exterior : 외모
privilege : 특권
affluent : 부유한
upright : 강직한

해 석

Stanislavski는 여러 가지 면에서 행운아였다. 그는 자신에게 다양한 교육의 이점과 국내외에서 무대 예술의 위대한 예술가들을 만날 수 있는 기회를 줄 수 있었던 부유한 남자의 아들이었다. 그는 위대한 명성을 얻었는데 그가 높은 목표를 세우고 그것들을 이끄는 힘든 길을 흔들림 없이 나아갔기 때문이다. 일에 대한 그의 개인적 진실성과 지칠 줄 모르는 능력은 그를 일류 전문 예술가로 만드는 데 기여했다. 또한 Stanislavski는 매력적인 외모와 우아한 목소리 그리고 천재적인 재능 같은 것을 풍부하게 타고났다. 배우, 연출가, 교사로서 그는 그와 함께 또는 밑에서 일하는 사람 또는 무대 위에 있는 그를 볼 수 있는 특권을 가졌던 사람들에게 영향을 주고 감동시킬 운명이었다.

① Stanislavski는 매력적인 외모를 가지고 태어났다.
② Stanislavski는 그의 일생을 통해 그의 동료들에게 영향을 주지 못하며 남아 있었다.
③ Stanislavski의 아버지는 그의 교육을 지원할 만큼 충분히 부유했다.
④ Stanislavski는 자신의 바른 성격과 지칠 줄 모르는 능력으로 최고의 배우가 되었다.

11 ②

단 어 ·

stick one's nose in(to something) : ～에 쓸데없이 참견하다

해 석

그건 사적인 겁니다. 당신은 왜 <u>참견했습니까</u>?

① 서두르다   ② 간섭하다
③ (코를) 쿵쿵거리다   ④ 물러나다

12 ③

단 어 ·

unprecedented : 전례 없는, 미증유의

해 석

뉴턴은 수학, 광학, 기계물리학에 <u>전례 없는</u> 기여를 했다.

① 평범한   ② 시사하는
③ 타의 추종을 불허하는   ④ 화를 돋우려는

13 ③

단 어 ·

demand : 요구하다

TIP

① Jessica is a <u>much</u> careless person ～. →Jessica is a <u>very</u> careless person ～.
　형용사 careless를 수식하기 위해 부사 very가 와야 한다. much는 비교급 등 특정 단어만을 수식한다.
② <u>But</u> he will co me or not is ～. →<u>Whether</u> he will come or not is ～.
　동사는 is이고 주어 자리에 명사절이 와야 하므로 '～인지 아닌지'를 뜻하면서 명사절을 이끄는 종속접속사 whether가 와야 한다. 비슷한 뜻을 나타내는 접속사 if는 절 안에서 or not과 함께 쓰이지 않으므로 올 수 없다. But은 문장과 문장을 이어주는 등위접속사이며, 의미상으로도 맞지 않다.
③ demand 등 요구, 주장 등을 나타내는 동사가 이끄는 목적절에는 'should+동사'가 온다. should는 생략될 수 있으므로 ～demanded that she (should) not leave ～는 맞는 표현이다.
④ <u>The more</u> a hotel is <u>expensiver</u>, ～. →<u>The more expensive</u> a hotel is, ～.
　expensive의 비교급은 more expensive이다. 또한, 'the 비교급 S+V, the 비교급 S'+V" 구문에서 비교급을 분리해서 쓸 수 없다.

14 ④

단 어 ·

interpret : 이해하다, 해석하다
tyranny : 폭정
tremendous : 거대한
humility : 겸손
alliance : 동맹
bitter : 맛이 쓴, 격렬한

인격이란 인간에 대한 존경이며 경험을 다르게 해석할 수 있는 권리이다. 인격이란 사리를 추구하는 것을 자연적인 특성으로 인정해 주며, 협력하려는 인간의 주저하면서도 가슴 따뜻한 본능에 대한 신념을 고정시키기도 한다. 인격은 독재에 대해서는 알레르기 반응을 보이며, 무지를 참지 못하며, 항상 상황의 개선에 열려 있다. 무엇보다도 인격이란 사실 앞에서의 거대한 겸허함이다. 그 겸허함이란 진실이 쓴 약인 상황에서조차 반사적으로 진실의 편에 서는 것을 말한다.

① 인격의 진실에 대한 저항
② 어떻게 등장인물들과 협력할 것인가
③ 인격에 대한 무지
④ 인격은 무엇을 의미하는가

15 ③

단 어 ●

underachieve : 자기 능력 이하의 성적을 내다
impede : 방해하다
equate to : ~와 같다, ~에 해당하다

☑ 해 설

학교에서 성취도가 낮은 학생들은 지능이 낮기보다는 기억능력이 나쁜 것일 수도 있다. 대학의 연구자들은 다양한 연령의 3,000명 이상의 초등학생들을 연구했고 그들 중 10%가 기억력이 좋지 않아 고생을 한다는 것을 밝혀냈는데, 이는 그들의 학습능력을 심각하게 방해했다. 전국적으로 이 숫자는 초등학교에 다니는 거의 오십만 명의 아이들이 영향을 받고 있다는 것이 된다. 연구자들은 또한 교사들이 아이들이 이렇게 기억력이 좋지 않은 것을 거의 알고 있지 못하며 이러한 문제가 있는 아이들을 부주의하거나 지능이 낮다고 치부해 버린다는 것을 밝혀냈다.

① 학교에서 아이들의 교사와의 공감능력
② 초등학교 아이들의 낮은 지능
③ 초등학교 아이들에게 끼치는 낮은 기억력의 영향
④ 아이들의 기억력 문제를 해결하려는 교사들의 노력

16 ④

단 어 ●

compelling : 설득력 있는
over the course of : ~ 동안
elevate : 고양시키다
tenfold : 10배
line : (~의 안에서) 막을 형성하다
obesity : 비만
counter : 반박하다

exaggerate : 과장하다
ingest : 섭취하다

☑ 해 설

하버드 연구자들의 새로운 연구는 캔에 든 수프나 음료를 당신의 식탁에서 치워버려야 하는 설득력 있는 근거를 제시할지도 모른다. 연구에 따르면 5일 동안 매일 1끼를 캔에 든 음식을 먹는 사람들은 대부분의 음식과 음료 캔에 포함된 물질인 비스페롤-A 또는 BPA의 수준이 10배 이상 엄청나게 증가했다. 미국의 공중보건 관련자들은 이를 규제하라는 압력을 더욱 받게 되었다. BPA에 대한 몇몇 연구가 보여주듯 이는 암, 심장병 그리고 비만의 위험을 더욱 높이는 것과 관련이 있다. 그러나 몇몇 연구자들은 건강 위험요소로서의 그 악명이 과장되었다고 반박한다. '미국의학협회지'에 발표된 그 새로운 연구는 사람이 캔에서 바로 딴 음식을 먹게 될 경우 섭취되는 BPA의 양을 측정한 최초의 연구이다.

17 ①

단 어 ●

sympathy : 동정심, 연민
irrelevant : 관련이 없는
morality : 도덕

☑ 해 설

당신의 문에 노크소리가 들렸다. 당신 앞에는 도움이 필요한 젊은이가 서 있다. 그는 다쳤고 피를 흘리고 있다. 당신은 그를 데리고 들어와 도와주고 그가 편하고 안전하게 느끼게 해주며 전화로 구급차를 불러준다. 이것은 분명 올바른 일을 한 것이다. 그러나 임마누엘 칸트에 의하면 만약 당신이 그가 불쌍하다는 마음에서 그를 도와줄 경우, <u>그것은 절대로 도덕적인 행동이 될 수 없다.</u> 당신의 동정심은 당신의 행동의 도덕성과는 관련이 없다. 그것은 당신 성격의 일부일 뿐, 옳고 그른 것과는 관련이 없다. 칸트에게 있어 도덕성이란 단지 당신이 무엇을 하는지에 대한 것이 아니라 당신이 왜 그러한 행동을 하는지에 대한 것이다. 올바른 일을 하는 사람은 단지 그들이 느끼는 감정 때문에 그 일을 하는 것이 아니다. 그 결정은 이성에 의하며, 그 이성은 당신에게 당신이 어떠한 감정을 느끼는 것과는 상관없이 당신의 의무가 무엇인지를 알려준다.

① 절대로 도덕적인 행동이 될 수 없다.
② 당신의 행동은 이성에 근거한다.
③ 당신은 도덕적인 행동을 보여주고 있다.
④ 당신은 그에게 정직한 사람이 되도록 격려하고 있다.

18 ③

☑ 단 어 •

pose : 제기하다
propositional : 명제로 이루어지는, 명제의
perceptual : 인식의

☑ 해 석

모든 동물들은 수면시간 동안 인간과 동일한 두뇌 활동을 보인다. 그들이 꿈을 꾸느냐 마느냐는 다음 질문을 제기함에 의해서만 대답할 수 있는 또 다른 문제이다. 동물들은 지각능력이 있을까?

(B) 오늘날 많은 과학자들은 동물들이 아마도 제한된 형태의 지각능력을 가지고 있다고 생각하는데, 언어가 부족하다는 점과 명제적이고 상징적인 사고능력이 부족하다는 점에서 우리(인간의) 지각능력과는 상당히 다르다.

(C) 동물들은 비록 그들이 꿈을 꾸더라도 꿈에 대해 분명히 이야기할 수 없다. 그러나 대체 어떤 애완동물 주인이 그 혹은 그녀가 사랑하는 동물 친구가 지각력과 기억, 그리고 감정을 갖고 있다는 것을 의심할까?

(A) 이것이 바로 지각능력의 세 가지 중요한 요소이다. 그리고 동물들이 우리와 같은 음성언어를 가지고 있는지 없는지와 상관없이 그들은 이러한 것들을 경험할 수 있다. 동물의 두뇌가 수면시간 동안 활동한다면, 동물들이 어떤 인식적이고 감정적인, 그리고 기억과 관련된 종류의 활동을 한다고 가정하지 않을 이유가 무엇이겠는가?

19 ④

☑ 단 어 •

handle : 다루다, 처리하다
sharpen : 향상되다, 선명해지다

☑ 해 석

옛말에 이르기를, 당신이 먹는 음식이 곧 당신이다. 당신이 먹는 음식들은 분명히 몸의 수행에 영향을 미친다. 그 음식들은 또한 뇌가 어떻게 과제를 처리하는지에도 영향을 준다. 만약 당신의 뇌가 과제들을 잘 처리한다면 당신은 더 명료하게 생각하고 더 감정적으로 안정되게 된다. 적절한 음식은, 당신이 집중하는 것, 계속 동기부여 된 상태를 유지하는 것, 기억을 예리하게 만드는 것, 반응속도를 빠르게 하는 것, 스트레스를 줄이는 것에 도움을 줄 수 있고, 심지어 당신의 뇌가 노화하는 것을 막는 것에도 도움을 줄 수 있다.

⊘ TIP

① As the old saying go → As the old saying goes
접속사 as가 이끄는 절에서 주어는 the old saying의 3인칭 단수 형태이다. 따라서 동사 go를 goes로 고쳐야 한다.

② ~ obvious affect ~ → ~ obviously affect ~
affect가 문장의 동사이고, 동사를 수식하는 단어는 부사이다.

③ ~ help you being concentrated, → ~help you (to) concentrate,
help는 5형식에서 목적보어로 to부정사 혹은 동사원형을 취한다. 또, 목적어 you가 '집중하는(능동)' 것이므로 수동태(be+p.p)로 쓰지 않는다.

④ 'prevent A from -ing : A가 -하는 것을 막다' 형태로 알맞게 쓰였다. prevent your brain from aging에서 age는 '나이가 들다'라는 동사의 뜻을 가진다.

20 ③

☑ 단 어 •

genera : (genus의 복수) 속(屬)
hop : (한 발로) 깡충깡충 뛰다
distress : 괴롭히다, 고통스럽게 하다
scale : 비늘
quill : 깃털
elongate : 길게 늘이다
branch into : ~이 갈라져 나오다
crude : 뭉툭한
reptilian : 파충류의
hitherto : 지금까지
invasion : 침투
solicitude : 배려
modification : 수정, 변경
bask : 햇볕을 쬐다

☑ 해 석

한 무리의 도약 파충류 속, 다시 말해 공룡 타입의 작은 생명체들은 경쟁과 천적의 위협에 의해 쫓겨나와 멸종에 대한 대안, 또는 적응의 방식으로 바다 옆이나 높은 언덕지대의 추운 지역으로 밀려난 것처럼 보였다. 이러한 곤경에 처한 종족 사이에서 새로운 형태의 비늘이 생겨나게 되었다. – 깃털의 형태로 길게 늘어져 나와 곧 깃털의 뭉툭한 끝의 형태로 갈라져 나오는 식의 비늘이다. 이러한 깃털과 같은 비늘이 서로 겹쳐 있어 지금까지 존재했던, 파충류들을 덮고 있던 비늘보다 훨씬 더 효율적인 열 보존 비늘을 형성하였다. 그래서 그들은 그렇지 않았더라면 거주하지 못했을 추운 지역으로의 침투가 가능했다. 아마도 이러한 변화와 함께 이들 생물체 안에서 그들의 알에 대한 엄청난 배려 역시 발생하게 되었다. 대부분의 파충류들은 그들의 알에 대해 매우 명백하게 관심이 없었으며, 알들은 부화되기 위해 태양과 계절에 남겨지곤 했다. 그러나 생명의 새로운 분과에 놓인 몇몇 다양한 종들은 그들의 알을 지키고 그들의 몸의 온도로 알을 따뜻하게 하는 습관을 가지게 되었다. 이렇게 추위에 적응하게 되면서 이러한 생물체를 탄생시킨 – 곧 따뜻한 피를 가지고 있어서 햇볕 쬐는 것에 의존하지 않아도 되는 원시 조류를 탄생시킨 – 다른 내적 변화들이 진행되었다.

① 부화를 성공하지 못하게 하는
② 그들을 혼자 햇볕을 쬐도록 버려두는
③ 그들 몸의 온도로 그들을 덥히는
④ 그들을 비늘에 쌓인 파충류에게로 운반하는

2016. 6. 18.
제1회 지방직 시행

---

1 ④

단 어

utterly : 완전히

해 석

두 개의 문화는 서로 완전히 <u>달라서</u> 그녀는 하나의 문화로부터 다른 문화로 적응하는 것이 어렵다는 것을 발견했다.

① 공통부분이 있는 　　　② 동등한
③ 결합의 　　　　　　　④ 이질적인

2 ③

단 어

allergic to : ~에 대해 알레르기가 있는

해 석

페니실린은 그것에 알레르기가 있는 사람에게 <u>부정적인</u> 효과를 가질 수 있다.

① 긍정의　　② 냉담한　　③ 부정적인　　④ 암시적인

3 ③

단 어

responsible for : ~에 책임이 있는

해 석

지난 해, 나는 그 극장에서 예술 이벤트를 무대에 올리는 데 책임이 있는 그 스태프와 이 공연을 할 수 있는 좋은 기회를 가졌다.

① turn into ~이 되다
② do without ~없이 견디다
③ put on 상연하다, 방송하다
④ give up 포기하다

4 ①

단 어

unwilling : 꺼리는, 싫어하는
misplace : 제자리에 두지 않다

TIP

① I'd rather relax at home than <u>going</u> to ~ → I'd rather relax at home than <u>go</u> to ~
would rather A than B(B하느니 A하는 것이 낫다)에서 A와 B 자리에는 동사원형이 와야 한다. 그리고 A와 B는 병렬 구조이다. 따라서 going을 go로 고쳐주어야 한다.
② be unwilling to 동사원형 : ~하기를 꺼리다
③ It's no use ~ing : ~하는 것은 소용이 없다
worrying의 형태로 알맞게 쓰였다. over which you have no control이 선행사 past events를 수식한다. which you have no control over에서 over가 which 앞으로 갔다.
④ so 형용사/부사 that ~ : 너무 (형용사/부사)해서 ~하다
that절 안에 ones는 목적어 keys의 반복사용을 피하기 위한 대명사로 쓰였다.

5 ②

단 어

outnumber : 수적으로 우세하다

TIP

① talk A out of B : A에게 B를 하지 않도록 설득하다
② I know no more than you <u>don't</u> about ~ → I know no more than you <u>know(do)</u> about ~
'no more A than B'는 'B가 아닌 것과 같이 A도 아니다'라는 뜻을 가진다. 즉, than 이하에 이미 부정의 뜻이 포함되어 있기 때문에 than you don't (know) about과 같이 부정문을 쓰지 않도록 주의한다.
③ outnumber는 타동사로 전치사 없이 목적어를 취하며 '~보다 수적으로 우세하다'는 뜻을 가진다. His army가 '수적 열세'라고 했으므로 was outnumbered 수동태를 취했다. (by) two to one에서 to는 비율을 나타내는 단어로 쓰였다.
④ a/an은 '같은 부류의, 같은'의 의미를 지니고 있어 of an age, of a mind에서 각각 '같은 나이의', '같은 마음의'라는 뜻으로 쓰였다. 또한, not always는 '항상 ~한 것은 아니다'라는 뜻을 나타낸다.

6 ③

단 어

mercury : 수은, 수은주 (cf. Mercury : 수성)
Fahrenheit : 화씨의
far-flung : 먼, 멀리 떨어진
glacier : 빙하
precipitation : 강수량
ice cap : 만년설

해 석

행성은 따뜻해지고 있다. 북극부터 남극까지, 그리고 그 사이에 있는 어디나. 전 세계적으로, 수은주는 이미 화씨 1도 이상 올라가 있고 그리고 심지어 민감한 극지에서는 더 올라가 있다. 그리고 온도 상승의 영향은 먼 미래를 기다려 주지 않는다. 그 영향들은 지금 일어나고 있다. 징조들이 전반적으로 나타나고 있고 그것들 중 몇몇은 엄청나다. 열기는 빙하와 해빙을 녹이고 있을 뿐만 아니라 그것은 또한 강수 패턴을 바꾸고 동물들이 이동하게끔 한다.

① 기후 변화에 대비하여 예방하는 방법
② 북극의 만년설의 녹아내림
③ 지구온난화 사인의 증가
④ 온도 상승의 긍정적 영향

7 ④

단 어

taint : (평판 등을) 더럽히다
subtle : 미묘한, 감지하기 힘든
liberal : 진보적인
connote : 함축하다
proceeds : 수익, 수입
fundamentally : 근본적으로
royal screwing : 몹시 가혹한 배반
incentive : 장려책
conservative : 보수적인
endearment : 애정을 담은 말
ultimate : 궁극적인
overgeneralization : 과잉 일반화
bias : 편견
competence : 능숙함
polarized : 양극화 된

해 석

'영리'라는 단어만큼 그렇게나 미묘한 얼토당토않은 말과 혼란에 의해 더럽혀진 단어는 거의 없다. 진보적인 내 친구들에게 그 단어는 근본적으로 존경받을 만하지 않고 가치가 없는 행동들에 대한 수익을 함축한다. 최소한으로 말하면 탐욕과 이기심이고, 최대한으로 말하면 수백만의 무력한 피해자들에 대한 매우 가혹한 배반이다. 영리는 가장 자격이 없는 행동들에 대한 장려책이

다. 내 보수적인 친구들에게, 그것은 가장 사랑스러운 말이고 효율성과 양식을 내포한다. 그들에겐, 영리는 훌륭한 행동에 대한 궁극적인 장려책이다. 물론, 두 가지의 함축은 어느 정도 가치를 가진다. 영리가 탐욕적이고 이기적인 행동으로부터도, 합리적이고 효율적인 행동으로부터도 나오기 때문이다. 그러나 한쪽의 편향으로 지나치게 일반화하는 것은 영리와 인간의 능력 사이의 관계를 이해하는 데 우리에게 조금도 도움이 되지 않는다.

① 영리와 정당 사이의 관계
② 누가 영리로 이득을 보는가
③ 이익을 내는 것이 바람직하지 않은 이유
④ 영리에 대한 양극화 된 인식

8 ④

단 어

drool : 침을 흘리다
setback : 차질
shake-up : (기업·조직 등의) 대대적인 개혁
ecstatic : 열광하는
affordable : (가격이) 알맞은
suspend : 중단하다

해 석

전기 자동차들은 항상 친환경적이고 조용하고 깨끗했다. 그러나 분명히 흥미롭지는 않았다. Sesta Speedking은 그런 것들을 바꿔왔다. $120,000에 팔리고 최고 속력이 125m.p.h(200km/h)인 배터리로 동력을 갖춘 스포츠카 Speedking은 그것이 처음에 발표된 이래로 클린 테크 사람들을 들뜨게 만들었다. 몇몇의 할리우드 유명인사들 또한 Speedking을 사려는 긴 웨이팅 리스트에 참여했다; Wired와 같은 매거진들은 그것에 열중했다. 수년간의 차질과 대대적인 개혁 끝에, 최초의 Sesta Speedking들이 올해 고객들에게 배송이 됐다. 리뷰들은 열광적이었다. 그러나 Sesta Motors는 재정적 위기로 큰 타격을 받았다. 가격이 적절한 전기 세단을 개발하는 계획은 연기되고 Sesta는 고용인들을 해고하고 있다. 그러나 비록 Speedking이 하나뿐인 히트작이 되더라도, 그것은 들뜨게 만드는 전기차이다.

① Speedking은 새로운 전기 세단이다.
② Speedking은 부정적인 피드백을 받았다.
③ Sesta는 고용인을 더 늘렸다.
④ Sesta는 신차 프로젝트를 중단하였다.

9 ③

단 어

versatile : 다용도의, 다목적의
cabbage : 양배추

antioxidant : 산화방지제

fiber : 섬유질

potassium : 칼륨

chunk : 큰 덩어리

☑ 해 석

콜라비는 주로 그 특이한 모양과 이상한 이름 때문에 많은 사람들이 피하는 채소들 중 하나이다. 그러나 콜라비는 맛있고, 다용도이고 당신에게 유익하다. 콜라비는 브로콜리와 양배추를 포함하는 배추속의 한 구성원이다. 배추속 식물들은 항산화능력이 크고 콜라비도 예외가 아니다. 또한 콜라비는 유용한 양의 vitamin C인 섬유질과 Vitamin B, 칼륨 그리고 칼슘도 함께 포함하고 있다. 콜라비는 날로 먹을 수 있다: 그것은 얇게 썰어서 샐러드에 섞어 먹을 때 맛있다. 당신은 또한 그 덩어리째로 오븐에 구워 먹거나 수프의 재료로 사용할 수 있다.

10 ④

단 어 •

demonstration : 설명

mere : 겨우 ~의

ideogram : 표의문자

duration : 지속, 계속

deliberately : 의도적으로

subliminal : 알지 못하는 사이 영향을 미치는

register : 기억하다

stimuli : (stimulus의 복수형) 자극

hence : 이런 이유로

recall : 기억해 내다, 상기하다

previously : 이전에

replicate : 복제하다, 모사하다

numerous : 수많은

robust : 확신에 찬

extensive : 광범위한

☑ 해 석

단순 노출 효과에 관련된 초기 설명에서, 실험의 참가자들은 일본어 문자들의 한 세트에 노출됐다. 대부분의 사람들이 아는 것처럼, 일본어 문자들은 그림들처럼 보이고 표의문자로 불린다. 그 실험에서, 각각 표의문자에 노출 지속 기간은 의도적으로 30밀리세컨드만큼 짧게 유지됐다. 그런 짧은 노출 지속 기간에-잠재 노출로 알려진- 사람들은 그 자극을 인식할 수 없었고, 이런 이유로 그 실험의 참가자들은 그 표의문자들을 본 것을 상기할 수 없었다. 그렇지만, 그들에게 문자들의 두 세트, 하나는 그들이 이전에 노출이 되었던 것이고 다른 하나는 그들이 노출이 되지 않았던 것들을 보여주었을 때, 참가자들은 전자에 대해 더 큰 호감도를 알려줬다, 그들이 그들을 본 것을 상기할 수 없었더라도! 이러한 결과들은 수차례 다양한 종류의 자극에 걸쳐 반복되어 나타났다. 그래서 그것은 확실하다. 단순 노출 결과들이 보여준 것은 <u>사람들이 익숙한 자극에 더 호감을 가진다는 것</u>이다.

☑ TIP

① 우리는 확장된 노출로 일본어를 배울 수 있다는 것이다

② 지속(시간)이 연구에서 확실한 결과를 가져오는 데 중요하다

③ 짧은 시간동안 그 자극을 기억하는 것은 불가능하다

④ 사람들은 익숙한 자극에 호감을 가지게 된다

11 ③

단 어 •

psychologist : 심리학자

intake : 섭취

☑ 해 석

• 그 심리학자는 학생들의 전반적인 인격 개발을 <u>설명하기</u> 위해 새로운 테스트를 사용했다.

• 과자는 청소년 사이에서 하루 섭취량의 25~30%를 <u>차지한다</u>.

① 계속 가다, 투덜대다

② 이해하다, 계산하다

③ 설명하다, (비율을) 차지하다

④ ~에 의존하다

12 ④

단 어 •

ramp : 경사로

autism : 자폐증

☑ 해 석

처음 내가 당신의 집에 당신을 방문하러 왔을 때 나는 당신의 아버지에 대해 꽤 좋은 느낌을 가지기 시작했다. 내가 방문하기 전에, 그는 나에게 나의 신체적인 어려움들에 대해 몇몇의 상세한 질문들을 해왔다. 그는 내 무거운 휠체어에 대해 알자마자, 어떻게 현관에 경사로를 만들 것인가 계획을 짜기 시작했다. 내가 그 집에 간 첫 날에 그가 직접 만든 경사로가 준비가 되어 있었다. 후에, 당신의 아버지가 당신의 남동생의 자폐증에 대해 알았을 때, 그는 내가 절대 잊지 못할 한 가지를 말했다. "만약 Sam이 학교에서 배울 수 없다면, 나는 2년간 일을 쉴 거고 우리는 세계를 향해할 거야. 나는 2년 동안 Sam이 알아야 할 필요가 있는 모든 것을 가르쳐 줄 거야." 그 말이 당신 아버지의 성격에 대한 모든 것을 말해 준다.

① 엄격하고 근엄한

② 재밌고 유머러스한

③ 게으르고 느긋한

④ 사려 깊고 신중한

13 ④

단 어 ▸

traditional market : 전통적 시장

해 석

John : 실례합니다. 남대문 시장이 어디에 있는지 알려줄 수 있나요?
Mira : 네. 앞쪽으로 쭉 가다 저기에 있는 택시 정류소에서 오른쪽으로 도세요.
John : 아, 알겠습니다. 저기가 시장이 있는 곳인가요?
Mira : 정확하진 않아요. 당신은 2블록 더 내려가야 돼요.

① 맞아요. 저기서 시장 방향으로 가는 버스를 타셔야 해요.
② 전통 시장에서 보통은 물건을 싸게 살 수 있어요.
③ 잘 몰라요. 택시기사님께 여쭤 보세요.
④ 정확하진 않아요. 두 블록 더 내려가셔야 해요.

14 ④

단 어 ▸

occasion : (특정한) 때, (특별한) 행사, 이유, 원인, 일

해 석

① A : 이번 주에 나랑 같이 저녁 먹으러 갈래요?
　 B : 네. 그런데 어쩐 일이세요?
② A : 우리 가끔 농구 게임하러 갈까?
　 B : 그래. 언제인지 말만 해 줘.
③ A : 당신은 남는 시간에 뭐하세요?
　 B : 난 그냥 집에서 쉬어요. 가끔씩 TV 보고요.
④ A : 내가 뭘 좀 도와 줄 수 있을까요?
　 B : 그래요, 내가 그러고 싶어요. 그거 좋지요.

15 ②

단 어 ▸

take a medicine : 약을 복용하다

해 석

① 당신이 수영하는 것을 좋아하든 걷는 것을 좋아하든 그 장소는 환상적이다.
② 그녀는 미팅 후에 저녁 먹으러 가길 제안했다.
③ 내가 당신에게 말한 그 댄서는 시내로 오고 있는 중이다.
④ 만약 그녀가 어제 약을 먹었다면, 그녀는 오늘 좀 더 나을 것이다.

TIP

① ~like swimming or to walk → ~like swimming or walking
　A or B 병렬구조이므로 ~ing or ~ing 로 형태를 일치시켜 준다.

② suggest는 3형식 동사로, 명사, 동명사, that절을 목적어로 취한다. going out~으로 시작하는 동명사구가 목적어로 왔으므로 올바른 표현이다.
③ The dancer that I told you about her ~ → The dancer that I told you about ~
　I told you about her(the dancer) 문장이 선행사 the dancer를 수식하는 형용사절이 되었다. 따라서 관계대명사 that이 이끄는 절에서 전치사 about의 목적어 (her)가 없어야 옳은 문장이다.
④ If she took the medicine last night, she would have been better today. → If she had taken ~, she would be better today.
　가정을 나타내는 if 종속절은 과거 시제(last night), 주절에서는 현재 시제(today)이므로 혼합가정법 문장이 되어야 함을 알 수 있다. 따라서 If S' had p.p ~, S +V(조동사 과거형)에 맞게, if절에서 took을 had taken으로, 주절에서 would have been을 would be로 고친다.

16 ①

단 어 ▸

occur : 일어나다, 발생하다

해 석

① 그 가난한 여자는 스마트폰을 살 수 없다.
② 나는 매일매일 일찍 일어나는 게 익숙하다.
③ 그 도시에서 일어난 화재들의 수는 매년 증가하고 있다.
④ Bill은 Mary가 결혼한 상태라고 가정하고 있어, 그렇지 않아?

TIP

① cannot afford to부정사 : ~할 여유가 없다
② I am used to get up~ → I am used to getting up~
　'be used to 동사원형'에서 to는 to부정사를 나타내며 '~하는 데에 이용되다'라는 수동태 구문이다. 반면, 'be used to -ing'에서의 to는 전치사로 뒤에 동명사를 취해 '~하는 데에 익숙하다'라는 뜻을 가진다. '나는 매일 일찍 일어나는 데 익숙하다'라는 뜻이 되어야 하므로 getting이 와야 한다.
③ The number of fires that occur ~ are growing → The number of fires that occur is growing ~
　the number of는 '~의 숫자'를 나타내는 단수 취급하는 명사이다. 따라서 동사 are growing을 is growing으로 고쳐준다. that절의 동사 occur는 선행사 fires를 수식하고 있으므로 수일치가 올바르다.
④ Bill supposes that~, isn't he? → Bill supposes that~, doesn't he?
　주절에 대해(Bill이 그렇게 생각하지?) 부가의문문의 형태를 완성하기 위해서, 주절에 쓰인 suppose(일반동사)에 맞춰 doesn't으로 써주어야 한다.

17 ③

단어

gradually : 서서히

해석

암에 대항하는 싸움에서 서서히 진전이 이뤄지는 중이다. ① 1900년대 초반에는 장기 생존의 희망을 가졌던 암 환자는 거의 없었다. ② 그러나 의료 기술의 발전으로 진전이 이루어져 현재 10명의 암 환자들 가운데 4명이 생존할 수 있게 되었다. (③ 흡연이 폐암의 직접적인 원인이라는 것이 증명되어 왔다.) ④ 그러나 그 싸움은 아직 이기지 못했다. 몇몇 형태의 암에 대한 치료법들이 발견됐다 하더라도, 다른 형태들의 암이 여전히 증가하고 있다.

18 ①

단어

make it : 성공하다
convince : 확신시키다
get through with : 끝내다
admirable : 감탄스러운, 존경스러운

해석

몇몇의 사람들은 삶이 단순히 풀려야 할 문제들의 연속이라고 확신한다. 그들이 더 빠르게 그들이 직면한 문제를 통과할수록, 그들은 더 빨리 행복할 것이다. 그러나 사실은, 당신이 성공적으로 이 문제를 통과한 후에도 직면할 다른 문제가 있을 것이다. 그리고 당신이 그 장애물을 극복한 후에, 극복해야 할 또 다른 것이 있을 것이다. 그리고 항상 올라야 할 또 다른 산이 있다. 이것이 목적지뿐 아니라 여정 자체를 즐겨야 하는 이유이다. 이 세상에서, 당신은 모든 것이 완벽하고 더 이상의 도전할 것이 없는 장소에 도착할 수 없을 것이다. 목표를 정하는 것 그리고 거기에 도달하는 것은 칭찬할 만하지만, 당신은 당신의 목표를 수행하는 것에 너무 집중해서 당신이 현재 있는 곳을 즐기지 못하는 실수를 해서는 안 된다.

19 ②

단어

frightening : 무서운
shoot a film : 영화를 촬영하다
get up the nerve : 용기를 내다
vividly : 생생하게

해석

여성들 혹은 다른 남자들은 어떨지 모르겠지만, 어렸을 때 나는 결혼에 대한 두려움을 가지고 있었다. 나는 그것이 죽음을 향한 큰 걸음이라고 생각했다. 그 생각이 나를 겁먹게 만들었기 때문에 나는 그것에 저항하기 위해 내가 할 수 있는 모든 것을 했다. 그러고 나서, 어느 날 나는 나의 첫 번째 영화를 촬영하는 중에 Jane을 만났다. 이것은 모든 것을 바꾸었다. Kentucky에서 온 Jane은 그때 종업원 일을 하고 있었고 나는 곧바로 그녀를 주목했다. 그녀는 정말로 아름다웠다. 그리고 그녀에게 데이트 신청할 용기를 내는 것은 하루 종일 걸렸다. 바로 그때, 영화 메이크업 담당자가 우리 둘의 사진을 찍었다. 약 2년 전에 그는 그것을 나에게 보내며 "여기 당신이 시골 소녀에게 데이트 요청을 하고 있다"고 말했다. 그는 그 시골 소녀가 내 부인이 된 걸 모른다. 나는 여전히 그 날을 생생히 기억한다.

20 ①

단어

term : (특정한 이름·용어로) 칭하다, 일컫다
cognitive : 인지의
stick to : 고수하다
turn out to be : ~로 판가름이 나다, 밝혀지다
discourage : 막다, 좌절시키다

해석

새로운 것들을 찾을 때 한 가지 잘 알려진 어려움은 인지심리학자인 David Perkins에 의해 'oasis trap'이라고 명명되었다. 지식은 풍요로운 발견의 '오아시스'에만 집중이 되고, 여전히 생산적이고 물이 풍부한 지역을 떠나기에는 너무 위험하고 비용이 많이 든다. 그래서 사람들은 그들이 알고 있는 것을 고수한다. 이것은 여러 세기에 걸쳐 중국에 어느 정도 있어 왔다. 중국에 있는 지식의 중심지들 간 엄청난 물리적 거리, 그리고 멀리 떨어져 있는 지식 중심지들이 서로 별반 다를 게 없는 것으로 드러난 사실은 탐험 의욕을 꺾었다.

① 그들이 알고 있는 것
② 미지의 세상
③ 그들의 꿈과 상상
④ 상황이 어떻게 변해 가는가

2016. 6. 25.
서울특별시 시행

---

1 ③

단어

rebellious : 반항적인
awkward : 어색한, 곤란한
outgrow : 나이가 들면서 ~을 그만두다

✓ 해석

부모들은 사회적으로 다루기 곤란해 보이거나 <u>반항적으로</u> 행동하는 아이들을 단념해서는 안 된다. 이것은 대부분의 청소년들이 통과하고 나이가 들면 결국에는 그만두게 되는 정상적인 단계이다.

① 수동적인　　　　② 기뻐 날뛰는, 의식이 혼미한
③ 반항하는　　　　④ 산발적인

2 ④

단 어 ·

prodigal : (돈 · 시간 · 에너지 · 물자를) 낭비하는

✓ 해석

그는 1800년대 뉴욕의 부유한 가정에서 태어났다. 이런 환경은 그에게 그의 삶의 대부분을 <u>호화로운</u> 상황에서 지내게 만들었다.

① 위증죄　② 불안정한　③ 치명적인　④ 호화로운

3 ①

단 어 ·

contemporary : 동시대의, 당대의
resurgence : 재기, 부활
engage in : ~에 참여하다

✓ 해석

미국 고등교육의 당대 현실에서 가장 괜찮은 점은 아마 학생들이 캠퍼스를 넘어서 시민생활에 참여하도록 하는 것에 대한 관심의 <u>부활</u>일 것이다.

① 복귀　　② 소멸　　③ 자극　　④ 결핍

4 ①

단 어 ·

acknowledge : 인정하다
harsh : 가혹한, 냉혹한

✓ 해석

그는 1940년대 동안 몇몇 지역에서 많은 한국인들이 가혹한 상황하에서 강제노동에 동원되었음을 인정했다.

✓ TIP

① the number → a number
that 절에서 were forced 복수 형태 동사가 쓰였으므로 a number of Koreans(많은 한국인)이라는 복수 주어로 고쳐야 한다. the number of는 '~의 수'라는 뜻으로 단수 형태이다.

5 ③

단 어 ·

get stuck : 꼼짝 못하게 되다, 끼이다

✓ 해석

Ann : 너 머리 멋지다.
Tori : 저 카페 옆에 있는 새로운 미용실에 키가 큰 미용사한테 머리를 잘랐어.
Ann : 내 머리가 드라이어에 끼었던 거기 말이야?
Tori : 아마도 그럴 거야. 그래, 거기야.
Ann : 허, 거기가 아직 영업 중이구나.

✓ TIP

③ got my head to stick → got my head (to be) stuck
get은 사역동사로 쓰일 때 목적보어로 to부정사를 취한다. 목적어와 목적보어가 수동의 관계에 있으므로 목적보어에 to be stuck으로 써주어야 한다. 'to+be동사'는 함께 생략될 수 있다.

6 ①

단 어 ·

original : 본래의, 독창적인
generate : 발생시키다, 만들어 내다

✓ 해석

창조성이란 문제에 대한 근본적이고, 실용적이면서 의미 있는 해결책을 이끌어 내는 방법으로, 또는 예술적 표현에 대한 새로운 아이디어나 형태를 <u>만들어 내는</u> 방법으로 생각하는 것이다.

✓ TIP

① or 전후로 관계대명사 that이 나란히 연결되어 ways를 수식한다.

7 ④

단 어 ·

across the board : 전반에 걸쳐
republican : 공화주의자
democrat : 민주주의자

✓ 해석

민주주의자들뿐만 아니라 공화주의자들에게까지 정치적으로 전반에 걸쳐 지지를 받았을 때에야 나는 내가 옳은 일을 하고 있다는 것을 알았다.

✓ TIP

④ 'It was when ~ that ~.'에서 when절을 강조하는 it -that 강조구문이다. 이 때 that절은 빠진 문장 성분 없이 완전한 문장 구조를 이룬다.

8 ②

skunk : 스컹크
striped : 줄무늬가 있는

해 석

일반적으로 수십 마리의 스컹크들이 함께 모여서 산다. 그러나 성장한 수컷 줄무늬 스컹크들은 여름 동안 혼자 지낸다.

① 야행성의　② 혼자 하는　③ 포식성의　④ 휴면기의

9 ①

단 어 •

prolific : 다작하는, 다산하는
rhubarb : 대황, 장군풀

해 석

언어와 철자는 변한다. 영국에서 가장 작품을 많이 쓰는 작가 중 하나인 Crystal은 이런 사실을 대중화하는 데 기여해 왔다. 그는 인터넷 이용이 암시하듯이, 만약 사람들이 "rhubarb"를 "rubarb"로 쓰기 시작한다면 그것은 언젠가 용인되는 대안이 될 것이라고 말한다.

① 대안　　② 의무　　③ 위험　　④ 질서

10 ④

단 어 •

reputation : 평판, 명성
chronicler : 연대기 작자
exaggerate : 과장하다
encouraged by : ~에 기운을 얻어

해 석

칭기즈칸의 완전히 무자비한 전사에 대한 명성은 실제보다 더 평판이 나빴을 수도 있다. 많은 정보들은 종종 사실을 과장하는 당시의 연대기 작자로부터 나온다. 그들이 잔인한 이야기를 과장하도록 몽골의 고용주들로부터 장려되었을 가능성이 있다. 몽골이 그들의 적들에게 더 무섭게 보이도록 하기 위해.

① 과장하는 이야기꾼
② 용감한 황제
③ 영향력 있는 인물
④ 완전히 무자비한 전사

11 ②

단 어 •

factual : 사실에 기반을 둔
entail : 수반하다
explicit : 분명한, 명쾌한
manipulate : 조종하다
context : 맥락

해 석

우리 뇌는 다른 방법으로 다른 종류의 정보를 처리하고 저장한다. 사실에 기반을 둔 정보에 대해 생각해 보자. 사실적인 정보는 이름, 얼굴, 단어들과 데이터 같은 명백한 정보의 학습을 수반한다. 그 정보는 우리의 의식적인 생각과 상징 및 언어를 다룰 수 있는 능력과 연관되어 있다. 사실 정보가 오랜 정보로 전환될 때 그들은 일반적으로 그들이 이미 알고 있었던 맥락과 함께 기억된다. 예를 들어 당신의 새로운 친구 Joe에 대해 생각하면, 당신은 아마도 그를 만났던 농구 경기에서의 Joe를 마음속에 그려볼 것이다.

12 ④

단 어 •

nest : 둥지, 보금자리
intruder : 불법 침입자
invader : 침략군
squeeze : 짜다
abdomen : 배, 복부
rupture : 파열하다
lethal : 치명적인

해 석

믿을 수 없는 말처럼 들리겠지만, 그들의 보금자리를 지키기 위해 스스로를 희생하는 몇몇 곤충들이 있다. Borneo의 Camponotus cylindricus 개미는 불법 침입자와 마주쳤을 때 침입자를 잡고 스스로 폭발할 때까지 쥐어 짤 것이다. 개미의 복부가 파열되면서 방어자와 공격자 둘 다에게 치명적인 끈적거리고 노란 물질을 뿜어내면, 영원히 그들이 붙으면서 공격자들이 그들의 보금자리로 들어오는 것을 막을 것이다.

① 저지르다　　　　② 대신하다
③ 드러내다　　　　④ 희생하다

13 ②

단 어 •

E-waste : 전자폐기물
keep up : 따라가다
have no(little) choice but to R.V : ~할 수 밖에 없다

전자폐기물들이 유래 없는 규모로 생산되고 있다. 컴퓨터들과 다른 전자 장비들은 고객들이 시대에 발맞추기 위해 새것을 구매할 수밖에 없도록 만들어서 몇 년 안에 <u>더 이상 쓸모가 없어진다</u>. 따라서 수천만 대의 컴퓨터, TV, 휴대폰들이 매년 <u>버려진다</u>.

① 능률적인 – 문서로 기록된
② 더 이상 쓸모가 없는 – 버리다, 폐기하다
③ 대단히 흥미로운 – 재생한, 재사용되는
④ 동일한 – 던져진

14 ③

amount to something : ~에 이르다
given : (이미) 정해진, 특정한
increment : 증가
accumulated : 축적된, 누적된
substantial : 상당한

지난 20년 동안 미국인들이 그들의 직업에 들이는 시간의 양은 꾸준히 증가해 왔다. 매년 그 변화는 작은데, 다해서 약 9시간이거나 혹은 하루 추가근무 시간보다 약간 더 많은 수준에 이른다. 어떤 특정한 해에 그러한 작은 증가는 아마 <u>감지하기 어려울</u> 수 있다. 하지만 지난 20년 동안 축적된 양은 상당하다.

① 눈부신   ② 취약한   ③ 감지할 수 없는   ④ 강제적인

15 ③

resident : 주민
pick-pocket : 소매치기
shop-lifting : 절도
border control : 출입국관리
pope : 교황
detention : 구금
trial : 재판

세계에서 범죄율이 가장 높은 국가는 바티칸이다. 주민 한 명당 1.5번의 범죄를 저지른다. 그러나 이런 높은 범죄율은 거의 840명 정도의 매우 적은 인구 때문이다. 소매치기와 절도를 포함한 범죄의 다수는 외부인들에 의해 <u>저질러졌을</u> 가능성이 있다. 바티칸은 범죄수사, 출입국관리, 교황 보호를 책임지고 있는 130명으로 이루어진 특별한 경찰력을 지니고 있다. 바티칸에는 재판 전에 잠시 범죄자들을 구금하는 몇 안 되는 감옥을 제외하고는 그 어떠한 감옥도 없다. 범죄자들의 다수는 이탈리아 법원에서 <u>재판을 받는다</u>.

① 조종하다 – 밀봉하다
② 지배하다 – 기각하다
③ 저지르다 – 재판을 받다
④ 지휘하다 – 집행하다

16 ①

relativity : 상대성
hypothesis : 가설, 추정
attempt : 시도
universe : 우주

앨버트 아인슈타인의 상대성 이론이 곧 100주년이 된다. 그리고 그의 혁명적인 가설은 그의 이론에 대한 <u>결함</u>을 찾아내려는 수많은 전문가들의 시도에도 불구하고 시험의 시간을 <u>견뎌 냈다</u>. 아인슈타인은 공간이나 시간과 같은 기본적인 것들에 대해 생각하는 우리의 방식을 바꿨다. 그리고 그것은 우주에 대해서, 그리고 블랙홀과 같은 우주 안의 여러 흥미로운 것들이 어떻게 작용하는지에 대해서 우리의 눈이 뜨이게 해 주었다.

① 견뎌 내다 – 결함   ② 저항하다 – 증명
③ 낭비하다 – 예시   ④ 낭비하다 – 위험

17 ③

cope with : ~에 대처하다
conversation : 대화, 회화

Casa Heiwa는 사람들이 중요한 삶의 기술과 새로운 환경에서 어떻게 삶에 대처해야 하는지를 배울 수 있는 아파트이다. 빌딩 매니저는 아파트에 살고 있는 아이들과 어른들에게 많은 프로그램을 제공하는 서비스를 한다. 아이들을 위해 오전 7시부터 저녁 6시까지 운영되는 어린이집이 있다. 또한 성인들이 이용 가능한 컴퓨터 처리와 영어회화 과정을 포함하는 교육 프로그램들이 있다.

① 교육 프로그램의 필요성에 대해 논의하기 위해서
② 아파트를 위한 고용인을 모집하기 위해서
③ 아파트 주민들을 프로그램들로 끌어들이기 위해서
④ 삶의 기준을 향상시키는 방법을 추천하기 위해서

18 ④

단 어

convict : 유죄를 선고하다
segregation : (인종·종교·성별에 따른) 분리, 차별
be accused of : ~로 비난받다
encroach : 침해하다
mien : 태도, 표정
fine : 벌금을 부과하다

해 석

ⓔ 1955년 12월 1일, Rosa Park는 그녀의 직장인 Alabama주 Montgomery 시내의 가게에서 집으로 가는 버스를 탔다.

ⓛ 그 시절 인종차별법에 따르면, 아프리카계 미국인인 Rosa Park는 버스 뒷자리에 앉도록 되어 있었다. 그녀는 백인 구역을 침범한 것으로 비난을 받았고 버스 기사는 법을 준수하라고 그녀를 설득했다.

ⓒ Rosa Park는 그의 말을 따르는 대신에 그녀의 태도를 유지한 채 자리를 지키고 있었다. 마침내, 기사가 경찰을 부르겠다고 그녀에게 경고했다. "그렇게 하세요. 그들을 부르세요."라고 Park가 답했다.

ⓐ Rosa Park는 체포되어 수감되고, 유죄 선고를 받아 벌금을 부과 받았다. 그녀는 벌금 내길 거부했다. 그녀의 일은 382일간의 Montgomery 시내버스 불매운동을 유발했다.

19 ③

단 어

entrepreneur : 사업가
delinquent : (돈이) 연체된, 비행의, 범죄 성향을 보이는

해 석

Ryan Cox가 US 패스트푸드 드라이브 스루인 Indiana에서 주문한 커피 값을 지불하려고 기다리고 있을 때, 그는 TV 뉴스에서 봤던 것 ─ 한 남자가 뒤 차 운전자의 커피 값을 지불했다. ─ 을 하려고 결심했다. 그 작은 행동이 젊은 Indianapolis 사업가를 기분 좋게 했고 그래서 그는 그의 경험을 Facebook에 공유했다. 한 오랜 친구가 사람들의 커피 값을 지불하기보다는 그 돈으로 학생들의 밀린 급식비를 지불하는 것을 돕기를 제안했다. 그래서 Ryan은 그 다음 주 조카의 학교식당을 방문했고 그가 몇 개의 계산서를 지불할 수 있는지를 물었고 100달러를 주었다.

① 우울한   ② 고요한
③ 감동적인   ④ 지루한

20 ②

단 어

respect : 측면
spherical : 구 모양의, 구체의
diameter : 지름
astronomical object : 천체
bulge : 가득 차다, 불룩하다
equator : 적도
undergo : 겪다
density : 밀도

해 석

달은 많은 측면에서 지구와 다르다. 첫째로, 달에는 생명체가 없다고 알려져 있다. 그리고 크기 면에서 지구보다 훨씬 작다. 당신은 아마도 이 두 천체가 동일한 구형의 모양이라고 생각할지도 모른다. 하지만 엄격히 말하면, 동일하지 않다. 달은 거의 완벽한 구형이다; 그 지름이 어느 방향으로든 결코 1% 이상 다르지 않다. 천체가 더 빨리 회전할수록, 그 천체는 적도 부근이 더 볼록해지게 되고, 극지방은 평평해진다. 달은 지구보다 더 느리게 회전하기 때문에, 거의 더 구형이다.

① 그래서 달과 지구를 제외한 회전하는 천체는 그들의 모양에서 어떤 변화를 겪는다.
② 달은 지구보다 더 천천히 회전하기 때문에, 거의 구형이다.
③ 더욱이, 달의 지름은 지난 수백 년간 변화되어 왔다.
④ 사실은, 달의 밀도와 중력을 고려하면, 달이 구형의 모양이라는 것은 오히려 예상 밖이다.

2017. 3. 18.
제1회 서울특별시 시행

---

1 ④

단 어

cardinal : 가장 중요한

해 석

판매원으로서 당신의 가장 중요한 원칙은 고객을 만족시키기 위해 당신이 할 수 있는 모든 것을 해야 한다는 것임을 기억해야만 합니다.

① 최종적인   ② 거대한   ③ 잠재적인   ④ 주요한

2 ①

단 어

surreptitious : 은밀한
indicate : 보여 주다, 암시하다

해 석

은밀하게 녹음된 소리는 참가자들이 녹음되는 것을 원치 않는다는 것을 명백히 보여 주었다.

① 은밀한 ② 법으로 정한 ③ 솔직한 ④ 천사 같은

3 ②

단 어

ought to ~ : ~해야 한다
mandatory : 법에 정해진, 의무적인

해 석

① A : 이 장치가 왜 제대로 작동하지 않나요?
   B : 먼저 코드를 꽂아야 합니다.
② A : 우리 집에서 그의 사무실까지 얼마나 걸릴까요?
   B : 바라건대 이번 주 후반까지입니다.
③ A : 휠체어를 어디에서 빌릴 수 있나요?
   B : 후문에서 빌려 보세요.
④ A : 당신은 이번 주말에 직원 교육에 참여할 예정이지요?
   B : 그건 필수입니다. 그렇지요?

4 ④

단 어

allium : 파속 식물(파/양파/마늘 등)
edible : 식용 가능한
bulb : 구근, 동그란 부분
cuisine : 요리
fundamental : 필수적인, 근본적인
dice : 깍둑썰기를 하다
replicate : 복제하다, 모방하다
standby : (필요하면 언제나 쓸 수 있는) 예비품

해 석

파속 식물들 – 양파, 마늘, 리크(부추) 등을 포함한 식용 가능한 봉우리들 – 은 전 세계의 거의 모든 요리에 등장한다. 파속 식물은 전통 요리의 기초 – 프랑스의 미르포아(깍둑썰기 된 양파, 셀러리, 당근), 라틴 아메리카의 저냐(양파, 마늘, 토마토) 그리고 케이준 삼총사(양파, 피망, 셀러리) - 에 필수적이다. 우리는 때때로 이러한 재료들을 당연시 여기지만, 파속 식물의 맛은 똑같이 만들어질 수 없다. 그리고 심장병이나 암을 예방해 주는 물질을 포함하고 있는 그들의 건강적인 이점 역시 흉내낼 수 없다.

TIP

① including이 edible bulbs를 수식하고 있으며, 뒤에 목적어(onions, garlic, and leeks)를 가지고 있고 능동의 뜻이기 때문에 –ing로 맞게 썼다.
② they는 앞 문장의 allium vegetables의 복수 명사를 나타내는 대명사로 바르게 쓰였다.
③ '~하는 반면에'라는 뜻으로 종속절을 이끄는 접속사 while이 바르게 쓰였다.
④ And neither their health benefits <u>can</u>, ~ → And neither <u>can</u> their health benefits, ~
부정어 neither가 문장 앞에 왔기 때문에 주어-동사가 도치되어야 한다.

5 ③

단 어

adolescent : 청소년
be cognizant of : ~을 인식하다
second-hand smoking : 간접흡연
release : 방출하다

해 석

① 청소년들과 성인들은 간접흡연의 위험성에 관해 인식해야 한다.
② 오찬 회의에서 그의 연설이 너무 훌륭해서 모든 청중들은 그를 지지했다.
③ 적절한 경험과 학문적인 배경이 그 직위의 지원자들에게 요구된다.
④ 식물, 동물 그리고 사람들에게 가장 큰 위협은 공기와 물로 방출된 독성 화학물이다.

TIP

① ~ should be cognizant <u>to</u> the risks ~ → ~should be cognizant <u>of</u> the risks ~
'~을 알고 있다'의 뜻으로 be cognizant of를 쓴다.
② ~was <u>such</u> great that ~ → ~was <u>so</u> great that ~
'너무 ~해서 ~하다' 구문으로 'so+형용사/부사+that~', 'such+명사+that~'이다. such는 명사 앞에서 쓰므로, 형용사 great 앞은 so가 맞다.
③ require가 수동형태 be required of ~(~에게 요구되다)로 쓰였다. 또한 주어가 appropriate experience and academic background이므로 and로 연결된 두 가지 개념으로 보아 복수로 취급하여 동사 역시 복수형태(are)로 썼다.
④ ~ toxic chemicals <u>releasing</u> into ~ → ~ toxic chemicals <u>released</u> into ~
독성 화학물질이 대기와 물에 '방출된' 것이므로 수동 형태인 released가 와야 한다.

6 ③

해 석

'늙은 개에게 새로운 재주를 가르칠 수 없다'는 말이 있다. 하지만 대부분의 경우 이 속담은 진실이 아니다. 현대 신경과학의 역사상, 성인의 뇌는 고정된 구조여서 한번 손상이 되면 치유할 수 없다고 믿어져 왔다. 하지만 1960년대 이후에 발표된 연구는 이 가정에 이의를 제기했다. 이 연구에서 뇌는 매우 유동적인 구조여서, 새로운 경험에 반응하여 스스로 변화를 하고 부상(상처)에 적응하게 되는데, 이는 신경가소성이라 불리는 현상이다.

① 제때의 한 땀의 바느질이 아홉 땀의 바느질을 던다.
② 유유상종 ; 같은 유형의 사람들은 서로 함께 모이는 경향이 있다.
③ 늙은 개에게 새로운 재주를 가르칠 수는 없다 ; 노인은 새로운 것을 배우기 어렵다는 뜻
④ 백지장도 맞들면 낫다. 한 사람이 하는 것보다는 두 사람이 하는 것이 낫다.

7 ③

해 석

만약 당신이 음식을 천천히 먹는다면, 훨씬 덜 먹게 되고 칼로리도 덜 섭취하게 되므로 휴일 식사 시에는 속도 조절을 하십시오.

8 ②

해 석

정부는 최근에 환경오염을 막기 위해 음식물 찌꺼기 처리기의 대안을 찾고 있다.

① 살며시 나가다   ② 차단하다, 저지하다
③ 출발하다   ④ ~을 훔쳐 달아나다

9 ④

해 석

50년 전 맑은 봄날 아침, 벨연구소에서 두 명의 젊은 천문학자들이 20피트짜리 뿔 모양의 안테나를 뉴저지 상공 하늘을 향해 조준하고 있었다. 그들의 목표는 지구의 고향인 우리 은하를 측정하는 것이었다. 놀랍게도 Robert W. Wilson과 Arno A. Penzias는 우리 은하 건너편으로부터, 그리고 모든 방향으로부터 계속되는 전자기파의 소리를 들었다. 그것은 우주 마이크로파 배경복사였고, 이는 138억 년 전 우주를 생겨나게 했던 에너지와 물체들의 원시 폭발의 잔여물들이었다. 과학자들은 1931년 George Lemaître에 의해 처음으로 제안된, 빅뱅이론을 확신할 수 있는 증거를 찾아냈다.

① 빛은 빅뱅이론을 배제시키는 것을 돕는다.
② 신비로운 신호는 우주의 변동 없는 상태를 의미한다.
③ 우주는 두드러진 시작도 없이 변동 없는 상태였다.
④ 복사는 Lemaître가 이론을 제시했던 폭발의 잔여효과이다.

10 ②

해 석

만약 우리가 우리 마음속에 있는 것을 직접적으로 직관하지 못한다면, 유일한 방법은 마치 새들이나 행성들과 같은 외부적인 것들을 조사하는 것과 같이 지식이나 마음 상태와 같은 내부적인 것들을 조사하는 것이다. 즉, 우리는 사실들을 만족스럽게 설명하기 위하여 분명한 이론을 고안해야만 한다. 우리는 직접적으로 마음 내부에 있는 것을 볼 수 없기 때문에, 우리가 해야 할 일은 우리가 외부로부터 관찰할 수 있는 것의 토대 위에서 내부에 있는 것을 알아내는 것이다.

① 대화 유추　　② 내부영역 관찰의 문제
③ 문제 영역의 분할　　④ 인류 언어의 비교

☑ TIP

보기 ②번의 black box는 보이지 않는 내부를 들여다보는 것을 의미한다.

11 ③

☑ 단 어

green revolution : 녹색혁명(품종 개량에 의한 식량 증산)
sequence : 연속적인 사건들
breakthrough : 돌파구
irrigation : 관개(물을 끌어들임)
resistance : 저항력
massive : 부피가 큰, 대량의
fertilizer : 비료
controversy : 논란

☑ 해 석

녹색혁명은 식량 생산 증대에 의해 굶주림에서 성공적으로 벗어나게 하는 과학적인 진보와 발달의 연속적인 사건들의 결과이다. 녹색혁명의 주요 구성요소는 새로운 씨앗, 화학물질의 사용, 적절한 관개 체계이다. ① 녹색혁명은 생산의 증대를 가져왔고 이는 농부들의 사고방식을 변화시켰다. ② 녹색혁명은 작물의 질병 저항력을 증대시켜 주었고, 산업과 농업 분야의 일자리 대방출을 가져왔다. (③ 그러므로 화학 비료의 환경비용과 무리한 관개사업은 상당한 논란을 불러 일으켰다.) ④ 식용곡물의 자급자족은 기획과정에도 영향을 주었고 이는 민주주의로 나아가는 국가적 자존감도 향상시켰다.

☑ TIP

이 글의 요지는 녹색혁명이 어떠한 과정으로 이루어지고 어떠한 이점을 가져 왔는지에 관련된 내용이므로 ③번은 흐름상 적절하지 못하다.

12 ①

☑ 단 어

ring a bell : 친숙하게 들리다
weird : 기묘한, 기괴한

☑ 해 석

내가 그 시를 들었을 때, 몇몇 구절들이 친숙하게 들렸다.

13 ③

☑ 단 어

referendum : 총선거
turnout : 참가자 수, 투표율
eligible : 자격 있는
step down : (요직에서) 물러나다
petition : 진정서

☑ 해 석

2016년 6월 23일, 영국에서 역사적인 총선이 치러졌다. 총선의 안건은 다음과 같았다. "영국이 EU 구성원으로 남을 것인가, 아니면 탈퇴할 것인가?" 영국이 EU를 떠날 가능성은 Brexit(브렉시트)라고 알려졌다. 3천만이 넘는 인원이 투표를 했다. 투표율은 영국의 지난 선거보다 더 높았다. 투표의 자격이 있는 사람들은 18세 이상의 영국에서 살고 있는 영국인, 아일랜드인, 영연방 시민들이었다. 6월 23일 투표자의 52퍼센트가 영국이 EU를 탈퇴할 것을 선택했다. 이는 전 세계에 충격을 주었다. 몇 시간 내로 영국의 통화인 파운드는 역사상 최저로 떨어졌고, 영국 수상인 Cameron은 사임했다. 총선 몇 주 후 수백만의 사람들이 재선을 요구하는 진정서를 냈다. 새로운 수상인 Theresa May는 시민들에게 "브렉시트는 브렉시트일 뿐"이라고 말했다. 탈퇴를 협상하는 데 거의 2년이 걸릴 것이다. EU에 살고 있는 영국 국민들의 권리와 지위 그리고 영국에 살고 있는 EU 국민들의 권리와 지위가 주요 관심사이다.

① 영국이 EU에 참여하는 것이 브렉시트라고 불린다.
② 영국에 있는 모든 사람이 투표를 했다.
③ 투표자의 52퍼센트가 영국이 EU를 떠나기를 원했다.
④ 선거 이후 유로의 가치가 올라갔다.

14 ④

☑ 단 어

respect : 존경하다

☑ TIP

① It was three years since ～ → It has been three years since ～
～이래로(since) 지금까지 3년이 흘렀다는 뜻이므로 현재완료형 have+p.p가 와야 한다.
② before the sun will set → before the sun sets
시간 부사절에서는 현재 시제가 미래 시제를 대신한다.
③ if she finishes the work ～ → if she will finish the work
이 문장에서 if절은 조건을 나타내는 절이므로, by tonight 시점에 맞게 미래형으로 써야 한다.
④ Although he made a mistake, he could be ～ 문장에서 부사절을 분사구문으로 바꾸어 (Although) making a mistake가 되었다.

15 ①

단어 •

that said : 그렇긴 하지만
religious : 종교의

TIP

① We asked him <u>about</u> this job → We asked him <u>to do</u> this job
'ask+A+to부정사'의 5형식 형태로 쓰여서 'A가 ~하도록 요청하다'의 뜻을 가진다. 목적보어로 to부정사를 취한다. ask (someone) about~은 '-에게 ~을 물어보다'의 뜻이다.
② everything but~에서 but은 '~를 제외하고'의 뜻을 가진다.
③ while eating이 삽입 구문으로 쓰였다.
④ that said는 '그렇긴 하지만의 뜻을 가진다.

16 ①

단어 •

misspell : 철자를 잘못 쓰다

해석

이름을 이야기할 때 철자를 체크하는 것이 매우 중요한데, 이는 그 누구도 본인 이름의 철자가 잘못 쓰이길 원치 않기 때문이다. 영어에서 발음은 똑같이 나지만 스펠링이 다르게 쓰이는 당혹스러운 경우들이 종종 있다. 이 이름들의 예로는 McIntosh와 Mackintosh, Stevenson과 Stephenson, Davis와 Davies, Frances(여자)와 Francis(남자) 등이 있다.

① 당황하게 하는 ② 설득의 ③ 영리한 ④ 외국의

17 ②

단어 •

contemplate : 고려하다, 생각하다
allegory : 풍자
enlightenment : 계몽하다, 계몽시키다
intelligible : 이해할 수 있는
dominate : 지배하다

해석

"국가론" 7권에서 플라톤은 그들에게 숨겨진 진실을 알지 못하는 평범한 사람들이 어두운 동굴에 갇힌 모습을 형상화했다. 한 명의 죄수가 동굴에서 풀려났을 때 그는 처음에는 눈이 보이지 않을 만큼 밝은 햇빛 때문에 고통스럽지만, 그의 눈이 적응을 하면 그는 진실을 보기 시작한다. 만약 그가 그의 동료 죄수들을 계몽시키기 위해 동굴로 돌아간다면, 동료들은 그를 믿지 않을 것이다. <u>이는 그들이 그들의 존재를 지배하는 어두움 너머의 세상을 상상할 수 없기 때문이다.</u> 플라톤의 풍자는 무지함과 깨달음 사이의 구분 – "보이는" 세상과 "이해할 수 있는" 영역 사이의 구분 – 을 생각하게 하는 강력한 유추이다.

① 이는 그들이 동굴 밖의 현실에 영감을 받을 수 있기 때문이다.
② 이는 그들이 그들의 존재를 지배하는 어두움 너머의 세상을 상상할 수 없기 때문이다.
③ 이는 그들이 태양의 빛 속으로 자신을 움직이기 때문이다.
④ 이는 그들이 그가 동굴 밖에서 볼 수 있었던 것들을 외면할 수 없기 때문이다.

18 ①

단어 •

drearily : 쓸쓸하게
tickle : 재미있게 하다, 간지럼을 태우다
suburbanity : 교외 거주자들
presently : 이내, 머지않아
unmistakable : 오해의 여지가 없는
flustered : 허둥지둥하게 만들다
preliminary : 예비의

해석

11월이었다. 비가 차갑게 그리고 쓸쓸히 내렸다. 그는 긴 레인코트의 단추를 채우고 그녀를 만나기 위해 나섰다. 그녀는 빨간 카네이션을 달고 나오겠다고 약속했다. 이는 그녀가 제안한 것이고 그를 매우 즐겁게 만들었다. 차가운 빗줄기 속에 붉게 상기된 얼굴의 교외 거주자들이 따뜻한 대기실로 들어왔고 그는 그녀를 찾아보았다. 이내 그는 그녀를 보았다. 오해할 여지가 없는 그의 키 때문에 그녀는 그의 앞으로 곧장 다가왔다. 그들은 신나서 허둥대며 이야기를 나눴지만 점차 서로에게 어떤 예감을 가지게 되었다.

① 그 남자와 그 여자는 처음으로 만나는 중이다.
② 그 남자는 교외 지역에 살았다.
③ 그 남자는 키가 크고 간지럼을 잘 탄다.
④ 그 남자는 그 여자가 꽃을 달고 나오기를 제안했다.

19 ②

단어 •

continental scale : 대륙적 규모
decline : 감소하다
conservation : 보존
latitude : 위도, 범위

corresponding : 상응하는
retreat : 후퇴하다
hospitable : (기후, 환경이) 쾌적한

☑ 해석

Science지에서 출간된 최근 연구에 따르면, 기후 변화는 최근 수십 년 동안 북미와 유럽에서 호박벌이 발견되는 범위를 좁혀왔다. [(B) 그 연구지는 1970년대부터 따뜻해지고 있는 기온이 호박벌 군수를 그 이동의 남쪽 경계로부터 190마일이나 후퇴시켰음을 시사한다. (A) 논리상으로는, 호박벌의 주 서식지의 북쪽 범위가 이에 상응하는 거리만큼 더 높은 위도로 이동해야 한다. (C) 그러나 그러한 일은 일어나지 않았고, 연구자들은 보다 북쪽의 서식지가 호박벌들에게 덜 쾌적할 수 있다고 생각하게 되었다.]
연구의 대표 연구자이며 캐나다 오타와 대학교의 보존생물학자 Jeremy T. Kerr는 "유럽과 북미의 호박벌은 대륙적 규모로 감소하고 있으며 우리의 자료는 기후 변화가 이러한 추세에서 어떤 주도적인 또는 아마도 분명히 주도적인 역할을 하고 있음을 시사한다."라고 기자회견에서 말했다.

☑ TIP

[ ] 이전의 문맥에서 언급된 recent study(최근의 연구)를 (B)의 The paper(그 연구지)가 받고 있으므로 (B)가 가장 먼저 온다. 그리고 (A)에서는 (B)의 내용을 논리적으로 설명을 하고 있으므로 (B) 다음에 (A)가 온다. (C)는 (A)의 내용을 반박하는 내용이 나오고 있으므로 글의 순서는 (B)-(A)-(C)가 된다.

20 ④

☑ 단 어

early period : 초기
refute : 논박하다, 부인하다
reproach : 비난하다, 책망하다

☑ 해석

당신의 사업을 운영하는 것의 금전적인 보상은 당신이 수많은 시간과 노동을 투자하기 <u>전에는</u> 나타나지 않을 수도 있다. 돈을 벌고자 하는 욕구만으로는 초기의 어려운 시기를 <u>계속해서 견뎌내기</u>에 충분치 못하다.

☑ TIP

(A)에는 not A until B (B하고 나서야 A하다) 구문이 쓰였다. (B)에는 목적보어로 분사 형태를 가질 수 있는 keep을 써서 '계속해서 ~하다 뜻을 나타낼 수 있다.

---

1 ②

☑ 단 어

absolutely : 극도로, 굉장히

☑ 해석

나는 밤늦게까지 깨어있는 것을 극도로 <u>싫어했다.</u>

① 방어하다 ② 혐오하다 ③ 확신하다 ④ 버리다

2 ①

☑ 단 어

uncanny : 이상한, 묘한

☑ 해석

나는 내가 이 장면을 이전에 어디선가 본 것 같은 <u>이상한</u> 감정을 느꼈다.

① 이상한   ② 계속 진행 중인
③ 분명한, 확실한   ④ 불쾌한, 모욕적인

3 ④

☑ 단 어

headquarter : 본사
abroad : 해외에
fluently : 유창하게
splendid : 훌륭한

☑ TIP

① as soon as(~하자마자) 시간 부사절에서 현재 시제가 미래 시제를 대신하므로 you will receive로 쓰지 않도록 한다.
② should have p.p 혹은 ought to have p.p를 써서 '~했어야 했는데 (안 했다)'는 가정법 문장을 쓸 수 있다.
③ 현재 완료형(have p.p)의 분사구문 형태(having p.p)로 바른 표현이다.
④ I <u>should</u> have achieved → I <u>couldn't</u> have achieved
If I had given up~ 가정법 if절에서 if가 생략되고 조동사 had가 앞으로 도치된 것으로 바른 형태이다. 그러나 의미상 should have achieved는 '성공했어야 했는데 (못했다)'는 뜻이 되어 보기 지문의 뜻과 맞지 않다. couldn't have p.p 형태로 써야 한다.

4 ①

> **단 어 ·**

refund : 환불

> **해 석**

A : 도와드릴까요?
B : 제가 이 드레스를 이틀 전에 샀는데, 저에게 좀 큰 것 같아요.
A : <u>죄송합니다만, 더 작은 사이즈는 없습니다.</u>
B : 그러면 환불을 하고 싶습니다.
A : 영수증 좀 보여주시겠어요?
B : 여기 있습니다.

① 죄송합니다만, 더 작은 사이즈는 없습니다.
② 그런데 제 생각에는 손님에게 딱 맞는 것 같은데요.
③ 그 드레스는 저희 가게에서 매우 잘 팔립니다.
④ 죄송합니다만 이 제품은 환불이 되지 않습니다.

5 ②

> **단 어 ·**

home blood pressure monitor : 가정용 혈압측정기
strap : 끈, 줄

> **해 석**

A : 제가 집에 있는 혈압측정기를 사용할 때마다 다른 결과를 얻게 됩니다. 제가 무엇인가를 잘못하고 있는 것 같은데요. 혈압측정기를 올바르게 사용하는 방법을 알려줄 수 있나요?
B : 물론입니다. 먼저 끈을 팔에 두르세요.
A : 이렇게요? 맞게 하고 있는 건가요?
B : 너무 꽉 조인 것 같습니다.
A : 그럼 지금은 어떤가요?
B : 이번에는 너무 느슨한 것 같습니다. 너무 꽉 조이거나 느슨하면 잘못된 결과를 얻게 됩니다.
A : <u>알겠습니다. 다음에는 무엇을 해야 하나요?</u>
B : 이제 버튼을 누르세요. 움직이거나 말을 해서는 안 됩니다.
A : 알겠습니다.
B : 잠시 후에 측정기의 화면을 읽어야 합니다.

① 오늘은 아무것도 보지 못했습니다.
② 알겠습니다. 다음에는 무엇을 해야 하나요?
③ 맞습니다. 저는 책을 좀 읽어야겠습니다.
④ 그들의 웹사이트를 체크해 봐야 할까요?

6 ①

> **단 어 ·**

determine : 알아내다, 결정하다

> **해 석**

① 그들은 그의 이야기를 믿지 않았고, 나 또한 믿지 않았다.
② 내가 가장 좋아하는 스포츠는 축구이다.
③ Jamie는 제1차 세계대전이 1914년에 일어났다는 것을 책에서 배웠다.
④ 두 가지 요소들은 과학자들이 지구상의 종의 수를 결정하는 것을 어렵게 만들어 왔다.

> **TIP**

① 부정문에 대해 '~역시 그렇다'라는 뜻을 나타낼 때는 neither를 쓴다. 또한 주어-동사 순서가 뒤바뀐다 (neither did I).
② in <u>that</u> I am most interested → in <u>which</u> I am most interested
   관계대명사 that은 선행하는 전치사와 함께 쓰일 수 없다.
③ that World War Ⅰ <u>had broken out</u> → that World War Ⅰ <u>broke</u> out
   과거의 역사적 사실에 대해서는 문장에서의 선후관계에 상관없이 과거 시제로 표현한다.
④ Two factors have made <u>scientists difficult to determine</u>~ → Two factors have made <u>it</u> difficult <u>for scientists to determine</u>~
   make는 5형식 동사로 쓰이므로 scientists-목적어, difficult-목적보어로 하게 되면, 과학자들을 어렵게 만든다는 뜻이 될 뿐 아니라, 뒤에 있는 to부정사 구조가 남게 된다. 의미상 '과학자들이 결정하는 것을 어렵게 만든다'는 뜻이므로, scientists는 to determine~의 의미상 주어가 된다. for scientists to determine~으로 써서 전체가 make의 목적어가 되는데 가목적어 it을 써서 문장의 뒤로 위치시킨다.

7 ②

> **단 어 ·**

in passing : 지나가는 말로

> **해 석**

① 지나가면서 들었던 몇 마디 말은 나를 생각에 잠기게 했다.
② 그녀가 집에 들어서자마자 누군가 불을 켰다.
③ 우리는 그 호텔로 운전을 했고, 그 호텔의 발코니에서 우리는 도시를 내려다 볼 수 있었다.
④ 노숙자들은 보통 일자리를 얻기가 어렵고 이로 인해 그들은 희망을 잃게 된다.

TIP

① words는 가산명사 이므로 a few를 쓸 수 있다(a few+ 가산명사/ few+불가산명사). words와 caught의 수동관계 또한 바르게 썼다.

② Hardly <u>did</u> she enter the house when ~ → Hardly <u>had</u> she <u>entered</u> the house when ~
S+had hardly p.p when S'+V'(S가 ~하자마자 S'가 V'하다) 구문이다. hardly가 있는 절에서 had p.p 과거완료형을 써야 한다는 점에 주의한다. 또 보기 지문에서 부정어 hardly(거의-하지 않는)이 문장 앞에 있으므로 주어-동사 순서가 뒤바뀌어야 한다.

③ We drove on to <u>the hotel</u>. + We could look down at the town <u>from the hotel's balcony</u>. 소유관계대명사 whose(=the hotel's)를 써서 두 문장을 연결하였다. 전치사 from을 관계대명사(whose) 앞에 위치시킬 수 있다.

④ the는 'the 형용사' 형태로 쓰여서 '(형용사가 묘사하는) 사물·사람들'을 뜻하는 명사(복수형)로 쓸 수 있다. 따라서 복수주어에 수일치를 시켜 동사-have, 뒤의 문장 주어에서 대명사-they로 쓴 것은 올바른 표현이다. have difficulty (in) -ing는 '~하는 데에 어려움이 있다'는 뜻이다. 전치사의 목적어 자리이므로 명사/동명사(구)를 쓴다.

8 ③

단어

on earth : 도대체
strangle : 목졸라 죽이다, 교살하다
globalization : 세계화
stem : 막다, 저지하다
disparity : 격차, 차이
undeniable : 부인할 수 없는
opponent : 반대자
proportionately : 균형적으로
at the expense of : ~의 희생으로
revive : 회복시키다, 활기를 되찾다

해석

만약 정부가 세계 경제의 세 가지 요소인 무역, 정보, 자금의 흐름을 막음으로써 세계화를 억압한다면 도대체 그것이 가난한 사람들을 어떻게 도울 수 있을까? 빈부의 격차가 여전히 크다는 것은 부인할 수가 없다. 하지만 세계화를 반대하는 사람들과 시장경제가 우리로 하여금 믿도록 만든 것처럼 경제 성장이 부유한 사람들에게만 득이 되고 가난한 사람들은 배제한다는 것은 진실이 아니다. 최근에 "경제성장이 가난한 자들에게 도움이 될까?"라는 제목으로 행해진 세계은행의 연구는 인구의 하위 5%의 소득과 1인당 GDP사이에 1:1 관계가 있음을 밝혀냈다. 다시 말해서

모든 분야의 소득은 같은 비율로 균형적으로 증가한다는 것이다. 그 연구는 해외 무역에의 경제 개방이 전체 경제에 이득을 주는 것과 똑같이 가난한 자들에게도 이득이 된다는 것을 보여준다.

① 세계화가 빈부 갈등을 심화시킨다.
② 세계 경제는 가난한 사람들의 희생으로 성장한다.
③ 세계화는 개인의 경제적 지위와 상관없이 이득이 될 수 있다.
④ 정부는 경제회생을 위하여 무역의 흐름을 통제해야 한다.

9 ③

단어

hover : 맴돌다
astute : 영리한, 약삭빠른
uncertainty : 불확실성
orient : (목적에) 맞추다
pitch in : 협력하다
prerequisite : 전제조건
empathy : 감정이입, 공감
responsiveness : 민감성
conduit : 전달자
altruism : 이타주의
heroism : 영웅적 행위
compel : 강요하다
intervene : 개입하다
clutch : 위기

해석

왜 빈곤선 근처를 맴도는 사람들이 그들의 동료를 더 잘 도와주는 경향이 있을까? Keltner는 가난한 사람들이 어려운 시기를 해결하기 위해 종종 서로 협력을 해야만 하는 것이 그 부분적 이유라고 생각을 한다 - 이는 아마도 그들을 사회적으로 훨씬 영리하게 만드는 과정일 것이다. "당신이 불확실함에 직면할 때, 그것은 당신이 다른 사람들에게 더 초점을 맞추게 한다. 당신은 이 강한 사회적 연결 관계를 형성하게 되는 것이다."라고 그는 말한다. 예를 들면, 가난하고 어린 엄마가 아기를 낳게 되면, 그 엄마는 음식, 물품, 아기 돌봄 등의 도움이 필요한데, 만약 그녀가 사회적으로 좋은 관계를 가지고 있었다면 그녀의 사회 구성원들이 협력을 하게 될 것이다. 그러나 제한된 수입원이 이러한 종류의 공감대와 사회적 민감성을 발달시키는 전제 조건은 아니다. 우리 은행 자산이 얼마이든지 상관없이, 고통은 이타주의 혹은 영웅적인 행위로 이끄는 전달자가 된다. 우리 자신의 고통이 다른 사람의 필요에 <u>더 주의를 기울이도록</u> 만들 때, 그리고 우리가 잘 아는 종류의 고난 위기에 있는 누군가를 보고 개입하도록 만드는 경우에.

① 덜 개입하다   ② 덜 사로잡히다
③ 더 집중하다   ④ 더 무관심하다

10 ④

단 어

amenity : 생활 편의 시설
exclusive : 독보적인
unveil : 모습을 드러내다
death-defying : 아슬아슬한, 죽음에 도전하는
turn up : 나타나다
brick-and-mortar : 소매
repurpose : 다른 목적에 맞게 고치다
thrive : 번영하다

해 설

상하이에 있는 Soleil 백화점 아웃렛은 현대 중국 소매업의 성공에 필요한 모든 시설을 갖춘 것처럼 보인다: 최고급 명품 브랜드들과 독보적인 위치. 그러나 이러한 이점에도 불구하고 그 백화점의 경영진은 고객을 유치하기 위해 무언가가 여전히 부족하다고 생각했다. 그래서 다음 주에 그들은 고객들이 5층 부티크 샵에서 1층 부티크 샵으로 아찔한 속도로 갈 수 있는 거대하고 비틀린 용 모양의 슬라이드를 공개한다. 소셜미디어 사용자들은 반농담으로 실제 그 슬라이드가 사람을 죽일 수도 있는지 궁금해하고 있다. 하지만 Soleil 측은 중국의 쇼핑몰들이 곧 완전히 사라질 것이라는 다른 걱정을 하고 있다. 중국의 소비자들이 겉보기에는 무한한 공급자처럼 보이지만, 늘어나는 온라인 쇼핑몰 때문에 더 이상 소매상을 찾지 않고, 명품을 사기 위해서는 해외로 갈 것이다. 그래서 다른 방법으로 시간과 돈을 쓰는 소비자들을 위해 이러한 거대한 공간들을 개조하는 것은 더 많은 창의성을 요구할 것이다. <u>5층짜리 용 슬라이드는 나쁜 출발점은 아닐 수 있다.</u>

① 명품 브랜드들이 Soleil에서 성황 중에 있다.
② Soleil은 과감한 조치에 반하는 결정을 했다.
③ 온라인 고객을 늘리는 것이 마지막 희망이 될 것이다.
④ 5층짜리 용 슬라이드는 나쁜 출발점은 아닐 수 있다. (좋은 출발점일 수도 있다)

TIP

이 글에서 소매상에서 고객을 유치하기 위해서는 더욱더 창의력이 요구된다는 내용이고, 이를 위해 Soleil 백화점은 상상할 수 없이 큰 슬라이드를 설치했다. 이는 고객을 유치하기 위한 창의성의 좋은 예일 수 있으므로 빈칸에는 ④번이 적절하다.

11 ①

단 어

devise : 고안하다, 창안하다
on the face of it : 보기에는
in hindsight : 지나고 나서 보면

dividend : 비상금, 상금
anticipate : 예측하다

해 설

미래 발전에 가능한 한 많은 시나리오들을 창안해 내는 것은 쉽고, 겉보기에는 각각의 시나리오가 거의 같아 보인다. 어려운 과업은 그 중 어떤 시나리오가 실제로 일어날 것인가이다. 지나고 나서 보면 그것은 보통 명백하게 보인다. 우리가 지난 시간을 돌이켜 보면, 각각의 사건은 명백히 그리고 논리적으로 앞 사건을 따라서 일어나는 것 같다. 그러나 그 사건이 발생하기 전에 가능성의 수는 끝없이 많아 보인다. 특별히 결정적인 요인이 알려져 있지 않고 어떤 한 그룹만의 통제를 받지 않는, 복잡한 사회 변화나 기술 변화 분야에서 성공적인 예측을 하기 위한 방법은 없다. 그럼에도 불구하고 <u>미래를 위해 합리적인 시나리오들을 만들어 내는 것</u>이 필요하다. 우리는 반드시 새로운 기술이 이점과 문제점 – 특별히 사회적인 문제점 – 을 가져올 것이라는 것을 알아야 한다. 이러한 문제점을 예측하려고 더 많이 노력할수록 우리는 그것들을 더 잘 통제할 수 있다.

① 미래를 위해 합리적인 시나리오들을 만들어 내는 것
② 미래 변화로부터 가능한 이점들을 정당화하는 것
③ 기술적 문제들의 여러 측면들을 배제시키는 것
④ 현재에 집중하는 것이 어떤 것인지 고려하는 것

12 ③

단 어

taste bud : 미뢰
mound : 무더기
petal : 꽃잎
wear out : 닳아버리다
palate : 구개
jade : 약해지다
keen : 예리한, 날카로운
adore : 아주 좋아하다
blunted : 무딘

해 설

미뢰는 19세기 독일의 과학자들인 Georg Meissner와 Rudolf Wagner에 의해 그 이름을 갖게 되었는데, 이 과학자들은 꽃잎처럼 겹쳐진 미각 세포들로 구성된 무더기를 발견했다. 미뢰는 일주일에서 열흘이면 닳아버려서 우리는 그것들을 새로운 것으로 대체한다. 하지만 45세 이상이 되면 그렇게 자주는 아니다. 우리의 구개는 나이가 들면서 정말 쇠퇴한다. 똑같은 수준의 감각을 느끼기 위해 더 강렬한 맛이 필요하고 어린이들은 가장 예민한 미각을 가지고 있다. 아기의 입안에는 어른보다 훨씬 더 많은 미뢰들이 있고 심지어는 볼에도 분포되어 있다. 아이들은 단 것을 아주 좋아하는데, 설탕에 더 민감한 그들의 혀끝이 – 뜨거운 수프가 식기 전에 먹어 보려고 함으로써 – 아직 둔감해지지 않은 것이 부분적인 이유이다.

82 ‖ 최근 7개년 기출문제

① 미뢰는 19세기에 발명되었다.
② 미뢰의 대체(교체)는 나이가 들어도 느려지지 않는다.
③ 아이들은 어른보다 훨씬 예민한 구개를 가지고 있다.
④ 미각은 차가운 수프를 먹음으로 쇠퇴한다.

13 ③

단 어

put up with : ~을 참다

해 석

이 회사에서, 우리는 그러한 행동을 용납할 수 없다.

① 수정하다
② 녹음하다
③ 참다, 용납하다
④ 평가하다

14 ④

단 어

former : 예전의, 과거의
take over : 인계 받다
take on : 떠맡다
take off : 이륙하다

해 석

① 나는 그의 이전 직위를 인계 받을 것이다.
② 나는 요즘 더 이상의 일을 맡을 수 없다.
③ 비행기는 짙은 안개 때문에 이륙할 수 없었다.
④ 나는 여동생을 돌봐야 해서 밖에 나갈 수 없다.

TIP

④번에서 take after는 '~를 닮다'의 의미로 이 문장에서
적절하지 않으며 take care of로 바꿔야 한다.

15 ②

단 어

engage in : 참여하다, 개입하다
depression : 우울증
beforehand : 미리
elaborate : 정교한
run off : 달아나다
inquisitive : 호기심 많은
get on with : ~을 해 나가다
dignity : 품격
dysfunction : 역기능

해 석

드라마는 행동하는 것이다. 드라마는 존재이다. 드라마는 매우
평범한 것이다. 우리가 매일매일의 어려운 상황에 직면할 때 우
리가 참여하게 되는 바로 그것이다. 당신이 아침에 일어나서 극
심한 두통이 있고 우울감이 몰려와도 당신은 아무렇지도 않은
체하며 다른 사람들을 만나고 하루를 보내야 한다. 당신이 중요
한 미팅이나 인터뷰를 앞두고 있을 때 당신은 미리 그 이야기를
해보고, 어떻게 자신감 있고 즐거운 얼굴로 발표를 하고, 무엇
을 입어야 하고 손은 어떻게 해야 하는지 등을 결정한다. 당신이
동료의 서류에 커피를 쏟으면 즉시 정교한 변명을 준비해야 한
다. 당신의 애인이 당신의 가장 친한 친구와 달아난다 해도, 당
신은 호기심 많은 학생들을 가르치는 것을 피할 수 없다. 만약
우리가 품격을 유지하고 다른 사람들과 조화를 이루는 삶을 유
지하기 원한다면, 하루하루의 삶은 우리에게 연속된 문명화된 가
면이 필요하게 한다.

① 드라마의 역기능
② 우리 일상의 드라마
③ 극예술로서의 드라마
④ 감정의 극적인 변화

16 ④

단 어

financial : 금융의
crisis : 위기
construct : 건설하다
distract : ~을 혼란시키다

TIP

① only after 부사구가 문장 앞에 있으므로 주어-동사 순
서가 도치(he realized → did he realize)되었다.
② insist와 같이 요구, 주장 등의 뜻을 나타내는 동사는 목
적어로 오는 that절에서 'should+동사원형'을 쓴다. 이
때 should는 생략될 수 있으므로 that 절에서 a bridge
(should) be constructed로 표현된 것은 바른 표현이다.
③ '(as) 형용사/부사 as +S +V' 구문에서 as는 though와 같
은 양보(~이긴 하지만)의 뜻을 가진다. though it was
a difficult task와 같은 뜻이다. 'as +형용사 +a 명사'의
순서도 as difficult a task로 바르게 쓰였다.
④ He was so distracted~ to know that~ → He was too
distracted~ to know that~
so distracted~ to know라고 하면 '너무 정신이 팔려서
알았다'라는 뜻으로 해석되고 의미상으로도 어색한 문장
이 된다. '너무 ~해서 ~하지 못하다'라는 표현이 되어야
하므로 too~to 구문을 써야 한다.

17 ④

단 어 •

contrast with : ~와 대조를 이루다
precisely : 정밀하게
calculate : 계산하다
handicap : 장애
notion : 개념
optic nerve : 시신경
assume : 추정하다
transmit : 전송하다
clear up : ~을 말끔히 정리하다
disseminate : 퍼뜨리다
sweep up : 쓸다, 쓸어담다

해 석

귀와 대조하여 눈에 의해 수집되는 정보의 양은 정확하게 계산되지 않았었다. 그러한 계산은 번역 과정을 포함하고 있을 뿐 아니라, 무엇을 계산해야 하는지 몰라서 과학자들도 어려움을 겪어왔다. 그러나 두 체계의 상관적인 복잡성의 일반적인 개념은 눈과 귀를 뇌 중심부에 연결하는 신경의 크기를 (A)비교해 봄으로써 얻어질 수 있다. 시신경이 달팽이관 신경보다 약 18배 많은 뉴런을 포함하고 있기 때문에, 우리는 눈이 더 많은 정보를 전달한다고 추정한다. 실제로, 정상적으로 경계하고 있는 피사체에서, 정보를 수집하는 데 있어서 눈이 귀보다 1,000배 더 효과적일 것이다.

18 ③

단 어 •

proliferate : 급증하다
contribution : 공헌
literature : 문학
outstanding : 뛰어난
put on hold : 보류하다

해 석

최근에 아동문학상이 급증하고 있다; 오늘날 다양한 조직에서 주는 100개도 넘는 다른 상들이 있다. ① 이 상들은 특별한 장르의 책에 주어지거나 혹은 단순히 정해진 기간 동안 출판된 아동 도서 중 최고의 작품에 수여될 수도 있다. 상은 아동 문학 세계에 평생 공헌을 한 작가나 특정한 책에 주어질 수도 있다. ② 대부분의 아동문학상은 어른들이 선정하지만, 최근에는 아이들이 선택한 문학상이 점점 더 많아지고 있다. 대부분의 국가에서 주어지는 더 큰 국가적인 상은 가장 영향력이 있고 어린 독자들을 위해 출판된 좋은 책들에 관한 공공의 인식을 높이는 데 상당한 도움을 주고 있다. (③ 출판 산업에서 뛰어난 서비스에 관한 시상식은 보류된다.) ④ 물론 독자들은 현명해서 수상 작품에 너무 많은 믿음을 가지진 않는다. 상이 반드시 좋은 독서 경험을 의미하지는 않지만 책을 고르는 데 있어 좋은 시작점이 될 수는 있다.

TIP

이 글은 아동문학상에 관한 내용이 주를 이루고 있는데 ③번은 출판업계의 시상식에 관한 내용이므로 이 글의 흐름에 어색하다.

19 ④

단 어 •

inequality : 불균형, 불평등
portion : 분배
distribution : 분배
to some extend : 어느 정도
kinfolk : 친족, 친지
net result : 최종결론
substantially : 상당히, 실질적으로
kinship : 친족
obligation : 의무
morality : 도덕성

해 석

한 동물이 사냥에서 죽었을 때 일어나는 단순한 분배 상황을 살펴보자. 누군가는 그 동물을 얻기 위해 각 사냥꾼이 일한 정도에 따라 사냥감이 분배될 것으로 기대할 수도 있다. ① 어느 정도까지는 이 원칙이 지켜지지만, 다른 사람들 또한 그들의 권리를 가질 것이다. ② 그 진영의 각각의 사람들은 사냥꾼들과의 관계에 따라 몫을 받을 것이다. ③ 예를 들어, 캥거루 한 마리가 사냥되었을 때 사냥꾼들은 제일 좋은 부분을 그들의 친족에게 주어야 하고 가장 안 좋은 부분들은 사냥꾼 자신이 가져야 한다. ④ 이러한 불평등은 그들이 다른 사람들의 사냥감으로부터 더 좋은 몫을 받게 됨으로 바로잡을 수 있다. 장기적으로 최종적인 결과는 각자의 사람에게 동등하다. 그렇지만 이러한 체계를 통해 친족관계의 의무원칙과 음식을 나누는 데 있어 도덕성이 강조되어 왔다.

TIP

주어진 문장의 this inequality(이 불평등)이 무엇인지를 먼저 찾아야 이 문장의 문단 내의 위치를 찾을 수 있다.

20 ②

단 어 •

innovative : 혁신적인
psychodrama : 심리극
brainchild : 발명품, 독창적인 생각
premise : 전제
alien : 외래의, 이질적인
psyche : 정신, 마음
solitary : 고독한, 혼자의
interaction : 상호작용
improvisation : 즉흥극

consciousness : 의식
persona : 모습
empathic : 감정이입의
impulse : 충동, 자극

☑ 해석

가장 혁신적인 집단치료법은 Jacob L. Moreno가 창안한 심리극이었다. 집단치료의 한 형태로서의 심리극은 정신질환이 본질적으로 정신 또는 마음에서 일어난다는 프로이드의 견해와는 다른 전제에서 출발한다.

(B) 주류 견해와 다른 그의 이론적 차이에도 불구하고, 20세기에 심리적 의식을 형성하는 데 있어 Moreno의 영향력은 상당했다. 그는 인간의 본성은 창의적이고 창의적인 삶을 사는 것이 인간 건강과 복지의 핵심이라고 믿었다.

(A) 그러나 그는 또한 창의성이 유일한 과정이 아니며 사회적인 상호작용에 의해 일어나는 어떤 것이라고 믿었다. 그는 창의성과 사회적 신뢰를 증대시키기 위한 수단으로 역할극과 즉흥극을 포함한 연극적인 기법에 상당히 의존했다.

(C) 그의 가장 중요한 연극적인 도구는 그가 역할 바꾸기라고 부르는 것인데, 이는 참여자들에게 다른 사람의 입장이 되어보도록 요청하는 것이다. 한 사람이 다른 사람의 입장에 있는 "것처럼" 하는 행동은 감정 이입되는 자극을 이끌어내는 것을 돕고 더 높은 수준으로 그것을 발달시키기 위해 고안되었다.

☑ TIP

(B)의 his theoretical difference에서 his는 주어진 글의 Moreno를 받고 있고 mainstream은 주어진 글에 Freudian worldview를 받고 있으므로 주어진 글 다음에 (B)가 먼저 와야 한다. (B)의 후반부에서 언급한 창의성(creative)을 (A)에서 다시 부연설명하고 있으므로 (B) 다음에 (A)가 온다. 그리고 (A)의 theatrical techniques를 (C)에서 좀 더 구체적인 예(역할바꾸기)를 들어 설명하고 있으므로 주어진 글 다음 순서는 (B)-(A)-(C)가 된다.

2017. 6. 17.
제1회 지방직 시행

---

1 ②

단 어

drift apart : 뿔뿔이 흩어지다
fume : 화가 나서 씩씩대다

☑ 해석

A : 나 오래된 고등학교 친구 중 한 명에게서 편지를 받았어.
B : 와 멋지다!
A : 응, 사실 그 친구로부터 소식을 들은 지 오래되었지.

B : 솔직히 말하면, 난 내 오랜 친구들과 연락을 못하고 있어.
A : 맞아. 사람들이 이사를 많이 가면 연락을 유지하기가 어려워.
B : 네 말이 맞아. <u>사람들은 뿔뿔이 흩어져.</u> 하지만 너는 친구와 다시 연락이 닿았다니 행운이다.

① 낮이 점점 길어지고 있어.
② 사람들은 뿔뿔이 흩어져.
③ 그것은 내가 들어본 것 중 제일 웃기다.
④ 내가 그의 이름을 들을 때마다 화가 나기 시작해.

---

2 ③

단 어

inkling : 눈치챔

☑ 해석

A : Ted 생일선물로 뭐 사줄꺼니? 나는 야구 모자 몇 개를 사주려고 해.
B : 나는 좋은 선물을 생각해 내기 위해 <u>머리를 쥐어짜고 있었어.</u> 나는 그가 필요한 것을 전혀 눈치채지 못하겠어.
A : 앨범을 사 주는 것은 어때? Ted는 사진을 많이 갖고 있잖아.
B : 완벽한데? 나는 왜 그 생각을 하지 못했지? 제안해줘서 고마워.

① 그에게 연락을 받아오다.
② 하루 종일 잠을 잤다.
③ 머리를 쥐어짜고 있다.
④ 사진 앨범을 모으고 있다.

---

3 ①

단 어

authorize : 권한을 부여하다
appoint : 임명하다
surrogate : 대리자

☑ 해석

새로운 법안 중 일부는 사람들이 필요할 때 그들을 위해 의학적 결정을 내려 줄 <u>대리인</u>을 임명할 수 있도록 권한을 부여한다.

① 대리인   ② 감시인   ③ 선배   ④ 약탈자

---

4 ④

단 어

keep one's feet on the ground : 기반을 굳히다, 현실적이다

☑ 해석

A : 그는 모든 것을 다 이룰 수 있다고 생각해.
B : 맞아, 그는 <u>현실적일</u> 필요가 있어.

① 그 자신만의 세계에 산다.
② 편안하게 즐기다.
③ 용기 있게 자신감을 갖다.
④ 삶에 관해 분별력을 갖고 현실적이다.

5 ④

단어·

on the fence : 애매한 태도를 취하는

해석

그녀는 루브르 박물관에 가서 모나리자를 볼 것인지 결정을 내리지 못하고 있다.

① 고뇌에 찬　　　　　　② 열정적인
③ 걱정하는, 염려하는　④ 결정하지 못하는

6 ②

단어·

reckless : 무모한
processed food : 가공식품

해석

① 너는 단순히 많은 야채를 먹는 것이 너를 완전히 건강하게 해줄 것이라고 생각하는지도 모른다.
② 학문적 지식이 항상 올바른 결정을 할 수 있도록 하는 것은 아니다.
③ 다치는 것에 대한 두려움도 그가 무모한 행동을 하는 것을 막지 못했다.
④ Julie의 의사는 그녀에게 너무 많은 가공식품을 먹는 것을 멈추라고 이야기했다.

TIP

① that절 안에서 eating a lot of vegetables가 주어이며, keep의 목적어, 목적보어로 각각 you, healthy(형용사)가 왔으므로 올바른 표현이다.
② ~ isn't always that leads you ~ → ~ isn't always what leads you ~
보기에 주어진 문장은 2형식 문장으로, be동사 다음에 오는 자리는 보어 자리이다. 따라서 1) that절 앞에 선행사가 오고 that절이 그 선행사를 수식하는 형용사절이 되거나, 2) that절 자체가 완전한 문장 구조를 가진 명사절로서 보어 역할을 하는 경우가 있다. 여기서는 that절 안에 주절의 주어 academic knowledge를 it으로 받아 따로 주어를 넣어주면 어색한 문장이 되므로, that을 선행사 역할을 포함하는 관계사 what(=the thing that)으로 고침으로써 바르게 표현할 수 있다.

③ prevent A from −ing(A가 ~하는 것을 막다, 예방하다) 구문으로 바른 표현이다.
④ tell A to R.V(A에게 ~하라고 하다), stop −ing(−하는 것을 그만두다)이 각각 바르게 쓰였다.

7 ④

단어·

Saturn : 토성
famine : 기근
enchanted : 마법에 걸린

해석

① 바다는 아직까지도 발견되지 않은 많은 생명체를 포함하고 있다.
② 토성의 링은 너무 멀리 있어서 망원경 없이 지구에서 볼 수 없다.
③ Aswan High 댐은 이웃 국가들의 기근으로부터 이집트를 보호해 왔다.
④ 다른 유명한 도서들 중 "마법에 걸린 말"은 이 시리즈에 포함되어 있다.

TIP

① that의 선행사는 forms(of life)로 복수이므로 that 이하의 동사는 단수동사 has가 올 수 없다.
→ The oceans contain many forms of life that have not yet been discovered.
② '너무 ~해서 ~할 수 없다'의 의미를 가지기 위해 too ~ ~to 구문 혹은 so ~ that can't 구문으로 표현해야 한다.
→ The rings of Saturn are too distant to be seen from Earth without a telescope.
→ The rings of Saturn are so distant that they can't be seen from Earth without a telescope.
③ 이 문장에서 'Aswan high 댐이 이집트를 보호한' 능동의 의미이므로 이 문장은 능동이 되어야 한다.
→ The Aswan High Dam have protected Egypt from the famines of its neighboring countries.
④ 형용사 보어 도치구문으로 분사인 Included를 강조하기 위해 문두로 가면서 주어와 동사의 도치가 이루어졌다.

8 ①

단어·

farmland : 경작지
carry away : 소실시키다, 빼앗다
erosion : 부식, 침식
formation : 형성
net loss : 절대 손실

agriculture : 농업
productivity : 생산성
churchyard : 교회경내

해 석

작물 재배를 위해 사용되는 경작지들의 토양은 물이나 바람의 침식으로 토양 형성의 속도보다 10배에서 40배 사이의 토양 침식 속도로 소실되고 있으며, 삼림 지역에서는 500배에서 10,000 배 사이의 토양 침식 속도로 소실되고 있다. 토양 소실 속도가 토양 형성 속도보다 훨씬 빠르기 때문에, 이는 토양의 절대 손실을 의미한다. 예를 들자면, 미국에서 가장 높은 농업 생산력을 지닌 Iowa주 상층부 토양의 반 정도가 지난 150년 동안 침식되어 왔다. 내가 가장 최근 Iowa주를 방문했을 때, 나를 초대한 사람이 나에게 그러한 토양 침식의 가장 극적인 예로 교회 경내를 보여 주었다. 한 교회가 19세기에 농장의 한 가운데에 지어졌고 그 이후로 그 주변 땅은 경작되어 온 반면에 그 교회는 계속 남아 있었다. 교회 경내보다 들판의 토양이 훨씬 더 빠르게 소실된 결과, 교회 경내 땅은 현재 그 주위를 두른 경작지라는 바다에서 10피트 올라온 작은 섬처럼 보인다.

① Iowa주의 교회 경내는 주변 경작지보다 높다.
② Iowa주의 농업 생산성은 토양 형성으로 가속화되었다.
③ 농작지에서 토양이 형성되는 속도가 토양 침식 속도보다 빠르다.
④ Iowa주는 지난 150년 동안 상층부 토양을 유지해 왔다.

TIP

이 글의 후반부에 보면 Iowa주의 교회 경내는 다른 지역보다 10피트 높게 올라와 섬처럼 보인다는 내용이 있으므로 이 글과 일치하는 것은 ①번이다.

9 ③

단 어

take a toll on : ~에 큰 피해를 끼치다
multitude : 다수, 일반 대중
physiological : 생리적인
marker : 표시(물)
reveal : 드러내다
reduction : 감소
athlete : 운동선수
dwindle : 줄어들다
slink : 살금살금 움직이다
decondition : 몸 상태가 안 좋아지다
a slew of : 많은

해 석

당신이 여행을 하든지, 가족에 집중을 하든지, 직장에서 바쁜 시기를 지내든지 간에, 헬스장에 14일을 가지 못한다면 그것은 당신의 근육뿐만이 아니라 당신의 수행능력, 뇌 그리고 수면에까지 피해를 가져온다. ① 대부분의 전문가들은 2주 안에 헬스장으로 돌아오지 않는다면 당신은 곤경에 처하게 될 것이라고 동의한다. "운동을 하지 않고 2주가 되면 건강 수준의 감소를 자연스레 보여주는 신체적인 지표들이 많아진다"라고 뉴욕을 근거지로 둔 생리학자이자 유명한 운동선수들의 트레이너인 Scott Weiss는 말한다. ② 결국, 인간 몸의 그 능력에도 불구하고, 아주 건강한 몸도 매우 예민한 체계를 가지며, 당신의 운동량이 줄어들면 근력이나 유산소 능력과 같은 신체적인 변화들이 사라지게 될 것이라고 그는 강조한다. 운동에 대한 욕구가 존재하지 않기 때문에, 당신의 몸은 원래 상태로 돌아가게 된다. ③ (더 많은 단백질이 당신의 몸 안에서 빠른 속도로 더 많은 근육을 만들기 위해 요구된다.) ④ 물론 당신의 몸이 얼마나 많이 그리고 빠르게 나빠지는지는 당신이 얼마나 건강한지, 당신의 나이가 어떤지 그리고 얼마나 땀 흘리며 운동해 왔는지 등의 다양한 요인들에 따라 달라진다. "두 달에서 여덟 달 운동을 하지 않는 것은 이전에 한 번도 운동을 안 해본 것처럼 당신의 운동능력을 떨어뜨릴 것입니다."라고 Weiss는 말한다.

TIP

이 글의 주제는 운동을 하다가 2주 동안 운동을 하지 않을 경우 나타나는 신체적인 변화이므로 ③번 '단백질과 근력의 관계'는 이 글의 전체 흐름상 어색하다.

10 ④

단 어

pact : 약속, 협정
ascribe : (성질, 특징을) ~에 속하는 것으로 생각하다(to), ~의 탓으로 돌리다
adversaries : 적
heretic : 이단자들, 이교도들
dissident : 반체제 인사
striking : 두드러진, 현저한, 빼어난
supernatural : 초자연적인
peasant : 소작농
confession : 고백
witchcraft : 마술
border : 가장자리를 이루다
heresy : 이단, 이교
masculine : 남자 같은
preserve : 전유물

해 석

15세기 이전에는, 마녀의 모든 4가지 특징들(밤에 나는 것, 비밀 모임, 해로운 마술, 그리고 악마의 계약)이 교회에 의해서 개별

적으로 혹은 일부 혼합되어, 그들의 적들 - 템플 기사단, 이교도들, 숙련된 마술사, 그리고 다른 반체제적 단체들을 포함해서 - 의 속성으로 여겨져 왔다. 초자연적인 힘에 대한 민간 신앙은 마녀 재판을 하는 동안 소작농들의 고백에서부터 생겨나게 되었다. 마법에 대한 대중적인 개념과 학술적인 개념의 가장 큰 차이는 마녀가 악마에게서 유래하지 않고 초자연적인 힘을 타고났다고 믿는 민간 신앙에 있다. 학식이 있는 사람들에게, 이것은 이단과 접해 있었다. 초자연적 힘은 절대 사람에게 있지 않을뿐더러, 마녀들 또한 학구적 마법의 전통으로부터 그들의 마술을 얻을 수 없었는데, 그러한 학구적 마법은 그 당시 남자들의 전유물이었던 대학에서의 학문적인 교육을 요구하는 것이었다. 마녀의 힘은 필연적으로 그녀가 악마와 맺은 계약에서 나온 것일 수밖에 없었다.

① 민간인들과 학자들은 마녀의 초자연적인 힘의 근원에 관해 다른 견해를 가지고 있었다.
② 민간인의 신앙에 따르면 초자연적인 힘은 마녀의 중요한 특징에 속한다.
③ 마녀의 4가지 특징은 교회에 의해서 반체제적 단체의 특징으로 여겨졌다.
④ 학식이 있는 사람들은 마녀의 힘이 대학의 학문적인 훈련에서 왔다고 믿었다.

✓ **TIP**

이 글 중 nor could witches derive their craft from the tradition of learned magic, which required a scholarly training at the university에서 보면 ④번의 마녀의 힘이 대학의 학문적인 훈련에서 왔다고 믿는 것은 이 글과 일치하지 않는다.

11 ③

단 어

inevitable : 피할 수 없는
companion : 동반자, 동행
dread : 두려워하다
lest ~ should : ~하지 않도록, ~할까 봐
supper : 저녁
snore : 코를 골다
seal : 봉하다

✓ **해 석**

여러 가지 일들이 내가 도착하기를 기다리고 있었다. 나는 소녀들이 공부하는 동안 함께 앉아있어야 했다. ① 그러고 나서 기도문을 읽고 학생들이 잠자리에 드는 것을 보는 건 내 차례였다. 그 후 나는 다른 선생님들과 식사를 했다. ② 우리가 마침내 잠자리에 들어갔을 때도, 나의 동료 Miss Gryce는 피할 수 없었다. 촛대의 초가 얼마 안 남았고 나는 그녀가 초가 다 타버리고 없어질 때까지 이야기를 할까 봐 두려워했다. ③ 하지만,

운 좋게도 그녀가 먹었던 엄청난 저녁식사 때문에 그녀는 피곤해졌고 곧 잘 준비를 마쳤다. 그녀는 내가 옷을 벗기도 전에 코를 골고 있었다. 여전히 1인치의 초가 남아 있었다. ④ 이제 나는 편지를 꺼냈다. 봉인된 곳에 이니셜 F가 있었다. 나는 그것을 떼었다. 그 내용은 간결했다.

12 ②

단 어

obscurity : 모호함
indispensability : 필수적인 것, 불가결한 일
disapproval : 반감, 반대

✓ **해 석**

두려움 그리고 그것과 함께 오는 고통은 적절히 이용되기만 하면 인간과 동물이 가진 가장 유용한 것들이다. 만약 불이 날 때 그 불이 다치지 않게 한다면, 아이들은 그들의 손이 데일 때까지 불을 가지고 놀 것이다. 유사하게, 고통은 있지만, 두려움이 없다면 아이는 계속해서 데이게 되는데, 이는 두려움이 그에게 이전에 그가 데였던 불을 조심하라고 경고하지 않을 것이기 때문이다. 정말 두려움이 없는 군인은 - 몇몇은 실제로 존재한다 - 좋은 군인이 아닌데, 이는 그가 곧 죽임을 당할 수 있기 때문이며, 죽은 군인은 군대에는 쓸모가 없다. 그러므로 두려움과 고통은 그것들이 없다면 인간 존재와 동물들은 곧 죽어 없어질지도 모르는, 두 보호자들이다.

① 군인에게 있어서 두려움과 고통의 모호함
② 두려움과 고통의 필수불가결성
③ 두려움과 고통에 대한 못마땅함
④ 두려움, 고통과 아이들과의 연관성

13 ④

단 어

grab : 붙잡다

✓ **TIP**

① make it a rule to 부정사 : ~하는 것을 습관으로 하다.
② grab 목적어 by the 신체부분 : (신체부분)을 잡다
③ owing to 명사 : ~때문에
④ 'prefer 동명사 to 동명사' 혹은 'prefer to 부정사 (rather) than to 부정사' 중 하나로 택해야 한다. 병렬구조에 맞춰준다.
  → I prefer staying home to going out on a snowy day.
  → I prefer to stay home than to go out on a snowy day.

14 ③

단어

tend : (환자, 어린이들을) 돌보다, 간호하다
wounded : 부상은 입은

TIP

① not A but B : A가 아니라 B다
② cannot ~ too : 아무리 ~해도 지나치지 않다
③ tend의 목적어로 명사(환자들, 부상자들)가 와야 한다.
  '형용사/분사' 앞에 정관사 the를 써서 '~하는 사람들'을 뜻하는 복수 명사를 만들 수 있다. the sick(=sick people), the wounded(=wounded people, the persons (who are) wounded)로 표현한다.
  →More doctors were required to tend the sick and the wounded.
④ to make matters worse 설상가상으로

15 ①

단어

condiment : 조미료

해석

메인 요리가 맛이 별로 없었지만, 나는 조미료를 첨가하여 요리를 좀 더 맛있게 만들었다.

① 맛있는   ② 분해할 수 있는
③ 마셔도 되는   ④ 민감한

16 ③

단어

undertake : 착수하다
layout : 구획, 배치
mastery : 숙달, 통달

해석

런던의 택시 운전자들은 운행 자격을 얻기 위해 몇 년에 걸쳐 "the knowledge"라고 알려진 강도 높은 훈련을 받아야 하는데, 이는 런던의 25,000개가 넘는 거리의 구획을 익히는 것을 포함한다. 한 연구가와 그녀의 연구팀은 택시기사들과 일반인들을 조사했다. 두 그룹은 아일랜드 한 마을의 익숙하지 않은 도로가 나오는 비디오를 보도록 요청 받았다. 그리고 나서 그들은 길을 스케치하는 것, 주요 건물들을 알아보는 것, 장소들 사이의 거리를 측정하는 것 등에 관한 테스트를 받았다. 두 그룹 모두 잘 해 주었지만, 새로운 길을 알아보는 것에 있어서는 택시 운전자들이 상당히 우수했다. 이 결과는 택시 운전사들의 통달이 새롭

고 모르는 지역에도 일반화될 수 있음을 보여준다. 세심한 연습을 통한 수년간의 훈련과 연습으로 그들은 잘 알지 못하거나 전혀 모르는 지역에서도 비슷한 문제를 수행하도록 준비를 갖추게 된다.

① 제한된   ② 전념한   ③ 일반화된   ④ 기여한

17 ④

단어

plain : 평원
trout : 송어

해석

나는 Lewis가 폭포를 발견했던 그 날을 기억한다. 그들은 해가 돌 때 야영장을 떠났고, 몇 시간 후 그들은 아름다운 평원을 만났고 그곳에서 이제껏 봤던 버팔로보다 더 많은 버팔로를 한 장소에서 보았다.
(C) 그들은 멀리서 폭포수가 떨어지는 소리가 들릴 때까지 계속 걸었고 멀리서 솟았다 사라지는 물줄기를 보았다. 그들은 그 소리를 따라갔고 소리는 점점 더 커졌다.
(B) 잠시 후 그 소리는 엄청났고 그들은 미시시피 강의 거대한 폭포에 있었다. 그들이 그곳에 갔을 때는 정오쯤이었다.
(A) 그날 오후 좋은 일이 일어났는데, 그들은 폭포 아래에서 낚시를 했고 6마리의 송어를 잡았고 그 크기가 16에서 23인치 길이의 훌륭한 물고기들이었다.

18 ④

단어

novelty : 새로움, 참신함
induce : 유도하다, 유발하다
phenomenon : 현상
estimate : 추정하다, 추산하다
repetitive : 반복적인
unremarkable : 평범한
moderately : 중간 정도로, 적당히
sufficient : 충분한
subjective : 주관적인
presumably : 짐작컨대
allocate : 할당하다
by-product : 부산물
give rise to : ~이 생기다

해석

새로움이 야기한 시간 확장은 실험실 조건에서 조사할 수 있는 잘 특징지어진 현상이다. 단순히 사람들에게 일련의 자극에 노출된 시간의 길이를 추정하도록 물어보는 것만으로 새로운 자극이 반복적이고 평범한 자극보다 더 오래 지속된다는 것을 알 수

있다. 사실, 적당히 반복되는 일련의 자극 중 첫 번째 자극이 되는 것은 주관적 시간 확장을 유도하기에 충분한 것처럼 보인다. 물론, 우리의 뇌가 이와 같이 작동하도록 발달한 이유를 생각하는 것은 쉽다. 짐작컨대 새롭고 색다른 자극은 익숙한 자극에 비해 더 많은 생각과 고려를 필요로 할 것이고, 그래서 뇌가 더 많은 주관적인 시간을 할당한다는 게 말이 된다.

① 자극에 반응하는 것은 뇌 훈련의 중요한 부산물이다.
② 자극이 반복될수록 그 강도는 커진다.
③ 자극에 대한 우리의 신체 반응은 우리의 생각에 영향을 끼친다.
④ 새로운 자극은 주관적인 시간 확장을 이끈다.

19 ③

단 어

highlight : 강조하다
nasty : 끔찍한, 형편없는
confirmation bias : 확증 편향

해 석

우리 마음이 하는 트릭 중 한 가지는 우리가 이미 믿고 있는 것을 확증하는 정보를 강조하는 것이다. 만약 우리가 라이벌에 관한 소문을 들었다면, "나는 그가 형편없는 줄 이미 알고 있었어."라고 생각하는 경향이 있고, 그 소문이 친한 친구에 관한 것이라면 우리는 "그건 소문일 뿐이야."라고 말하는 편이다. 당신이 확증 편향이라 불리는 이 정신적인 습관에 관해 알게 된다면 그것을 모든 곳에서 보기 시작한다. 이것은 우리가 더 나은 결정을 하기 원할 때 문제가 된다. 확증 편향은 우리가 옳을 때는 괜찮겠지만, 그러나 우리는 너무 자주 틀리며 너무 늦은 경우에는 단지 결정적인 증거에만 주목한다. 어떻게 우리가 우리의 결정을 확증 편향으로부터 보호할 수 있는지는 심리학적으로 확증 편향이 왜 발생하는지에 대한 우리의 인식에 달려있다. 여기에 두 가지 그럴듯한 이유가 있다. 하나는 우리의 상상력에 사각지대가 있기 때문이고 다른 하나는 우리가 새로운 정보에 대해 의문을 제기하지 못하기 때문이다.

① 우리의 라이벌이 우리를 믿게 만드는지
② 우리의 사각지대는 우리가 더 나은 결정을 하도록 도와주는지
③ 우리가 우리의 결정을 확증 편향으로부터 보호할 수 있는지
④ 우리가 정확히 똑같은 편견을 발달시키는지

20 ②

단 어

preservative : 방부제
let alone : ~커녕
unwillingness : 본의 아님, 자발적이 아님
inability : 무능

해 석

소비재 브랜드에 있어서 많은 큰 회사에게 해외의 노동력과 그 지역 입맛에 맞추어 물건을 생산하고 수출하는 것은 옳은 일이다. 그렇게 함으로써, 그 회사들은 그들의 가격 구조를 향상시킬 수 있는 방법과 신흥공화국에서 소비자 시장을 빠르게 성장시킬 수 있는 방법을 찾았다. 그러나 Sweet Co.는 여전히 국내 시장에 머물러 있다. 그 생산품이 방부제와 함께 적재되는데도 – 이것은 멀리 있는 시장까지 가는 장거리 여행을 견딜 수 있는 걸 뜻한다 – Sweets Co.는 해외생산은커녕 <u>거의 수출을 하지 않는다</u>. 변화하는 세상에서 사업 전략과 생산품을 향상시키려는 것에 게으르고 무능력한 것은 분명히 그 회사에 손해를 끼치고 있다.

① 수입에 몰두하기
② 수출을 거의 하지 않는 것
③ 기업들을 간소화하기로 결정하다
④ 신흥국가로 확장을 하는 것

TIP

밑줄 친 부분의 앞부분에 Sweet Co. remains stuck in domestic market의 내용을 보면 Sweet 회사는 국내 시장에만 몰두하고 있다는 내용이므로 빈칸에는 수출을 거의 하지 않는다는 내용인 ②번이 적절하다.

2017. 6. 24.
제2회 서울특별시 시행

---

1 ①

단 어

inextricably : 불가분하게
look to : ~에 기대를 걸다

해 석

지도력과 힘은 <u>뗄래야 뗄 수 없이</u> 서로 연관되어 있다. 우리는 지도자로서 강인한 사람들을 찾는데 이는 강인한 사람들이 우리 그룹에게 닥치는 위협으로부터 우리를 보호해 줄 수 있기 때문이다.

① 분리할 수 없게　　　② 생명이 없이
③ 헛되게, 무능하게　　④ 인정머리 없게, 경솔하게

2 ②

단어

prudence : 신중, 조심
dictate : 지시하다
transient : 일시적인, 순간적인

해석

사실상, 신중함은 오래전에 설립된 정부가 사소하고 <u>일시적인</u> 원인으로 변경될 수 없다는 것을 암시할 것이다.

① 투명한, 명백한　　　② 순간적인, 잠깐의
③ 기억할 만한　　　　④ 중요한

3 ④

단어

allocate : 할당하다
access : 입장, 입학
have something to do with : ~와 관련이 있다
pursue : 추구하다
unjust : 불공정한

해석

대학 입학에서 할당제도의 정의가 대학들이 올바르게 추구하는 선과 관련이 있다는 생각은 입학 허가를 파는 것이 왜 불공정한 지를 설명해 준다.

TIP

이 문장의 주어는 the idea로 단수이므로 3인칭 단수 주어에 맞춰 explains가 되어야 한다. 문장에서 explains 앞부분은 주어인 the idea를 수식하고 있다.

4 ③

단어

expanse : 넓게 트인 지역
grassland : 풀밭, 초원
associated with : ~와 관련된

해석

이상하게 보일지 모르지만, 사하라 사막은 한때 아프리카 평원과 관련된 동물들의 생태를 지지하는 광활한 초원이었다.

TIP

두 번째 줄에서 광활한 초원이 동물들의 삶을 지지하는 능동의 의미이므로 ③번의 supported는 supporting이 되어야 한다.

5 ③

단어

loan : 대출
stocks : 주식
bonds : 채권
guarantor : 보증인

해석

A : 제가 대출을 받을 수 있을까요?
B : 글쎄, 상황에 따라 다릅니다. 자산 소유하고 있는 거 있으신 가요? 주식이나 채권 같은 거 있나요?
A : 없습니다.
B : 그렇군요. 그럼 담보물이 없는 거네요. 아마도 당신의 대출 을 위해 서명해 줄 사람인 보증인이 있어야 할 것 같습니다.

① 수사, 조사　　② 짐승　　③ 담보물　　④ 영감

6 ②

단어

immigrant : 이민자
Revolutionary War : 독립 전쟁
colony : 식민지
passage : 구절
posterity : 후세, 후대
melting pot : 용광로, 도가니

해석

1782년 독립전쟁 동안 유럽으로 돌아가기 전에 뉴욕에 정착했던 프랑스 이민자 헥터 세인트 존 드 크레브쾨르는 북미에서 영국의 식민지 삶에 관한 수필집「미국 농민의 편지」를 출판했다. 이 책은 영국, 프랑스, 미국에서 즉각적인 성공을 거두었다. 그 책에서 가장 유명한 구절 중 하나에서 크레브쾨르는 다른 배경을 가지고 다른 나라에서 온 사람들이 식민지에서의 그들의 경험에 의해 변화되는 과정을 기술했고 "그렇다면 미국인이란 무엇인가?"라는 질문을 했다. "미국에서 모든 나라의 각 개인들이 새로운 인종으로 녹아들고, 이 새로운 인종의 노동과 그 후세들이 언젠가는 세계에서 거대한 변화를 가져올 것이다"라고 크레브쾨르는 말한다. 크레브쾨르는 나중에 "용광로(멜팅팟)"라고 불리게 될 미국의 유명한 개념의 최초 창시자였다.

① 크레브쾨르의 책은 영국에서 즉각적인 성공을 거두었다.
② 크레브쾨르는 그의 책에서 용광로의 개념을 만들어 냈다.
③ 크레브쾨르는 미국의 개인주의에 관해 기술했고 논했다.
④ 크레브쾨르는 그의 책에서 미국인들이 어디에서 왔는지 를 설명했다.

7 ②

단어 •

light on : 우연히 보다
unfavorable : 나쁜, 호의적이지 않은
serviceable : 쓸 만한
courteous : 공손한
obliging : 친절한
meddler : 간섭하려는 사람
belong to : ~에 속하다

해석

우리는 한때는 좋은 의미로 사용되었지만, 지금은 나쁜 의미로 사용되는 단어들을 계속해서 보게 된다. 18세기 후반까지 이 단어는 '쓸 만한, 친근한, 매우 공손하고 친절한'의 의미로 사용되었다. 그러나 요즘에는 '거들먹거리는' 사람이란 '그/그녀와 관련되지 않은 사건에 주제넘게 나서서 간섭하기 바쁜 사람'을 의미한다.

① 굽실거리는   ② 거들먹거리는
③ 사교적인   ④ 아부하는

8 ②

단어 •

faint : 희미한
odor : 냄새
vinegar : 식초
grimace : 얼굴을 찡그리다

해석

암모니아 또는 식초의 희미한 냄새는 1주 된 신생아들의 얼굴을 찡그리게 하고 머리를 피하게 만든다.

① (말등의) 마구를 채우다   ② 피하다
③ 감싸다   ④ 떠올려보다

9 ④

단어 •

trade : 무역
commerce : 상업

해석

서구 유럽의 최초 커피하우스는 무역과 상업의 중심지가 아닌 옥스퍼드 대학가에 있었다. 이는 1650년 Jacob이라는 이름의 레바논 사람이 세운 상점이었다.

TIP

'~라고 이름 지어진'의 의미는 수동의 의미이므로 ④번 naming은 named로 바뀌어야 한다.

10 ③

단어 •

remind : 상기시키다

해석

① John은 Mary에게 그의 방을 청소할 거라고 약속했다.
② John은 Mary에게 그가 일찍 떠날 것이라고 이야기했다.
③ John은 Mary가 행복할 것이라고 믿었다.
④ John은 Mary에게 그 장소에 일찍 가야 한다는 걸 상기시켰다.

TIP

③ John believed Mary that she would be happy. → John believed that Mary would be happy.
believe는 4형식 동사로 쓸 수 없다.
① promise ② tell ④ remind 모두 4형식 동사로도 쓰이며, that절을 직접목적어로 취할 수 있다.

11 ④

단어 •

commitment : 약속

해석

A : Mr. Kim, 오늘 제가 당신에게 점심을 대접해도 될까요?
B : 그럴 수 있으면 좋겠지만, 오늘은 다른 약속이 있습니다.

① 아니요, 그것은 저에게 좋은 시간이 될 것입니다.
② 좋습니다. 제가 잊지 않도록 달력에 적어두겠습니다.
③ 좋아요. 월요일에 함께 체크해 봅시다.
④ 그럴 수 있으면 좋겠지만, 오늘은 다른 약속이 있습니다.

12 ①

단어 •

gaze : 응시하다
vibrant : 활기찬, 선명한
sparkling : 불꽃
Big Dipper : 북두칠성
culprit : 범인, 장본인
obscure : 보기 어렵게 하다
astrotourism : 천문관광
stargaze : 별을 관찰하다

해석

수 세기 동안 해가 진 뒤 하늘을 응시하는 사람들은 선명하게 반짝이는 수천 개의 별들을 볼 수 있었다. 그러나 요즘은, 만일 당신이 북두칠성을 볼 수 있다면 운이 좋은 것이다. 이 주범은

바로 가정과 가로등에서 쏟아져 나오는 전자 빛들인데, 그 밝기가 밤하늘을 보기 어렵게 한다. 미국에서 소위 빛공해라 불리는 것이 매우 심해져서 한 추산에 따르면 오늘날 태어난 아이들 10명 중 8명은 은하수를 볼 수 있을 만큼 충분히 <u>어두운</u> 하늘을 마주하지 못할 것이다. 그렇지만 희망이 존재하는데, 그건 바로 세계의 가장 어두운 곳에서 별을 관찰하는 것에 중점을 둔, 작지만 성장하고 있는 천문관광 산업이다. 대부분 국립공원 안에 있는 이런 외딴 장소들은 야영지 비용에 지나지 않은 비용으로 별 관측을 제공한다. 그리고 그 산업을 운영하는 사람들은 주변 지역의 빛공해를 줄이기 위해 애를 쓴다. 비록 별 관광이 일부 관광처럼 호화롭지 <u>않을지 모르지만,</u> 여행자들은 신경 쓰지 않는다.

✓ **TIP**

첫 번째 빈칸은 은하수를 보려면 하늘이 충분히 어두워야 하므로 dark가 되어야 하고 두 번째 빈칸은 별 관광을 즐기는 사람들은 시설이 호화롭지 않더라도 개의치 않는다는 내용이 되어야 하므로 접속사 Although가 적절하다. ④의 in that은 '~라는 점에서'라는 뜻을 가진다.

13 ④

단 어

watery : 희미한, 물기가 많은
stinging : 찌르는, 쏘는
pounding : 쿵쿵 두드리는 소리
sinus : 부비강(두개골 속의, 코 안쪽으로 이어지는 구멍)
refuge : 피난, 도피처
scour : 샅샅이 뒤지다
debilitate : 쇠약하게 하다
outrage : 격분, 격노
scrutiny : 정밀 조사, 철저한 검토
impel : ~해야만 하게 하다
inactive : 활발하지 않은
visibility : 가시성

✓ **해 설**

ⓔ 2013년도에 위험하게 높은 공해도 때문에 발생한 베이징의 비상사태가 교통체계에 혼돈을 일으켰고, 낮은 가시도로 인하여 항공사들이 비행을 취소하게 되었다.

ⓒ 학교와 기업들이 문을 닫았고, 베이징 시 정부는 사람들에게 집안에 머물면서, 공기정화기를 작동시키고 실내 활동을 줄이고 가능한 한 움직이지 말라고 경고했다.

ⓖ 눈물이 나고, 눈이 따끔거리고, 쿵쿵거리는 두통을 겪고, 부비강에 문제가 생기고, 목이 간질거리는 고통을 겪는 수백만 명의 사람들은 공기정화기와 마스크를 찾아 상점들을 샅샅이 뒤져 심신을 쇠약하게 만드는 공기로부터 피신했다.

ⓛ 중국 거주민들의 분노와 세계 미디어의 정밀 조사가 중국 정부로 하여금 국가의 공기오염 문제를 다룰 수밖에 없게 만들었다.

✓ **TIP**

ⓔ은 2013년도를 언급하며 공기오염에 관한 글의 도입부를 이끌고 있다. ⓒ에서 공기오염으로 인한 결과를 설명하고 있고 ⓖ에서는 이 공기오염에 대한 개인들의 대처방법들이 나오고 있다. 마지막으로 ⓛ에서는 국가차원의 해결이 필요하다는 것으로 결론을 짓고 있다.

14 ①

단 어

fiction : 허구
prose : 산문
narrative : 서술
exotic : 이국적인

✓ **해 설**

소설과 로맨스는 둘 다 다양한 등장인물들을 가진 상상의 허구 작품이지만, 거기서 그들의 유사성은 끝난다. 소설은 현실적이지만, 로맨스는 그렇지 않다. 19세기에 로맨스는 상징적이고, 상상적인 그리고 비현실적인 방식으로 주제와 등장인물들을 다루는 허구의 이야기를 말하는 산문이었다. <u>전형적으로</u> 로맨스는 시간과 장소에서 독자들로부터 이국적이고 먼, 명백히 상상적인 이야기들과 사람들을 다룬다.

① 일반적으로　　　　　② 반면에
③ 그럼에도 불구하고　④ 경우에 따라서는

15 ③

단 어

oft-cited : 자주 인용되는
discouraging : 낙담시키는
erode : 침식시키다, 약화되다

✓ **해 설**

정의는 특별히 아이들에게 <u>도움이 되지 않는다</u>. 자주 인용되는 1987년 연구가 있는데, 그 연구에서 5학년 학생들은 사전적 정의를 듣고, 정의된 단어를 사용하여 자신의 문장을 만들어 보라고 요청받았다. 그 결과는 낙담스러웠다. erode라는 단어를 받은 한 아이는 "우리 가족은 많이 침식한다"라고 썼는데, 이는 주어진 정의가 "eat out(외식하다), eat away(먹어 치우다, 침식하다)'였기 때문이다.

① 이득이 되는　　　② 무례한
③ 도움이 되지 않는　④ 쉽게 잊혀질

✓ **TIP**

discouraging의 단어에서 힌트를 얻을 수 있으므로 적절한 단어는 ③번 unhelpful이 된다.

16 ①

단 어

safeguard : 보호하다
turn to : 의지하다
goldsmith : 금세공인
vault : 금고
redeem : 되찾다
due : 지불 기일이 된
payee : 수취인
depositor : 예금자

해 설

현대의 은행은 고대 영국에서 그 기원을 갖는다. 그 시절에 그들의 금을 보호하기를 원했던 사람들은 두 가지 선택이 있었다. 그것을 매트리스 밑에 숨기거나 안전한 보관을 위해 그것을 누군가에게 맡기는 것이었다. 보관을 위해 의지할 수 있는 합당한 사람들은 바로 그 지역의 금세공인이었다. 왜냐하면 금세공인들은 가장 강력한 금고를 가지고 있었기 때문이었다. 금세공인들은 보관을 위한 금을 받아들였고, 그 소유주에게 후일에 금을 되찾을 수 있다고 쓰인 영수증을 주었다. 지불 만기가 되었을 때 소유주는 금세공인에게 가서 금의 일부를 되찾고, 그것을 수취인에게 주었다. 결국 그 수취인은 안전한 보관을 위해 금세공인에게 금을 다시 줄 가능성이 매우 높았다. 점차적으로, 물리적인 금 교환에 시간과 노력을 들이는 대신 사업가들은 <u>금세공인의 영수증을 지불수단으로 교환하기 시작했다.</u>

① 금세공인의 영수증을 지불수단으로 교환하기 시작했다.
② 이런 방식에서 소득을 내는 잠재성을 보았다.
③ 예금자에게 그들의 금을 되찾지 말라고 경고했다.
④ 수수료를 받고 다른 누군가에게 금을 빌려주었다.

17 ②

단 어

norm : 규범
hospitality : 친절, 환대
thoughtlessness : 생각이 모자람, 인정 없음

해 설

한국과 이집트 같은 일부 문화에서는 누군가에게서 먹을 것이나 마실 것을 제공받았을 때 공손함의 규범으로 거절을 해야 한다. 그러나 그러한 거절이 다른 문화에서는 누군가의 친절에 대한 거절로, 그리고 인정이 없는 걸로 종종 여겨진다. 특히나 그 거절에 대해 어떠한 변명도 없을 때는 더 그렇다. 예를 들어 미국인들과 캐나다인들은 합리적인 변명이 수반되는 거절을 기대한다.

① 역할   ② 변명   ③ 선택   ④ 상황

18 ④

단 어

sincerity : 진심어림
extension : 연장, 확대
colleague : 동료
supportive : 지지하는
comprise : ~로 구성되다
notable : 주목할 만한
reward schema : 보상금제도
senior position : 상급직

해 설

① 직업만족도와 생산성 사이에는 분명한 연관이 있다. 그러나 직업만족도는 조직의 서비스 문화에도 달려있다. ② 이러한 문화는 사업체를 독특하게 만들어 주며 그곳 근무자들이 그곳에서 일하는 것에 자부심을 가지도록 하는 것들로 이루어져 있다. ③ Fortune지가 "일하기 좋은 10대 회사"의 직원들에게 왜 그들이 이러한 회사를 위하여 일하는 것이 좋은지 물어보았을 때, 그들이 월급, 보상제도, 상급직으로의 승진 등을 언급하지 않은 것은 주목할 만하다. ④ <u>대신, 그들은 직장에서 관계의 진실성을 가장 먼저 말했다. 즉, 그들의 직장 문화가 가정의 연장선같이 느껴지며, 그들의 동료들이 힘이 된다는 것이다.</u>

TIP

Instead는 대조를 나타낼 때 쓰이며 이 글에서 ③번에서 직장이 좋은 이유로 월급, 보상제도, 승진 등으로 대답을 하지 않고 대조적으로 ④번의 관계의 진실성을 답하고 있다는 것이 흐름상 적절하므로 주어진 문장은 ④번에 들어가야 한다.

19 ④

단 어

scatter : 분산
powerhouse : 동력실
maritime : 해양의
rebellion : 반란
annihilation : 전멸, 소멸
prosperity : 번영, 번창

해 설

모든 장소 중에 왜 Orkney일까? 스코틀랜드 북쪽 끝에 위치한 이 분산된 섬들이 어떻게 그러한 기술적, 문화적, 정신적 동력실이 되었을까? 우선, 당신은 Orkney가 멀리 떨어져 있다고 생각하지 말아야 한다. 역사의 대부분의 시간 동안, Orkney는 중요한 해양 중심지로서 모든 곳으로 갈 수 있는 장소였다. 그곳은 또한 영국의 비옥한 농토와 멕시코 만류의 영향 때문에 온화한 기후를 가진 축복받은 곳이었다.

① Orkney 사람들은 많은 사회적, 자연적 불리함을 극복해
  야만 했다.
② 그 지역은 궁극적으로 그곳의 시민화의 소멸을 이끈 반
  란의 중심지 중 한 곳이었다.
③ Orkney는 본토에서 멀리 떨어져 있었기 때문에 그 자원
  을 최대한 활용하지 못했다.
④ Orkney는 그 지리학적인 이점과 자연 자원 덕분에 번영
  했다.

20 ①

단 어 ·

parchment : 양피지
scroll : 두루마리
unroll : 펼치다
vertically : 수직으로
horizontally : 수평으로
scribe : 필경사, 필기자
refrain from : ~을 삼가다
mark off : (선을 그어) 표시하다
column : 열, 세로단
struggle : 몸부림치다, 애쓰다

해 석

처음에 파피루스와 양피지는 원고의 방향에 따라 수직으로 또는
수평으로 펼쳐지는 두루마리로 보관되었다. 수평의 형태가 더
흔했는데, 이는 두루마리가 길어질 수 있어서 필경사가 전체 길
이를 가로질러 한 줄로 쓰는 것을 삼가고, 그 대신 적절한 너비
의 열을 표시했기 때문이다. 이러한 방식으로 독자는 읽는 동안
한 면은 펼치고 다른 면은 말 수 있었다. 그럼에도 불구하고 지
속적으로 두루마리를 말아야 하는 것이 이 형태의 가장 큰 단점
이었는데, 우리가 책의 특정한 페이지로 건너뛰는 방식으로 두루
마리에서는 다양한 위치로 이동하는 것이 불가능했다. 더욱이 두
루마리를 펼치고 있기 위해서는 양손이(또는 추들이) 필요했기
때문에 읽는 동안 메모하기 위해서는 상당히 애를 써야 했다.

① 두루마리의 불편함
② 책의 진화
③ 쓰기와 읽기의 발달
④ 두루마리의 단점을 극복하기 위한 방법들

1 ①

단 어 ·

subsidy : 보조금
demand : 수요
vastly : 대단히

해 석

두 차례의 세계 대전 동안 정부 보조금과 새로운 항공기에 대한
수요가 그 설계와 구조의 기술을 대단히 발전시켰다.

① 재정 지원   ② 장기 계획
③ 기술 지원   ④ 비제한적인 정책

2 ③

단 어 ·

premiere : 개봉, 초연, 개봉하다
strike a balance (between A and B) : (A와 B 사이에서) 균형
을 유지하다
convoluted : 대단히 난해한
character-driven : 인물 중심
dimension : 차원, 관점, 크기, 치수

해 석

화요일 밤 TV 쇼 시즌 첫 방송은 복잡한 신화와 좀 더 인간적
인 인물 중심의 관점 사이에서 쇼의 균형을 유지하려고 노력한
것으로 보인다.

① 고대의   ② 관련 없는   ③ 복잡한   ④ 내세의

3 ③

단 어 ·

wind up : 마무리 짓다

해 석

우리가 대화를 마무리 지을 때쯤에는, 나는 내가 제네바로 가지
않을 것이란 것을 알았다.

① 착수시키다   ② 재개하다
③ 끝내다   ④ 방해하다

4 ④

단어 .

sergeant : 병장, 경사
dismay : 경악하게 만들다, 크게 실망시키다
promotion : 승진, 진급

해 석

15년 경력의 한 경찰 경사가 젊은 경관을 선호하는 진급시험에서 제외되어 크게 실망하였다.

① (차로) 치고 가다　　② 데이트를 신청하다
③ 수행하다　　　　　　④ 무시하다, 제외시키다

5 ①

단어 .

sneeze : 재채기하다
cough : 기침하다

해 석

지난주에 나는 독감에 걸렸었다. 아버지는 내가 재채기하고 기침하는 것을 들었을 때, 내 침실 문을 열고 뭔가 필요한 것이 있는지 물어 보았다. 그의 친절하고 상냥한 얼굴을 보고 정말 기뻤지만, 그가 독감을 없애기 위해 할 수 있는 일은 아무것도 없었다.

② that I needed anything → if I needed anything
　'내가 무엇이 필요한지 아닌지'를 물었다는 의미이므로 that이 아니라 if가 와야 한다.
③ anything he could do it → anything he could do
　선행사 anything 뒤에 목적격 관계대명사 that이 생략된 형태이다. 선행사 anything이 do의 목적어 역할을 하여 '그가 할 수 있는 어떤 것'을 의미하는데 뒤에 목적어 it이 중복하여 나왔으므로 it을 빼 준다.
④ to go away → go away
　make는 사역동사로 목적어인 the flue와 목적격 보어인 to go away의 관계는 능동이다. 이때 사역동사의 목적격 보어로는 원형부정사만이 가능하다.

6 ①

단어 .

increasingly : 점점 더, 갈수록 더

해 석

① 모든 사무실 직원들에게 일주일간의 휴가가 약속되었다.
② 그녀는 다른 사람들을 섬기는 삶을 살 운명이다.

③ 아이들을 키우기에 큰 도시보다는 작은 도시가 더 좋아 보인다.
④ 최고의 소프트웨어 회사들은 선두를 유지하는 것이 점점 더 어려워지고 있다는 것을 알고 있다.

TIP

② destine은 '운명으로 정해지다'란 의미의 타동사로 '~할 운명이다'로 표현하려면 수동형인 'be destined to'의 형태로 써야 한다.
③ preferable than → preferable to : ~보다 더 좋은
④ finding increasingly challenging → finding it increasingly challenging
　동사 are finding의 목적어로 보이는 명사가 없다. challenging 뒤에 있는 to stay ahead를 목적어로 보기 위해서는 원래 목적어 자리에 가목적어 it이 있어야 한다. increasingly challenging은 목적보어가 된다.

7 ③

단어 .

drawback : 결점, 문제점

해 석

A : 새 동네는 어때?
B : 대부분 훌륭해. 깨끗한 공기와 녹지 환경이 좋아.
A : 살기 좋은 곳으로 들리네.
B : 응, 그렇지만 단점이 없지는 않아.
A : 어떤?
B : 하나는, 많은 다양한 상점들이 없어. 예를 들어, 슈퍼마켓이 하나뿐이야. 그래서 식료품이 매우 비싸.
A : 문제가 좀 있어 보이네.
B : 내 말이 그 말이야. 하지만, 다행이야. 시에서 지금 새 쇼핑센터를 짓고 있거든. 내년이면 선택지가 더 많아질 거야.

① 거기 슈퍼마켓이 몇 개나 있어?
② 거기 쇼핑할 곳이 많아?
③ 문제가 좀 있어 보이네.
④ 나 너희 동네로 이사 가고 싶어.

8 ④

단어 .

on the cutting edge of : ~의 최첨단에
unpredictable : 예측할 수 없는
astonished by : ~에 놀란

해석

최신 현대 과학의 한 이야기는 19세기 스웨덴 북부의 어느 고립된 지역에서 시작되었다. ① 스웨덴의 그 지역은 19세기 상반기에 예측하지 못한 수확을 거두었다. 수확에 실패했던 수년 동안 사람들은 굶주렸다. 하지만 수확이 잘 된 해에는 상황이 좋았다. ② 수확이 형편없는 시기에 굶주렸던 사람들은 수확이 잘 된 해에는 두드러지게 많이 먹었다. 한 스웨덴 과학자는 이러한 식습관이 장기적으로 어떤 영향을 끼칠지 궁금했다. 그는 그 지역의 수확과 건강 기록과의 관계를 연구했다. 그는 그가 알아낸 것에 놀랐다. ③ 수확이 잘 된 해에 과식을 했던 소년들은 거의 먹지 못했던 소년들의 자녀와 손주보다 약 6년 정도 빨리 사망하는 자녀와 손주를 낳았다. 다른 과학자들은 소녀들에 있어서도 동일한 결과를 발견했다. (④ 수확이 좋은 해의 소년과 소녀들은 모두 커다란 혜택을 받았다.) 과학자들은 과식이라는 단 한 가지 원인이 세대에 걸쳐 계속되는 부정적 영향을 가질 수 있다는 결론을 내리게 되었다.

9 ②

단어

wait on : 시중을 들다
shortly : 곧, 얼마 안 되어

해석

A : 그래서 Wong 선생님, 뉴욕시에는 얼마나 오래 사셨습니까?
B : 약 7년 정도 여기 살고 있습니다.
A : 직장 경험에 대해 이야기해 주시겠습니까?
B : 지난 3년 동안 pizzeria에서 일해 왔습니다.
A : 거기서 무슨 일을 하셨나요?
B : 고객들을 자리에 앉히고 식사를 도왔습니다.
A : 본인의 일에 대해 어떻게 생각하십니까?
B : 좋습니다. 모든 사람들이 정말 친절합니다.
A : 그렇다면, 왜 이 일에 지원하셨습니까?
B : 단지 좀 더 정규적인 환경에서 일하고 싶습니다.
A : 좋습니다. 덧붙일 말씀이 있으십니까?
B : 저는 사람 관계가 정말 좋습니다. 그리고 이탈리아어와 중국어도 할 수 있습니다.
A : 알겠습니다. 감사합니다. 곧 연락 드리겠습니다.
B : 곧 소식 듣길 바랍니다.

① 그래서, 거기 환경은 어떻습니까?
② 그렇다면, 왜 이 일에 지원하게 되셨습니까?
③ 그런데, 어떤 외국어를 잘하십니까?
④ 여기서 일하시려면 어떤 자질이 필요하다고 생각하십니까?

10 ④

단어

accompany : ~와 동반하다, 동행하다

TIP

① haven't → hadn't
과거에 대한 가정이므로 가정법 과거 완료로 써야 한다.
② bored → boring
bore는 감정유발동사로 영화가 지루함을 느끼게 한 것이므로 현재분사를 써야 한다.
③ accompany with → accompany
accompany는 타동사로 전치사 없이 목적어를 취한다.
④ stop + ~ing는 '~하는 것을 멈추다'의 의미이고 stop + to부정사는 '~하기 위해 멈추다'의 의미이다. 컴퓨터가 작동하는 것을 멈춘 것이므로 stopped working으로 쓰는 것이 맞다.

11 ①

단어

originally : 원래, 본래

TIP

① originally expecting → originally expected
주절의 주어인 비교대상 the budget이 than 뒤에서 생략되어 있다.
② work는 셀 수 없는 명사이므로, a lot of work에서 복수형 works를 쓰거나 복수형 동사 are로 쓰지 않도록 주의한다. 또한 work는 do의 수동 관계에 있으므로 to be done의 수식을 받아 '해야 될 일'의 뜻을 나타낸다.
③ 'it takes+시간+(for 사람)+to부정사 : ~하는 데 ~시간이 걸리다' 구문이 맞게 쓰였다.
④ 문장의 주어는 the head of ~이다. 관계사절의 receives, 주절의 has 동사 모두 단수 주어에 맞는 형태로 쓰였다. 또한, twice the salary는 '배수사+명사' 순서로 쓰여 '두 배의 월급'이라는 뜻이다.

12 ④

단어

domestic : 국내의
adoption : 입양
contraception : 피임
pervasive : 만연하는
postponement : 연기
childbearing : 출산

abortion : 낙태

stigmatize : 오명을 씌우다, 낙인을 찍다

count on : ~에 의지하다

prospective : 장래의, 유망한

resort to something : (다른 대안이 없어서, 좋지 못한 것에) 기대다

as a consequence : ~의 결과로서

선진국에서 국내 입양이 감소한 것은 단순히 국내의 입양 가능한 아이들의 공급이 줄어든 결과이다. 그러한 나라들에서는 대부분 낙태를 법적으로 허용하고 있을 뿐만 아니라 출산을 미루는 분위기가 만연한데, 여기에 안전하고 믿을 만한 피임이 널리 가능하기까지 해서 이는 결과적으로 원치 않는 출산의 급격한 감소로 이어졌고, 따라서 입양 가능한 아이들의 수도 줄어들게 되었다. (A) <u>게다가</u> 미혼모는 더 이상 과거에 그랬던 것만큼 낙인찍히지 않으며, 그들의 자녀들을 키울 수 있도록 국가의 원조에 의지할 수 있다. (B) <u>결과적으로</u> 선진국에서는 아이를 입양하기 바라는 사람들을 위한 충분한 입양아가 없게 되었고, 아이를 입양하기 바라는 양부모들은 점점 더 해외에서 아이를 입양하는 것에 의존해 왔다.

13 ③

단 어

distinguish : 구별하다

medium : 매체

definition : 정밀도

meager : 빈약한, 결핍한, 메마른

classify : 분류하다

해석

라디오와 같은 핫 미디어와 전화와 같은 쿨 미디어, 또는 영화와 같은 핫 미디어와 텔레비전과 같은 쿨 미디어를 구별하는 기본적인 원칙이 있다. 핫 미디어는 한 단일한 감각을 고도의 정밀도로 확장하는 것이다. 고도의 정밀도라는 것은 데이터로 충실히 채워져 있는 상태를 말한다. 사진은 시각적으로 "높은 정밀도"이다. 만화는 단순히 매우 적은 시각적 정보가 제공된다는 이유로 낮은 정밀도에 있다. 전화는 쿨 미디어이고 낮은 정밀도를 갖는데, 그 이유는 귀가 적은 양의 정보를 받기 때문이다. 말은 낮은 정밀도의 쿨 미디어인데, 그 이유는 너무 적은 정보가 주어지고 듣는 사람에 의해 많은 것들이 채워져야 하기 때문이다. 반면에 핫 미디어는 시청자에 의해 메워지거나 완성되도록 많은 것들을 남기지 않는다.

① 미디어는 핫 미디어와 쿨 미디어로 분류될 수 있다.
② 핫 미디어는 데이터로 충분히 채워져 있다.
③ 전화는 높은 정밀도로 여겨진다.
④ 쿨 미디어는 듣는 사람에 의해 많은 부분이 메워지도록 남긴다.

14 ④

단 어

humpback whale : 혹등고래

iconic : 상징적인

sanctuary : 보호 구역

spot : 발견하다, 알아채다

call about : ~의 조사를 위해 방문하다

a handful of : 소수의

calculate : 계산하다, 추산하다

해석

12월은 하와이에서 혹등고래의 계절이 시작되는 달이다. 그러나 전문가들은 혹등고래의 귀환이 늦어지고 있다고 말한다. 이 거대한 고래들은 섬의 겨울의 상징적인 부분이며 여행 안내원들을 위한 수입원이다. 하지만 혹등고래 해양보호 구역 전문가들은 지금까지 고래를 발견하기 어렵다는 보고를 받고 있다고 한다. "한 가지 이론은 이런 일들이 고래가 증가할 때 발생했다는 겁니다. 이는 성공(개체 수 증가)의 부산물이죠. 더 많은 개체수로 인해, 그들은 먹이 자원을 얻는 것에 경쟁하고 있습니다. 그리고 돌아오는 긴 여정을 위해 비축되었던 에너지를 씁니다."라고 마우이 섬 자원보호 담당자이자 보호구역 대응 코디네이터인 Ed Lyman은 말했다. 괴로워하는 새끼 고래에 대해 문의하는 연락에 응답하면서 "우리는 정말 소수의 고래만을 보아왔다"고 말하며 그는 그가 본 그 동물들(고래들)이 얼마나 적었는지에 놀랐다. 전 보호구역 공동 매니저인 Jeff Walters에 따르면, 공무원들이 고래의 실질적 수를 파악하기까지는 오랜 시간이 걸릴 거라고 한다. 왜냐하면 고래 수에 대한 연간 카운트는 1월, 2월, 3월 마지막 토요일이 되어서야 진행되기 때문이다.

① 하와이의 혹등고래 시즌은 보통 연말에 시작한다.
② 혹등고래는 하와이의 여행 안내원들에게 있어 수익성이 좋다.
③ 하와이에서 발견된 혹등고래의 수가 감소한 것은 그들의 성공 때문일 것이다.
④ 이번 고래 시즌에 하와이로 돌아오는 혹등고래의 수는 공식적으로 집계되었다.

15 ②

단 어

drowsy : 졸리는

cultivate : 경작하다, 기르다

consciousness : 의식

knack : 기교, 요령, 재주

take over : 빼앗다, 인수하다

exert : (권력, 영향력을) 행사하다

clarify : 명확히 하다

perceptible : 인지의

해석

사전은 어휘를 학습하는 데 있어 가장 믿을 만한 자원들이다. 그러나 그것을 사용하는 습관은 길러져야 한다. 물론 책을 읽는 것을 중단하고 단어를 찾는 것은 성가신 방해라고 느낄 수 있다. 당신은 아마도 계속 읽다보면 결국 문맥으로부터 이것을 이해하게 될 것이라고 스스로 말할 수도 있다. 실제로 독해 학습 안내서들은 종종 바로 그렇게 조언을 한다. 그러나 이해를 하지 못한다면 곧 졸고 있는 당신을 발견하게 될 것이다. 잠에 대한 욕구가 생기는 게 아니라 보통 점진적인 의식의 상실이 나타난다. 여기에서의 요령은 졸음이 오기 전, 즉 단어 공부를 위해 사전을 잡을 수 있는 충분한 의지력을 행사하기가 좀 더 쉬울 때, 단어 혼동의 신호를 일찍 알아채는 것이다. 비록 이런 특별한 노력이 필요함에도 불구하고, 일단 의미가 명확해지기만 한다면 충분히 느낄 수 있는 안도감이 그 노력을 가치 있게 만들어준다.

TIP

주어진 글은 독해를 하는 과정에서 모르는 단어가 나올 때는 졸리게 된다는 의미이다. 따라서 이 졸림이라는 말에 대한 설명이 나오는 문장 앞에 나오는 것이 가장 바람직하다. ② 뒤에서 보면 그것이 잠에 대한 욕구가 아니라 의식의 상실이라는 말로 그 졸음을 설명하고 있으므로 이곳에 들어가는 것이 가장 바람직하다.

16 ③

단어

diverse : 다양한
genetics : 유전학
composer : 작곡가
playwright : 극작가
universality : 일반성, 보편성
sculptor : 조각가
what we call : 소위, 이른바
reproducible : 재생 가능한
subjective : 주관의, 주관적인
give rise to : 불러일으키다
distinctive : 독특한, 특유의
feature : 특징, 기능

해석

사람들이 만들어 내는 다양한 것들을 보고 그들의 차이점을 설명하는 것은 쉽다. 확실히 시는 수학적인 공식과 다르다. 그리고 소설은 유전학의 실험이 아니다. 작곡가는 확실히 시각적인 예술가들의 언어와는 다른 언어를 사용하며, 화학자들은 극작가들이 하는 것보다는 매우 다양한 것들을 혼합시킨다. 그러나 그들이 만든 다양한 사물로 사람들을 특징짓는 것은 그들이 어떻게 창조하는가에 대한 보편성을 놓치는 것이다. 왜냐하면 창조과정의 단계에서는 과학자, 예술가, 수학자, 작곡가, 작가 그리고 조각가가 소위 우리가 말하는 공통된 "사고의 도구"를 사용하기 때문이다. 그것에는

감정적 감각, 시각적 이미지, 육체적 감각, 재생 가능한 패턴, 비유 등이 포함된다. 그리고 모든 창의적인 사상가들은 이러한 주관적인 사고의 도구들로부터 창조된 생각들을 자신들의 통찰력을 표현하기 위해 대중적인 언어로 번역하는 것을 배운다. 그리고 이를 통해 다른 사람들의 정신에 새로운 사고를 불러일으킬 수 있다.

① 창의적인 사고의 방해물들
② 예술과 과학 사이의 차이점
③ 창조 과정의 공통성
④ 다양한 전문직종의 고유한 특징

17 ②

단어

straightforward : 직접의, 간단한
probe : 탐구하다
nuance : 미묘한 차이
starve : 굶기다, 굶겨 죽이다
deflate : 수축시키다
deprivation : 박탈, 결핍, 몰수
intuition : 직관
observation : 관찰

해석

과학에는 단순한 대답은 거의 없다. 심지어 간단해 보이는 문제들도 사람들이 증거를 찾아 탐구할 때 더 많은 질문을 낳는다. 그런 질문들은 미묘한 차이, 여러 겹의 복잡성, 그리고 우리가 예상했던 것보다 더 자주 초기의 직관과는 모순되는 결론으로 이어진다.
1990년대에 과학자들은 "우리는 어떻게 산소에 굶주린 암세포와 싸우는가?"라는 질문을 하며 명백한 해결책을 제안했다. 혈액의 공급을 차단하여 그들로부터 산소를 제거하여 죽이는 것이다. 그러나 Laura Beil이 "암을 굶겨죽이기"에서 설명하듯이 산소를 부족하게 만드는 것은 실제로 암이 커지고 퍼지게 만든다. 과학자들은 새로운 전략을 찾으면서 대처해 왔다. 예를 들어 콜라겐 교통로 차단하기, 또는 Beil이 썼듯이 세포에 "혈액을 더 적게 주는 것이 아니라 더 많이 공급하기" 등이다.

① 실현되지 않고 끝나는 계획
② 초기의 직관과는 모순되는 결론
③ 주의 깊은 관찰로 시작되는 위대한 발명
④ 과학적 발전을 방해하는 오해들

18 ③

단어

distribute : 배포하다, 나눠주다
leaf through : (책 등을) 대충 획획 넘겨보다

grasp : 이해하다, 파악하다
to one's disappointment : 실망스럽게도
elaborate : 설명하다

강연이 시작하기 전에, 오늘의 연사는 각 관중들에게 자신의 논문의 복사본을 나누어 주었다. 나도 한 부를 받았고 훑어보면서 이 글의 주제를 파악했다. 그가 시작하기를 기다리면서 나는 이 연사가 그 주제에 대해 그가 알고 있는 내용을 관중들에게 단순히 읽어주는 것이 아니라 그 자신의 의견을 연설로 해주기를 조용히 기도했다. 그러나 너무나 실망스럽게도 그는 <u>그의 장황하면서도 잘 준비된 논문을 충실하게 읽어나가기 시작했다</u>. 곧 나는 내가 손에 있는 종이 위에 인쇄된 단어들을 기계적으로 따라가고 있다는 것을 알아차렸다.

① 그의 강연이 너무 형식적이 될까 두려워했다.
② 그의 논문을 보지 않고 그의 이론을 설명했다.
③ 그의 장황하면서도 잘 준비된 논문을 충실하게 읽어나가기 시작했다.
④ 청중들의 관심을 이끌어내기 위해 많은 유머러스한 몸동작을 사용했다.

19 ③

liberal : 진보적인, 개방적인
hark back to : ~를 상기하다
lyric : 서정적인, 서정시
hedgehog : 고슴도치, 호저
prism : 프리즘, 분광기
exclusively : 전적으로, 독점적으로, 배타적으로
overlook : 간과하다, 못보다
mold : 틀, 틀에 넣다
variegate : 변화를 주다, 변화 있게 하다
take : 몫, 의견, 생각
skeptical : 회의적인, 부인하는
complication : 복잡, 합병증
articulate : 똑똑히 발음하다, 설명하다

진보적인 철학자 Isaiah Berlin 경은 Tolstoy에 관한 유명한 에세이에서, 그리스 서정시인인 Archilochus(BC 7세기)의 말이라고 생각되는 고대의 속담을 상기시키며, 두 종류의 사상가들을 구분하였다 ; "여우는 많은 것을 알지만, 고슴도치는 큰 한 가지만 안다." 고슴도치들은 하나의 중심 생각을 가지고 세계를 전적으로 그 개념의 프리즘을 통해서만 본다. 그들은 복합적 문제들과 예외들을 간과하거나, 그것들을 틀에 넣어 그들의 세계관에 맞춘다. 모든 시대와 모든 환경에 맞는 하나의 진정한 답만 있다는 것이다. Berlin이 더 크게 공감했었다는 여우들은 세계에 대

해 더 다양한 의견을 가지고 있는데, 이는 여우들이 <u>하나의 큰 슬로건을 내세우지</u> 못하도록 한다. 그들은 세계의 복잡성이 일반화를 막는다고 느끼기 때문에 그들은 하나의 완전한 이론에 대해 회의적이다. Berlin은 Shakespeare를 여우로 생각한 반면, Dante를 고슴도치라고 생각했다.

① 합리적으로 행동하는 것을
② 다양한 해법을 찾는 것을
③ 하나의 큰 슬로건을 내세우는 것을
④ 세계의 복잡한 문제를 파악하는 것을

20 ①

defense : 변호, 방어
fertile : 비옥한
fallow : 휴경지
clear : 개간하다
peripheral : 주변적인
figure : 인물, 특징
aristocratic : 귀족의
be entitled to : ~할 권한이 있다
landholding : 토지의 소유
bourgeoisie : 중산층, 자본가 계층
bourgeois : 중산층의, 자본가의
pass ~ by : (아무런 영향을 주지 않고) ~을 스쳐 지나가다
elevation : 향상, 높임
be bound to : 반드시 ~하다
transition : 전환
essential : 필수적인

로크의 사유재산의 옹호에서 중요한 요점은 우리가 신이 내려준 토지에 우리의 노동이 결합할 때 어떤 일이 일어나는가에 있다. 우리는 노동을 함으로써 그 땅에 가치를 더하게 된다 ; 우리는 예전에는 놀고 있던 땅을 비옥하게 만든다. 이런 의미에서 우리의 노동력은 가치의 원천, 혹은 토지에 부과된 가치인 것이다. 이러한 가치를 창조하는 나의 노동력은 내가 개간함으로써 가치 있게 만들었던 일부 토지를, 내가 파서 완성시켰던 우물을, 그리고 내가 키워 살찌운 가축들을 내가 소유하는 것에 정당성을 부여한다. 로크에게 호모 파베르-노동의 인간-는 처음으로 정치 사상의 역사에 있어 주변적인 인물이 아니라 중심적인 인물이 된다. 로크의 세계에서 신분과 명예는 여전히 귀족들에게로 흘러갔으며, 귀족들은 광대한 토지를 소유할 권리를 가지고 있었지만 그들은 역사가 신분과 명예에 아무 영향도 주지 않고 스쳐 지나가도록 하고 있었다. 그 정확한 이유는 새로운 경제적 현실이 노동을 통해 실질적으로 가치를 창조하는 부르주아들에게 부를 전환시키고 있었기 때문이다. 시간이 지난 후, 로크의 노동의 중요성에 대한 찬양은 부상하는 부르주아들의 관심을 끌 수밖에 없었다.

① 재산의 소유권은 노동으로부터 온다.
② 노동은 귀족 사회에서 가장 이상적이다.
③ 사유재산의 축적은 행복의 원천이다.
④ 자본주의 사회로의 원활한 전환은 사회의 진전에 필수적이다.

2018. 3. 24.
제1회 서울특별시 시행

---

1 ①

단어

integral : 필수적인, 완전한
key : 필수적인, 핵심적인
incidental : 부수적인
interactive : 상호적인

해석

윤리적인 고려는 생명공학 규제를 위한 <u>필수적인</u> 요소가 될 수 있다.

2 ④

plasticity : 가소성
make up for : 보상하다, 만회하다
accuracy : 정확도
systemicity : 체계성, 계통성, 조직성
obstruction : 방해, 장애물
suppleness : 유연성

해석

만약 언어와 관련된 뇌의 부분이 파괴된다면, 뇌는 손상된 세포를 대체하는 방법으로서 원래는 언어와 관련되지 않은 뇌의 다른 부분이 그 능력을 배우도록 <u>유연성</u>을 사용한다.

3 ④

단어

mere : 겨우 ~의, ~에 불과한
do : 충분하다
genuine : 진짜의, 진실한
reciprocal : 상호간의
verbal : 말로 된, 구두의

해석

Mephisto는 서명과 계약을 요구하고 있다. 단지 <u>구두</u> 계약으로는 충분하지 않을 것이다. Faust의 말처럼, 그 악마는 서면으로 된 모든 것을 원한다.

4 ①

단어

tentative : 잠정적인, 자신 없는
amid : 가운데에
deteriorating : 악화되어가고 있는, 악화 중인
ameliorating : 개선되는
leveling : 평등화

해석

노사는 양쪽 모두 사업 환경이 좋지 않은 가운데 회사의 영업 이익 <u>악화</u>를 심각하게 받아들이면서 올해 임금 협상에서 잠정적인 합의에 도달했다.

5 ①

단어

from scratch : 맨 처음부터

해석

나는 호박케이크를 (시중에 나와 있는 패키지) 케이크 박스로 만드는 것보다 처음부터 만드는 것이 훨씬 쉬울 거라고 확신했다.

TIP

① convinced → am convinced/was convinced
convince는 '~을 확신시키다'라는 뜻을 가진 타동사이다. convince A of B 혹은 convince A that S'+V'를 써서 'A에게 ~을 확신시키다'로 나타낸다. 보기 지문에서는 convince 뒤에 목적어 A 없이 that절이 왔고, 내가(I) 목적어 that절을 확신하고 있다는 뜻이 되어야 하므로 수동태 be+p.p형으로 고쳐 준다.
② from scratch는 '맨 처음부터'라는 뜻의 관용어구이다.
③ even은 much, still, (by far) 등과 마찬가지로 비교급 앞에서 '훨씬'의 뜻으로 쓰여 비교급을 강조하는 역할을 한다.
④ 비교급에서 비교대상끼리 형태가 동일해야 하므로 making pumpkin과 동일하게 동명사 making을 써서 나타내었다.

6 ④

단어

amusement park : 놀이공원

해석

텔레비전에 광고된 놀이공원에 갈 수 없는 이유를 여섯 살짜리 딸에게 설명할 방법을 찾다가 당신의 혀가 꼬이는 것을 발견하면, 그때 당신은 우리가 기다리는 걸 어렵게 생각하는 이유가 무엇인지 이해할 것이다.

✅ **TIP**

① find your tongue twisted에서 find는 5형식 동사로 쓰일 수 있으므로 your tongue는 목적어, twisted는 목적보어가 된다. 목적어와 목적보어가 수동관계(혀가 꼬이는 것)에 있으므로 p.p형 twisted로 쓴 것이 맞다.

② six-year-old는 '여섯 살짜리, 여섯 살의' 형용사로 쓰였으며, 하이픈(-)으로 이어져 하나의 한정용법으로 쓰이는 단어를 이룰 때 year를 복수명사로 쓰지 않는 것에 주의한다.

③ 주어가 선행사 the amusement park로 쓰인 관계대명사절이며, 관계대명사 that이 바르게 쓰였다.

④ wait → to wait

목적어로 쓰인 why 명사절에서 it은 가목적어로 쓰였다. 진목적어는 to부정사의 형태를 취하므로 to wait으로 고쳐준다.

7 ②

📌 **단 어**

foreman : 감독
operation : 수술
wound : 상처
suffering : 고통
shard : 조각, 파편
penetrate : 관통하다
abdomen : 배, 복부
hopper : 호퍼(V자형 용기. 곡물·석탄·짐승 사료를 담아 아래로 내려 보내는 데 씀)

☑️ **해 석**

중소기업 대표이자 건설현장 감독인 Lewis Alfred Ellison은 1916년 100파운드짜리 얼음 덩어리가 호퍼로 운반되는 도중 그것이 떨어져 그 얼음의 날카로운 부분이 그의 복부를 관통하여 고통 받다가 내부 상처를 치료하기 위한 수술을 받은 후 사망하였다.

✅ **TIP**

① and를 기준으로 두 명사(a small-business owner, a construction foreman)가 주어를 수식하고 있다. 각각의 명사에 부정관사 a가 오는 것이 가능하다.

② suffering → suffered

wounds를 수식하면서 능동형 suffering으로 쓰기 위해서는 suffering from ~(~로 고통 받다)이 되거나 타동사로서 목적어를 취해야 한다. 그러나 목적어 없이 after부사절이 왔으므로 목적어를 가지는 타동사로는 쓸 수 없다. 따라서 wounds를 수동의 의미로 수식해주는 suffered가 되어야 맞는 표현이 된다.

③ 접속사로 쓰인 after절에서 주어는 shards, 동사는 penetrated이다. 과거시제 능동형으로 알맞게 쓰였다.

④ while 절에서 주어 it(=the 100-lb ice block)을 생략하고, 동사 load는 (주어와 수동의 관계이므로) be+p.p(be loaded)에 -ing를 써줌으로써 while being loaded~로 시작하는 분사구문이 되었다.

8 ④

📌 **단 어**

dust down : (먼지 등을 없애려고) ~을 털다
rip (사람) off : ~에게 바가지를 씌우다

☑️ **해 석**

A : 당신은 중고차에 대해 모르잖아. Ned, 어위! 7만 마일이나 되네.
B : 오, 너무 많이 달렸네! 우리가 엔진, 도어, 타이어 등 모든 것을 자세히 살펴보아야 할 것 같아.
A : 이건 너무 비싸잖아. Ned, <u>바가지 쓰고 싶지 않아.</u>
B : 중고차 판매상을 조심해야 해.

① 이걸로 사자.
② 내가 먼지를 털어낼게.
③ 원하는 모델이 뭐니?
④ 바가지를 쓰고 싶지 않다.

9 ②

📌 **단 어**

bionic : 생체 공학적인
artificial : 인공의, 인위적인
capability : 능력, 역량
imbue : 가득 채우다

☑️ **해 석**

그 단어는 두 가지 개념, 즉 생명체에게 생체 공학적 팔과 같이 인공적인 능력을 주는 것을 의미하는 "생명 공학" 개념과 생명체에 새로운 능력으로 가득 채우기 위해 사용될 수 있는 100 나노미터보다 작은 입자들을 <u>가리키는</u> "나노" 개념을 결합시킨다.

① 길들이다, 침입하다, 끼어들다
② 나타내다, 언급하다, 지칭하다
③ 기원하다, 비롯되다, 생기다
④ 머물다, 덮어씌우다

10 ①

단어

applaud : 박수를 치다, 갈채를 보내다
consumption : 소비

해석

① 그 상품이 내일까지 배송되지 않는다면, 그들은 그것에 대해 불만을 나타낼 것이다.
② 그는 그의 학급에서 다른 어떤 야구 선수들보다 실력이 더 좋다.
③ 바이올리니스트가 연주를 끝내자마자 관객들은 일어서서 박수를 쳤다.
④ 제빵사들은 밖으로 나와, 밀 소비의 촉진을 요구했다.

TIP

① if절에 tomorrow가 쓰였고, '혹시라도 ~한다면'의 희박한 가능성을 나타내기 위해서 가정법 미래를 썼다. 가정법 미래는 'if S'+should/were to V'(원형), S+조동사 과거형+V' 구문으로 쓴다.
② any other baseball players → any other baseball player
'비교급+than any other 단수명사' 구문은 '다른 어떤 ~보다도 더 ~한'의 뜻으로 최상급의 표현이다.
③ Hardly has the violinist → Hardly had the violinist
'hardly had p.p +when/before S+과거V'는 '~하자마자 ~하다'의 뜻으로 쓰이는 구문이다.
④ have been made come out → have been made to come out
사역동사 have는 능동형으로 쓰일 때 목적보어로 동사원형(수동의미일 때는 과거분사형)을 취하지만, have 동사가 수동태로 쓰여 목적어 없이 보어만 남게 되면 to부정사로 쓴다.

11 ②

단어

exceptional : 이례적일 정도로 우수한, 극히 예외적인
receptive : 수용적인

해석

동물들은 건강하고 먹을 게 충분히 있다면 항상 행복하다. 사람들이 느끼기에 사람도 반드시 그래야 한다고 생각하지만 현대 사회에서는 그렇지 않다. 적어도 대다수의 경우에는 말이다. 만약 당신 자신이 불행하다면, 당신은 아마도 이 점에 있어서 극히 예외적인 사람이 아니라는 것을 인정할 준비가 되어 있을 것이다. 만약 당신 자신이 행복하다면, 당신의 친구들에게 얼마나 그러한지 물어보아라. 그리고 당신이 친구들을 살펴 볼 때, 그들의 표정을 읽는 기술을 길러보아라 ; 일상 중에 당신이 만나는 사람들의 기분을 받아들이도록 해라.

12 ②

단어

tight : 엄격한
spill over : 번지다, 넘치다
restrictive : 제한하는
taxation : 조세
regulatory : (산업ㆍ상업 분야의) 규제(단속)력을 지닌
smuggling : 밀수, 밀반입
infringement : 침해행위, 위반
intellectual property right : 지적재산권, 지적소유권

해석

담배 제품에 대한 더 엄격한 규제는 주류, 탄산음료, 그리고 다른 소비제품으로 번져갔고, 이것은 소비자의 선택권을 제한하고 상품들을 더 비싸게 만드는 요인이 되었다. ① 여러 국가들은 지난 40년 동안 담배 제품에 대해 조세, 그림으로 된 건강 경고문구, 그리고 광고와 홍보 금지 등을 포함해 더욱 제한적인 조치를 취해 왔다. (② 규제 조치들은 국민 건강을 증진시키는 데 실패했고, 결과적으로 담배 밀수를 증가시켰다.) ③ 담배에 먼저 규제를 가하고 그 다음에 다른 소비재 제품에 규제를 가하는 것은 도미노 효과 즉, 다른 산업들에 대해 "미끄러운 경사"를 만들어 냈다. ④ 미끄러운 경사의 가장 극단적인 사례는 모든 상표, 로고 및 특정 브랜드 색상이 제거된 단순한 포장인데, 이것은 의도하지 않은 결과와 심각한 지적 재산권의 심각한 침해를 초래하고 있다.

13 ④

단어

migration : 이주, 이송
fertile : 비옥한, 풍부한
displace : 대체하다, 쫓아내다
on account of : ~때문에
circumstance : 환경, 상황
succumb : 굴복하다
persist : 지속되다

해석

언어는 한 언어의 사용자가 다른 언어 또는 여러 언어의 사용자와 접촉할 때 변한다. 이것은 아마도 그들이 더 비옥한 땅으로 이주하거나 전쟁, 가난, 질병 때문에 쫓기나 이주하는 것 때문일 것이다. 또한 그들이 침략을 당했기 때문일 수도 있다. 상황에 따라 모국어는 침략자들의 언어에 완전히 굴복할 수도 있는데, 그 경우 우리는 대체 언어에 대해 이야기한다. 그렇지 않으면, 모국어는 침략자들의 언어와 나란히 지속될 수도 있고, 정치적 상황에 따라 지배적인 언어가 될 수도 있다.

① 일반적으로, 늘 그렇듯이
② 지속적으로, 항상
③ 비슷하게, 유사하게
④ 그 대신에, 그렇지 않으면

14 ③

단어 •

notion : 개념, 관념, 생각
branding : 브랜드 명(제품 이미지) 부여 작업
appraise : 평가하다
entirely : 전적으로, 완전히, 전부
no more A tnan B : B가 아닌 것처럼 A도 아니다

해 석

브랜드를 가리고 테스트한 제품이 다소 더 객관적으로 평가되고 있다는 생각은 완전히 잘못 이해한 것이다. 현실에서 우리가 구매하는 제품에 부착된 브랜드와 그 제품 상자의 모양과 느낌, 가격 등을 무시하지 않는 것처럼, 눈을 감고 코를 부여잡은 채 제품을 평가하지도 않는다.

① 정확한, 옳은   ② 믿을 수 있는
③ 잘못 이해한   ④ 편견 없는

15 ③

단어 •

relaxation : 휴식, 완화
worthwhile : 가치 있는, ~할 가치가 있는

해 석

미국에 가는 많은 방문객들은 미국인들이 자신들의 운동과 여가활동을 지나치게 고려한다고 생각한다. 미국인들은 종종 사업 약속을 잡는 것처럼 그들의 여가 시간을 계획한다. 그들은 매일 같은 시간에 조깅을 하고, 일주일에 두세 번 테니스를 치고, 매주 목요일마다 수영을 한다. 외국인들은 종종 이런 종류의 여가활동이 휴식이라기보다는 오히려 일처럼 보인다고 생각한다. 그러나 많은 미국인들에게 그들의 여가 활동은 편안하고, 즐길 만하고, 최소한 건강과 신체적 단련에 기여하기 때문에 가치가 있다고 여겨진다.

① 건강과 신체단련
② 미국의 인기 있는 여가 활동
③ 여가 활동에 대한 미국인의 접근법
④ 여가 활동의 정의

16 ③

단어 •

bedrock : 기반
overburden : 과중한 부담을 주다
myriad : 무수함, 무수히 많음
unstoppable : 막을 수 없는
die down : 차츰 잦아들다
mournful : 애절한

requiem : 진혼곡
sorrow : 슬픔

해 석

고통이나 기쁨의 감정 혹은 그 사이의 어떤 상태는 우리 마음의 기반이다. 우리는 종종 이러한 단순한 현실을 인식하지 못하는데, 그 이유는 우리를 둘러싸고 있는 사물과 사건들의 정신적 이미지가 그것들을 묘사하는 단어와 문장들의 이미지와 함께 우리의 과도한 관심을 너무 많이 쓰기 때문이다. 그러나 무수한 감정과 관련된 상태의 느낌이 존재한다. 우리 마음에 계속되는 음악적 선율, 우리가 잠자리에 들 때 비로소 잦아드는 가장 보편적인 멜로디의 울림, 우리가 기쁨으로 가득 차 있을 때 완전한 노래가 되는 콧노래 또는 슬픔이 가득 찰 때의 애절한 진혼곡이.

① 감정은 음악과 밀접한 관련이 있다.
② 감정은 고통과 기쁨으로 이루어져 있다.
③ 감정은 우리 마음 속 어디에나 있다.
④ 감정은 사물과 사건의 정신적 이미지와 관련이 있다.

17 ③

단어 •

deject : 낙담시키다
pebble : 조약돌, 자갈
claw : (발톱으로) 할퀴다
pavement : 인도, 보도, 노면

해 석

나는 경기에 참가하기를 바라며 지역 학교 운동장에 간다. 하지만 아무도 없었다. 그물 없는 농구 골대 밑에서 낙담한 채 모두 어디에 있는 건지 궁금해하며 몇 분을 우두커니 서 있은 후에 나를 기다릴 거라고 생각되는 사람들의 이름들이 내 마음을 채우기 시작했다. 나는 몇 년 동안 이런 장소에서 놀아보지 못했다. 그게 뭐였을까? 나는 무엇 때문에 여기에 온 건가? 어렸을 때, 나는 놀기 위해 학교 운동장에 갔다. 이미 오래전 일이다. 이곳의 어떤 아이도 나를 알지 못할 것이다. 사실 내 주변에는 자갈, 빈병 그리고 내가 발로 차서 인도에서 무시무시한 소음을 내고 있는 맥주캔 말고는 아무것도 없다.

① 평온하고 평화로운   ② 즐겁고 기쁜
③ 황량하고 외로운   ④ 끔찍하고 무서운

18 ①

단어 •

magnate : 거물, 왕, 큰손
emigrate : 이민을 가다, (다른 나라로) 이주하다
textile : 직물, 옷감

종종 <u>전형적인</u> "무일푼에서 부자가 되기" 이야기로 알려진 철강업계 재벌 Andrew Carnegie의 출세 이야기는 1835년 스코틀랜드 던퍼믈린에 있는 작은 방 하나짜리 집에서 시작된다. 궁핍한 노동자 가정에서 태어난 Carnegie는 1848년 그의 가족이 미국으로 이민가기 전까지 거의 교육을 받지 못했다. 펜실베이니아에 도착해서 그는 곧 직물 공장에서 일자리를 얻었는데, 그는 그곳에서 일주일에 겨우 1달러 20센트밖에 벌지 못했다.

① 본질적인, 전형의 - 극빈한, 궁핍한
② 제외의, 예외적인 - 독실한
③ 흥미로운 - 꼼꼼한, 세심한
④ 해로운, 유해한 - 빈곤한, 결핍된

19 ②

단 어

arbitrary : 임의적인, 제멋대로인
sphere : 영역, 구체
sovereignty : 자주권, 독립
division : 분할, 분열
ratify : 승인하다
borderland : 국경지방, 중간
blend into : (구별이 어렵게) ~와 뒤섞이다
prefigure : 예시하다
nationalism : 민족주의
terrain : 지형, 지역
signify : 의미하다

해 석

이전에는 멕시코 북쪽이었던 미국 남서부에서 앵글로-아메리카인들은 히스패닉 아메리카인들과 만났다. 그 만남에는 언어, 종교, 인종, 경제, 정치라는 변수들이 포함되었다. 히스패닉 아메리카와 앵글로 아메리카의 경계는 시간이 흐르면서 바뀌었지만, 한 가지 사실은 변하지 않았다 : 하나는 자주권이 있는 두 영역 사이에 임의적인 지형학적 선을 긋는 것이고, 다른 하나는 사람들에게 그것을 존중하도록 설득하는 것이다. 1848년 멕시코-미국 간의 전쟁에서 승리한 미국은 멕시코의 절반을 차지했다. 그 결과로 초래된 영토 분할은 자연의 지형을 조금도 따른 것이 아니었다. 국경지방은 완전한 생태학적 공간이 되었고, 민족주의를 조장하지 않으며 멕시코 북동쪽 사막은 미국 남동부의 사막과 어우러졌다. 자연이 제공한 단 하나의 경계는 리오 그랑데 강이었는데 이어져 있는 지형을 가로질러 흐르기는 해도 지형을 실제로 분할하지는 않았다.

① 미국과 멕시코 사이의 국경은 하나의 주권의 긴 역사를 의미한다.
② 자연은 선을 긋지 않았지만 인간 사회는 확실히 그렸다.
③ 멕시코-미국 간의 전쟁은 사람들이 국경을 존중하는 것

을 가능하게 했다.
④ 리오 그랑데 강은 임의적인 지정학적 경계로 간주되었다.

20 ③

단 어

trigger : 계기, 도화선
coupled with : ~와 결부된
traffic congestion : 교통 혼잡
startle : 깜짝 놀라게 하다
take evasive action : 회피 작전을 쓰다
violation : 위반, 방해
attempt : 시도, 도전
negligent : 태만한, 부주의한
inconsiderate : 사려 깊지 못한

해 석

ⓔ 난폭 운전은 하나의 교통위반 혹은 지나치게 붙어서 따라가거나 과속하기, 안전하지 못한 차선 변경, 차선 변경을 위한 신호를 보내지 않는 것, 그리고 부주의하거나 사려 깊지 못한 여러 형태의 운전과 같은 위반 행위들의 결합이다.
ⓐ 난폭 운전자를 유발하는 요인은 시간 맞추기가 거의 불가능한 일정과 겹친 교통 혼잡이다.
ⓒ 결과적으로 난폭 운전자는 부족한 시간을 보충하기 위해 여러 가지 위반을 저지르게 되는 것이 일반적이다.
ⓑ 불행하게도, 이러한 행동들은 우리를 위험에 빠뜨린다. 예를 들어, 도로 갓길을 이용하여 추월하는 난폭 운전자는 다른 운전자를 깜짝 놀라게 만들고 더 큰 위험이나 심지어 충돌을 초래하게 되는 회피적인 행동을 취하게 할 수 있다.

2018. 4. 7.
인사혁신처 시행

---

1 ①

단 어

cut it close : 시간이 아슬아슬하다

해 석

A : 부탁 하나만 드려도 될까요?
B : 네, 뭔가요?
A : 제가 출장 때문에 공항에 가야 하는데 차가 시동이 걸리질 않네요. 태워다 주실 수 있을까요?
B : 그럼요. 언제까지 도착해야 하나요?
A : 늦어도 6시까지 도착해야 합니다.

B : 지금이 4시 30분이네요. <u>시간이 아슬아슬하네요.</u> 지금 당장 출발해야겠어요.

① 시간이 아슬아슬하네요.
② 저는 가장 중요한 것에서 눈을 뗐습니다.
③ 반짝이는 모든 것이 금은 아니다.
④ 이미 다 지나간 일이다.

2 ④

단 어

take measures : 조치를 취하다
indefinitely : 무기한으로
be with : ~에 지지하다
perspective : 관점
embrace : 포용하다
fluctuation : 변동
averse to : ~을 싫어하는
be inclined to : ~하는 경향이 있다
dwell on : 숙고하다, 곱씹다

해 석

손실에 대한 두려움은 인간의 가장 기본적인 부분이다. 뇌에게 손실은 위험이며, 우리는 자연스럽게 그것을 피하려는 조치를 취한다. 그러나 우리는 무기한으로 그것을 피할 수는 없다. 손실을 마주하는 한 가지 방법은 주식 거래자의 관점을 갖는 것이다. 주식 거래자들은 손실의 가능성을 경기의 목적이 아닌 게임의 일부로 받아들인다. 이런 생각을 이끄는 것은 포트폴리오 접근법이다 ; 즉, 이익과 손실은 둘 다 일어날 것이지만, 가장 중요한 것은 전체적인 포트폴리오의 결과이다. 당신이 포트폴리오 접근법을 수용하게 되면, 그것들이 더 큰 그림을 위한 작은 부분이라는 것을 알고 있기 때문에 당신은 <u>개별적인 손실을 깊게 생각하는 경향이 더 적어질 것이다.</u>

① 주식 시장의 변동에 더 민감해질 것이다
② 손실을 더 싫어하게 될 것이다
③ 당신의 투자에 관심을 거의 갖지 않을 것이다
④ 개별적 손실을 깊게 생각하는 경향이 더 적어질 것이다

3 ②

단 어

the minute (that) : ~하자마자
manifest : 나타나다, 분명해지다
construct : 건설하다 ; 구성체, 구조물, 개념
relevant : 관련있는, 사람들의 (삶 등에) 의의가 있는
conceive : 마음속으로 그리다
legacy : 유산

manifestation : 명시, 징후
futuristic : 초현대적인

해 석

지난 몇 년 동안의 여행을 통해, 나는 우리 인간이 얼마나 많이 과거 속에 살고 있는지를 관찰했다. 어떤 것이 나타나자마자 그것이 과거가 된다는 것을 고려해보면, 과거는 계속해서 우리 주변에 머문다. 우리의 주변 상황, 우리의 집, 우리의 환경, 우리의 건축물, 우리의 물건들 모두 과거의 구성물이다. 우리는 우리 시대의 일부이며, 우리의 공동체 의식의 일부, 우리의 삶에서 만들어진 것들과 함께 살아야 한다. 물론 우리는, 살아가는 동안 우리 주변의 모든 것들을 의미있게 하거나 구상할 수 있도록 선택하거나 통제할 수는 없지만, 우리가 통제하는 것은 그 시간─ 우리가 존재하고 있고 현재를 전하는─을 돌아보는 것이어야 한다. 현재는 우리가 가진 모든 것이며, 우리가 그것들에 의해 둘러싸여 있으면 있을수록, 더욱 더 우리 자신의 존재와 참여에 대해 알게 된다.

① 여행 : 과거의 유산들을 추적하는 것
② 지금 당신을 둘러싸고 있는 시간을 되돌아보라
③ 숨겨진 삶의 징후
④ 초현대적인 삶의 건축학

4 ③

단 어

take ~ for granted : ~을 당연하게 생각하다
estimate : 추정
deforestation : 삼림 벌채
wilderness region : 환경 보전 지역
temperate rainforest : 온대 강우림

해 석

숲의 아름다움과 풍요로움이 없는 삶을 상상하는 것은 어려울 것이다. 그러나 과학자들은 우리가 우리의 숲을 당연한 것으로 여길 수 없다고 경고한다. 일부 추산에 따르면, 삼림 벌채는 세계 자연림의 80%에 달하는 상실을 초래해 왔다. 현재, 삼림 벌채는 태평양 연안의 온대 우림과 같은 환경 보전 지역에 영향을 미치는 세계적인 문제이다.

TIP

① it은 가주어이고, 진주어로 to부정사(to imagine)가 왔으므로 맞는 문장이다.
② take ~ for granted는 '~을 당연하게 여기다' 뜻의 관용어구이다.
③ has <u>been</u> resulted in → <u>has resulted in</u>
　 result는 자동사로만 쓰이므로 수동태 형식이 불가능하다. 'result from (원인) : ~의 결과로 발생하다/result in (결과) : ~을 야기하다'와 같이 쓰인다.

④ 분사구문으로, 생략된 의미상 주어는 deforestation이다. wilderness regions에 영향을 주는 능동의 의미이므로 현재분사로 표현하였다. 또, affect 동사 자체가 '~에 영향을 미치다'라는 뜻을 가진 타동사이므로 목적어 앞에 전치사를 쓰지 않도록 주의한다.

5 ④

단어

indigenous : 토착의, 토종의
itinerant : 순회하는, 전전하는
impoverished : 가난해진, 허약해진
ravenous : 배가고파 죽을 지경인

해석

전설적인 다큐멘터리 영화 제작자인 Robert J. Flaherty는 어떻게 토착민들이 음식을 모았는지를 보여주려고 노력했다.

① 떠돌아다니는　　　　② 빈곤한
③ 배가고파 죽을 지경인　④ 토박이의

6 ②

단어

talent : 재능, 재주

해석

음악을 듣는 것은 록 스타가 되는 것과는 전혀 다른 것이다. 누구나 음악을 들을 수 있지만 음악가가 되는 것은 재능을 필요로 한다.

① ~와 동등한　　　② ~와 현저히 다른
③ ~여하에 달린　　④ ~의 서막

7 ④

단어

submerge : 가라앉다
deprive : 박탈하다
oxygen : 산소
wither : 시들다
perish : 죽다
prolong : 연장하다, 지연시키다
susceptible : 취약한
flooding : 홍수
prone : 당하기 쉬운
annually : 매년
waterlogged : 물에 잠긴

rice paddy : 논
hardy : 강인한
bumper harvest : 풍작
dreadful : 끔찍한, 지독한
vulnerable : 취약한, 연약한
urbanization : 도시화
yield : 생산
staple : 주된, 주요한

해석

생물학자들은 벼가 현재보다 일주일 더 긴 2주일 동안 물속에 잠긴 상태로 생존할 수 있게 하는 유전자를 발견해 냈다. ― 일주일 이상을 물속에 있는 식물들은 산소가 부족하여 시들어서 죽게 된다. ① 과학자들은 그들의 발견이 홍수에 취약한 지역에서 농작물 수확하는 것을 지연시킬 수 있기를 바란다. ② 아시아의 홍수에 취약한 지역에 있는 쌀 재배자들은 과도하게 물에 잠긴 논 때문에 매년 10억 달러의 손실을 보고 있다. ③ 그들은 이 새로운 유전자가 태풍과 장마철에 발생되는 재정적인 피해를 줄여주고 더 강인한 쌀 종자를 만들어서 풍작을 초래하기를 희망한다. (④ 이것은 도시화의 희생자이고 농작물이 부족한 취약한 지역에 살고 있는 사람들에게 끔찍한 소식이다.) 쌀 수확량은 향후 20년 동안 30% 가량 증가해서 10억 명이 쌀을 주식으로 먹을 수 있도록 보장되어야 한다.

8 ③

단어

learner's permit : 임시 면허증
behind the steering wheel : 운전하다
take a rain check : 다음을 기약하다

해석

A : 운전할 줄 아세요?
B : 물론이죠. 운전 잘 합니다.
A : 운전하는 방법을 알려주실 수 있나요?
B : 임시면허증이 있습니까?
A : 네, 지난주에 받았습니다.
B : 운전해본 적 있습니까?
A : 아뇨. 하지만 빨리 시작하고 싶습니다.

① 펑크 난 타이어를 갈다　② 엔진오일을 교체하다
③ 시작하다　　　　　　　④ 다음을 기약하다

9 ②

단어

scale : 비늘
aerospace : 우주항공
shortfin mako : 청상아리

great white shark : 대백상어
taper : 점점 가늘어지다
flatten : 납작해지다
drag : 항력, 끌림

해석

상어는 이빨과 같은 물질로 만들어진 비늘로 덮여 있다. 이 유연한 비늘은 상어를 보호해주고 물에서 빨리 헤엄칠 수 있도록 도와준다. 상어는 헤엄치면서 비늘을 움직일 수 있다. 이러한 움직임은 물의 저항력을 줄여준다. Alabama대학의 항공우주 산업 기술자인 Amy Lang은 대백상어와 친척관계인 청상아리의 비늘을 연구했다. Lang과 그녀의 팀은 청상아리 비늘이 몸의 부위마다 크기와 유연성이 다르다는 것을 발견했다. 예를 들면, 몸의 측면에 있는 비늘은 한쪽 끝에서 가늘다가 넓어지고 다른 끝에서는 좁아진다. 비늘들이 더 가늘어지기 때문에 이러한 비늘들은 매우 쉽게 움직인다. 이것들은 상어 주변 물의 흐름에 따르고 항력을 줄이기 위해서 위로 향하거나 평평해질 수 있다. Lang은 상어 비늘은 비행기와 같이 저항을 겪는 기계들의 디자인에 영감을 줄 수 있다고 생각한다.

① 상어는 수영할 때 자신을 보호하기 위해서 항상 움직이지 않는 비늘을 가지고 있다.
② Lang은 청상아리의 비늘이 물속에서 저항을 줄이기 위해 사용된다는 것을 밝혀냈다.
③ 청상아리는 몸 전체에 걸쳐 똑같은 크기의 비늘을 가지고 있다.
④ 비행기의 과학적 디자인들은 상어 비늘에서 영감을 받았다.

10 ③

단어

entrepreneur : 사업가
combine A with B : A와 B를 결합하다
ingenuity : 독창성
dichotomy : 이분
optimistic : 낙관적인
pessimistic : 비관적인
pass by : 지나치다

해석

집중은 할 일을 하는 것을 의미한다. 많은 사람들이 뛰어난 아이디어를 가지고 있지만 그것을 실천하지는 않는다. 예를 들어, 나에게 있어 사업가란, 혁신과 독창성을 새로운 아이디어에 실행하는 능력과 결합할 수 있는 사람이다. 몇몇 사람들은 삶에서 가장 중요한 이분법이 당신에게 흥미를 일으키거나 걱정을 끼치는 일들에 대해 당신이 긍정적인지 혹은 부정적인지에 대한 것이라고 생각한다. 낙관적인 시선을 갖는 것이 좋은지 또는 비관적인 시선을 갖는 게 좋은지에 관한 의문에 많은 관심이 쏠리고 있다. 내 생각에 더 나은 질문은 당신이 그것에 대해 무엇인가를 할 것인지 아니면 그냥 지나가게 할 것인지이다.

TIP

① get은 사역의 의미로 쓰일 때 목적보어 자리에 to부정사 혹은 과거분사(수동 의미일 경우)를 쓰는데 stuff와 do에서 수동의 의미이므로 done이 맞다. 또한 동사 mean의 목적어로 동명사가 올 수 있다.
② interest와 concern 모두 타동사로서 전치사 없이 목적어를 바로 취한다. 또한 that 절 안에서 주어였을 선행사 the issues 복수 명사에 맞춰 복수형 동사로 맞게 쓰였다.
③ paying to this question → paid to this question
pay attention to라는 구문에서 pay의 목적어였던 명사 attention이 앞으로 나가면서 pay가 뒤에서 수식하게 되었다. attention이 pay의 주체가 아니고 객체이므로 paid로 고쳐주어야 한다.
④ whether you are going to do ~ or let에서 or를 기준으로 병렬을 이루고 있다. you are going to do ~ or (you are going to) let ~에서 공통부분은 생략되었다. 또 let은 사역동사로 쓰여 목적어로 동사원형을 취하므로 pass by역시 맞게 쓰였다. 대명사 you는 '동사+부사'로 이루어진 동사구에서 목적어가 되며 동사와 부사 사이에 올 수 있다.

11 ④

단어

treasure : 귀중히 여기다
tolerate : 인내하다
generality : 일반론

해석

대부분의 사람들은 말하는 것은 좋아하지만 듣는 것을 좋아하는 사람은 거의 없다. 그러나 잘 듣는 것은 모든 사람들이 소중하게 여겨야 하는 ① 귀중한 재능이다. 훌륭한 청취자들은 더 많은 것을 듣기 때문에, 대부분의 사람들보다 그들 주변에서 일어나는 것들을 더 많이 알고 그것들에 더욱 민감하게 반응하는 경향이 있다. 게다가 남의 말을 잘 듣는 사람들은 판단하거나 비판하는 것보다는 차라리 받아들이거나 인내하는 경향이 있다. 따라서 그들은 대부분의 사람들보다 적이 ② 거의 없다. 사실, 그들은 사람들 중 가장 사랑받는 이들일 것이다. 그러나 이러한 일반화에도 ③ 예외들은 있다. 예를 들어 John Steinbeck은 훌륭한 청취자였다고 알려져 있지만, 그는 그의 글에서 언급했던 몇몇 사람들에게 미움을 받았다고 한다. 틀림없이 그의 청취능력은 그의 글쓰기 능력에 기여했다. 그럼에도 불구하고 그의 경청의 결과는 그를 ④ 인기 없게(→ 인기 있게) 만들지는 못했다.

TIP

④ unpopular → popular

good listeners는 the most beloved of people이라고 하면서, 예외로 John Steinbeck을 들고 있다. he was hated 등으로 보아 그는 인기가 없었음을 알 수 있다. 마지막 문장이 부정문(didn't make)임을 주의해야 한다.

12 ①

단어 ★

clutter : 혼란
energize : 북돋우다
ingrained : 뿌리 깊은
have a fit of : ~이 북받치다
dwell on : ~을 깊이 생각하다
originate from : ~에서 비롯되다

해석

걱정은 흔들 목마와 같다. 당신이 아무리 빨리 가도 당신은 아무데도 가지 않는다. 걱정은 완벽한 시간 낭비이며, 마음 속에 너무나 많은 혼란을 만들어 내기 때문에 어떤 것도 분명하게 생각할 수 없게 된다. 걱정을 그만두는 것을 배우는 방법은 당신이 집중하는 것이 무엇이든지 그것에 에너지를 쏟아야 한다는 것을 먼저 이해하는 것이다. 그러므로 당신이 스스로 걱정을 하면 할수록, 더 많은 것들이 잘못될 것이다. 걱정하는 것은 몸에 깊이 밴 습관이어서 그것을 피하기 위해서는 스스로 그렇게 하지 않도록 훈련을 해야 한다. 당신이 걱정으로 가득찬 것을 알아챌 때마다 멈추고 생각을 바꿔라. 당신이 일어나길 원하는 것에 대해 더 생산적으로 집중하고 당신의 인생에 일어났던 멋진 것을 계속 곱씹으면 더 멋진 일들이 당신에게 일어날 것이다.

① 어떻게 걱정에 대처할까?
② 언제 우리는 걱정해야만 할까?
③ 걱정은 어디에서 발생하는 걸까?
④ 걱정은 삶에 어떤 영향을 미칠까?

13 ③

단어 ★

founder : 창립자
nation-building : 국가건설
satellite : (인공)위성
aspiring : 야망을 가진
familiarized : ~에 친숙한

해석

뭄바이의 Everonn 교육의 창시자인 kisha Padbhan은 그의 사업을 일종의 국가건설로 여긴다. 인도의 2억 3천만 명(유치원에서 대학까지)의 학생 인구 수는 전 세계에서 가장 큰 규모 중 하나다. 정부는 교육에 830억 달러를 쓰고 있지만 심각한 격차가 존재한다. "교사와 교사 양성 기관이 충분하지 않다"라고 kisha는 말한다. "인도의 먼 지역에 사는 학생들에게 부족한 것은 좋은 선생님을 만나고 양질의 콘텐츠를 접하는 것이다." Everonn의 해결책은? 그 회사는 가상 교실을 통해서 그 격차를 메우기 위해 양방향 비디오와 오디오를 갖춘 위성 네트워크를 사용한다. 그것은 인도의 28개 주 중 24개 주에 있는 1,800개의 대학과 7,800개의 학교에 이른다. 이것은 디지털화된 학교 수업에서부터 장래의 기술자들을 위한 입학시험 준비까지 모든 것을 제공해주고 구직자들을 위한 교육도 제공한다.

① 전국에서 능력 있는 교사를 발굴하도록
② 학생들이 디지털 기술에 익숙해지도록 하는 것
③ 가상 교실을 통해 차이를 좁히는 것
④ 교사 훈련 기관의 질을 향상시키는 것

14 ②

단어 ★

service academy : 사관학교
conservatory : 음악학교
compromise : ~을 위태롭게 하다, 타협하다, (원칙 등을) 굽히다
stella : 뛰어난
scholarship : 장학금

해석

MHC의 학생들은 비싼 수업료에 스트레스를 받지 않는다. 왜냐하면 수업료가 무료이기 때문이다. MHC와 소수의 다른 사관학교들, 워크 칼리지, 단과대 학교들과 음악학교들에서는 학생들 100%가 4년 동안 수업료 전액 장학금을 받는다. MHC 학생들은 또한 연구와 서비스 경험, 해외 연수와 인턴십을 할 수 있게 해줄 노트북과 7,500달러의 "기회 펀드"를 받는다. "정말 중요한 것은 무료 학비가 아니라 돈에 대한 부담 없이 자유롭게 공부하는 것이다"라고 MHC의 학장 Ann Kirschner는 말한다. 그녀는 부채 부담이 학생들이 대학에서 하는 결정들을 방해하고 있고, 그래서 우리는 그들에게 그것으로부터 자유로워질 기회를 제공하고 있다고 말한다. 모든 학생들에게 무료 수업료를 제공하는 학교는 매우 드물지만, 점점 더 많은 기관들이 높은 학점으로 입학한 학생들에게 장학금을 제공하고 있다. Indiana University Bloomington과 같은 기관에서는 뛰어난 평점과 우수한 등급 순위를 가진 학생들에게 자동으로 상을 수여한다.

TIP

MHC 학생들은 노트북과 기회펀드 형태로 7,500 달러를 받는다고 했으므로 ②는 옳지 않다.

15 ①

단 어 •

spend A ~ing : ~하는 데 A를 소요하다
determine : 밝히다
malefactor : 악인
culprit : 범인, 원인
dilettante : 호사가
pariah : 버림받는 사람
demagogue : 정치 선동가

해 석

경찰은 7개월 동안 범죄사건을 조사했지만, 결국 범인의 신원을 밝혀낼 수 없었다.

16 ①

단 어 •

at first glance : 언뜻 보기에는
leech : 거머리

해 석

처음에는 그의 친구들이 거머리처럼 보이긴 하지만, 그들은 **좋을 때나 안 좋을 때나** 그가 의존할 수 있는 사람들임을 알게 된다.

① 좋을 때나 나쁠 때나 ② 행복한 순간에
③ 이따금 ④ 당장에

17 ④

단 어 •

intensely : 강렬하게
dialect : 방언
accommodate to : ~ 에 맞추다
stand out : 눈에 띄다
perception : 이해
norm : 표준
temporary : 일시적인
fit in : 어울리다
debate : 토론

해 석

언어에 대한 우리의 인식과 생성은 시간에 따라 변한다. ①만약 우리가 오랜 기간 동안 고향을 떠나게 된다면, 우리 주위의 새로운 억양이 낯설다는 우리의 인식은 일시적일 뿐이다. ② 차츰, 우리는 다른 사람들이 억양이 있다는 생각을 안 하게 되고 우리의 말투를 새로운 표준에 맞추어 적응하기 시작할 것이다. ③ 모든 사람들이 같은 정도로 이렇게 되는 것은 아니다. ④ 어떤 사람들은 그들의 언어 습관을 고쳐 빠르게 새로운 환경에 적응

하며 더 이상 "눈에 띄지 않게" 되는 반면에, 어떤 사람들은 자신의 고향 억양과 사투리, 어구, 그리고 몸짓들을 여전히 매우 자랑스러워한다. 그들이 이것을 의식적으로 하는지 그렇지 않은지는 논쟁의 여지가 있지만 개인에 따라 다를 수 있다. 그러나 언어와 관련이 있는 대부분의 과정에서처럼 우리가 그것을 의식하기 전에 변화는 발생하며, 만약 우리가 의식한다면 그것은 발생하지 않을 것이다.

18 ②

단 어 •

insomnia : 불면증
transient : 일시적인
acute : 급성의
chronic : 만성의
disorder : 질환, 질병
impaired : 손상된
psychomotor : 정신운동의
deprivation : 부족
initiate : 착수시키다
adequate : 적절한
weariness : 피곤함
hallucination : 환각
fatigue : 피로
double vision : 복시
solely : 오로지

해 석

불면증은 일시적이거나 급성이거나 만성적인 것으로 분류된다. 일시적인 불면증은 일주일 미만의 기간 동안 지속된다. 그것은 다른 질병이나, 수면 환경의 변화, 수면 시간의 선택, 극심한 우울증, 혹은 스트레스에 의해서도 야기된다. 졸음이나 손상된 정신운동수행과 같은 이것의 영향은 수면 부족의 영향과 같다. 급성 불면증은 한 달 이하의 기간 동안 지속적으로 잠을 자지 못하게 한다. 급성 불면증은 잠이 드는 것 혹은 잠을 계속 자는 것에 어려움이 있을 때 혹은 수면이 상쾌하지 않은 경우이다. 이러한 문제들은 수면의 충분한 기회와 환경에도 불구하고 발생하며, 낮 동안의 기능에 방해가 될 수 있다. 급성 불면증은 또한 단기간의 불면증 혹은 스트레스 관련 불면증으로도 알려져 있다. 만성 불면증은 한 달 이상 지속된다. 그것은 다른 질환에 의해 생길 수도 있거나 이것이 주요한 질병일 수도 있다. 시토카인 수치의 변화나 스트레스 호르몬의 높은 수치를 가진 사람들이 다른 사람들보다 만성 불면증을 겪을 가능성이 더 많다. 이 만성 불면증의 영향은 원인에 따라 다르다. 그 원인으로는 근육 피로, 환각, 혹은 정신적 피로들이 있다. 만성 불면증은 또 복시를 야기할 수 있다.

① 불면증은 지속 기간에 따라 분류될 수 있다.
② 일시적 불면증은 오로지 적절치 않은 수면 환경 때문에 발생한다.

③ 급성 불면증은 일반적으로 스트레스와 관련된 것으로 알려져 있다.
④ 만성 불면증 환자는 환각을 겪을 수 있다.

19 ③

단어

autonomic : 자율적인
involuntary : 본의 아닌
biofeedback : 생체 자기 제어
attach : 붙이다
variable : 가변적인 변수
trigger : 유발하다

해석

이러한 기능들(자율적이거나 비자율적인 신체 기능들)의 전자적 측정치를 관찰함으로써 개인이 자율적이거나 혹은 비자율적인 신체 기능들에 어떤 자발적 조절 능력을 얻도록 하는 기술을 바이오피드백(생체자기제어)이라고 한다.
(B) 전자 센서는 심장박동, 혈압, 체온 등과 같은 변수들을 측정하기 위해 신체의 다양한 부분에 붙여진다.
(A) 이러한 가변적인 변수가 원하는 방향(예 : 혈압 강하)으로 이동하면 텔레비전 세트, 측정기나 조명과 같은 장치에 시각적 또는 청각적 신호를 유발시킨다.
(C) 생체 자기 제어 훈련은 표시장치를 촉발시킨 생각의 패턴이나 행동을 재현하여 원하는 반응을 도출하도록 가르친다.

20 ④

단어

stingy : 인색한
turn out : ~인 것으로 드러나다

TIP

① be good at(~를 잘하다)에서 전치사(at) 뒤에는 명사가 와야 하므로 동사 get을 동명사 getting으로 바르게 표현하였다. 또한 get across (to somebody)는 '(의미가) ~에게 전달되다, 이해되다'라는 뜻으로 쓰인다.
② 'more ~ than ~ any other 단수명사' 비교급으로 최상급 의미를 나타냈고, 비교 대상 the traffic jams를 than 뒤에서 those로 받아 복수형 수일치가 바르게 이루어졌다.
③ 주어 역할을 하는 명사구 Making eye contact with the person you are speaking to에서 the person (whom/who) you are speaking to는 관계대명사가 생략되고 you are speaking to가 선행사 the person을 뒤에서 수식하고 있다. 관계대명사가 생략될 때 전치사 to는 관계대명사 앞으로 가지 않고 함께 생략되지도 않는다. 동명사구 전체를 단수 동사 is로 받은 것 또한 맞다.

④ not so <u>stingier</u> as → not so <u>stingy</u> as
'as(so) 형용사/부사 as'로 쓰인 원급비교 구문이다. 비교급 형태로 쓰인 형용사 stingier를 원급 형태로 고쳐주어야 한다.

**2018. 5. 19.
제1회 지방직 시행**

---

1 ①

단어

paramount : 다른 무엇보다 중요한

해석

의사의 <u>가장 중요한</u> 의무는 해를 끼치지 않는 것이다. 치료와 같은 그 밖의 모든 것은 2순위이다.

① 주된   ② 선서를 한   ③ 성공적인   ④ 의문의

2 ②

단어

get cold feet : 겁이 나다, 용기를 잃다

해석

사람들이 북극으로 여행하는 것에 대해 <u>겁을 먹는 것</u>은 이상한 일이 아니다.

① 야심적이게 되다   ② 겁을 먹다
③ 기진맥진하다   ④ 슬픔을 느끼다

3 ④

단어

integrity : 진실성
post : 지위

해석

Mrs. Ferrer에 대한 문의를 요청하신 데에 대한 답장을 씁니다. 그녀는 지난 3년 동안 저의 비서로 일했고 훌륭한 직원이었습니다. 저는 그녀가 당신의 직무기술서에 언급된 모든 요구 조건들을 충족시키고 정말로 여러 면에서 그것들을 능가한다고 믿습니다. 저는 결코 그녀의 완전한 성실성을 의심할 이유를 가져본 적 없습니다. 그러므로 저는 Mrs. Ferrer를 당신이 공고하는 그 자리에 추천합니다.

TIP

① has worked 현재완료형과 맞춰 for the last three years는 '지난 3년간'이라는 뜻으로 맞게 쓰였다.

② believe의 목적절 that절 안에서 동사는 meets이므로 mentioned는 동사가 될 수 없고 all the requirements를 수식하는 형용사구로 쓰였다. 또 따로 목적어를 가지고 있지 않고, 의미상으로도 '언급된 모든 요구사항들'이 되어야 하므로 과거분사 형태로 수동의 뜻을 나타내었다.

③ 동사 have never had, 목적어 reason의 3형식에서 앞의 명사 reason을 수식하는 형용사 용법으로 쓰인 to부정사이다.

④ for the post <u>what</u> you advertise → for the post <u>that/which</u> you advertise
관계대명사 what(=the thing that 등)은 선행사를 포함하고 있는 개념으로 선행사 없이 그 자체로 명사절을 이끌 수 있다. 여기서는 앞에 the post라는 선행사가 있고 뒤에서 수식하는 형용사절이 되어야 하므로 that 혹은 which로 바꾸어준다.

4 ④

단어

apologize : 사과하다

TIP

① information은 셀 수 없는 명사이다. 따라서 all of information에서 informations로 쓸 수 없고, 동사 또한 단수형(was)으로 써주어야 한다.

② should have p.p(~했어야 했다) 가정법 구문이 바르게 쓰였다.

③ 주절의 주어가 when we arrived 보다 더 과거임(already)을 알 수 있으므로 과거완료형을 써서 had started로 나타내었다.

④ Being cold outside → <u>It</u> being cold outside
분사구문을 만들 때 주절의 주어와 일치할 때에만 분사구문 내에서 주어를 생략할 수 있다. Being cold outside로 표현하게 되면 주절의 주어 I가 생략된 것으로 보아, 주어진 '바깥 날씨가 춥다' 지문과 다른 뜻이 된다. 날씨를 나타낼 때는 비인칭 주어 it을 써서 It was cold outside로 나타내므로, 주절의 주어와 같지 않아서 생략할 수 없다.

5 ④

단어

state-of-the-art : 최첨단의
approach : 접근법
intimidating : 위협하는

해석

최신식 접근법이 <u>위협적이라고</u> 생각하는 학생들은 그들이 구식 방법으로 배운 것보다 덜 배우게 된다.

① 재미있는 　② 친근한 　③ 편리한 　④ 위협하는

6 ③

단어

electric fan : 선풍기

해석

에어컨이 현재 수리 중이기 때문에, 사무실 직원들은 오늘 하루 동안은 <u>아쉬운 대로 선풍기를 써야 한다</u>.

① ~을 제거하다 　　　② ~를 놓다
③ ~으로 임시 변통하다 　④ ~와 헤어지다

7 ②

단어

extinct : 멸종한
attempt : 시도하다

해석

① 제가 지난주에 알려드린 이메일 주소로 연락 부탁드립니다.
② 물이 없다면, 지구상의 모든 살아있는 생물들은 멸종할 것이다.
③ 노트북 컴퓨터는 사무실 밖에서도 계속해서 일을 할 수 있도록 해 준다.
④ 그들이 자신들의 실수에 대해서 설명하려고 하면 할수록, 그들의 이야기는 더 안 좋게 들렸다.

TIP

① <u>contact to</u> me → <u>contact</u> me
contact는 전치사를 취하지 않는 완전타동사이다. 목적어 me가 전치사 없이 바로 와야 한다.

② Were it not for~는 '~이 없다면'의 가정을 나타내는 구문이다. 원래 형태는 if it were not for이다. 주절에서 '조동사 과거형(would)+동사원형'이 쓰여 가정법 과거로 알맞게 쓰였다. 가정법 과거완료형에서 '~이 없다면' 조건절 구문은 had it not been for로 쓴다.

③ people who is away from → people who are away from
선행사 people(복수형)에 맞춰 관계사절 안의 동사 또한 복수형으로 수일치를 해주어야 한다. allow people ~ to continue에서는 allow A to B(동사원형)의 형태로 바르게 쓰였다.

④ the more ~, the worst → the more ~, the worse
'the 비교급, the 비교급(~할수록 ~하다)' 구문이므로 bad-worse-worst에서 최상급 worst가 아닌 비교급 worse로 써야 한다.

8 ①

단 어

see off : ~를 배웅하다

TIP

① 며칠 전(a few days ago)이라는 특정 과거 시점이므로 과거 시제(went)가 맞다.

② made it believe → made believe
'~인 체하다' 뜻은 make believe (that)으로 나타낸다.

③ looking forward to go → looking forward to going
looking forward to(~하기를 고대하다, 기다리다)에서 to는 전치사이다. 따라서 뒤에 오는 동사 형태는 동명사이어야 한다.

④ anything interested → anything interesting
'재미, 흥미를 느끼게 하다' 동사 interest의 주체가 anything이므로 현재분사 형태(-ing)로 써준다.

9 ③

단 어

definite : 확실한
hierarchy : 계급, 위계질서
elaborate : 정교한
banquet : 연회
scalco : 식탁에서 고기를 잘라주는 사람
steward : 집사장
in charge of : ~을 맡아서
supervise : 감독하다
butler : 집사
silverware : 은제품
linen : 아마 섬유, 리넨
undercook : (휘하 요리사), 설익히다
pastry cook : 페이스트리 요리사

해 설

르네상스 시대 주방에는 정교한 만찬을 만들어내기 위해서 함께 일하는 조력자들의 명확한 위계질서가 있었다. ① 우리가 보아왔던 것처럼 꼭대기에는 집사 또는 집사장이 있었고 그는 주방 뿐 아니라 식당까지도 책임을 지고 있었다. ② 식당은 집사에 의해서 감독되었다. 그는 은식기와 식탁용 리넨제품을 담당하고 있었으며 연회를 시작하고 마치는 요리, 즉 식사를 시작할 때는 차가운 요리, 샐러드, 치즈, 과일을, 그리고 식사를 마칠 때는 스위츠와 단 음식들을 서빙했다. (③ 이렇게 정교한 장식과 접객은 레스토랑에서 "FoH"라고 불리는 것이다.) ④ 그 주방은 수석 주방장에 의해서 감독되었으며, 그는 휘하 요리사들과 페이스트리 요리사들, 주방 보조들을 감독했다.

TIP

③은 주방과 식당의 책임자들에 대한 설명과 어울리는 문장이 아니다.

10 ②

단 어

pique : 불쾌하게 하다, 언짢게 하다
advance one's career : 출세하다

해 설

나의 학생들은 종종 더 중요한 사람들을 만나면 그들의 업무 성과가 좋아질 거라고 생각한다. 하지만 당신이 먼저 이 세상에 무언가 가치를 더하지 않은 이상 이런 사람들과 관계를 맺는 것은 상당히 어렵다. 이것이 바로 조언자들과 후원자들의 호기심을 불러일으키는 것이다. 성취는 당신이 무언가를 그저 취하는 것뿐만 아니라 무언가 줄 것이 있다는 것을 보여준다. 물론 우리가 살아가면서 꼭 필요한 사람들을 만나는 것은 도움이 된다. 하지만 이들이 얼마나 여러분을 위해 팔을 걷어붙일지, 얼마나 큰 위험을 감수할지는 당신이 그들에게 무엇을 제공할 수 있느냐에 달려있다. 강력한 인맥을 구축하는 것은 당신으로 하여금 인맥 전문가가 되기를 요구하는 것은 아니다. 단지 어떤 분야에서 전문가가 되어야 한다는 것을 의미한다. 좋은 사람들과 관계를 맺으면 당신은 출세할지도 모른다. 당신이 대단한 성과를 낼 수 있다면 이러한 좋은 사람들과 더 쉽게 이어질 수 있다. 당신의 명함이 아닌 통찰력과 결과물이 당신의 실력을 대변할 수 있도록 해라.

① 후원은 성공적인 경력을 쌓기 위해 필수적이다.
② 좋은 인맥을 구축하는 것은 당신의 성취로부터 시작된다.
③ 영향력 있는 인맥은 당신의 성취를 위한 전제조건이다.
④ 인맥 쌓기의 전문가가 되면 당신의 통찰력과 결과물도 커지게 된다.

11 ②

단어

shut down : 멈추다
charge : 충전하다

해석

A : 내 컴퓨터가 이유도 없이 멈췄어. 심지어 다시 켤 수도 없네.
B : 충전했어? 배터리가 거의 방전됐을지도 몰라.
A : 물론 충전도 다시 해봤지.
B : 그럼 가장 가까운 서비스센터를 가봐.
A : 그래야 하는데, 내가 너무 게을러.

① 어떻게 네 컴퓨터를 고쳐야 할지 모르겠어.
② 그럼 가장 가까운 서비스센터를 가봐.
③ 글쎄, 문제에 대한 걱정 그만하고 자러 가.
④ 내 동생이 기술자니까 네 컴퓨터 고쳐 보라고 할게.

12 ①

단어

white as a sheet : 백지장처럼 창백하다
convincing : 설득력 있는
tornado : 분출
curb : 억제하다, 제한하다
proctor : 시험 감독관
desperately : 필사적으로
arithmetic : 연산
scramble : 허둥지둥 해내다
doom : 운명
declare : 선언하다
algebraic : 대수학
swim : 빙빙 돌듯 보이다
geometric : 기하학

해석

내 얼굴은 창백해졌다. 나는 시계를 쳐다보았다. 지금쯤 시험은 거의 끝나갈 것이다. 나는 완전한 공황상태로 시험장에 도착했다. 나는 내 사정을 이야기하려고 노력했지만 내 말과 설명하려는 몸짓이 너무 혼란스러워 나는 감정이 폭발하는 상황에서 설득력 있는 무엇도 전달할 수 없었다. 나의 산만한 설명을 제지하고자 시험 감독관은 나를 빈 좌석으로 이끌었고 시험지를 내 앞에 놓아두었다. 그는 미심쩍게 나로부터 시계로 눈을 돌렸고, 걸어서 나로부터 멀어져갔다. 나는 필사적으로 놓친 시간을 만회하려고 했고, 미친 듯이 허둥지둥 유사점들과 문장 완성들을 이어갔다. "15분 남았습니다." 운명의 목소리가 교실을 울렸다. 대수 방정식과 산술계산, 기하학도표가 내 눈앞에서 빙빙 도는 것 같이 보였다. "끝. 연필 내려놓으세요."

① 긴장되고 걱정하는　　② 흥분되어 들뜬
③ 차분하고 단호한　　④ 편안하고 안전한

13 ②

단어

device : 장치
the moment S+V : ~하자마자

해석

건강상태를 모니터링하고 추적하는 장치가 모든 연령층에서 인기를 얻고 있다.
(B) 하지만 살던 곳에서 노후를 맞이하는 노인들, 특히 가정 내에 돌보는 사람이 없는 경우에 이러한 기술들은 생명을 구할 수도 있다.
(A) 예를 들어, 낙상은 65세 이상 성인들에게 있어 사망의 주된 원인이다. 낙상 경고 장치는 수년 동안 있어 왔던 대중적인 노인을 위한 양로 기술이지만 지금은 개선되었다.
(C) 이 간단한 기술은 노인이 넘어지자마자 자동으로 911 또는 가까운 가족에게 알려준다.

TIP

제시된 글은 건강을 감시 및 추적하는 장치들이 인기를 얻고 있다고 했다. (B)의 'these technologies'는 이런 장치들을 뜻한다. (A)는 낙상 경보 기술이 필요한 이유를 설명하고, (C)에서는 낙상 경보 기술을 연결하여 설명하고 있다.

14 ①

단어

neither of : ~의 어느 쪽도 아니다

해석

A : 신혼여행 어디 가고 싶어?
B : 우리 둘 다 한 번도 간 적 없는 곳으로 가자.
A : 그럼 하와이에 가는 거 어때?
B : 나도 늘 그곳에 가고 싶었어.

① 난 늘 그곳에 가고 싶었어.
② 한국은 살기 좋은 곳 아니니?
③ 좋았어! 지난번에 갔던 여행은 정말 멋졌어!
④ 오, 넌 하와이에 벌써 가본 게 틀림없구나.

15 ④

단어

commitment : 약속, 헌신, 책무
impede : 지연시키다, 방해하다
unforeseen : 예측하지 못한
get in the way : 방해되다
distraction : 부주의

성공한 사람들의 비결은 대개 그들은 한 가지 일에 완전히 집중할 수 있다는 데에 있다. 그들은 그들의 머릿속이 복잡하더라도 이 많은 일들이 서로 방해하기는커녕 훌륭한 내적 질서를 이루도록 하는 방법을 찾아냈다. 그리고 이러한 질서는 매우 단순하다 : <u>가장 중요한 것 먼저</u>. 이론상으로 이것은 매우 명확해 보인다. 그러나 일상의 삶에서 이것은 다소 다른 것 같다. 당신은 우선순위를 결정하려고 시도했을지도 모른다. 하지만 당신은 일상의 사소한 문제와 예측하지 못한 방해요소들로 인해 실패했을 것이다. 예를 들어, 다른 사무실로 탈출하여 산만한 상황들에서 벗어나라. 당신이 당신의 우선순위에 있는 한 가지 과제에 집중할 때, 당신은 심지어 당신이 갖고 있으면서도 알지도 못했던 당신의 에너지를 발견할 것이다.

① 바쁠수록 좋다
② 안 하는 것보다 늦게라도 하는 것이 낫다
③ 눈에서 멀어지면 마음에서도 멀어진다
④ 가장 중요한 것이 먼저다

16 ③

abundance : 풍부
fluctuation : 변동
fishery : 어장
mackerel : 고등어
sustainable : 유지 가능한
blue whale : 흰 긴수염 고래
halibut : 큰 넙치
deplete : 고갈시키다

과학자들의 도움으로 상업적 어업은 어획을 계속하려면 과학적으로 수행해야 한다는 사실을 알아냈다. 물고기 개체 수에 대한 어획의 압력이 없다면, 물고기의 개체 수는 예측 가능한 풍부한 수준에 도달하고 그대로 유지될 것이다. 유일한 변동은 음식의 가용성, 적절한 온도 등과 같은 자연적인 환경 요인 때문일 것이다. 만일 어업이 이러한 물고기를 잡도록 발전하고, 어획량이 적다면, 그것의 개체 수는 유지될 수 있다. 북해의 고등어가 좋은 예이다. 우리가 매년 어업을 늘리고 물고기를 더 많이 잡는다면, 해마다 우리가 잡는 모든 물고기를 대체할 수 있는 이상적인 수준 이하로 개체 수를 줄이지 않도록 주의해야 한다. 만약 우리가 '최대 유지 생산량'이라고 하는 이러한 수준에서 물고기를 어획한다면, 우리는 가능한 최대의 생산량을 매년 유지할 수 있다. 너무 많이 잡는다면 우리가 어업을 할 수 없게 되기까지 물고기의 수는 매년 줄어들 것이다. 과도하게 남획된 물고기의 사례로는 대서양의 흰 긴수염 고래와 북대서양의 넙치가 있다. 최대 연간 산출량을 유지하기 위해 꼭 정확한 양의 물고기를 잡는 것은 과학인 동시에 기술이다. 우리로 하여금 물고기

개체 수를 더 잘 이해하고 개체 수를 고갈시키지 않으면서 최대한 활용하는 방법에 대한 연구는 끊임없이 진행되고 있다.

① 상업적 어업을 거부하라
② 수산업으로 간주되는 양식 어업
③ 어업에 과학이 필요한 이유는 무엇인가?
④ 남획된 물고기들 : 불법 어업의 사례들

17 ①

tactical : 전술적인
thereby : 그렇게 함으로써
take place : 발생하다
ensure : 반드시 ~하게 하다, 보장하다
coverage : 보도
significant : 중요한
empire : 제국

테러는 정말 효과가 있는 것인가? 9·11 테러는 알카에다에게는 엄청난 전술상의 성공이었는데, 그 이유 중 하나는 세계의 미디어 수도와 미국의 실제 수도에서 일어난 공격들과 관련있었기 때문이었고, (A) <u>그것으로 인해</u> 이 사건의 가능한 한 가장 광범위한 보도를 보장했기 때문이다. 만약 테러가 많은 사람들이 보고 싶어하는 극장의 한 형태라면 9·11 테러보다 인류 역사상 더 많은 전 세계 관객들에게 알려진 사건은 없었을 것이다. 그 당시에는 9·11 테러가 진주만 공격과 얼마나 유사한지에 대해 많은 논의가 있었다. 그것들은 둘 다 미국을 심각한 전쟁으로 몰아 넣은 기습 공격이었기 때문에 정말 비슷했다. 하지만 그것들은 다른 의미에서도 비슷했다. 진주만 공격은 제국주의 일본의 커다란 전술적인 성공이었지만, 그 전략은 커다란 전략적 실패로 이어졌다. 진주만에서 4년 만에 일본 제국은 완전히 파괴되어 폐허가 되었다. (B) <u>마찬가지로</u> 9·11 테러는 알카에다에게 커다란 전술적 성공이었지만, 오사마 빈 라덴에게는 전략적으로 큰 실패로 판명되었다.

18 ①

human embryo : 인간 배아
descendant : 자손
germline : 생식세포계열
modification : 수정, 변경
eugenics : 우생학
weigh in : ~에 끼어들다, 거들다
endorse : 지지하다, 보증하다
embryo editing : 배아 수정
aim at : 겨냥하다
be wary of : ~을 조심하다

우리는 중국의 과학자들이 잠재적으로 치명적인 혈액 질병을 – 단지 아이에게서뿐만 아니라 아이의 자손 모두로부터 – 제거하기 위해 인간 배아를 변형시켰을 때 하나의 종으로서 새로운 국면에 접어들었다. 연구자들은 이 과정을 유전자 변형이라고 부른다. 언론은 "designer babies(맞춤 아기)"라고 부르길 좋아한다. 그러나 우리는 그것을 있는 그대로 "우생학"이라고 불러야 한다. 그리고 우리 인류는 그것을 사용하길 원하는지 아닌지 결정해야 한다. 지난달 미국의 과학계가 관여하였다. 국립 과학원과 국립 의학연구원 합동위원회는 "합리적 대안이 없을 때" 심각한 질병을 일으키는 유전자를 겨냥하는 배아 수정을 승인했다. 하지만 이미 건강한 아이들을 더 강하거나 더 키가 크게 만드는 것 같은 "향상"을 위한 수정에 대해 더 신중해야 한다. 위원회 측은 공개 토론을 권고하면서 "의사들은 이 시점에서 진행해서는 안 된다"고 말했다. 이 위원회는 신중을 강요할 충분한 이유가 있었다. 우생학의 역사는 억압과 불행으로 가득하다.

① 의사들은 향상을 위한 배아 수정을 즉시 진행할 것을 권고 받았다.
② 최근에 미국의 과학계가 우생학에 대한 논의를 시작했다.
③ 중국 과학자들은 심각한 혈액 질환을 예방하기 위해 인간 배아를 변형시켰다.
④ "Designer babies"는 일반 수정 과정에 대한 또 다른 용어이다.

19 ④

eliminate : 제거하다
brink : (어떤 상황이 발생하기) 직전, 끝, 벼랑
glorify : 미화하다, 찬미하다
wrestling : 레슬링
leather : 가죽
stud : 징, 못
gouge : 찌르다
contender : 경쟁자
collapse : 무너지다, 붕괴되다
surrender : 항복하다, 투항하다

고대 올림픽은 현대 경기와 마찬가지로 선수들에게 그들의 체력과 우월성을 증명할 수 있는 기회를 제공했다. ① 고대 올림픽 경기들은 약한 자들을 제거하고, 강한 자를 찬양하기 위해 만들어졌다. 우승자들은 벼랑으로 내몰렸다. ② 현 시대와 마찬가지로 사람들은 극한 스포츠를 좋아했다. 가장 좋아하는 경기들 중 하나가 33회 올림픽 경기에 추가되었다. 판크라티온이라는 것으로 레슬링과 복싱의 극단적인 조합이었다. 그리스어로 판크라티온은 전제적인 힘을 의미한다. 선수들은 징이 박힌 가죽 끈을 착용했는데 이것이 상대방을 처참하게 엉망으로 만들어버릴 수

있었다. ③ 이 위험한 형태의 레슬링은 시간과 체중 제한이 없었다. 이 경기에서는 오직 두 가지 규칙만이 적용되었다. 첫째, 레슬러는 엄지손가락으로 눈을 찌르는 것이 허용되지 않았다. 둘째로, 그들은 깨물 수 없었다. 그 외에는 어떤 것이라도 공정한 경기로 간주되었다. 그 경기는 권투와 동일한 방식으로 결정되었다. 경쟁자는 두 사람 중 하나가 쓰러질 때까지 경기를 계속했다. ④ 만일 어느 쪽도 항복하지 않으면, 두 사람은 한 사람이 쓰러질 때까지 주먹을 휘둘렀다. 가장 강하고 가장 결의 있는 선수들만이 이 경기에 참가했다. 상대의 손가락을 부러뜨려 "Mr. Fingertips"라는 별명을 얻은 선수와 레슬링 한다는 것을 상상해 보아라.

20 ①

rule over : 지배하다
in place of : ~를 대신하여
physics : 물리학
atomic : 원자의
fission bomb : 원자 폭탄
hydrogen : 수소
transcend : 초월하다
appendix : 맹장, 부록
empower : 권한을 주다

우리 시대에 자체적인 생명력을 가지고 인간을 지배하는 것은 시장의 법칙만 그런 것이 아니라 과학과 기술의 발전 역시 그러하다. 여러 가지 이유로, 오늘날 과학의 문제들과 구조는 과학자가 그의 문제점들을 선택하는 것이 아니라 문제점들이 과학자에게 그들 자신을 받아들이도록 강요하는 그런 것이다. 그가 하나의 문제를 해결하면, 그 결과로 그가 더 안심하고 확신하게 되는 것이 아니라 열 가지 다른 새로운 문제들이 해결된 한 문제를 대신하여 나타나게 된다. 그것들은 그 과학자에게 그것들을 해결할 것을 강요한다 ; 그는 전례 없이 빠른 속도로 계속해야 한다. 산업 기술 분야에서도 그렇다. 과학의 속도는 기술의 속도에도 영향을 준다. 이론 물리학은 우리에게 원자력 에너지를 강요한다 ; 원자 폭탄의 성공적인 생산은 우리에게 수소 폭탄 제조를 강요한다. 우리가 우리의 문제를 선택하지 않으며, 우리가 우리의 생산품을 선택하지 않는다. 우리는 강요받고, 강요받는다. – 무엇에 의해서? 그것을 초월하는 목표와 목적이 없는, 그리고 인간을 그것의 부속물로 만드는 시스템에 의해서.

① 인간을 그것의 부속물로 만드는
② 보안에 대한 거짓된 관념을 창조하는
③ 창조적인 도전 과제들로 인간에게 영감을 주는
④ 과학자들에게 시장 규칙을 통제할 권한을 주는

2018. 6. 23.
제2회 서울특별시 시행

1 ③

> **단 어**

disobedient : 반항하는, 거역하는
authority : 당국, 관계자
muzzle : 재갈을 물리다, 억압하다

> **해 석**

인간은 새로운 사상을 <u>퍼뜨리지 못하게 한</u> 정부 당국에도, 그리고 변화를 무의미한 것으로 선언한 오랫동안 확립된 의견의 권위에도 계속해서 복종하지 않았다.

① 표현하다, 나타내다　　② 주장하다
③ 진압하다, 억제하다　　④ 펼치다, 퍼뜨리다

2 ①

> **단 어**

pompous : 젠체하는, 거만한
informal : 일상적인, 편안한
colloquial : 구어의, 일상적인 대화체의
teaching assistant : 조교

> **해 석**

<u>잘난 척하지 마십시오.</u> 당신은 당신의 글이 너무 일상적인 구어체가 되는 것을 원하지 않겠지만, 예를 들어 여러분의 교수, 상사 같은 사람이나 로즈 장학생 조교 같이 당신이 아닌 다른 사람처럼 말하고 싶지도 않을 겁니다.

① 주제넘은, 건방진　　② 무심한, 평상시의
③ 정중한, 형식적인　　④ 진짜의, 진실한

3 ②

> **단 어**

call it a day : ~을 그만하기로 하다
initiate : 개시되게 하다, 착수시키다

> **해 석**

외과 의사들은 그들의 일에 적합한 도구를 찾을 수 없었기 때문에 어쩔 수 없이 그 날 일을 끝낼 수밖에 없었다.

4 ③

> **단 어**

reservation : 예약

> **해 석**

① A ; 내일 날짜로 예약을 하려고 합니다.
　 B ; 물론이죠. 시간을 말씀해 주시겠어요?
② A ; 주문하시겠습니까?
　 B ; 네, 수프를 주시겠어요.
③ A ; 리소토는 어떤가요?
　 B ; <u>네, 버섯과 치즈를 곁들인 리소토가 있습니다.</u>
④ A ; 후식 드시겠습니까?
　 B ; 전 괜찮습니다. 감사합니다.

5 ②

> **단 어**

alter : 변하다, 바꾸다
discussion : 논의

> **해 석**

1961년 독립 이후 수년 간 그의 생존은 실질적인 정책 결정에 대한 공개적인 논의가 거의 일어나지 않았다는 사실을 바꾸지 않는다. 사실, Nyerere가 국가집행위원회를 통해 논쟁해 왔던 많은 중요한 정책에는 항상 문제가 있었다.

> **TIP**

② hardly 자체에 '거의 ~ 아니다'라는 부정의 의미가 포함되어 있기 때문에 never와 같은 부정부사를 중복하여 쓰지 않는다.

6 ③

> **단 어**

fall ill : 병에 걸리다
mostly : 주로, 일반적으로

> **해 석**

지난 3주 동안 주로 홍콩과 베트남에 사는 150명 이상의 사람들이 병에 걸렸다. 전문가들은 중국 광동성에 사는 다른 300명의 사람들이 11월 중순부터 같은 병을 앓고 있는 것으로 의심하고 있다.

> **TIP**

① have fell ill → have fallen ill
　 fall-fell-fallen으로 형태 변화가 일어난다.

② are suspected → suspect/have suspected

주어 experts가 주체가 되어 행하는 것이므로 능동이어야 한다. 또한 suspect는 진행형으로는 쓰이지 않으므로 전체 문맥에 맞게 현재형 또는 현재완료형으로 나타낸다.

③ another 자체로는 단수개념을 가진 명사이지만, 다른 명사를 꾸며주는 형용사로 쓰일 때는 복수명사 역시 수식할 수 있다. 300이라는 수에 맞춰 복수명사 people이 왔고 '또다른 300명'의 뜻이 되었다.

④ begin in → beginning

that절 안에서 동사는 had이므로 또다시 본동사 형태로 올 수 없다. 형용사구나 부사구 형태로 바꿔줘야 한다. beginning in mid-November로 표현하여 '11월 중순부터 시작하여'라는 뜻으로 나타낼 수 있다.

7 ④

단어

counter-aggression : 반격
coercive : 강압적인
aversive : 혐오의, 회피적인
elicit : (반응을) 끌어내다
perpetuate : 영구화하다, 영속시키다

해석

사회적 학습 이론가들은 가정에서 폭력을 경험한 아이들이 보이는 반격행동에 대해 다른 설명을 제시한다. 공격적인 행동과 강압적인 가족에 대한 광범위한 연구는 피하려고 한 결과가 오히려 공격적인 반응을 이끌어 내고 계속적인 강압 행동을 가속화할 수도 있다는 결론을 내린다. 공격적인 행동의 피해자들은 모델링을 통해 결국 공격적인 행동교환을 시작하도록 배운다. 이러한 사건들은 공격적인 행동의 사용을 영속시키고 아이들에게 어른으로서 행동하는 방법을 훈련시킨다.

① 멈추다
② 약화시키다, 희석시키다
③ 혐오하다
④ 착수시키다, 접하게 하다

8 ③

단어

a close-knit : 긴밀하게 조직된 공동체
pious : 경건한, 독실한
orthodox : 정통의, 전통적인
Jewish : 유대인의, 유대교인인
philosophy : 철학
supervision : 감독, 지휘
take trouble : 수고하다, 노고를 아끼지 않다
nephew : 조카

retain : 간직하다, 보유하다
utmost : 최고의, 극도의
admiration : 감탄, 존경
doctrinaire : 교조적인

해석

프랑스 사회학자인 마르셀 모스는 로레인의 에피날(보주)에서 태어났는데, 그곳에서 그는 친족들로 이루어진 경건하며 정통적인 유대인 가정에서 자랐다. 에밀 뒤르켐은 그의 삼촌이었다. 18살까지 모스는 유대적 신앙에 반대하는 반응을 나타냈다. 그는 결코 종교인이 아니었다. 그는 보르도에서 뒤르켐의 지휘 아래 철학을 공부했다. 뒤르켐은 조카의 학업을 지도하는 데 끊임없이 매진하였으며 심지어 모스에게 가장 유용할 것 같은 강의 주제를 선택했다. 그래서 모스는 처음에는 (대부분의 초기 뒤르켐주의자들과 마찬가지로) 철학자였으며, 철학에 대한 신념은 무엇보다도, 그가 항상 최고로 존경했던 뒤르켐에게 직접 영향을 받았다.

① 그는 유대인 출생이다.
② 그는 삼촌의 지도를 받았다.
③ 그는 교리를 믿었다.
④ 그는 철학적 배경을 가진 사회학자였다.

9 ④

단어

satisfy : 충족시키다, 채우다
gradually : 서서히

해석

ⓓ 사람들이 나무를 베는 것에는 새로울 것이 없다. 고대에는 그리스, 이탈리아 그리고 영국이 숲으로 덮여 있었다. 수 세기를 거치면서 그 숲들은 서서히 축소되었다. 지금까지 거의 남아 있는 것이 없다.

ⓐ 하지만 오늘날 나무들은 훨씬 더 빠르게 잘려 나가고 있다. 매년 약 2백 만 에이커 면적의 숲이 벌채되고 있다. 그것은 영국 전체의 면적과 동일하다.

ⓒ 나무를 베는 데는 중요한 이유가 있지만, 지구상의 생명체에는 위험한 결과가 따르기도 한다. 현재 파괴의 주요 원인은 목재에 대한 전 세계적인 수요이다. 산업화된 국가에서는 사람들이 종이를 사용하기 위해 목재를 점점 더 많이 사용하고 있다.

ⓑ 이 나라들에는 수요를 충족시킬 만큼 목재가 충분하지 않다. 따라서 목재 회사들은 아시아, 아프리카, 남미, 심지어 시베리아의 숲에서 목재를 벌채하기 시작했다.

10 ①

단어

contemporary : 현대의, 당대의
fresh from : ~를 갓 나온
integral : 필수적인, 완전한
enthusiasm : 열광, 열정
surly : 성질 못된, 무례한

해석

현대 미술은 실제로 오늘날 중산층 사회의 필수적인 부분이 되었다. 심지어 스튜디오에서 갓 나온 예술 작품들에도 열광하게 된다. 그들은 꽤 빨리 인정받게 되는데, 무례한 비평가들 취향에 비해 너무 빠르다. 물론, 모든 작품을 즉시 구입할 수 있는 것은 아니지만, 확실히 새로운 예술 작품을 구입하는 것을 즐기는 사람들의 수가 증가하고 있다. 빠르고 값비싼 자동차 대신 그들은 젊은 예술가들의 그림, 조각품, 사진 작품을 산다. 그들은 현대 미술이 그들의 사회적 명성을 높여 준다는 것을 안다. 게다가, 예술은 자동차처럼 마모와 파손에 노출되지 않기 때문에, 훨씬 더 나은 투자이다.

11 ④

단어

prerequisite : 전제 조건
fertilization : 수정, 수태
pollination : 수분
breed : 재배하다, 새끼를 낳다

해석

수정을 위한 전제 조건으로, 수분은 과일과 종자식물의 생산에 필수적이며, 번식을 통해 식물을 개량하기 위해 고안된 프로그램에서 중요한 역할을 한다.

① 중대한, 결정적인　　② 필수적인
③ 필요한, 필수품　　④ 편재하는, 어디에나 있는

12 ④

단어

object to : ~에 반대하다
proposal : 제안, 제의
principle : 원칙, 신조

해석

존슨 씨는 그 제안이 잘못된 원칙에 근거하고 있다는 이유로, 그리고 때때로 불편하다는 이유로 반대했다.

① 불완전한, 잘못된 - 바람직한, 가치있는

② 긴요한, 위엄 있는 - 합리적인, 적정한
③ 따르는, 순응하는 - 개탄스러운
④ 잘못된, 틀린 - 불편한, 곤란한

13 ③

단어

fit : 맞다, 가봉하다

해석

나는 내가 충분한 옷을 가지고 있어서 기쁘다. 미국 사람들은 일반적으로 일본 사람들보다 커서 시카고에서 나에게 맞는 옷을 찾기가 매우 어렵다. 일본에서의 M사이즈가 여기에서는 S사이즈이다.

TIP

① please는 동사로 쓰일 때 '~을 기쁘게 하다'라는 뜻을 가진다. 주어(I)가 기쁜 것이므로 be pleased 형태를 써서 주어의 감정을 나타낸다.
② 뒤에 나오는 to find clothes~가 보어 difficult의 진주어이므로 가주어 it을 쓴 것이 맞다.
③ fits → fit
that fits me 관계사절에서 선행사는 clothes이다. 복수명사이므로 동사 역시 수 일치시켜 fit으로 고쳐준다.
④ what is medium size in Japan까지가 주어이며 명사절이다. what은 선행사 없이 명사절을 이끌 수 있으므로 맞는 표현이다.

14 ④

단어

heartbroken : 비통해 하는
extent : 정도, 크기

해석

BBC가 제작한 자연 다큐멘터리인 블루 플래닛 II는 플라스틱이 어느 정도까지 바다에 영향을 미치는지 보여 준 후 시청자들에게 비통함을 남겼다.

TIP

① 삽입구에서 a nature documentary를 수식하는 것으로, 과거분사형 produced로 써서 수동의 의미를 잘 나타내었다.
② leave는 5형식의 형태로 쓰일 때 '(목적어)를 (목적보어)한 상태로 있게 놔두다'라는 뜻이며 목적보어에는 to부정사, 동명사, 형용사 등이 올 수 있다. left viewers heartbroken에서 viewers의 목적보어로 heartbroken 형용사가 왔다.

③ plastic affects the ocean to the extent에서 the extent는 선행사로 쓰이고 관계사절 which로 연결되었다. the extent which plastic affects the ocean to에서 전치사 to는 관계사 which 앞에 위치할 수 있다.
④ affects on → affects
affect는 그 자체로서 '~에 영향을 미치다'라는 뜻을 가진 타동사로 전치사 없이 바로 목적어를 취한다.

15 ①

단어

preparation : 준비
Quincentenary Jubilee : 500주년 기념일
anniversary : 기념일
harbinger : 조짐
reckless : 무모한, 난폭한
exploitation : 착취
slavery : 노예제도
reinforce : 보강하다, 강화하다
reversal : 반전, 역전
revealing : 흥미로운 사실을 드러내는
integrate : 통합시키다, 통합되다
divinely : 거룩하게
ordain : (성직자로) 임명하다

해석

그러나 '500주년 기념일'을 준비하면서 1980년대에 명확해진 것은 많은 미국인들이 그 기념일을 '기념일'로 보는 것이, 불가능한 것은 아니지만, 힘들다는 것을 발견하게 되었다는 것이다. 콜럼버스의 유산을 기념할 만한 것은 아무것도 없었다. 많은 비평가들에 따르면, 콜럼버스는 진보와 문명의 선구자가 아니라 노예제도와 환경의 무모한 착취의 선구자였다.

① 많은 비평가들에 따르면, 콜럼버스는 진보와 문명의 선구자가 아니라 노예제도와 환경의 무모한 착취의 선구자였다.
② 1893년 시카고 세계 박람회는 미국의 발견과 진보의 힘 사이에 서술적인 관련성을 강화시켰다.
③ 19세기 콜럼버스의 신화의 이러한 반전은 흥미로운 사실을 보여주고 있다.
④ 따라서 콜럼버스는 미국의 진보가 거룩하게 이루어졌다는 믿음인 매니 페스트 운명에 통합되었다.

16 ③

단어

imprisonment : 투옥, 감금
run-down : 황폐한
rodent : 설치류
be supposed to : ~하기로 되어 있다, ~할 의무가 있다

해석

그의 아버지가 투옥된 후, 찰스 디킨스는 학교를 떠나 템즈 강 옆에 있는 구두 닦는 공장에서 일할 수밖에 없었다. 폐허가 되고 설치류가 들끓는 공장에서, 디킨스는 벽난로를 청소하는 데 사용되는 물질인 "블래킹" 항아리에 라벨을 붙이면서 일주일에 6실링을 벌었다. 그게 그가 가족을 부양하는 것을 도울 수 있는 최선이었다. 그 경험을 돌아보면서 디킨스는 "그가(디킨스 자신이) 그렇게 너무 쉽게 버려질 수 있는가"에 대해 의아해하면서 그 시절을 어린 시절의 순수함에 작별을 고하는 순간으로 보았다. 그는 자신을 돌봐줄 의무가 있었던 어른들에게 배신감을 느꼈다.

① 버려진, 유기된   ② 배신당한, 저버린
③ 지지된, 힘을 실어 주는   ④ 무시된, 묵살된

17 ④

단어

adopt : 입양하다, 채택하다
handle : 다루다, 만지다
disability : 장애
abuse : 학대하다
neglect : 방치하다
prospective : 곧 있을, 유망한
foster : 위탁 양육하다
temporary : 일시적인, 임시의

해석

아이를 입양하고 싶어하는 가정은 먼저 입양 기관을 선택해야 한다. 미국에는 입양을 돕는 두 종류의 기관이 있다. 공공 기관은 일반적으로 나이 든 어린이, 정신적 또는 신체적 장애가 있는 어린이, 또는 학대 당하거나 방치된 어린이들을 다루고 있다. 곧 아이를 입양할 부모들은 공공 기관에서 아이를 입양할 때 보통은 비용을 지불할 것으로 예상하지 않는다. 임시 입양의 형태인 위탁 양육 역시 공공 에이전시를 통해 가능하다. 민간 기관은 인터넷에서 찾을 수 있다. 그들은 국내와 국제 입양을 다룬다.

① 공공 입양 기관은 민간 기관보다 낫다.
② 부모들은 위탁 가정으로부터 아동을 입양하기 위해 엄청난 비용을 지불한다.
③ 도움이 필요한 아이들은 공공 기관을 통해 입양될 수 없다.
④ 민간 기관은 국제 입양을 위해 연락될 수 있다.

18 ①

단 어 ·

moth : 나방
Lepidoptera : 인시목(나비나 나방류를 포함하는 곤충강의 한 목)
numerous : 많은
diurnal : 주행성의
flatten : 반반하게 만들다
spread : 펼치다

해 석

나방과 나비는 모두 인시목에 속하지만 두 곤충 유형 사이에는 많은 물리적 및 행동상의 차이가 있다. 행동 측면에서, 나방은 <u>야행성</u>이고 나비는 주행성(낮에 활동적인)이다. 휴식을 취하는 동안, 나비는 보통 날개를 뒤로 접는 반면, 나방은 날개를 몸에 반반하게 만들거나 "제트기" 자세로 날개를 펼친다.

① 야행성의　　② 합리적인　　③ 영원한　　④ 반원형의

19 ③

단 어 ·

clown : 광대
frightening : 무서운
lure : 유인하다
violence : 폭행, 폭력
sighting : 목격

해 석

광대가 사람들을 무섭게 한다는 생각이 미국에서 힘을 얻기 시작했다. 예를 들어, 사우스캐롤라이나 주에서는 사람들이 종종 밤에 광대 복장을 하고 숲속이나 도시에 숨어있는 이상한 사람들을 보았다고 보고했다. 어떤 사람들은 광대들이 아이들을 빈 집이나 숲으로 유인하려 한다고 말했다. 곧, 어린이와 어른들 모두를 무섭게 하려는 위협적인 모습을 한 광대에 대한 보고가 있었다. 일반적으로 폭력에 대한 보고는 없었고, 보고된 많은 목격들이 나중에 거짓인 것으로 밝혀졌지만, 이것은 <u>전국적으로 공황을 일으켰다.</u>

① 서커스 산업에 이득이 되었다.
② 광고에 광대의 사용을 장려했다.
③ 전국적으로 공황을 일으켰다.
④ 행복한 광대의 완벽한 이미지를 형성했다.

20 ②

단 어 ·

impose : 부과하다
blatant : 노골적인, 뻔한
breach : 위반, 파기
non-intervention : 내정 불간섭, 불개입
institution : 기구, 제도
referenda : (referendum의 복수형) 국민 투표, 총선거
legitimize : 정당화하다
dictatorship : 독재 국가
restraint : 규제
consensus : 의견 일치, 합의
confrontation : 대립

해 석

우리의 민주주의 체제가 최고라고 믿는 것과 다른 나라에 그것을 강요하는 것은 전혀 다른 문제다. 이것은 독립 국가의 국내 문제에 개입하지 않는다는 유엔 정책에 대한 노골적인 위반이다. 서구 시민들이 그들의 정치 제도를 위해 싸운 것처럼, 다른 나라의 시민들도 원한다면 그렇게 할 것이라고 믿어야 한다. 민주주의는 절대적인 용어도 아니다. – 나폴레옹은 오늘날 서아프리카와 동남아시아의 지도자들처럼 권력 장악을 정당화하기 위해 선거와 투표를 이용하였다. 국내 질서를 유지하는 것에 너무 많은 관심을 두는 완전히 비선출적인 독재국가들보다 부분적인 민주주의를 취하고 있는 국가들이 종종 더 공격적이다. 민주주의의 서로 다른 유형들은 어떤 규범을 도입할지 결정하는 것을 불가능하게 한다. 미국과 유럽 국가들은 정부에 대한 규제 면과 합의와 대립 사이의 균형 면에서 모두 다르다.

① 남의 떡이 더 커 보인다.
② 갑의 약은 을에게는 독이 된다(사람마다 기호가 다르다).
③ 예외 없는 법칙 없다.
④ 로마에 가면 로마법에 따르라.

2018. 8. 25.
국회사무처 시행

---

1 ②

단 어 ·

peculiar : 특유한

해 석

우리는 민주주의 시대에 살고 있다. 지난 세기를 걸쳐 세계는 모든 것들을 뛰어 넘어 '민주주의의 대두'라는 한 가지 트렌드로 틀이 잡혀졌다. 1900년대에 어떤 한 국가도 오늘날 우리가 민주주

의라고 생각하는 부분, – 예를 들면 성인인 시민이 투표해서 선거로 세워진 정부 – 을 갖고 있지 못했다. 오늘날 이것은 전 세계 60% 이상의 국가에서 행해지고 있다. 한때 대서양 북부 근처 몇몇 주들의 고유한 관례였던 것이 인류 정부의 표준 형태가 된 것이다.

✓ **TIP**

every adult citizen could vote in elections에서 elections가 생략되었으므로 in which가 되어야 한다.

2 ⑤

단어 ·

grapple : 붙잡고 싸우다

해석

그는 운이 없는 피해자를 <u>붙잡고 싸우기</u> 위해 군중 속으로 뛰어들었다.

① 확인하다
② 회피하다
③ 환기시키다
④ 착취하다
⑤ 움켜잡다, 폭력으로 장악하다

3 ④

단어 ·

conciliatory : 회유하기 위한
compensation : 보상

해석

사과나 보상을 하는 것 같은 회유의 행동들은 충돌 후 화를 달래고 용서를 베풀도록 하는 것으로 나타났다.

① 장담하는
② 처벌을 위한
③ 아첨하는
④ 달래주는
⑤ 묵인하는

4 ⑤

단어 ·

opulent : 부유한
renowned : 유명한

해석

영국의 호화로운 바닷가 마을 중 한 곳에 집을 마련하는 것은 적당히 부유한 사람들 조차 오랫동안 어림없는 일이었다. 하지만 작년 일 년 동안 가장 세련된 리조트 두 곳에서 집값이 상당히 폭락한 것으로 보인다. Halifax에 따르면 Devon 남쪽의 Salcombe의 보트선착장에서도 8.2%가 떨어졌고, 또 Dorset에 있는 영국에서 가장 비싼 리조트로 유명한 Sandbanks에서 그 값이 5.6% 하락했다.

✓ **TIP**

문장의 주어는 prices이고, 밑줄 친 부분은 본동사가 되어야 한다. 작년 동안 집값이 연속적으로 하락하고 있는 사실을 나타내고 있으므로 have p.p로 나타내어 have been down 이 옳다.

5 ③

단어 ·

adorn : 꾸미다
norm : 규범

해석

남성들은 항상 관심을 끌고 개인적인 과시욕을 채우기 위해 패션을 이용해왔다. 여성들만 그들의 신체를 향상시키고 꾸미고, 달라보이게 하기 위해 옷에 의지한 것이 아니다. 그럼에도 불구하고 사회적 규범은 오랫동안 패션에 대한 남자들의 관심이 <u>세심하게 균형 잡히기</u>를 요구해왔다. 패션과 외모에 관한 너무 과한 관심은 허영뿐 아니라 남자답지 못하다고 이해되는데, 반대로 너무 관심이 없어도 똑같이 미심쩍게 여겨진다.

① 철저히 문서화 된
② 완전히 제거된
③ 세심하게 균형이 잡힌
④ 본래부터 무시된
⑤ 공정하게 보상받은

✓ **TIP**

패션에 관한 과한 관심과 부족함 모두 지양되기를 요구되는 사회규범이 마지막에 설명되었으므로, carefully balanced 가 알맞다.

6 ①

☑ 해석

거의 모든 아기들은 아주 어린 나이에서 웃기 시작한다. 어떤 사람은 아기들이 다른 사람을 관찰하고 그들이 보게 되는 얼굴 표정을 따라하면서 웃는 것을 배운다고 생각할지도 모르지만 증거가 이런 생각을 부정한다. 한 연구에서 2004년 장애인올림픽 경기에서 메달을 받은 운동선수들 세 그룹의 얼굴 표정을 비교했다. 한 그룹은 선천적으로 시각 장애를 가지고 있었고, 두 번째 그룹은 이제는 완전히 시각 장애를 가지고 있지만, 몇 년 동안은 시각적으로 경험을 했었고, 세 번째 그룹은 정상적인 시각을 가지고 있었다. 그 연구는 이 그룹들 사이에 얼굴 표정의 <u>차이</u>가 기본적으로 없었다고 밝혔다.

① 차이   ② 변화
③ 경기   ④ 영향
⑤ 연결

☑ TIP

빈칸의 내용은 아기들이 타인의 미소를 시각적으로 관찰하고 모방했을 것이라는 주장을 반박하는 내용이므로 세 집단 간의 '차이'가 없는 것이 적절하다.

7 ⑤

단 어

obligated : 의무가 있는
pursuit : 취미

☑ 해석

"여가"는 우리가 일이나 생활비를 벌어야 하는 책임에서 자유로운 시점인 "의무가 없는 상태"를 지칭한다. (A) <u>따라서</u>, 집에 학생들의 과제를 점수 매기려고 가져온 한 선생님은 여가활동과 관련 없는 사람이다. 또한 잔디 깎기와 장보기도 여가활동이 아니다. 왜냐하면 그것들은 필수적인 유지 업무이기 때문이다. (B) <u>반면에</u> 야구경기에 참여하기, 상점에서 윈도쇼핑, 영화 보러 가기, 연못에서 오리 먹이주기가 여가활동이다. 왜냐하면 우리가 이런 것들은 꼭 해야 할 의무가 있는 것이 아니기 때문이다.

☑ TIP

   (A)   /   (B)
⑤ Thus 따라서 / On the other hand 반면에

8 ②

단 어

gigantic : 거대한
statistically : 통계상으로
bias : 성향
let alone : ～은 고사하고
correlation : 연관성
impediment : 장애

☑ 해석

데이터는 폭설의 만큼이나, 빠른 속도로 거대한 양으로 쌓이고 있다. 당신은 좋다고 생각할 수도 있다. 더 많은 자료는 더 많이 믿을만한 통찰을 의미한다고 말이다. 하지만 현실에서는 매우 많은 양의 자료가 꼭 실행력 있는 통찰을 의미하지는 않는다. 때론 당신이 모든 정보를 담고 있는 자료를 갖고 있다 하더라도, 통계상으로 그것들은 <u>당신이 분석해야 하는 자료를 대표하는 표본</u>이 아니다. 예를 들어, 트위터의 의견들과 인류전반에 걸친 사람들의 의견들이 그러하다. 이전의 성향들은 고사하고, 전체 인구의 관점조차 포함하지 못한다. 예를 들어 노인들이나 성격이 내성적인 사람들은 자주 포함되지 못한다. 이런 식으로 당신은 쉽게 잘못된 분석결과를 얻게 된다. 그밖에 '폭설'과 같이 쉽게 말해 어쨌든 쓸모가 없는 자료를 제거하느라, 당신이 필요로 하는 것을 찾는 것은 더 힘들어진다.

① 인구와의 연관성을 찾기 충분히 최신식
② 당신이 분석해야 하는 자료를 대표하는 표본
③ 지정된 문제를 해결하는 당신의 방법에서 장애물
④ 정리된 정보로 인하여 중요한 결론에 이르도록 분석할 수 있는
⑤ 일부 핵심정보가 이미 제거되어졌기 때문에 완전한

☑ TIP

본문 전반적으로 정보가 아무리 많더라도 그 점이 당신이 생각한 만큼 좋은 것은 아니라는 결론지어지고 있다. 따라서 갖고 있는 많은 정보가 찾고 있는 표본이 아닐 확률이 높기 때문에 ②번이 알맞다.

9 ③

단 어

hasten : 서둘러 하다
utterly : 완전히
benign : 유순한
banish : 제거하다
void : ～이 전혀 없는
indecipherable : 이해할 수 없는
margin : 여백
benevolent : 자애로운

☑ 해 석 ⌐⌐⌐⌐⌐⌐⌐⌐⌐

옛 시대의 세계지도들은 탐험되어야 할 빈자리를 환상의 생명체들, 용들, 바다괴물들, 날개달린 무서운 야수들로 채우곤 했었다. 인간의 심성은 그렇게 많은 공백을 참을 수 없었다. 우리가 알지 못하는 곳, 우리가 지어낸 곳, 우리가 지어낸 것은 우리가 알지 못하는 것에 대한 두려움을 반영한다. 요정들은 그런 두려움으로 탄생한다. 마을 지도에 있는 알지 못하는 곳들 역시 채워져야 했다. 나무, 산, 바다, 개울로는 결코 지도를 채울 수 없다는 사실을 직면할 때, 인간은 빈자리를 알게 됐고, 그 공백은 여러 다른 이름이 주어진 존재들의 다양성으로 서둘러 채웠다. 그렇더라도 요정같이 모든 알아볼 수 있는 형태로 말이다. 우리가 아는 요정들은 전구, 고속도로, 휴대전화가 인적이 드문 시골의 공포를 사라지게 하는 오늘날이 되어서야 아주 유순하게 되었다. 유순한 요정에 익숙해졌기 때문에, 우리가 과거의 요정들을 이해하기는 아주 힘든 일이다.

① 인간은 비어있고 채워지지 않은 것을 보고 싶어하지 않는다.
② 요정은 자연에 있는 이해할 수 없는 것들에 대한 인간의 공포를 반영한다.
③ 요정에 대한 인간의 인식은 역사적으로 큰 변화는 없었다.
④ 지도의 여백들은 보통 환상의 생명체들로 꾸며진다.
⑤ 자애로운 요정들에 대한 생각은 아주 현대적이다.

☑ TIP

본문에서 요정들은 인간의 두려움을 바탕으로 만들어졌지만, 문물의 발달로 그 두려움이 사라지고 존재가 유순해졌다고 언급하고 있으므로 ③번 글의 내용과 거리가 멀다.

10 ①

☑ 해 석 ⌐⌐⌐⌐⌐⌐⌐⌐⌐

A : 너 오늘 시장에 갈거니?
B : 아니. 오늘 병원에 가야 해. 왜? 뭔가가 필요하니?
A : <u>오, 신경 쓰지마.</u> 내가 내일 갈게.
B : 아니야, 집에 가는 길에 시장에 들러도 돼.

① 오, 신경 쓰지마.
② 응. 나도 병원에 가야 해.
③ 아니, 나는 필요한건 없어.
④ 달걀 좀 사다줄 수 있니?
⑤ 달걀을 좀 사다준다면 고맙겠어.

☑ TIP 마지막 문장 B의 대답으로 보아 A는 B가 신경 쓰지 않고 자신의 계획대로 하길 바랐을 것이다. 따라서 ①번이 적절한 표현이다.

11 ③

단 어 ·

laudable : 칭찬할 만한

☑ 해 석 ⌐⌐⌐⌐⌐⌐⌐⌐⌐

의사들이 건강을 향상시키고 생명을 보존해 준다고 기대해서, 죽음에 대한 의학적 저항은 완전 <u>칭찬할 만한</u> 것으로 보인다.

① 눈을 뗄 수 없는   ② 두려움을 모르는
③ 칭찬할 만한   ④ 대담한
⑤ 현명한

12 ②

☑ 해 석 ⌐⌐⌐⌐⌐⌐⌐⌐⌐

결국 민주주의는 단지 일련의 관행이 아니라 문화이다. 민주주의는 정당과 무기명투표와 같은 공식적인 구조일 뿐 아니라, 직감과 시민들의 기대 속에서 행해진다. 직업, 전쟁, 외국과의 경쟁 같은 객관적인 상황은 정치적 문화로 형태를 갖추며, 지도자들의 말과 행동 역시 마찬가지이다.

☑ TIP

② in so formal mechanisms은 명사구로서 such+명사구로 사용되어야 하므로 in such formal mechanism이 되어야 한다.

13 ④

☑ 해 석 ⌐⌐⌐⌐⌐⌐⌐⌐⌐

① 당신이 요청했던 문서 파일이 첨부되어 있습니다.
② 내 인생에서 그런 아름다운 여인을 본적이 없다.
③ 더 많은 정보가 필요하다면 나에게 연락 주세요.
④ 그 상황은 지금보다 더 심각해질 수 없어요.
⑤ 지금이 당신이 항상 꿈꿔오던 삶을 살기 시작할 때다.

☑ TIP

④ Hardly has the situation more serious than now는 부정어구 도치구문으로 the situation 의 동사로 내용상 현재완료가 사용되어야 하고 more serious가 형용사이므로 been이 자리해야 한다. Hardly has the situation been more serious than now가 알맞다.

14 ⑤

단 어 •

inertia : 타성, 관성

inert : 기력이 없는

fervor : 열정

해 석

타성이 당신의 삶에 자리잡는 것을 바라지 않을 것이다. 나는 당신이 자신을 <u>무기력한</u> 상태로 둔다면 당신의 목표를 포기하게 될 거라고 강력히 말하고 싶다.

① 산만한   ② 취약한

③ 매력있는   ④ 무책임한

⑤ 무기력한

15 ①

단 어 •

anecdote : 일화

cohesion : 화합

abound : 풍부하다

delve into : ~을 철저히 조사하다

throb : 고동치다

해 석

코끼리에 대한 일화에는 집단 내 유대감과 그들의 충성심에 대한 사례가 (A) <u>아주 많이 있다.</u> 이런 종류의 단란함을 유지하기 위해서는 좋은 의사소통 시스템을 필요로 한다. 우리는 이제 겨우 이 시스템이 (B) <u>얼마나</u> 복잡하고 광범위한지 그 진가를 알아보기 시작했다. 연구가 Katharine Payne은 포틀랜드에 있는 워싱턴 동물원을 방문한 이후로 처음 코끼리의 의사소통을 철저히 조사하기 시작했다. 그녀는 코끼리 우리에 서서 공기가 (C) <u>고동치는</u> 진동을 느끼기 시작했고, 잠시 후 그 요동이 코끼리들 때문이라는 것을 깨달았다. Katharine은 그 무언가를 느낀 후 초저주파 불가음이라 불리는 초저파수 소리형태 연구를 시작했다.

① (A)abound 풍부하다 / (B)how 얼마나 / (C)throbbing 고동치는

TIP

(A) abound는 '아주 많다, 풍부하다'의 의미를 가진 자동사로 능동의 형태로 쓴다.

(B) How가 이끄는 의문절이 간접의문문 형태로 삽입되면서, 의문문의 본래 어순(How+형용사+동사+주어)에서 주어와 동사가 서로 도치된 것이다.

(C) 의미상 진동이 '고동치는' 것이므로 능동의 의미를 갖도록 동명사 형태 throbbing을 써야 한다.

16 ④

해 석

당신이 만약 어딘가에 가거나 무언가를 하는데 어려움이 있다면, 포기하지 마라. 당신은 그저 최선의 해결책을 찾지 못했거나 맞는 사람을 아직 만나지 못한 것이다. 잘 될 리 없다고 말하는 사람들 말을 듣지 마라. <u>인내</u>가 성과를 낸다. 나는 내가 원하는 것이 불가능하다고 몇 번이나 들었는지 당신에게 말할 수는 없지만, 나중에 내가 포기하지 않고 계속했을 때 그것이 틀렸다는 것을 결국 증명하게 된다고 말할 수는 있다.

① 불안   ② 협력

③ 추측   ④ 인내

⑤ 관습

17 ③

단 어 •

complication : 문제, 합병증

defeatist : 패배주의자

reluctant : 꺼려하는

interpersonal : 인간관계에 관련된

해 석

평등과 사회정의는 우리가 다양한 사회에서 살아가고 일하며 그러한 다양성은 해결되어야 할 문제라기보다 귀중한 자산이라는 것을 인식하는 데에 달려있다. 하지만, 이것은 의사소통에 관한 약간의 복잡한 문제가 보인다. 이것은 의사소통이 사람들이 비슷하거나 적어도 비슷한 파장일 때 최고로 잘 이루어지는 것처럼 보이기 때문이다. 그렇다면 우리는 의사소통과 다양성 사이에 갈등이 있다는 것을 인정해야 한다. 우리는 쉽게 포기하는 사람이 되지 말고, 이런 갈등에 도전해봐야 한다. 이것은 다양성의 가치가 <u>효과적인 의사소통을 위하여 포기되면 안 된다</u>는 것을 의미한다.

① 사회적인 조화의 관점에서 인정되는 것이 꺼려진다.

② 다른 언어와 문화로 추구되어져야 한다.

③ 효과적인 의사소통을 위하여 포기되면 안 된다.

④ 인간관계에 관한 상호작용에서 작용하는 충돌이 생긴다.

⑤ 사회에서 우리의 의사소통 노력에 반하여 효과가 나타날 수 있다.

TIP

다양성이 의사소통과 상충할 수 없을 것 같지만, 사회적 평등과 정의를 위하여 포기하지 말고 추구해야 한다는 문맥을 따라 ③번이 가장 적절한 표현이다.

18 ⑤

단어 ·

ambiguous : 애매모호한
retiring : 내성적인

해석

회색은 검은색도 흰색도 아니지만 이 두 가지 반대색들의 조합이고 애매모호하며 정의되지 않는 색이다. 회색은 옅고 짙은 안개, 연기, 황혼기 같은 흐릿한 모양과 색의 상태를 나타낸다. 위아래 회색인 의상은 Virginia Woolf의 소설 '등대로'에서 Lily Briscoe처럼, 수수하고 내성적인 사람, 눈에 띄는 것을 선호하지 않는 사람 혹은 주변에 섞여 조용히 있던 혹은 그것을 바라는 그런 사람들을 나타낼 수 있다. 더 활기차고 예쁜 소녀가 방으로 들어왔을 때, 서술자는 Lily Briscoe가 "작은 회색 드레스를 입고서 평소보다 <u>더 눈에 안 띄게 되었다</u>"라고 말했다.

① 더 낭랑한, 공감을 일으키는
② 더 구별되는
③ 더 침울한
④ 더 교양 있는
⑤ 눈에 더욱 잘 안 띄는

TIP

회색의 이미지와 비슷한 lily Briscoe가 활기차고 예쁜 소녀와 대조적으로 눈에 띄지 않았다는 내용이 자연스럽기 때문에, ⑤번이 적절한 표현이다.

19 ②

단어 ·

barrage : 연속

해석

많은 사람들에게 대학의 요구들은 그들이 여태껏 직면한 가장 큰 시험대이다. 매일 학생들은 그들이 늘 마감기간을 맞추기 위해 완전히 이해해야 하는 쏟아지는 새로운 개념에 노출된다. 이 (A) <u>끊임없는</u> 과정은 일, 경제적 어려움, 다른 인간관계 문제와 일정의 충돌로 더욱 어려워진다. 다수는 그런 일로 완전히 어쩔 줄 몰라 하지만, 일부 사람들은 자퇴하는 반면에 해마다 사람들은 졸업한다. 대부분의 경우에, 오직 한 가지 것이 졸업하는 사람과 자퇴하는 사람을 구분 짓는다. 졸업하는 사람들은 (B) <u>끈기</u>를 가지고 있다. 그들은 어려운 장애물 때문에 맞닥뜨리거나 심지어 그들이 실패할 때도 그만두지 않을 것이다. 그 점은 성공한 사람들에게서 공통으로 발견되고, 그런 사람들은 실패에서 조차 이점을 찾는다.

	(A)		(B)
①	unflinching 위축되지 않는	/	versatility 융통성
②	unrelenting 끊임없는	/	tenacity 끈기
③	impeccable 흠 잡을 데 없는	/	flexibility 융통성
④	irreversible 되돌릴 수 없는	/	punctuality 정확함
⑤	unprecedented 전례 없는	/	conformity 순응

20 ①

단어 ·

wills : 유언
forensic : 범죄 과학 수사의

해석

사람의 필적은 오랫동안 개인의 신원 확인 형식으로 공인되어 왔다. 이 점이 사람들이 수표, 유언장, 계약서에 서명하도록 요청 받은 이유이다. <u>친필로 신원 확인 하는 것은 어떤 범법 상황에서 중요한 역할을 해왔다.</u> 예를 들어, 연쇄살인마 Ted Bundy는 그 희생자들을 살해할 때 여러 방법들을 이용했다. 당국은 먼저 그 희생자들이 다른 몇몇의 살인자들에게 당했다고 생각했다. 필적으로 신원 확인하는 것이 도움이 되어, 나중에 경찰관들은 그들이 한 연쇄살인마를 쫓고 있다는 것을 깨달았다. 나치전범 Josef Mengele은 미 남부로 이동해서 다른 독일 남성의 신원을 취했다. 그가 죽은 후에 이 남자와 Mengele의 필적이 같다는 것이 밝혀졌다. Mengele은 그의 이름, 직업, 지문을 포함하여 전부 바꿨지만, 그는 그의 필적은 바꿀 수 없었다.

① 친필로 신원 확인 하는 것은 어떤 범법 상황에서 중요한 역할을 해왔다.
② 의문이 제기 되는 필적이 유언장이나 계약서, 편지에서 발견될 수도 있다.
③ 필적을 이용한 신원 확인은 법정 필적감정가에 의해 개발 되었다.
④ 의문이 제기되는 서명의 한 종류는 의도적으로 고친 서명이다.
⑤ 요청 받아 적는 것과 그냥 적는 두 가지 종류의 쓰기가 있다.

TIP

연쇄살인마와 나치전범의 예를 들어 범죄를 다룰 때에도 필적으로 신원확인이 이용되는 사실을 보여주었으므로 ①번이 적절한 문장이다.

1 ③

단 어

predispose : 하는 성향을 갖게 하다
vigilant : 바짝 경계하는
physiological : 생리학의
jerky : 갑자기 움직이는

해 석

최근 연구는 어떤 사람들은 유전적으로 수줍은 성향이 있다고 밝혔다. 다른 말로, 어떤 사람들은 수줍은 성향으로 태어난 것이다. 연구가들은 15%와 20% 사이의 신생아들이 부끄러워하는 신호를 보인다고 말한다. 그들은 더 조용하고 더 경계한다. 연구가들은 사교적인 아기들과 수줍은 많은 아기들 사이에 이미 생 후 두 달 안에 나타나는 생리학적인 차이점들을 밝혀왔다. 한 연구에서, 후에 수줍음 많은 어린이로 밝혀진 두 달 된 아기들은 이동하는 물체와 녹음된 사람 목소리 같은 자극에 심장박동과 갑작스런 팔 다리의 움직임, 과도한 울음의 증가 같은 스트레스를 받는다는 신호로 반응했다. 수줍음에 관한 유전적으로 더 강한 증거는 수줍음 많은 아이들의 부모와 조부모들이 안 그런 아이들의 부모, 조부모들 보다 그들이 어렸을 때 수줍음이 많았었다고 더 빈번하게 말한다는 점이다.

TIP

③번이 있는 문장의 주어는 two-month-olds who were later identified as shy children이고 ③번은 동사자리이며 문맥상 reacted가 알맞다.

2 ③

단 어

wield : (권력) 행사하다
tangible : 유형의
surge : 감정) 치밀어 오름
decline : 감소
delegate : 대표
tremendous : 엄청난
boost : (신장시키는)힘
stagnation : 침체

해 석

남한은 전 세계에서 대중문화를 세계적으로 이끄는 수출국가가 되는 목표에 공을 들이는 몇 안되는 국가들 중 하나이다. 그것은 한국이 'soft power'를 발달시키는 방식이다. 'soft power'는 군사적 힘 또는 경제적 힘을 통하기 보다는 국가의 이미지를 통해 권력을 행사하는 (A) 무형의 힘을 나타낸다. 한류는 처음 중국과 일본으로 퍼졌고, 나중에는 세계적으로 남부 아시아와 몇몇 국가들로 나아갔다. 2000년도에, 50년 동안 교류가 금지되었던 한국과 일본 사이의 대중문화는 부분적으로 열렸고, 그것은 일본인들 사이에 한국 대중문화 (B) 열풍을 일으켰다. 한국의 방송 관계자들은 몇몇 국가들로 TV프로그램들과 문화 컨텐츠들을 홍보하기 위해 대표들을 보내고 있다. 한류는 한국과 한국의 사업, 문화, 나라 이미지에 축복이 되어왔다. 1999년 이후 한류는 아시아 전역에서 가장 큰 문화 현상이 되었다. 한류는 2004년 한국의 GDP의 0.2%, 18억 7천 달러 가까이 기여하는 엄청난 효과를 보여 왔다. 더 최근인 2014년에는 한류가 한국 경제에서 116억 달러의 (C) 신장을 일으킨 것으로 추산되었다.

TIP

③ (A)intangible – (B)surge – (C)boost

3 ③

단 어

operatically : 오페라 풍으로
flamboyant : 이색적인
the bulk of : ~의 대부분

해 석

1975년에 Queen의 오페라 스타일의 보헤미안 랩소디 싱글이 발매되었고, 9주 동안 영국 음반 순위에서 계속 1위를 유지했다. ①Freddie가 고집했던 곡이지만, 곡의 길이와 남다른 스타일로 인해 거의 발매되지 못하고 있던 한 곡이 연주되자마자 즉시 눈에 띌 만한 히트를 했다. ②그 당시 Freddie의 특별한 재능들은 분명해지고 있었고, 주목할 만한 음역의 목소리와 무대 존재감은 그룹 Queen에 다채롭고 예측할 수 없으며 이색적인 성격을 더했다. (③Bomi와 Jer Bulsara의 아들인 Freddie는 그가 다녔던 성 베드로 기숙학교가 있는 인도에서 유년시절 대부분을 보냈다.) ④Queen의 인기는 아주 빨리 그들이 차트를 기록한 영국의 경계를 넘어 확장됐고, 유럽과 일본, 미국에서 대성공을 거뒀다. 그리고 그곳에서 그들은 1979년에 Freddie의 곡 'Crazy Little thing Called Love'으로 차트에서 1위를 차지하였다.

TIP

③번 문장은 지문과 어울리지 않는 Freddie의 어린 시절을 담고 있으므로, 전체 흐름과 관계 없는 문장이다.

4 ③

단 어

persona : 모습
distinctive : 독특한

① 건물 유지비용을 줄이기 위해 새로운 디자인이 채택된다.
② 사무 건물들이 주거용으로 재개발 되어야 한다는 여러
   계획들
③ 주거용 건물들이 상업용으로 전환되어야 한다.
④ 우리는 가능한 많은 상점들을 계획하고 내놓는다.

6 ②

✓ 단 어
psychologist : 심리학자
prenatal : 태아기의
maturity : 성숙함

✓ 해 석

아동 심리학자들은 출생부터 11세까지 개인에 관한 연구에 공을
들인다. 발달 심리학자들은 태아기부터 성인기, 노년기에 이르
는 행동과 성장 패턴을 연구한다. 많은 임상 심리학자들은 어린
이들의 행동장애를 다루는데 특화되었다. 아동 심리 연구는 때
때로 근로 행태를 밝히는데 도움이 된다. 예를 들어, 한 연구는
아동 학대와 방치를 당한 사람들은 장기간 그 결과로 고통을 받
을 것이라고 밝혔다. 그들 중 일부는 더 낮은 IQ와 독해능력을
가졌고, 더 많은 자살시도를 하고, 실직자수가 더 많으며 더 낮
은 연봉의 직업을 가진다. 오늘날 많은 사람들이 인간 발달에서
성인 시기 연구에 관심을 갖게 되었다. 발달 심리학의 연구는
중년의 위기 같은 중년에 나타나는 문제들에 대한 관심을 넓히
는데 앞장선다. 발달 심리학자들에게 직무 관련 관심사는 왜 그
렇게 많은 임원들이 은퇴 후에 기대한 것 보다 일찍 죽는지에
대한 것이다.

✓ TIP

② 발달심리학자들은 인간의 일생의 행동과 성장을 연구한다.

7 ①

✓ 단 어
virtually : 사실상
perceive : 감지하다
salient : 핵심적인

✓ 해 석

결정하는데 영향을 끼치는 표현 요소는 대조적 효과가 있다. 예
를 들면 70달러의 스웨터가 처음에는 그렇게 좋은 거래로 보이
지 않지만, 만약 당신이 그 스웨터가 200달러에서 값이 떨어졌
다는 것을 알게 되면 갑자기 엄청 싸게 보일 것이다. "거래를
성사시킨 것"은 대조이다. 비슷하게 나의 가족은 Massachusetts
에 살아서 추운 날씨에 아주 익숙하다. 하지만 우리가 추수감사
절에 Florida에 있는 이모와 삼촌을 보러 방문했을 때, 그들은
밖이 60도인데 아이들에게 모자를 쓰라고 강요했다. 사실상 아

✓ 해 석

많은 산업 전문가들이 만화영화 성우 연기의 창시자로 여기는
Mel Blanc은 1927년에 한 지역 라디오 프로그램에서 성우로 일
을 시작했다. 프로듀서들은 많은 성우들을 고용할 자금이 없어
서 Mel Blanc은 라디오 쇼를 위해 필요에 따라 다른 목소리와
모습들을 만들어 캐릭터들을 살렸다. 그는 The jack Benny
Program에서 고정이 되었고, 그는 인간, 동물, 조율이 필요한
자동차처럼 살아있지 않은 사물 같은 많은 역할들을 위해 연기
하였다. Porky Pig에서 그가 만들어낸 독특한 목소리는
Warner Bros에서 그의 성공을 더욱 부추겼다. 곧 Blanc은
Hanna-Barbera 스튜디오의 캐릭터들 뿐 아니라 스튜디오에서
잘나가는 다수의 만화 스타들과 밀접한 관계를 맺게 되었다. 그
의 가장 오랜 더빙은 약 52년간 Daffy Duck 캐릭터를 연기한
것이다. Blanc은 그의 작업에 심하게 방어적이었는데, "목소리
연기-Mel Blanc"라는 크레딧 영상이 나온다는 조건이 그의 계
약 조건에 항상 포함되었다.

✓ TIP

(A) / (B) / (C)
③ creating / where / were
restored 뒤의 to는 전치사이고 뒤에 명사구가 와야 하므로
(A)에는 동명사 creating, 그리고 (B)를 포함한 문장을 보
면 The jack Benny Program이 중복되어 생략 되었고 문
장 마지막이나 which 앞에 on이 사라졌으므로 관계부사 계
속적 용법으로 where이 적절하다. (C)에서 screen credits
가 복수주어이므로 were가 알맞다.

5 ②

✓ 단 어
plummet : 급락하다
at full tilt : 전속력으로

✓ 해 석

최근 사무실 건물의 시장 수요 급락의 결과로 비어있는 건물들
이 발생하였고, 우리는 미래에 거주시설과 상업시설 혹은 사무
용 건물들 사이에 전환을 쉽게 해 줄 계획을 세울 필요가 있다.
이런 공실은 기록적인 단계에 이르렀다. 현재 네덜란드의 큰 마
을들은 500만 평방미터의 비어있는 사무실들이 있는 반면에 집
은 16만 채가 부족한 상황이다. 네덜란드의 부동산 개발자 협회
에 따라 적어도 100만 평방미터가 공실로 있을 거라 예상할 수
있다. 주요 도시들 근방에 갑자기 생겨나는 빈 사무 건물들의 '
유령 마을'에 대한 실제적인 위험이 있다. 이런 전망에도 불구하
고, 사무 건물들이 고 수익률 시기 동안에 계획되었기 때문에
사무 건물 건설은 빠른 속도로 계속되고 있다. 그러므로 사무
건물들이 주거용으로 재개발 되어야 한다는 여러 계획들이 이제
필수적이다.

이들 관점에서는 수영복을 입어야 하는 날씨였는데도 말이다. 연구는 심지어 사람들이 큰 접시에 음식을 두고 먹을 때 작은 접시에 먹을 때 보다 더 많이 먹는다는 것을 보여준다. 같은 양의 음식이 큰 접시보다 작은 접시에서 간단히 더 크게 보이고, 우리는 감지된 부분의 크기를 우리가 배부를 때 그렇다고 말해주는 신호로서 사용한다.

↓

[대조적 효과는 (B) 이전 경험과 가장 눈에 띄는 비교에 의존하는 여러 방식으로 자극을 (A) 감지하는 성향이다.]

☑ **TIP**

   (A) /   (B)

perceive / previous experience 이전 경험

provide / predictive future 예측 가능한 미래

perceive / unexpected events 예상치 못한 사건들

provide / initial impressions 첫 인상

8 ③

☑ **단 어**

be prone to : ~하기 쉽다

halt : 세우다

skid : 미끄러지다

forthcoming : 다가오는

☑ **해 석**

대부분의 치명적인 사고들은 과속으로 발생한다. 과속하는 것은 인간의 자연스런 무의식적인 정신이다. 만약 인간에게 기회가 주어진다면 분명 무한대로 속도를 낼 것이다. 하지만 우리가 다른 운전자들과 도로를 공유하고 있을 때 우리는 항상 어떤 운송 수단이든 다른 차량들이 뒤에 있음을 기억해야 할 것이다. 속도를 ① 높이는 것은 사고 위험과 사고 도중 부상의 심각성을 증가시킨다. 빠른 차량은 저속 운행 차량보다 사고 나기가 더 쉽고, 사고의 심각성 또한 빠른 차량들의 경우가 더 심할 것이다. ② 더 고속일수록 더 큰 위험이 존재한다. 고속 주행하는 차량은 정지하기 위해 더 긴 거리, 즉 차간거리가 필요하다. 저속으로 운행하는 차량은 즉시 세우게 되는 반면 고속 운행 차량이 제1 운동 법칙 때문에 정지하기 위해 긴 거리가 필요하고 ③ 긴 거리를 미끄러진다. 고속으로 이동하는 차량은 충돌 도중 엄청난 충격을 받을 것이고 이런 이유로 더 심한 부상을 낼 것이다. 앞으로 다가올 상황을 판단하는 능력 또한 더 빠른 속도로 운전하는 동안 ④ 감소하게 되며, 판단의 착오를 야기하고 마침내 충돌에 이르게 된다.

☑ **TIP**

③ short distance는 차량이 고속으로 주행할 때 더 긴 거리가 필요하고 더 멀리 미끄러진다는 내용과 맞지 않으므로 쓰임이 적절하지 않다.

9 ②

☑ **단 어**

endeavor : 시도, 노력

earnestly : 진지하게

faculty : 능력

vicious : 악랄한

carper : 혹평가

enlightened : 깨우친

☑ **해 석**

읽어 볼 가치가 있어 보이는 어떤 것이든 흥미가 생기도록 노력하는 것이 먼저 필요하다. 학생들은 다른 사람들이 훌륭한 점이 있다고 찾아낸 것을 발견하려고 진지하게 노력해야 한다. 모든 독자들은 명작이라 할지라도 좋아하거나 싫어할 자유가 있다. 하지만 그 사람은 그 명작이 왜 존경받는지 그 진가를 알아보기 전까지는, 그 명작에 대해 의견까지 표현할 처지는 아니다. 그 사람은 그 책에서 무엇이 별로인가가 아닌 무엇이 훌륭한가를 스스로 깨달아야 한다. 단점을 발견하려는 정신적 훈련을 통해 비판적인 능력이 가장 잘 개발된다는 흔한 이론은 거짓처럼 악랄하다. 어떤 혹평가라도 훌륭한 작품에서도 오점을 찾아낼 수 있다. 그 작품의 모든 장점을 발견할 수 있는 사람은 오직 계몽된 사람뿐이다. 훌륭한 책의 진가를 볼 수 있는 진정한 노력이 독자가 관심을 잃도록 하는 일은 거의 일어나지 않는다.

① 책의 명성에 흠을 낼 단점에 집중하라.

② 그 책을 판단하기 전에 읽는 동안 그 책의 가치를 이해하려고 노력해라.

③ 당신이 흥미가 있는 책뿐 아니라 그렇지 않은 책들도 읽어봐라.

④ 책을 다 읽을 때까지 주제에 비판적 시점을 유지해라.

10 ④

☑ **해 석**

[대다수 미국인들은 재래식 재배 농산물 보다 유기농 재배 농산물이 더 건강하다고 말한다.]

대부분의 미국인들은 건강을 생각해서 유기농 음식을 구매하고 있다. ① 대중의 반 이상이 사람의 건강에 유기농 과일과 채소가 재래식 재배 농산물보다 더 좋다고 말한다. ② 40% 이상은 유기농 농산물이 사람의 건강에 더 좋지도 나쁘지도 않다고 대답하고 가장 적은 수가 유기농 농산물이 사람의 건강에 더 좋지 않다고 말한다. ③ 그 보다 적은 수의 미국인들은 유기농 농산물이 재래식 재배 농산물보다 맛이 더 좋다고 답한다. ④ 미국 성인의 약 ⅓이 유기농 농산물의 맛이 더 좋고, ⅖ 넘는 사람들은 유기농과 재래식 재배 농산물의 맛이 같다고 말한다.

☑ **TIP**

표를 보면 taste about the same-맛에 차이가 없다고 말한 비율이 ⅔를 넘지 못하기 때문에, over가 사용되어 ④번이 일치하지 않는 문장이다.

11 ②

🔲 **단어**

brush ~off : ~를 무시하다

☑ **해설**

의사와 환자 사이의 많은 의사소통은 개인적이다. 당신의 의사와 원만한 관계를 갖기 위해 당신이 부끄럽거나 불편하더라도 섹스나 기억력 문제 같은 민감한 주제들에 관해 이야기하는 것이 중요하다. 대부분의 의사들은 개인적인 문제에 관해 이야기를 나누는 것에 익숙하고 당신의 불편함을 덜어주려 노력할 것이다. 많은 노인들이 이런 주제와 관련되어 있다는 것을 명심해라. 당신은 당신이 의사와 이야기 할 때 민감한 주제를 꺼내는데 도움이 되도록 소책자와 다른 자료들을 활용할 수 있다. 기억력 문제, 우울증, 성기능 문제, 요실금이 불가피한 의 정상적인 증상이 아님을 이해하는 것이 중요하다. 훌륭한 의사는 이런 화제에 관해 당신의 걱정들을 진지하게 다루고, 그것들을 무시하지 않을 것이다. 만약 당신이 의사가 당신의 걱정을 진지하게 듣지 않는다고 생각된다면, 당신의 감정을 의사에게 말하던지 새로운 의사를 찾는 것을 고려해봐라.

① 당신과 민감한 화제를 의논하다.
② 당신이 갖고 있는 걱정들을 무시한다.
③ 당신이 말하는 것에 편안해하다.
④ 불변한 주제를 진지하게 다루다.

12 ①

🔲 **단어**

hypothesis : 가설
linguist : 언어학자

☑ **해설**

언어학자 Edward Sapir와 Benjamin Lee Whorf가 제안한 유명한 가설에 따르면, 우리 모두가 세상을 감지하기 위한 동일한 신체 기관-보기 위해서 눈, 듣기 위해 귀, 냄새를 맡기 위해 코, 느끼기 위해 피부, 맛을 보기 위해 입을 갖고 있다 하더라도, 세계를 인지하는 것은 우리가 말하는 언어에 상당부분 달려 있다. 그들은 언어가 특정한 방식으로 세상을 "보게"끔 하는 안경과 같다고 가정했다. 언어와 인지의 연관관계의 전형적인 예는 '눈'이라는 단어이다. 에스키모 언어는 눈을 무려 32가지나 되는 다른 단어들로 가지고 있다. 예를 들어, 에스키모인들은 내리는 눈, 땅 위의 눈, 얼음만큼 단단히 쌓인 눈, 바람에 날리는 눈, 그리고 우리가 '옥수수가루눈'이라고 부를지도 모르는 것을 뜻하는 다른 단어들이 있다. 반대로 멕시코의 고대 아즈텍 언어는 눈, 추위, 얼음을 뜻하는 단 하나의 단어를 사용했다. 따라서 Sapir와 Whorf의 가설은 옳다면, 우리는 우리가 갖고 있는 단어들이 뜻하는 것들만 인지할 수 있다. 아즈텍 사람들이 눈, 추위, 얼음을 <u>동일한 현상</u>으로 받아들인 것처럼 말이다.

① 동일한 현상
② 서로 구별되기
③ 사물들을 고유의 특징들로 분류
④ 특정 신체 기관으로 감지한 것

☑ **TIP**

위 언급된 가설에 따라 아즈텍 사람들이 눈, 추위, 얼음을 오직 한 단어를 사용해 표현한 것은 그들이 그 현상을 모두 동일한 현상으로 받아들였기 때문이다.

13 ③

🔲 **단어**

coercion : 강제
deputy : ~부
provoke : 유발하다
contradict : 부인하다
legitimate : 합법적인
component : 요소

☑ **해설**

[그와 반대로 '소프트 파워'는 강요나 벌금 보다는 유도와 설득력으로 목적을 성취하는 힘이다.]
'소프트 파워'의 개념은 미국 정치학자이자 Clinton 행정의 국방부원인 Joseph Nye Jr.에 의해 1990년 초에 형성되었다. 미국인 교수인 J. Nye의 개념들은 '파워'의 개념 이해에서 새로운 관점으로 보게 하였고, 과학적 논란을 일으켰으며 국제 정치학의 실용적 측면을 고무시켰다. (①) 그가 밝혀낸 작업에서는 그는 권력의 두 유형으로 '하드 파워'와 '소프트 파워'를 구별했다. (②) 그는 '하드 파워'를 '타인의 본질적 선호와 전략을 반대되는 방식으로 타인을 동하게 하는 함'으로 정의했다. (③ 그와 반대로 '소프트 파워'는 강요나 벌금 보다는 유도와 설득력으로 목적을 성취하는 힘이다.) '소프트 파워'의 실정은 세계 정치협상 과정에서 다른 참가자들 '마음을 사기', 고유의 문화로 이목 끌기와(어떤 상황에서 다른 사람들 마음을 끈다) ,정치적 가치, 외국인 정책(도덕적으로 정당하고 합법적으로 고려될 때)을 보여 줄 능력이 있음을 말한다. (④) '소프트 파워'의 주요 요소들은 문화와 정치적 가치, 외국인 정책이다.

③번 이전 문장에서 '하드 파워'에 대하여 설명하고 그와 대조되는 '소프트 파워'를 ③번 자리에서 설명하는 것이 적절하다.

14 ②

단어 ·

deployment : 배치
retail giant : 대형 할인마트
passenger aircraft : 여객기
autonomous : 자율적인

☑ **해석**

여러 다른 분야들에서 인공지능의 배치 속도는 몇 가지 중요한 요인에 달려있다. 소매업체가 특히 몇 가지 이유로 적합하다. 첫 번째는 시험하고 측정하는 능력이다. 적절한 안전장치로 대형 할인마트는 인공지능을 배치하고 소비자 반응을 확인하고 측정할 수 있다. 그들은 또한 최종 결산의 결과를 정말 빠르게 측정할 수 있다. 두 번째는 실수의 비교적 작은 결과들이다. 여객기를 착륙시키는 한 인공지능 에이전트는 사람이 죽을 수도 있기 때문에 절대 실수할 수 없다. 한 인공지능 에이전트는 매일 수 없이 많은 결정을 해야 하는 소매업체에 투입했고 전반적인 결과가 긍정적인 한, 실수를 좀 해도 괜찮다. 어떤 스마트 로봇 기술은 이미 소매업체에서 활용되고 있다. 하지만 가장 중요한 변화의 대다수가 물리적 로봇이나 자율주행차량 보다는 인공지능의 배치에서 일어날 것이다.

① 인공지능 에이전트의 위험
② 소매업체가 인공지능에 적합한 이유
③ 소매 기술과 접대
④ 인공지능 개발의 중요한 요소

✅ **TIP**

글 전반적으로 소매업체에서 인공지능 활용이 얼마나 적합한지 설명하고 있으므로 ②번이 글의 주제로 적절하다.

15 ④

단어 ·

collective : 집단의
manifest : 나타나다

☑ **해석**

"남에게 한 대로 되받게 된다."는 카르마가 어떻게 작용하는지에 대한 기본 이해이다. 카르마라는 단어는 문자 그대로 '활동'을 의미한다. 카르마는 좋은, 나쁜, 개인적인, 집단적인 같은 몇 가지 간단한 종류로 나눌 수 있다. 사람의 행동에 따라, 그런 행

동들의 열매를 거둘 것이다. 그 열매들은 행해진 행동들의 성질에 따라 달거나 신 맛이 날것이다. 한 그룹이 함께 특정한 활동이나 행사를 할 때, 열매도 집단적인 방식으로 수확될 수 있다. 우리가 말하고 행동하는 모든 것들이 미래에 우리에게 무슨 일이 일어날지 결정한다. 우리가 정직하게, 정직하지 않게, 도움이 되게 혹은 타인을 해하던지, 그것 모두가 기록되고 이번 생이나 다음 생에서 카르마 반응으로 드러난다. 모든 카르마 기록은 영혼과 함께 다음 생과 그 육체로 옮겨진다.

① 불운은 한꺼번에 닥친다.
② 제 때의 한 땀이 나중 아홉 땀을 던다.
③ 일손이 많으면 일이 가벼워진다.
④ 남에게 한 대로 되받게 된다.

✅ **TIP**

우리가 말하고 행동하는 대로 그 결과를 거두게 된다는 카르마의 개념을 설명하고 있으므로 ④번이 빈 칸에 들어갈 말로 적절하다.

16 ④

단어 ·

empower : 권한을 주다
accountability : 책임
fall short of : 미흡하다

☑ **해석**

독창적으로 생각하도록 도와주는 문화를 만드는 것은 궁극적으로 사람들이 더 나아가도록 동기부여 하고 변화하도록 권한을 주는 일이다. 당신은 리더로서 변화가 힘든 그런 시기에 지원을 해줘야 한다. 그리고 그런 지원은 당신이 격려한 행동들과 보상받을 성취들이 당신이 보여 줄 예이다. 먼저, 당신이 설정한 예들에 관해 생각해 보라. 당신은 스스로 지속적으로 독창적인 행동의 모범이 되도록 하고 있는가? 당신은 나아가 의무와 책임을 다하고 문제 해결에 집중하며, 호기심을 보이는가? 그 다음, 틀에서 벗어날 준비가 된 사람들을 격려하고 힘을 실어줄 방법을 찾아라. 그들에게 당신이 그들의 노력을 보아왔음을 알게끔 해라. 그들이 그들의 생각들을 개선하도록, 위험을 감수할 가치가 있는 것을 결심하도록 도와줘라. 그리고 가장 중요한 것은, 당신이 보상해 줄 성취들을 강하게 상기시켜 줘라. 당신은 단지 탈 없이 행동하는 사람들만 인정하는가? 아니면 당신은 또한 다소 높은 목표에 미치지 못하지만 기꺼이 나아가고 독창적인 행동을 보여 줄 의지가 있는 사람들에게 보상을 하고 있는가?

✅ **TIP**

리더로서 팀원들이 독창적인 사고를 할 수 있도록 도와야 함을 강조하는 글이므로 필자가 주장하는 바는 ④번이 적절하다.

③ 후반전의 승자들
④ 긍정적 사고의 기법

[17~18]

단 어

asthma : 천식
chronic : 만성적인
bring oneself to : ~할 생각이 나게하다
dissect : 해부하다
scalpel : 메스
futile : 헛된
contempt : 경멸, 무시
slit : 길게 자르다
impediment : 장애

해 석

사전에서 '이기는 것'은 경쟁에서 다른 사람들을 제치고 승리를 취하는 것이나 상을 받는 것, 성취를 보상하는 것으로 정의한다. 하지만, 내 인생에서 가장 뜻 깊은 승리 중 일부는 다른 사람을 이기거나, 받게 될 상이 있었을 때가 아니다. 내게 승리는 장애물을 극복하는 것을 의미한다.

나의 처음 승리한 경험은 초등학교 체육관에서 일어났다. 거의 매일 팔굽혀펴기와 버피로 준비운동을 한 후에, 우리는 이어 달리기를 지시 받았다. 비록 나는 어렸을 때 천식 때문에 힘들었지만, 나의 팀은 많은 경기에서 우승했다. 이런 경기들을 나갈 때마다 나의 가슴은 몇 분 동안 아주 심하게 타는 듯 아팠지만, 내가 다른 선수들을 이겨서가 아니라 나의 불리한 조건을 극복했기 때문에 벅찬 자랑스러움으로 이겨낼 가치가 있었다. 나는 그런 식으로 11살에 나의 만성질환에서 (A) 벗어났다.

고등학교 시절, 나는 또 하나의 승리의 경험을 했다. 비록 나는 생물학 공부하는 것을 좋아했지만, 나는 실험실에서 개구리를 해부할 생각이 들지 않았다. 나는 뭔든 죽은 냄새가 싫었고, 해부되어 배가 갈린 개구리 상상은 날 (B) 역겹게 했다. 내가 개구리 쪽으로 메스를 가져가려고 할 때 마다, 내 손은 떨리고 위는 뒤집어졌다. 그 중 최악은, 생물학 선생님이 나의 헛된 시도에 경멸하는 반응을 보인 것이다. (C) 놀라운 몇 주가 지난 후에 나는 나 자신에 대해 알아가기로 결심했다. 나는 내가 과민반응하고 있었다는 것을 깨달았다. 나는 투지를 갖고서 다음 실험시간에 들어가 탁자로 다가가서 개구리를 단번에 잘라 열었다. 그 일 이후 나는 생물학을 (D) 더 잘하게 되었다. 나는 나 자신의 알지 못하고 발견하지 못했던 새로운 두려움을 정복하게 되었다. 나는 또 이겨냈다.

이런 경험들을 통해 나는 장애물들을 극복하기 위해 참아내야 할지라도 내가 삶을 더 제대로 인식하고 있음을 이제는 안다. 그것이 나에게 긍정적으로 작용했고 그게 바로 승리 정신이다.

17 ①

TIP

① 승리란 나에게 무엇인가
② 행복의 추구

18 ③

TIP

③번 (C) amusing은 화자가 생물학 실험에서 힘든 시간을 보냈던 이야기와 어울리지 않으므로 적절하지 않다.

19 ③

단 어

python : 비단뱀
slither : 매끄럽게 기어가다
innate : 선천적인

해 석

한 고전적인 심리학 연구에 엄마들과 12 개월 된 아기들이 포함되었다. 각 엄마와 그녀의 아기는 연구 내내 함께 있었지만, 엄마들은 A와 B 두 집단으로 나뉘었다. A와 B 집단 모두 같은 상황에 노출되었고, 딱 하나 다른 점은 B집단의 엄마들은 아기들이 그들 앞에 놓여 있는 것을 가지고 계속 놀도록 긍정적으로 호응해줘야 했지만, 집단 A의 엄마는 아기들이 무엇을 가지고 놀던 원래 본인들이 하던 대로 하면 되었다.

이 아기들은 무엇을 가지고 놀았을까? 그건 바로 정말 크지만 길들여진 비단뱀이었다. 그 연구는 다음과 같이 진행되었다. A집단에 있던 아이들은 바닥에 있었고 그래서 비단뱀이 어린이들 사이를 스르르 기어 다닐 수 있었다. 뱀에 대한 공포를 인간은 타고 나지만, 2살까지는 그 공포심이 거의 나타나지 않기 때문에, 이 아이들은 그 비단뱀을 커다란 장난감으로 보았다. A집단의 아이들이 그 살아있는 비단뱀을 가지고 놀기 시작할 때, 그들은 자신들의 엄마가 무엇을 하고 있는지 보려고 고개를 들었다. 본인 자체로 있어보라고 지시 받은 엄마들은 자연히 공포에 질려 보였다. 엄마 얼굴의 공포를 보자 아이들은 울기 시작했다. B집단의 차례가 되었고, 지시받은 대로 엄마들은 웃으며 아이들이 계속 비단뱀과 놀도록 장려했다. 결과적으로 이 아이들은 그 비단뱀을 잡아들고 물고 있었다. 왜냐하면 자신들의 엄마가 그들의 새 장난감을 지지했기 때문이다.

↓

[(A) 모든 공포증은 아이들이 보통 부모의 특정한 것에 대한 (B) 반응을 보면서 학습된다.]

TIP

(A)	/	(B)
게임의 규칙들	/	지지
장난감 선호	/	참여
모든 공포증	/	반응
다양한 감정	/	격려

20 ②

단어 •

revalue : 평가 절상하다
inversely : 반대로
urbanization : 도시화
disperse : 해산시키다
devalue : 평가 절하하다

해석

노화의 근대적 이론에 따르면, 사회가 더 현대화됨에 따라 노년층의 지위는 하락한다. 노년기의 지위는 사냥 채집 시절에도 낮았지만, 안정된 농경사회에서 부쩍 ①올랐고 노인들이 토지를 관리했다. 산업화가 진행되면서, 현대사회는 노인들을 ②평가 절하하는 경향이 있다고 한다. 노화의 근대적 이론은 노인들의 역할과 지위가 기술 진척과 ③반비례적으로 관련되어 있다고 말한다. 도시화와 사회적 유동성 같은 요인들은 가족을 해체시키는 반면, 기술 변화는 노인들의 지혜와 인생 경험을 평가 절하하게 만들었다. 어떤 투자자들은 현대화의 기본적인 요소가 사실상 여러 사회에서 노인들의 지위 ④하락과 대체적으로 관련되어 있다는 것을 발견하였다.

TIP

본문은 시대가 변화하며 노인들의 지위가 오르기도 내리기도 하지만, 현대사회에 이르며 그들에 대한 평가가 낮아지고 그것이 현대화와 관련되어 있다고 보여주므로 ②번 revalue는 쓰임이 적절하지 않다.

21 ④

단어 •

stalk : 줄기
kernel : 알맹이
germinate : 싹트다
mutant : 변종
nurture : 양성하다
cultivar : 품종

해석

쌀의 줄기는 무르익을 때 머리를 낮추고, 옥수수 알맹이는 다 익었을 때도 생장상태 그대로 남는다. 이것은 낯설어 보이지 않지만, 현실적으로 쌀이나 옥수수 타입은 자연에서 살아남아선 안 된다. 보통, 이 작물들이 무르익었을 때, 씨앗이 발아하기 위해 땅으로 떨어져야 한다. 하지만 현재 쌀과 옥수수는 변종이고, 편리하고 효율적인 수확을 위해 씨앗이 ①붙어있도록 개량되었다. 인간들은 꾸준히 ②이런 현상이 나타나도록 품종 개량 기술을 통해 그런 변종을 선택하고 개량해왔다. 씨앗을 손상 없이 유지하기 위해 ④개량해가며, 이런 변종 씨앗들은 의도적으로 확산되었고, ③그리고 이 사실은 식물들이 자연에 없는 인공적인 종이 되어왔음을 의미한다. 이런 품종들을 장려함으로 가장 선호하는 씨앗들이 생산된다.

TIP

어법상 틀린 부분은 ④번 having bred이고 이것은 분사구문으로 생략된 주어는 위의 these mutant seeds이다. 능동으로 사용되어 틀렸으므로 수동인 having been bred가 되어야 한다.

22 ③

단어 •

unassertive : 내성적인

해석

첫인상 편견은 우리가 처음 받는 인상이 그 사람에 관련되어 우리가 모은 나중 정보가 처리되고, 기억되고, 생각하게끔 틀을 설정함을 의미한다. 예를 들어, 수업시간에 Ann-Chinn을 관찰한 한 것을 바탕으로 Loern은 그녀를 전형적인 아시아 여성으로 생각하고, 그녀가 조용하고 열심히 공부하며 내성적이라고 짐작할지도 모른다. 이런 결론에 이르렀기 때문에, 옳든 그르든 그는 이제 기본형태를 정하고 Ann-Chinn의 행동을 이해하고 해석하기 위해 구상을 한다. 시간이 지나고 그는 그가 생각한 그녀의 모습과 처음 그가 이미 그녀라는 사람의 틀을 형성한 그 인상과 일관되게 그녀의 행동을 끼워 맞추고 있다. 그는 그가 고른 범퍼에 붙인 스티커를 그녀가 미덥지 못하다고 표현하는 것을 알아차렸을 때, 그는 간단히 그 일을 넘겨버리거나, 그녀의 천성에서 이상하게 제외되는 일로 볼지도 모른다. 왜냐하면 그 일이 그가 생각하는 그녀의 이미지에 맞지 않기 때문이다.

TIP

③ (A) by which – (B) Having reached – (C) that

(A)에서 which 이하의 주어 later information we gather about this person이고 동사는 수동태로 이어지고 있으므로 뒤에 이 동사의 주체가 생략되어도 by는 남아 있어야 한다.
(B) 분사구문으로 As he have reached these conclusions 에서 as he가 생략되며 Having reached가 되어야 한다.
(C) 관계대명사 what은 선행사를 가질 수 없기 때문에 that이 적절하다.

23 ③

단어 •

acquisition : 습득
analogy : 유사점
salient : 현저한
tremendous : 대단한
cognitive : 인지의
affective : 정서적인

아동 언어 습득에 관한 연구의 물결은 언어 교사들과 교사 트레이너들로 하여금 모국어 습득과 제2언어 습득 사이의 유사점을 그리고 심지어 제1언어 학습 원리에 기초하여 특정한 교수법과 기법을 정당화하려는 목적으로 그러한 연구의 일반적인 발견의 일부를 연구하게 했다. 표면적으로, 유사점을 만드는 것을 완전히 합리적이다. 정상적인 발달 환경에서 모든 아이들은 그들의 모국어를 유창하고 효율적이게 습득한다. 게다가 그들이 언어에 대한 상당한 노력과 주의가 없는 것은 아니지만, 그것을 특별한 지도 없이도 자연스럽게 습득한다. 그러나 직접적 비교는 주의 깊게 다뤄져야 한다. 모국어와 제2언어 습득 사이에는 수 십 개의 두드러진 차이점이 있다. – 성인이 제2언어를 배우는 경우 가장 눈에 띄는 차이점은 어른과 어린이 사이의 엄청난 인식과 정서적 대조이다.

TIP

③ despite가 어법상 틀렸다. 양보부사절 it is not without에서 it is가 생략된 절이고, not without은 전치사 despite 뒤에 목적어로 올 수 없기 때문에, 접속사 although가 적절하다.

24 ④

단 어

physiology : 생리학
distort : 왜곡하다
logarithm : 로그
justifiably : 정당화되어
linear : 순차적

해 설

미국 생리학자인 Hudson Hoagland는 어디에서나 과학적 미스터리를 보았고, 그것들을 푸는 것이 그의 소명이라고 느꼈다. 한번은 그의 아내가 열이 났을 때, Hoagland는 그녀에게 아스피린을 사다주려고 약국으로 운전해 갔다. 그는 재빨리 갔다 왔지만, 그가 돌아 왔을 때 보통은 ① 합리적인 그의 아내가 그가 너무 느렸다며 화나서 불평했다. Hoagland는 그녀의 열이 그녀 내부의 시계를 ② 왜곡시켰는지 궁금했고, 그래서 그는 그녀의 체온을 측정하고, 그녀가 일 분 길이를 어림하도록 했으며 아스피린을 주고서 열이 떨어질 때까지 그녀가 일 분씩 어림해 보도록 시키기를 계속했다. 그녀의 체온이 정상으로 돌아오자 그는 로그를 짜고 그 결과가 ③ 순차적이라는 것을 발견했다. 후에도 그는 그가 옳다고 확신할 때까지 실험자들 체온을 인위적으로 높이고 낮추면서, 그의 실험실에서 연구를 계속했다. 더 고온인 체온은 신체시간이 더 빨리 가도록 만든다. 그리고 그의 아내는 ④ 정당하게 짜증이 났었던 것이 아니다.

TIP

체온이 오르면 신체시간이 더 빨리 가는 것처럼 느껴지기 때문에 글쓴이의 아내는 남편이 약국에 오래 걸려 갔다 온 것처럼 느꼈을 것이다. 그래서 그녀가 짜증이 난 것이 정당하지 않다고 나타낸 ④번이 적절하지 않다.

25 ②

단 어

preoccupied : 사로잡힌
sculptor : 조각가
contend : 겨루다
semblance : 외관
omnipotent : 전능한

해 설

성 바울은 보이지 않는 것은 보이는 것에 의해 이해되어야 한다고 말했다. 그것은 히브리인의 사고가 아니고, 그리스인의 사고이다. 고대 사회에서도 오직 그리스에서만 사람들은 보이는 것에 집착했다. 그들은 그들 주위의 세계에 실존하는 것에서 자신들의 욕구의 만족을 찾고 있었다. 조각가는 경기를 겨루고 있는 선수들을 지켜보고, 그들의 강하고 젊은 육체만큼 아름다운 것을 상상할 수도 없음을 느꼈다. 그래서 그는 아폴로 조각상을 만들었다. 작가는 그가 길에서 지나쳤던 사람들 중에서 헤르메스를 발견했다. 그는 "젊음이 가장 아름다운 시기의 젊은이들처럼"이라고 호머가 말한 것처럼 그 신을 보았다. 그리스의 예술가와 시인들은 사람이 얼마나 아름답고 올곧고, 재빠르며 강할 수 있는지 깨달았다. 그는 아름다움을 찾는 그들의 성취였다. 그들은 자신들 마음속에 있는 상상의 형태를 만들어낼 생각이 없었다. 그리스의 모든 예술과 사고는 <u>인간을 중심에 두었다</u>.

① 현실의 모습이 없었다.
② 인간을 중심에 두었다.
③ 전능한 신에 관심을 가졌다.
④ 초능력의 갈망을 나타낸다.

TIP

그리스에서 예술가들과 시인들이 인간에서 아름다움을 발견한 예를 보여주고 있기 때문에 ②번 인간이 중심에 있다는 말이 가장 적절하다.

1 ①

단어 •

subscriber : 구독자

accurate : 정확한

reliable : 믿을 만한

figure : 수치, 숫자

discern : 알다, 식별하다

concern : 관련시키다, 영향을 미치다

해석

Natural Gas World 구독자들은 산업에서 무슨 일이 일어나고 있는지에 대해 정확하고 믿을 만한 중요한 사실과 수치를 받게 될 것입니다. 그래서 그들은 그들의 사업과 관련된 것을 충분히 알 수 있습니다.

① 구별하다, 알아보다   ② 강화하다

③ 약화시키다   ④ 포기하다

2 ②

단어 •

event : 경기

stand out : 두드러지다

해석

여자 1,500미터 경기에서 은메달을 딴 West는 경기 내내 두각을 나타냈다.

① 압도되었다   ② 인상적이었다

③ 우울했다   ④ 낙관적이었다

3 ④

단어 •

be used to N : ~에 익숙해지다

get accustomed to N : ~에 익숙해지다

keep one's fingers crossed : 행운을 빌어주다

해석

① A : 나는 해외 여행을 할 계획이지만, 나는 다른 나라에 머무르는 게 익숙하지 않아.

　　B : 걱정하지마, 곧 익숙해질 거야.

② A : 나는 사진 콘테스트에서 상을 받고 싶어.

　　B : 네가 받게 될 거라고 확신해. 행운을 빌어줄게.

③ A : 친한 친구가 세종시로 이사했어. 나는 그녀가 매우 그리워.

　　B : 그래, 네가 어떤 느낌인지 알겠어.

④ A : 잠깐 당신과 얘기 좀 나눌 수 있을까요?

　　B : 네, 괜찮습니다. 나는 지금 매우 바쁩니다.

4 ②

단어 •

dim sum : 딤섬

pork : 돼지고기

chop : 잘게 썰다

dip : 담그다

sauce : 소스

해석

A : 딤섬 좀 드시겠습니까?

B : 네, 감사합니다. 맛있어 보이는군요. 안에 뭐가 들어 있나요?

A : 이것들은 돼지고기와 잘게 썬 야채가 들어 있고, 저것들은 새우가 들어 있습니다.

B : 음, 그러면 이것들을 어떻게 먹나요?

A : 이렇게 젓가락으로 하나를 들어서 소스에 찍어서 먹으면 됩니다. 쉽습니다.

B : 알겠습니다. 한번 먹어보죠.

① 그것들은 얼마나 많은가요

② 이것들을 어떻게 먹나요

③ 그것들은 얼마나 맵나요

④ 어떻게 요리하나요

5 ②

단어 •

lurk : 잠복하다

coral reef : 산호초

summit : 정상

TIP

① I told you about이 the new teacher를 수식하고 있다. about의 목적어인 the new teacher가 선행사로 가고 관계대명사(who/whom)가 생략되어 있는 형태이다.

② shy of는 '~이 부족한, 모자라는'의 뜻이다. five minutes shy of midnight은 '자정이 되기 5분 전'으로 해석될 수 있으므로 보기 지문의 '5분이나 지난 후'라는 뜻과 맞지 않다.

③ what appeared to be a shark가 주어로 쓰였다. what(=the thing which)은 선행사 없이 관계사절을 이

끌 수 있다. appear (to)는 '~인 것 같다'는 뜻으로 쓸 수 있다.

④ reach는 타동사로 '~에 닿다, 도달하다' 뜻을 가진다. 따라서 전치사 없이 목적어를 바로 취해야 한다. 16-year-old는 명사 friend를 수식하는 형용사구로 쓰였다. 복수형태 years로 쓰지 않도록 주의한다.

6 ①

단 어 •

wooden : 나무로 된, 목재의
retire : 은퇴하다

TIP

① per person은 '1인당'이라는 뜻이다. 개인용 컴퓨터는 personal computers이다.

② 동사는 was이며 그 앞까지 what절이 명사절로서 주어 역할을 하고 있다. what 절 안에는 불완전한 문장이 와야 하는데 주어가 나타나 있지 않으므로 옳은 문장이다.

③ 앞 문장에 긍정하면서 '~도 그러하다'는 뜻을 나타내기 위해 'so+동사+주어'의 표현을 쓴다. and 이하의 원래 문장은 plastic bottles are excellent toys for children, too이다. and so are plastic bottles에서 주어가 복수(plastic bottles)이므로 동사 are를 맞게 썼으며, 순서가 도치되어 맞는 표현이다.

④ since가 '~이후로'의 의미로 쓰였고, 은퇴 이후 계속 해오고 있으므로 현재완료진행형으로 썼다. since 구/절은 특정 과거 시점을 나타내는 표현으로 쓴다.

7 ②

단 어 •

domesticated : 길들인
take off : 제거하다
strain : 무거운 짐
utilize : 이용하다
considerably : 상당히
supplementary : 보충의, 추가의
foodstuff : 식료품
burden : 짐

해 석

가축은 인간에게 이용 가능한 가장 초기의 그리고 가장 효과적인 '기계'이다. 그들은 인간의 등과 팔의 무거운 짐을 덜어준다. 다른 기술들과 함께 이용될 때, 동물들은 보충 식량제(육류에서의 단백질과 우유)로서 그리고 물건을 나르고 물을 길어 올리고 곡식을 갈기 위한 기계로서 매우 상당히 인간의 삶의 수준을 향

상시킬 수 있다. 그들은 너무 명백하게 유용했기 때문에, 우리는 인간이 수 세기 동안 그들이 보유한 동물의 수와 품질을 향상시켰을 거라고 기대할지도 모른다. 놀랍게도, 이것은 대개 그렇지만은 않았다.

TIP

① "형용사/부사"를 묻는 문제이다. 앞에 있는 machines를 수식할 수 있는 형용사가 오는 것이 적절하다. available 앞에 "which are"가 생략된 것으로 볼 수 있다.

② "능동태/수동태"를 묻는 문제이다. utilize의 목적어가 없는 것으로 봐서 수동태의 형태가 오는 것이 적절하다. utilized로 고쳐야 한다.

③ 앞에 있는 machines을 수식해주는 to carry의 형태가 적절하다. to 부정사의 형용사적 용법이다.

④ "of + 추상명사"는 형용사의 역할을 한다. 따라서 of great benefit은 very beneficial과 같은 의미이다.

8 ④

단 어 •

narrative : 이야기
embody : 구현하다
philosophical : 철학적인
moral : 도덕적인
political : 정치적인
supernatural : 초자연적인
occurrence : 사건
contrary to : ~와 반대로
usage : 사용, (단어의) 용법
falsehood : 거짓
regardless of : ~와 상관없이
accuracy : 정확성
frequently : 빈번히
refer to A as B : A를 B로 부르다(지칭하다)

해 석

신화는 문화의 종교적, 철학적, 도덕적, 정치적인 가치를 구현하는 – 몇몇 경우에 있어서는 이를 설명하는 데 도움을 주는 – 이야기이다. 신과 초자연적인 존재에 대한 이야기를 통해서, 신화는 자연에서 사건을 이해하려고 노력한다. 대중적으로 사용되는 의미와는 다르게, 신화는 거짓을 의미하지 않는다. 가장 넓게 보면, 신화는 사실이거나 혹은 부분적으로 거짓이기도 하며 부분적으로 사실일 수도 있는 이야기 – 대개는 이야기들의 전체적인 묶음들 – 이다. 하지만 그들의 정확함의 정도와 상관없이, 신화는 빈번하게 한 문화의 가장 깊은 믿음을 표현한다. 이러한 정의에 따르면, 일리아드와 오디세이, 코란, 구약과 신약 모두 신화로 간주될 수 있다.

TIP

① helps의 주어는 a myth로서 3인칭 단수 주어로 받아서 helps가 되는 것이 적절하다.

② try to v 는 '~하려고 노력하다'라는 의미로서 적절한 표현이다.

③ that은 주격 관계대명사로서 앞에 첫 번째 하이픈 앞에 있는 stories를 선행사로 받는 것으로서 적절한 표현이다.

④ refer to A as B는 'A를 B로 부르다'라는 표현으로서 문장에 있는 주어(일리아드와 오디세이, 코란, 구약과 신약)가 '불려지는' 것이기 때문에 수동태 be referred to as로 고쳐야 한다.

9 ④

단어 •

application : 응용 프로그램
molecular : 분자의
genome : 유전체
geophysicist : 지구물리학자
core : 핵
oceanographer : 해양학자
imaginary : 가상의
hazard : 위험
computerization : 컴퓨터화
virtual reality : 가상현실
artificial : 인공의
realm : 영역
cartography : 지도 제작법
definition : 정의
employ : 이용하다
resemble : ~을 닮다
frontier : 경계, 한계

해석

매핑(mapping) 기술은 많은 새로운 응용분야에 사용되고 있다. 생물학 연구자들은 DNA의 분자 구조를 분석("유전체 지도 작성")하고 있고, 지구물리학자는 지구의 핵의 구조를 지도화하고 있고, 해양학자는 해양 바닥을 지도화하고 있다. 컴퓨터 게임은 규칙, 위험, 그리고 보상이 바뀌는 다양한 가상의 땅과 고도를 가지고 있다. 컴퓨터화는 이제 특별한 상황을 불러일으키는 인공적인 환경인 "가상 현실"로 현실세계에 도전하는데, 이는 훈련과 오락에 유용할지도 모른다. 매핑 기술은 생각의 영역에서도 사용된다. 예를 들어서, 생각들 간의 관계가 개념지도라고 불리는 것을 통해서 표현될 수 있다. 일반적이거나 중심적인 사고로부터 시작해서 관련 아이디어들이 연결될 수 있고, 주된 개념 주위에 망을 만든다. 이것은 어떤 전통적인 정의에 의한 지도는 아니지만, 지도 제작법의 도구와 기법이 그것을 만들어 내기 위해서 이용되고 있고 어떤 면에 있어서 그것은 지도를 닮아 있다.

① 컴퓨터화된 지도 대 전통적인 지도
② 지도제작법은 어디서 시작되었나?
③ DNA 비밀로 가는 길을 찾아서
④ 새로운 미개척 분야들의 매핑

TIP

첫 번째 문장 'Mapping technologies are being used in many new applications.'을 통해서 ④번 '새로운 미개척 분야들의 매핑'이 정답이라는 것을 알 수 있다.

10 ③

단어 •

performance : 수행
recipient : 받는 사람
estimate : 추정치
frequency : 빈도
prod A into B : A를 재촉해서 B하게 하다
corrective : 바로잡는
sap : 약화시키다
initiative : 진취성
adequate : 적당한
settle into : 자리잡다
advancement : 발전
reliable : 믿을 만한
steady : 꾸준한
sanction : 제재
lay off : 해고하다
fire : 해고하다
explicit : 명백한

해석

수행 결과에 대한 피드백을 줄 때, 당신은 그것의 빈도, 양, 내용을 설계하는 데 있어서 (피드백을) 받는 사람의 과거 수행과 그 또는 그녀의 미래 잠재력에 대한 추정치를 고려해야 한다. 성장을 위한 잠재력을 가지고 있는 높은 수행자들에게는, 피드백이 그들을 재촉해서 수정할 수 있는 조치를 취할 정도로 충분히 빈번해야만 하지만, 그것이 통제하는 것으로 받아들여지고 그들의 진취성을 약화시킬 정도로 빈번해서는 안 된다. 일에 자리잡고 발전에 제한된 잠재력을 가지고 있는 적당한 정도의 수행자들에게는 매우 적은 피드백만이 필요하다. 왜냐하면 그들은 자신의 일을 알고 어떤 일이 수행되어야 할지 알고 있으며, 과거에 믿을 만하고 꾸준한 행동을 보여 왔기 때문이다. 형편없는 수행자, 즉 만약 그들의 실적이 향상되지 않는다면 해고될 필요가 있을 사람들에게, 피드백은 빈번하고 매우 구체적이어야 하고, 피드백대로 행동하는 것과 휴직이나 해고와 같은 부정적인 제재 사이의 관계는 명확해야 한다.

① 피드백의 시기를 잘 맞춰라
② 부정적인 피드백을 그 사람에게 맞춰라
③ 피드백을 그 사람에게 맞춰라
④ 목표 지향적인 피드백을 피하라

☑ TIP

첫 번째 문장(When giving performance feedback, you should consider the recipient's past performance and your estimate of his or her future potential in designing its frequency, amount, and content.)을 통해서 정답이 ③번 "피드백을 그 사람에게 맞춰라"라는 것을 알 수 있다.

11 ④

단 어

pursue : 추구하다
academic discipline : 학과
publish : 출판하다
experimental : 실험적인
incorporate : 포함시키다
authentic : 진짜의
dialect : 방언
adapt : 각색하다, 조정하다
poetic : 시적인
embrace : 포용하다
cadence : 억양
character : 등장인물
lower-class : 하층 계급
fuse : 융합하다
racial : 인종적인
prejudice : 편견
witty : 재치있는

☑ 해 석

Langston Hughes는 Missouri주, Joplin에서 태어났고, 많은 아프리카계 미국 학생들이 학업을 추구하는 링컨 대학을 졸업하였다. 18살의 나이에, Hughes는 그의 가장 잘 알려진 시집 중 하나인, "Negro Speaks of Rivers(흑인, 강에 대해 말하다)."를 출간했다. 창의적이고 실험적인 Hughes는 그의 작품에 진짜 방언을 포함시켰으며 블루스와 재즈의 억양과 분위기를 포용하기 위해 전통적인 시적 형태를 각색하였고 하층민의 흑인들의 문화 요소를 반영하는 등장인물과 주제를 만들어 내었다. 유머러스한 스타일과 진지한 내용을 융합할 수 있는 그의 능력으로, Hughes는 자연스럽고 재치 있게 인종 편견을 공격하였다.

☑ TIP

마지막 문장에서 인종편견을 자연스럽고 재치 있는(natural and witty) 방식으로 공격하였다고 하였다.

12 ②

단 어

concern : 관심, 우려
staggering : 믿기 어려운
rational : 이성적인
status : 지위
make a bet : 내기(도박)를 하다
excessively : 과도하게
risky : 위험한
complicated : 복잡한
derivative : 파생상품
virtual : 가상의
currency : 화폐, 통화
crisis : 위기
breakdown : 붕괴
make progress : 발전하다
address : 다루다
capitalize : 자본화하다
regulator : 규제자

☑ 해 석

2007년에, 우리의 가장 큰 염려는 "실패하기엔 너무 크다"는 것이었다. Wall Street에 있는 은행들은 믿기 어려운 규모까지 성장했고 금융 시스템의 건전성에 너무 중요해져서, 어떠한 이성적인 정부도 그 은행들이 실패하도록 놔둘 수 없었다. ①그들의 보호받는 지위를 알고, 은행들은 주택시장에서 과도하게 위험한 도박을 하고 더 복잡한 파생상품을 만들어 냈다. (②비트코인과 이더리움과 같은 새로운 가상 화폐는 돈이 어떻게 작동할 수 있고 어떻게 작동해야 하는지에 대한 이해를 빠르게 바꿔놓고 있다.) ③그 결과는 1929년의 경제 붕괴 이후 최악의 금융 위기로 나타났다. ④2007년 이후로 몇 년 동안, 우리는 너무 커서 실패할 수 없는 딜레마를 다루는 데 큰 발전을 이뤄왔다. 은행들은 이전보다 더 자본주의화되었다. 우리의 규제당국은 거대 기관들을 대상으로 정기적인 스트레스 테스트를 수행한다.

☑ TIP

위의 글은 은행들이 너무 커져서 생기는 문제점에 관한 글로 ②번은 비트코인과 이더리움과 같은 가상화폐에 관한 글로 주제와는 거리가 멀다.

13 ③

단 어

pretty : 꽤
over the course of~ : ~하는 동안
hierarchy : 계급, 서열
attain : 획득하다
eliminate : 제거하다
alternative : 대안
explanation : 설명

foreignness : 이질성
pronounce : 발음하다
simplicity : 단순함
feature : 특징
determine : 결정하다
outcome : 결과

해설

두 사람이 같은 날 법률회사에서 일을 시작한다고 상상해 봐라. 한 사람은 매우 단순한 이름을 가지고 있다. 다른 사람은 매우 복잡한 이름을 가지고 있다. 우리는 그들의 다음 16년간 경력의 과정 동안 더 단순한 이름을 가지고 있는 사람이 더 빨리 법조계 서열을 올릴 만한 꽤 타당한 증거를 가지게 된다. 그들은 그들의 경력을 쌓는 중간쯤에 더 빨리 파트너십을 얻게 된다. 그리고 로스쿨을 졸업한 후 대략 8년 또는 9년이 지났을 쯤에 더 단순한 이름을 가지고 있는 사람들은 파트너가 될 가능성이 7~10퍼센트 더 많은데, 이것은 놀라운 효과이다. 우리는 모든 종류의 다른 대안적 설명을 제거하려고 노력한다. 예를 들어서 우리는 외국 이름들은 발음하기에 더 힘든 경향이 있기 때문에 그것이 이질성에 대한 것이 아니라는 것을 보여주려고 노력한다. 하지만 비록 당신이 정말로 진정한 내집단에 있는 영미의 이름을 가진 백인 남성을 볼지라도, 당신은 백인의 이름을 가진 그러한 백인 남성들 중에서 만약에 그들의 이름이 우연찮게 더 단순하다면 그들이 더 올라갈 가능성이 있다는 것을 발견한다. 그래서 단순함은 이름에 있어서 다양한 결과를 결정하는 하나의 중요한 특징이다.

① 법률상의 이름의 발달
② 매력적인 이름의 개념
③ 단순한 이름의 이점
④ 외국 이름의 근원

TIP

We've got pretty good evidence that over the course of their next 16 plus years of their career, the person with the simpler name will rise up the legal hierarchy more quickly.의 문장을 통해서 ③번 "단순한 이름의 이점"이 정답임을 알 수 있다.

14 ③

단어

compulsory : 강제적인
attendance : 출석
vary : 다양하다

해설

학교교육은 미국에서 모든 아이들에게 <u>강제적</u>이지만, 학교 출석이 요구되는 나이의 범위는 주마다 다르다.

① 보완적인　② 체계적인　③ 강제적인　④ 혁신적인

15 ①

단어

turmoil : 혼란
disclose : 말하다, 폭로하다

해설

비록 그 여배우는 그녀의 경력에 있어서 많은 혼란을 경험했지만, 그녀는 결코 누구에게도 그녀가 행복하지 않다는 것을 <u>폭로하지</u> 않았다.

① 말하다　② 발사하다　③ 약해지다　④ 내리다

16 ①

단어

visionary : 선지자
segment : 분야
fundamentally : 기본적으로
competitive : 경쟁하는
leverage : 차입금을 이용하여 투자하다
come about : 발생하다
discover : 밝혀내다
extensive : 광범위한
reference : 참조
turn off : 끄다, 잠그다
indicate : 나타내다
at any rate : 어쨌든
pragmatist : 실용주의자
value : 소중하게 여기다

해설

선견지명이 있는 사람들은 그들의 산업 분야에서 새로운 기술의 잠재력을 볼 수 있었던 최초의 사람들이다. 기본적으로 그들은 그들 자신을 경쟁 회사에서의 상대방보다 더 똑똑하다고 여긴다. 그리고 꽤 자주, 그들은 실제로 그러하다. 사실, 그들이 경쟁력 있는 이점으로 이용하여 투자하려고 했던 것이 바로 사물을 처음으로 볼 수 있는 그들의 능력이었다. 그 이점은 오직 어느 누구도 그것을 발견하지 못한 경우에서만 생길 수 있다. (A) <u>그러므로</u> 그들은 광범위한 목록의 산업계에서 검증한 참조를 가지고 있는, 잘 검증된 상품을 사는 것을 기대하지 않는다. 사실 만약 그러한 참조 기반이 존재한다면, 그것은 사실 어쨌든 이러한 기술에 대해 그들은 이미 늦었다는 것을 나타내며, 그들을 기능하지 못하게 만들지도 모른다. (B) <u>반면에,</u> 실용주의자들은 다른 회사에 있는 그들의 동료들의 경험을 매우 소중하게 여긴다. 그들은 구매할 때, 광범위한 참조를 기대하고 굉장히 많은 수의 상품이 그들 자신의 산업 분야에 있는 회사에서 나오기를 원한다.

17 ④

단어

ailment : 질병
short-lived : 일시적인
long-lasting : 장기간 지속되는
wonder : 궁금하게 여기다
realm : 영역
astronomer : 천문학자
sustain : 유지하다
extraterrestrial : 외계의
astronaut : 우주비행사
atmosphere : 대기
physiological : 생리학의
psychological : 심리학의
motion sickness : 멀미
gravity : 중력
differentiate : 구별하다
nausea : 메스꺼움

해석

수 세기 동안 인간들은 하늘을 올려다보고 지구의 영역 위에 무엇이 존재하는지 궁금하게 여겼다. 고대 천문학자들은 우주에 대해 더 많은 것을 알고자 희망하면서 밤 하늘을 연구했다. 더 최근에는, 어떤 영화들은 외계의 생명체의 형태가 우리의 행성을 방문했는지 의문을 제기한 반면에, 몇몇 영화들은 바깥 세계에서 인간의 삶을 유지할 수 있는 가능성을 탐구했다. 우주 비행사 Yuri Gagarin이 1961년에 우주를 여행한 최초의 인간이 된 이래로, 과학자들은 지구 너머의 상태가 어떤 상태일지, 그리고 우주여행이 인간 신체에 어떤 영향을 미칠지를 연구해 왔다. 비록 대부분의 우주 비행사들이 단지 몇 개월 미만의 시간을 우주에서 보내지만, 많은 우주비행사들은 지구에 돌아올 때 심리적인 그리고 생리적인 문제들을 경험한다. <u>몇몇 이런 질병은 잠깐 지속이 되지만 다른 질병들은 오래 지속될지도 모른다.</u> 모든 우주비행사들의 3분의 2 이상이 우주에서 이동하는 동안 멀미로 고통 받는다. 중력이 없는 환경에서, 신체는 위아래를 구분할 수 없다. 신체의 내부 균형 체계는 혼란스러운 신호를 뇌로 보내고, 그 결과 며칠씩이나 지속되는 멀미를 야기한다.

TIP

physiological and psychological problems를 주어진 문장에서 some of these ailments로 이어지기 때문에 ④번에 들어가는 것이 가장 적절하다.

18 ③

단어

fragment : 조각
literature : 문학
gene : 유전자
physics : 물리학
evolution : 진화
sociologist : 사회학자
disorientation : 혼미
meaninglessness : 무의미함
anomie : 사회적 무질서
despair : 절망
suicide : 자살
disenchantment : 각성
unified : 통일된
enchantment : 황홀감
inevitable : 피할 수 없는
rationality : 이성
modernity : 현대성

해석

왜 모든 역사에 대해서 신경을 쓰는가? <u>오늘날 우리는 우리의 세계에 대해서 단편적으로 가르치고 배운다.</u> 문학 수업에서 당신은 유전자에 대해서 배우지 않는다. (마찬가지로) 물리학 수업에서 당신은 인간의 진화에 대해서 배우지 않는다. 그래서 당신은 세상을 부분적인 시각으로 보게 된다. 그것이 교육에 있어서 '의미'를 찾는 것을 어렵게 만든다. 프랑스 사회학자 Emile Durkheim은 이 혼미와 무의미함을 아노미(사회적 무질서)라고 불렀고 그는 그것이 절망과 심지어 자살을 초래할 수 있다고 주장했다. 독일 사회학자 Max Weber는 세계의 각성에 대해서 얘기했다. 과거에 사람들은 대개 그들 자신의 종교적 전통의 기원이 되는 이야기에 의해 제공된 시각인, 그들의 세계에 대한 통일된 시각을 가졌다. 그 통일된 시각은 목적, 의미, 그리고 심지어 세상과 삶에 대한 각성에 대한 의미를 주었다. 하지만, 오늘날 많은 작가들은 무의미에 대한 의식이 과학과 이성의 세계에서 불가피하다고 주장한다. 현대성은 무의미함을 의미하는 것처럼 보인다.

① 과거에, 역사 연구는 과학으로부터의 각성을 요구했다.
② 최근에, 과학은 우리에게 많은 기발한 비법과 의의를 주었다.
③ 오늘날, 우리는 우리의 세계를 부분으로 가르치고 배운다.
④ 최근에, 역사는 여러 개의 범주로 나누어진다.

TIP

빈칸문장 뒤에 나오는 So you get a partial view of the world.라는 문장을 통해서 ③번이 정답이라는 것을 알 수 있다.

19 ②

단 어

Great Depression : 대공황
surplus : 과잉(의)
agricultural : 농업의
commodity : 상품
explosion : 폭발
fuel : 가속화하다
shift : 옮기다
federally : 연방 차원에서
steadily : 꾸준히
function : 기능(하다)
nutritious : 영양분이 풍부한
underprivileged : 불우한
if anything : 오히려
replacement : 대체(물)

해 석

가장 초기의 정부 음식 서비스 프로그램은 유럽에서 대략 1900년도에 시작되었다. 미국에서의 프로그램은 대공황으로 거슬러 올라가는데, 그때 과잉의 농업 상품을 사용하고자 하는 필요가 가난한 집 아이들을 먹이고자 하는 관심과 결합되었다. 제2차 세계대전 기간 동안 그리고 그 후에, 노동할 수 있는 여성의 수가 폭발적으로 증가하면서 더 광범위한 프로그램의 필요성이 대두되었다. 한때 가족의 기능이었던 것 – 점심을 제공하는 것 – 이 학교 음식 서비스 시스템으로 옮겨왔다. 전국적인 학교 급식 프로그램이 이러한 노력들의 결과이다. 그 프로그램은 취학 나이의 아이들에게 연방 차원에서 지원받는 식사를 제공하도록 설계되었다. 제2차 세계 대전이 끝날 때부터 1980년대 초반까지, 학교 급식 서비스에 대한 자금조달이 꾸준히 확대되었다. 오늘날 그것은 미국 전역에서 거의 10만 개 학교의 아이들을 먹이는 데 도움을 준다. 그 첫 번째 기능은 모든 학생들에게 영양이 풍부한 점심을 제공하는 것이다. 두 번째 기능은 혜택을 못 받는 아이들에게 아침과 점심에 영양이 풍부한 음식을 제공하는 것이다. 오히려, 한때 가족의 기능을 위한 대체물이었던 학교의 음식 서비스의 역할이 확대되어 왔다.

① 일하는 여성 수의 증가가 음식 서비스 프로그램의 확장을 촉진시켰다.
② 미국 정부는 음식 부족에도 불구하고 대공황 동안 가난한 아이들을 먹이기 시작했다.
③ 미국 학교 음식 서비스 시스템은 현재 가난한 가정의 아이들을 먹이는 데 도움을 준다.
④ 점심을 제공하는 기능은 가정에서 학교로 옮겨져 왔다.

TIP

두 번째 문장인 Programs in the United States date from the Great Depression, when the need to use surplus agricultural commodities was joined to concern for feeding the children of poor families.에서 음식 부족이 아닌 과잉의 음식을 사용하기 위해서 가난한 아이들을 먹였다는 것을 알 수 있다.

20 ④

단 어

boast of : ~을 뽐내다, 자랑하다
wired : 네트워크를 사용할 수 있는 환경의
addiction : 중독
drop dead : 급사하다
exhaustion : 탈진
for days on end : 여러 날 동안
shockingly : 깜짝 놀랄 만큼
self-destructive : 자기 파괴적인
intensely : 심하게
competitive : 경쟁적인
embrace : 포용하다
come at a price : 대가가 따르다
legion : 군단, 부대, 무리
obsessed : 중독된, 빠진
tear away : 떼어놓다

해 석

남한은 지구상에서 인터넷이 가장 잘 보급된 나라가 된 것을 자랑스럽게 여긴다. (B) 사실, 아마 다른 어떤 나라들도 그렇게 완전하게 인터넷을 포용하진 않았을 것이다. (C) 하지만 많은 중독된 사용자들이 그들의 컴퓨터 스크린으로부터 그들 자신을 떼어낼 수 없다는 것을 발견하면서 그러한 즉각적인 웹 접근성은 대가가 따르게 되었다. (A) 사용자들이 며칠 동안 쉬지 않고 온라인 게임을 한 후에 지쳐서 급사하기 시작하면서, 이러한 중독이 최근 몇 년 동안 한국에서 국가적 문제가 되었다. 점점 더 많은 학생들이 인터넷에 접속해 있기 위해 학교를 빠지고 있는데, 이는 이렇게나 심각한 경쟁적인 사회에서 말도 안 되게 자기 파괴적인 행동이다.

TIP

주어진 문장에 인터넷이 가장 잘 보급된 내용이 제시되고 (B)에서 다른 나라들은 이러한 인터넷을 갖추지 못했다는 내용이 이어진다. 또 (C)에서는 이러한 인터넷의 많은 보급이 온라인 게임에 중독된 사용자들에 대해 언급하고 (A)에서 그것이 사회적인 문제가 된다는 내용으로 마무리가 된다.

1 ①

단 어

relic : 유물, 유적
sensibility : 감성, 정서
buried : 파묻힌
excavate : 발굴하다
exhume : 파내다, 발굴하다
pack : (짐을)꾸리다

해 석

나는 이 문서들을 이제 죽어서 파묻힌 감성의 유물로서 보게 됐는데, 그것은 발굴될 필요가 있었다.

2 ①

단 어

joy ride : 폭주
anticipation : 기대
strap : ~를 끈으로 묶다
sheer : 완전한, 순전한

해 석

롤러코스터를 타는 것은 감정의 폭주일 수 있다. 다시 말해서, 당신이 좌석벨트를 맬 때의 초조한 기대감, 당신이 높이, 높이, 높이 올라갈 때 오는 의문과 후회, 그리고 롤러코스터가 첫 번째 하강할 때의 완전한 아드레날린의 쇄도와 같은 것들 말이다.

① 완전한   ② 무서운   ③ 가끔   ④ 관리할 수 있는

3 ④

해 석

① A: 우리 몇 시에 점심 먹나요?
  B: 정오 전에는 준비가 될 거예요.
② A: 제가 당신에게 여러 번 전화했었어요. 왜 안 받았어요?
  B: 아, 제 핸드폰이 꺼졌던 것 같아요.
③ A: 올 겨울에 휴가 가실 건가요?
  B: 아마도요. (하지만) 아직 결정하지 않았어요.
④ A: 여보세요. 전화를 못 받아서 미안해요.
  B: 메시지를 남기시겠습니까?

4 ③

단 어

exchange : 환전하다
currency : 통화
exchange rate : 환율
commission : 수수료

해 석

A: 안녕하세요. 제가 돈을 좀 환전해야 해요.
B: 그래요. 어떤 통화가 필요하세요?
A: 달러를 파운드로 바꿔야 해요. 환율이 어떻게 되죠?
B: 환율은 달러당 0.73파운드입니다.
A: 좋아요. 수수료를 받으시나요?
B: 네, 우리는 4달러의 약간의 수수료를 받습니다.
A: 재매입 방침은 어떻게 되나요?
B: 우리는 당신의 통화를 무료로 바꿔드려요. 그냥 영수증만 가져오세요.

① 이거 얼마입니까?
② 제가 그것을 어떻게 결제하면 됩니까?
③ 재매입 방침은 어떻게 되나요?
④ 신용카드도 되나요?

5 ④

단 어

pedestrian : 보행자
constitute : 구성하다
fatality : 사망자, 치사율
proportion : 비율
grief : 슬픔

해 석

매년 270,000명 이상의 보행자들이 전 세계의 도로에서 생명을 잃는다. 많은 사람들은 어떤 날에 (평소처럼) 떠나듯이 그들의 집을 나서지만 결코 집에 돌아오지 못한다. 전 세계적으로, 보행자들은 모든 도로 교통 사망자 중에 22%를 차지하고, 몇몇 국가에서는 이 비율이 모든 도로 교통 사망자의 3분의 2만큼 높다. 수백만 명의 보행자들이 치명상을 당하지는 않는다 - (하지만) 그들 중 일부에게는 영구적인 장애가 남게 된다. 이런 사고들은 경제적 어려움뿐만 아니라 많은 고통과 슬픔을 야기한다.

TIP

① 주어 more than 270,000 pedestrians가 복수 주어이기 때문에 복수형 동사인 lose가 올바르다.
② never to는 '결코 ~하지 못하다'라는 뜻으로, to부정사의 부사적 용법 중 결과를 의미한다. 올바른 표현이다.

③ as ~ as 사이에 들어갈 수 있는 품사는 형용사와 부사의 원급이다. high가 올바르게 쓰였다.
④ 주어인 millions of pedestrians가 부상을 당하는 것이므로 능동(injuring)이 아니라 수동(injured)이 되어야 한다.

6 ②

단어

utmost : 극도의, 최고의
suspicion : 의심, 혐의
arouse : 불러일으키다

해석

① 그 신문은 그녀를 그녀 자신의 목적을 위해 회사의 돈을 사용한 것으로 기소했다.
② 그 조사는 의심을 사지 않기 위해서 매우 주의 깊게 다뤄져야만 했다.
③ 그 과정의 속도를 높이는 또 다른 방법은 새로운 체계로의 변화를 만드는 것일 것이다.
④ 화석연료를 태우는 것이 기후변화의 주요한 원인들 중 하나다.

TIP

① use → using
charge A with B는 'B라는 이유로 A를 비난하다'라는 뜻이며 전치사 with 뒤에는 명사가 와야 한다. 보기 지문에서 use가 the company's money를 목적어로 취하고 있어 동사 역할도 하고 있으므로 동명사 형태 using으로 써주어야 한다.
② 부사절 접속사인 lest는 'lest S(주어) (should)+동사원형'의 형태로 사용되어 '~하지 않도록 하기 위해'라는 부정의 의미를 나타낸다. 보기 지문에서는 should가 생략되고 be동사가 원형의 형태로 남았다. 올바른 표현이다.
③ made → to make
be made를 수동태로 본다면 the shift가 목적어로 남게 되어 문법상 틀리게 되며, 해석 또한 어색하다. to부정사 형태를 취해 be동사의 보어로 오게 할 수 있으며 'S (주어)+be동사+to부정사' 형태가 되어 'S는 ~이다/~하는 것이다' 뜻이 된다.
④ one of the lead cause → one of the leading causes
'one of 복수명사'로 써주어야 한다. cause는 셀 수 있는 명사이므로 복수형이 가능하다. lead는 causes라는 명사를 수식하므로 형용사 형태인 leading으로 쓰는 것이 적절하다.

7 ②

단어

haunt : 출몰하다, 괴롭히다
weigh down : 무겁게 짓누르다
discipline : 학문, 훈련, 훈육
deliberately : 고의로
strip down : 해체하다, ~를 벗겨내다
representation : 설명, 발표
phenomenon : 현상
relevant : 관련있는
contemporary : 동시대의
causal : 인과관계의
exclude : 배제하다
interact : 상호작용하다

해석

우리를 괴롭힐 수 있는 생각이 있다: 모든 것들이 아마도 다른 모든 것들에 영향을 주고 있는데 어떻게 우리가 사회 세계를 이해할 수 있을까? 그러나 만약 우리가 그런 걱정으로 짓눌린다면, 우리는 나아가지 못할 것이다. (A) 내가 익숙한 모든 학문들은 그것(세상)을 이해하기 위해 세상의 캐리커처를 그린다. 현대의 경제학자들은 모델(모형)을 만듦으로써 세상을 이해하는데, 여기에는 바깥 세상의 현상들에 대한 설명이 의도적으로 배제되어 있다. (C) 내가 "벗겨냈다(배제했다)"라고 말할 때, 나는 정말 '벗겨냈다'는 걸 뜻하는 거다. 우리 경제학자들 사이에서는 우리가 현실의 바로 그러한 측면들이 어떻게 작용하고 상호작용하는지 이해할 수 있게 해주기를 바라면서, 한두 개의 인과 관계에만 초점을 맞추고, 다른 것들을 배제하는 것은 드문 일이 아니다. (B) 경제학자 John Maynard Keynes는 우리의 주제를 다음과 같이 묘사했다: "경제학은 동시대와 관련있는 모델을 선별하는 기술과 연관되어 있는 모델 관점으로 사고하는 과학이다."

TIP

주어진 문장의 the social world를 (A)의 make sense of it에서 it으로 받고 있다. (A)의 후반부에 나오는 stripped down을 (C) 첫 문장에서 에서 다시 언급하고 있고 (B)에서 경제학자 John, When I say "stripped down,"이라는 말로 풀어 설명하는 것으로 (C)가 뒤따름을 알 수 있다. (B)에서 경제학자 John Maynard Keynes의 말을 인용해 마무리를 짓고 있다.

8 ②

단 어 •

prehistoric : 선사시대의
distinguish : 구분하다
disorder : 장애
abnormal : 비정상의
inhabit : 살다
afflicted : 고통받는
demonic possession : 악령 빙의
sorcery : 마법, 마술
behest : 명령, 훈령
offend : 기분 상하게 하다
ancestral : 조상의
demonology : 귀신학
misfortune : 불운
surgical : 외과의
trephine : 머리수술을 하다
chip away : 조금씩 잘라내다
crude : 막된, 대충의

해 석

약 오십만 년 전쯤의 선사시대의 사회들은 정신적 질환과 신체적 질환들을 정확히 구분하지 못했다. 단순한 두통에서 경련성 발작까지의 비정상적인 행동은 고통 받는 사람의 몸에 살거나 통제하는 악령들의 탓으로 여겨졌다. 역사가들에 따르면, 이 고대 사람들은 많은 형태의 질병들을 악령 빙의, 마법, 또는 화가 난 조상의 영혼의 명령 탓으로 돌렸다. 귀신학이라고 불리는 이런 신념 체계 안에서, 희생자는 대개 최소한 부분적으로 그 불행에 대한 책임이 있었다. 석기시대의 동굴 거주자들은 행동 장애를 trephining(머리수술)이라고 불리는 외과적 (수술) 방법으로 치료했을지도 모르는데, 그 외과 수술에서 두개골의 일부가 악령이 도망갈 수 있는 구멍을 만들어 내기 위해 잘려졌다. 사람들은 악령이 떠날 때, 그 사람이 정상 상태로 돌아올 것이라고 믿었을지도 모른다. 놀랍게도, 두개골 시술을 받은 두개골들이 치료된 것으로 밝혀졌는데, 이것은 일부 환자들이 이렇게 극도로 조잡한 수술에서 생존했었다는 것을 나타낸다.

① 정신 장애들은 신체장애와 분명히 구분되었다.
② 비정상적 행동들은 사람에게 영향을 미치는 악령으로부터 기인한다고 믿어졌다.
③ 악령이 들어올 수 있도록 두개골에 구멍이 만들어졌다.
④ 어떤 동굴 거주자들도 머리수술로부터 생존하지 못했다.

TIP

① 첫 번째 문장에서 정신 장애와 신체장애는 명확히 구분되지 않았다고 했다.
③ 다섯 번째 문장에서 악령이 들어오는 게 아니라 나가도록 구멍을 뚫었다고 했다.
④ 마지막 문장에서 생존한 경우가 발견되었다고 하였다.

9 ②

단 어 •

upend : 근본적인 영향을 주다
frequency : 빈도
immigration : 이주, 이민
at the top of the hour : 매 정시에
at the bottom of the hour : 매시 30분에
presidential : 대통령의
convention : 전당 대회, 관습

해 석

디지털 혁명이 전국적으로 뉴스룸에 근본적으로 영향을 주면서, 여기 기자들을 위한 나의 충고들이 있다. 나는 25년 동안 기자였다. 그래서 여섯 번의 기술적 라이프 사이클을 겪었다. 가장 극적인 변화들은 마지막 6년 동안에 왔다. 그것은 내가 점점 증가하는 빈도로 순조롭게 진행하면서 무엇인가를 만들어가고 있다는 것을 의미한다. 뉴스 업계에서의 많은 시간 동안, 우리는 우리가 하고 있는 것에 관해 모른다. 우리가 아침에 나타나면, 누군가 "세금 정책, 이민, 기후변화 중 하나 골라서 글을 써 주실 수 있나요?"라고 말한다. 신문이 하루에 한 번씩 마감이 있었을 때, 우리는 기자가 아침에는 배우고 밤에는 가르칠 것이라고들 말했다 — 24시간 전에는 그 기자도 전혀 알지 못했던 주제에 관해 내일의 독자에게 알려줄 수 있는 이야기를 기사로 쓰는 것이다. 이제 이것은 마치 매 정시에 배워서 같은 시간 30분마다 가르치는 것과 같다. 예를 들어, 나는 정치 팟캐스트도 운영하고 있는데, 대선 전당대회 기간 동안 실시간 인터뷰를 하기 위해서 어디에서든 그것을 이용할 수 있어야만 한다. 나는 점점 더 대본 없이 일하고 있다.

① 교사로서의 기자
② 기자와 즉흥성
③ 정치학에서의 기술
④ 저널리즘과 기술의 분야들

TIP

마지막 문장인 I am just increasingly working without a script.를 통해서 정답이 ②번이라는 것을 알 수 있다.

10 ④

단 어 •

wilderness : 황무지
stream : 시내, 개울
vacant : 텅빈
spontaneous : 자발적인
vacate : 비게 하다
roam : 배회하다
creek : 개울
counterpart : 상대물
sedentary : 앉은 채 있는

해설

전 역사에 걸쳐서 아이들의 놀이터는 시골의 황야와 들판, 개울, 언덕이었고 마을과 도시의 도로, 거리, 공터였다. ① 놀이터라는 용어는 아이들이 그들의 자유롭고 자발적인 게임을 하기 위해서 모이는 모든 장소들을 일컫는다. ② 아이들이 비디오 게임, 문자 메시지, 소셜 네트워크에 대한 그들의 커져가는 과도한 사랑을 위해서 자연의 놀이터를 비워둔 것은 단지 지난 몇십 년에 불과했다. ③ 심지어 미국 시골에서도 어른과 함께하지 않고 자유롭게 돌아다니는 아이들이 거의 없다. (④ 학교 밖에 있을 때, 그들은 모래를 파거나, 요새를 짓거나, 전통 게임을 하거나, 등산을 하거나, 공놀이를 하면서 동네에서 흔히 발견된다.) 그들은 계곡, 언덕, 그리고 들판의 자연 지형에서 빠르게 사라지고 있고, 도시 아이들처럼 오락을 위해 실내에서, 앉아서 하는 사이버 장난감으로 향하고 있다.

TIP

자연 속에서 뛰어 놀던 과거와는 달리 현대 사회의 아이들은 실내 오락에 파묻혀 있다는 내용의 글이다. 따라서 모래를 파는 것과 같은 전통적인 게임을 한다는 ④번의 내용은 주제와 거리가 멀다.

11 ④

단 어

slow to a trickle : 눈곱만큼으로 줄어들다
engross : 몰두시키다
apathetic : 무관심한, 심드렁한
stabilize : 안정되다, 안정시키다
preoccupy : 뇌리를 떠나지 않다, 사로잡다

해설

시간은 지루한 오후 강의 동안에는 눈곱만큼 줄어드는 것 같고, 뇌가 매우 재미있는 것에 몰두할 때에는 빠르게 가는 것 같다.

12 ①

단 어

keep abreast of : ~을 잘 챙겨 알아두다
keep A under control : A를 통제하다

해설

이러한 매일의 업데이트는 정부가 그들을 통제하려고 시도하면서 독자들이 시장을 잘 아는 것을 돕기 위해서 고안됐다.

① ~을 잘 알다
② ~에 의해 영감을 받다
③ ~에 믿음을 갖다
④ ~와 밀리 하다

13 ③

단 어

famine : 기근
approximately : 대략
shortage : 부족
dehydration : 탈수, 건조
deport : 강제 추방하다
immigrate : 이민을 오다
starvation : 기아, 굶주림
emigrate : 이민 가다
fatigue : 피로, 피곤함
detain : 구금하다, 억류하다

해설

1840년대에, 아일랜드 섬은 기근을 경험했다. 아일랜드는 국민들을 먹여 살릴 만큼의 충분한 식량을 생산할 수 없었기 때문에, 약 백만 명의 사람들이 (A)굶어 죽었다. 그들은 살아있을 만큼 충분히 먹지 못했다. 그 기근은 또다른 125만 명의 사람들이 (B)이민을 가도록 야기했다. 많은 사람들은 그들의 고국인 섬을 떠나 미국으로 갔고, 나머지는 캐나다, 호주, 칠레, 그리고 다른 나라들로 갔다. 기근 이전에 아일랜드의 인구는 대략 6백만 명이었다. 엄청난 식량 부족 이후에는 약 4백만 명이 되었다.

14 ④

단 어

component : 구성요소
on one's way to~ : ~로 가는 길에
affordable : 가격이 적당한
convincingly : 설득력 있게
break apart : 망가지다
may as well : ~하는 것이 낫다
inadequate : 부적합한
by contrast : 대조적으로
consequently : 결과적으로
similarly : 마찬가지로

해설

오늘날 가상현실(VR) 경험의 시각적 구성요소를 만들 수 있는 기술은 널리 접근 가능하고 가격이 저렴해지는 중에 있다. 그러나 강력하게 효과가 있기 위해서는, 가상현실은 시각적인 것 이상이 될 필요가 있다. (A) 만약 당신이 듣고 있는 것이 시각적인 것과 설득력 있게 들어맞지 않는다면, 가상현실은 엉망이 된다. 농구 시합을 생각해 보라. 만약 선수들, 코치들, 아나운서들, 그리고 관중들 모두가 그들이 미드코트에 있는 것처럼 들린다면, 여러분은 텔레비전으로 경기를 보는 게 낫다 – 여러분은 그곳에 있는 기분처럼 느낄 것이다. (B) 불행히도, 오늘날의 청각 장비와 널리 사용되는 녹음 그리고 재생 포맷은 먼 거리 행성의 전쟁터, 코트사이드의 농구 경기, 혹은 거대한 콘서트홀의 첫

번째 줄에서 들리는 교향곡의 소리를 설득력 있게 재창조하는 일에는 그저 부적합하다.

15 ④

단 어

that being the case : 사정이 그렇다면
associate : 관련짓다
incremental : 증가하는
enormity : 거대함
profession : 직업

해 석

행복한 두뇌는 단기간에 집중하는 경향이 있다. 사정이 그렇다면, 결국에는 장기적인 목표를 성취하도록 만드는, 우리가 해낼 수 있는 단기 목표는 무엇일지 고려하는 것이 좋다. 예를 들어, 만약 당신이 6개월 안에 30파운드를 감량하기를 원한다면, 어떤 단기 목표를 그 목표에 이르게 해 줄 더 작은 무게 증가분을 빼는 것과 연관시킬 수 있는가? 아마도 그것은 매주 당신이 2파운드를 감량할 때 당신 자신에게 보상하는 것만큼 간단한 일이다. 동일한 생각이 직장에서의 성과를 향상시키는 것과 같은 어떤 종류의 목표에서도 적용될 수 있다. 전체적인 목표를 더 작고 단기적인 부분으로 나눔으로써, 우리는 우리의 직업에서 목표의 거대함에 의해 압도되는 대신에 점진적인 성취에 초점을 맞출 수 있다.

TIP

주어진 문장에 '그 같은 생각(the same thinking)'이 ④번 앞에 있는 2파운드와 같은 작은 목표로 시작하는 것을 의미한다. 따라서 삽입문장이 ④번에 들어가는 것이 가장 알맞다.

16 ③

단 어

decade : 10년

TIP

① just in case(~인 경우에 한해서, 혹시라도 ~인 경우에)는 접속사로, 절을 이끌 수 있다.
② be busy ~ing(~하느라 바쁘다) 표현이 바르게 쓰였다.
③ has married to → has been married to
marry는 전치사 없이 목적어를 바로 취하는 타동사이다. 따라서 능동태에서는 marry 동사 다음에 목적어가 와야 한다. 수동형으로 쓴다면, be married to로 써서 '~와 결혼하다, ~와 결혼생활을 하다'라는 뜻으로 쓸 수 있다. for more than two decades이므로 현재완료형 표현과 함께 나타내어 has been married to로 쓰는 것이 알맞다.

④ to read의 주체가 주절의 주어 I가 아니므로 의미상의 주어를 나타내기 위해 for my son을 써 주었다.

17 ①

단 어

fancy : 멋진
pass along : 전하다, 알리다
quarters : (하인)숙소
adopt : 채택하다
antiseptic : 방부제
momentously : 중요하게
scrapes : 찰과상, 긁힌 자국

해 석

19세기에, 가장 존경받는 건강 의학 전문가들 모두 질병은 "miasma(독기)" – 나쁜 공기에 대한 멋진 용어 – 에 의해 야기된다고 주장했다. 서구 사회의 건강 체계가 이 가정을 토대로 하였다: 질병을 막기 위해, 창문은 방 안에 또는 바깥에 더 많은 miasma가 있는지에 따라서 열려 있거나 닫힌 상태를 유지했다. 귀족들은 나쁜 공기가 있는 숙소에 거주하지 않았기 때문에 의사들은 병을 전하지 않는다고 믿어졌다. 그러고 나서 세균이라는 개념이 나왔다. 어느 날, 모든 사람들은 나쁜 공기가 당신을 아프게 한다고 믿었다. 그런 다음 거의 하룻밤 사이에 사람들은 병의 진짜 원인인 병원균과 박테리아라고 불리는 보이지 않는 것들이 있다는 것을 깨닫기 시작했다. 이 새로운 병의 관점은 의사들이 소독약을 채택하고 과학자들이 백신과 항생제를 발명하면서 약에서의 광범위한 변화를 가져왔다. 그러나 같은 중요도로, 병원균이라는 개념은 일반 사람들에게 자신들의 삶에 영향을 주는 힘을 주었다. 이제 건강을 유지하기를 원한다면, 손을 씻거나, 물을 끓이거나, 음식을 완전하게 조리하거나 베이거나 긁힌 상처를 요오드 용액으로 깨끗이 할 수 있다.

① 19세기에 창문을 여는 것은 miasma의 밀도와는 관계가 없었다.
② 19세기에 귀족은 나쁜 공기가 있는 장소에서는 살지 않는다고 믿어졌다.
③ 백신은 사람들이 병원균과 박테리아가 병의 진짜 원인이라는 것을 깨달은 이후에 발명되었다.
④ 베인 상처와 긁힌 상처를 깨끗이 하는 것은 사람들이 건강을 유지하는 데 도움을 줄 수 있을 것이다.

TIP

① 두 번째 문장에서 miasma가 방 밖에 많은지 아니면 방 안에 많은지에 따라 문을 열거나 닫은 상태로 둔다고 했다. 따라서 본문의 내용과 다르다.

18 ③

단 어

subordinate : 부하, 하수인
obediently : 복종적으로
restrict : 제한하다
exert : 발휘하다

해석

추종자들은 리더십 방정식의 중요한 부분이지만, 그들의 역할이 항상 인식되어 온 것은 아니다. 사실, 오랫동안 "리더십에 대한 공통된 관점은 리더들은 적극적으로 이끌고, 나중에 추종자로 불리는 부하들은 수동적으로 그리고 복종적으로 따른다는 것이었다." 시간이 지나면서, 특히 지난 세기에, 사회적 변화가 추종자들에 대한 사람들의 관점을 형성했고, 리더십 이론들은 점차 추종자들이 리더십 과정에서 적극적이고 중요한 역할을 한다는 것을 인식했다. 오늘날 추종자들이 하는 중요한 역할을 받아들이는 것은 중요하다. 리더십의 한가지 측면은 특히 이러한 점에 있어서 주목할 만한 가치가 있다는 것이다: 다시 말해, 리더십은 한 그룹의 모든 구성원들 사이에 공유되는 사회적 영향 과정이다. 리더십은 특정한 위치나 역할에 있는 누군가에 의해 행사되는 영향에만 제한되지 않는다; 따르는 사람들 역시 리더십 과정의 일부분이다.

① 오랜 기간 동안, 리더들은 적극적으로 이끌고, 따르는 사람들은 수동적으로 따르는 것으로 이해되었다.
② 종속자들에 대한 사람들의 관점은 사회적 변화에 의해 영향을 받았다.
③ 따르는 사람들의 중요한 역할은 오늘날에도 여전히 부정되고 있다.
④ 리더와 따르는 사람들 모두 리더십 과정에 참여한다.

TIP

③ 네 번째 문장에서 따르는 사람들 또한 리더십에서 중요한 역할을 한다고 하였다.

19 ①

단 어

proper : (명사 뒤에서 쓰여) 엄밀한 의미의
coherent : 일관된
sequence : 순서, 연속성
sparrow : 참새

해석

엄밀한 의미의 언어는 그 자체로 두 개의 층을 이루고 있다. 개별적 소음들은 단지 가끔씩만 의미가 있다; 대개 다양한 말의 소리가 중복되는 고리들과 결합되었을 때에만 일관성 있는 메시지를 전달하게 되는데, 다양한 색깔의 아이스크림이 서로 서로 녹아 들어가는 것과 같다. 새소리에 있어서도, <u>개별적 음들은</u>

<u>종종 거의 의미가 없다</u>: 순서가 중요한 것이다. 인간과 새 둘 다에게 있어, 이러한 특화된 음성 체계에 대한 조절은 뇌의 절반, 주로 왼쪽 절반에 의해 행하여지며 그 체계는 비교적 삶의 초기에 학습된다. 그리고 인간의 많은 언어가 방언을 가지고 있듯이, 몇몇 새들의 종도 그러하다: 캘리포니아에서 흰줄무늬 참새는 지역마다 너무 다른 노랫소리를 갖고 있어서 캘리포니아 사람들은 아마도 이러한 참새 소리를 듣고 자신이 그 주의 어디에 있는지를 구별할 수 있을 것이다.

① 개별적 음들은 종종 거의 의미가 없다.
② 리듬감 있는 소리가 중요하다.
③ 방언이 중요한 역할을 한다.
④ 어떤 소리 체계도 존재하지 않는다.

TIP

빈칸 앞 문장 the various speech sounds convey coherent messages only when combined into an overlapping chain의 내용으로 보아 개별적 음들은 아무런 의미가 없다는 내용이 들어가야 한다.

20 ②

단 어

upend : 뒤집다
alter : 바꾸다
evaluate : 평가하다
outline : 개요를 잡다
strategic : 전략적인
gut : 배짱
intuition : 직관
analyze : 분석하다
attribute : 특성
separately : 별개로
holistic : 총체적인
possess : 소유하다
facilitate : 가능하게 하다

해석

노벨상 수상자이자 심리학자인 Daniel Kahneman은 인간이 이성적 의사결정자라는 개념을 뒤엎으며, 세계가 경제학에 관해 생각하는 방식을 변화시켰다. 그 과정에서, 그의 학문 전반에 걸친 영향력은 의사들이 의학적 결정을 내리는 방식과 투자가들이 월 스트리트에서 위험을 평가하는 방식을 변화시켰다. 한 논문에서, Kahneman과 그의 동료들은 큰 전략적 결정을 내리기 위한 과정의 개요를 만들었다. 'Mediating Assessments Protocol(조정 평가 프로토콜)', 혹은 MAP이라고 이름 붙여진 그들이 제시한 접근법은 한 가지 간단한 목표를 가진다: 하나의 선택이 다수의 별개 요소들에 의해 알려질 때까지 배짱에 근거한 의사결정을 지연시키는 것이다. "MAP의 가장 본질적인 목표 중 하나는 기본적으로 직관을 미루는 것이다."라고 Kahneman

은 최근 〈포스트〉와의 인터뷰에서 말했다. 이러한 구조화된 과정은, 그것들 각각을 개별적으로 논의하고 나서, 그들에게 상대적인 백분점수를 부여하고 마지막으로 총체적 판단을 위해 그 점수를 사용하면서, 이전에 선택된 여섯 개에서 일곱 개의 특성들에 근거하여 하나의 결정을 분석하는 것을 요구하는 것이다.

✓ **TIP**

빈칸 앞 문장 To put off gut-based decision-making until a choice can be informed by a number of separate factors.에서 의사 결정을 미룬다(put off)는 내용을 통해서 ②번이 정답이라는 것을 알 수 있다.

2019. 6. 15
제2회 서울특별시 시행

---

1 ④

단어

see eye to eye : 견해가 일치하다
quarrel : 다투다
dispute : 논쟁하다
part : 나누다

☑ **해석**

적어도 고등학교 때 그녀는 마침내 그녀의 부모님과 견해가 일치하는 하나의 결정을 내렸다.

2 ①

단어

justification : 변명
account : 설명, 해석
in question : 논쟁 중인
deny : 부인하다
pejorative : 가치를 떨어뜨리는, (낱말·발언이) 경멸적인
associated with : ~랑 관련된

☑ **해석**

변명은 사람이 논쟁 중인 행위에 대해서 책임은 받아들이지만, 그것과 관련된 가치를 떨어뜨리는 본질을 부정하는 말이다.

① 가치를 떨어뜨리는　② 외향적인
③ 강제적인　④ 여분의

3 ①

단어

rule out : 배제하다
sanitation : 위생
yellow fever : 황열병
suspected : 의심되는
uncivilized : 미개한

☑ **해석**

검사는 황열병의 원인으로 먼지와 나쁜 위생을 제외했고, 모기가 의심 가는 매개체였다.

4 ②

단어

life expectancy : 기대수명
smallpox : 천연두
diphtheria : 디프테리아
preventable : 예방할 수 있는
curable : 치료할 수 있는
eradicate : 근절하다
curtail : 생략하다
hover : 하늘에 멈춰 떠 있다
initiate : 시작하다
aggravate : 악화시키다

☑ **해석**

일반적으로 말해서, 당신이 현대를 전체적인 인류 역사에 비교해 봤을 때, 2018년에 사는 사람들은 꽤 운이 좋다. 기대 수명은 약 72세 정도 위에서 맴돌고, 한 세기 전만 해도 널리 퍼져 있고 치명적이던 천연두와 디프테리아 같은 질병들은 예방할 수 있거나, 치료할 수 있거나, 혹은 완전히 근절되었다.

5 ②

단어

concrete : 구체적인
project : 투영하다
certainty : 확실성
fulfill : 수행하다
hallucination : 환각
template : 본보기
inquiry : 질문
commotion : 동요

☑ **해석**

우리의 삶과 결정을 위한 본보기를 제공할 수 있는, 과거 사건들에 구체적인 패턴이 있다고 상상하는 것은 그것이 수행할 수 없는 확실성에 대한 희망을 역사에 투사하는 것이다.

6 ④

☑ 해석

① A : 토요일 영화는 어땠나요?
   B : 좋았어요. 정말 재밌게 봤어요.
② A : 안녕하세요. 셔츠 몇 벌 다림질하기를 원합니다.
   B : 네, 얼마나 빨리 그것들이 필요하신가요?
③ A : 싱글룸으로 하시겠습니까, 더블룸으로 하시겠습니까?
   B : 아, 나만을 위한 것이요. 그래서 싱글룸이 좋겠어요.
④ A : Boston으로 가는 다음 비행기는 몇 시인가요?
   B : Boston에 가는 데 약 45분 걸릴 것입니다.

7 ①

☑ 단 어

sewing machine : 재봉틀
cannibal : 식인종
spear : 창

☑ 해석

발명가 Elias Howe는 재봉틀의 발견을 그가 식인종에게 붙잡힌 꿈의 탓으로 돌린다. 그는 그들이 그 주위에서 춤을 출 때 창 끝에 구멍들이 있다는 것을 알아차렸고, 그는 이것이 그가 이 문제를 풀기 위해서 필요로 했던 디자인의 특징이라는 것을 깨달았다.

☑ TIP

① for a dream → to a dream
   attribute A to B는 'A를 B의 탓으로 돌리다'라는 뜻을 가진 표현이다.
② he was captured by cannibals in a dream 문장을 a dream를 선행사로, which를 관계대명사로 하여 앞 문장과 연결하면, ~ for a dream which he was captured by cannibals in이 된다. 전치사 in을 which 앞으로 위치시킬 수 있으므로 ~ for a dream in which(=where) he was captured by cannibals로 쓸 수 있다.
③ notice의 목적어로 that절이 왔다. as they danced around him은 중간에 삽입된 부사절이다.
④ '~하기 위해서' 뜻을 나타내기 위해 쓰인 to부정사의 부사적 용법이다.

8 ①

☑ 단 어

embark on : ~에 착수하다
coexistence : 공존
whereby : (그것에 의해) ~하는
confrontational : 대립하는

☑ 해석

1955년쯤 Nikita Khrushchev는 USSR(소비에트 사회주의 공화국 연방)에서 스탈린의 후계자로 나타났고, 그는 "평화공존 정책"에 착수했는데, 그것에 의해 동서양은 그들의 경쟁을 계속 하긴 했어도 덜 대립하는 방식으로 하였다.

☑ TIP

① emerge는 '나타나다'라는 의미의 자동사이기 때문에 수동태로 쓸 수 없다.
② embark (on)은 '~에 착수하다, 관계하다'는 의미로 맞는 표현이다.
③ whereby는 관계사의 의미로 '(그것에 의해) ~하는' 이라는 의미이다.
④ were to continue는 to부정사의 be to 용법으로 '예정, 가능, 당연, 의무, 의도' 등을 나타낸다.

9 ③

☑ 단 어

cuttlefish : 오징어
cephalopod : (오징어, 문어와 같은) 두족류 동물
pigment : 인료, 색소

☑ 해석

(작은) 오징어, 문어 그리고 오징어는 모두 두족류 동물의 종류이다. 이 동물들의 각각은 색소, 즉 색깔을 띠는 색소를 포함하는, 피부 밑 특별한 세포를 가지고 있다. 두족류 동물은 이 세포들을 피부 쪽으로 또는 피부로부터 멀리 이동시킬 수 있다. 이것은 두족류 동물이 그 외양의 패턴과 색깔을 바꾸도록 한다.

☑ TIP

① 모든 종류의 두족류 동물들을 의미하는 "all types of cephalopods"는 맞는 표현이다.
② each는 형용사와 대명사의 쓰임 모두 가능하다. 문제에서는 대명사로 쓰였다.
③ 관계대명사 that의 선행사가 skin이 아닌 cells이기 때문에 수 일치시켜 contains를 contain으로 고쳐준다.
④ allow는 목적보어로 to 부정사를 취해야 한다. to change는 맞는 표현이다.

10 ④

단어

bathrobe : 실내복

해 설

도시를 유지하는 것보다 심각한 문제들이 있다. 혼자 일하는 게 더 편하게 되면서, 사람들은 덜 사회적으로 될지 모른다. 편한 운동복이나 실내복으로 집에 머무르는 것이 다른 사업상의 미팅을 위해서 갖추어 입는 것보다 더 쉽다.

TIP

① 비교 대상이 주어인 명사구 (a more serious problem) 이기 때문에 (동)명사구 maintaining the cities는 맞는 표현이다.
② 양, 정도의 비교급을 나타내는 less가 형용사 앞에 쓰였다. 맞는 표현이다.
③ 뒤에 나오는 than과 병치를 이루어서 비교급 easier가 맞는 표현이다.
④ 비교대상이 집에 머무르는 것(to stay)과 옷을 갖추어 입는 것(getting dressed)이기 때문에 비교대상의 형태를 일치시켜 (to) get dressed가 되어야 한다.

11 ②

단어

marginal cost : 한계비용
substantial : 상당한
negligible : 무시할 만한
implication : 암시, 영향
markup : 가격인상

해 설

경제학자들은 정보재의 생산이 높은 고정비용과 낮은 한계비용을 포함한다고 말한다. 정보재의 초고를 제작하는 비용은 상당할지도 모른다. 하지만 추가적인 사본을 제작(또는 재제작)하는 비용은 무시해도 될 정도다. 이런 종류의 비용 구조는 많은 중요한 영향을 가지고 있다. 예를 들어, 비용을 기반으로 하는 가격책정은 효과가 없다: 단가가 0일 때, 단가에 대해 10퍼센트 혹은 20퍼센트의 가격인상은 말이 되지 않는다. 당신은 당신의 생산비가 아니라, 소비자 가치에 따라 당신의 정보재의 가격을 책정해야 한다.

① 저작권 확보하기
② 정보재 가격 책정하기
③ 지적재산권으로서의 정보
④ 기술적 변화의 비용

TIP

마지막 문장인 "You must price your information goods according to consumer value, not according to your production cost."를 통해서 정보재의 가격 책정이 제목이라는 것을 알 수 있다.

12 ③

단어

a claim to fame : 명성을 얻을 자격
wield : 휘두르다, 사용하다
bend : 구부리다
lash out : 채찍질하다, 강타하다
extraordinary : 대단한, 비상한
velocity : 속도
snap : ~를 탁하고 닫다, 물다
secretive : 숨기는
subterranean : 지하의

해 설

드라큘라 개미들은 그들이 때때로 자기 새끼의 피를 마시는 방식 때문에 그들의 이름을 얻었다. 하지만 이번 주, 이 곤충들은 명성을 얻을 새로운 자격을 얻었다. Mystrium camillae 종의 드라큘라 개미들은 그들의 턱을 아주 빠르게 부딪칠 수 있어서, 당신이 눈을 깜빡이는 데 걸리는 시간에 5,000번의 타격을 맞출 수 있다. 이것은 이번 주에 Royal Society Open Science지에 발표된 한 연구에 따르면, 피를 빨아먹는 그들이(개미들이) 자연에서 가장 빠른 것으로 알려진 동작을 사용한다는 것을 의미한다. 흥미롭게도, 이 개미들은 단순히 그들의 턱을 너무 세게 부딪쳐서 그것들이 구부러지게 함으로써, 그들의 기록적인 부딪침을 만들어 낸다. 이것은 한쪽 턱이 다른 쪽 턱을 미끄러지면서 지나가 엄청난 속도와 힘 – 다시 말해 시속 200마일 이상의 최대 속도에 도달하는 – 으로 강타할 때까지, 스프링처럼 한쪽 턱에 에너지를 저장한다. 그것은 당신이 손가락을 탁 칠 때 발생하는 것과 같은데, 1,000배 더 빠를 뿐이다. 드라큘라 개미들은 그들이 낙엽 밑이나 지하 터널 안에서 사냥하는 것을 더 좋아하기 때문에 비밀스러운 포식자들이다.

TIP

①, ②, ④는 개미를, ③은 개미의 턱(their jaws)을 가리킨다.

13 ①

해 설

나는 독일의 한 기차에서 편지를 쓰고 있는데, 바닥에 앉아서 쓰고 있습니다. 기차는 붐비고, 모든 좌석은 차 있습니다. 하지만, 이미 앉은 사람들이 그들의 자리를 포기하도록 할 수 있는 "comfort customers"라는 특별한 등급이 있습니다.

TIP

빈칸 앞 문장 Conscientious people have a tendency to organize their lives well. A disorganized, unconscientious person might lose 20 or 30 minutes rooting through their files to find the right document, an inefficient experience conscientious folks tend to avoid.의 내용으로 보아 스트레스를 비켜 간다는 의미인 ④번이 정답이라는 것을 알 수 있다.

TIP

빈칸 앞에 있는 사역동사 make로 인해 빈칸은 동사원형 자리이다. 따라서 ① 또는 ②가 올바른데, 문맥상 이미 앉아 있는 사람이 자리를 '차지하는 것'이 아니라 '포기한다'고 하는 것이 맞다.

14 ③

단어

house 수용하다

해석

한 나라의 부는 교육에 있어서 중심적인 역할을 해서, 국가로부터의 자금과 자원의 부족은 시스템을 약화시킬 수 있다. 사하라 사막 이남 아프리카의 정부들은 세계 공공 자원의 2.4퍼센트만을 교육에 지출하지만, 취학 연령 인구의 15퍼센트가 그곳에 산다. 반면에 미국은 전 세계적으로 교육에 지출되는 모든 돈의 28퍼센트를 지출하지만, 취학 연령 인구의 고작 4퍼센트만을 수용한다.

① 그럼에도 불구하고   ② 더욱이, 게다가
③ 반대로   ④ 마찬가지로

15 ④

단어

conscientious : 양심적인, 성실한
owe A to B : A는 B의 덕분이다
hygiene : 위생
tendency : 경향
root : 뒤지다, 찾다
folks : 사람들
setback : 차질
thorough : 빈틈없는, 철두철미한
sidestep : 비켜 가다

해석

"매우 성실한 직원들이 나머지 우리보다 일련의 일들을 더 잘한다"고 성실함을 연구하는 Illinois 대학 심리학자 Brent Roberts는 말한다. Roberts는 그들의 성공을 '위생' 덕분이라고 생각한다. 성실한 사람들은 그들의 생활을 잘 정리하는 경향이 있다. 체계적이지 못하고 불성실한 사람은 올바른 서류를 찾기 위해 그들의 파일들을 구석구석 찾는 데 20분이나 30분을 허비할지도 모르는데, (이것은) 성실한 사람들은 피하는 경향이 있는 비효율적인 경험이다. 근본적으로, 성실함으로써, 사람들은 그들이 만약 그렇지 않았다면 스스로 만들었을지도 모를 스트레스를 비켜 간다.

16 ②

단어

deforestation : 삼림 벌채
biodiversity : 생물 다양성
era : 시대
anthropocene : 인류세
underpin : 지지하다
far from : 전혀 ~이 아닌
devastation : 황폐
inequality : 불평등
capitalism : 자본주의
accumulation : 축적
viable : 실행 가능한, 성공할 수 있는

해석

기후변화, 삼림 벌채, 만연한 공해 그리고 생물다양성의 6차 대멸종은 모두 오늘날 우리 세계, 즉 - '인류세'로 알려지게 된 시대 - 에 '산다'는 것을 말한다. 이러한 위기는 세계적인 생태계의 한계를 크게 초과하는 생산과 소비에 의해 뒷받침되고 있는데, 비난은 전혀 고르게 분산되지 않는다. 세계에서 가장 부유한 42명의 사람들이 가장 가난한 37억 명의 사람들이 소유한 것만큼 소유하고, 그들은 훨씬 큰 환경적 영향을 미친다. 그래서 일부의 사람들은 생태학적인 황폐화와 증가하는 불평등의 이 시대를 묘사하기 위해 '자본세'라는 용어를 사용하기를 제안했는데, (그것은) 무한 성장과 더 적은 수의 주머니 안으로 부가 축적되는 것에 대한 자본주의의 논리를 반영하는 것이다.

① 여전히 우리 손이 닿는 더 나은 세상
② 더 적은 수의 주머니 안으로 부가 축적되는 것
③ 기후변화에 대한 효과적인 대응
④ 더 성공적인 미래를 위한 불타는 욕망

TIP

빈칸 바로 앞 문장 The world's 42 wealthiest people own as much as the poorest 3.7 billion, and they generate far greater environmental impacts.를 통해서 ②번이 정답이라는 것을 알 수 있다.

17 ④

단 어

haunt : 출몰하다
revenger : 복수하는 사람
borderline : 국경선
barbarity : 야만, 만행
mercy : 자비
exact : 가하다
vengeance : 복수
take action : 조치를 취하다
perpetrator : 가해자, 범인
murderous : 살인의
deed : 행위
redemption : 구원, 구함
deprave : 타락하게 하다
atrocity : 잔혹 행위
accountability : 책임, 의무

해 석

고대 그리스 비극 시대 이후로 지금까지, 서양 문화에는 복수자의 인물이 등장해 왔다. 그 또는 그녀는 그 모든 일련의 경계선에 서 있는데, 다시 말해서 문명과 야만 사이에, 그 또는 그녀 자신의 양심에 대한 개인의 책임과 법규에 대한 공동체의 요구 사이에, 상충되는 정의와 자비의 요구 사이에 서 있다. 우리는 우리의 사랑하는 사람들을 파괴한 사람들에게 복수를 가할 권리가 있는가? 아니면 우리는 복수를 법이나 신들에게 맡겨야 하는가? 그리고 만약 우리가 정말 스스로 조치를 취한다면, 우리는 우리 자신을 살인 행위의 원래 가해자와 같은 도덕적 수준으로 낮추는 것이 아닌가?

① 타락한 상황으로부터의 복수자의 구원
② 인간의 잔학한 행위에 대한 신의 복수
③ 부패한 정치가들의 도덕적 타락
④ 그 또는 그녀 자신의 양심에 대한 개인적 책임

TIP

위에 나오는 Do we have a right to exact revenge against those who have destroyed our loved ones? Or should we leave vengeance to the law or to the gods? 의 두 개의 문장을 통해서 ④번이 정답이라는 것을 알 수 있다.

18 ③

단 어

assemble : 모으다, 조립하다
material : 자료, 내용
irrelevant : 관련없는
metaphor : 은유
register : 나타내다, 등록하다
association : 연합

해 석

나에게는 네 종류의 독서를 명명하는 것이 가능한 것처럼 보이는데, 각각은 특징적인 형식과 목적을 가지고 있다. 첫 번째는 정보를 위한 독서 – 무역, 정치, 또는 무언가를 성취하는 방법에 관해서 배우기 위한 독서이다. ① 우리는 이런 식으로 신문을 읽거나, 대부분의 교과서 또는 자전거를 조립하는 방법에 관한 설명서를 읽는다. ② 대부분의 이러한 자료를 가지고, 그가 필요로 하는 것을 생각해 내고 문장의 운율 또는 은유의 사용 같이 그에게 관련없는 것을 무시하면서, 독자는 페이지를 빨리 훑어보는 것을 배울 수 있다. (③ 우리는 또한 은유와 단어의 연상을 통해서 감정의 경로를 나타낸다.) ④ 속독에 관한 강좌는 눈이 페이지를 가로질러 빠르게 건너뛰도록 훈련시키면서, 우리가 이 목적을 위해 읽도록 도와줄 수 있다.

TIP

글의 주제는 독서의 종류에는 4종류가 있다고 설명해주는 첫 문장 It seems to me possible to name four kinds of reading, each with a characteristic manner and purpose. 이다. 따라서 "은유와 단어의 연상을 통해서 감정의 경로를 나타낸다."는 내용의 ③번은 주제에 관한 내용이 아니다.

19 ③

단 어

manifest : 나타내다, 분명해지다
obligation : 의무
comprise : 구성하다
accumulate : 축적하다
collectivistic : 집산주의적인
fulfill : 성취하다
individualistic : 개인주의적인
separate A from B : A를 B와 구분하다

해 석

일의 의미에서 문화적 차이는 다른 측면에서도 나타날 수 있다. 예를 들어, 미국 문화에서는, 일을 단지 돈을 모으고 생계를 꾸리는 수단으로 생각하기 쉽다. 다른 문화, 특히 집산주의적 문화에서, 일은 더 큰 그룹에 대한 의무를 성취하는 것으로서 더 여겨질지도 모른다. 이러한 상황에서 우리는 그 또는 그녀가 속한 직장 조직을 향한, 그리고 그 조직을 구성하고 있는 사람들

에 대한 개인의 사회적 의무 때문에 한 직장에서 다른 직장으로 이동하는 것이 덜할 거라고 예상한다. 개인주의적 문화에서는, 직업을 자신과 분리하는 것이 더 쉽기 때문에 한 직업을 떠나 다른 직업으로 가는 것을 고려하는 게 더 쉽다. 다른 직업도 그만큼 쉽게 같은 목표를 달성할 것이다.

☑ **TIP**

삽입 문장 앞에 나오는 이러한 상황(this situation)은 앞 문장에서 나왔던 '일이 그룹에 대한 의무를 성취하는 것으로 여겨지는' 상황을 의미한다. 따라서 정답은 ③이다.

20 ②

☑ **단 어**

navigate : 항해하다, 조종하다, 길을 찾다
microbat : 작은 박쥐류
emit : 발산하다
squeak : 찍찍 울다
echo : 메아리
instantaneous : 동시의
spot : 발견하다
echolocation : 반향 정위
sonar : 음파 탐지기
exactness : 정확함
perceive : 지각하다, 인식하다
nocturnal : 밤의

☑ **해 설**

ⓛ 북미에서 발견되는 작고, 곤충을 잡아먹는 박쥐인 소형박쥐들은 어둠속에서 길을 찾고, 먹이를 발견하는 데에 좋지는 않을 것 같은 작은 눈을 갖고 있다. ⓔ 그러나, 사실, 소형박쥐들은 쥐와 다른 작은 포유류만큼 잘 볼 수 있다. 박쥐들의 야행성 습관은 밤에 먹이를 먹는 것과 날아다니는 것을 우리가 생각하는 것보다 훨씬 더 쉽게 만들어주는 특별한 능력인, 그들의 반향 정위의 힘에 의해 도움을 받는다. ⓐ 어둠 속에서 길을 찾기 위해, 소형박쥐는 인간이 들을 수 없는 고음의 찍찍거리는 소리를 내면서, 입을 벌린 채 날아다닌다. 이러한 소리 중 일부는 나뭇가지와 그들 앞에 놓여있는 다른 장애물뿐만 아니라 날아다니는 곤충들로부터도 반향된다. 박쥐는 그 메아리를 듣고, 그것의 앞에 있는 물체의 즉각적인 형상을 뇌에 얻는다. ⓒ 음파탐지기라고도 불리는 반향정위로, 소형박쥐는 모기나 다른 어떤 가능한 먹이에 대해 상당히 많이 알 수 있다. 극도의 정확성으로, 반향 정위는 소형박쥐들이 움직임과 거리, 속도, 이동, 그리고 모양을 인식하도록 해 준다. 박쥐들은 또한 인간의 머리카락만큼 가다란 물체를 감지하고 피할 수 있다.

☑ **TIP**

소형박쥐가 작은 눈을 가지고 있어서 잘 못 볼 것 같다는 내용이 ⓛ에서, 그러나 예상과는 달리 잘 볼 수 있다는 내용이 ⓔ에서 이어진다. ⓐ에서 반향 정위를 그 원리와 함께 설명하고 ⓒ에서 반향 정위의 정확성 등에 대해 부가적으로 설명하고 있다.

2019. 8. 24.
국회사무처 시행

---

1 ①

☑ **단 어**

conspicuous : 눈에 잘 띄는
altruism : 이타심

☑ **해 설**

가장 흔하고 <u>뚜렷한</u> 동물의 이타심의 행동들은 부모들에 의해 행해지는데, 특히 자신들의 아이들을 향한 어머니들이 그러하다.

① 가장 두드러진   ② 적절한
③ 감추어진   ④ ~의 여부에 달린
⑤ 가장 기본적인

2 ③

☑ **단 어**

neoliberal : 신자유주의의
intact : 온전한
vicious : 공격적인
legislation : 제정법
countervail : 상대하다
thrall : ~에 좌우되는

☑ **해 설**

집단에 있어 신자유주의의 타격은 유럽보다 덜 하지만 미국에서도 온전히 남아있다. 자동화가 주된 이유도 아니고 산업화도 끝나지 않았다. 그저 거리가 벌어졌을 뿐이다. 금융화도 물론 신자유주의 시대 동안 큰 확장을 해왔고, 일반적인 관례들도 성격상 상당히 세계적인 것으로 민간과 기업의 힘을 향상시키도록 <u>설계되어</u> 왔다. 이것은 앞으로 과정을 이끌어갈 법제정과 행정상의 관례들을 차례로 만들어내는 악순환으로 나아가고 있다. 상쇄할 만한 힘이 존재하고 그들은 더 강력하게 될 수도 있다.

만약 Trump가 호소하는 백인노동 계층이 그들 계급의 적에게
속하지 않고 그들의 진정한 이익에 집중하도록 정리될 수 있다
면 우리가 Sanders와 심지어 Trump의 정치운동에서 볼 수 있
듯 잠재력 또한 있다고 본다.

✓ TIP

designed의 주어가 the general practies이고 financialization
has exploded와 상응하여 has designed가 적절하다.

3 ③

단 어

undocumented : 허가증 없는
legitimate : 합법적인
Individual Taxpayer Identification Number : ITIN 납세자 번호

☑ 해 설

그 글의 작성 시점에서 이민자 관리법에 관해 일반적으로 이번
행정부의 계획인 무엇인지는 불분명하다. 사용된 모든 이름들은
허가 없는 공동연구자들의 신분을 보호할 가명들이다. 이러한
사실들은 미등록 이민자들이 그들의 임금에 대한 세금을 내지
않는다는 일반적인 생각과는 반대로 작용한다. 그와 반대로 미
등록 근로자들은 해마다 위조된 서류들에 사용되는 소득세에 수
십억 달러를 지불한다.

✓ TIP

The undocumented는 복수이므로 do가 적합하다.

4 ②

단 어

reauthorize : 다시 권한을 부여하다, 다시 재가하다
deprive : 박탈하다
dilute : 희석하다, 약화시키다
undermine : 약화시키다

☑ 해 설

미국 의회는 법이 다시 권한을 부여하지 않는 한, "소수 민족과
언어 소수 시민은 투표권을 행사할 기회를 박탈당하거나 그들의
표를 약화시켜 지난 40년 동안 소수 민족들이 벌어들인 중요한
이득을 손상시킬 것이다."라고 결론지었다.

① 냉담한   ② 제한된
③ 적대적인   ④ 논쟁을 초래할
⑤ 파격적인

✓ TIP

diluted는 문맥 상 제한된(restricted)과 가까운 의미를 갖
고 있다.

5 ④

단 어

morsel : 작은 조각
proportional : 비례하는

☑ 해 설

많은 아기새들이 둥지에서 그들의 부모가 공급하는 먹이를 먹는
다. 그들 모두가 입을 벌리고 소리치면 부모새들이 그 중 하나
의 벌려진 입에 벌레나 다른 음식 조각을 떨어트린다. 각 새끼
들이 소리치는 소란함은 얼마나 배가 고픈지에 완벽히 비례한
다. 한 마리가 충분히 먹었을 때 더는 크게 울지 않기 때문에,
그 부모가 항상 가장 크게 우는 새끼에게 먹이를 준다면 새끼들
은 모두 공평한 양을 얻게 될 것이다. 하지만 우리의 이기적인
유전자 개념을 고려하면 우리는 개개인들이 <u>자신들이 얼마나 배
고픈지에 대해 거짓말할 것이라고</u> 예상하게 된다.

① 그들의 새끼들에게 먹일 것이다.
② 그들 각 공평한 양을 얻게 될 것이다.
③ 그렇게 크게 소리 지르지 않을 것이다.
④ 그들이 얼마나 배고픈지에 대해 거짓말할 것이다.
⑤ 항상 가장 크게 소리 내는 자에게 음식을 줄 것이다.

✓ TIP

마지막 문장은 but으로 시작하여 앞에서 설명한 새의 경우
와 다른 내용이 와야 하기 때문에, ④번이 정답이다.

6 ⑤

단 어

staggering : 충격적인
bluntly : 직설적으로

☑ 해 설

지난 주, 세계 야생동물 기금에서 그들의 살아있는 지구 보고서
를 발표했고, 그것은 포유류, 파충류, 양서류, 조류, 어류를 포
함한 야생동물 개체수가 1970년과 2014년 사이에 60%까지 떨
어졌다고 추정했다. 이것은 인간이 아닌 동물들의 생명과 생태
학적인 유산의 충격적이고 비극적인 손실을 보여준다. 하지만
WWF에 따르면 야생동물의 손실은 그것 이상의 의미를 지닌다.
보고서에 따르면 "우리의 건강, 음식, 안전은 (A) <u>생물의 다양성</u>
에 달려 있다". 그리고 연구가들은 "건강한 자연 체계가 없이 인
류 발전의 지속이 가능할 것인지에 대해 의문을 제기하고 있다."
그 보고서의 저자들 중 하나인 Mike Barrett은 가디언의 인터뷰
에서 더 직설적으로 표현했다. "이것은 그저 자연의 경이를 잃
는 것 훨씬 이상이고 몹시도 슬픈 일이다. 실제로 이 일은 이제
인간의 미래를 (B) <u>위태롭게 하고 있다.</u> 자연은 단지 '가져서 좋
다'가 아닌 우리의 생명자원체계이다."

(A)   /   (B)
① instrumentality 수단 / negating 무효화하는
② relativity 상대성   / enhancing 향상시키는
③ dissimilarity 차이점 / preserving 보존하는
④ productivity 생산성 / eradicating 근절하는
⑤ biodiversity 생물의 다양성 / jeopardizing 위태롭게 하는

7 ②

단 어

attribute : 속성
counter : 논박하다
stereotype : 정형화하다
cognitive : 인지의
constraint : 통제

해 석

잘 알려진 심리학 연구의 결과를 살펴보자. 사람들이 성별의 고정관념을 확정, 반박 혹은 회피하는 인간속성을 묘사하는 단어를 읽게 된다. 그 후에 그들은 한 이름을 받고 그것이 남성인지 여성인지 판단하도록 요구 받는다. 사람들은 <u>정형화된 속성이 이름과 관련 지어졌을 때 그렇지 않을 때 보다</u> 더 빨리 반응했다. 그래서 사람들은 '강한 Jane'과 '상냥한 John'보다 '강한 John', '상냥한 Jane'일 때 더 빠른 자극을 받는다. 피 실험자들에게 적극적으로 그 고정 관념에 대항해보라고 요청하고 낮은 수준의 인지적 통제(충분한 시간)를 가진다면 사람들은 이러한 반사적인 반응을 넘어설 수 있다.

① 그들이 그렇지 않을 때 보다 고정관념을 논박하도록 요구받았을 때
② 정형화된 속성이 이름과 관련 지어질 때가 그렇지 않을 때 보다
③ 단어가 성별 고정관념에 중립적일 때 그렇지 않을 때 보다
④ 그들은 그렇지 않을 때 보다 성별 고정관념을 피하게 되었을 때
⑤ 충분한 시간이 있을 때 그렇지 않을 때 보다

8 ④

단 어

acceleration : 가속
approximately : ~가까이

해 석

과학은 그 이론들이 분명한 상황 하에 '참이고 입증된' 것이라고 간주한다. 과학은 절대 완벽한 확실성을 가지고 무언가를 진술할 수 없다. 이 점이 우리 모두에게 문제를 일으킨다. 우리는 우리의 작업을 수행하기 위해 분명한 생각들이 사실로 입증되도록 할 필요가 있다. 우리는 종종 실질적인 이유로 계속적인 질문없이 그들의 상태를 특정한 것으로 받아들이는 합의점에 도달한다. 예를 들어, 우리는 중력이 물체가 9.8㎨ 비율로 지상으로 하강하는 것을 의미하고 있다는 것을 받아들인다. 우리는 이것이 평균적인 측정임을 이해한다. 학교 과학에서 그것은 자주 10㎨로 반올림된다. 중력으로 인한 가속도의 현실은 그 수치가 지역에 조건에 따라 달라질 수 있다. 예를 들어, 태평양 연안지역보다 인도 남부해안에서 중력은 더 적다. 당신이 측정할 질량은 평균에 비교할 때 인도해안에서 1% 가까이 적다.

① 완벽한 진실을 추구하기
② 사회 체계로서의 과학
③ 과학에서 해야 할 일
④ 과학적 진리의 상대성
⑤ 과학적 개혁의 구조

9 ①

단 어

inclusivity : 포용력
peripheral : 주변장치
advocate : 지지하다
saturate : 포화시키다
buoy : 부표

해 석

게임을 하기 위해 분투하는 사람에게 참여하는 능력과 화면에 비추어지는 능력을 부여하는 것은 정말로 중요한 표현의 일부이다. (A) <u>접근성</u>과 포용성 같은 메시지의 다른 부분이다. 영국의 Special Effect와 미국의 Able Gamers와 같은 자선단체들이 장애인 선수를 (B) <u>돕기</u> 위해 장비와 주변 장치를 세우고 산업 전반에 걸쳐 더 나은 지원을 지지하는 중요한 이유가 그것이다. 게임은 유년시절과 십대의 삶에 (C) <u>습관적인</u> 요소이며, 다른 능력이나 배경을 가진 사람들이 게임을 할 수 없고, 그들을 대표하는 아바타를 가질 수 없다는 것을 알게 되는 것은 고립을 양산한다. 그것은 당신이 필사적으로 소비하고 참여하고 싶은 문화에서 생각되거나 고려되지 않는 것을 고립시키고 있다. 미디어가 포화된 환경에서 소속의 메시지가 TV, 소셜 미디어 및 스마트 폰을 통해 끊임없이 전송되는 곳에서 포용성은 생명의 부표이다. 만약 당신이 넷플릭스, 인스타그램, 게임, 포럼에서 자신을 볼 수 없다면, 당신은 어디에 있는 것인가? 무슨 뜻인가? 그것이 문제이다.

(A)   /   (B)   /   (C)
① accessibility 접근성 / assist 돕다 / habitual 습관적인
② allegation 협의 / encourage 격려하다 / benign 유순한
③ commitment 헌신 / exclude 제외하다 / manic 정신없는
④ counterculture 반체제 / pursue 추적하다 / terse 간결한

⑤ misrepresentation 허위진술 / involve 관련시키다 / widespread 광범위한

10 ④

단 어

diagnose : 진단하다
equivalent : 등가물
contract cancer : 암에 걸리다

해 석

Sorbonne Paris Cite University의 연구원들인 Wednesday는 발행된 연구에서 100% 과일 주스를 포함한 당이 든 청량 음료의 소비량이 "전반적인 암의 위험요소와 상당히 관련되어 있다."고 밝혔다. 그들은 다이어트 소다 같이 인공적으로 달게 한 음료수들은 암발생 위험 증가와 관련이 없다는 것을 발견했다. 그 보고서의 저자들은 5년 동안 101,257명의 성인들을 추적하며 설탕과 인공감미료가 든 음료의 섭취를 모니터링 했다. 설탕이 든 음료를 설탕 5% 이상을 함유한 음료로 정의했고, 설탕이 첨가되지 않은 과일 주스도 포함시켰다. 연구 기간 중 2,193건의 암이 참여자들 중에서 진단되었고, 그것은 사람 1,000명 당 약 22건에 상당하는 것이다. 이러한 경우의 대부분이 설탕이 든 음료를 정기적으로 마시는 사람들 중에 있었다.

① 오렌지주스와 같이 단 음료는 암 걸릴 위험을 증가시킬 수도 있다.
② 연구원들은 5년 동안 참가자들의 설탕이 포함되었거나 인공감미료가 들어간 음료 섭취를 기록했다.
③ 연구원들은 설탕이 든 음료를 설탕 5% 이상인 음료라고 정의했다.
④ 오랜 기간 동안 설탕이 첨가되지 않은 오렌지주스를 섭취하는 것은 암 걸릴 확률을 줄일 수도 있다.
⑤ 연구 기간 동안 약 2.2% 의 연구 참가자들이 암환자로 진단 받았다.

TIP

본문에서 과일음료도 Sugary Drinks로 정의하였기 때문에 ④번이 일치 하지 않다.

11

단 어

acrimony : 악감정

해 석

Biff와 Travor는 그들 사이에 어떤 여자도 끼어들 수 없다고 맹세했지만, 사랑스러운 Teresa와 둘 모두 사랑에 빠진 후 그들의 우정을 넘어서는 정도가 아니라 <u>악감정</u>까지 가질 수 밖에 없었다.

① 적의 ② 무모함
③ 진심 ④ 연민
⑤ 기억

12 ⑤

단 어

torso : 몸통
wingspan : 날개폭

해 석

Michael Phelps는 역대 가장 잘 갖춰진 운동선수들 중 하나이다. 올림픽 5개 팀에서 대표선수 자리를 얻은 최초의 올림픽 수영선수이자 올림픽 금메달을 획득한 가장 나이 많은 개인부 수영선수로서, 그는 'Flying fish'라는 별명을 얻었다. 수영선수들은 평균적인 사람들보다 긴 상체와 짧은 다리를 가진 경향이 있다. 6피트 4인치를 기준으로 했을 때, Phelps는 6피트 8인치의 상체와 8인치 더 짧은 다리를 가지고 있다. 이중관절인 팔꿈치는 그가 물속에서 더 많이 아래로 내려가는 힘을 만들도록 했다. 또한 그의 커다란 손은 패들 같은 역할을 한다. 그의 보통보다 긴 팔 폭까지 더해 그의 팔은 프로펠러처럼 그가 물살을 헤쳐 힘 있게 나아가게 도와준다.

TIP

⑤ 주어가 his arms 이므로 shoot의 목적어로 him이 적절하다.

13 ③

해 석

학생들이 공부할 때 무엇을 하는지에 대하여 질문을 받을 때, 그들은 흔히 그들이 배우기 위해 애썼던 대로 밑줄 긋기, 하이라이트 표시 외에 다른 재료로 표시한다고 전한다. 우리는 이러한 기술들을 개념적으로 볼 때, 같은 방식으로 작업해야 한다는 점에서 동등하게 취급한다. 이 기술은 이용하기에 간단하고, 훈련을 수반하지 않으며 독해에 요구되는 것 이상의 시간을 투자할 필요가 없기 때문에 학생들에게 매력적이다. 여기서 우리가 물어볼 질문은 이렇게 사용하기 복잡한(→ 단순한) 기술이 학생들이 배우는데 도움이 될것인가 하는 것이다. 우리는 하이라이트 표시나 밑줄 긋기에 구체적인 어떤 이점이 있는지 이해도록 적극적으로 본문에 표시하는 것과 노트 필기 같은 다른 보통의 기법들을 병행하는 학습들은 고려하지는 않고 있다. 비록 많은 학생들이 여러 가지 기법들을 함께 사용한다고 말했지만, 각 기법들은 성공에 어떠한 것들이 중요한지 독립적으로 평가되어져야 한다.

① 상당하는 ② 수반하다
③ 복잡한 ④ 병행하는

⑤ 자주적으로

TIP

③문맥상 사용되는 기법들이 학습을 돕기에 적합한지에 대하여 반문하는 문장이므로 complicated는 어울리지 않는다.

14 ②

단 어

sensible : 합리적인
imperishable : 불멸의
inviolable : 신성한
indiscriminate : 무분별한
irrepairable : 수리 불가능한
decomposable : 분해할 수 있는
refuse : 쓰레기

해 석

그 최근 보고서는 대서양이 심각하게 오염되어 가고 (B) 썩지 않는 인간들의 쓰레기를 버릴 국제 쓰레기장이 식물과 동물 종들의 실제 생존과 생산성에 (C) 돌이킬 수 없는 영향을 끼치기에, 전 세계 바다를 계속적으로 (A) 무분별한 남용을 하고 있다는 경고를 주는 사실에 주의를 환기시키는 것 외에는 다른 목적이 없었다.

TIP

(A) indiscriminate 무분별한 – (B) imperishable 불멸의 –
(C) irrepairable 수리 불가능한

15 ②

단 어

sensorially : 감각기관으로
deprive : 박탈하다
neurological : 신경의
stunted : 성장을 저해당한
acquainted : 접한적 있는
refined : 교양 있는

해 석

한 대표적인 연구에서, 새끼 쥐들을 감각적으로 빈곤한 환경에 놓았다. 또 다른 그룹은 감각적으로 풍부한 환경에서 키워졌다. 감각적으로 제한된 그룹은 뇌의 발달에 지장을 초래했다. 그들은 간단한 미로를 통과할 수 없었고 공격적이고 폭력적인 사회 행동의 경향이 있었다. 감각적으로 풍부한 환경의 쥐들은 더 크고 좋은 연계형 뇌가 발달되었다. 그들은 복잡한 미로들을 빨리 익혔고 함께 행복하게 어울려 놀았다. 쥐들의 신경 시스템이 우리의 신경과 유사성을 보여주기 때문에 이 같은 실험에 사용되었다. 그러므로 지궁에서 시작하여 가정에서 뇌에 영양

을 공급하는 환경을 만들기 위해 모든 노력을 다해라. Dr. Thomas Verny 와 다수의 다른 연구가들에 의한 연구는 예를 들어 모차르트 음악을 들을 때와 같이 당신의 태아가 긍정적으로 영향 받는 것을 보여준다. 일단 아이들이 태어나면 당신의 자녀들을 위한 풍부하고 교양있는 감각적인 환경을 조성할 모든 기회를 놓치지 마라. 자주 사랑이 담긴 손길과 안아주는 행동은 당신의 성장하는 자녀들의 신경과 감정적 발달에 특히 중요하다.

① 그들이 클래식 음악의 역사를 알게 하기 위해
② 당신의 자녀들을 위한 풍부하고 교양 있는 감각적 환경을 조성하기 위해
③ 감각적인 자극 없이 상냥한 손길과 포용을 향상시키기 위해
④ 안전한 환경을 제공함으로 건강한 뇌 발달을 보장하기 위해
⑤ 신체 발달을 위해 당신의 자녀들에게 교육적인 환경을 제공하기 위해

16 ④

단 어

obliterate : 없애다
succumb : 굴복하다
trilobite : 삼엽충

해 석

1840년대에 이첩기의 화석 특징을 정의한 지질학자들은 그들이 그 시기 말에 있었던 많은 멸종의 흔적들을 언급하지 못했기 때문에 Lyell의 비평을 두려워했음에 틀림없다. 그들이 그것을 쉽게 간과했다고 보여지지는 않는다 이첩기의 멸종은 오늘날 지구 못지않게 복잡한 생태계를 지워버렸다. 육지에서 3미터 길이의 사브르치아파충류들은 없어지고 풀, 뿌리유충, 곤충을 먹는 도마뱀들은 그들이 먹은 식물이나 벌레들과 마찬가지로 사라졌다. 바다에서 생명으로 바글바글하던 암초들은 헐벗은 골격이 되었다. 이첩기는 사라져가던 삼엽충(어쩌면 포식공룡 시대의 한 유명 종이었던) 조차 멸종시켰다.

① 발달되었다   ② 비틀었다
③ 구했다   ④ 사라졌다
⑤ 번창했다

17 ④

단 어

throng : 인파
engulf : 휩싸다
belfry : 종탑
relic : 유물

소방관들이 월요일에 파리 노트르담 대성당의 큰 화재를 진압했다. 관광객 인파와 지역주민들이 12세기 명소가 큰 불에 휩싸이는 장면을 보고 촬영하기 위해 근처로 모여들었다. 파리 소방 사령관인 Jean-Claude Gallet은 수백 명의 소방관들이 북쪽 종탑으로 번지는 화염을 막을 수 있었고, 구조물은 완전한 파괴로부터 지켜졌다고 말했다. 주요 보수는 수사관들이 화재 원인이라 생각하는 바닥에 난 균열을 해결하기 위해 대대적으로 진행하고 있다. 대성당 내부의 많은 예술작품들에는 3장의 장미 스테인드글라스 창문이 포함된다. 대성당 성유물인 가시면류관은 사순절을 위해 전시되었고, 그것이 바로 이번 주가 시작이었다. "나는 우리 국민 모두와 같이 오늘 밤 우리 일부가 타는 것을 보게 되어 슬픕니다."라고 프랑스 대통령 Emmanuel Macron은 트윗으로 전했다. 하지만 그는 성당은 국가 모금 운동으로 재건될 것이라고도 말했다.

① 놀란 관중들이 공포 속에서 지켜봤다.
② 성당은 대중에게 제한되어 왔다.
③ 균열은 바닥에서 나타나기 시작했다.
④ 구조물은 완전한 붕괴에서는 지켜졌다.
⑤ 예술작품 중 일부는 실제로 제거되지 않았다.

18 ①

단 어

latitude : 위도
longitude : 경도
nautical : 항해의

☑ 해석

A : David, 나는 이 도표 읽는게 어려워.
B : 뭐가 문제인데?
A : 내가 위도랑 경도는 이해하는 것 같은데 분과 초를 완전하게 이해를 못해.
B : 글쎄, '분과 초'는 항해용어에서 다른 것을 의미해. 그것들은 보통 용어와 같지 않아.
A : 무슨 말이야?
B : 음, 항해시간은 거리를 측정해

① 그것들은 보통 용어와 같지 않아.
② 그들은 다양한 항해 기술을 사용해.
③ 그것들은 GPS를 어떻게 사용하는지에 따라 달라.
④ 사람들은 학생들이 자신의 고유의 도표를 그리도록 훈련시켰어.
⑤ 사람들은 초기 인류 역사 이후로 다른 기술을 사용해왔어.

19 ②

단 어

distortion : 왜곡
formulate : 나타내다

☑ 해석

금붕어들에게 있어 실제 모습은 우리들이 보는 것과 다르지만 우리는 그것이 덜 실제적이라고 확신할 수 있을까? ① 금붕어의 시야는 우리와 다르지만, 금붕어는 금붕어들이 관찰하는 수조 밖 물체의 움직임을 운용하는 과학법칙을 나타낼 수 있다. ② 예를 들면, 왜곡으로 인해 우리가 직선으로 움직이는 것으로 관찰되는 자유이동물체가 금붕어에게는 곡선로를 따라 이동하는 것으로 관찰된다. 그렇다 하더라도 항상 참을 유지하고 금붕어들이 수조 밖 물체들의 앞선 움직임에 관해 예측하도록 할 수 있게 해주는 왜곡된 틀로부터 과학법칙을 공식화 할 수 있다. ③ 그들의 법칙은 우리 틀 안에 있는 법칙보다 더 복잡할 것이다. ④ 하지만 그 단순함은 취향의 문제이다. ⑤ 만약 금붕어가 그러한 이론을 만들어 낸다면 우리는 현실의 타당한 모습으로서 금붕어의 시야를 인정해야 한다.

☑ TIP

②번 앞 문장에서 금붕어와 우리의 차이를 언급 후 주어진 예문을 넣고 그 뒤에 금붕어의 시야에 보이는 모습이 과학법칙에서 참이라는 보충을 Nevertheless 뒤에서 언급하고 있다.

20 ⑤

단 어

rhetoric : 발언
accompany : 동반하다

☑ 해석

전 세계에서 (A) 반무역풍의 발언 급증은 세계 무역 기구(WTO)에서 경고해 왔던 세계 주요 경제 강국에 의한 보호무역론자 방안의 도입의 발생과 동반하게 되었다. WTO는 화요일에 나온 보도에서 작년 10월 중반과 2016년 5월 중반 사이에 시작하며 G20 금융정상회담이 2008년 금융 위기 이후 가장 빠른 속도로 새 보호무역방안을 도입했으며 매주 5개에 해당하는 조치를 취했다고 밝혔다. 그 트렌드는 5년째 해인 지금 세계무역의 둔화와 함께 일어났다. 게다가, 그것은 세계 경제의 지속적인 느린 성장에 원인이 되고 있고, 전 세계 보호무역 정책방안의 (B) 증가와 동시에 일어난다는 사실이 우려되어진다고 WTO는 밝혔다.

	(A)	/	(B)

① hostile 적대적인 / plummet 급락하다
② democratic 민주적인 / embargo 수출금지하다
③ emotional 정서적인 / initiative 진취성
④ banal 시시한 / restraint 규제
⑤ antitrade 반대무역의 / increase 증가

2020. 2. 22.
법원행정처 시행

---

1 ②

단 어

dangle : 매달리다
slip : 메모용지

해 석

지식과 사실을 동일시하고 싶지만, 모든 사실들이 지식의 하나는 아니다. 동전 하나가 들어있는 밀봉된 골판지상자를 흔든다고 상상해보라. 당신이 그 상자를 내려놓았을 때, 상자 안의 동전은 앞면이나 뒷면으로 내려졌을 것이다. 이것을 사실이라고 하자. 하지만 누군가가 상자 안을 들여다보지 않는 한 이 사실은 알 수 없는 상태로 남는다. 그렇다면 그것은 아직 (A) 지식의 영역 안에 있지 않다. 또한 글로 쓰인다고 간단히 사실이 지식이 되지도 않는다. 만약 당신이 종이쪽지에 '동전이 앞면으로 착지했다.'라는 문장을 쓰고 다른 쪽지에는 '동전이 뒷면으로 착지했다.'라고 쓴다면, 당신은 쪽지들 중 하나에 사실을 적게 된 것이지만 당신은 아직 동전던지기 결과에 대한 지식을 파악할 수 없을 것이다. 지식은 어떤 식으로든 실제하는 것에서부터 사실에 접근할 것을 요구한다. 그러한 사실에 접근할 마음이 (B) 없다면, 도서관이나 데이터베이스에 무엇이 저장되어 있던지 그것은 지식이 되지 못할 것이고, 그거 잉크자국이나 전자적 흔적일 뿐이다. 어떠한 지식에 대해서, 한 개인에게 이런 접근은 특별하거나 아닐 수도 있다. 그 같은 사실을 아는 사람과 알지 못하는 사람들이 있을 수도 있다는 말이다. 상식은 다수의 사람이 공유할 수 있지만, 어떤 실체에도 (C) 속하지 못하는 지식은 없다.

TIP

② knowledge 지식 / without ~하지 않고 / unattached 소속되지 않는

---

2 ①

단 어

impressionable : 쉽게 외부 영향을 받는
sales rep : 영업 사원

해 석

민감한 청년들만 동료집단의 압박을 받는 것은 아니다. 우리들 대부분은 아마 판매직원에게 압박을 받은 경험이 있을 것이다. 당신은 영업 사원이 당신에게 '당신의 경쟁사들의 70%가 그들의 서비스를 이용하고 있는데 당신은 왜 그렇게 하지 않는가'라고 말하면서 '사무용품'을 판매하려고 한 적이 있는가? 하지만 만약 당신의 경쟁사들 중 70%가 바보들이라면? 아니면 그들이 꽤 고가의 무료부가상품을 받게 되거나 그들이 그 기회를 저버릴 수 없을 만큼 낮은 가격을 제안 받았다면? 그런 영업방식은 오직 한가지, 당신이 구매하도록 압박할 그 목적으로 계획된 행동인 것이다. 당신이 뭔가 좋은 기회를 놓치고 있는지도 모르고 당신만 모르고 다른 모든 사람들은 알고 있다고 느끼게 만들기 위해서 말이다.

① 동료들에게 받는 사회적 압력
② 충동구매
③ 괴롭히기 작전
④ 치열한 경쟁

---

3 ②

단 어

compound : 타협하다
opt for : ~을 선택하다
conversely : 정반대로
compensate : 보상하다
attribute : ~의 결과로 보다

해 석

높은 자존감을 가진 사람들은 그들의 기술과 능력에 자신감을 갖고 인생이 그들에게 주는 도전을 직면하는 것을 즐긴다. 그들은 자신에게 확신이 있고 팀에 기여할 기회를 갖는 것을 즐기기 때문에 (A) 기꺼이 팀에서 일한다. 하지만 낮은 자존감을 가진 사람들은 불편하고 부끄러움을 느끼고 자신을 표현하지 못하는 경향이 있다. 그들은 자주 문제를 회피하는 방법을 선택함으로써 그들의 문제와 타협한다. 왜냐하면 그들은 자신들이 어찌됐건 실패로 결론지어 질 것이라는 신념을 (B) 가지고 있기 때문이다. 정반대로 그들은 스스로의 가치 없다는 느낌을 덮기 위해 허세를 부리거나 거만한 행동으로 부족한 자존감을 채우려할지도 모른다. 게다가, 그런 사람들은 그들 외부에 있는 이유들을 찾음으로 그들의 성공을 해명지만, 반면에 높은 자존감을 가진 사람들은 그들의 성공을 내적인 기질의 (C) 결과로 본다.

② (A) willingly – (B) hold – (C) attribute

4 ④

단어

devise : 고안하다
intricate : 복잡한
elaborate : 정교한
skyscraper : 고층 건물
manipulate : 다루다
unprepossessing : 매력 없는
fang : 송곳니

해석

분명한 것은, 숭고한 것에서 황당하고 말도 안 되는 것까지 어떤 다른 종도 새롭고 독창적인 뭔가를 고안하는 우리의 능력을 자신들도 갖고 있다고 주장할 수 없다. 다른 동물들도 분명 여러 가지를 만들었다. 새들은 복잡한 둥지를 조립해 짓고, 비버들은 댐을 지으며 개미들은 정교한 터널 네트워크를 뚫는다. Fuentes는 "하지만 비행기, 희한하게 기울어진 고층건물이나 Chica Pets는 꽤 인상적입니다."라며 진화적 관점에서 "창의력은 직립보행하고 큰 뇌를 갖고 도구를 다룰 수 있는 또 정말 좋은 손을 가진 것만큼 도구를 사용하는 우리의 중요한 대단한 부분입니다."라는 말을 더했다.
다른 눈에 띄는 큰 어금니나 발톱, 날개 또는 다른 뚜렷한 신체적 장점은 없는 영장류에게 창조력은 대등하게 해주었다. 그리고 더하자면 인류가 적어도 이제까지 생존하도록 보장해주고 있었다.

① 인간의 창조력은 어디에서 온 것일까?
② 영장류의 신체적 특징은 무엇인가?
③ 다른 종에 비교하여 인류의 신체적 장점들
④ 창조력 : 인류가 생존을 위해 가진 독특한 특성

TIP

생존을 위해 인간만이 갖고 있는 창조력에 대해 정리한 ④번이 제목으로 적절하다.

5 ①

단어

instantaneous : 직관적인
sequence : 순서, 연속

해석

"대부분의 조류 식별은 새들이 이동하는 방식과 다른 각도에서 순간의 모습, 다양한 모습들의 연속에 관한 대상의 고유한 특징

을 바탕으로 한다. 새가 머리를 돌릴 때, 새가 날 때, 또 새가 주위를 돌 때, 당신은 연속된 다양한 모습과 각도를 보게 된다." Sibley는 "모든 것들이 결합하여 따로 분리시킬 수 없고, 말로 표현할 수 없는 조류의 한 독특한 모습을 만들어 낸다. 새를 관찰할만한 들판이 있는 곳으로 가보면, 당신은 새를 바로 분석하게 되고, 새가 이런 저런 것을 보여주기 때문에 그 새가 이 종이다 라고 말 할 수 있다. 그 작업은 더 자연스럽고 직감적이다. 많이 연습한 후에 당신이 새를 보면 그 새가 당신 뇌의 작은 스위치를 자극한다. 그렇다. 당신은 한눈에 그것이 무엇인지 알아볼것이다."라고 말했다.
[Sibley에 따르면 조류 식별은 (B) 개별적인 분석 보다는 (A) 직관적인 인상에 근거한다.]

① 직관적인 인상 – 개별적 분석
② 객관적인 조사 – 주관적인 판단
③ 신체적 모습 – 행동적 특성
④ 면밀한 관찰 – 원거리 관찰

6 ①

단어

leasing : 임대
correspond : 부합하다
exterior : 외부의
derive : 유래하다

해석

[자동차가 인간에 대한 의존도가 낮아짐에 따라, 차량 공유와 단기 리스 프로그램에 더 높아진 참여율로 자동차가 소비자들에 의해 사용되어지는 수단과 상황 또한 분명한 변화를 겪을 가능성이 있다.]
(A) 그리 멀지 않은 미래에, 무인자동차가 당신에게 필요할 때가 올 수 있고, 사용 후 주차할 공간을 찾을 필요 없이 떠나면 된다. 차량 공유와 단기 리스의 증가는 또한 이에 상응하게 자동차 외부 설계의 중요성 감소와 관련될 가능성이 있다.
(C) 자동차 외관은 맞춤 개조와 개성의 한 수단으로 쓰이기 보다는, 점점 더 광고와 Free Car Media가 제공하는 것 같은 브랜드 홍보를 포함하는 홍보 활동들을 대표하게 되었다.
(B) 결과적으로, 자동차에서 파생된 상징적 의미와 자동차와 소비자의 자아정체성과 지위와의 관계도 변하게 될 것 같다.

7 ①

단어

executive : 임원
mallet : 망치
sheepishly : 소심하게
accumulate : 모으다

✓ 해 석

[일본의 생산라인을 보려고 일본으로 갔던 미국의 자동차 임원들의 한 그룹에 관한 놀라운 이야기가 하나 있다. 미국에서와 마찬가지로 그 라인 끝에서 자동차 문에 경첩이 달렸다.]

(A) 하지만 무언가가 생략되었다. 미국에서 생산 근로자는 문이 완벽히 맞아 떨어지도록 고무망치를 가지고 문의 가장자리를 두드린다. 그런 작업은 일본에서는 존재하지 않는 듯 했다.

(B) 혼란스러운 상태로 미국 자동차 임원은 그들이 자동차 문이 완벽히 맞는지 언제쯤 확인하는지 질문했다. 일본 가이드들이 그들을 보고 겸연스레 웃었다. "우리는 우리가 차를 디자인 할 때 이미 문이 꼭 맞도록 확인합니다."

(C) 일본 자동차 공장에서, 그들은 최선의 방법을 알아내기 위해 그 문제를 시험하거나 데이터를 축적하지 않았다. 그들은 시작 시점부터 그들이 원하던 결과를 고안했다. 만약 그들이 바라던 결과를 얻지 못한다면, 그들은 그것이 그들이 과정의 시작부터 했던 결정 때문이라고 이해할 것이다.

8 ①

📖 단 어

nonverbal : 비언어적인, 말로 할 수 없는
deception : 속임, 사기
leakage : 누출
date back to : ~까지 거슬러 올라가다
reliance : 의존
assess : 평가하다
infer : 추론하다

✓ 해 석

Ekman의 논문과 들통 이라는 그의 발상까지 거슬러 올라가 속임수에 대한 비언어적 단서들에 관한 많은 연구가 존재해왔다. 사람들이 거짓말을 알아내는 방법으로 다른 사람들의 비언어적 행동들을 이용한다는 점은 문서로 잘 기록되어있다. 나의 연구와 많은 다른 이들의 연구는 사람들이 정직에 대해 가늠할 때, 다른 사람들의 비언적 행동에 대한 관찰에 의존한다고 강력히 지지해 왔다. (A) 하지만 다양한 비언어적 행동들과 거짓의 행동의 관계를 조사한 사회과학연구는 그 둘의 연결이 전형적으로 아주 강력하거나 일관적이지는 않다고 시사한다. 나의 연구에서 나는 한 거짓말쟁이가 보이는 비언어적 신호가 두 번째 거짓말쟁이에게 받은 것과는 다르다는 것을 알게 되었다. (B) 게다가 비언어적 행동과 속임에 연결된 과학적 증거는 시간을 거듭하며 약해졌다. 사람들은 다른 사람들이 얼마나 비언어적으로 자신을 표현하는 지에 근거하여 정직을 추론하지만, 그것은 아주 제한된 유용성과 타당성을 지닌다.

　　　(A)　 / 　(B)
① 하지만 / 게다가
② 결과로 / 반대로
③ 하지만 / 그렇다 하더라도
④ 결과로 / 예를 들어

9

📖 단 어 · ③

sales force : 판매 조직
administrative : 행정상의

✓ 해 석

신규업체가 법인등록을 하려고 하자마자, 은행 계좌가 필요하고 급여계좌의 필요도 곧 따른다. 은행들은 아주 작은 사업체와 시작하더라도 급여지불과 관련된 세금 부기 업무 서비스에 매우 경쟁적이다. 이것이 바로 사업체가 최고급의 서비스와 받을 수 있는 한 많은 무료 회계 도움을 원하는 부분이다. 변하는 급여지불세 법률은 정기적으로 따라잡기 골칫거리이다. 특히 50주의 영업부서에서 영업을 해야 할 때 그렇다. 그리고 요구되는 보고서들은 회사의 추가 행정 직원에게 부과되는 부담이다. 이러한 서비스는 종종 은행원들에 의해 가장 잘 제공된다. 이런 분야에서 은행들의 증빙서류는 ADP 같은 급여관리 서비스 대안 업체와 비교되어야 한다. 하지만 앞으로와 장기적인 관계라는 점을 결정이 내려질 때 꼭 염두에 두어야 한다.

✓ TIP

③번 requiring은 현재분사로 수식되는 reports가 능동으로 받을 수 없기 때문에, 수동의 의미로 required가 적절하다.

10 ①

📖 단 어

elements : 비바람
distraught : 심란한

✓ 해 석

많은 사람들이 동물보호센터에 가는 것이 슬프고 우울한 일임을 느끼기 때문에 방문하려 하지 않는다. 정말 많은 운 좋은 동물들이 그들이 처해 있던 교통사고의 위험, 다른 동물들이나 사람들에 의한 공격, 비바람의 문제가 있던 거리의 위험한 삶에서 구해지기 때문에 사람들이 그렇게 유감을 가질 필요가 없다. 마찬가지로 많은 길 잃은 애견들도 동물보호센터로 보내졌기 때문에 놀라서 제정신이 아닌 주인들이 간단히 발견해 되찾아진다. 가장 중요하게도, 입양 가능한 애견들은 살 집을 찾게 되고, 아프거나 위험했던 동물들은 인도적으로 그들이 받던 고통들을 덜게 된다.

✓ TIP

동물보호센터를 방문하는 일은 우울함을 일으키는 원인이므로 능동으로 현재부사 depressing이 되어야 한다. 따라서 ① depressed가 어법상 틀렸다.

11 ②

단어 ·

reliable : 믿을 만한
extraordinary : 비범한

해석

EQ테스트는 믿을 만한 테스트방법으로 수행될 때 당신에게 자신에 대한 유용한 정보를 제공할 수 있다. 나는 수많은 사람들을 테스트 해오면서 많은 수가 자신들의 결과에 약간 놀란다는 것을 알게 되었다. 예를 들어, 자신이 매우 사회적 책임감이 높고 타인에 대해 관심이 크다고 믿었던 한 사람은 그 영역에서 (A) 평균인 점수가 나왔다. 그녀는 그녀의 점수에 꽤 실망했다. 그녀가 사회적 책임에 대해 아주 높은 기준을 갖고 있었고, 따라서 그녀는 그녀가 스스로에 대해 평가를 할 때 자신에 대하여 엄청나게 (B) 엄격했다는 것이다. 실제로 그녀는 대부분의 사람보다 (C) 더 많은 사회적 책임감을 갖고 있지만 그녀는 자신이 지금 하는 것 보다 훨씬 더 잘할 수 있다고 믿었던 것이다.

TIP

② (A) 평균의 – (B) 엄격한 – (C) 더 많은

12 ②

단어 ·

conceal : 감추다
enthusiast : 열성팬

해석

한 사람이 자신에게 유리한 증거를 들어가며 확실한 믿음을 주려 할지도 모른다. 한 어머니가 그녀의 아들에게 "이번 학기에 영어는 어떠니?"라고 묻자, "오, 저는 시험에서 95점을 막 받았어요."라고 그는 활기차게 대답한다. 그 진술은 그가 모든 시험을 낙제했고 그의 실제 평균은 55점이라는 사실을 숨기고 있다. 하지만 그녀가 만약 더 이상 그 문제에 대해 계속 묻지 않는다면, 그녀는 그녀의 아들이 잘하고 있는 것이 기쁠지도 모르겠다. Linda가 Susan에게 "Dickens 책을 좀 읽어봤니?"라고 묻자, Susan은 "오, Pickwick Papers는 내가 가장 좋아하는 소설 중에 하나야."라고 대답한다. 그 대답은 Pickwick papers가 Susan이 읽었던 Dickens의 유일한 소설이라는 사실을 숨기고 있고, 그 진술은 Linda에게 Susan이 Dickens의 엄청난 열성팬이라는 인상을 줄 수도 있다.

① 여분의 돈을 벌다.
② 확실한 믿음을 가져오다.
③ 기억력 문제를 숨기다.
④ 다른 사람들이 죄책감을 느끼게 만들다.

13 ①

단어 ·

complement : 보완하다
reinforcement : 강화
occasional : 가끔의
sweeping : 포괄적인
enthusiastic : 열렬한
downfall : 몰락

해석

우리는 잘 꾸민 외모, 잘 가꾼 정원, 우리가 잘 차린 저녁식사, 혹은 사무실에서 업무, 이 중 어느 것에 대한 칭찬이든, 그 일을 잘 해냈다고 인정받는 것은 언제나 만족스러운 일이다. 확실히, 강화이론에서 가끔씩 칭찬하는 것은 새로운 기술을 배우는 데 도움을 주는 도구라고 하지만, 어떠한 증거는 더 나은 성과를 위해 칭찬을 하는 것에 대하여 포괄적인 일반화를 만들지 말라고 주의하고 있다. 칭찬이 특정한 일에서 성과를 향상시키는 반면, 다른 영역에서 그것은 대신 나쁜 결과를 낼 수도 있다. 열성팬이 승리를 기대하며 홈팀을 응원한 것이 그 팀의 몰락을 가져 온 상황을 상상해보라. 이런 상황에서 칭찬은 운동선수들에게 부담을 주고 그들의 실적에 지장을 준 것으로 보인다.
[(A) 칭찬이 성과에 도움을 주거나 해를 끼치는 것은 주어진 (B) 일의 유형에 달려 있다.]

14 ③

단어 ·

consumption : 소비

해석

우리가 익명의 사회적 관계의 맥락에서 미디어 사용을 고려해 볼 때, 술집 같은 공공장소에서 텔레비전을 보는 것, 콘서트나 댄스클럽에 가는 것, 혹은 버스나 지하철에서 신문을 읽는 것과 같이 낯선 사람들이 있는 것을 포함하는 모든 경우를 지칭한다. 우리가 우리 주위의 낯선 사람들 그리고 미디어 제품들과 보통 어떻게 소통하는지 통제하는 사회적 규칙들이 있다. 예를 들어, 다른 사람의 어깨 너머로 읽거나 공공장소에서 일어나 설치된 TV의 채널을 바꾸는 것은 우리 문화에서 무례하다고 여겨지거나 최소 공격적이라고 여겨진다. 음악을 좋아하는 사람이라면 특정한 형태의 콘서트에서 어떤 행동이 적절한지 알고 있다. 관계가 완전히 개인적이지 않다는 사실에도 불구하고, 타인의 존재는 종종 설정과 그에 따른 미디어 소비의 활동을 정의하는데 중요하다.

TIP

③번 read는 등위 접속사 or 뒤에 to get up and change와 병렬로 to read가 알맞다.

15 ③

단 어

amnesia : 기억 상실
inability : 불능
portray : 묘사하다, 연기하다
exceedingly : 대단히
intact : 온전한

해 석

우리 중 다수는 기억 상실증, 즉 갑작스런 기억 손실이 그 사람의 이름과 정체성을 기억하는 능력을 상실하는 결과를 야기한다고 믿는다. 이런 믿음은 보통 기억 상실증이 영화, 텔레비전, 문학에서 묘사된 방식을 반영한 것일 수 있다. 예를 들어, 우리가 영화 'The Bourne Identity'에서 Matt Damon 역할을 볼 때, 우리는 그가 자신이 누구인지, 왜 그가 그런 능력을 가졌는지, 혹은 어디 출신인지에 대하여 전혀 기억이 없다는 것을 보게 된다. 그는 영화의 많은 시간을 이런 질문들의 대답을 찾기 위해 보낸다. 하지만 당신의 이름과 정체성을 기억하지 못하는 것은 현실에서는 무척 보기 힘든 일이다. 대게 기억 상실증은 환자가 과거 대부분의 기억은 온전히 지닌 채로 새로운 기억은 할 수 없게 만드는 뇌손상으로 주로 유발된다. 우리가 정말 좋아하는 Memento 같은 일부 영화들은 꽤 흔한 이 신드롬을 섬세하게 그려낸다.

TIP

③번에는 to remember의 수식을 받은 the inability가 주어이기 때문에 단수동사 is가 적합하다.

16 ②

단 어

subconsciously : 잠재의식적으로
occurrence : 발생

해 석

현재는 자연 재해와 그 피해가 사람들과 그들의 재산에 끼친 부정적인 영향에 관한 많은 것이 잘 알려져 있다. 논리적인 사람이라면 잠재적인 자연재해의 영향을 회피하거나, 그런 피해를 최소화하기 위해 그들의 행동이나 속성을 최소한 변경하는 것은 명백해 보일 것이다. 하지만, 인간은 항상 이성적이지 않다. 어떤 사람이 개인적인 경험을 하거나 그런 경험을 겪은 사람을 알기 전까지, 대부분의 사람들은 잠재의식적으로 "여기서는 그런 일이 일어나지 않을 거야." 혹은 "나에게는 일어날리 없어."라고 믿는다. 위험성, 재해의 발생 가능성, 사고피해비용을 잘 아는 총명한 과학자들조차 항상 적절하게 행동하지는 않는다.

① 침묵하기를 거부한다.
② 항상 적절하게 행동하지는 않는다.
③ 유전적 요소를 우선으로 적용한다.
④ 자연 재해를 정의하기가 어렵다.

17 ③

단 어

infrastructure : 사회 기반 시설
specialization : 전문화
densely : 밀집하여
exclusive : 독점적인
mediocre : 썩 좋지 않은

해 석

도시와 국가가 생겨나고 교통시설의 발달은 전문직을 위한 새로운 기회를 야기했다. 인구 밀도가 높은 도시들은 전문적인 구두 제조인, 의사뿐 아니라 목수, 성직자, 군인, 변호사도 정규직 일자리를 제공했다. 정말 질 좋은 와인이나 올리브 오일, 도자기 생산으로 명성을 얻은 마을들은 그 생산품을 거의 독점적으로 특화하고, 그들이 필요로 하는 다른 모든 상품들을 얻기 위해 다른 정착민들과 거래하는 것이 시간적 가치가 있다는 것을 알아냈다. 이것은 정말 기발한 생각이었다. 각 기후와 토양이 다르기에 만약 당신이 토양과 기후가 포도나무에 훨씬 더 적합한 곳에서 온 더 괜찮은 와인을 살 수 있다면 왜 당신의 텃밭에서 온 그저 그런 와인을 마시겠는가? 만약 당신 텃밭의 진흙이 더 단단하고 더 예쁜 화분을 만들 수 있다면, 당신은 맞교환하면 된다.

① 기후와 토양이 지역 상품에 어떤 영향을 끼치나.
② 지역 특산물에서 좋은 평판을 얻는 방법들
③ 무엇이 사람들을 특산품에 관심을 갖고 무역을 하게 만들었나.
④ 도시의 융성과 전문직 종사자를 위한 정규직화

TIP

지문의 시작에서 특산품 생산 시작의 원인을 보여주며, 이후에 다른 지역 사람들과 왜 거래하게 되었는지 글 전반에서 설명하고 있다. 따라서 ③번이 제목으로 알맞다.

18 ④

단 어

penalize : 부당하게 대우하다
empathy : 공감

해 석

9살 인 Ryan Kyote가 그 뉴스를 봤을 때 그는 California Napa에 있는 집에서 아침식사를 하고 있었다. 그 뉴스는 인디애나의 한 학교가 한 여섯 살짜리 아이의 급식계좌에서 급식비가 부족하자 그녀의 식사를 가져가 버렸다는 내용이었다. Kyote는 만약 그런 일이 그의 친구들에게 일어날 수 있는지 물었다. 그의 엄마가 이를 알아내기 위해 교육청에 연락했을 때, 그녀는 그 학군의 학생들에게 통 틀어 급식비 25,000 달러 정도의 미납이 있다는 사실을 알게 되었다. 그 교육청에서는 절대 미납된 학생들을 부당하게 대우하지 않았다고 말하지만, Kyote는 그가 모은 용돈을 그의 학년의 미납금 약 74달러를 지불하는데 사용하기로 결정했고 이것은 급식비 미납을 해결하려는 운동의 시작이 되었다. 10월에 California 주지사 Gavin Newsom은 '부끄러운 점심식사' 혹은 미납 때문에 '질 낮은 급식 제공'을 금지하는 법안에 서명했을 때, 이런 문제에 대한 인식을 높이는 데 있어서 Kyote가 보여준 "그의 공감과 용기"에 감사를 표했다. Kyote는 이렇게 말한다. "영웅들은, 다양한 연령에서 나옵니다."

① 주지사가 급식비 미납인 학생들에게 점심 메뉴를 줄이라는 법안에 서명했다.
② Kyote가 급식비가 부족했기 때문에 그는 급식을 받지 못했다.
③ 재정적 부담이 있던 교육청은 양질의 급식을 제공하지 못한 예산을 삭감했다.
④ 급식비를 낼 수 없었던 그 지역의 많은 학생들은 급식비 미납인 상태였다.

☑ TIP

Kyote가 뉴스를 접하고 자신의 지역 학생들의 상황에 관심을 갖고 그의 어머니가 알아봤을 때, 그 지역에 상당한 급식비 미납 상황이 있음이 드러났고 급식비 미납상황으로 인해 곤란할 학생들을 돕기 위한 활동이 시작됨을 암시하는 글이다. 따라서 ④번이 the issue가 가리키는 내용이다.

19 ④

■ 단 어

ken : 시야, (지식의) 범위, 지식, 알다
mating : 교미
penetrating : 날카로운
yearning : 갈망

☑ 해 석

세상에서 가장 큰 심장은 청고래 안에 있다. 그것은 7톤 이상의 무게가 나간다. 그리고 방 하나만큼 크다. 이 생명체는 20피트의 길이와 4톤의 무게로 태어난다. 그 새끼 고래는 당신의 차보다 훨씬 더 크다. 그리고 매일 100갤런의 엄마 모유를 마시고 하루에 무게가 200파운드씩 늘어난다. 그리고 이 새끼 고래가 7-8살이 되면 상상을 초월한 사춘기를 보내고, 그 후 사실상 인간 지식의 영역에서 사라져버리는데, 그 이후의 교미 습성, 이동 형태, 식습관, 무리생활, 언어, 사회구조, 질병에 대해서는 알려진 점이 없어서이다. 여태껏 우리에게 거의 알려진 바 없는 가장 큰 동물이자, 지구 상 모든 바다에 서식하는 약 만 마리의 청고래가 살고 있다. 하지만 우리는 전 세계에서 가장 큰 심장을 가진 그 동물들이 일반적으로 쌍으로 이동하고, 그들의 귀청을 찢고 갈망하는 듯한 언어로 울부짖는 신음 소리는 바다 밑 멀리에서도 들을 수 있다는 것은 알고 있다.

☑ TIP

지문에서 청고래가 보통 쌍으로 이동한다고 언급했기 때문에 ④번에서 혼자서 이동한다는 말은 맞지 않다.

20 ④

■ 단 어

carbon dioxide : 이산화탄소
optimal : 최적의

☑ 해 석

신선한 농산물을 취급할 때 온도를 조절하는 것 외에도 대기의 조절이 중요하다. 공기 중 약간의 수분은 보관 중에 건조를 막기 위해 필요하지만, 과한 수분은 곰팡이 성장을 촉진할 수 있다. 어떤 상업저장창고는 신중히 이산화탄소와 수분 모두 신중하게 통제하는 수준으로 대기를 관리해 오고 있다. 에틸렌 가스 같은 다른 가스들이 때때로 바나나와 다른 신선한 농산물들이 최상의 질에 이르는데 도움이 되도록 통제된 수준에서 도입될 수 있다. 가스와 습기의 조절과 관련된 것은 저장된 음식들 사이에서 공기의 순환이 어느 정도 필요하다는 것이다.

① 대기 중 유해기체 관리의 필요성
② 식물과 과일 성장에서 수분 양을 관리하는 최선의 방법
③ 전 세계에서 해마다 증가하는 탄소 배출량의 심각성
④ 식품을 저장할 때 가스와 수분을 분명한 단계로 관리하는 중요성

☑ TIP

본문 전반에서 공기의 질과 수분 조절의 중요함을 강조하고 있다. 따라서 ④번이 주제로 적절하다.

21 ④

■ 단 어

vanity : 허영
undermine : 기반을 약화시키다
outweigh : 더 크다
accelerate : 가속화되다

☑ 해 석

거짓말이 특정 상황에서 어떤 유해한 영향을 끼치지 않더라도, 여전히 도덕적으로 옳지 않은 것은, 만약 거짓말이 밝혀진다면 인간이 의사소통하며 신뢰하는 진실 전달의 일반적인 관행을 약화시키기 때문이다. 예를 들어, 내가 허영심 때문에 내 나이에 대해 속이고 그 거짓말이 밝혀진다면, 그것이 비록 심각한 해가 행해지는 것은 아닐 지라도, 나는 기본적으로 당신의 신뢰 기반을 ①약화시킬 것이다. 이런 경우 당신은 내가 앞으로 말하는 어떤 것이든 믿을 가능성이 훨씬 더 적어질 것이다. 그러므로

모든 거짓말은 발견되었을 때 간적접인 ② 유해를 끼친다. 하지만, 아주 가끔 이런 유해한 상황들은 거짓말로 발생하는 ③ 이로운 점보다 적을 수도 있다. 예를 들어, 만약 누군가가 심각한 병이 들었을 때, 그들에게 자신들의 생명 기대치에 대하여 하는 거짓말은 어쩌면 그들에게 더 오래 살 기회를 줄 수도 있다. 반대로 그들에게 진실을 말해주는 것은 아마도 환자의 몸 상태 악화를 촉진하는 우울증을 ④ 유발할 수도 있다.

✅ **TIP**

④번이 있는 문장 전에 하얀거짓말의 순기능이 나왔기 때문에 그 뒤에는 그렇게 하지 않았을 때 더 악화된 상황이 있을 수 있다는 문장이 적절하다. 따라서 prevent는 적절하지 않다.

22 ②

🔲 **단 어**

sustain : 지속시키다
transparency : 투명성
integral : 완전한
attribute : 속성

☑ **해 석**

바닷물의 몇몇 일반적인 특성은 바다 서식 동물들의 생존과 복지에 아주 중요하다. 물은 대부분의 해양 생명체의 80~90% 양을 차지한다. ① 물은 생명체가 헤엄치고 떠다니기 위한 부력과 체중을 지지하는 힘을 공급하고, 무거운 골격의 필요성을 줄여준다. ② 물은 또한 생명이 계속 살아가는데 필요한 대부분의 화학적 반응을 위한 매개체이다. 해양 생물들의 생태활동은 결국 바닷물의 투명도와 화학적 구성요소를 포함한 바닷물의 기본적인 물리적, 화학적 속성을 바꾸고, 생명체가 전반적인 해양 환경의 필수적인 부분이 되도록 한다. ③ 생명체와 그들이 사는 해양 환경 사이의 상호작용을 이해하는 것은 바닷물의 더 주요한 물리적, 화학적 속성에 관한 간단한 조사가 필요하다. ④ 순수한 물과 바닷물의 특징은 어떤 점에서 다르기 때문에 우리는 순수한 물의 기본 속성을 고려하고 그 후에 그 속성이 바닷물과 어떻게 다른지 검토해야 한다.

✅ **TIP**

②번 앞 문장에서 물의 한 기능을 설명하고 있기 때문에 주어진 문장이 ②번에 들어가 물에 다른 기능을 보여주는 것이 알맞다.

23 ③

🔲 **단 어**

advent : 출현
diminish : 약하게 하다
deem : 여기다

☑ **해 석**

훨씬 더 놀라운 일이 여기에 있다. 인공지능의 출현이 순전한 인간 고유의 능력으로 체스를 두는 선수의 실력을 (A) 약하게 하지 못했다는 것이다. 정반대이다. 값싸고 매우 성능 좋은 프로그램이 그 어느 때보다 더 많은 사람들이 체스를 두고, 더 많은 체스 대회가 생기고 선수들이 전 보다 체스를 더 잘 두도록 (B) 영감을 주었다. Deep Blue가 Kasparov를 처음 이겼을 때 보다 두 배 더 많은 그랜드 마스터가 활동하고 있다. 요즘 최상위의 체스 선수인 Magnus Carlsen은 인공지능으로 훈련했고 모든 선수들 중에 가장 컴퓨터 같은 선수로 여기어져 왔다. 그는 또한 시대를 통틀어 (C) 가장 높은 순위의 그랜드 마스터이다.

✅ **TIP**

③ diminish – inspired – highest

24 ③

🔲 **단 어**

aesthetic : 미학의
elicit : 끌어내다
facilitate : 가능하게 하다
inherently : 본질적으로
regardless of : ~에 상관없이

☑ **해 석**

유행하는 아이템에서 미적가치는 예술작품에서의 미적가치와 같이 자기지향적이다. 소비자들은 매력적으로 보이고 싶고 매력적인 다른 사람들이 자신들을 둘러싸기를 바라는 욕구를 가진다. 하지만, 예술작품이 받는 미적가치와는 달리 패션에서의 미적가치는 타인 지향적이기도 하다. 외모로 이목을 끄는 것은 타인의 반응을 끌어내고 사회적인 상호작용을 가능하게 하는 한 가지 방법이다.

↓

패션 아이템에서의 미적가치는 자신과 타인 둘 다를 지향한다.

① 본질적으로 온전히 자기중심적인
② 다른 것들과 달리 단지 타인 지향적인
③ 자신과 타인 둘 다를 지향하는
④ 원래 속성과 상관없이 정의하기 어려운

✅ **TIP**

패션 아이템의 미적가치는 예술작품에 주어지는 미적가치와 같이 자기중심적인 특성 뿐 아니라 예술작품과는 달리 타인 지향적이기도 하다.

25 ④

단 어

nocturnal : 야행성의
irrelevant : 무관한
integral : 필수적인

해 석

어떤 이들은 꿈꾸는 것이 가치 없다고 믿지만, 밤에 꾸는 이런 드라마들을 무관한 것으로 묵살하는 것은 옳지 않다. 꿈을 기억하는 것에서 얻어지는 무언가가 있다. ① 우리는 더 연결되어져 있고, 더 완벽하게, 제대로 된 길로 가고 있다고 느낄 수 있다. 우리는 또 영감, 정보, 안정감을 받기도 한다. Albert Einstein은 그의 상대성 이론이 꿈에서 영감을 받았다고 말했다. ② 사실, 그는 꿈이 그가 발견한 많은 것들에 영향을 끼쳤다고 주장했다. ③ 우리가 왜 꿈을 꾸는지 묻는 것은 우리가 왜 호흡하는지 질문하는 것과 통한다고 할 수 있다. 꿈꾸는 것은 건강한 삶의 필수적인 부분이다. ④ <u>좋은 소식은 우리가 꿈을 기억하든 못하든 이것이 사실이라는 것이다.</u> 다수의 사람들이 비록 그 구체적인 꿈은 기억하지 못하더라도, 잠에서 깨어나면서 한 문제에 대한 새로운 접근을 떠올리게 되었다고 말한다.

TIP

우리가 꿈을 꾸고 꿈을 통해 여러 부분 도움을 받는데, 그것은 우리가 꿈을 기억하지 못하더라도 가능할 일이라는 점을 ④번 뒤 마지막 문장에서 예로 제시하였다. 그래서 ④번에 주어진 문장이 들어가는 것이 적합하다.

2020. 5. 30.
제1차 경찰공무원(순경) 시행

---

1 ③

단 어

struggle : 고군분투하다
contain : 억제하다
epidemic : 전염병
include : 포함하다
suffer from : ~로부터 고통 받다
prevent the spread of : ~의 확산을 막다
transmit : 보내다

해 석

비록 의사들은 전염병을 <u>억제하기</u> 위해 애썼지만, 그것은 전 세계를 휩쓸었다.

2 ②

단 어

take risk : 위험을 무릅쓰다
wind up : ~을 끝내다
blow up : 화내다
end up : ~로 끝나다, 결국 처하게 되다
make up : 구성하다
use up : 다 쓰다

해 석

그런 위험을 감수하면 결국 죽음에 <u>처하게 될거야.</u>

3 ④

단 어

detective : 형사
scrutinize : 면밀히 조사하다
clue : 단서
hit-and-run : 뺑소니
arrest : 체포하다
criminal : 범죄자
obliterate : 말살하다
distort : 왜곡하다
compliment : 칭찬하다

해 석

형사들은 뺑소니 사고의 단서를 <u>면밀히 조사했고</u> 진짜 범인을 체포하는 데 성공할 수 있었다.

4 ③

단 어

square : 똑바로
unbreak : 치유하다
court : 법정
overhead : 머리위에
square a circle : 불가능한 일을 하다

해 석

나는 그녀의 얼굴을 <u>똑바로</u> 바라보았다.
내 마음을 치유하는 것은 원을 <u>사각형으로</u> 만들려고 노력하는 것과 같았다. 즉, 그것은 불가능했다.

5 ④

단 어

complicated : 복잡한
request : 요청하다

sanction : 제재, 승인
work out : 해결하다
habitually : 습관적으로
blatantly : 뻔뻔스럽게
violate : 위반하다
sanction in relation to : ~에 관하여

☑ 해석
• 이번 사건은 우리가 예상했던 것보다 더 복잡해 보이기 때문에, 이를 해결하기 위해 경찰의 승인을 요청해야 한다.
• 지금까지 북한은 핵무기 개발 문제와 관련하여 유엔의 제재를 습관적이고 뻔뻔스럽게 위반했다.

6 ②

단 어
suggestion : 제안
practical : 실용적인
providing : 만약 ~라면
mind : 꺼리다

☑ 해석
① 아픈 것 같아요. 그렇게 많이 먹지 말았어야 했어요.
② 회의에서 제시된 제안들은 대부분 실용적이지 않았다.
③ 방이 깨끗하다면 어느 호텔에 묵든 상관없다.
④ 우리는 30분 정도 테니스를 치고 있었는데 비가 많이 오기 시작했다.

☑ TIP
"most of the 명사"가 주어가 되는 경우, 명사에 수일치한다. ②번에서 주어는 most of the suggestions이다. 따라서 동사는 was가 아닌 were가 되어야 한다.

7 ②

☑ 해석
① 나를 보자마자 그는 도망쳤다.
② 그가 나에게 거짓말을 했다는 것을 꿈에도 생각하지 못했다.
③ 평범한 영어로 쓰여진 이 책은 많은 사람들에 의해 읽혀졌다.
④ 처음 만났을 때, 나는 그녀와 사랑에 빠지지 않을 수 없었다.

☑ TIP
②번에서 부정어구 little 이 문두에 나왔기 때문에 주어/동사 가 도치되어야 한다. 문장의 동사가 일반동사이기 때문에

일반동사가 나올수 없고, did가 나와야 한다. 따라서 Little did I dream that ~의 형태의 문장이 되어야 한다.

8 ④

☑ 해석
① A : 오, 나는 내 전화기를 다시 잊어 버렸습니다!
   B : 늘 이런 식이야! 당신은 항상 전화기를 잊어버리고 있네요.
② A : 셔츠를 뒤집어 입었니? 솔기가 보이네.
   B : 사실, 원래 보이는 거야.
③ A : 값싼 컴퓨터를 어디서 구할 수 있습니까?
   B : 온라인 쇼핑이 가장 좋은 방법이야.
④ A : 딸기 쇼트케이크 드시겠습니까?
   B : 물론이죠, 더 많이 드세요.

9 ①

☑ 해석
A : 오늘 밤 파티를 위해 와인을 몇 병 준비해야 합니까? 손님이 많을 거라고 들었습니다.
B : 더 많을수록 좋습니다. 하지만 안타깝게도 오늘 밤 제 사무실에서 긴급한 일이 있어서 파티에 같이 있을 수 없습니다. 대신, 다음번에 가도 될까요?
A : 물론입니다! 당신은 언제나 환영입니다.

① 다음번에 가도 될까요?
② 그들에게 안부 전해 주겠어요?
③ 집에 가도 될까요?
④ 당신은 기다리고 있나요?

☑ TIP
① raincheck : 다음을 기약하다(우천 교환권)

10 ②

☑ 해석
① 그들은 참 친절한 사람들이야! → They're so kind people!
② 그녀는 곰 인형을 하나 가지고 있었는데, 인형 눈이 양쪽 다 떨어져 나가고 없었다. → She had a teddy bear, both of whose eyes were missing.
③ 가장 쉬운 해결책은 아무 일도 하지 않는 것이다. → The most easiest solution is to do nothing.
④ 애들 옷 입히고 잠자리 좀 봐 줄래요? → After you've got the children dress, can you make the beds?

TIP

① 'so+형+관사+명사', 'so+형용사'의 형태로 사용되며 'so+수량형용사(many, much, few, little)+명사'의 형태로는 사용하나, 'so+일반형용사+명사'의 형태로는 표현하지 않는다. 'such+관사+형+명사'의 어순으로 사용되므로 'so'를 'such'로 바꿔야 한다.

③ easy의 최상급은 easiest이므로 most를 제거해야 한다.

④ get은 to부정사, 현재분사, 과거분사를 목적격 보어로 취한다. 아이들이 옷을 스스로 입는 것이 아니라 옷이 입혀진다는 의미를 가지므로 목적어와 목적격 보어의 관계가 수동이 되어 dressed라는 과거분사가 목적격 보어로 와야 한다.

11 ①

단어

cue : 신호
recall : 생각해내다
strengthen : 강화하다
remarkably : 놀랍게도
radish : 무
retrieval : 만회, 복구
litter : 쓰레기, 어지르다
irrelevancy : 무관계
interfere with : 방해하다

해석

붉은/혈액, 음식/무와 같은 단어 쌍을 연구한 후에, 당신에게 신호로 빨간색이 주어지고 피가 그것과 함께 나왔다는 것을 상기한다고 상상해보라. 이 기억 행위는 함께 나타나는 두 단어에 대한 기억을 강화시켜 다음 번에 빨간색이 주어지면 피를 기억하는 것이 더 쉬워질 것이다. 하지만 놀랍게도, 피가 빨간색과 함께 나왔다는 것을 상기하는 것은 나중에 음식이 주어졌을 때 무를 기억하는 것을 더 어렵게 만들 것이다! 빨간색/혈액을 연습할 때는, 피 이외의 최근에 접하게 된 '빨간 것'의 생각을 억제해야 한다. 그래서 당신의 마음은 당신이 찾는 단어의 회상을 방해할 수 있는 관련성이 없는 것들로 뒤죽박죽이 되지 않도록 해야 한다. 그러나 무와 같은 원치 않는 품목의 회수를 억제하는 데는 대가가 따른다. 그것들은 미래에 상기할 때, 심지어 "빨간색"과는 아무 상관이 없는 것처럼 보이는 단서(음식)도 전보다 잘 떠오르지 않는다.

① 단어 쌍 학습의 장점과 단점
② 단어 쌍을 매치 시키는 기술
③ 단어 쌍의 기억의 중요성
④ 단어 쌍을 실행하는 적절한 방법

12 ③

단어

responsibility : 책임
adversity : 역경
confusion : 혼란
strain : 긴장
lever : 레버
threaten : 위협하다
unbalance : 균형을 깨뜨리다
floor : 바닥에 쓰러뜨리다
cumulative : 축적적인
sustain : 지탱하다
resistance : 저항
equanimity : 평정
exceed : 초과하다

해석

최고의 지도자라도 자신의 감정적 균형을 잃을 때가 있다. 리더십은 책임감을 수반하고, 책임감은 극심한 역경이 닥칠 때 감정적인 혼란과 긴장을 가져온다. 이런 의미에서 책임감은 지렛대와 같아서, 그것은 역경이 한쪽 끝을 강하게 누를 때 지도자의 감정적 균형을 깨뜨릴 수 있다. 역경이 충분히 위협적이거나 예고 없이 닥칠 때, 그것은 단박에 지도자의 균형을 잃게 할 수 있다. 심지어 링컨만큼 위대한 지도자도 이런 식으로 한 번 넘게 곤혹을 겪었다. 다른 경우에는 그 영향이 누적되는데, 한쪽 끝에 압력이 가해지고 반대쪽 끝에 저항이 가해지는, 지속되는 높은 긴장감의 시기 뒤에 나타나다가, 결국에는 지도자의 평정이 무너지기 시작한다. 요지는, 모든 지도자에게는 각자의 감정적인 한계가 있으며, 그것을 넘어가는 것에 대해 부끄러울 건 없다는 것이다.

13 ③

단어

establish : 입증하다, 밝히다
beyond a doubt : 의심의 여지없이
indefinitely : 무기한으로
postpone : 연기하다
prevention : 예방
maintain : 유지하다
risk : 위험
be linked with : ~와 연관되다
intake : 섭취량, 섭취
body mass-index(BMI) : 체질량 지수(체중을 신장의 제곱으로 나누어 비만도를 가늠하는 지수)
junk food-junkie : 정크 푸드 중독자
metabolic rate : 신진대사율
restriction : 제한
exert : (영향을)주다, 미치다
age-accelerating : 노화를 가속하는

generate : 생성하다,

과학자들은 단지 우리가 섭취하는 음식과 칼로리의 양을 줄임으로써 노화와 그것에 동반되는 모든 못된 것들이 무기한 연기될 수 있다는 것을 언젠가 의심의 여지없이 입증하기를 바란다. 알츠하이머 병을 예방하는 데 이상적인 체중을 유지하는 것이 충분하지 않을 수 있다는 것에 주목하라. 연구들은 알츠하이머 병의 위험이 체중이나 체질량 지수(BMI)보다 칼로리 섭취량과 더 밀접히 연관되어 있다는 것을 보여주었다. 이것은 체중이 늘어나지 않게 해주는 높은 신진대사율을 갖는 복을 받은 정크 푸드 중독자에게 기억력 문제가 생길 위험이 여전히 더 높을 수 있다는 것을 의미한다. 칼로리 제한이 몸과 마음에 어떻게 이로운 영향을 주는지를 설명하는 논리를 생각해 보면, 이 말은 정말 일리가 있다. 우리의 식단에서 생성되는 노화를 가속하는 활성산소의 양은 우리의 몸무게가 아니라 우리가 섭취하는 칼로리의 양과 관련이 있다. 따라서 더 많은 칼로리를 섭취하는 높은 신진대사율을 지닌 사람이 더 느린 신진대사율을 지닌 사람보다 실제로는 더 많은 유해한 형태의 산소를 만들고 있을지도 모른다.

① BMI와 알츠하이머병의 관계
② 알츠하이머병의 위험 감소 방법의 교육
③ 칼로리 섭취가 신체와 정신에 미치는 영향
④ 정크푸드를 먹는 것이 인간대사에 미치는 부작용

14 ④

hazard : 위험
starvation : 기아, 굶주림
menace : 위협하다
medicinal herb : 약초
valor : 용기, 용맹
naught : 무
crude : 조악한
pronounce : 선언하다, 선고하다, 발음하다
urge : 열망 충동
anchor : 정착시키다, 자리 잡다

삶은 위험으로 가득 차 있다. 질병과 적, 굶주림은 항상 원시인들을 위협한다. 경험은 그에게 약초, 용기, 격렬한 노동이 종종 아무런 결과를 가져오지 못한다는 것을 가르치지만 보통 그는 살아 남아서 삶의 좋은 것들을 즐기고 싶어 한다. 이런 문제와 맞닥뜨렸을 때 그는 자신의 목적에 적합해 보이는 방법이라면 무엇이든 전념한다. 종종 그의 방법이 비슷한 비상사태에 우리의 이웃이 어떻게 행동하는가를 기억하기 전까지는 우리 현대인들에게는 믿을 수 없을 만큼 조악해 보이기도 한다. 의학이 그에게 치유 불가능하다고 선고할 때 그는 운명을 감수하며 따르지 않고 회복의 희망을 약속하는 근처 돌팔이 의사에게 달려간다. 자기 보전에 대한 그의 열망은 수그러들지 않으며 세계의 교육 받

지 못한 민족들의 열망도 마찬가지이다. 초자연적인 힘에 대한 믿음은 살고자 하는 강렬한 의지에 자리 잡고 있으며, 이는 과거에도 현재에도, 알려진 민족들 사이에서 절대적으로 보편적이다.

① 그 지지자들의 수는 급격히 증가했다
② 고대 문명이 현대 문명으로 발전하게 한 것
③ 의학에 긍정적인 영향을 미친 것
④ 이는 과거에도 현재에도, 알려진 민족들 사이에서 절대적으로 보편적이다

15 ①

measure : 측정하다
exposure : 노출
curvilinear relationship : 곡선관계
adversity : 역경
predict : 예측하다
intermediate : 중간의
moderate : 적당한
resilience : 회복
follow-up study : 후속연구
response : 반응
laboratory : 실험의
stressor : 자극요인, 스트레스 요인
predictive : 예언하는
grapple : 잡다, 파악하다

참가자들의 서른일곱 가지 주요 부정적인 사건 경험을 측정한 한 연구는 생애에서 겪은 역경과 정신 건강 사이의 곡선 관계를 발견했다. 높은 수준의 역경은 예상대로 나쁜 정신 건강을 예측했지만, 중간 수준의 역경에 직면했던 사람들은 역경을 거의 경험히 않았던 사람들보다 더 건강했는데, 이것은 적당한 양의 스트레스가 회복력을 촉진할 수 있음을 보여준다. 후속 연구는 생애에서 겪은 역경의 양과 피실험자들이 실험 중 주어진 스트레스 요인에 반응하는 것 사이에서 비슷한 관계를 발견했다. 중간 수준의 역경이 가장 큰 회복력을 예측했다. 따라서 적당한 양의 스트레스를 해결하기 위해 노력해야 하는 것은 미래에 스트레스를 직면할 때의 회복력을 길러 줄 수 있다.

16 ①

salient : 현저한, 두드러진
moral agent : 도덕적 행위자, 도덕적 행위자로서의 인간
uncontested : 명백한, 논쟁의 여지가 없는
uncontroversial : 논란의 여지가 없는
flesh-and-blood : 현재 살아 있는, 현실의

as opposed to : ~와는 대조적으로
ridiculously : 우스꽝스럽게, 터무니없이
multiple : 다양한
perspective : 시간, 견지
bear : 품다, 지니다
one-size-fits-all : 널리[두루] 적용되도록 만든

☑ 해석

도덕적 행위자로서의 인간의 가장 명백한 두드러진 특징은 이성적인 사고를 할 수 있는 능력이다. 이성적인 사고를 할 수 없는 사람들은 그들의 행동에 대해 도덕적인 책임을 질 수 없다고 우리 모두 받아들이기 때문에 이것은 어떤 유형의 도덕적 행위자로서의 인간에게 있어서도 논쟁의 여지가 없이 필요한 조건이다. ㉠하지만 이렇게 논란의 여지가 없는 두드러진 특징을 넘어서면, (터무니없이 이상적인 것과는 대조적으로) 실제로 현재 살아있는 도덕적 행위자로서의 인간 각자의 가장 두드러진 특징은 분명히 어떤 도덕적인 문제가 있는 상황에서도 도덕적 행위자로서의 인간이라면 누구든지 지니고 있는 다양한 견해를 제시한다는 사실이다. ㉡즉, "도덕적 행위자로서의 인간이 다른 사람들에게 영향을 미치는 기본적인 방법은 무엇인가?"라는 질문에 대해 두루 적용되도록 만들어진 답은 없다. 오히려, 도덕적 행위자로서의 인간은 이러한 "다른 사람들"이 누구냐에 따라서 다양한 방식으로 "다른 사람들"에게 영향을 미치기를 바란다.

	㉠	/	㉡
①	하지만	/	즉
②	게다가	/	그렇지 않으면
③	간단하게 말하면	/	결국
④	특히	/	심지어

17 ②

단어

core : 핵, 중심부
contract : 수축하다
evaporate : 증발하다
runaway : 통제 불능의
damp : 습한 축축한
transformation : 변화, 변형
shelter : 보호하다
break down : 분해하다, 부수다

☑ 해석

태양이 그 핵이 수축하고 가열되면서 서서히 더 밝아지고 있다. 10억 년 후에는 태양이 오늘보다 약 10 퍼센트 더 밝아져서 불편할 정도로까지 지구를 가열하게 될 것이다. 태양으로부터 ㉠증발하는 물은 지구를 습한 금성의 형태로 바꾸게 되는 통제 불능의 온실 효과를 유발하여 지구가 영원히 두꺼운 흰 구름 막에 둘러싸여 있게 할 수도 있다. 혹은 그 변화가 어느 정도 시

간이 걸리고 더 온화하여서 한동안은 미생물 생명체를 보호해 줄 수 있는 점점 더 무덥고 구름 낀 대기를 유지할 수도 있다. 어느 쪽이 되었든지 물은 성층권 속으로 달아나 자외선에 의해 산소와 수소로 분해될 것이다. 산소는 성층권에 남아서 어쩌면 외계인들이 지구가 여전히 생명체가 살고 있다고 ㉡착각을 하게 만들 수도 있지만 수소는 아주 가벼워 우주 공간으로 달아나게 될 것이다. 그래서 우리의 물은 점차 새어 없어지게 될 것이다.

	㉠	/	㉡
①	축적하는	/	오해하는
②	증발하는	/	오도하는
③	흐르는	/	설득하는
④	스미는	/	추방하는

18 ④

단어

ankle : 발목
heel : 뒤꿈치
ailment : 병
sprain : 염좌, 삠
bruise : 타박상
anti-inflammatory : 항 염증의
alleviate : 완화하다
elevate : 올리다
above all : 무엇보다도

☑ 해석

발목과 발뒤꿈치 통증은 발 전문의에게 가장 흔한 질병인데, 주자와 농구나 테니스와 같은 짧은 거리를 전력 질주하는 선수들 사이에서 특히 그렇다. ㉡일부 발부상은 심각하여 의사의 진료를 필요로 할 수 있지만, 대부분의 경미한 염좌는 집에서 치료할 수 있다. ㉣스포츠 의사들은 멍든 부위를 얼음 찜질하고, 발을 부드럽게 스트레칭하고 마사지하고, 통증을 완화하기 위해 항염증제를 복용할 것을 권고한다. ㉢그들은 또한 가능할 때 발을 높이고 많은 지지가 있는 편안한 신발을 신도록 할 것을 제안한다. ㉠무엇보다 부상이 완치될 때까지 쉬면서 진정하는 것이 가장 중요하다.

19 ②

단어

insight : 통찰(력)
restructure : 재구성하다
get stuck : 꼼짝 못하게 되다
represent : 표현하다, 나타내다
claim : 주장하다

specific : 특정한
attain : 얻다, 획득하다
break away from : ~에서 벗어나다
wander : 돌아다니다
analytical : 분석적인
contribute to : ~에 기여하다
perspective : 시각

☑ 해석

몇몇 심리학자들은, 통찰력이란 어떤 사람이 과거의 경험에 너무 집중해서 꼼짝 못하는 것이라고 믿어지는 정체 상태 후에 문제를 재구성한 결과라고 믿는다. 그 문제를 표현하는 새로운 방식이 갑자기 발견되어 지금까지 예측되지 않은 해결책으로 가는 다른 길로 이어진다. 문제의 상황에서 통찰력을 얻기 위해서는 어떤 특정한 지식이나 경험도 요구되지 않는다고 주장되어 왔다. 사실은 경험에서 벗어나 마음이 자유로이 돌아다니도록 해야 한다. 그럼에도 불구하고 실험 연구들은 통찰력이란 실제로 평범한 분석적 사고의 결과라는 점을 보여주었다. 문제를 재구성하는 것은 그 문제를 해결하는 데 실패한 시도에 의해 야기되어 그 사람이 생각하고 있는 동안 새로운 정보가 들어오는 것으로 이어질 수 있다. 새로운 정보는 해결책을 찾는 데 있어서 완전히 색다른 시각에 기여해서 '아하!' 체험을 만들어 낼 수 있다.

20 ①

☑ 단어

all-time : 전대 미문의, 시대를 초월한
selection bias : 선택 편향
headline : 제1면의 큰 표제
opponent : 상대, 대항자
poll : 여론조사; 여론조사를 하다
go to press : 편집을 마감하다
editor : 편집자
statistician : 통계 전문가, 통계학자
in advance of : ~에 앞서
energize : 열기[활기]를 북돋우다
conduct : 실시하다, 처리하다
infamous : 불명예스러운, 수치스러운, 악명 높은
accidental : 우발적인, 우연의
stakeholder : 이해관계자
hop on the bandwagon : 시류에 편승하다, 지지하다, 편애하다

☑ 해석

거의 틀림없이 전대 미문의 가장 큰 선택 편향의 사례였던 것은 'Dewey가 Truman을 물리치다'라는 당황스러운 1948년 'Chicago Tribune'의 제1면 큰 표제의 결과를 낳았던 것이다. 실제로는, Harry Truman이 그의 상대를 완파했다. 그 당시 모든 주요 정치 여론조사는 Thomas Dewey가 대통령으로 선출될 것이라고 예측했다. 'Chicago Tribune'은 선거 결과가 들어오기 전에 편집을 마감했는데, 왜냐하면 그 편집자들은 여론조사가 정확할

것이라고 확신했기 때문이었다. 통계 전문가들은 두 가지 이유로 틀렸다. 첫째, 그들은 선거에 훨씬 앞서 여론조사 하는 것을 중단했고, Truman은 선거 전 마지막 며칠 간 사람들에게 열기를 북돋우는 데 특히 성공했다. 둘째, 실시된 전화 여론조사는 Dewey를 지지하는 경향이 있었는데, 왜냐하면 1948년에 전화기는 전반적으로 더 부유한 가정에 한정되어 있었고, Dewey는 엘리트 유권자들 사이에서 주로 인기가 있었기 때문이었다. 불명예스러운 'Chicago Tribune'의 제1면 큰 표제를 초래한 선택 편향은 우발적이었지만, 그것은 다른 사람들을 시류에 편승하도록 조장함으로써 마음과 정신에 영향을 미치기를 원하는 이해관계자에게는 선택 편향의 위험과 잠재적 힘을 보여준다.

2020. 6. 13.
제1회 지방직 / 제2회 서울특별시 시행

---

1 ②

☑ 단어

heat up : 뜨거워지다
insulate : 절연하다, 단열하다
sanitary : 위생의, 보건상의
recyclable : 재활용할 수 있는
waterproof : 방수의

☑ 해석

플라스틱 병의 문제는 그것들이 절연되지 않는다는 것이다, 그래서 온도가 오르기 시작하면, 여러분의 물도 가열될 것이다.

2 ④

☑ 단어

strategy : 전략
adopt : 채택하다
alleviate : 완화하다
overload : 과부하
complement : 보완하다
accelerate : 촉진시키다
calculate : 계산하다, 생각하다
relieve : 완화하다

☑ 해석

작가가 글쓰기 과정에서 채택하는 전략은 주의력 과부하의 어려움을 완화시킬 수 있다.

3 ②

sight : 광경
touch off : 촉발하다
enter : 떠오르다, 들어가다
look after : ~를 돌보다
give rise to : ~을 유발하다
make up for : ~을 보상하다
keep in contact with : ~와 접촉을 유지하다

해 석

그 잔인한 광경은 그렇지 않았다면 그녀의 마음속에 떠오르지 않았을 생각을 <u>촉발했다</u>.

4 ①

단 어

bully : 불량배
shun : 피하다
avoid : 피하다
warn : 경고하다
punish : 처벌하다
imitate : 모방하다

해 석

학교 불량배는 반의 다른 학생들에게 <u>외면당하는</u> 것이 어떤 것인지 알지 못했다.

5 ③

단 어

hatch : 부화하다
lose track of time : 시간가는 줄 모르다

해 석

① Of the billions of stars in the galaxy, how much(→ many) are able to hatch life?
② The Christmas party was really excited(→ exciting) and I totally lost track of time.
③ I must leave right now because I am starting work at noon today.
④ They used to loving(→ love) books much more when they were younger.

① 은하계의 수십억 개의 별들 중 얼마나 많은 별들이 생명을 잉태시킬 수 있을까?
② 크리스마스 파티는 정말 흥분됐고 나는 완전히 시간 가는 줄 몰랐다.

③ 오늘 정오에 일을 시작하니까 지금 당장 떠나야 해.
④ 그들은 어렸을 때 책을 훨씬 더 좋아했었다.

TIP

① 별들이 셀 수 있는 명사이기 때문에 many로 바꾸어야 한다.
② 크리스마스 파티가 흥분시키는 것이기 때문에 exciting이 되어야 한다.
④ ~하곤했다, ~했었다, ~이었다의 의미를 가지고 있는 used to RV의 형태로 고쳐야 한다.

6 ④

단 어

make a case : 주장하다
uncomfortable : 불편한
fall on : ~을 엄습하다
grandiose : 거창한, 웅장한
object to : ~에 반대하다
dream about : ~을 꿈꾸다
suggest : 주장하다

해 석

프란체스카가 여름 휴가 동안 집에 머무르는 것을 <u>주장한</u> 후, 저녁 식탁에는 불편한 침묵이 흘렀다. 로버트는 지금이 자신의 거창한 계획에 대해 그녀에게 말할 적기인지 확신할 수 없었다.

7 ③

단 어

amass : 수집하다, 모으다
declare : 선언하다
finest : 질 높은, 좋은
bring in : 가져오다, 벌어들이다
possessions : 소지품
bejeweled : 보석으로 장식한
timepiece : 시계
serpent : 뱀
coil : 감다, 똘똘 말다
wrist : 손목
hypnotic : 최면을 거는 듯한
discreet : 신중한

해 석

엘리자베스 테일러는 아름다운 보석에 대한 안목을 가지고 있었고, 몇 년 동안 놀라운 작품들을 수집하였으며 한 때 "여자라면 더 많은 다이아몬드를 가질 수 있다"고 선언했었다. 2011년 그녀의 가장 훌륭한 보석들이 1억 1천590만 달러를 벌어들인 저녁

경매에서 크리스티에 의해 팔렸다. 저녁 경매 중에 판매된 가장 소중한 소유물 중에는 Bulgari가 1961년 보석으로 장식된 시계가 있었다. 머리와 꼬리를 다이아몬드로 덮고 두 개의 최면 에메랄드 눈을 가진 손목을 감기 위한 뱀으로 디자인된, 조심스러운 메커니즘은 작은 석영 시계를 드러내기 위해 사나운 턱을 연다.

✓ TIP

③ 도치된 문장으로서 동사 뒤에 있는 a 1961 bejeweled timepiece가 실제 주어이다. 단수주어이기 때문에 were를 was로 바꾸어야 한다.

① "a girl can always have more diamonds."을 목적어로 '선언하는' 것이기 때문에 능동의 decaring이 옳은 표현이다.

② an evening auction을 선행사로 받는 관계대명사 that은 옳은 표현이다.

④ 머리와 꼬리가 다이아몬드로 덮어진 것이기 때문에 수동을 의미하는 covered가 옳은 표현이다.

8 ②

단어 •

warranty : 품질 보증서
expire : 만료되다, 만기가 되다
questionnaire : 설문지

✓ TIP

① 보증이 만료되어서 수리는 무료가 아니었다.
→Since the warranty had expired, the repairs were not free of charge.

② 설문지를 완성하는 누구에게나 선물카드가 주어질 예정이다.
→A gift card will be given to whomever(→ whoever) completes the questionnaire.

③ 지난달 내가 휴가를 요청했더라면 지금 하와이에 있을 텐데.
→If I had asked for a vacation last month, I would be in Hawaii now.

④ 그의 아버지가 갑자기 작년에 돌아가셨고, 설상가상으로 그의 어머니도 병에 걸리셨다.
→His father suddenly passed away last year, and, what was worse, his mother became sick.

②번에서 whomever뒤에 completes 동사가 있기 때문에 주어 역할을 할 수 있는 whoever가 들어가야 한다.

9 ①

단어 •

behavior : 행동
stand up for : ~을 옹호하다, 지지하다
appropriate : 적절한
assertive : 단호한, 적극적인
interpersonal : 대인관계에 관련된
violate : 위반하다
exhibit : 보여주다
maintain : 유지하다
subservient : 종속적인
interrupt : 방해하다, 침해하다
sarcasm : 빈정댐, 비꼼
verbal abuse : 언어폭력, 욕설, 악담

☑ 해석

적극적 행동은 자신의 권리를 옹호하고 자신의 생각과 감정을 다른 사람의 권리를 침해하지 않는 직접적이고 적절한 방식으로 표현하는 것을 포함한다. 그것은 상대방이 당신의 관점을 이해하도록 하는 문제다. 적극적 행동능력을 보여주는 사람들은 좋은 대인관계를 유지하면서 갈등상황을 쉽고 확실하게 처리할 수 있다. (A) 이와는 대조적으로 공격적인 행동은 자신의 생각과 감정을 표현하고 다른 사람의 권리를 공공연히 침해하는 방식으로 자신의 권리를 방어하는 것을 포함한다. 공격적인 행동을 보이는 사람들은 다른 사람들의 권리가 자신의 권리에 종속된다고 믿는 것 같다. (B) 따라서 그들은 좋은 대인관계를 유지하는 데 어려움을 겪는다. 그들은 통제력을 유지하기 위해 방해하고, 빠르게 말하고, 다른 사람들을 무시하고, 빈정거림이나 다른 형태의 언어적 학대를 사용할 가능성이 있다.

10 ③

단어 •

employ : 고용하다, (기술, 방법 등을) 이용하다
feature : ~을 특징으로 하다
translate : 변환하다
command : 명령(하다)
resistive : 저항력 있는, 저항성의
electrify : 전기를 통하게 하다
pass through : ~을 관통하다, 거쳐 가다
interpret : (의미를)설명하다, 해석하다
carry out : 수행하다
capacitive : 용량성의, 전기 용량의

☑ 해석

태블릿 컴퓨터에서 사용할 수 있는 전자책 애플리케이션은 터치스크린 기술을 사용한다. 일부 터치스크린은 마주보고 놓인 두 개의 전기를 띤 금속 막을 덮는 유리패널을 특징으로 한다. 스크린이 터치되면 두 개의 금속 표면이 압력을 느끼고 접촉한다.

이 압력은 컴퓨터에 전기 신호를 보내며 터치를 명령으로 변환시킨다. 터치 스크린의 이 버전은 화면이 손가락의 압력에 반응하기 때문에 저항성 화면으로 알려져 있습니다. 다른 태블릿 컴퓨터는 유리 패널 아래에 하나의 전기화된 금속층을 특징으로 한다. 사용자가 화면을 터치하면 일부 전류가 유리를 통과하여 사용자의 손가락으로 전달된다. 전력이 전송되면 컴퓨터는 전력 손실을 명령으로 해석하고 사용자가 원하는 기능을 수행한다. 이러한 유형의 화면은 용량성 화면이라고 한다.

① 사용자가 새로운 기술을 배우는 방법
② 전자책이 태블릿 컴퓨터에서 작동하는 방법
③ 터치스크린 기술이 작동하는 방법
④ 터치스크린이 진화해 온 방식

11 ②

단 어

junk email : 스팸 이메일
weed out : 제거하다

해 석

A : 아, 하나 더! 정크메일 너무 많아!
B : 알아. 나는 하루에 10통 이상의 정크 이메일을 받아.
A : 정크 메일을 차단하는 방법이 없을까?
B : 나는 그들을 완전히 차단하는 것이 불가능하다고 생각해.
A : <u>우리가 할 수 있는 일이 없을까?</u>
B : 음, 설정에 필터를 설정할 수 있어.
A : 필터?
B : 응. 필터가 정크 메일 중 일부를 걸러낼 수 있어.

① 당신은 자주 이메일을 쓰나요?
③ 어떻게 이 훌륭한 필터를 만들었습니까?
④ 이메일 계정 설정을 도와줄 수 있는가?

12 ①

단 어

regret to V : ~해서 유감이다
regret Ving : ~를 후회하다
remind A of B : A에게 B를 상기시키다

TIP

① 나는 네 열쇠를 잃어버렸다고 네게 말한 것을 후회한다.
→ I regret to tell you that I lost your key.
② 그 병원에서의 그의 경험은 그녀의 경험보다 더 나빴다.
→ His experience at the hospital was worse than hers.

③ 그것은 내게 지난 24년의 기억을 상기시켜준다.
→ It reminds me of the memories of the past 24 years.
④ 나는 대화할 때 내 눈을 보는 사람들을 좋아한다.
→ I like people who look me in the eye when I have a conversation.

①번에서 regret to V 는 '~하게 돼서 유감이다'라는 의미이다. 후회한다는 regret Ving가 와야 한다. 따라서 to tell 은 to telling으로 고쳐야 한다.

13 ②

단 어

be off to 장소 : ~로 향하다

해 석

① A : 지금 몇 시인지 알아?
  B : 미안, 요즘 바빠.
② A : 이봐, 어디가는 거야?
  B : 우리는 식료품점에 가.
③ A : 이것 좀 도와줄래?
  B : 좋아. 박수를 쳐줄게.
④ A : 누가 내 지갑을 봤습니까?
  B : 오랜만입니다.

14 ④

단 어

greatness : 위대함
lodge : 오두막, 소규모 별장
palace : 궁전
enormous : 거대한
canal : 운하
drain : 배수하다
marshland : 습지대
elaborate : 정교한
throne : 왕좌
statue : 동상
Jupiter : 제우스, 목성
Neptune : 포세이돈, 해왕성

해 석

루이 14세는 자신의 위대함에 걸맞은 궁전이 필요해서, 작은 사냥용 오두막이 서 있던 베르사유에 거대한 새 집을 짓기로 결심했다. 거의 50년의 노동 끝에 이 작은 사냥용 오두막은 길이가 4분의 1마일인 거대한 궁전으로 변모했다. 운하는 강에서 물을 가져오고 습지대를 배수하기 위해 파냈다. 베르사유는 17개의 커다란 창문 맞은편에 17개의 거대한 거울이 서 있는 유명한 거울의 전당과 단단한 은색 왕좌가 서 있는 아폴로의 살롱과 같은 정교한 방들로 가득 차 있었다. 아폴로, 제우스, 포세이돈 같은 그리스 신들의 동상 수백 개가 정원에 서 있었다. 각각의 신은 루이스의 얼굴을 가지고 있었다!

① 그리스 신들의 진정한 얼굴
② 거울의 전당 vs 아폴로의 살롱
③ 운하가 베르사유에 물보다 더 많은 것을 가져다 주었는가?
④ 베르사유 : 초라한 오두막집에서 대궁까지

15 ③

단어

anthropology : 인류학
anthropologist : 인류학자
philosophy : 철학
influential : 영향력 있는
contemporary : 현대의, 동시대의
take into account : 고려하다
specialize in : ~을 전문으로 하다
illustrate : 묘사하다
conceptual : 개념의
epistemological : 인식론의
distinction : 구분
criticize : 비판하다
ethical : 윤리의
implication : 함축, 함의
inspiration : 영감
experimental : 실험상의
rarely : 거의 ~않다
fieldwork : 야외연구

해석

철학자들은 인류학자들이 철학에 대해 가지고 있는 것만큼 인류학에 관심이 없었다. ① 영향력 있는 현대 철학자들은 그들의 작품에서 인류학적 연구를 고려하지 않는다. ② 사회과학 철학을 전공하는 사람들은 인류학적 연구의 예를 고려하거나 분석할 수 있지만, 대부분 개념적 포인트나 인식론적 구별을 설명하거나 인식론적 또는 윤리적 의미를 비판하기 위해 그렇게 한다. (③ 사실 우리 시대의 위대한 철학자들은 인류학이나 심리학 같은 다른 분야에서 영감을 얻었다.) ④ 철학 학생들은 인류학에 대해 진지한 관심을 보이거나 공부하는 경우가 거의 없다. 그들은 과학에서 실험적인 방법에 대해 배울 수도 있지만, 인류학적 현장연구에 대해서는 거의 배우지 않는다.

16 ③

단어

inherit : 상속받다, 물려받다
property : 재산, 소유물
heirloom : 가보
concrete : 구체적인, 실체가있는
tangible : 실재하는, 유형의, 만질 수 있는
moral : 도덕적인

해석

우리 모두는 무언가를 물려받는다. 어떤 경우에는 돈, 재산 또는 할머니의 웨딩 드레스 또는 아버지의 공구 세트와 같은 가보일 수도 있다. 하지만 그 너머에 우리 모두는 다른 것, 훨씬 덜 구체적이고 유형적인 것, 심지어 우리가 완전히 알지 못하는 것을 물려받는다. 그것은 일상의 일을 하는 방법일 수도 있고, 특정한 문제를 해결하거나 우리 자신을 위해 도덕적인 문제를 결정하는 방법일 수도 있다. 특정 날짜에 소풍을 가는 것은 휴일이나 전통을 유지하는 특별한 방법일 수도 있다. 그것은 우리의 사고에 중요하거나 중심적인 것일 수도 있고, 우리가 오랫동안 무심코 받아들인 사소한 것일 수도 있다.

① 우리의 일상 생활과는 전혀 무관한 것
② 우리의 도덕적 기준에 반하는
③ 훨씬 덜 구체적이고 유형적
④ 매우 금전적으로 가치가 있는

17 ①

단어

evolutionarily : 진화론적으로
goody : 좋은 것들
breeder : 사육사
warrior : 전사
leave over : ~을 남겨두다
contribute : 기여하다
life expectancy : 기대수명
consume : 소비하다
materially : 물질적으로
behaviorally : 행동으로, 행실로
tumult : 소란, 소동
swirl : 빙빙 돌다, 소용돌이치다

해석

진화적으로, 살아있기를 원하는 어떤 종이라도 자원을 주의 깊게 관리해야 한다. 그것은 식량과 다른 좋은 것이 우선적으로 그들이 기여하는 것보다 더 많이 소비하는 것으로 보여 질지도 모르는 노인들에게 많이 남아있지 않은 채, 사육업자, 전사, 사냥꾼, 경작자들, 건설업자, 그리고 확실히, 아이들에게 간다는 것을 의미한다. 그러나 현대 의학이 기대 수명을 연장하기 전부터 일반 가정은 조부모와 증조부모까지 포함했다. 그것은 노인들이 물질적으로 소비하는 것을, 그들이 행동으로 되돌려 주기 때문이다 – 종종 그들 주위에 휘몰아치는 소동에 평등하게 하고 정당화하는 중심을 제공하면서 말이다.

① 노인들이 그 가족에게 기여를 하고 있다.
② 현대의학은 노인의 역할에 초점을 맞추었다.
③ 한 가정에서 자원을 잘 할당하는 것은 그 번영을 결정한다.
④ 대가족은 제한된 자원의 희생으로 온다.

18 ③

dominate : 지배하다
industrialization : 산업화
mechanical : 기계적인
immediately : 즉시
fashionable : 유행하는
decorative : 장식적인
province : 지방
reset : 재설정하다
repeatedly : 반복적으로
confusion : 혼란

해 석

요즘 시계가 우리의 삶을 너무 지배해서 시계가 없는 삶은 상상하기 어렵다. 산업화 이전에, 대부분의 사회는 시간을 알리기 위해 태양이나 달을 사용했다. (B) 기계 시계가 처음 등장했을 때, 즉시 인기가 있었다. 시계나 손목시계를 가지고 있는 것은 유행이었다. 사람들은 시간을 알려 주는 새로운 방법을 언급하기 위해 '시계의' 또는 '시간'라는 표현을 발명했다. (C) 이 시계들은 장식적이었지만 항상 유용하지는 않았다. 마을, 지방, 심지어 이웃 마을들도 시간을 알 수 있는 다른 방법을 가지고 있었기 때문이다. 여행자들은 한 곳에서 다른 곳으로 이동할 때 시계를 반복적으로 재설정해야 했다. 미국에서는 1860년대에 약 70개의 다른 시간대가 있었다. (A) 철도망의 성장으로 시간 기준이 없다는 사실은 재앙이었다. 종종, 몇 마일 떨어진 역들은 다른 시간에 시계를 맞추었다. 여행객들에게는 많은 혼란이 있었다.

19 ④

Millennials : 밀레니얼세대
label : ~로 분류하다
burden : 부담(을 지우다)
staggering : 충격적인, 엄청난
boot : 게다가, 더구나
accumulate : 축적하다
primarily : 주로, 기본(우선)적으로
net : 순자산
retirement : 은퇴

해 석

밀레니얼(1980~2000 사이에 태어난 사람)은 종종 현대에서 가장 가난하고 재정적으로 부담이 많은 세대로 분류된다. 그들 중 많은 수가 대학을 졸업하여 미국이 본 최악의 노동 시장 중 하나로 들어가는데, 게다가 엄청난 학생 부채와 함께. 놀랄 것도 없이, 밀레니얼들은 X세대가 비슷한 단계에서 했던 것보다 적은 부를 축적해왔는데, 주로 그들 중 더 적은 수가 집을 소유하고 있기 때문이다. 그러나 지금까지 다른 세대의 미국인들이 무엇을 절약하는지에 대한 가장 상세한 그림을 제공하는 새로 사용된 데이터는 그 평가를 복잡하게 한다. 그렇다, 1965년에서 1980년 사이에 태어난, X세대들은 더 높은 순자산을 가지고 있다. 그러나 1981년부터 1996년 사이에 태어난 밀레니얼들은 같은 나이인 22세에서 37세 사이의 X세대보다 은퇴를 위해 더 적극적으로 저축하고 있다는 분명한 증거도 있다. 그리고 그것은 그들이 많은 사람들이 생각하는 것보다 더 나은 재정 상태를 갖게 할 수도 있다.

20 ④

carbonate : 탄산염 모래
accumulate : 축적하다
breakdown : 고장, 붕괴, 분해
coral reef : 산호초
sensitive : 민감한
absorb : 흡수하다
carbon dioxide : 이산화탄소
acidify : 산성화하다
dissolve : 용해시키다
emit : 발하다
acidity : 산도
overlie : ~위에 가로 놓이다
acidification : 산성화
dissolution : 용해
reflect : 반영하다
modify : 수정하다
adjust : 적응하다

geochemical : 지구화학적인

adapt : 적응하다

산호초와 다른 암초 유기체의 붕괴로부터 수천 년 이상 축적된 탄산염 모래는 산호초의 틀을 위한 건축 자재다. 그러나 이 모래들은 바닷물의 화학적 구성에 민감하다. 바다가 이산화탄소를 흡수하면서, 그들은 산성화되고, 어느 시점에서는 탄산 모래가 그냥 녹기 시작한다. 세계 해양은 인간이 배출하는 이산화탄소의 약 3분의 1을 흡수했다. 모래가 용해되는 속도는 위에 있는 해수의 산성과 강하게 관련되어 있었으며 해양 산성화에 대한 산호 성장보다 10 배 더 민감했다. 즉, 해양 산성화는 산호초의 성장보다 산호초 모래의 용해에 더 큰 영향을 미칠 것이다. 이것은 아마도 산호의 환경을 수정하고 부분적으로 해양 산성화에 적응하는 능력을 반영하는 반면, 모래의 용해는 적응할 수 없는 지구 화학적 과정이다.

① 산호초의 틀은 탄산염 모래로 만들어진다.

② 산호는 해양 산성화에 부분적으로 적응할 수 있다.

③ 인간이 배출한 이산화탄소는 세계 해양 산성화에 기여했다.

④ 해양 산성화는 산호초 모래의 용해보다 산호의 성장에 더 많은 영향을 미친다.

2020. 6. 20.
소방공무원 시행

---

1 ③

Choking : 숨막힘, 질식

lodge : 박히다, 들어가다

swallow : 삼키다

sore throat : 후두염

heart attack : 심장발작

food poisoning : 식중독

질식은 이물질이 목구멍에 박혀 공기의 흐름을 차단할 때 발생한다. 어른들의 경우, 음식 한 조각이 종종 원인이다. 어린 아이들은 종종 작은 물건들을 삼킨다.

2 ④

drown : 익사하다

deck : 갑판, 덱

---

consciousness : 의식

supervision : 감독

superstition : 미신

foundation : 설립, 기초

collision : 충돌

수영 실력이 어떻든 간에, 아이들이 어떤 물속이나 물 근처에 있을 때는 항상 가까이서 아이들을 지켜봐라. 수영을 할 줄 아는 아이들도 익사할 위험이 있다. 예를 들어, 아이는 수영장 덱에 미끄러져 넘어지고 의식을 잃고 수영장에 빠져 익사할 수도 있다. 감독은 수상 안전을 위한 규칙 1호이다.

3 ①

emergency : 응급상황

unconscious : 의식이 없는

bleed : 피를 흘리다

A : 119입니다. 무슨 응급상황이세요?

B : 교통사고가 났어요.

A : 어디 있어요?

B : 잘 모르겠어요. 해밀턴 로드 어딘가에 있어요.

A : 누가 다쳤는지 알 수 있나요?

B : 운전자 중 한 명은 의식을 잃고 바닥에 누워 있고 다른 한 명은 피를 흘리고 있어요.

A : 선생님, 전화 끊지 말고 기다리세요. 지금 구급차를 보내겠습니다.

B : 네, 하지만 서둘러 주세요!

4 ④

contain : 방지하다, 억제하다

incident : 사건

cordon : 저지선

Auxiliary Fire Service : 보조 소방서

blitz : 대공습

bomb : 폭격하다

in a row : 연속으로

런던 소방대가 현장으로 달려갔고 소방관들은 한 노인이 저지선에 접근할 때 그 사건을 진압하고 있었다. ①그는 대원 중 한 명에게 제2차 세계 대전 중 런던의 보조 소방서의 일원으로 소방관이었다고 말했다. 현재 93세인 ②그는 런던이 57일 연속 폭격을 당했던 기간인 대공습 기간 동안 화재와 싸웠던 것을 여전히 기억했다. ③그는 소방관에게 도울 일이 없냐고 물었다.

그 소방관은 그 자신이 그 순간 적절한 대응을 할 준비가 되어 있지 않다는 것을 알았고 ④그는 단지 그가 저지선을 통과하도록 도왔다. 나중에 그는 그를 소방서에 초대하여 차를 마시게 하고 그의 이야기를 나누게 했다.

✅ **TIP**

①②③은 93세의 노인을, ④는 the officer를 가리킨다.

5 ①

단 어

presence : 존재
audible : 청취할 수 있는
input : 입력
automatic : 자동의
manual : 수동의
activate : 활성화시키다
corresponding : 상응하는
notification : 통지
in addition : 게다가
initiate : 시작하다
adequate : 적절한
measure : 조취
requirement : 요구사항
significantly : 상당히
occupancy : 점유
classification : 분류
in question : 논의되고 있는
fire sprinkler : 화재 스프링클러
standpipe : 급수탑
smoke control system : 연기 제어 시스템

☑ **해 석**

그것들은 화재의 발생에 대해 건물을 감시하여 화재가 감지되면 청각 및 시각 신호를 생성한다. 제어부는 모든 화재 감지 장치로부터 자동 또는 수동으로 입력을 수신하고, 해당 알림 시스템을 활성화한다. 또한 그것들은 화재가 감지되면 적절한 대응 조치를 시작하는 데 사용할 수 있다. 논의 중인 해당 건물의 사용 구분에 따라 그것들의 요건이 크게 변경된다는 것을 주목하는 것이 중요하다. 올바른 요구 사항 집합을 따르는 것이 코드 준수 설계의 첫 번째 단계다.

6 ③

단 어

discriminate : 차별하다
applicant : 지원자
fairness : 공정성
screening test : 선발 검사
have little to do with : ~와 거의 관련이 없다

ensure : 보장하다
candidate : 후보자
be eligible to : ~할 자격이 있는

☑ **해 석**

브루클린의 니콜라스 판사는 흑인과 히스패닉계 지원자를 차별하는 시험을 바탕으로 뉴욕시가 소방관을 고용하는 것을 막음으로써 매우 필요한 충격 치료를 제공했다. 당시 도시 자체가 27%의 흑인임에도 불구하고 소방관의 2.9%만이 흑인이었다. 공정성에 가장 큰 장애물 중 하나는 직무 수행과 거의 관련이 없는 추상적 추론 기술을 측정하는 형편없게 설계된 선발 시험이었다. 따라서 소방관의 직업에 중요한 기술과 성격 특성을 진정으로 반영하는 새로운 테스트를 설계하고 개발해야 할 때다. 소방사업과 더 밀접하게 연계되고 채용될 자격이 있는 모든 후보자들이 흑인이든 아니든 소방관으로서 역할을 할 수 있다는 것을 보장한다면 더 공정할 것이다.

7 ①

단 어

play a part : 역할을 하다
drought : 가뭄
occur : 발생하다
contribute to : 기여하다
humidity : 습도
control : 통제하다
determine : 결정하다
bush : 수풀
pine needle : 솔잎
abound : 풍부하다
ignite : 불을 붙이다

☑ **해 석**

산불이 얼마나 멀리, 얼마나 빨리 번질지 결정하는 데 날씨가 큰 역할을 한다. 가뭄의 시기에는 풀과 식물이 건조하기 때문에 산불이 더 많이 발생한다. 바람은 산불 확산에도 기여한다. 야외 온도와 공기 중의 습도도 산불을 진압하는 데 한몫을 한다. 불이 연소하려면 연료, 산소, 열원이 있어야 한다. 연료의 양은 산불이 얼마나 오래 그리고 빨리 연소할 수 있는지를 결정한다. 많은 큰 나무, 덤불, 솔잎, 풀들이 연료를 위해 숲에 넘쳐난다. 갑작스런 화재는 마른 풀, 덤불, 작은 가지에서 발생한다. 그들은 빨리 불이 붙어서 큰 나무에서 훨씬 더 무거운 연료에 불을 붙일 수 있다.

8 ②

단 어

urgent : 긴급한
head on : 정면으로
procrastination : 지연 · 미룸

laziness : 게으름
sort out : 분류하다
priority : 우선순위
proper : 적절한
recover : 회복하다
blame : 비난하다
embrace : 받아들이다

☑ 해석

지구상의 모든 사람들은 적어도 한 번은 해야 할 급한 일이 있을 상황에 처했을지 모르지만, 정면으로 도전하는 대신, 가능한 한 오랫동안 이 일을 하는 것을 미룬다. 여기서 설명된 현상을 미루기라고 한다. 많은 사람들이 믿는 것에 익숙해진 것과 달리, 미루기는 게으름이 아니라, 오히려 여러분을 늦추고 여러분의 우선순위를 정리하고, 중요한 결정을 내리기 전에 정보를 수집하거나, 다른 사람과의 관계를 회복하기 위해 적절한 단어를 찾는 충분한 시간을 주는 심리적 메커니즘이다. 따라서, 당신은 미루는 것에 대해 자신을 비난하는 대신에, 적어도 때때로 그것을 받아들이고 싶을 것이다.

① 일을 미루지 말고 효율성을 높여라.
② 지연은 걱정해야 할 나쁜 일이 아니다.
③ 도전은 당신이 다른 사람과의 관계를 고치는 데 도움이 될 수 있다.
④ 중요한 결정을 내리기 전에 우선순위를 분류하라.

9 ④

단어

application : 응용프로그램
participate : 참여하다
interaction : 상호작용
medium : 매체
handle : 다루다
carelessly : 부주의하게

☑ 해석

소셜 미디어는 사람들이 소셜 네트워킹에 참여하거나 의사 소통을 지원하는 일부 웹사이트 및 응용 프로그램이다. ① 즉, 사회적 상호작용을 허용하는 모든 웹사이트는 소셜 미디어로 간주된다. ② 우리는 페이스북, 트위터 등 거의 모든 소셜 미디어 네트워킹 사이트에 익숙하다. ③ 그것은 우리를 소셜 세계와 쉽게 의사소통하게 한다. (④ 만약 우리가 그것을 부주의하게 다루면 큰 피해를 줄 수 있는 위험한 매체가 된다.) 우리는 우리가 수년 동안 이야기하지 않았을지도 모르는 우리 주변의 사람들과 즉시 연결되어 있다고 느낀다.

10 ①

단어

retail business : 소매 업체
fulfill : 성취하다
line : 일렬로 늘여 세우다
eventually : 결국
abandon : 포기하다

☑ 해석

한때 식당, 신발 가게, 식료품점과 같은 모든 소규모 소매 업체는 개인 소유였다. 그들은 종종 가게들에 루시의 커피숍과 같은 그들만의 이름을 지어주었다. 어떤 사람들은 창업으로 독립적인 소유에 대한 평생의 꿈을 성취하기도 했다. 다른 사람들은 몇 세대 전으로 거슬러 올라가는 가족 사업을 계속했다. 이 사업체들은 도시와 작은 마을들의 거리를 일렬로 늘여 세우곤 했다. 이와는 (A) 대조적으로 오늘날 일부 국가의 작은 독립 상점들은 거의 모두 사라졌고, 대형 체인점들은 그것들을 대체하기 위해 이사했다. 대부분의 소규모 독립기업들은 거대 체인점들과 경쟁할 수 없었고 결국 실패했다. (B) 하지만 많은 소유주들이 소매 판매를 완전히 포기하지는 않았다. 그들은 프랜차이즈를 통해 다시 한번 소상공인이 되었다.

② 게다가 / 더욱이
③ 대조적으로 / 그러므로
④ 게다가 / 그럼에도 불구하고

11 ②

단어

predict : 예측하다
in advance : 미리
imprecise : 부정확한
accurate : 정확한
implicit : 암묵적인
integrate : 통합하다

☑ 해석

지진과 같은 자연 재해를 미리 예측하는 것은 이용 가능한 데이터가 제한되어 있기 때문에 부정확한 과학이다.

12 ④

단어

reminder : 생각나게 하는 사람(것)
catastrophe : 큰 재해
devastate : 황폐화시키다
derive : 유래하다
deploy : 배치하다
deviate : 벗어나다

빠르게 번지는 불길과 발코니에서 솟아오르는 연기는 2014년 멜버른에서 발생한 라크로스 건물 화재를 떠올리게 하는 끔찍한 계기가 되었다. 그것은 또한 우리에게 런던의 그렌펠 타워 화재를 생각나게 한다. 이 재앙은 72명의 목숨을 앗아갔고 더 많은 사람들의 삶을 <u>황폐화시켰다.</u>

13 ③

단 어

put out : 끄다
rescue : 구조하다
besides : 이외에
wreck : 난파선
collapse : 붕괴하다
endanger : 위험에 빠뜨리다
imperil : 위태롭게 하다
recommend : 추천하다

☑ 해석

소방관들은 불을 끄고 사람들을 <u>구출하는</u> 일을 하는 사람들이다. 화재 외에도 소방관들은 부서진 차, 붕괴된 건물, 멈춘 엘리베이터 및 기타 많은 비상 사태로부터 사람과 동물을 구한다.

14 ①

단 어

proceed : 나아가다, 전진하다
crumple : 구기다, 찌부러 뜨리다
ground : 지상에 떨어지다
worthless : 가치없는

☑ 해석

잘 알려진 한 연설가는 20달러짜리 지폐를 들고 세미나를 시작했다. 200명이 있는 방에서 그는 "누가 이 20달러짜리 지폐를 좋아합니까?"라고 물었다. 손이 올라가기 시작했다. 그는 "제가 여러분 중 한 분께 이 20달러를 드릴 겁니다. 그런데 우선 제가 이렇게 하도록 하죠."라고 말했다. 그는 계속해서 달러 지폐를 구겨버렸다. 그러고 나서 그는 "누가 아직도 이것을 원합니까?"라고 물었다. 여전히 손은 공중에 들려 있었다. "나의 친구들이여, 제가 이 돈에 어떤 행동을 했든 간에, 그것의 가치가 감소하지 않았기 때문에 여러분들은 여전히 그것을 원했습니다. 그것은 여전히 20달러의 가치가 있습니다. 우리는 살면서 여러 번 우리가 내리는 결정과 우리에게 닥쳐오는 상황에 의해 떨어지고, 구겨지고, 진흙탕으로 좌초됩니다. 우리는 마치 우리가 가치 쓸모없다고 느낄 것입니다. 그러나 무슨 일이 일어났든, 무슨 일이 일어나든 결코 여러분은 <u>가치를 잃지</u> 않을 것입니다. 여러분은 특별합니다. 절대 잊지 마십시오."

15 ③

단 어

front : 전선
cease : 그만두다
explosion : 폭발
evaporate : 증발하다
remain : 남다
char : 까맣게 태우다
surrender : 항복하다

☑ 해석

제2차 세계대전에서 일본은 독일과 이탈리아와 힘을 합쳤다. 그래서 이제 유럽 전투 지역과 태평양에 있는 섬 두 개의 전선이 있었다.
(B) 1941년 말, 미국, 영국, 프랑스는 독일과 일본에 대항하는 싸움에 참가했다; 미군은 두 전선에 모두 파견되었다.
(C) 1945년 8월 6일 오전 8시 15분, 미군 비행기가 일본 히로시마 상공에 원자 폭탄을 투하했다. 순식간에 8만 명이 목숨을 잃었다. 히로시마는 그저 존재하지 않게 되었다. 폭발의 중심에 있던 사람들이 증발했다. 남은 것은 건물 벽에 새까맣게 그을린 그림자뿐이었다.
(A) 3일 후, 미국은 다른 도시 나가사키에 폭탄을 투하했다. 일본은 곧 항복했고, 제2차 세계대전은 마침내 끝났다.

16 ③

단 어

trivial : 사소한
productivity : 생산성
in this regard : 이러한 측면에서
category : 범주
demanding : 요구가 많은
prone : ~하기 쉬운

☑ 해석

에어컨이나 신선한 물이 든 쿨러, 유연한 일정, 동료들과의 좋은 관계 등의 사소한 것들은 물론 많은 다른 요소들도 직원들의 생산성과 업무 질에 영향을 미친다.
(B) 이런 점에서 가장 중요한 요인 중 하나는 업무 프로세스를 지휘하는 관리자 또는 상사이다.
(C) 상사가 다루기 어려운 사람들의 범주인 것은 비밀이 아니다. 그들 중 많은 사람들은 부당하게 요구하고, 책임을 다른 노동자들에게 전가시키기 쉽다.
(A) 동시에, 직원들의 생산성을 높은 수준으로 유지하면서도 잘 대해주고 함께 일하기에 즐거운 상사들도 많다.

17 ②

단 어 ·

ravage : 황폐화시키다

bushfire : (잡목림 지대의) 산불

blaze : 화염

deadly : 치명적인

rage : 격노, 격정

reservist : 예비군

contain : 억제하다

fan : 부채질하다

persistent : 지속적인

intensity : 강도

해 석

호주는 수십 년 만에 최악의 산불 시즌에 의해 파괴되어 불타고 있다. 지금까지, 총 23명의 사람들이 화재로 인해 전국적으로 사망했다. 9월부터 맹위를 떨치고 있는 이 치명적인 산불은 이미 약 500만 헥타르의 땅을 불태우고 1,500채 이상의 집을 파괴했다. 주와 연방 당국은 화재 진압을 위해 3,000명의 육군 예비군을 배치했지만 캐나다를 포함한 다른 나라들의 소방 지원에도 불구하고 어려움을 겪고 있다. 불길을 부채질하는 것은 지속적인 더위와 가뭄으로, 많은 사람들이 올해 자연재해 강도의 핵심 요인으로 기후변화를 지적한다.

TIP

② 관계대명사 that은 콤마 뒤에 계속적 용법으로 쓰일수 없다. 따라서 which로 바꾸어야 한다.

① 수동 분사구문으로 being은 옳은 표현이고, 생략도 가능하다

③ struggle은 '고군분투하다'는 자동사의 의미로 쓰여서 올바른 표현이다.

④ '~로서'라는 의미의 전치사로 쓰였다.

18 ③

단 어 ·

blanket : 담요

definite : 분명한

해 석

특히 춥거나 비가 오는 날에는 아침에 어려울 수 있다. 담요는 너무 따뜻하고 편안하다. 그리고 우리는 보통 수업이나 사무실에 가는 것에 흥분하지 않는다. 여기 일찍 일어나는 것을 쉽게 만드는 몇 가지 묘수가 있다. 우선 일찍 일어나려면 확실한 결정을 내려야 한다. 다음으로, 필요한 시간보다 한 시간 일찍 알람을 설정하라. 이렇게 하면, 당신은 뛰어다니지 않고 아침에 휴식을 취할 수 있다. 마지막으로, 우리가 아침에 침대에서 일어나기 싫은 주된 이유 중 하나는 우리가 밤중에 잠을 잘 자지 않기 때문이다. 그래서 우리는 잠에서 잘 깨지 못하는 것이다. 가능한 한 방을 어둡게 유지하도록 하라. 야간 조명, 디지털 시계, 휴대폰 전원 빛은 모두 좋은 휴식을 막을 수 있다.

TIP

③ 주어, 동사의 수 일치를 묻는 문제로서 주어는 one이고, 동사는 are이다. 따라서 are를 is로 바꾸어야 한다.

① 분사를 묻는 문제로서 주어가 사람(we)이기 때문에 excited 가 옳다.

② 수량형용사 + 명사 수 일치를 묻는 문제로서 tricks가 셀 수 있는 명사 복수이기 때문에 a few가 맞는 표현이다.

④ That's why는 뒤에 결과가 나와야 된다. 우리가 잠에서 잘 깨지 못한다는 결과의 내용이기 때문에 맞는 표현이다.

19 ④

단 어 ·

protest : 시위하다

demand : 요구하다

take action : 조치를 취하다

go on strike : 파업하다

parliament : 의회

pressure : 압박하다

eliminate : 제거하다

carbon footprint : 탄소 발자국(온실효과를 유발하는 이산화탄소의 배출량)

해 석

툰버그(16)는 기후변화에 항의하고 전 세계 정부들이 <u>더 많은 조치를 취할 것</u>을 요구하는 전 세계 젊은이들의 목소리가 됐다. 2018년 8월, 툰버그는 학교에서 파업을 벌이며 스웨덴 의회 건물 앞에서 시위를 벌이기로 결정했다. 그녀는 정부가 온실가스를 줄이고 지구 온난화와 싸우기 위해 좀 더 구체적인 일을 하도록 압력을 가하기를 원했다. 사람들은 그녀의 항의에 툰버그와 합류하기 시작했다. 이 단체가 규모가 커지면서, 그녀는 정부가 온실가스를 줄이기 위한 목표를 달성할 때까지 매주 금요일 시위를 계속하기로 결정했다. 그 시위는 미래를 위한 금요일로 알려지게 되었다. 툰버그가 시위를 시작한 이후, 60개 이상의 나라들이 2050년까지 탄소 발자국을 제거하겠다고 약속했다.

① 사람들을 두려워 하도록

② 자유 연설을 하도록

③ 더 많은 돈을 절약하도록

20 ②

단 어 ·

misprint : 오인, 오식

correction : 수정

inconvenience : 불편함

해 설

친애하는 영업사원분들께,

The Brooktown Weekly 최신호에 실은 우리 광고에 오자(誤字)가 있었습니다. 그것은 우리의 반값 세일의 종료를 12월 1일이 아닌 12월 11일로 기재했습니다. 다음 호에는 수정 사항이 나오겠지만, 우리 고객 모두가 오류를 인지하지는 못할 것으로 예상됩니다. 따라서 12월 2일에서 11일 사이에 구매자들이 판매에 대해 물어본다면, 먼저 불편함을 사과한 후 매장이나 온라인에서 구매하고자 하는 물품에 대해 10% 할인 쿠폰을 제공해 주십시오.

총괄 매니저

2020. 7. 11.
인사혁신처 시행

---

1 ①

단 어

extensive : 광범위한
microwave oven : 전자레인지
candid : 솔직한
range : 범위
appliance : 가전제품
comparison : 비교
frank : 솔직한
logical : 논리적인
implicit : 함축적인
passionate : 열정적인

해 설

솔직한 고객 리뷰 및 가격 범위와 함께 전자레인지 모델과 스타일의 광범위한 목록을 가전제품 비교 웹사이트에서 이용 가능하다.

2 ④

단 어

volcanic : 화산작용의
volcano : 화산
conspicuous : 눈에 띄는
passive : 수동적인
vaporous : 증발되는
noticeable : 눈에 띄는

해 설

옐로스톤은 자연에서 화산이었다는 것은 오랫동안 알려져 있었고 화산의 한 가지는 그들이 일반적으로 눈에 잘 띈다는 것이다.

3 ③

단 어

inside out : 안팎으로, 철저하게
eventually : 결국
culturally : 문화적으로
thoroughly : 철저하게
tentatively : 임시로, 시험삼아

해 설

그는 도시를 속속들이 알고 있기 때문에 그곳에 어떻게 가야 하는지를 당신에게 말해 줄 수 있는 최고의 사람이다.

4 ①

단 어

homespun : 소박한
pay atribute to : 찬사를 보내다
etch : 새기다
honor : 경의를 표하다
compose : 구성하다, 작곡하다
publicize : 공표하다

해 설

그 길 내내 마분지, 눈, 건설용지에 새겨진 메시지를 포함하여 팀에 경의를 표하려는 수천 건의 소박한 시도가 있었다.

5 ④

단 어

expensive : 비싼
be related to : ~과 관련된

해 설

① 대도시의 교통은 작은 도시의 교통보다 더 바쁘다.
② 다음 주에 해변에 누워 있을 때 너를 생각해 볼게.
③ 건포도는 한때 값비싼 음식이었고, 부유한 사람들만이 그것들을 먹었다.
④ 색의 강도는 색상이 얼마나 많은 회색을 포함하는지와 관련이 있다.

TIP

① 지시 대명사 those는 traffic을 받고 있기 때문에 that으로 바뀌어야 한다.
② 시간을 나타내는 부사절에서는 현재시제가 미래시제를 대신한다. 따라서 will be를 am으로 바뀌어야 한다.
③ 형용사 앞에 the가 오면 일반 복수 명사가 된다. 따라서 the wealth를 the wealthy로 바꾸어야 한다.
④ 올바른 문장이다.

6 ②

단 어

due to : ~에 기인하는, 때문에
committee : 위원회
construction : 건설, 공사

TIP

① raise는 타동사이기 때문에 have been raised로 바뀌든지, 자동사인 아니면 have arisen으로 바뀌어야 한다.
② cease앞에 should가 생략되었다.
③ 싸운시점이 과거이기 때문에 바람이 분 시점도 과거가 되어야 한다. 따라서 will blow가 blew가 되어야 한다.
④ survive는 살아남다는 의미의 타동사이다. 씨앗이 살아남는 것이기 때문에 are survived by가 survive로 바뀌어야 한다.

7 ③

단 어

have no choice but to~ : ~할 수 밖에 없다
assemble : 모이다, 조립하다

TIP

③ 그가 부회장으로 승진되는 것이기 때문에 promoting을 being promoted로 바뀌어야 한다.
① 주어와 목적어가 같을 경우 목적어 자리에 재귀대명사를 쓰는 데 옳게 쓰였다. "adapt A to B"는 'A를 B에 적응시키다'라는 뜻이다.
② "have no choice but to RV"는 '~할 수 밖에 없다'라는 뜻의 관용어구로 옳게 쓰였다.
④ easy가 포함된 난이형용사 구문이 옳게 쓰였다.

8 ②

단 어

remain : ~인 상태를 유지하다
intact : 완전한
air out : 공개 토론하다
breathe : 호흡하다
foundational : 기본의
speak up : 분명한 어조로 말하다
bang : 세게 두드리다
pot : 단지
pan : 후라이팬
prerequisite : 전제 조건
echo : 메아리치다, 그대로 흉내내다

worn-out : 낡아빠진
hand-me-down : 만들어 놓은, 기성품의
pre-fab : 조립식의
authentically : 진정으로
courteously : 예의바르게
perspective : 관점
uninterrupted : 끊임없는
discernment : 인식

해 석

누군가의 생각을 듣는 것은-당신 자신과 세상 안에 있는 당신의 위치에 대해서 뿐만 아니라-세상에 대해 당신이 믿는 이야기가 온전한 상태로 남아 있는 것인지 아닌지를 알 수 있는 유일한 방법이다. 우리 모두는 우리의 신념을 검토하고 그것들을 공개적으로 토의하고 그것들로 하여금 호흡하도록 둘 필요가 있다. 다른 사람들이 특히 우리가 기본적이라고 여기는 개념에 대해서 말해야 하는 것을 듣는 것은 우리 마음과 우리의 가슴의 창문을 여는 것과 같다. 분명한 어조로 말하는 것은 중요하다. 그러나 듣지 않고 분명한 어조로 말하는 것은 냄비와 팬을 함께 두드리는 것과 같다. 비록 그것이 당신에게 관심을 갖게는 할지라도, 당신을 존중하게 하지는 못할 것이다. 대화가 의미있게 되기 위한 세가지 전제조건이 있다. 1. 당신이 무엇에 대해 말하고 있는지 알아야 하는데, 이것은 당신이 독창적인 논점을 가지고 있고 진부하거나 미리 만들어진 주장을 그대로 흉내 내지 않는다는 것을 의미한다. 2. 당신은 당신이 대화하고 있는 사람들을 존중하고 비록 당신이 그들의 입장에 동의하지 않는다 해도 기꺼이 진정으로 그들을 예의 바르게 대하려고 하는 것이다. 3. 당신은 끊임없는 좋은 유머와 분별력을 가지고 주제에 대한 자신의 관점을 다루면서 상대방이 말하는 것을 들을 정도로 똑똑하고 지식이 많아야 한다.

① 우리는 다른 사람들을 설득하는 데 좀 더 단호해져야 한다.
② 우리는 대화를 잘하기 위해서 듣고 의견을 말해야 할 필요가 있다.
③ 우리는 우리가 보는 세상에 대한 믿음을 바꾸는 데 주저한다.
④ 우리는 우리가 선택한 것만 듣고 다른 의견들을 무시하려고 애쓴다.

9 ①

단 어

demographics : 인구통계
geopolitics : 지정학
inescapable : 피할 수 없는
wrestle with : 해결하려고 애쓰다, 싸우다
anthropocene : 인류세(인류로 인한 지구온난화 및 생태계 침범을 특징으로 하는 현재의 지질학적 시기
identity politics : 정체성 정치학

environmentalism : (인격 형성의)환경 결정론

anonymity : 익명성

authenticity : 진실성

collective : 집단의

experiential : 경험상의

미래는 불확실하지 모르지만, 기후 변화, 바뀌는 인구 통계, 지정학 같은 어떤 것들은 명백하다. 유일한 보장은 변화가 있을 것이라는 점인데 그 변화는 멋질 수도, 끔찍할 수도 있다. 현재와 미래에 예술이 어떤 목적을 제공할지 뿐만 아니라 이러한 변화에 예술가들이 어떻게 반응할지는 고려해볼 가치가 있다. 보고서는 2040년까지 인간이 초래한 기후 변화의 영향은 피할 수 없을 것이고, 20년 후 예술과 삶의 중심에서 큰 이슈가 될 것이라고 제시하고 있다. 미래의 예술가들은 포스트 휴먼과 포스트 인류세의 가능성 -인공지능(AI), 우주에 있는 인간의 식민지, 그리고 잠재적 파멸과 씨름할 것이다. #미투(Me Too)와 흑인 민권 운동(Black Lives Matter 흑인 생명도 중요하다)을 둘러싼 예술에서 볼 수 있는 정체성의 정치학은 환경 결정론, 경계 정치, 이주가 훨씬 더 뚜렷해지면서 성장하게 될 것이다. 예술은 점점 더 다양해질 것이고 우리가 기대하는 것만큼 "예술처럼 보이지"않을 수도 있다. 미래에, 모두가 보는 온라인에서의 가시적인 우리의 삶에 우리가 싫증나게 되고 우리의 사생활이 거의 없어지면, 익명성이 명성보다 더 바람직할지도 모른다. 수천 또는 수백만의 '좋아요'와 '팔로워'들 대신에, 우리는 진실성과 관계에 굶주리게 될 것이다. 예술은 결국 개인보다는 좀 더 집단적이고 경험적이게 될 수 있다.

① 예술은 미래에 어떤 모습일까?

② 지구 온난화는 우리의 삶에 어떤 영향을 미칠까?

③ 인공지능이 환경에 어떤 영향을 미칠까?

④ 정치운동으로 인해 어떤 변화가 일어날까?

10 ④

militia : 시민군

bear : 지니다

infringe : 어기다, 범하다

cite : 말하다

amendment : 변경, 수정헌법

uphold : 지지하다, 유지시키다

firearm : 화기

confirm : 확인하다

strike down : 폐지하다

ban : 금지하다

handgun : 권총

disassemble : 해체하다

advocate : 옹호자

birthright : 타고난 권리

heritage : 유산

homicide : 살인

proponent : 제안자, 발의자

statistics : 통계

indicate : 나타내다

overturn : 뒤집다

미국 헌법 수정 제2조는 "자유국가의 안전에 필요한 잘 규제된 시민군, 무기를 보유하고 소지할 수 있는 국민의 권리는 침해되지 않는다"고 명시하고 있다. 대법원의 판결은 이 개정안을 인용하면서, 총기 규제 국가의 권리를 지지했다. 그러나 2008년 개인의 무기 보유권을 확인한 판결에서 법원은 권총을 금지하고 집에 있는 권총은 자물쇠로 잠그거나 분해하도록 요구하는 워싱턴 D.C. 법을 기각했다. 많은 총기 옹호자들은 소유권을 타고난 권리이자 국가 유산의 필수적인 부분이라고 생각한다. 스위스에 본부를 둔 소형 무기 조사의 2007년 보고서에 따르면, 세계 인구의 5% 미만인 미국은 세계 민간 소유 총기의 약 35~50%를 보유하고 있다. 1인당 총기 1위다. 미국은 또한 세계에서 선진국들 중에서 가장 높은 총기 살인율을 가지고 있다. 그러나 많은 총기 권리 지지자들은 이러한 통계가 인과관계를 나타내지 않으며 1990년대 초 최고치 이후 미국의 총기 살인 및 기타 총기 범죄의 비율이 감소했다는 점에 주목한다.

① 2008년 미국 대법원은 권총 금지법인 워싱턴 D.C.를 뒤집었다.

② 많은 총기 옹호자들은 총을 소유하는 것은 타고난 권리라고 주장한다.

③ 가장 발전된 국가 중 미국이 총기 살인율이 가장 높다.

④ 미국의 총기 범죄는 지난 30년 동안 구준히 증가했다.

11 ④

check~ in : ~을 부치다

① A : 지불 기한은 언제입니까?

　　B : 다음 주까지는 돈을 내야 합니다.

② A : 이 수하물을 부쳐야 하나요?

　　B : 아닙니다. 비행기에 가지고 탑승할만큼 충분히 작습니다.

③ A : 언제 어디서 만날까요?

　　B : 8시 30분에 당신 사무실에서 데리러 갈게요.

④ A : 요리 경연 대회에서 상을 받았습니다.

　　B : 당신이 없었다면 난 할 수 없었을 거예요.

12 ③

해 석

A : 로얄 포인트 호텔 예약 부서에 전화해 주셔서 감사합니다. 제 이름은 샘입니다. 어떻게 도와드릴까요?

B : 안녕하세요, 방을 예약하고 싶은데요.

A : 우리는 두 가지 방 유형이 있습니다. 디럭스 룸과 스위트 룸입니다.

B : 두 개의 차이점은 무엇인가요?

A : 우선, 그 스위트룸은 매우 큽니다. 침실 외에도 부엌, 거실, 식당이 있습니다

B : 비싸게 들리는군요.

A : 하룻밤에 200달러 더 비쌉니다.

B : 그렇다면 디럭스 룸으로 하겠습니다.

① 다른 건 필요하세요?

② 방 번호를 알려주시겠습니까?

③ 두 개의 차이점은 무엇인가요?

④ 애완 동물이 허용되나요?

13 ②

단 어

advocate : 옹호자

secure : 안전한

psychologist : 심리학자

establish : 확립하다

enable : 할 수 있게 하다

critic : 비평가

peer : 동료

though : 하지만

in terms of : ~의 관점에서

guidance : 지도

raise : (문제를) 제기하다

해 석

홈스쿨링 옹호자들은 아이들이 안전하고 사랑스런 환경에 있을 때 더 잘 배운다고 믿는다. 많은 심리학자들은 집을 가장 자연스러운 학습 환경으로 보고 있으며, 원래 집은 학교가 설립되기 훨씬 전부터 교실이었다. 홈스쿨 학부모들은 자녀의 교육을 감시하고 전통적인 학교 환경에서 부족한 관심을 줄 수 있다고 주장한다. 학생들은 또한 무엇을 공부할 것인지, 언제 공부할 것인지를 고르고 선택할 수 있어서, 그들로 하여금 자신의 속도로 배우게 할 수 있다. (A) 이와는 대조적으로, 홈스쿨링에 대한 비판자들은 교실에 있지 않은 아이들이 또래들과의 상호작용이 거의 없기 때문에 중요한 사회적 기술을 배우는 것을 놓친다고 말한다. 그러나 몇몇 연구는 가정 교육을 받은 아이들이 다른 학생들과 마찬가지로 사회 및 정서적 발달 면에서도 잘 하는 것처럼 보이며, 그들의 복지에 관심을 갖는 부모들의 지도와 함께

그들의 집의 편안함과 안전에 더 많은 시간을 보냈다는 것을 보여주었다. (B) 이러한 것에도 불구하고, 홈스쿨링에 대한 많은 비평가들은 그들의 아이들을 효과적으로 가르칠 수 있는 부모들의 능력에 대한 우려를 제기했다.

14 ③

단 어

obsession : 강박

burnout : 소진

gender inequity : 성 불평등

besides : ~이외에

paycheck : 봉급

push back : 밀리다

flexibility : 유연성

remotely : 멀리서

meditation : 명상

해 석

많은 사람들에게, 일은 강박관념이 되었다. 사람들이 급여를 받기 위해 하는 일 외에 아이를 위한 시간이나 열정, 애완동물, 또는 어떤 종류의 삶을 위한 시간을 찾기 위해 애쓰기 때문에, 그것은 소진, 불행, 그리고 성별 불평등을 야기시켰다. 그러나 점점 더 젊은 노동자들이 반발하고 있다. 그들 중 더 많은 사람들이 유연성을 요구하고 기대한다. 예를 들어 새로 태어난 아기를 위한 유급 휴가, 원격으로 일할 수 있는 능력, 늦게 오거나 일찍 떠나거나 운동이나 명상을 할 수 있는 시간 같은 일상적 일과 함께 관대한 휴가 시간을 요구한다. 그들의 삶의 나머지는 어떤 장소나 시간에 묶여 있지 않고 전화로 일어나는데, 왜 일은 달라야 하는가?

① 급여를 인상하는 방법

② 불평등을 줄이기 위한 집착

③ 업무 유연성 요구 증가

④ 긴 휴가가 있는 삶의 장점

15 ③

단 어

frequent : 빈번한

psychological : 심리학적

significant : 중요한

cardiovascular : 심장 혈관의

stressor : 스트레스 요인

anxiety : 불안

accompany : 동반하다

on a daily basis : 매일

ease : 완화하다

relieve : 완화하다

☑ 해 석

과거의 연구는 잦은 심리적 스트레스를 경험하는 것이 심혈관 질환의 중요한 위험 요인이 될 수 있다는 것을 보여주었는데, 이것은 미국 20세 이상의 사람들 거의 절반에 영향을 미치는 질환이다. (C) 잦은 스트레스의 한 원천은 교통 체증과 관련된 스트레스 요인이나 경험이 없는 운전자와 종종 동반되는 불안 때문이다. (A) 하지만 이것은 매일 운전하는 사람들이 심장 질환을 일으키도록 설정되어 있다는 것을 의미하는가, 아니면 운전의 스트레스를 완화시키는 간단한 방법이 있는가? (B) 새로운 연구에 따르면, 간단한 방법이 있다. 연구원들은 운전을 하면서 음악을 듣는 것이 심장 건강에 영향을 미치는 스트레스를 완화시키는 데 도움이 된다고 언급했다.

16 ④

단 어

perceive : 인식하다
immediate : 인접한
initiate : 시작하다
a string of : 일련의
release : 내보내다
bloodstream : 혈류
prompt : 자극하다
adrenal gland : 부신
kidney : 신장
lookout : 감시
skeletal : 골격의
lash : 채찍질하다
fight-or-flight respose : 공격 도피 반응
consciously : 의식적으로
regulate : 조절하다
ignore : 무시하다
reason : 추론하다

☑ 해 석

뇌가 인접한 환경에서 위협을 감지하면, 그것은 신체에서 복잡한 일련의 사건들을 시작한다. 그것은 다양한 분비선, 즉 화학 호르몬을 혈류로 방출하는 기관에 전기 메시지를 보낸다. 혈액은 이 호르몬들을 다른 장기로 빠르게 운반하고, 그 장기들은 다양한 것들을 하도록 자극받는다. 신장 위의 부신은, 예를 들어, 신체의 스트레스 호르몬인 아드레날린을 펴낸다. 아드레날린은 위험의 징후를 경계하기 위해 눈을 넓히고, 혈액과 여분의 호르몬이 흐르도록 심장을 더 빨리 펌프질하고, 골격 근육을 긴장시켜 위협으로부터 채찍질하거나 도망칠 준비가 되도록 하는 등의 일을 하면서 온몸을 여행한다. 이 모든 과정은 몸의 전투를 준비하거나 목숨을 걸고 달려갈 준비를 하기 때문에 투쟁도주 반응이라고 불린다. (인간은 다양한 호르몬의 방출을 조절하기 위해 의식적으로 분비선을 조절한다.) 일단 반응이 시작되면, 호르몬을 논리적으로 설득할 수 없기 때문에 그것을 무시하는 것은 불가능하다.

17 ④

단 어

flask : 병
astonishment : 놀람
shatter : 산산이 부서지다
retain : 보유하다
residue : 나머지, 찌꺼기
phenomenon : 현상
windshield glass : 앞유리
apply : 바르다
thereafter : 그로부터

☑ 해 석

1903년 프랑스 화학자인 에두아르 베네딕토스는 어느 날 유리 플라스크를 단단한 바닥에 떨어뜨려 깨뜨렸다. 그러나 놀랍게도 플라스크는 산산조각이 나지 않았고 여전히 원래의 모양을 유지했다. 그가 병을 조사했을 때, 그는 병이 함유하고 있던 콜로디온 용액에서 남은 잔여물인, 필름 코팅이 안에 들어 있다는 것을 발견했다. 그는 이 특이한 현상을 메모했지만, 몇 주 후 날아오는 자동차 앞 유리에 다친 자동차 사고가 난 사람들에 대한 기사를 신문에서 읽었을 몇 주가 지날때까지 그것에 대해서 전혀 생각하지 못했다. <u>그가 그때 유리병을 사용한 경험이 생각났고, 그만큼 빨리 유리 앞유리에 특수 코팅을 발라 깨지지 않게 할 수 있을 것이라고 상상했다.</u> 얼마 지나지 않아 그는 세계 최초의 안전 유리판을 만드는 데 성공했다.

18 ③

단 어

mess : 혼란
attraction : 관광명소
medieval : 중세의
absorb : 흡수하다
legion : 군단
miasma : 불길한 분위기
tank-top-clad : 탱크탑을 입은
march : 행진하다
limestone : 석회암
proactive : 진취적인
curb : 억압하다
perpetual : 영속적인
swarm : 무리
to make matters worse : 설상가상으로
lure : 유혹하다
inspire : 영감을 주다
authentic : 진짜의

☑ 해 석

Croatia의 Dubrovnik는 혼란 상태이다. 그것의 주요 관광명소가 80피트의 중세 벽으로 둘러싸인 그것의 해안가의 Old Town

이기 때문에, 이 Dalmatian Coast 도시는 방문객들을 매우 잘 흡수하지 못한다. 그리고 유람선들이 여기에 정박할 때면 관광객 군단은 Old Town을 탱크톱을 입은 관광객들이 마을의 석회암으로 포장된 거리를 확보하는 불길한 분위기로 바꾼다. 그렇다, Dubrovnik 시에서는 유람선 관광을 억제하기 위해 주도적이었지만, 어떠한 것도 Old Town을 영속적인 관광객 무리로부터 구하지 못할 것이었다. 설상가상으로, 여분의 돈을 벌도록 하는 유혹은 Old Town의 많은 집주인들이 그들의 장소를 Airbnb로 바꾸도록 고무시켰고, 마을의 벽으로 둘러싸인 지역을 하나의 거대한 호텔로 만들었다. 당신은 Old Town에서 지역주민들처럼 '진정한' Dubrovnik를 경험하기를 원하나? 당신은 이곳에서 그것을 발견하지는 못할 것이다. 절대로.

① Old Town은 80피트 중세 시대 벽으로 둘러싸여 있다.
② 크루즈 배가 정박할 때면 많은 여행객이 Old Town 거리를 확보한다.
③ Dubrovnik 시는 크루즈 여행을 확대하려고 노력해 왔다.
④ Old Town에서는 많은 집이 여행객 숙소로 바뀌었다.

19 ①

☑ **단어**

carbon dioxide : 이산화탄소
radioactive : 방사선의
detector : 감지기
radiation : 방사선
give off : 내뿜다
determine : 결정하다
decay : 썩다
archaeologist : 고고학자
approximate : 대략의

☑ **해석**

유기체가 살아있을 때, 그것은 주위의 공기로부터 이산화탄소를 흡수한다. 그 이산화탄소의 대부분은 탄소-12로 만들어지지만, 작은 부분은 탄소-14로 구성되어 있다. 그래서 살아있는 유기체는 항상 매우 적은 양의 방사성 탄소인 탄소-14를 함유하고 있다. 살아있는 유기체 옆에 있는 감지기는 유기체의 탄소-14에 의해 방출된 방사선을 기록할 것이다. 유기체가 죽으면 더 이상 이산화탄소를 흡수하지 않는다. 새로운 탄소-14는 추가되지 않고, 오래된 탄소-14는 천천히 질소로 붕괴된다. 탄소-14의 양은 시간이 지남에 따라 서서히 (A) 감소한다. 시간이 지남에 따라 탄소-14로부터의 방사선이 점점 더 적게 생성된다. 따라서 유기체에 대해 검출된 탄소-14 방사선의 양은 유기체가 (B) 죽은 지 얼마나 되었는지를 측정하는 것이다. 유기체의 나이를 결정하는 이 방법을 탄소-14 연대 측정이라고 한다. 탄소-14의 붕괴는 고고학자들이 한때 살아 있던 물질의 나이를 찾을 수 있게 해준다. 남은 방사선의 양을 측정하는 것은 대략적인 나이를 알려준다.

20 ②

☑ **단어**

extinct : 멸종된
vanish : 사라지다
inevitably : 불가피하게
exploit : 이용하다
emerge : 나타나다
multicellular : 다세포의
evolve : 진화하다
immense : 거대한
naturalist : 박물학자
speciation : 종 형성
taxonomist : 분류학자
status : 지위
constitute : 구성하다
acceptable : 받아들여질 수 있는
definition : 정의

☑ **해석**

과거와 현재를 막론하고 모든 생명체는 사라졌거나 멸종될 것이다. 그러나 지구에서의 지난 38억 년의 생명의 역사에 걸쳐 각 종들이 사라지면서, 새로운 종들은 필연적으로 그들을 대체하거나 새로 생겨난 자원을 이용하기 위해 나타났다. 아주 단순한 몇 가지 유기체에서, 많은 수의 복잡한 다세포 형태가 이 거대한 기간 동안 진화했다. 19세기 영국의 자연주의자 찰스 다윈 Charles Darwin이 '미스테리 중의 미스테리'라고 일컬었던 새로운 종의 기원은 인간이 지구를 공유하는 생물의 다양성을 만들어내는 것을 담당했던 자연적인 종분화 과정이다. 분류 학자들은 현재 150만 종의 살아있는 종을 인정하지만 실제 숫자는 아마도 1,000만 종에 가까울 것이다. 이런 다수의 무리의 생물학적 지위를 인식하는 것은 종을 구성하는 것에 대한 명확한 이해가 필요하며 진화 생물학자들이 보편적으로 허용되는 정의에 아직 동의하지 않았다는 점을 감안할 때 쉬운 일이 아니다.

① 생물학자 기술
② 생물의 다양성
③ 멸종된 생물의 목록
④ 멸종위기종의 수집

2020. 8. 22.
국회사무처 시행

1 ①

단 어

attainment : 성취

해 석

현재 가장 문명화된 나라들에서 언론의 자유는 당연하게 여겨지고 지극히 간단한 일로 보인다. 우리는 그 사실에 매우 익숙해져서 언론의 자유를 자연스러운 권리로 여긴다. 하지만 이 권리는 꽤 근대에 이르러서야 겨우 얻게 되었고, 그 <u>성취</u>로 가는 길은 피바다를 지나 놓여있었다.

① 획득   ② 공급   ③ 요건
④ 절차   ⑤ 범죄

2 ②

단 어

conductivity : 전도율
odor : 냄새
eradication : 근절
slay : 죽이다
wavelength : 파장

해 석

나노 과학자들은 은, 금, 연필심 같은 요소들이 가장 작은 입자로 줄여나갈 때 매우 효율적인 전도율, 고감도의 독극물 탐지, 완전한 악취 제거, 박테리아 DNA 박멸, 빛의 파장에서 전기를 내는 것과 같은 강력한 힘을 갖게 된다는 사실을 발견했다. 만약 당신이 예를 들어 비닐랩이라는 일반적인 물질에 독을 감지하는 초소재를 더한다면, 상한 음식을 감별하고 라벨 색의 변화로 경고해 줄 수 있는 "스마트한 비닐랩"을 만들어낼 것이다.

TIP

② reducing to their smallest 는 분사구문으로 사용되었지만, 생략된 주어 certain elements가 수동으로 사용되어 being reduced 혹은 being을 생략하고 reduced가 적절하다.

3 ②

단 어

cellular : 세포의
intricate : 복잡한
constitute : 되다

해 석

동물 저항력 훈련의 세포성 효과에 관한 한 참신한 연구에 따르면, 우리가 무거운 것을 들어 올리기 시작할 때, 처음에 우리 몸의 근육들은 강화되거나 변하지 않지만, 신경계는 강화되고 변화한다. 여러 번의 한 팔 턱걸이와 맞먹게 재주를 부리는 원숭이들을 포함한 그 연구는 강화 훈련이 우리 대다수가 생각했던 것보다 더 생리학적으로 복잡하고, 무엇이 힘이 되는지에 대한 우리의 이해가 너무 편협할지도 모른다고 시사하고 있다.

TIP

② that 앞에는 쉼표가 있고 이것은 관계대명사 계속적용법임을 보여준다. 계속적용법에 that은 쓰일 수 없으므로 which가 알맞다.

4 ⑤

단 어

yearn : 동경하다
torment : 고통을 주다

해 석

Frank McCourt의 유년 시절은 고통으로 가득했다. 음식이 절대적으로 부족했다. 그들의 집은 작고 더럽고 겨울에는 매우 추웠다. 비가 오면 바닥에 물이 찼다. Frank와 그의 형제들은 더 나은 삶을 간절히 바랐다. 하지만 Frank는 그의 괴로운 유년시절에서 벗어날 방법이 있었다. 그는 독서를 좋아했다. 그의 다 <u>허물어져 가는</u> 집은 전기도 없었기 때문에 그는 차라리 집 밖의 가로등 아래에서 책을 읽었다.

① 가로 누운   ② 흐트러진
③ 휘갈긴   ④ 간단명료한
⑤ 허물어져 가는

5 ④

단 어

prospective : 장래의, 유망한
self-indulgence : 방종

해 석

일생에 대한 미래 연구들은 알콜중독 이론들이 옳지 않다고 빈번하게 밝힌다. 왜냐하면 그 이론들이 알콜중독 원인의 <u>연관성</u>을 혼동했기 때문이다. 예를 들어, 현재있는 증거를 기반으로 알콜중독인 부모가 있는 가정에서 성장한 것이 알콜중독과 관련은 있지만 원인이 되는 것은 아니라고 보여진다. 마찬가지로, 알콜중독은 우울증과 관련은 있지만 우울증에 때문은 아니고(적어도 남자들의 경우), 유년 시절 방종과 빈곤, 방치도 관련은 있지만 원인은 되지 못한다. 오히려 개인에게서 알콜중독이 빈번히 우울증과 불안증을 일으킨다. 실제로 알콜중독을 자가치료하는 것은 우울증에 차도는커녕 우울증을 더 악화시킨다.

① 증거　　② 알콜중독의　　③ 우울증
④ 연관　　⑤ 자기치료

6 ②

Iraqi : 이라크의

☑ 해설

전 세계에서 중요한 사건들이 일어날 때, 대부분의 사람들은 CNN과 BBC 같은 전통 언론 매체의 취재들에 의지한다. 하지만 2003년 초 미국과 동맹국들의 이라크 침범 기간에 상당히 많은 사람들이 자칭 "Salam Pax"인 한 익명의 이라크 시민의 관점으로 그 전쟁을 지켜봤다.

① 나타나다　　② 의지하다　　③ 변하다
④ 뒤집다　　⑤ 쫓아내다

7 ①

단 어

landfill : 쓰레기 매립지
disposal : 처리
compost : 퇴비
fertilizer : 비료

☑ 해설

점점 더 많은 사람들과 지역사회들이 환경을 보호하기 위해 그들의 습관을 바꾸고 있다. 쓰레기 매립지 공간이 부족해져서 쓰레기 처리가 어렵게 된 점이 이런 변화의 한 이유이다. (A) 그결과로 재활용, 재사용, 쓰레기 줄이기의 실천이 더 평범한 일이 되어가고 있다. 어떤 나라들에서는 쓰레기 처리나 제거를 위한 기술이 실제로 큰 사업이 되고 있다. 또한 개인들은 매립지 쓰레기를 줄이기 위한 실천을 한다. 예를 들어, 사람들은 신문을 재활용하고 옷가지를 자선단체에 기부하고 있다. (B) 게다가 어떤 사람들은 남은 음식을 가져다 채소밭과 꽃밭의 훌륭한 비료인 비옥한 정원 퇴비로 바꾸었다.

(A) / (B)
① 결과로 / 게다가
② 하지만 / 일반적으로
③ 그런데 / 대체로
④ 따라서 / 예를 들어
⑤ 그래서 / 특히

8 ④

☑ 해설

미국의 설립자들은 "민주주의"보다 "공화국"이라는 용어를 더 선호했다. 왜냐하면 자신들을 투표로 뽑아준 사람들에게 책임이 있는 더 유식하거나 부유한 시민들이 일반 사람들의 이해관계를 대변하고 있었고, 공화국이 그들이 일반적으로 선호하던 시스템을 보여주기 때문이었다. 오늘날 우리는 "공화국"과 "민주주의"라는 용어를 바꿔 사용하는 경향이 있다. 널리 알려진 대표적인 민주주의 비판은 그 대표하던 자들이 일반 시민들과 좀처럼 소통하지 않는 "엘리트들"이 되었다는 것이고, 심지어 그들이 당선되더라도 정말로 일반 시민들을 대표하는 정부는 실제로 존재하지 않는다.

① 진정한　　② 책임있는　　③ 보편적인
④ 대표하는　　⑤ 빈번한

9 ③

단 어

bidis : 담배의 일종

☑ 해설

많은 십대들에게 인기를 끄는 유행은 문신하는 것이다. ① 부모들은 보통 자신들의 아이들 피부에 영구적으로 남을 이런 문신을 끔찍해 하지만, 많은 젊은 사람들은 그것을 패션감각으로 여긴다. ② 2000년대가 되면서 자녀들의 유행이 일시적인 유형으로 손이나 발, 목, 다리에 겨우 약 3주만 남는 아름다운 그림을 그리는 방법으로 새로운 유행이 바뀌었을 때 일부 부모들은 아주 안심하게 된다. ③ 이 새로운 유행은 실제 아주 오래된 것이다. 인도에서 수백 년 동안 신부의 친구들이 그녀의 결혼을 축하해 주기 위해 신부를 색칠해 주었다. 하지만 인도에서 유래한 또 다른 유행이 부모들이 비디스를 걱정하게 만든다. 어린이들과 어린 십대들이 오렌지, 초콜릿, 망고, 라즈베리 같은 사탕 맛의 얇은 담배에 끌린다. 문제는? 비디스는 일반 담배 보다 더 많은 니코틴을 함유하고 있다. ④ 불행히도 많은 아이들이 비디스를 정말 "멋진" – 즉 유행이라고 생각한다. ⑤ 그래서 새로운 유행이 올 때까지, 한 라디오 아나운서가 말한 것처럼 "인도 스타일이 인기다"

cardiac arrest : 심박 정지
recurrent : 반복되는
angina : 협심증

해 석

심장마비를 겪는 모든 사람들이 같은 증상이나 심각한 증상을 갖지는 않는다. 어떤 사람들은 가벼운 통증이 있고 다른 사람들은 더 극심한 통증이 있다. 어떤 사람들은 증상이 없다. 다른 사람들은 갑작스러운 심박 정지가 첫 신호 일지도 모른다. 하지만 더 많은 신호와 증상이 있을수록, 당신에게 심장마비가 올 확률이 커진다. 어떤 심장마비는 갑자기 일어나지만, 많은 사람들이 이미 전부터 시간, 일 또는 주마다 경고의 신호와 증상이 있었다. 초기 경고는 흉부 통증이나 신체활동으로 유발되고 휴식으로 완화되는 재발성 흉통이나 압박일 수 있다. 상황의 반복일 것이다. 협심증은 심장으로 흐르는 혈류의 일시적인 감소로 일어난다.

TIP

"the+비교급~, the+비교급~"은 '~하면 할수록, ~하다'의 뜻으로 해당 문장에서 ③은 the greater로 바뀌어야 한다.

12 ①

해 석

만약 경찰이 사람들의 새 드론을 작동시키기 위한 면허증을 보여달라고 요구했다면, 주요한 범죄와의 투쟁에서 성공(A) 했을 것이다. 불행히도 경찰관들은 그러지 않았고 그 결과 그들이 촬영한 차를 훔치는 장면에 담긴 그 청년은 잡히지 않았을 것이다. "당신들이 면허증을 가지고 있는 한 드론들을 사용하는데에 문제가 없습니다."라고 한 변호사가 말했다. "(B) 만약 그들이 적합한 허가를 받은 카메라를 사용했다면, 문제 없습니다."

TIP

(A) would have been / 가정법 과거분사 문장으로 if 주어 had p.p~, 주어 조동사과거 have p.p~.
(B) had they used / 가정법 과거분사 문장에서 if가 생략되어 if they had used~에서 had they used로 도치된 문장이다.

13 ④

해 석

그 이후, 친애하는 국민여러분, 미래는 우리의 손에 달려 있습니다. 우리의 건국자들께서는 우리의 자유와 연합을 보존하는 일은 책임감 있는 시민정신에 달려있다고 가르쳐주었습니다. 그리고 우리는 새로운 세기를 위한 새로운 책임감이 필요합니다.

TIP

③번 이전 문장에서 신체에 색이나 그림을 입히는 유행이 나오고 ③번 이후에는 인도에서 유래한 또 다른 유행을 언급하므로 ③번에 주어진 문장이 들어가는 것이 적절하다.

10 ⑤

단 어

lending : 대출
metrics : 지표
down payment : 계약금, 보증금
social security : 사회보장제도

해 석

우리는 빈부격차를 좁히는 일에 더 깊이 생각할 필요가 있다. 만약 대다수의 사람들, 특히 더 낮은 소득을 받는 사람들과 소수자들이 주거에 그들 재산의 대부분을 둔다면, 우리는 대출 관례를 재고하고, 그간 백인들 위주였던 신용 지표를 더 넓은 범위로 허용해 주어야 하며, 성실한 채무자에게는 보증금도 낮춰야 한다. 우리의 은퇴 정책을 재고하는 것도 중요하다. 퇴직 수당은 주로 백인들과 부유한 사람들을 위해 역할을 한다. 소수자들과 빈곤한 가정들이 음식점이나 탁아소 같은 덜 정규적인 분야의 여러 직업에 있다는 부분적인 이유로 직장 은퇴 계획을 갖게 되기가 더욱 쉽지 않다. 벌써 행해졌어야 할 또 다른 해결책으로, 우리는 급여세를 최대치로 높여 사회보장제도를 확장시켜 부유한 사람들이 다른 모든 사람들과 마찬가지로 그들 수입의 동등한 지분을 기여하게 한다. 그 (A) 둘 다를 하는 것은 훌륭한 첫걸음이 될 것이다. 그렇지만 앞으로 경제적, 인종적 공평성은 더 이상 (B) 분리된 쟁점으로 여기면 안된다.

```
        (A)    /    (B)
① 둘 다 아닌 / 나눈
② 둘 다      / 균등
③ 둘 중 하나 / 사회적인
④ 둘 다 아닌 / 수입
⑤ 둘 다      / 분리된
```

TIP

본문에서 제시한 두가지 방법이 둘다 실천되어야 한다는 논점에서 (A) both, 경제와 인종에서의 공평성이 연관성이 있다는 맥락에서 (B) separate가 알맞다.

해야 할 일이 있는데, 그 일은 바로 아이들에게 읽기를 가르치고 복지 수혜인인 사람들을 고용하는 일 같이 정부가 혼자 할 수 없는 일입니다.

① 복종　　② 권고　　③ 황폐
④ 보존　　⑤ 완화

14 ⑤

단 어 ⦁

falsehood : 거짓말

해석

New Youk에 있는 Cornell 대학에서 한 팀이 이메일과 문자 메시지의 거짓말 탐지를 목표로 하는 소프트웨어를 개발해왔다. 전통적인 거짓말 탐지기는 사람의 심박수를 측정하여 작동한다. 그 기계들은 사람의 맥박이 사람들이 진실을 말하지 않을 때 주는 강한 신호인 긴장과 스트레스를 받을 때 더 빨라진다는 사실에 의지한다. 새로운 소프트웨어는 훨씬 더 영리하다. 그것은 전기적 신호를 살피고, 들려지는 거짓말이 보여주는 다양한 단서들을 찾는다. 연구원들은 이런 수 많은 단서들이나 거짓말 지표를 확인했고, 3인칭 대명사를 많이 사용하는 것부터 부정적 의미의 형용사와 동사의 빈번한 사용까지 다양했다. 지원자들 중 한 팀이 진실되고 정직하지 못한 이메일 둘 다를 연구원들에게 보냈다. 그들은 그 이메일들을 비교함으로 수 많은 특성들을 마주했다. 예를 들어, 그들은 진실된 이메일들은 보통 짧고 첫 번째 사람에게 쓰여진다는 것을 알아차렸고, 문자 시작을 '나는'을 많이 사용하는 1인칭으로 쓰였다는 것을 알아차렸다. 정직하지 못한 이메일들은 정직한 이메일 보다 평균 28% 더 길다. 왜냐하면 사람들이 설득력있게 들리지 않을 것을 걱정하기 때문에, 그들은 거짓말 할 때 더 자세한 세부사항을 주려는 경향이 있다. 그리고 거짓말하는 사람들은 사람들이 자신들의 이야기에 넘어오길 원하기 때문에, 어쩌면 읽는 사람의 동조를 얻기 위한 시도로, '보다', '느끼다' 같은 더 많은 감각동사를 사용하기 쉽다.

TIP

거짓말 하는 사람들이 더 설득력 있게 말하기 위해 자세한 설명을 한다는 내용이 언급되어 있기 때문에 ⑤번이 옳지 않다.

15 ②

William Tell의 집은 산중에 있었고, 그는 유명한 사냥꾼이었다. 지상에서 누구도 그처럼 뛰어나게 활과 화살을 쏠 수 없었다. Gessler는 이 사실을 알았고 그래서 그는 그 사냥꾼 자신의 실력이 본인에게 불행을 가져오게 만들 잔인한 계획을 생각해냈다. 그는 Tell의 어린 아들을 마을 광장에서 사과를 그의 머리에 둔 채로 서있도록 시킨 후 Tell에게 그의 화살 중 하나로 사과를 쏘라고 말했다.

② (A) bring　　(B) to stand　　(C) shoot

TIP

(A) 5형식에서 [사역동사 make+목적어+동사원형]의 형태가 필요하다. 따라서 to bring이 아니라 동사원형 bring이 적절하다.

(B) that 뒤에 5형식 수동태문장이다. 사역동사 make가 사용되었지만 수동태로 변하며 동사원형으로 쓰였을 stand가 to stand로 변해야 한다.

(C) suggest와 같이 제안하는 동사 뒤의 that절에는 shoud+동사원형이 와야하는데 should가 생략되고 he suggested (that) Tell (should) shoot ~로 사용되었다.

16 ④

단 어 ⦁

magnitude : 지진 규모
tremor : 떨림
ripple : 파장을 일으키다
epicenter : 진원지
impoverished : 빈곤한
seismic : 지진의

해석

Gorkha는 좋은 표적이었다. Nepal 수도 북부의 Kathmandu 산림지대에 있는 대부분의 집들은 진흙으로 돌이나 벽돌을 붙여 지어진 것에 지나지 않았다. ①이 말은 4월 25일 정오 전에 진도 7.8 규모의 지진의 진동이 그 지역에 파장을 일으켰을 때, 8,000명의 사람이 죽을 정도로 쉽게 파괴되었다는 것을 의미했다. ②5월 5일쯤 Time지의 사진작가 James Nachtwey가 지진 진원지 근처 Gorkjha 북부인 Barpak의 외딴 마을에 도착했을 때, 그는 "남아 있는 것이 많지 않다."고 말했다. ③진동은 "기본적으로 건물구조를 산산조각 냈고", 한때는 집이었던 곳에 울퉁불퉁한 돌 더미와 뒤틀린 나무틀들이 남겨졌다. (④당신 발 아래 땅이 언제든 움직일 수 있을 때, 어떻게 재건하겠는가?) ⑤가장 심각한 것은, 닥칠 지진이 더 있다는 것이다. Nachtwey가 Nepal을 떠나고 다행히 구조팀들이 히말라야의 빈곤한 국가들로 마침내 파견된 후에 두 번째 지진 타격이 있었다. 5월 12일에 7.3 규모의 지진이 이전 진동을 일으켰던 같은 구역의 지질 단층 동쪽 끝에서 일어났다.

TIP

지진이 일어난 지역에 방문한 사진작가가 그곳 상황을 전하고 있는 중에 ④번 문장은 맥락에 어울리지 않는다.

17 ④

pessimism : 비관주의
cognitive : 인식의
skepticism : 회의론
outperform : 능가하다

해 석

① 비관론은 때때로 더 나은 지도자들을 만들기도 하는데, 사회적 변화가 점화될 필요가 있는 곳에서 특히 그러하다. ② 그들의 회의론은 그들을 과장된 선전과 허위 광고에 더 저항하게끔 만든다. ③ 한 개인이나 그룹에 의해 느껴지는 비관론의 정도는 자주 그들의 개인적 삶과 사회 속의 정치적, 경제적 상황에 연결될 수 있다. ④ 게다가 방어적인 비관주의는 어떤 사람들에게는 유용한 인식적 전략임이 입증되었다. 그들은 기대치를 낮게 설정한 후 미리 넓은 범위에서 부정적 결과를 철저히 준비하여 그 기대치를 능가한다. ⑤

TIP

④번 뒤 문장에서 주어진 문장에 언급된 cognitive strategy의 경우를 보여주고 있다.

18 ①

devastating : 대단히 파괴적인
asteroid : 소행성
emission : 배출
methane : 메탄
meteor : 유성

해 석

지구 역사를 통틀어, 몇 번의 멸종 사건들이 발생해왔다. 가장 큰 사건은 'the Great Dying'이라 불리고 약 2억 5천 년 전에 일어났다. 과학자들은 단 하나의 파괴적인 사건이 지구상 대부분의 생명체들을 죽였다는 가설을 세웠다. 연이은 거대 소행성의 충돌, 온실효과 가스 메탄의 해저층에서 엄청난 양의 방출이나, 현재 러시아의 770,000 평방 마일을 덮어버린 시베리안 트랩을 만들어낸 화산 분출과 같이 증가한 화산 활동이 있어왔을 수 있다. 대규모의 멸종이 끝났을 때, 모든 동물 군의 57%와 모든 생물 종의 83%가 지구에서 사라져버렸고, 그 생명들이 회복하는데 1000만년이 걸렸다.

① 대규모 죽음으로 영향 받은 지구
② 거대한 화산 폭발
③ 지구 위 생명의 시작
④ 지구와 유성의 큰 충돌
⑤ 화산활동으로 인한 대규모 생명체 멸종

19 ③

demise : 종말
reserve currency : 준비통화
hand over first : 아주 엄청나게
recession : 불황
greenback : (미국)지폐
detrimental : 해로운
roil : 휘젓다
treasury : 재무부
hold by : ~에 따르다

해 석

[세계적으로 가장 대중적인 준비통화의 실패 기록들은 대단히 과장되었다.]

(B) 2008-2009년 경제위기 이후로, dollar의 실패 예측들이 어마어마하게 나오게 되었다. 미국 경제가 불황으로 침체 되어 미국 지폐가 세계 최고 준비통화로서 오랫동안 그 입지를 유지할 수 있었던 그 자신감도 그렇게 가라앉았다.

(C) Beijing, Moscow 외 다른 지역에서도, 국회의원들이 세계 안정에 해롭다는 이유로 dollar가 지배하는 세계 금융 시스템에 격분했고, 대체할 것을 찾기로 서약했다. 신흥국의 중앙 은행장들은 dollar 우선이 자신들의 시장과 통화를 혼란스럽게 만들어 미국 경제 활동이 세계 경제에까지 영향을 끼쳤다며 항의했다.

(A) 하지만 이 순간 우리는 금융 위기 6년 후이고, dollar는 그저 실제로 얼마나 만능인지 보여주고 있다. 다른 통화 대비 가치를 책정하는 dollar 인덱스가 최근 4년 만에 최고에 다다랐다. 그리고 dollar를 격렬히 비판하던 국회의원들은 dollar를 내치는데 조금도 관심이 없어 보인다. 미국 재무부 채권 금액은 중국을 따랐는데, 예를 들어, 2008년보다 75% 이상인 1조2천7백억 달러에 달한다.

20 ②

proliferation : 확산

해 석

스마트폰은 작은 사이즈, 사용의 용이함, 무료 혹은 저렴한 어플들의 확산과 끊김없는 접속에도 불구하고, 우리가 노트북을 경험했던 것을 넘어서는 방식으로 컴퓨터와 우리 관계를 변화시킨다.

① 감소 　② 확장 　③ 전망
④ 획득 　⑤ 이용

2020. 9. 19.
제2차 경찰공무원(순경) 시행

1 ②

단어

surveillance : 감시

해석

경찰서장은 감시 카메라가 범죄를 <u>억제</u>하는 데에 이바지 할 수 있다고 주장한다.

① 체면　② 억제　③ 연약함　④ 일탈

2 ①

해석

㉠<u>자백</u> : 사람이 말한 진술, 그 남자 혹은 그녀가 어떤 범죄에서 유죄임을 인정하는 것: 경찰이 심문한 후, 그 여자는 완전히 ㉡<u>자백</u>했다.

① 자백　② 감금　③ 적합　④ 논박

3 ②

단어

Athenian : 아테네의

identify A with B : A와 B를 동일시하다, 확인하다

해석

㉠ 과학자들은 다이어트와 암 사이의 관련성을 <u>확인했다</u>.
㉡ Tom과 동명의 아테네 화가를 <u>동일시하도록</u> 유도하고 있다.
㉢ 승객들은 비행기에 탑승하기 전에 자신들의 짐을 <u>확인하도록</u> 요구 받았다.

① 관련시키다
② 확인하다 / 동일시하다
③ 분별하다
④ 상기하다

4 ①

단어

steam locomotiv : 증기기관차

ingenious : 독창적인

arousing : 자극적인

ingenuous : 순진한

해석

• 지난번 미팅의 회의록에서 ㉠<u>유발되는</u> 어떠한 문제가 있습니까?
• 증기기관차는 산업혁명 시기에 개발된 ㉡<u>독창적인</u> 장치이다.

TIP

arouse는 타동사, arise는 자동사로 목적어가 없는 상황에서 arise가 적절하다.
device를 수식하는 형용사로 ingenious 독창적인이 어울린다.

5 ②

단어

patent : 특허권

해석

㉠ improvement(s) 향상
㉡ membership 회원
㉢ agreement(s) 합의
㉣ ownership 소유권

특허권은 개발자들과 정부 사이에 있는 <u>합의</u>이고, 개발자들에게 일정 기간 동안 그들의 창작물에 대한 <u>소유권</u>을 부여한다. 미국 특허법은 발명은 새롭고 유용한 절차, 기계, 제조의 사안이거나 그것들에 있어 새롭고 유용한 <u>향상</u>이라고 명시한다.

6 ③

단어

criminal suspect : 피의자

해석

① 나는 Siwoo에게 20달러를 빌려달라고 물었다.
② 매니저는 그가 그 회의를 취소했던 이유를 우리에게 설명하기를 거절하였다.
③ 만약 그 환자가 어젯밤 약을 먹었다면, 그는 오늘 회복했을 것이다.
④ 그 피의자는 경찰에게 심문을 받을 때 답변하기를 거절했다.

TIP

③번은 가정법 과거완료 문장으로 'if+주어+had p.p~, 주어+조동사 과거+have p.p~'에 맞춰 'he would have been better today.'가 알맞다.

7 ④

☑ 해 석

① 그는 나에게 "내가 너의 휴대폰을 사용해도 될까?"라고 말했다.
 → 그는 나에게 그가 나의 휴대폰을 사용해도 되는지 물어봤다.
② 그는 졸음이 오지 않도록 진한 커피를 마셨다.
 → 그는 그가 졸음이 오도록 진한 커피를 마셨다.
③ Everest산은 세상에서 가장 높은 산이다.
 → Everest산은 세상에서 어떤 산보다도 더 높다.
④ 나는 나의 지갑과 휴대폰을 내가 집에 도착할 때까지 분실하지 않았다.
 → 내가 지갑과 휴대폰을 분실했던 때는 집에 도착할 때까지는 아니었다.

✓ TIP

① 직접화법에서 간접화법으로 전환할 때, 피전달문에서 의문사가 없는 의문문인 경우에는 if나 whether을 넣어야 한다.
② lest는 '~하지 않도록'으로 사용되었으므로 바뀐 문장에서 so that 뒤에는 부정문이 되어야 한다.
③ 최상급의 다른 표현으로 비교급 than any other+단수 명사가 오도록 해야 한다.
④ it-that 강조구문으로 바뀌어 it+be동사 뒤에 시간 부사구가 강조된 적절한 문장이다.

8 ④

【단 어】

property developer : 부동산 개발업자

☑ 해 석

내가 처음 그 낡은 집을 보았을 때, 나는 그 지역으로 막 이사 했었다. 그 집은 대략 일 년 동안 비어있었고 약간의 수리가 필요했지만, 그 집은 정확히 내가 원했던 곳이었다. 하지만 내가 충분한 돈을 모았을 때에, 나는 부동산 개발업자가 그 집을 구매해 호텔로 바꿀 계획이라는 것을 알게 되었다.

✓ TIP

④ ㉣ 본문의 화자가 알게 되기 전에 부동산 개발업자가 이전에 그 집을 구매하고 계획을 세웠기 때문에 that 뒤에는 had bought~ and ~planned ~. 과거 완료가 적절하다.

9 ②

✓ TIP

① advice는 셀 수 없는 명사이므로 부정관사 an이 사용될 수 없다.
② 부정빈도부사 scarcely가 문두로 오며 주어와 동사가 도치된 문장으로 적절하다.
③ recede는 능동의 형태로 수동의 의미를 갖기 때문에 was없이 receded가 적절하다.
④ ~만큼 'as ~ as' 용법으로 as intimately as bees and flowers가 알맞다.

10 ③

☑ 해 석

① A : Seohee, 어디 가는데?
 B : 나 경주로 떠나.
② A : Yusoo, 우리 롤러코스터 타자.
 B : 그건 내 취향이 아니야.
③ A : 너무 비싸다. 바가지 쓰기 싫어.
 B : 이미 다 지나간 일이야.
④ A : Sohyun, 너 운전해본 적 있니?
 B : 아니, 그런데 너무 기대된다.

11 ③

【단 어】

collate : 수집하다
relay : 전달하다
quarantine : 격리

☑ 해 석

〈감염병 확산 방지를 위한 경찰 업무 설명서〉

	Tasks	Details
①	공항과 항만 관리 위원회와 협력 강화	주거 당국과의 더 많은 협력과 정보 공유
②	지역, 관계 당국과 자료 공유와 반포	보건복지부, 지역 자치와 협력 및 정보 수집, 전달
③	지휘 계통 확보	격리 구역에서 접근 통제
④	형법 강화	범법 행동에 대한 범죄 수사

✓ TIP

단체 행동을 통솔하는 지휘 계통 확보라는 임무와 격리 구역 통제는 관계가 없으므로 ③이 적절하지 않다.

12 ④

단 어 ·

gift certificate : 상품권

intensity : 강도

markedly : 현저하게

해 석

이 두 가지 각본을 생각해보자. 먼저 당신이 Saks 500\$ 상품권을 탔다는 것을 알게 된 것이다. 당신은 이 사실에 대해 꽤 기분이 좋을 것이다, 안 그렇겠는가? 두 번째 각본은, 당신이 500\$가 들어있는 지갑을 분실한 것이다. 당신은 이 사실에 대해 얼마나 불쾌할까? 위험 부담 연구에 따르면, 이런 경험들에 대한 당신의 반응 강도가 현저하게 다르다. 과학자들이 언급한 뇌의 <u>부정적 성향</u>으로 인한 결과 때문에, 500\$를 잃은 결과로 겪을 고통이 당신이 상품권을 탔을 때 느낀 기쁨을 훨씬 넘어설 것이다.

① 확신　　② 중립　　③ 가능성　　④ 부정적 성향

TIP

밑줄 친 부분이 있는 문장 뒤에 부정적인 상황이 더 크게 영향을 끼친다는 문장이 따라오므로 뇌의 부정적 성향이 결과에 영향을 미친다는 내용이 적절하다.

13 ④

단 어 ·

euphemism : 완곡어법

counterpart : 대응물

해 석

모든 문화에서, 직접적으로 말하기 어려운 주제들이 있다. 사람들은 자주 이런 주제들을 완곡한 표현들을 사용해 말한다. 사람들이 완곡 표현들을 사용하는 이유는 그들이 ㉠<u>완곡한 표현들</u> 뒤로 불쾌함이나 불편함을 숨길 수 있기 때문이다. 그래서 사람들은 직접적으로 그런 생각들을 꺼내 다른 사람들 기분을 상하게 할 필요가 없다. 하지만 완곡어법은 외국어로서 영어를 배우고 있는 사람들에게 추가적인 부담을 제기한다. 배우는 사람들은 다른 상황마다 어떤 표현들이 적절한지 학습해야 한다. 완곡어법들은 또한 영어를 배우는 사람들에게 문제가 많다. 왜냐하면 ㉡<u>완곡한 표현</u>에는 빈번하게 ㉢<u>그것들의</u> 더 직접적인 표현보다 더 어려운 단어들이 있기 때문이다. 예를 들어, 영어를 배우는 사람들은 나이 든 사람이 "어르신"으로 언급될 수 있고, 경찰관을 "경관"으로 나타낼 수 있음을 외워야만 한다. 또한 ㉣<u>영어를 배우는 사람들</u>은 "키 작은"을 쓸 수 있을 때에도 "땅딸보" 같은 완곡한 표현 사용을 배워야만 한다.

TIP

㉣의 they는 앞 문장의 주어인 Learners of English와 동일하다.

14 ①

단 어 ·

classify : 분류하다

irrigation : 관개

precipitation : 강수량, 침전

evaporation : 증발

spatially : 공간적으로

temporal : 시간의

arid : 매우 건조한

해 석

물과 전기 소비 사이의 한 가지 차이점은 물은 여러 번 재사용이 가능한데 비해 전기는 그럴 수 없다는 점이다. 결과적으로 물은 "소비되는" 혹은 간단히 "끌어온"으로 분류될 수 있다. 이전에 물은 그 수원에서 제거되고 증발(발전 장치를 식히거나 담수 관개의 경우), 혹은 증산(바이오 작물 재배에서)을 통해 손실되었다. ㉠<u>반면에</u> 끌어온 물은 원래 있던 수원으로 돌아갈 수 있다. 결국 수문학적 순환에 따라 모든 급수는 강수로 돌아온다는 주장이 나올 수 있고 그러므로 "소비되"는게 아니다. ㉡<u>하지만</u> 증발과 강수 둘 다 공간적, 시간적으로 고르지 않다. 특히 매우 건조하고 비가 적게 오는 지역에서 구할 수 있는 물은 물 사용자의 즉각적인 필요를 만족시켜주지만 반면에 같은 지역에서나 바라던 시기에 향후 강수가 없을 수도 있다.

㉠　　　　/　　　　㉡

① on the other hand 반면에 / However 하지만

② however 하지만　　　　/ Thus 그러므로

③ for instance 예를 들어　/ As a result 결과적으로

④ as a result 결과적으로　/ For example 예를 들어

15 ②

단 어 ·

alignment : 동조

evolve : 발달하다

impose : 도입하다

legitimacy : 합법성

strive : 분투하다

courteous : 정중한

uphold : 인정하다

procedural : 절차상의

해 석

총리 Robert Peel 원칙에 동조하는 입장에서, 치안 유지 활동은 대체적으로 국민의 승인, 존중, 협조와 협동으로 발달되어왔다. 경찰권은 자주 "동의에 의한 치안 유지"로 언급되고, 정부의 다양한 부서들에 의해 도입되기 보다는 일반 국민들의 공동 합의를 지닌다. 공정성에서의 신념은 경찰의 합법성으로 이끄는데, 경찰이 갈등을 해결하기 위해 그들의 권력을 운용하는데 허가를 받아야 한다는 국민에 의한 일반적인 신념은 사회질서를

유지하고 지역사회의 문제들을 해결한다. 하지만, 경찰의 합법성을 유지하기 위해 경찰직원은 임무를 수행할 때, 정중하고 공평하며 존중하기 위해 노력해야만 한다. 치안 유지 활동에 의한 국민의 만족은 지역사회가 신뢰하고 확신하도록 세우고 유지하도록 돕는다. 경찰관들과 그들을 고용하는 경찰 기관들의 행동 합법성은 모든 개인의 권리를 가치있게 여기고 절차상 법의 감시에 의해 인정받는다.

① 권력과 공정성
② 치안 유지와 합법성
③ 동의와 정책
④ 신뢰와 관계

16 ③

단 어

universality : 보편성
analogy : 비유

해 석

사람들이 만든 다양한 것들을 보고 그들의 차이점을 묘사하기는 쉽다. ㉠ 분명히 시는 아주 정확한 공식이 아니고, 소설은 유전학 실험이 아니다. ㉡ 작곡가들은 확실하게 시각 예술가와 다른 언어를 사용하고, 화학자들은 극작가들 보다 매우 다른 것들을 결합한다. ㉢ 하지만, 사람들이 이룬 여러 다른 것들로 그들을 특징짓는 것은 어떻게 창조하는가에 관한 보편성을 지나치는 것이다. 창의적인 과정의 단계를 위해 과학자들과 예술가들, 수학자들, 작곡가들, 작가들, 조각가들은 우리가 "생각을 위한 도구"라 부르는 것에서 보편적인 설정을 사용하고, 감정적으로 느끼는 것과 시각적 이미지, 신체적 감각, 재현 가능한 양식, 비유를 포함한다. ㉣ 그리고 창의적으로 생각하는 모든 사람들은 그들의 통찰력을 전달하기 위해 이런 주관적인 생각 도구들로 생각을 대중적인 언어로 옮기고, 타인의 마음에 새로운 생각들 불러일으킬 수 있다.

TIP

③ ㉢이전 문장들을 통해 다양성을 나타냈지만, 주어진 〈보기〉를 ㉢에 넣어 그 이후 문장과 자연스럽게 보편성에 대해 다룰 수 있도록 했다.

17 ①

단 어

immeasurably : 헤아릴 수 없을 정도로
underlying : 근본적인
accumulation : 축적
pneumatic : 공기가 가득한
interchangeability : 호환성
laboriously : 힘들게

해 석

자동차 산업이 어떻게 수많은 취업 기회를 만들고 더 높은 삶의 기준에 헤아릴 수 없을 만큼 기여했는지 쉽게 알 수 있지만, 우리는 이런 모든 가능성을 만든 근본적인 요인을 간과하는 경향이 있다.

㉡ 그것은 그저 최근에 발명된 자동차와 공기 타이어, 전기 헤드라이트 발명품의 축적 그 이상이다. 호환성과 대량 생산은 처음으로 자동차 산업으로 결합된 두 가지 기본적인 제조업 기술들이고, 그것들이 오늘날 평균적인 임금의 노동자들이 차를 소유할 수 있게 해준 현실적인 이유이다.

㉠ 그것들 없이는, 모든 차 한 대마다 손으로 힘들게 만들어져야만 하고 그 비용은 너무 엄청나서 오직 부유한 사람들만 값을 치룰 수 있었을 것이다.

㉢ 그러나 근로자의 재능들을 수많은 유닛들을 모두 정확히 똑같이 생산하는데 전념하고 동력과 특별한 기계들을 통해 자동차는 존재할 수 있고 수백만 대가 생산된다.

18 ④

단 어

dialectical : 변증적인
dialectical : 결정적인, 결승의
presuppose : 예상하다
revolve : 회전하다
axis : 축
prerequisite : 전제조건
combustion : 연소

해 석

Engel은 실재하지 않더라도 중요하고, 모든 일은 변증법칙을 따른다고 믿었다. 하지만 언제든지 이 말이 진실이라고 결정할 방법이 없었기 때문에, 그가 전제로 했던 법칙들은 일반적인 과학법칙과 같지 않다. 자연과학에서 명시된 관계인 "일반적인" 법칙들의 경우조차 보편적인 진술로서 완전한 증명이 되어야 하는 것은 아니라고 인정돼야 한다. 예를 들어, 섭씨 100도에서 물이 끓지 못하는 경우는 절대 없을 것이라고 말할 수 없다. 하지만 그러한 법칙의 위배가 일어날 때, 측정 한계 내에서, 주목할 만한 무언가가 발생하는 일이 일어나는 것이 분명하다.

① 지구는 축을 중심으로 회전한다.
② 지구는 중력을 가진다.
③ 산소는 연소를 위한 전제조건이다.
④ 물은 섭씨 100도에서 끓지 못한다.

TIP

물이 엄청난 고압에서는 100도씨에서 끓지 못하는 경우가 있으므로 자연법칙에서 검증으로 다 나타낼 수 없는 예외를 보여주기 때문에 ④번이 적절하다.

19 ③

단어

inherent : 내재하는
contradiction : 모순
marginalize : 하찮은 존재로 만들다
enclave : 소수민족 거주지
real estate : 부동산
privileged : 특혜를 받는
dualism : 이원론
invariably : 예외없이
utilization : 활용
marginal : 주변부의
recoverable : 땅에서 얻을 수 있는
riverbed : 강바닥
threatened : 멸종할 위기에 놓인
hamper : 방해하다

해석

우리 사회의 대부분은 다수의 내재적 갈등들과 모순들이 있는 핵심적인 가치 변화들을 수반하는 도시화 과정을 겪고 있다. 만약 개발의 과정이 적절히 처리되지 않는다면, 빈곤과 과밀 거주 등을 야기하는 다수의 소외화에 이르게 될 것이다. 도시 사회에서 더 활동적인 구성원들이 번영한 소수민족 거주지의 부동산을 이루어낸 반면에, 대부분 도시의 현장은 소외당하는 사람들의 모습이다. 이원론은 역설적이다. 왜냐하면 사회에서 가장 소외당하는 사람들이 으레 가장 많은 돈을 도시 환경에 지불하고, 대체로 그들이 대부분의 환경 비용을 부담해야만 하기 때문이다. 대도시들에는 필연적으로 주변 구역의 활용이 초과되고, 때때로 안전 한계치와 그 땅에서 낼 수 있는 수용력을 넘어선다. 보통 거주가 불가능한 저지대, 강바닥, 습지 등이 인간을 위한 거주지가 된다. 따라서 환경적으로 민감한 지역들이 사라질 위기에 직면하고 실제 개발 과정을 방해할 수도 있는 도시 환경의 불균형의 결과에 이른다.

→ 이 기사는 <u>도시화가 빈부 격차의 결과를 낼 수 있다</u>고 서술한다.

① 도시 구역들은 환경을 훼손할 수 있다.
② 주변 지역의 활용은 생활비를 줄일 수 있다.
③ 도시화가 빈부 격차의 결과를 낼 수 있다.
④ 도시화는 도시와 지방 사이의 균형을 유지할 수 있다.

TIP

③ 도시화 과정 중에 일어나고 있는 도시의 소외 지역과 소수자들의 그늘진 상황이 기사 전반에 걸쳐 보이고 있다. 따라서 ③번이 요약의 일부로 적절하다.

20 ④

단어

come across as : ~라는 인상을 주다
competence : 역량
exceptional : 특출난
infer : 추론하다
deteriorate : 악화되다
broaden : 넓히다

해석

대부분의 사람들이 그들의 낙관적 성향에 갇혀 긍정적인 피드백에는 귀를 기울이고 부정적인 피드백은 무시하는 경향이 있다. 이것이 그들을 타인에게 자신감있는 인상을 주도록 도울지라도, 역량의 영역(예를 들면, 교육이나 사업, 스포츠, 공연 예술)에서 성취는 10%의 수행과 90%의 준비에 있다. 따라서 당신이 당신의 약점을 더 인지할수록, 더 잘 준비될 것이다. 낮은 자신감은 당신을 비관주의자로 바꿀지도 모르지만, 비관론이 포부와 하나가 될 때, 빈번히 눈에 띄는 성과를 낸다. 어떤 것에서든 최고가 되기 위해 당신 스스로 가장 가혹한 비평가가 될 필요가 있고, 당신의 시발점이 높은 자신감에 있을 때 그것은 거의 불가능하다. 특출한 성취도를 보이는 사람들은 항상 낮은 수준의 자신감과 자존감을 경험하지만, 그들은 만족스러운 역량에 이를 때까지 열심히 단련하고 끊임없이 연습한다.

→ 우리는 낮은 자존감이 성공의 원천이 될 수 있음을 추론할 수 있다.

① 긍정적인 피드백을 받아들이는 것은 역량을 낮출 수 있다.
② 높은 자존감은 마음 돌보는 폭을 넓힐 수 있다.
③ 약점의 인지는 당신을 비관주의자로 이끌 것이다.
④ 낮은 자존감이 성공의 원천이 될 수 있다.

TIP

지문에서 자신의 약점을 인지하고 자존감이 낮아졌을지라도, 성취를 이룬 사람들의 예에서 볼 수 있듯이 더 노력하여 더 뛰어난 역량에 이룰 수 있음을 보여주고 있다. 따라서 ④번이 유추할 수 있는 요지로 적절하다.

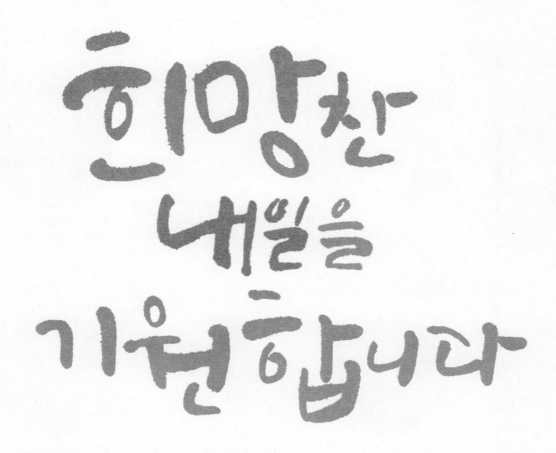

수험서 전문출판사 서원각

목표를 위해 나아가는 수험생 여러분을 성심껏 돕기 위해서 서원각에서는 최고의 수험서 개발에 심혈을 기울이고 있습 니다. 희망찬 미래를 위해서 노력하는 모든 수험생 여러분을 응원합니다.

공무원 대비서   취업 대비서   군 관련 시리즈   자격증 시리즈   동영상 강의

수험서 BEST SELLER

공무원

9급 공무원 파워특강 시리즈

국어, 영어, 한국사, 행정법총론, 행정학개론,
교육학개론, 사회복지학개론, 국제법개론

5, 6개년 기출문제

영어, 한국사, 행정법총론, 행정학개론, 회계학
교육학개론, 사회복지학개론, 사회, 수학, 과학

10개년 기출문제

국어, 영어, 한국사, 행정법총론, 행정학개론,
교육학개론, 사회복지학개론, 사회

소방공무원

필수과목, 소방학개론, 소방관계법규,
인ㆍ적성검사, 생활영어 등

자격증

사회조사분석사 2급 1차 필기

생활정보탐정사

청소년상담사 3급(자격증 한 번에 따기)

임상심리사 2급 기출문제

NCS기본서

공공기관 통합채용

9급 공무원 7개년
기출문제
영어

초판인쇄 2021년 1월 6일 / **초판발행** 2021년 1월 8일 / **편저자** 공무원시험연구소 / **발행처** ㈜서원각

등록번호 1999-1A-107호 / **교재주문** 031-923-2051 / **학습문의** 031-923-2053

영상문의 070-4233-2505 / **팩스** 031-923-3815 / **고객센터** 1600-6528

주소 경기도 고양시 일산서구 덕산로 88-45

정가 **20,000원**

13740

9 791125 733157

ISBN 979-11-257-3315-7